LANDMARK CASES IN THE LAW OF PUNITIVE DAMAGES

Punitive damages are private law's most controversial remedy. This book traces the development of the jurisdiction from the foundational decisions of *Huckle v Money* and *Wilkes v Wood* in England, to leading modern cases such as *Harris v Digital Pulse Pty Ltd* in Australia, *Whiten v Pilot Insurance Co* in Canada, *Couch v AG (No 2)* in New Zealand, *PH Hydraulics & Engineering Pte Ltd v Airtrust (Hong Kong) Ltd* in Singapore and *Mathias v Accor Economy Lodging, Inc* and *State Farm Mutual Automobile Insurance Co v Campbell* in the United States. Many of the decisions addressed are not only landmarks regarding punitive damages but are among the most important judgments delivered concerning private law more generally.

The essays, which are written by leading scholars from a wide range of jurisdictions, cast new light on the cases covered. They do so by examining their historical antecedents and the impact that they have had on the development of the law. The full spectrum of issues regarding punitive damages is addressed including the insurability of punishment, constitutional constraints on the remedy's availability and whether the award should be confined to particular causes of action. The collection will be of interest to all scholars and students of private law. It concentrates on common law cases although civilian perspectives, drawn from France and Germany, are also offered.

Landmark Cases in the Law of Punitive Damages

Edited by
James Goudkamp
and
Eleni Katsampouka

•HART•
OXFORD • LONDON • NEW YORK • NEW DELHI • SYDNEY

HART PUBLISHING

Bloomsbury Publishing Plc

Kemp House, Chawley Park, Cumnor Hill, Oxford, OX2 9PH, UK

1385 Broadway, New York, NY 10018, USA

29 Earlsfort Terrace, Dublin 2, Ireland

First published in Great Britain 2023

A catalogue record for this book is available from the British Library.

A catalogue record for this book is available from the Library of Congress.

Library of Congress Control Number: 2023943771

ISBN: HB: 978-1-50996-700-1
ePDF: 978-1-50996-702-5
ePub: 978-1-50996-701-8

Typeset by Compuscript Ltd, Shannon

Preface

THIS BOOK WAS envisaged around one year before the COVID-19 pandemic struck. It was, alas, necessary repeatedly to postpone a workshop at which the essays that comprise it were to be presented, and we are grateful to the contributors for their patience, many of whom had made significant headway in relation to their research only to have the event shunted off. The workshop ultimately took place, however, across two days in early October 2022 at Keble College, Oxford. Given the quality of the debates, we feel that the decision to wait until it was possible to meet to discuss the essays in person was justified. We were very fortunate to have in attendance distinguished observers who contributed much to the dialogue, namely, Nicholas McBride, Jason Neyers, Donal Nolan, Nelson Rosenvald, Robert Stevens and Rafael Peteffi da Silva. We received very helpful comments regarding the structure of the book from Paul Mitchell and from Hart Publishing's anonymous referees. We gratefully acknowledge financial assistance provided by Keble College, Oxford, Christ's College, Cambridge and the Oxford Law Faculty, without which the workshop would not have been possible. Amelie Berz provided us with excellent research assistance. Finally, we are indebted to Hart Publishing for enthusiastically supporting this project and for its characteristic efficiency during the publication process.

We should say a few words regarding the book itself. The first point concerns terminology. In some jurisdictions, the language of 'exemplary damages' tends to prevail whereas in others the preference is generally to speak of 'punitive damages'. We have deferred to contributors' choices in this regard, which we feel is also consistent with the fact that the essays concern the law in a wide range of jurisdictions. However, we needed to opt for one label rather than the other as regards the title of the book. We alighted on 'punitive damages' for two main reasons. The first reason is that it seems to us that it better captures the purposes of the remedy as defined by the courts both in England and elsewhere. The other reason concerns the fact that in some countries the label 'punitive damages' is used almost exclusively. This is particularly true in the United States and Canada.

Secondly, this book is the first in the Landmark Cases series that is focused on a particular doctrine rather than an area of law. We did not find this methodological approach to be problematic. On the contrary, we consider that the book's theme is clearly defined, and it was, as a result, immediately clear which cases were plausible candidates for inclusion within it, and which fell beyond its scope. Our experience editing the present volume suggests that similar books addressed to other forms of damages, and other remedies more generally, could work well.

Thirdly, although certain cases were clearly far too significant to the subject not to be covered by a book such as the present – for example, *Rookes v Barnard* [1964] AC 1129 (HL) and *Cassell & Co Ltd v Broome* [1972] AC 1027 (HL) – we largely left it up to contributors to select the decisions on which they wished to focus, although we liaised with them in this regard and proposed an indicative list for their consideration. Inevitably, there were a good number of cases that we would have addressed but for the exigencies of space and other constraints. Decisions that fell into this category include *Australian Consolidated Press Ltd v Uren* [1964] AC 1129 (PC), *Aquaculture Corporation v New Zealand Green Mussel Co Ltd* [1990] 3 NZLR 299 (CA), *BMW of North American Inc v Gore* 517 US 559 (1996), and *Exxon Shipping Co v Baker* 554 US 471 (2008).

Fourthly, the reader will note that the book contains two chapters which address cases from France and Germany respectively. This is controversial given that those jurisdictions do not formally acknowledge the institution of punitive damages. Conversely, it might be thought, as some have argued, that the formal position is a distortion of the truth, and that punitive damages are concealed within other doctrines. In any event, and as both of the relevant chapters demonstrate, even in jurisdictions where, as a matter of black-letter law, punitive damages are not available, issues regarding punitive damages nevertheless arise in connection with the recognition and enforcement of foreign judgments. Punitive damages also fall to be considered in other ways as concerns the conflict of laws, most obviously in relation to applicable law.

James Goudkamp
Eleni Katsampouka
6 May 2023

Contents

Contributors

TT Arvind is a Professor of Law at the University of York.

Kit Barker is a Professor of Law at the TC Beirne School of Law, University of Queensland.

Ellen M Bublick is the Dan B Dobbs Professor of Law, University of Arizona James E Rogers College of Law.

Iain Field is a Senior Lecturer, TC Beirne School of Law, University of Queensland and an Honorary Associate Professor, Bond University.

Emily Gordon is a Lecturer in Law at University College London.

James Goudkamp is Professor of the Law of Obligations at the University of Oxford and a Fellow of Keble College, Oxford.

David Ibbetson is formerly the Regius Professor of Civil Law at the University of Cambridge and President of Clare Hall, Cambridge.

Eleni Katsampouka is a Lecturer in Law at King's College London.

Pey-Woan Lee is a Professor of Law at the Singapore Management University.

Mark Leeming is a Judge of Appeal of the Supreme Court of New South Wales and Challis Lecturer in Equity, University of Sydney.

Mark Lunney is a Professor of Tort Law, Dickson Poon School of Law, King's College London; Adjunct Professor, School of Law, University of New England.

Felicity Maher is a Senior Lecturer in Law at the University of Western Australia.

Solène Rowan is Professor of Contract Law at King's College London and Honorary Professor at the Australian National University.

Catherine M Sharkey is the Segal Family Professor of Regulatory Law and Policy at New York University School of Law.

Zoë Sinel is an Associate Professor of Law at the University of Western Ontario.

Jenny Steele is a Professor of Law at the University of York.

Stephen Todd is a Professor of Law at the University of Canterbury.

Johannes Ungerer is the Erich Brost Lecturer in German Law and European Union Law at the University of Oxford and St Hilda's College, Oxford.

Table of Cases

Argentina

Australia

Canada

European Court of Human Rights

European Union

France

Germany

India

Ireland

Jamaica

New Zealand

Singapore

Trinidad and Tobago

United Kingdom

United States

Table of Legislation

Argentina

Australia

Canada

European Union

France

Germany

New Zealand

United Kingdom

United States

1

Huckle v Money (1763) Exemplary Damages and Liberty of the Subject

TT ARVIND AND JENNY STEELE*

I. INTRODUCTION

Our purpose in this chapter is to present a reappraisal of *Huckle v Money*.[1] We seek, specifically, to use the case's contemporary context to shed new light on the concerns that motivated the award of exemplary damages against the defendant, and to examine what those concerns tell us about the place of exemplary damages within tort law. *Huckle v Money* is in many ways a particularly appropriate case for a re-examination of exemplary damages. It is one of two cases from 1763, both of which arose out of the same set of politically charged events, which are seen as origin cases for exemplary damages in English law. Neither case introduced the practice of awarding exemplary damages: it is now generally conceded that non-compensatory damages had been previously recognised; and the Chief Justice expressed himself as though he thought such damages were normal, as well as justified. Such points about origins have been explored by others and are not the concern of this particular paper.[2] Nevertheless, the cases appear to be the first in which the

* Previous versions of this chapter were presented at a symposium at Keble College, Oxford, in October 2022, as well as at a seminar at York Law School, University of York. We are grateful to participants in both events for their useful comments, as well as to the editors for their comments on an earlier draft. We owe a particular debt to Ailbhe O'Loughlin for her comments on our engagement with theories of criminalisation and to Caroline Hunter for her suggestions on the use of exemplary damages in wrongful eviction cases.

[1] *Huckle v Money* (1763) 2 Wils KB 205, 95 ER 768.

[2] See, eg, J Taliadoros, 'The Roots of Punitive Damages at Common Law: A Longer History' (2016) 64 *Cleveland State Law Review* 251. In a paper that appeared when this volume was in production, Sinanis suggests that Camden's statements in *Huckle* simply expressed his 'personal view that … the Huckle jury had done justice in a substantive sense' and did not comprise an explicit articulation of a novel doctrine: N Sinanis, 'The North Briton No. 45 and the Doctrinal

term 'exemplary damages' was used, and the position which they, unlike their predecessors, continue to occupy in the common law story of exemplary damages suggests that lawyers and commentators see something distinctive about these cases.

It is to that question of distinctiveness that this chapter is directed. Our purpose, therefore, is to examine what explains not just the refusal of the court to use its power to award a new trial, but also the Chief Justice's forthright and positive recognition of the jury award as legitimate and justified on the facts, and to explore the implications of these in understanding tort as well as its remedies. As our subtitle suggests, we approach *Huckle v Money* as turning on the law's response to interference with the liberty of the subject. 'Liberty of the subject' is a compound idea in which freedom is not a property of abstract individuals in general but of subjects in particular, and is hence concerned with the definition of the terms of government. Exemplary damages were expressly considered a legitimate response to interference with liberty defined in these terms.

We therefore take an approach based on identifying the concerns that appear to have motivated the court in this case. In doing this, the context of political debate and controversy in its time, and the terms of that debate, are helpful resources. We suggest that tort law as a whole is a product of the law's responses to, and attempt to regulate, a variety of relationships.[3] It is possible to consider the development of the law in primarily doctrinal terms or as seeking rules and principles of general application: for example, it could be suggested that exemplary damages may be available for particular types of wrongdoing (how bad is the behaviour required to be?), perhaps in respect of particular 'torts' or causes of action, and not others. That is the kind of activity that was retrospectively attempted by later courts including the House of Lords in *Rookes v Barnard*.[4] But while tracing general rules and principles might help to set boundaries, it does not in itself advance an understanding of the remedy and its uses. That sort of understanding is needed to propose the applicable rules. We hope to indicate how differences in the concerns attached to underlying relationships may be as important as shared features in one particular aspect of the law's response, such as motive or behaviour.

Origins of Exemplary Damages' (2023) *CLJ* (forthcoming) 17. Editorial constraints prevent a fuller engagement with Sinanis's argument but, in summary, our position in this chapter is that Camden's statement represented a more widely held juristic position as to the role of exemplary damages within the legal system, which exercised an important influence over legal thinking in his day and after. Our argument is therefore different from the one advanced by Sinanis, but we do not make the argument he dismisses, namely that the two cases of *Huckle* and *Wilkes v Wood* had a distinctive law-making function.

[3] In this respect we continue the themes explored by J Steele, 'Regulating Relationships? The Regulatory Potential of Tort Law Revisited' in J Goudkamp, M Lunney and L McDonald (eds), *Taking Law Seriously: Essays in Honour of Peter Cane* (Oxford, Hart Publishing, 2022).

[4] *Rookes v Barnard* [1964] AC 1129 (HL).

Naturally, in determining the validity of a particular jury award in 1763, the court did not attempt to explain when such damages are and are not available. It is important to explore the court's construction of why exemplary damages should be recognised as legitimate in *Huckle v Money*. In doing this, we will seek to show why exemplary damages in this case are best understood in terms of regulation of a relationship, rather than as focusing either on behaviour (punishing egregious behaviour, spite or malice), or on the general rights of individuals irrespective of the identity of a transgressor. We point out a focus on the relationship between government and subject, explaining that it is in this specific relationship that the justification of exemplary damages in *Huckle* is expressly found. Whether similar thinking can help to explain the potential for exemplary damages in other cases, especially in the current context, is a subject for reflection later in this paper.

It is obvious that the case is a long way from the relationships with which the tort of negligence deals today. Exemplary damages are a contribution to tort law with origins in a much less studied and theorised area of the law of tort, and a valuable opportunity to think about tort theory without putting negligence at the centre. This too helps us to consider some general questions about understanding tort law, and its remedies. We take seriously the variety of relationships to which tort applies, but suggest that this variety itself can be productively studied.

At the same time, it is tempting to approach remedies as a separate subject, with a logic independent of actionability. Given that we consider the concerns of the court in responding to the relationships in hand to be central, we propose (or endorse) caution in extrapolating from these early cases to any general statement about the availability or basis of exemplary damages. Exemplary damages in some other contexts will be at best by analogy with those in *Huckle v Money*. In some contexts, an entirely different explanation or theory is needed. This illustrates that there is a danger in seeing remedies as a separate and independent subject, or in seeking to 'join the dots' to make pictures that do not fit underlying concerns.

II. EXEMPLARY DAMAGES WERE EXPRESSLY NOT ABOUT COMPENSATING FOR INJURY; NOR ABOUT PUNISHMENT FOR PARTICULARLY BAD BEHAVIOUR

In this section, we distinguish the award in *Huckle v Money* from either compensatory (including aggravated) or punitive (behaviour-based) reasoning. We emphasise that the damages in *Huckle v Money* were expressly stated by Camden to not be compensatory,[5] and were also not due to aggravation

[5] See, eg, Camden's remarks in *Huckle* (n 1).

of any injury suffered. Equally, it has been tempting to theorise exemplary damages in general as responding to particularly bad behaviour in the form of a punishment – hence the common assumption that 'punitive' is a synonym for 'exemplary'. The 'punitive' reasoning takes the law in a different direction from the award of damages in *Huckle v Money*, which was not concerned with particularly bad behaviour any more than it was concerned with compensation for harm.

The decision in *Huckle v Money* was issued in the context of an argument for a new trial on account of the excessiveness of the damages awarded by the jury.[6] The crux of the argument was that the award of £300 was excessive for the injury, given that the plaintiff had only been held for a few hours, in which he had suffered no particular distress. He was treated well, having been entertained in the messenger's house at no expense to himself and been supplied with beef and beer.[7]

Camden's decision upheld the award,[8] and rejected the motion for a new trial. In part, this was based on the well-established rule that a jury's award of damages would only be interfered with if the sum was so outrageous that 'all mankind at first blush must think so.'[9] But Camden's decision goes beyond that. Camden held not only that the damages were not outrageous, but that they were wholly justified, and that the jury had 'done right in giving exemplary damages.'[10] It is this latter aspect of Camden's reasoning that has given *Huckle* an enduring value as a precedent on exemplary damages (rather than being simply another case on when it was appropriate for a judge to interfere with a jury's award), and it is accordingly on that that this chapter will focus.

Camden's reasons for holding exemplary damages to be justified on the facts of *Huckle* were complex, and will be discussed in greater detail in the next section. Before proceeding to that discussion, however, it is important to note three things the damages were not. Firstly, the damages were not a response to injury. According to Wilson's report of the case, Camden accepted that if damages were to be based on the injury Huckle suffered, they might be estimated at about £20.[11] Nor was this seen by contemporaries as a minor point. The law on when fresh trials would be granted for excessive damages was seen at the time as not being settled, and *Huckle* was almost immediately taken up in one of the leading treatises on damages, by Joseph Sayer, as one of the principal cases on the point. Sayer specifically quotes Camden on the point that £20 would

[6] There is no known surviving account of the directions given to the jury at the actual trial.
[7] TNA TS 11/923, A State of the Causes against the late Secretaries of State and the Messengers (undated).
[8] Lord Camden was at this stage referred to as Pratt CJ.
[9] *Huckle* (n 1); Wils KB 207, ER 769.
[10] ibid.
[11] ibid 206, 768.

have sufficed if the damages were a simple response to injury.[12] That, however, was not what the damages were awarded for.

Secondly, the award of exemplary damages in *Huckle v Money* was not a response to a particularly egregious arrest by the standards of the day. Searches, seizures and arrests were controversial, and could be violent. A report by a messenger of a search and arrest against the printers of the *London Evening News* a decade before the events of *Huckle*, for example, describes doors being broken down after the printers refused to open them, the messengers being opposed 'force for force' by the printers' servants, and threats to shoot the officials conducting the search through the head.[13] In comparison, the arrests that were at issue in *Huckle* were a much more gentlemanly affair. As discussed above, the central plank of the challenges to the size of the award that was advanced in *Huckle v Money*, and repeated in the other cases arising out of the same set of searches and arrests, was that Huckle had been treated well, in that he had been held at Money's own house and provided refreshment including beer and food. The decision does not contest this as a factual matter. Rather, the damages were held to be within the jury's discretion even though Huckle had been treated well.

Equally, the arrests are also notable for not having engaged in what a contemporary pamphlet memorably termed a 'politico-legal game'. It was not unknown for the Attorney-General in cases against publishers of state libel to initiate prosecutions, enter a *nolle prosequi* just before trial, then initiate another prosecution, and enter another *nolle prosequi* as before, purely with a view to subjecting the accused to ruinous expenditure.[14] Similarly, officials often used the tactic of repeatedly moving detainees between the custody of different authorities in order to frustrate writs of *habeas corpus*.[15] These tactics were notably absent in Huckle's arrest.

Thirdly and finally, whilst the arrest of Huckle and the other printers was controversial, it is far from straightforward to treat them as having been carried out in contumelious disregard of their rights.[16] It was common ground that the practice of issuing general warrants was a long-established one, and that the Government had acted in full accordance with that practice: the arrest of

[12] J Sayer, *The Law of Damages* (London, Strahan and Woodfall, 1770) 220.

[13] TNA T 1/357, Carrington's Account of the Evening News, October 1754.

[14] *A Letter Concerning Libels, Warrants, Seizure of Papers, and Security for the Peace*, 5th edn (London, J Almon, 1765) 8–9.

[15] *A Letter from Candor to the Public Advertiser*, 2nd edn (London, J Almon, 1764) 34–35.

[16] Before *Rookes v Barnard*, the language of 'contumelious disregard of the plaintiff's rights' was commonly used in legal treatises to describe when an award of exemplary damages was appropriate. See, eg, JW Salmond, *The Law of Torts: A Treatise on the English Law of Liability for Civil Injuries* (London, Stevens & Haynes, 1907) 102; H McGregor, *Mayne and McGregor on Damages* (London, Sweet & Maxwell, 1961) 207. The phrase continues to be used in Australia, where the High Court has refused to follow *Rookes v Barnard*: see *Uren v John Fairfax & Sons Pty Ltd* (1966) 117 CLR 118 (HCA); *Gray v Motor Accident Commission* (1998) 196 CLR 1 (HCA) [14].

Huckle did not assert a novel power going beyond that practice. Both sides had their advocates, and the House of Commons had tacitly endorsed the practice by refusing to debate a resolution condemning it. Even some of the more strident voices arguing that general warrants were unconstitutional acknowledged that the issue needed judicial resolution so that, as one contemporary pamphlet put it, persons 'may know exactly how the law stands, and be fully apprized of his danger; so that all may provide against it the best they can'.[17] It was not a situation in which the Government engaged in a practice that was universally regarded as illegal or even borderline illegal.

III. HOW DID LORD CAMDEN (PRATT CJ) EXPRESS THE JUSTIFICATION OF THE DAMAGES?

If the previous section explains what the damages were not, how were the damages in fact justified? Lord Camden identified that what appeared to the jury in the most striking light was not the injury to the claimant, but the 'great point of law touching the liberty of the subject'.[18] The case before him involved a magistrate over all the King's subjects exercising arbitrary power and making a 'tyrannical' effort to uphold the legality of the warrant. Apart from being (unconvincingly) 'worse than the Spanish inquisition', this was 'a most daring public attack made upon the liberty of the subject'. The jury was right to award exemplary damages.[19]

Why do we see this centrally in terms of its relationship, and why does this matter? While certainly there is a focus on 'power', power is not simply an abstract concept here. It is exercised over the subject, and is enmeshed in the relationship between ruler and subject. This framing of the relationship draws attention to public acts, and the limits of power properly exercised over subjects. Sayer's treatise, citing a contemporary MS report, reports the damages as having been awarded because the false imprisonment was 'an Attack upon *publick* Liberty'.[20] In other words, as contemporaries understood it, Camden's reference to 'the liberty of the subject' did not simply mean a public attack on Huckle's *personal* liberty. The case involved something more than that, touching on the idea of the liberty of the public. It is not the abstract wrong of 'false imprisonment' or assault, but rather its association with an abuse of power by the Government over an individual, seen specifically as a *subject* and a member of the public, that justifies the exemplary damages awarded. Perhaps it is partly for this reason that the damages departed from the usual expectation, that they

[17] *A Letter to the Right Honourable the Earls of Egremont and Halifax on the Seizure of Papers* (London, J Williams, 1763) 30.

[18] *Huckle* (n 1) Wils KB 207, ER 769.

[19] ibid.

[20] Sayer (n 12) 220 (emphasis added).

would reflect the means of the plaintiff.[21] The award was entirely out of line with the earnings and status of the individual affected.

We can, it is suggested, understand the defence of the jury award better by attending to some features of the political context. The late eighteenth century was a time of bitter political controversy over the forms, ends and limits of government, and Camden's words should be seen against the backdrop of that controversy, which implicated not just the specific government policies that were the subject of the publications that led to Huckle's arrest, but also the broader question of the tactics used by the Government against its political opponents and the impact of those tactics on the ability of politically engaged members of the public to participate in critical debates on public affairs. *Huckle* itself related to the political controversy around the Government's policy in the Seven Years War, which was seen as too soft by more radical factions within the Whigs. The controversy culminated in a scathing criticism, published in issue 45 of *The North Briton* (an anti-Bute weekly paper), of the King's speech opening Parliament, in which the King defended the Treaty of Paris. In response, Lord Halifax as Secretary of State issued a general warrant to four messengers, including John Money, to 'authorize and require' them

> to make strict and diligent Search for the Authors Printers and Publishers of a seditious and treasonable Paper Intitled the North Briton Number XLV … and them or any of them having found to apprehend and seize together with their Papers and to bring in safe Custody before me to be examined concerning the Premises and further dealt with according to Law.[22]

Around 50 arrests were made under this warrant including not just journeymen printers like Huckle, but also the MP John Wilkes, who was the main mover behind *The North Briton*. As Stiles has pointed out, the arrests were seen by contemporaries as being targeted not just against one group of political commentators, but as 'an assault against one particular vision for the future of Britain and its empire', as well as a statement that dissent over imperial management would not be tolerated.[23] The controversy gave rise to debates in Parliament, and also spawned an extensive pamphlet literature that challenged the legality of general warrants more widely, with the chain of events arising out of *The North Briton* seen as instantiating the deeper constitutional problems with the practice. Two of the most influential pamphlets took the form of letters published under the pseudonyms 'Candor'[24] and 'Father

[21] Note that the judgment refers to 'the inconsiderableness of his station and rank in life', along with the absence of substantial material damage, as a factor outweighed in the minds of the jury by 'great points of law touching the liberty of the subject'.

[22] Quoted from a copy of the warrant in the National Archives, TS 11/923.

[23] D Stiles, 'Arresting John Entick: The *Monitor* Controversy and the Imagined British Conquests of the Spanish Empire' (2014) 53 *Journal of British Studies* 934, 935.

[24] *A Letter from Candor to the Public Advertiser*, 2nd edn (London, J Almon, 1764) ('First Letter').

of Candor',[25] respectively. Camden was believed by some contemporaries to have been their author, and at least some modern scholars agree that he contributed to them in collaboration with their publisher, John Almon.[26] A close reading of these pamphlets gives us a deeper insight into the nature of the concerns to which Camden saw exemplary damages as being capable of responding. Regardless of whether Camden was the author, the content of the pamphlets suggests that they were at the very least written by one of his supporters, and the concerns of these pamphlets therefore give us more to go on when interpreting the concerns of the day.

A central concern in the Candor letters is a particular conception of the relationship between the Government and the public. It saw the individual subject as a *liber homo*[27] who, motivated by public virtue, played an active part in the life of a polity.[28] Unless one adopted a conception of society in which private men had no business 'to write or to speak about publick matters',[29] it was inevitable that their writings would come into conflict with government policy. The letters argue that the proceedings for state libel which underpinned the general warrants and the arrests at issue in these cases were, 'ninety-nine times out of a hundred', no more than 'a dispute between the minister and the people.'[30] And here, the wide powers of arrest, search and seizure that general warrants would give to the Government so heavily tilted the balance against the subject that they became 'the means of great persecution' and 'a power necessary for no good purpose, and capable of being put to a very bad one.'[31] By using the full range of powers criminal libel gives the state (as opposed to the relatively weaker powers available to a private person under ordinary common law libel, which was at that time only actionable in case rather than in trespass *vi et armis*),[32] demanding exorbitant sums as bail,[33] playing procedural games for the sole purpose of bankrupting a person accused of state libel,[34] and using the power of their office to 'prevent and baffle the most regular pursuits of Justice',[35] the Government was, in effect, creating a state of affairs where hardly anybody would dare publish a stricture on the administration.[36]

[25] *A Letter Concerning Libels, Warrants, Seizure of Papers, and Security for the Peace*, 5th edn (London, J Almon, 1765) ('Second Letter').
[26] See, eg, A Patterson, *Nobody's Perfect: A New Whig Interpretation of History* (New Haven, Yale University Press, 2002) 44–45.
[27] *First Letter* (n 24) 29–30.
[28] ibid 19.
[29] ibid 11.
[30] *Second Letter* (n 25) 14.
[31] ibid 8.
[32] ibid 19.
[33] ibid 20–21.
[34] ibid 8–9.
[35] *First Letter* (n 24) 26.
[36] *Second Letter* (n 25) 9.

It is against this background that Camden's references to general warrants being an 'attack on publick liberty', 'tyrannical', and raising fundamental issues about 'the liberty of the subject' should be understood. Camden's underlying concern was not as much with the wrong done to the individual plaintiff as a rights-bearer as it was with the impact that purported exercise of power had on the relationship between the Government of the day and the politically engaged subject. The issue, as the Candor letters put it, was 'nearly and intimately' connected with the constitution and 'the liberty of every man living under it.'[37] This liberty was a political liberty, to participate in debate and comment about public affairs. It was this wider relational impact that made the actions at stake in *Huckle* an attack on *public* liberty and of fundamental importance to the constitution, and it was the Government's insistence in claiming and exercising that power that made the case one in which an award of exemplary damages was justifiable.

IV. THE LIBERTY OF THE SUBJECT AND RELATIONALITY

In this section, we delve deeper into the relational justification of exemplary damages in *Huckle v Money* and particularly the relational notion of liberty that is in operation.

In a recent essay on the perception of relationships in private law,[38] we argued that the way in which law perceives relations can be mapped along two axes. The first axis captures perceptions of how symmetric relations are, ranging from relations perceived as wholly symmetric at one end, to wholly asymmetric at the other. The second axis looks at how embedded relations are perceived as being, with relations that are wholly autonomous of society at one end and those that are wholly embedded in society at the other end. These axes give us a bit more insight into the court's perceptions of the nature of the relationship that was at issue in *Huckle v Money*. The case certainly draws attention to asymmetry – the protagonists are of very different status and the one holds power over the other. This is not the interaction of equal parties as might be seen, for example, in the idea of 'give and take', or in the equivalent of classical contract theory transferred to tort in terms of reciprocal limits on freedom. But the perception is also one that is embedded in the particular characteristics of a society and a polity, and particular relation between the parties, rather than being based in

[37] *First Letter* (n 24) 35.

[38] Our work related specifically to mapping perceptions of market relations in the law of contract: TT Arvind and J Steele, 'Remapping Contract Law: Four Perceptions of Markets' in TT Arvind and J Steele (eds), *Contract Law and the Legislature* (Oxford, Hart Publishing, 2020). Freedom of contract is strongly associated with autonomy of and symmetry between parties, for example. Our identification of the two axes was influenced by the work of Mary Douglas, as we discuss in the essay cited above.

simple inequality of power (as we may see, for example, where consumers deal with corporations). The perception of the court – and allegedly the jury – in *Huckle v Money* is not one that is focused on 'autonomy' in the sense of lack of legal coercion so much as embeddedness of these parties in particular roles and a particular form of relationship.

A. Autonomy, Dominion and Liberty

How can we deny centrality to 'autonomy' when the very thing protected is liberty of the subject? As we have argued in the previous section, liberty of the subject here is a relational idea, focused specifically on tyranny. The 'public' roles played by both subject and magistrate are rich and significant. That is not to say no other role would attract a similar response; but these features are part of the perception of the relationship which justifies the award. And both aspects of the relationship are key to the perception of liberty – of the subject – and tyranny – the excess of power by those who govern, over those they govern.

As Quentin Skinner has shown, between the early modern period and the late eighteenth century, political and juristic thought in England (and also elsewhere in Europe) had within it two very different conceptions of liberty. One is the familiar conception of negative liberty, which is focused on autonomy in the sense of lack of legal coercion, and sees liberty as consisting of a state of non-interference in which private persons are left in a position of freedom from constraint. The other conception to which Skinner draws our attention is one he terms 'neo-Roman liberty' (or 'republican liberty'), which sees liberty as consisting of a state of non-domination in which private persons are free not just from actual constraint, but from the possibility of constraint. In this conception, being in a position of dependence is in itself a source of constraint. A person who is aware that they live subject to the arbitrary power of a power-holder will, in this conception, be inherently subject to a non-trivial limitation on their liberty even if that power is not in fact exercised. The awareness that one's freedom depends on the goodwill of another has the effect of reducing one to servitude.[39]

As the discussion in the previous section proposed, it is exactly this conception of liberty that we see at work in Camden's approach to the question in *Huckle*, and in his contribution to the wider political debate. The nature of the power the Government wielded through a general warrant ran counter to the basic principles of the British constitution precisely because, by subjecting the individual to the constant threat of searches, arrests, and 'politico-legal

[39] Q Skinner, *Liberty Before Liberalism* (Cambridge, CUP, 1998) esp 84–96; Q Skinner, 'A Third Concept of Liberty' (2002) 117 *Proceedings of the British Academy* 237, 247ff.

games', it reduced members of the public to a condition where 'no man would venture to utter a syllable in print against any power of office ... however illegally usurped.'[40] It was this potential implicit in the essential character of a relationship of arbitrary dominion that justified the award of exemplary damages in a case where that dominion was exercised, even if the impact on the plaintiff in the particular case was relatively minor. As the Candor letters put it, to ask whether a prisoner of state was treated well was of little relevance, and the fact that the prisoner had been given comforts was 'too ridiculous to be noticed.'[41] The issue was not personal reparation for the bodily injuries the prisoner had sustained, but the consequences for relations between the Government and its subjects of its insistence on asserting the existence of arbitrary executive power over their person and property.

The understanding of *Huckle* we have advanced is not incompatible with general understandings of autonomy which build on richer conceptions of freedom, such as the freedom to plan a life or 'self-authorship'; at the same time, nor is it necessarily opposed to understandings of tort law built on negative liberty. As Skinner pointed out, the 'neo-Roman' understanding of liberty can potentially be understood within the framework of negative liberty, but even so, a theory of negative liberty as non-domination is radically different from, and wholly incommensurable with, a theory of liberty as non-interference.[42] Similarly, whilst the understanding of *Huckle* we have argued for in this chapter is not incompatible with the idea of autonomy, it does at a deeper level demonstrate that the type of autonomy that exemplary damages defended in this instance is one that is built on and embedded in an understanding of the need for the law to be attentive and responsive to the distinctive challenges posed by relationships characterised by arbitrary power.

B. Relationality and the Civil Order

Placing the focus on the republican conception of liberty and on the relational context in which the possibility of arbitrary power arises also highlights the manner in which the understanding of *Huckle* we have advanced differs from punishment-oriented accounts of exemplary damages. Punitive theories of exemplary damages treat them as concerned with punishment in the sense of the imposition of burdensome or painful consequences as retribution for (or deterrence against) particularly egregious types of wrongful conduct. The availability of a remedy of this type in tort is typically justified either on the basis of the wider social costs of the wrong in question,[43] or the need for

[40] *Second Letter* (n 25) 14.
[41] *First Letter* (n 24) 34–35.
[42] Skinner (n 39) 261–62.
[43] See, eg, C Sharkey, 'Punitive Damages as Societal Damages' (2003) 113 *Yale Law Journal* 347.

the legal system to be able to prevent a bad actor from treating harm to others merely as part of the cost of doing business,[44] or because the wilful or malicious character of the wrong gives the claimant 'a right to be punitive'.[45] The account of *Huckle* we have advanced differs significantly from these theories. Nevertheless, it is in sympathy with recent work in criminal law that grounds criminalisation and criminal sanctions not in punitivity in its traditional sense, but in wider principles of civil and constitutional ordering.

Antony Duff has argued that a fundamental purpose of criminalising conduct is to respond to actions that violate a polity's civil order: its shared aims and values, as well as how people should behave towards each other as members of the polity.[46] Criminal law serves an expressive or communicative role, by declaring the core values of that polity, and creating the ability to call to public account persons who violate those norms.[47] Sanctions, on this account, are expressive of 'the equal respect and concern that citizens owe each other', and become an expression of civic responsibility rather than of retribution or deterrence.[48] The court is dealing with a member of the polity who has erred rather than an enemy to be subjugated, and the sanction serves the purpose of being a process of two-way communication, 'from polity to offender and from offender to polity.'[49]

Implicit in Duff's account is a relational conception of criminal law and sanctions, which are seen as reflecting the obligations arising out of the relations between members of a polity. *Huckle* fits much better with this understanding of the role of sanctions than it does with the theories of punishment that have dominated tort scholarship on exemplary damages. Camden's judgment makes explicit his view that the Government's actions were threatening fundamental principles of the civil order, by challenging and seeking to overturn the essential character of the relationship between the Government and the subject in a free polity. The wider context we have discussed also demonstrates that there was a felt need for an expressive judicial statement of what the Government could and could not do against persons who questioned its policies, and how its agents should conduct themselves in dealing with such persons. It was to these ends, rather than to deterrence or retribution, that Camden's judgment in *Huckle* was directed.

It is also easy to see, against this background, why Camden held these considerations to justify the award of exemplary damages. Tort law, and the law

[44] See, eg, M Galanter and D Luban, 'Poetic Justice: Punitive Damages and Legal Pluralism' (1993) 42 *American University Law Review* 1393.

[45] See, eg, B Zipursky, 'A Theory of Punitive Damages' (2005) 84 *Texas Law Review* 105.

[46] RA Duff, 'Criminal Law and the Constitution of Civil Order' (2020) 70 *University of Toronto Law Journal* 4, 13.

[47] ibid 15, 17, 20.

[48] RA Duff, *The Realm of Criminal Law* (Oxford, OUP, 2018) 224.

[49] RA Duff and SE Marshall, 'Civic Punishment' in AW Dzur, I Loader and R Sparks (eds), *Democratic Theory and Mass Incarceration* (Oxford, OUP, 2016) 48.

of obligations more generally, is familiar with the notion that the type of relationship influences both the content of the obligation and the remedy granted for its breach. Much as professionals are held to different standards of care than laypeople in today's law, and relationships of trust and confidence generate distinctive remedies, a relationship in which one person holds arbitrary power over another raises distinctive issues which require a distinctive remedy. In a polity that sees non-domination as a fundamental part of its civil order (as eighteenth-century England arguably did), it is unsurprising that relationships perceived as being those of asymmetric and arbitrary power are seen as a particularly severe violation of the polity's civic order, requiring the stronger communicative and expressive value that the award of exemplary damages carries.

V. SOME OBSERVATIONS ON CURRENT LAW

The 'origin story' of *Huckle v Money* is highly specific. It gives no support for the equivalence of 'exemplary' damages with punishment in the narrow sense explored in Part 3(B); nor for their generalisation across the law of tort. Nevertheless, in making these points about the particular context of *Huckle v Money*, we are not attempting to support limiting categories, or to defend the specific category-based approach to exemplary damages taken in cases like *Rookes v Barnard*. Our point is a wider one. Skinner pointed out that a central contribution of intellectual history is to bring to light neglected riches from our intellectual heritage, as a trigger for reflection on normative concepts we might otherwise take for granted. *Huckle v Money*, as we have sought to show in this chapter, presents precisely such riches, in the relationally rich, embedded perception it evidences of the action and the remedy awarded. In addition, the fact that it continues to be seen as a case with present-day (and not merely historical) relevance to our understanding of the ends and purposes of tort law means that the riches it contains continue to be of relevance and utility to the way the role of damages in tort law is perceived.

Huckle presents a contrast with modern human rights jurisprudence under the ECHR, where exemplary damages are not awarded – at least, not explicitly[50] – but there is more freedom to compensate for distress, including distress at the violation, as an element of 'restitutio in integrum'. *Huckle*, in contrast, is structured around the misuse of power rather than solely the impact on the rights-bearer – a structure that relevant modern common law actions arguably continue to reflect. In *Huckle*, the framing of the relationship was very

[50] In her chapter on *Kuddus v Chief Constable of Leicestershire Constabulary* [2001] UKHL 29, [2002] 2 AC 122 in this volume, Katsampouka argues that UK courts have awarded damages that are de facto punitive in several human rights cases: see Katsampouka, ch 10 of this volume, p 221.

important to the understanding of why this award was thought to have been chosen by the jury, and why it was legitimate. The events smack of tyranny.

What, then, are the implications of this for exemplary damages in the present day? A full analysis is well beyond the scope of this chapter, but three broad points can be made.

Firstly, at one level, our analysis suggests that attempts to limit the availability of exemplary damages to certain causes of action may be off the mark. The problem of relationships of domination and arbitrary power to which *Huckle* sought to respond does not occur only in the context of particular causes of action, and cause of action limitations are only intuitively attractive, if at all, to the extent that they are proxies for the types of relationship that might be in play. In this, our argument is in sympathy with the approach taken in recent cases such as *Kuddus*[51] and, indeed, can perhaps be seen as fleshing out in greater detail what leads certain types of actions to be legally regarded as so outrageous as to lead to the award of exemplary damages.

Nevertheless, and secondly, our analysis does suggest that the idea of reasoning through different categories may not be wholly inappropriate. Not all types of relationships and not all cases of exemplary damages will necessarily have the same justification, and attempts to create a general set of rules applicable across all contexts are unlikely to be able to deal adequately with the full range of factors that apply across different contexts. Arguably, a reliance on conventional awards that cut across different categories of relationships somewhat blunts the edge which the award in *Huckle* had by reason of being significantly larger than the actual harm suffered. If, as we have argued, exemplary damages respond to actions that violate a polity's civil order in the context of a relationship of arbitrary and asymmetric power, then it is obvious that they will need to be tailored to the considerations that are specific to a particular type of relationship. Categories may well provide a useful, heuristic guide to reasoning through the diversity of considerations that apply across different types of relationship. Certainly, the discussion above may be taken to have shown that the first category in *Rookes* has perhaps more substance, and the focus on particularly bad behaviour perhaps less, than the critics of *Rookes* have necessarily allowed.

Thirdly and finally, framing exemplary damages as a communicative and expressive response to the exercise of arbitrary, asymmetric power, and the ability to call to account those who use that power to challenge a polity's civil order, highlights the continuing role these damages could play within tort law and even private law more broadly. Certainly, this framing suggests that their importance extends beyond cases involving the executive. Conceivably, some 'private' parties could be judged to have acted tyrannically. For example, the

[51] *Kuddus* (n 50).

exercise of total power by traffickers over their victims in an instance of modern slavery may be approached in the same way, even without the 'public' nature of the attacks – and, indeed, viewing it in these terms gives a far clearer sense of why the award of exemplary damages in a case like *AT v Dulghieru*[52] was both appropriate and in keeping with the purpose these damages serve. Equally, it suggests that there may be a need to reconsider whether the rejection of exemplary damages in cases that arguably did involve the assertion and exercise of arbitrary power, such as *Constantine v Imperial Hotels Ltd*,[53] was appropriate or necessary.

But even in less extreme contexts, the everyday actions of powerful economic entities can and do lead courts to award exemplary damages against them. In *Ramzan v Brookwide Ltd*,[54] for example, the defendant forcibly incorporated into its own property a storeroom belonging to the claimants, which left them unable to use a significant portion of their property. The courts found as a matter of fact that they did so on the assumption that it was unlikely that an aggrieved party was likely to be prepared to 'take on an opponent of Brookwide's size, financial backing, and acumen'.[55] The Court of Appeal held that exemplary damages were appropriate because Brookwide's conduct was so egregious that it was 'a totally unacceptable way of resolving the issues as to the ownership of property in a democratic society subject to the rule of law.'[56]

The approach we have advanced also helps us to make sense of the body of case law relating to the use of exemplary damages as a response to unlawful evictions of tenants by landlords. The damages in these cases are awarded in tort for trespass rather than for breach of the tenancy agreement itself, and they are usually justified with reference to the second category in *Rookes*, namely, conduct calculated to make a profit. Nevertheless, a closer examination of their facts suggests that they are influenced by the fact that the cases involved the exercise of arbitrary power in an asymmetric relationship. The leading case of *Drane v Evangelou*[57] – which was one of the first cases to recognise the possibility of awarding exemplary damages for unlawful eviction – involved the forceful invasion of the tenanted property to remove the tenant and their belongings without their consent in a manner that the judge at first instance described as 'monstrous'. But, crucially, the courts have also been willing to award exemplary damages in cases where the exercise of arbitrary power took a non-violent form. In *Design Progression Ltd v Thurloe Properties Ltd*,[58] the exercise of arbitrary power took the form of a breach of the statutory duty to respond within

[52] *AT v Dulghieru* [2009] EWHC 225 (QB).
[53] *Constantine v Imperial Hotels Ltd* [1944] KB 693 (KBD).
[54] *Ramzan v Brookwide Ltd* [2011] EWCA Civ 985, [2012] 1 All ER 903.
[55] ibid [75] (Arden LJ).
[56] ibid [83] (Arden LJ).
[57] *Drane v Evangelou* [1978] 1 WLR 455 (CA). See also *McMillan v Singh* (1985) 17 HLR 120 (CA).
[58] *Design Progression Ltd v Thurloe Properties Ltd* [2004] EWHC 324 (Ch), [2005] 1 WLR 1.

a reasonable time to a request to assign a lease.[59] Here, too, the defendant's actions were expressly directed towards frustrating the claimant's legitimate expectations and to obtaining possession through an abuse of power rather than through negotiation, in a manner that led the court to conclude that it was necessary 'to mark a disapproval'.[60]

Of course, the types of cases discussed above – whether relating to modern-day slavery or to rogue landlords – are also likely to be imbued with bad motive, profit motive and aggravated injury. But whilst these may be contributing factors, the fact that they were not the case in *Huckle v Money* itself, as we have shown above, suggests that they are not essential to the conception of exemplary damages that underpins that case. Nevertheless, these diverse cases may illustrate that the relational approach and concern with power that underpins the decision in *Huckle* can resurface in a range of different contemporary contexts. On the conception we have advanced, it is, in each of these contexts, to the task of regulating relationships of arbitrary power in a manner that communicates and upholds the polity's civil order that the award of exemplary damages is directed.

VI. THE VARIETY OF TORT'S RELATIONS

Timothy Endicott has suggested that landmark cases are cases that serve as guides to the legal landscape.[61] In that sense, as we have sought to argue in this chapter, *Huckle v Money* fully deserves its place as a landmark case on the law of exemplary damages. It serves as a guide to the legal landscape in at least two ways.

Firstly, it does so by providing a better guide to the portion of the legal landscape that involves exemplary damages. The issues that gave rise to the litigation in *Huckle* were important and contested ones, and the decision in *Huckle* represented a considered intervention in those issues. A closer focus on the issues and the nature of the intervention sheds light not just on why *Huckle* was decided in the way it was, but more broadly on the factors and considerations that underpin the award of exemplary damages, and their relationship to the wider issues and concerns with which tort law is called upon to deal. It sheds light, in particular, on the centrality of relational considerations to the award of exemplary damages, and it suggests a need to focus more closely on the ways in which exemplary damages are closely bound up with the roles of tort law in regulating

[59] Landlord and Tenant Act 1988, s 108.
[60] *Design Progression* (n 58) [146] (Smith J).
[61] T Endicott, 'Was *Entick v Carrington* a Landmark?' in A Tomkins and P Scott (eds), *Entick v Carrington: 250 Years of the Rule of Law* (Oxford, Hart Publishing, 2015).

relationships, and in responding to the challenges that power, asymmetry and dominion present to the civil order of a liberal polity.

Secondly, and perhaps more importantly, it provides a guide to the methodological challenges involved in drawing on legal theory to analyse a challenging area of law. Exploration of *Huckle v Money* allows the shining of light on a less visited area of tort theory. Tort as a whole has proved resistant to being theorised simply and coherently with equal respect for all areas. Negligence, for example, is either treated as the core of tort, or as entirely peripheral. Part of the solution to this problem lies in recognition of variety, not merely in legal frameworks and tests (which may be seen as 'accidents of history' or different ways to put together a wrong), but in relationships in which the law of tort is called upon for a response. There is no one perception of all tort's relations which underlies the entirety of the law. Different perceptions may be reasonably well aligned with some substantive causes of action or remedies, but only to an extent. There is no substitute, we suggest, for seeking to understand the legal rules and principles in relation to the concerns which motivated their development. *Huckle v Money* represents the law's response, in its day, to the question of the role of damages in respect of a failure to abide by restriction on government power to detain a subject in accordance with law. It is only through an examination of that context that we can achieve a fuller appreciation of its relevance to the present day.

2

Wilkes v Wood (1763) General Warrants and Punitive Damages

DAVID IBBETSON

IT IS NOT at all clear that *Wilkes v Wood*[1] is a landmark case on exemplary or punitive damages. It is without doubt a major constitutional case, and it certainly seems to be a case where exemplary damages were awarded in which the propriety of the award was in issue. But for all that, the measure of damages is simply passed over almost in silence in the judgment, and it may be the very fact that the measure of damages is not seen as an especially important issue is what makes it an interesting case on the subject. But much more revealing about the courts' attitudes to the whole subject is a follow-up, unreported, case, *Wilkes v Lord Halifax*.

In this chapter I will deal first with the development of the law relating to damages in tortious claims at common law, and then move on to the cases themselves.[2]

The starting point for the common law, explicit by the sixteenth century, was that damages fell to be assessed by the jury. In the Middle Ages the only exception to this was found in cases of maim – serious personal injury – where the judges could see the extent of the injury for themselves. This is not to say that the judges were powerless, for they might express a view to the jury of what they should do; but in the nature of the surviving records and reports, this is something which we cannot easily see. The action on the case for defamation in the sixteenth century provides the best illustration of what might happen when damages were at large and opinions might differ

[1] *Wilkes v Wood* (1763) Lofft 1, 98 ER 489. I have relied also on newspaper reports from the British Newspaper Archive (www.britishnewspaperarchive.co.uk), which are replete with details not found in Lofft.

[2] D Ibbetson, 'Tortious Damages at Common Law' in R Gamauf (ed), *Ausgleich oder Busse als Grundproblem des Schadenerstazrechts von der Lex Aquilia zur Gegenwart* (Vienna, Manz, 2016) 97–107.

as to what the proper measure of damages was. If the judges thought that the damages awarded were too small and they were able to assess them themselves, they might increase the amount awarded to the injured party in order to get closer to what they thought was an appropriate level of compensation. If the judges thought that the damages awarded were too high, they might simply refuse to enter judgment unless the plaintiff 'voluntarily' remitted part of the award.[3]

In the seventeenth century we begin to see the judicial perception of the criteria which should be applied in the assessment of damages. The jury might take into account not merely the injury suffered by the plaintiff but also the wickedness of the defendant's conduct. As Thomas Hobbes put it, seemingly reflecting the language of Grotius, the purpose was not to punish the defendant but to give both reparation and satisfaction.[4] Damages were purely plaintiff-oriented.

At the very start of the eighteenth century Sir John Holt CJ stressed that although the assessment of damages was a matter for the jury they were nonetheless under the control of the court, and the jury could be asked to give reasons why they had assessed the damages at a particular level. This is illustrated in the case of *Ash v Ash*.[5] A girl brought an action against her mother claiming that the mother and an apothecary had administered medicine to her, insisting that she was mentally deranged. The jury found in her favour and awarded damages of £2,000. Holt CJ thought this was clearly excessive – it was obviously an enormous sum – and when the jury refused to explain why they had so acted he ordered a new trial. Damages were undoubtedly a matter for the jury, but the judges were not powerless. Lord Mansfield CJ, later in the century, discussed how far this could go:

> I should be sorry to say that in cases of personal torts no new trial should ever be granted for damages which manifestly show the jury to have been actuated by passion, partiality or prejudice. But it is not to be done without very strong grounds indeed; and such as carry evidence of intemperance in the minds of the jury. It is by no means to be done where the court may feel that if they had been on the jury they would have given less damages.[6]

The judges would only intervene if the damages were 'flagrantly outrageous',[7] but if they did meet this threshold judicial intervention was appropriate. The result of this was that damages might be awarded on a non-compensatory basis

[3] eg, *Lassells v Lassells* (1595) British Library MS Add 25198 f.12v (court refuses to enter judgment when jury awarded £250 in a defamation suit by a father against his son); *Bonham v Sturton* (1554) Dyer 105, 73 ER 230.

[4] T Hobbes, *The Art of Rhetoric, With A Discourse of the Laws of England* (London, William Crooke, 1681) 46.

[5] *Ash v Ash* (1701) Comb 357, 90 ER 526.

[6] *Gilbert v Burtenshaw* (1774) 1 Cowp 230, 231; 98 ER 1059, 1060.

[7] ibid (Lord Mansfield CJ).

where it was not outrageous to do so. And the term coming to be used for such non-compensatory but not outrageous damages was that they were exemplary. This had been explained by Lord Mansfield shortly before *Wilkes v Wood*: 'The damages are for public example as well as private recompence.'[8] Against that background we can turn to *Wilkes v Wood* itself.

The facts of the case are very well known. John Wilkes, publisher of *The North Briton*, was the plaintiff. His house had been entered without his permission, pursuant to a general warrant issued by the Secretary of State, Lord Halifax, authorising the arrest of the writer or publisher of number 45 of *The North Briton* and the seizure of papers. Wilkes himself was placed into custody, his house was searched and his papers impounded. From a constitutional point of view, the case is significant as one of that group of cases in the 1760s dealing with the legitimacy of general warrants, or more generally of the power of arbitrary search and seizure by the state. And from that point of view, it fits well into the history of exemplary damages for egregious conduct by officers of the state.

The case is reported at length in Lofft's reports. It was an action of trespass for entry into the plaintiff's house, breaking his locks and seizing his papers. The form of action therefore was unexceptionable: trespass to land and trespass to goods, with the plaintiff's damages being laid at £5,000. It is worth noting at the start that it was not an action of trespass to the person, suggesting clearly that Wilkes' intention was to get a ruling on the legitimacy of the general warrant as a basis for seizing property. The first step that was taken by Wilkes' friends was to seek a writ of *habeas corpus*. After a brief delay, in which a new warrant was issued naming Wilkes himself, this was heard in the court of Common Pleas (though we might notice in passing that it would be more regular to hear this in the King's Bench). At this hearing Chief Justice Pratt, significantly, is reported to have held that general warrants were not unlawful in themselves, but this was irrelevant on the facts; Wilkes was a Member of Parliament, and that made his arrest unlawful.[9] Parliamentary privilege allowed the arrest of a Member only in limited cases, and the alleged publishing of a libel was not one of those.

Some two weeks later Wilkes initiated actions for trespass to land and trespass to goods against the two secretaries of state, Lord Halifax and the Lord Egremont, their deputies, Wood and Webb, and the Royal messengers who had carried out the search.[10] The case with which we are concerned here was the one against Wood. As a deputy of the secretaries of state (although, on the evidence, he was responsible to Lord Egremont rather than Lord Halifax), he was in some position of authority, but he had not been present for the whole time of the

[8] *Wilford v Buckley (Berkeley)* (1758) 1 Burr 609, 97 ER 472 quoted by J Oldham, *Trial by Jury* (New York, NYU Press, 2006) 71.

[9] *Derby Post*, 5 May 1763.

[10] *Salisbury Journal*, 16 May 1763; *Aris's Birmingham Gazette*, 30 May 1763.

search nor was he the person who had issued the warrant for it. He was at best in the middle of the line of authority. That the action proceeded against him personally while all the other actions were delayed may perhaps indicate that he had been selected as the fall guy to test the law. But this is not clear.

The first problem in the action against him was that he too was a Member of Parliament. It appears that at first he pleaded his parliamentary privilege, but at some stage this was withdrawn, replaced by a general plea of not guilty or in the alternative a special justification based on the legitimacy of the general warrant. This was in November 1763, more than six months after the seizure of the papers.[11] Significantly, the brief newspaper report of this hearing allowing the change of plea is immediately followed by an equally brief report of *Huckle v Money*, specifically on the issue of the measure of damages which had been awarded. The case against Wood, therefore, could proceed.

At this point we can turn to the arguments in the case as reported in Lofft's reports. Sergeant Glyn laid it on thick, stressing the interference with the liberty of the subject that was involved in the breaking into a man's house and seizing his papers, not just the liberty of Wilkes himself but the liberty of all English people. It was, it is true, exacerbated in Wilkes' case, since as a member of Parliament he might be thought to have had confidential papers in his desk; but this was not allowed to detract from the fundamental point that general warrants were ineffective in themselves. They were not simply an outrage to Wilkes, but an outrage to the very Constitution. A Secretary of State had no greater power than the meanest justice of the peace, and a justice of the peace would have no power to issue a search warrant without naming either the suspect or the crime suspected. It was at this point that he turned to the measure of damages:

> That the constitution of our country had been so fatally wounded, that it called aloud for the redress of a jury of Englishmen. That their resentment against such proceedings was to be expressed by large and exemplary damages; that trifling damages would put no stop at all to such proceedings: which would plainly appear, when they would consider the persons concerned in the present prosecution, persons, who by their duty and office should be the protectors of the constitution, instead of the violators of it.[12]

Sergeant Glyn was followed by James Eyre, the recorder of London. He dealt with precedents for such general warrants, which had been in use since 1662, dismissing their relevance to the present situation. Given that Pratt CJ had held in the *habeas corpus* suit that general warrants were lawful, we should see the recorder's argument as being the one which was most fundamental as a matter of law; nothing was said by him as to the measure of damages.

[11] *Ipswich Journal*, 19 November 1763.
[12] *Wilkes* (n 1) Lofft 2–3, ER 490.

Wood's case was put by the Solicitor General. Somewhat ingenuously, he asked why the action was brought against Wood and not against one of the secretaries of state. 'If the constitution had been in such an egregious manner attacked, why not bring the secretaries of state themselves in the court?'[13] There was an easy answer to that as the Solicitor General no doubt knew. Lord Halifax had been using every trick known to the well-advised litigant to avoid entering an appearance in order to answer Wilkes' claim.[14] Moreover, he argued, it was not for an individual citizen to seek to defend the Constitution; that was a public matter which would in appropriate circumstances be a matter for the criminal law. He took issue with the recorder of London's argument that there were no relevant precedents of such general warrants and argued that Wilkes was in fact guilty of sedition in the publication of the relevant issue of *The North Briton*. Finally, he turned, apparently briefly, to the question of damages. Wilkes was not worthy of exemplary damages, but was an incendiary and a blackguard. 'Damages should always be reckoned according to the injury received. A jury that ever acted on any other principles certainly forswore themselves.'[15]

After further argument Pratt CJ summed up to the jury. His focus was on whether it had been satisfactorily proved that Wilkes was in fact the author or publisher of the relevant issue of *The North Briton*. He then turned to the question whether the Secretary of State had the power to issue a general warrant in this form, something that was not open to an ordinary magistrate. And it was this that gave rise to the question of the appropriate measure of damages.

> Notwithstanding what Mr solicitor general has said, I have formerly delivered it as my opinion on another occasion, and I still continue of the same mind, that a jury have it in their power to give damages for more than the injury received. Damages are designed not only as a satisfaction to the injured party, but likewise as a punishment of the guilty, to deter from any such proceeding for the future, and as a proof of the detestation of the jury to the action itself.[16]

The jury took heed of his words. After deliberating for 30 minutes they brought in a verdict for Wilkes with damages of £1,000.

We might just summarise at this point the functions of exemplary damages:

- They make it possible for the jury to express their extreme disapproval of the defendant's conduct, and for Sergeant Glyn this disapproval might stem from the arbitrary misuse of power by a public official.
- They can act as a deterrent to the defendant and others from acting in this way in the future.

[13] ibid Lofft 8, ER 493.
[14] The various steps taken are detailed in *Aris's Birmingham Gazette*, 10 September 1764.
[15] *Wilkes* (n 1) Lofft 10, ER 494.
[16] ibid Lofft 18–19, ER 498–99.

- According to Pratt CJ, though perhaps not for Sergeant Glyn, they can have the effect of punishing the defendant.

We could leave *Wilkes v Wood* at that point, but it is not by any means the end of the story. Wilkes was prosecuted for seditious libel, and found guilty. However, by this time he was in Paris, and was convicted *in absentia*. Following the normal procedure, a convicted criminal who had escaped punishment by flight was outlawed. The consequence of his outlawry was that all other actions which had been brought by him were stayed. In particular, this meant that the action he had been pursuing against Lord Halifax since 1763, but in which he had met with the defendant's delaying tactics, was brought to a halt. But it was only a temporary halt. In the middle of 1768 Wilkes returned to England and brought a common form writ of error to reverse his outlawry.[17] Once he was no longer an outlaw he was able to recommence his suit against Lord Halifax, and the case was revived in the June of that year. There were, not unexpectedly, further delays and the case only came up for trial before Wilmot CJ in November 1769.[18]

The case is unreported, but the newspaper reports enable us to reconstruct the proceedings with some confidence.

Very substantial damages were sought, far greater than had been recovered in the action against Wood. As the trial was looming Wilkes is said to have been advised not to assign his prospective damages to anyone for less than £15,000. In this suit, it appears that the damages were the primary issue; the facts were not really in dispute. Wilmot CJ directed the jury that the damages they awarded, assuming they found for the plaintiff, should be 'liberal but not excessive'.[19] The jury no doubt took heed of this and awarded Wilkes £4,000.

We cannot regard this sum as in any way compensatory. Presumptively, the damages which had been awarded against Wood five years previously had dealt with the compensation, which in any event must surely have been fairly small. Moreover, contrary to what Pratt CJ had said in the earlier case, there could have been no element of punishment of Lord Halifax here. In 1765 he had been given an indemnity by the Crown, in the person of the Lord Privy Seal, against any damages which should be awarded against him;[20] the £4,000 was not going to come out of his pocket.

Could they be seen as a deterrent? Would a future minister be put off doing what he thought was the right thing, albeit something illegal, by the prospect of a large damages award which would in fact be met by somebody else? We may rather doubt it.

All we are left with is that the award of damages allowed the jury to express their justified disapproval of the defendant's high-handed conduct. This fits the

[17] *Stamford Mercury*, 28 April 1768; *Derby Mercury*, 6 May 1768.
[18] *Kentish Gazette*, 11 November 1769; *Aris's Birmingham Gazette*, 13 November 1769.
[19] *Gilbert* (n 6) Cowp 231, ER 1060 (Lord Mansfield CJ).
[20] *Kentish Gazette*, 11 November 1769.

approach in the case into the framework of the law which was developing in the eighteenth century. Damages fell to be assessed by the jury and it was only if they were 'manifestly outrageous' in the eyes of the judge that a new trial should be awarded. The exemplary damages awarded here, liberal no doubt but in the eyes of the Chief Justice not excessive, were not manifestly outrageous in the sense demanded by the law.

3

Bell v Midland Railway Company (1861)
The Curious Case of Disputing Directors

EMILY GORDON

I. INTRODUCTION

IN MODERN LIFE, we are accustomed to the idea of bodies corporate 'acting' in a separate capacity from the people who make the decisions for them. However, this was a relatively new concept that courts were increasingly forced to confront during the nineteenth century as railway companies proliferated and transformed life and trade in the United Kingdom. The focus of this chapter[1] is *Bell v Midland Railway Company*,[2] a decision of the Court of Common Pleas concerning deliberate interference by a railway company with the use of a private railway siding. This is a case that features in *Rookes v Barnard*[3] and the change of direction in the law of exemplary damages brought about there. The nature of the actionable wrong in *Bell* is not clearly articulated in the reports.[4] There are some indicators that it was considered to

[1] I am grateful to Mr Dave Harris and Dr Roger Brettle, of the Midland Railway Society, for their guidance and provision of information about the railway and its directors. I was greatly assisted by the article in the *Midland Railway Society Journal* on this dispute: R Brettle and C Rouse, 'The Strange Dispute between John Fox Bell and the Midland Railway Company' (2003) 24 *Midland Railway Society Journal* 1. I am also grateful to Professor Paul Mitchell for his very helpful comments on an early draft of this chapter. Any errors or oversights are my own.

[2] *Bell v Midland Railway Company* (1861) 10 CB (NS) 287, 142 ER 462.

[3] *Rookes v Barnard* [1964] AC 1129 (HL).

[4] See *Bell* (1861) 10 CB (NS) 287, 142 ER 462; (1861) SC 30 LJCP 273; (1861) 4 LT 293; (1861) 9 WR 612. Some reports contain the assertion that this was not a case of trespass: (1861) 4 LT 293, 296; (1861) 9 WR 612, 614.

be a form of nuisance.[5] It might also have been an instance of breach of a statutory duty.[6] Whatever the nature of the wrong, it is the *Bell* court's comments on remedies in this case that demand attention.

Before *Rookes*, malicious, insolent, dishonest or 'contumelious'[7] conduct might result in an award of exemplary damages – that is, damages over and above an amount that reflected or compensated the loss suffered. The defendant's motive would be of central importance in a court's decision to award such damages.[8] The purpose was generally said to be punitive, which Lord Devlin in *Rookes* described as 'confus[ing] the civil and criminal functions of the law', the civil law being concerned with compensation rather than punishment.[9] However, he appeared to feel forced by precedent to recognise three categories of case in which such damages were available.[10] The nature of these categories has been considered in more detail elsewhere in this volume. Discussion in this chapter will be confined to Lord Devlin's second category.

Bell was treated by Lord Devlin as the beginning of a line of authority compelling recognition of a category of case in which exemplary damages may be awarded: cases of conduct calculated to make a profit exceeding compensation payable to the plaintiff.[11] Though upheld by the House of Lords some years later,[12] Lord Devlin's reasoning has been subjected to much criticism.[13] Less than a decade after *Rookes*, the Court of Appeal in *Cassell & Co Ltd v Broome*[14] decided that it should not be followed.[15] There is some irony in that a key finding in taking this drastic position was that there was insufficient authority for the categories Lord Devlin felt compelled to recognise – according to Salmon LJ, they were 'conjured out of the air … with the most strange and unfortunate results'.[16]

[5] In one report, counsel for the defendant railway company relies on various authorities for the proposition that 'to entitle a reversioner to maintain an action for a nuisance or obstruction to his tenants, the thing done must be of a permanent character': *Bell* (n 2) CB (NS) 301, ER 468. In Kerr's 1878 treatise, *A Treatise on the Law and Practice of Injunctions*, *Bell* is cited in the part entitled 'Injunctions for Nuisance', for the proposition that for a reversioner to be able to bring an action for a nuisance, it is necessary for the act done to be injurious to the reversion – by being permanent in nature or operating as a denial of a right: WW Kerr, *A Treatise on the Law and Practice of Injunctions*, 2nd edn (London, W Maxwell and Son, 1878) 170.

[6] The declaration referred to 'breaches of duty'.

[7] See *Cassell & Co Ltd v Broome* [1971] 2 QB 354 (CA) 379 (Lord Denning MR) (hereafter '*Broome* (CA)').

[8] This had been confirmed in, eg, *Emblen v Myers* (1860) 6 Hurl & N 54, 158 ER 23. See discussion in P Mitchell, *The Making of the Modern Law of Defamation* (Oxford, Hart Publishing, 2005) 64–67.

[9] *Rookes* (n 3) 1221.

[10] ibid.

[11] ibid 1123, 1126.

[12] *Cassell & Co v Broome* [1972] AC 1027 (HL) ('*Broome* (HL)').

[13] See, eg, discussion in Mitchell (n 8) 68–69 and sources there cited.

[14] *Broome* (CA) (n 7).

[15] As noted above, this was overturned by the House of Lords in *Broome* (HL) (n 12).

[16] *Broome* (CA) (n 7) 391.

This chapter considers the peculiar story of Mr Bell's action against the Midland Railway Company, and the extent to which *Bell* can be considered to support Lord Devlin's second category. It will be suggested that, on a close reading of the reasoning in *Bell*, and upon consideration of further features of the story, *Bell* ought not, in fact, be considered a landmark decision in the law of exemplary damages. As a case of a court allowing an inflated damages award in response to malicious behaviour by the defendant, it was simply another example of a principle that was well established in the nineteenth century – that conduct motivated by malice or in contempt of authority or another's rights might be addressed by a higher award of damages. The decision in *Bell* certainly did not compel Lord Devlin's creation of the second category. It will be argued that profit-making may have been a part of the motivation for the defendant's conduct, but it was neither the principal focus of the court in allowing the award to stand, nor was it likely to have been the principal focus of the defendant in choosing a course of conduct. This was not simply a dispute between commercial parties; it was a dispute between long-standing colleagues: Mr Bell, the plaintiff, was a director of the defendant railway company at the time during which the latter obstructed the use of his siding. *Bell* was likely not truly about money at all; instead, it is a case reflecting both the directors' and the court's concerns with commercial morality.

It is hoped that this chapter will shed light on the true nature of this case and its uneasy role in establishing the restrictive rule in *Rookes*.

II. THE DISPUTE IN *BELL*

A. Outline of Events

The basic facts as reported in the various law reports[17] are as follows. The plaintiff, Mr Bell, owned land near Leicester railway station. In 1839, he had built a coal wharf on his land and, in accordance with the Act of incorporation of the defendant railway company (at the time, called Midland Counties Railway) and with the consent of that company by resolution,[18] installed a short track known as a 'siding' on his land on the side of the railway line. This was done to connect the railway to the plaintiff's wharf. Mr Bell had sold land to the defendant when it built the line through Leicester, and he remained the owner of land adjoining the railway.[19] He had also flattened a hill on his property and sold to the company the corresponding earth for use in building embankments; according to Mr Bell, this was done at the request of the company's engineer and in return

[17] See n 4.
[18] *Bell v Midland Railway Co* (1859) 3 De G&J 673, 676, 44 ER 1429, 1430.
[19] See, eg, ibid De G&J 676, ER 1430; R Brettle and C Rouse, 'The Strange Dispute between John Fox Bell and the Midland Railway Company' (2003) 24 *Midland Railway Society Journal* 1.

for permission to build the siding near Leicester station.[20] It was on the flattened site that the plaintiff chose to build the wharf.[21]

In May 1844, Midland Counties Railway was dissolved and joined other companies to form the Midland Railway Company (MRC). It continued to carry goods along the railway line and the siding for the plaintiff and his wharf tenants until 1857. However, in 1857, the MRC constructed its own wharf on the opposite side of the railway to the plaintiff's. In what the jury found was a deliberate step to draw trade away from the plaintiff's wharf and into its own, the MRC informed the plaintiff by letter in June 1857 that it would from 30 September no longer provide engine-power to carry goods to the plaintiff's wharf. On 1 October, when waggons intended for the plaintiff's wharf reached the siding, rather than stopping at the junction and sending them down the siding, as it had been doing previously, the MRC had them carried to its own wharf and left them there.[22] When one of the plaintiff's tenants went with horses to retrieve the waggons, access to the MRC wharf was refused.[23]

During further correspondence, the defendant denied that the plaintiff held a right to a communication by the siding with the railway.[24] It was alleged that the chairman of the MRC, Mr Ellis, had said to the plaintiff, 'That wharf shall never be a wharf again if I can help it'.[25] Eventually carriages were placed across the junction to prevent access to the plaintiff's wharf by the railway, and then, in December 1857, a wooden platform was erected to completely block the siding.[26] This physical obstruction persisted until the plaintiff obtained an injunction.[27] It seems the MRC courted the plaintiff's tenants, suggesting that they move their business to its wharf. The plaintiff ceased to receive royalties for goods transported through the wharf, and his tenants left the wharf – at least one took their business to the MRC wharf.[28]

B. Before the Courts

i. Bell v Midland Railway Company *(1859): The Claim for Injunctive Relief*

When attempts failed by Mr Bell to dissuade the company's (other) directors from their course,[29] he sought the assistance of the courts in 1858.[30]

[20] *Bell* (n 18) De G&J 680, ER 1432; Brettle and Rouse (n 19) 1.
[21] *Bell* (n 18) De G&J 680, ER 1432. See also Brettle and Rouse (n 19) 1.
[22] *Bell* (n 2) CB (NS) 292, ER 464.
[23] *Bell* (n 4) (1861) 9 WR 612, 613.
[24] See *Bell* (n 18) De G&J 680, ER 1431; *Bell* (n 2) CB (NS) 291–92, ER 464.
[25] *Bell* (n 2) CB (NS) 292, ER 464.
[26] ibid CB (NS) 292–93, ER 465.
[27] See discussion below accompanying nn 30–39.
[28] *Bell* (n 2) CB (NS) 293, ER 465.
[29] See, eg, *Bell* (n 4) WR 613. See also discussion below accompanying nn 134 and 139.
[30] *Bell* (n 2) CB (NS) 305, ER 470.

He was granted a perpetual injunction by Vice-Chancellor Wood to restrain the MRC from obstructing the link between the railway line and his wharf.[31] The defendant company appealed this decision but was ultimately unsuccessful.[32] It argued that there was no right to a physical link with the railway or to use that link, that the siding had been created under a misapprehension, and if there was such a right then the exercise of the right claimed by Mr Bell would 'be attended with the utmost danger to the public', as traffic had increased 'greatly beyond its extent at the date of the resolution'.[33]

Turner LJ was not convinced by the defendant's arguments; even if there had been a misunderstanding in its creation, the company had permitted the exercise of the right for nearly 20 years.[34] He found that there was no power in the company's Act of incorporation to revoke consent to the creation of the branch once it had been introduced;[35] this was a case concerning a right 'conferred by the Act of Parliament', not one of licence.[36] As to the 'public danger' argument, he commented wryly that the siding had been used for 17 years with no danger being 'apprehended', but disposed of the point by saying that the courts had no power to interfere on this ground under the Act.[37] Turner LJ's decision is based principally on the 'true construction of the Act'.[38]

In a short declaration asserting his agreement with Turner LJ, Knight-Bruce LJ added the following rebuke to what he saw as a dishonest corporate defendant:[39]

> I hope and believe that not one of the directors would, as an individual, or for the sake of his private interests, have been capable of conduct such as that which the directors, associated together and acting in a kind of corporate capacity, have persuaded themselves not to be inconsistent with fair and upright dealing: but it is, at least, as necessary for directors as for others to be convinced, and to act upon the conviction, that dishonesty is the worst policy.

The Lords Justices' handling of this case is consistent with attitudes generally held by the judiciary towards large corporations and the separate corporate body at the time.[40] In the mid-Victorian period, judges were often suspicious and cautious about the scope of corporate power and tended towards strict

[31] See *Bell* (n 18).
[32] ibid.
[33] ibid De G&J 682, ER 1432.
[34] ibid De G&J 684–85, ER 1433.
[35] ibid De G&J 685–86, ER 1433–34.
[36] ibid De G&J 689, ER 1435.
[37] ibid De G&J 687–88, ER 1434.
[38] ibid De G&J 683, ER 1433.
[39] ibid De G&J 689, ER 1435.
[40] See RW Kostal, *Law and English Railway Capitalism 1825–1875* (Oxford, Clarendon Press, 1994) 218–19.

construction of the legislation establishing companies.[41] A narrow construction of the powers that the statute permitted the railway company was certainly employed in this instance. Knight-Bruce LJ's comments also suggest that he thought the directors had perhaps acted less honestly than they might otherwise have done, had they been acting as individuals rather than as a group hidden behind the corporate veil. That it was said to be *at least as necessary*, if not more, for directors of a corporation to behave with honesty, does rather indicate some concern for unchecked corporate power and what the 'corporate body' might persuade otherwise fair-minded individuals to do. Newspaper reports of the proceedings contain further interesting details of the exchange between counsel and the bench. In one such report, Knight-Bruce LJ appears to joke about the abolition of directors of railway companies for the good of society.[42] Concern for the propensity of the incorporated association to be used for dishonest conduct (and thereby to shield directors from its consequences) persisted even to the end of the nineteenth century; in 1895 the Court of Appeal delivered a stinging criticism of, and would not permit, a sole trader's use of incorporation to protect himself from bankruptcy.[43]

ii. Bell v Midland Railway Company *(1861): The Claim for Damages*

We come now to the decision that is the principal focus of this chapter. The plaintiff's wharf was rendered 'useless'[44] by the defendant's conduct. He subsequently sold the wharf and claimed £5,000 in damages from the MRC for losses incurred. The evidence as to losses incurred was that one tenant, Nutt, had provided a minimum rent of £200 per year, with a royalty on all coal sold. Another tenant, Gould, paid £180 per year. It was also suggested that the plaintiff had received an offer from a Mr Harris for the remaining portion of the wharf for £300 per year, but that the negotiation failed due to the actions of the defendant.[45]

[41] ibid 219. Lord Eldon had said in 1825: 'when I look upon these Acts of Parliament, I regard them all in the light of contracts made by the Legislature, on behalf of every person interested in any thing to be done under them; and I have no hesitation in asserting that, unless that principle is applied in construing statutes of this description, they become instruments of greater oppression than any thing in the whole system of administration under our constitution' (*Blakemore v Glamorganshire Canal Navigation Company* (1832) 1 My & K 154, 39 ER 639).

[42] See 'The Midland and North Western Railways', *Leicester Journal*, 25 February 1859, 3. This report, as well as other newspaper reports referred to below, is available through the *British Newspaper Archive* (British Library), <www.britishnewspaperarchive.co.uk/> accessed 7 May 2023.

[43] See *Broderip v Salomon* [1895] 2 Ch 323 (CA). See also M Lobban, 'Joint Stock Companies' in WR Cornish et al (eds), *The Oxford History of the Laws of England, Vol XII: 1820–1914 Private Law* (Oxford, OUP, 2010) 668–70. However, the House of Lords upheld the sole trader's appeal: *Salomon v Salomon* [1897] AC 22 (HL).

[44] *Bell* (n 2) CB (NS) 293, ER 465.

[45] ibid.

Erle CJ, before whom the action was tried, asked the jury to decide whether or not the defendant company had intentionally obstructed access to the plaintiff's wharf by its railway, and prevented the plaintiff and his tenants from using the railway. He warned the jury not to give the plaintiff any damages which the tenants would have the right to recover, but directed them to consider loss of royalties and any diminution in the value of the wharf.[46] The jury decided that the defendant had intentionally obstructed the plaintiff and awarded £1,000 in damages.

Counsel for the MRC obtained a rule *nisi* to enter a verdict for the defendant company, or a nonsuit, on several grounds. Mr Kelly QC, for the MRC, argued that there had been no obstruction, merely a 'cesser, on notice' to carry coals for the plaintiff along the railway.[47] It was said that the plaintiff was never in a position to be obstructed in the exercise of rights as he had never provided his own locomotive power to use along the railway line and siding.[48] The plaintiff had only ever had a right, it was said, 'to use the railway with the siding for the conveyance of his own waggons by means of his own locomotive power, on payment of proper tolls, and subject to arrangement with the company'.[49] Of interest for present purposes is also the objection as to the damages awarded – it was said that the plaintiff, as a reversioner, was not entitled to several categories of award, including 'damages for any injury to the tenants, or unless upon some permanent obstruction necessarily injurious to him as reversioner'.[50] As the carriages were moveable, there had been no permanent obstruction. It was argued that the only party who sustained damage was a tenant. The plaintiff remained entitled to recover rent and royalties from the tenants.[51] The damages awarded were said to be excessive.

Erle CJ was asked to consider this dispute a second time on the rule *nisi*. He was not convinced by the defendant's suggestion that there was no obstruction and no right in existence to obstruct. He noted that the plaintiff was plainly entitled under the MRC's Act of incorporation to a right of passage from the railway to his siding.[52] The blockage, he said, while technically 'moveable', was 'calculated and intended by the company to be permanent, and to entirely destroy the communication' and had only been moved when the plaintiff had sought the help of the court of Chancery.[53] Comments that had been made by the MRC's chairman, Mr Ellis, were also indicative of an intention permanently

[46] ibid CB (NS) 295, ER 466.
[47] ibid CB (NS) 299, ER 467.
[48] ibid CB (NS) 299–301, ER 467–68.
[49] ibid CB (NS) 300, ER 468.
[50] ibid CB (NS) 296, ER 466.
[51] ibid CB (NS) 301, ER 468.
[52] ibid CB (NS) 302, ER 468.
[53] ibid CB (NS) 302, ER 469.

to deprive. As to the argument that the plaintiff was not in a position to claim the right, Erle CJ noted that it would have been entirely pointless for the plaintiff to obtain his own locomotive power after it had been intimated that any waggons would not be permitted to pass.[54] In the Chief Justice's view, injury was clearly demonstrated and was nothing to do with failure to supply locomotive power.[55] Erle CJ rejected the suggestion that damages were excessive. He pointed to the 'conduct of the company', which had set up a wharf of its own and, 'careless whether they were doing right or wrong, prevented all access to the plaintiff's wharf, for the purpose of extinguishing his trade and advancing their own profit'.[56] Such conduct rendered the plaintiff entitled to 'ample compensation' – indeed, Erle CJ noted that under these circumstances, it would be a 'very bold proposition' to say that £1,000 was not 'very temperate damages'.[57]

Willes J agreed with Erle CJ. He rejected arguments that the plaintiff had not sustained any injury and that he could not complain of obstruction unless it was permanent in nature. As to damages, he concluded in strong terms:[58]

> I must say, that, if ever there was a case in which the jury were warranted in awarding damages of an exemplary character, this is that case. The defendants have committed a grievous wrong with a high hand and in plain violation of an act of parliament; and persisted in it for the purpose of destroying the plaintiff's business and securing gain to themselves.

Byles J was the third judge sitting in judgment in *Bell*. He agreed with Erle CJ and Willes J, adding that he agreed that 'where a wrongful act [was] accompanied by words of contumely and abuse, the jury are warranted in taking that into their consideration, and giving retributory damages'.[59]

III. *BELL* AND LORD DEVLIN'S SECOND CATEGORY

A. *Bell* and *Rookes*

Why did *Bell* come to hold an important place in *Rookes*? Despite the express reference by the judges in *Bell* to exemplary damages, it is not at all obvious that such damages were, in fact, awarded in *Bell*. The precise nature of the damages given to the plaintiff is obscured; it was only in the twentieth

[54] ibid CB (NS) 303, ER 469.
[55] ibid.
[56] ibid CB (NS) 304, ER 469.
[57] ibid.
[58] ibid CB (NS) 307, ER 470.
[59] ibid CB (NS) 308, ER 471.

century that courts began to offer detailed breakdowns of damages awards. Nineteenth-century damages awards in tort cases were largely in the discretion of the jury,[60] and there was no requirement to account for, or explain the calculations behind, the lump sum. Judges did not typically set down rules as to damages for the jury before leaving the case in its hands;[61] the reason for Erle CJ attempting to do so in *Bell* (in his instruction to confine damages to those losses suffered by the plaintiff) may be, at least in part, because of the nature of the defendant – as well as to ensure that any award reflected the plaintiff's loss as opposed to his tenants' loss. As Lobban has noted, in themid-nineteenth century there was a tendency for juries to give high damages against railway companies.[62] Kostal has suggested that the classlessness of the danger posed by the new railways – that derailments and collisions might kill both 'barrel-makers and barristers' – churned up widespread anti-railway sentiment.[63] Railway companies were painted, particularly in newspapers, as able but unwilling to protect passengers from harm.[64] Kostal asserts that 'many Victorian commentators continued to assert that railway directors thought more of profit than of the safety of their patrons'.[65]

Of course, the *Bell* dispute did not concern the safety of the railways or a claim for personal injury. Nevertheless, it is not unlikely that a jury would be inclined to come down very hard on railway companies behaving ruthlessly in the mid-nineteenth century – even if the 'victim' was another commercial (and railway) person.[66] Indeed, railway monopolism was also considered something in need of constraint by judges and juries of the time.[67] This case could be understood as another instance of a railway company seeking to oust a smaller competitor.

Whether or not the damages awarded to Mr Bell actually contained a punitive element, as was said in *Broome*,[68] Lord Devlin in *Rookes* 'founded his second category on a sequence of cases beginning with *Bell v. Midland Railway*'.[69] After reviewing several authorities and some legislation, Lord Devlin decided that he could not, 'without a complete disregard of precedent', refuse to 'recognise

[60] See M Lobban, 'The Development of Tort Law' in WR Cornish et al (eds), *The Oxford History of the Laws of England, Vol XII: 1820–1914 Private Law* (Oxford, OUP, 2010) 900–02.

[61] ibid 902.

[62] ibid.

[63] Kostal (n 40) 280–82. See generally ch 7.

[64] ibid.

[65] ibid 282.

[66] Though, as Kostal has shown, there is a disparity between the treatment of injured workers and injured passengers; the former were treated far more harshly by the law: see ibid ch 7.

[67] See ibid ch 5.

[68] *Broome* (HL) (n 12) 1078 (Lord Hailsham LC).

[69] ibid. See also *Rookes* (n 3) 1221ff in which Lord Devlin asserted that the important comments in *Bell* were dicta, but nevertheless appeared to identify *Bell* as the starting point of a clearly identifiable category.

the exemplary principle'.[70] He went on to identify specific categories of case in which exemplary damages were useful 'in vindicating the strength of the law and thus affording a practical justification for admitting into the civil law a principle which ought logically to belong to the criminal.'[71] The important feature of these earlier cases was therefore that in them, exemplary damages had served to 'vindicat[e] the strength of the law'. He explained further the nature of the second category:[72]

> Where a defendant with a cynical disregard for a plaintiff's rights has calculated that the money to be made out of his wrongdoing will probably exceed the damages at risk, it is necessary for the law to show that it cannot be broken with impunity.

He concluded this discussion with the assertion that exemplary damages might be awarded where 'it is necessary to teach a wrongdoer that tort does not pay'.[73] This second category was said to be established as part of the common law.[74] Lord Devlin did not appear to consider his decision to be creating great changes in the law: he suggested that he was restating well-established (and therefore, to his dismay, unassailable) principles.[75] However, he did acknowledge that his decision would impose some limits 'not hitherto expressed'.[76]

These sentiments were the subject of particular criticism in the Court of Appeal in *Broome*. Lord Denning MR described Lord Devlin's decision as having 'knocked down the common law as it had existed for centuries' and laid down a new doctrine.[77] He noted that other supreme courts in countries of the Commonwealth had declined to follow the authority of *Rookes*; the High Court of Australia had subjected the 'new doctrine to devastating criticism'.[78] This 'wholesale condemnation' was said to justify the Court of Appeal in reconsidering the place of *Rookes* in the law.[79] Lord Denning described the rules laid down in *Rookes* as 'hopelessly illogical and inconsistent'.[80] As to the second category, he queried the emphasis on 'cold cynical calculation for profit':[81]

> It makes me ask this question: Which of these two men is worse: the man who says to himself: 'I reckon I will sell enough copies of this publication to pay any damages for libel'; or the man who says: 'I will smash this professional man whatever it costs me'?

[70] *Rookes* (n 3) 1226.
[71] ibid.
[72] ibid 1227.
[73] ibid.
[74] ibid.
[75] ibid 1227. See also at 1230: 'it will not … make much difference to the substance of the law …'.
[76] ibid 1226.
[77] *Broome* (CA) (n 7) 380 (Lord Denning MR).
[78] ibid (Lord Denning MR referring to *Uren v John Fairfax & Sons Pty Ltd* (1966) 117 CLR 118 (HCA) among other authorities). Salmon LJ used the same expression at 385.
[79] *Broome* (CA) (n 7) 380 (Lord Denning MR).
[80] ibid 381.
[81] ibid.

Salmon LJ thought that Lord Devlin's formulation, taken as a whole, appeared to mean that if the defendant were not a servant of the Government or liable under statute (and therefore falling within the first or third categories), exemplary damages were available only in cases of cynical calculation by the defendant that profit would exceed any damages payable in tort.[82] For this, he said, there was no authority and it was contrary to the law before *Rookes*. The key factor had always been the 'outrageous circumstances' in which the tort was committed, rendering it in the public interest that such conduct be punished and others deterred.[83]

The House of Lords in the further appeal in *Broome*[84] said that it had not been open to the Court of Appeal to say that *Rookes* should not be followed. The majority of the Law Lords appeared to see Lord Devlin's categories as having a firm foundation in earlier case law.[85]

It is striking to see such a stark difference in treatment and understanding of the existing legal landscape between the Court of Appeal and the House of Lords. Looking specifically at Lord Devlin's second category: was this principle set out, or supported, by *Bell*?

B. *Bell*: Economic Calculation?

i. The Meaning of 'Calculation'

When read closely, *Bell* does not appear to be a case of express or precise calculation by the defendant that profits were likely to outweigh any legal consequences. But what kind of 'calculation' is required, in order to fall within Lord Devlin's second category?

It was confirmed by the House in *Broome* that the relevant 'calculation' did not need to be precise or express. Viscount Dilhorne rejected the idea that Lord Devlin intended that the plaintiff show 'mathematical calculation by the defendant' of the profit likely to ensue, the consequent risk of being sued and the likely damages award.[86] However, he approved of a statement of principle by Widgery J to the effect that the defendant must have been knowingly or recklessly committing a wrong, with the 'cynical and calculated' knowledge that profit would likely outweigh loss.[87]

[82] ibid 387.
[83] ibid.
[84] *Broome* (HL) (n 12).
[85] See, eg, ibid 1087–88.
[86] ibid 1101.
[87] ibid, quoting Widgery J in *Manson v Associated Newspapers Ltd* [1965] 1 WLR 1038 (QBD) 1040–41.

Lord Hailsham advised:[88]

> It is not necessary that the defendant calculates that the plaintiff's damages if he sues to judgment will be smaller than the defendant's profit. This is simply one example of the principle …
>
> What is necessary is that the tortious act must be done with guilty knowledge for the motive that the chances of economic advantage outweigh the chances of economic, or perhaps physical, penalty.

The need for 'guilty knowledge' suggests that cases of carelessness (or lack of thought) as to the legality of the conduct may not suffice. Lord Hailsham did suggest, however, that *reckless* disregard for the legality or illegality of an act would also be sufficient.[89]

Lord Morris expressed the principle another way, which seems to require even less in the way of 'calculation' but still some contemplation of the possibility of having to pay damages:[90]

> The situation contemplated is where someone faces up to the possibility of having to pay damages for doing something which may be held to have been wrong but where nevertheless he deliberately carries out his plan because he thinks that it will work out satisfactorily for him. He is prepared to hurt somebody because he thinks that he may well gain by so doing even allowing for the risk that he may be made to pay damages.

Even if express or precise mathematical calculation of expected profit against potential liabilities is not required, it seems clear that Lord Devlin's second category has been understood as requiring: 1) that the defendant turned their mind to the possibility of having to pay damages when embarking upon the conduct (it must be 'cynical' conduct); and 2) that economic or physical gain was the dominant motive. On the latter point, in 2022 it was held that a claim for exemplary damages failed where there was the possibility (and insufficient evidence to decide either way) that the defendant's behaviour was motivated simply by the desire to be difficult, rather than by economic strategy or attempt to make a material gain.[91] On this interpretation, a more nebulous 'gain' in the form of general satisfaction is not sufficient. This is consistent with Lord Denning's criticism that the second category was unprincipled because it would catch the cool-headed defendant motivated by profit but would not cover the defendant motivated by the desire to 'smash' another person.

Returning, then, to *Bell*: at first glance, the dispute in *Bell* may indeed appear to be a case of a large railway corporation deciding that any damages payable to Mr Bell did not outweigh the likely financial gain involved in extinguishing

[88] *Broome* (HL) (n 12) 1079.
[89] ibid.
[90] ibid 1094.
[91] See *Gabb v Farrokhzad* [2022] EWHC 212 (Ch), [2022] 1 WLR 2842, particularly [118]–[121]. At the time of writing an appeal is outstanding in *Gabb*.

his coal wharf business and redirecting his trade to the MRC's own wharf. However, considering carefully the reasoning of the Court of Common Pleas in *Bell*, and looking in more depth at the relationship between the parties, to what extent does *Bell* actually form a convincing example of a case belonging to Lord Devlin's second category?

ii. The Bell *Reasoning*

The court considering the *Bell* dispute appears not to have treated the 'wrong' here as involving cynical weighing of legal consequences against potential gain. Instead, the different members of the bench offered various characterisations and interpretations of the 'bad' behaviour engaged in by the defendant railway (and, therefore, bases on which exemplary damages might be awarded). Some of these are, in fact, inconsistent with any cynical weighing of potential legal consequences against likely gain.

When it came to the claim for damages, Erle CJ, as trial judge, had instructed the jury not to compensate the plaintiff for his tenant's losses. On the rule *nisi* he found that £1,000 was not excessive, and his comments (characterising the sum as 'temperate') indicate that he thought perhaps the plaintiff might have been deserving of an even higher sum. He emphasised the company's wrongdoing in expressing this view – it had been careless as to the rights or wrongs of the situation, and had acted to 'extinguish' the plaintiff's venture and to further its own profits. Erle CJ was not against railways pursuing profits – just two years after this decision, Erle CJ would deliver a noteworthy dissent in *Baxendale v Great Western Railway*,[92] which swam against the tide of judicial opinion at the time and suggested that economic monopolism by large corporations was not something which the courts should try to prevent.[93] In *Bell*, however, the corporate defendant had gone beyond the legitimate pursuit of its economic interests. Nevertheless, it is not clear that Erle CJ considered the defendant to have acted cynically, in the expectation or contemplation that damages may be awarded against it. In several reports,[94] he refers to its having been *careless* as to the right or wrong of the situation. If we take this to mean *reckless*, then perhaps it sits comfortably with the requirement of some awareness of wrongdoing from the outset in Lord Devlin's second category.[95] However, Erle CJ is also noted in one report as having said that he found that the defendant, in placing the obstacles over the junction, had acted 'intentionally, and under the belief that [the company] had a right to stop up the passage'.[96] Erle CJ's analysis of the

[92] *Baxendale v Great Western Railway* (1863) 14 CB (NS) 1, 143 ER 343.

[93] See discussion in Kostal (n 40) 220.

[94] *Bell* (n 2) (CB) NS 304, ER 469; *Bell* (n 4) LJCP 280.

[95] See J Goudkamp and E Katsampouka, 'An Empirical Study of Punitive Damages' (2018) 38 *OJLS* 90, 93.

[96] *Bell* (n 4) LJCP 279.

situation, then, taken as a whole, seems not to be that the defendant company acted cynically and calculatedly in the hope that profits would outweigh any damages likely to be paid – on his finding, it is unlikely that the directors considered the possibility of paying damages at all in their conviction that Mr Bell had no rights.

Erle CJ and Willes J both clearly considered that the defendant company (or, rather, its directors) had been motivated by profit – at least in part. In one report, Willes J is said to have expressly asserted that the 'quarrel' in 1857 arose not from any misconduct by Mr Bell, but because the railway company was 'desirous of having a wharf of [its] own' and of directing the former's trade to its own wharf.[97]

However, that does not mean that *profit-seeking* was the sole (or even principal) ground upon which the Court of Common Pleas was prepared to award exemplary damages. Willes J also identified further bad behaviour by the defendant company. Willes J expressed 'astonishment' that the MRC had, before the present court, denied that it ever had any intention of obstructing or contesting the plaintiff's right, when in earlier proceedings before Vice-Chancellor Wood (and the appeal court) it had vigorously argued that the plaintiff had no right and that it was justified in causing an obstruction.[98] One report is particularly revealing as to Willes J's thoughts on the railway company's handling of the dispute and subsequent litigation:[99]

> [I]t is said that the company are not bound by what was said by the chairman; and for a long time I was under the impression that I had misunderstood the counsel, and that all that they meant to do was that they would not carry any longer, and that this obstruction was accidental or done by the chairman and not by the company at all; but I looked at the judgment in the case in Chancery … and on both those occasions it was contended by the company that they had a right to block up the siding, and that Bell had no right to the siding at all …

He described the railway company's denial as 'entire misrepresentation'.[100] The MRC, he noted, had done all it could to obstruct the siding and Mr Bell's business.[101] Willes J was not convinced by the company's attempts to distance itself from the aggressive words of its chairman. This was no accidental obstruction but a deliberate course of conduct undertaken by the company, not just its chairman. Some of Willes J's comments as to damages are set out above. It is useful now to return to one part, in particular: 'The defendants have committed a grievous wrong with a high hand and in plain violation of an act of parliament; and

[97] ibid 280.
[98] *Bell* (n 2) CB (NS) 305–06, ER 470.
[99] *Bell* (n 4) LJCP 280.
[100] *Bell* (n 2) CB (NS) 305–06, ER 470. The language varies across the reports; in one report the words are 'entire mistake': *Bell* (n 4) LJCP 280.
[101] See, eg, *Bell* (n 2) CB (NS) 306, ER 470; *Bell* (n 4) LJCP 280.

persisted in it for the purpose of destroying the plaintiff's business and securing gain to themselves.'[102] The high-handedness of the defendant's conduct, the fact that it violated an act of Parliament and that it was done not just to secure gain but to 'destroy' the plaintiff's business, appear, from this report of Willes J's reasoning, at least as important as the fact that the defendant sought to make a profit.

As was noted above, Byles J in *Bell* emphasised the appropriateness of additional damages where a wrong was accompanied by 'contumely and abuse'.[103]

In the reasoning of Willes J and Byles J (and particularly the latter) it is possible to discern importance being placed on the idea of the defendants having acted not just deliberately but with contempt or insolence. Byles J was express in this opinion – contumelious conduct, which might also mean contemptuous or insulting, was the core of the Roman delict of *iniuria*,[104] and it seems that Byles J may have been inspired by the Romans in focusing on such conduct.[105] Although Willes J did not so obviously use the language of the Roman delict, the punishment-worthy conduct identified in his reasoning is a perfect example: acting in contempt of both the will and authority of Parliament and the rights of the plaintiff. If authority were necessary for this position, Willes J said, *Emblen v Myers*[106] would assist. That case concerned damage caused by the defendant to neighbouring property when a building had been pulled down on the defendant's land without sufficient care. The defendant in *Emblen* had sought to purchase the plaintiff's neighbouring premises but had been refused. He was required by the police to pull down his own premises. He engaged labourers to do this deconstruction and they did the work in such a way that a large piece of timber fell through (and destroyed) the plaintiff's stable roof, while his wife was in the stable, causing damage to a horse and cart as well. Though the plaintiff confronted the defendant, the defendant nevertheless told the labourers to continue with the work, which caused more damage. It was said that the defendant, in so acting, hoped the plaintiff would give up the stable. Pollock CB, Bramwell B, Channell B and Wilde B confirmed that that the defendant's motive was relevant, and that wilful misconduct (and particularly if, according to Pollock CB, accompanied by 'expressions of contempt'[107]) might justify damages beyond those required to cover losses.[108] Bramwell B seemed to approve of damages being given for

[102] *Bell* (n 2) CB (NS) 307, ER 470.
[103] ibid CB (NS) 308, ER 471.
[104] See, eg, E Descheemaeker (ed), *The Roman Law of Obligations* (Oxford, OUP, 2016) ch 10.
[105] See also Mitchell (n 8) 66.
[106] *Emblen v Myers* (1860) 6 Hurl & N 54, 158 ER 23.
[107] ibid Hurl & N 59, ER 25 (Pollock CB).
[108] ibid. See also Lobban (n 60) 902.

the 'insult as well as the actual injury'.[109] *Emblen* thus also appears to be based on contemptuous or contumelious conduct.

Treatise writers took up these ideas in reflecting on the circumstances in which exemplary damages might be awarded. For example, Frederick Pollock, writing in 1887, said:[110]

> The kind of wrongs to which [exemplary damages] are applicable are those which, besides the violation of a right or the actual damage, import insult or outrage, and so are not merely injuries but *iniuriae* in the strictest Roman sense of the term.

For this principle, *Merest v Harvey*[111] was cited (among other authorities) – a case in which it is particularly clear that it was the outrageousness of the conduct and the gravity of the defendant's contempt for the plaintiff that was thought to justify a large award. The plaintiff was awarded £500 in damages when the defendant, apparently drunk, had belligerently invited himself onto the plaintiff's land to join a shooting party despite the plaintiff's request for him to leave. Intriguingly, this badly behaved defendant was a Member of Parliament and magistrate,[112] and had threatened the plaintiff on that account. Gibbs CJ asked: 'I wish to know, in a case where a man disregards every principle which actuates the conduct of gentlemen, what is to restrain him except large damages?'[113] There is more than a hint of this sentiment in the court's reasoning in *Bell*: the directors of the defendant company had, in the eyes of the court, acted in an ungentlemanly, dishonest manner and in contempt of the plaintiff's rights.

iii. Ellis and the MRC: Calculated Profit-chasing or Personal Agenda?

It has been suggested in the preceding discussion that the court in *Bell* was not focused on the profit-seeking of the defendant railway company in suggesting that exemplary damages might be appropriate. However, it is also possible that the company was not even motivated principally by profit. There are further features of these events that are worthy of attention but largely overlooked in the law reports. However, these additional features add colour which suggests a motivation beyond cynical calculation for profit on the part of the directors of the defendant railway. It is also likely that the courts dealing with this dispute were aware of these features.[114]

[109] *Emblen* (n 106) Hurl & N 59, ER 25.

[110] F Pollock, *The Law of Torts* (London, Stevens and Sons, 1887) 162. See also Mitchell (n 8) 66–67.

[111] *Merest v Harvey* (1814) 5 Taunt 442, 128 ER 761.

[112] See C Harvey, Member Biographies, <www.historyofparliamentonline.org/volume/1790-1820/member/harvey-charles-1756-1843> accessed 7 May 2023.

[113] *Merest* (n 111) Taunt 443, ER 761.

[114] The appeal court in 1859 was certainly aware of Mr Bell's position in the company. Reports of the appeal proceedings concerning the injunction in regional newspapers suggest that submissions were made which centred on this feature: see, eg, 'The Midland and North Western Railways', *The Leicestershire Mercury*, 26 February 1859, 6.

Mr Bell, at the time of receiving the letter and of the MRC's obstruction of the siding, was a director of the defendant railway company.[115] He remained a director until 5 January 1859, when the Board of Directors accepted his resignation of the post.[116] Before holding the post as director, he had been company secretary of the Midland Counties Railway since its inception.[117] He was a central and important figure in the bringing-to-life of this enterprise. Mr Bell is listed as 'Secretary' (and therefore responsible for collecting applications for shares) in 1835 newspaper notices concerning the formation of the new Midland Counties Railway.[118] From 1844 until he joined the Board as a director, Bell was also secretary of the MRC.[119] The plaintiff was therefore intricately involved in the establishment and subsequent operation of the MRC. Mr Bell was no mere commercial competitor of the MRC, and these are not parties at arm's length: this is a dispute between long-standing colleagues.

The steering mind of the actions of the MRC at the time of the obstruction of the siding seems to have been that of the chairman. He (at one time, a Member of Parliament for Leicester) had also been involved with the defendant railway company since its formation, and so must have known Mr Bell for many years at the time of the relevant events.[120] As noted above, the various reports of the *Bell* litigation contain the allegation of the rather aggressive assertion by Mr Ellis. However, rendering that allegation most surprising, Mr Ellis appears to have had a reputation as a generous and philanthropic man. An obituary published in 1862 notes that he was a prominent Quaker, and 'distinguished for his philanthropy and public spirit, and much respected for his active charities'.[121] He was said to take an interest in 'all measures which tended to improve the social condition of the people'.[122] Of course, people are usually praised extensively in obituaries. Nevertheless, when he announced his resignation of the chairmanship in December 1857, the Board of Directors – including Mr Bell who was present at the meeting[123] – unanimously adopted a minute

[115] See, eg, list of directors in *Herapath's Railway Journal*, 15 August 1857, p 841. See also Meetings of Board of Directors of Midland Railway Company, 1857–1858, RAIL 491/18, The National Archives, Kew, London.

[116] Meeting of Board of Directors of Midland Railway Company, 5 January 1859, RAIL 491/18, The National Archives, Kew, London.

[117] See, eg, *Bell* (n 18) De G&J 676, ER 1430; 'Midland Counties Railway', *Nottingham Journal*, 11 August 1837, 2. Before the Act for the incorporation of the company had been passed, he was secretary of the Provisional Committee of the Midland Counties Railway and played an important role in obtaining subscriptions: see Brettle and Rouse (n 19) 1.

[118] See, eg, 'Midland Counties Railway', *The Leeds Intelligencer*, 24 January 1835, 1.

[119] Brettle and Rouse (n 19) 1. See also, eg, 'Railway Appointments', *The Durham Chronicle*, 26 August 1853, 5.

[120] See, eg, 'Obituary', *Northampton Mercury*, 1 November 1862, 3; *The Home News for India, China and the Colonies*, 3 November 1862, 14.

[121] See, eg, 'Obituary', *Northampton Mercury*, 1 November 1862, 3; *The Home News for India, China and the Colonies*, 3 November 1862, 14.

[122] See, eg, 'Obituary', *Northampton Mercury*, 1 November 1862, 3.

[123] See Minute of Meeting of Board of Directors of Midland Railway Company, 2 December 1857, RAIL 491/18, The National Archives, Kew, London.

recording their 'deep pain' on learning of his resignation and the hope that he would continue to play an active role in the running of the company.[124] It is a glowing review, praising Mr Ellis for steering the company through a period of 'unusual difficulty and mistrust'[125] when other railway companies faced ruin, and emphasising the 'personal esteem' and affection of colleagues for him.[126] Mr Ellis finally quit the position in 1858; the newly elected chairman, Mr Paget, had died unexpectedly so Mr Ellis continued in the role for an additional period.[127] A dinner was held in his honour in July 1858, at which he was presented with retirement gifts including a portrait to celebrate his service.[128] Interestingly, Mr Bell is reported to have been present at the event at which toasts were proposed not just in celebration of Mr Ellis, but also to a lawyer representing the company against Mr Bell's action.[129] It seems that this event took place after the injunction proceedings were commenced.[130]

It seems clear that the purpose of the obstruction was to discourage trade at Mr Bell's wharf and redirect it to the new MRC wharf. This would, of course, have benefited the MRC to the extent that royalties and rents received by Mr Bell would be received by the MRC instead. It has also been suggested that Mr Ellis may have benefited personally from the new wharf[131] – his will confirms that he certainly had a coal business in Leicester.[132] While Mr Ellis was the leading mind and mouthpiece in the early stages of the dispute, the obstruction continued into 1859 – well after Mr Ellis's retirement as chairman. Of course, he was still on the Board as a director and was no doubt influential. However, given the timing, it does seem likely that there was wider support for the obstruction of the siding, and subsequent refusal to negotiate a deal, among the directors (excluding Mr Bell).

Given the attempt by the MRC to justify its actions on the basis of 'public safety' due to vastly increasing traffic around Leicester station, one wonders whether the course of action that would secure maximum profit for the MRC

[124] ibid. See also, eg, 'Retirement of Mr John Ellis from the Chairmanship of the Midland Railway Company', *Leicester Journal*, 11 December 1857, 5.

[125] This may be a reference to the crash of the railway securities markets in 1845 (see Kostal (n 40) ch 2) or the turmoil surrounding the downfall and disgrace of the MRC's previous chairman, George Hudson.

[126] ibid.

[127] It seems that Mr Ellis presided until March 1858: see Minute of Meeting of Board of Directors of Midland Railway Company, 3 March 1858, RAIL 491/18, The National Archives, Kew, London.

[128] See, eg, 'Testimonial to John Ellis, Esq, Late Chairman of the Midland Railway Company', *Leicester Journal*, 9 July 1858, 8.

[129] ibid.

[130] See 'Law Notices', *The Times*, 10 May 1858, 11 (obtained from *The Times Digital Archive, 1785–2019*, Gale) in which Mr Bell's action against the Midland Railway Company is listed before Vice-Chancellor Wood.

[131] Brettle and Rouse (n 19) 2.

[132] The Last Will and Testament of John Ellis, dated 1 October 1855. Obtained from General Register Office <www.gov.uk/general-register-office> accessed 7 May 2023.

might well have been to allow Mr Bell's wharf to continue to bring traffic along the line while also operating a wharf on the opposite side. Carriage of goods through Mr Bell's wharf brought benefits to the MRC. It was noted by the court in the appeal concerning the injunction that the railway company benefited financially from the tolls and charges involved in the carriage of goods along the railway when a wharf or mining concern invested in a siding to communicate with the principal railway.[133]

In any event, even if it were a profitable move to run Mr Bell out of business, the connection between the parties and certain features of the dispute makes it likely that some personal disagreement fuelled the MRC's policy with respect to Mr Bell's wharf. I have been unable to uncover its cause. However, there are clues that this is not truly a dispute about money. Some reports offer additional information which shows the unreasonably rigid position adopted by the defendant: while the injunction proceedings were on foot, Mr Bell's solicitor, a Mr Reeve, had applied to the MRC's solicitor, Mr Morris, for permission for the passage to be opened for just five minutes every day – without prejudice, until the matter was decided.[134] This request was refused. Something beyond cynical exploitation of a commercial situation is most clearly in evidence in the alleged statement by Ellis, variously reported as: 'That wharf shall never be a wharf again if I can help it',[135] and 'You shall never have a wharf there again, as long as I live, if I can help it'.[136] These are not words of cool calculation and instead are suggestive of bitter commitment to destruction.

Even if the MRC's actions were motivated principally by profit, was this a case of acts done 'with guilty knowledge for the motive that the chances of economic advantage outweigh the chances of economic … penalty'?[137]

On the one hand, certain actions of the Chairman's Committee of the MRC Board of Directors might be understood as preparations for litigation from the very moment of issuing the notice to Mr Bell in June 1857. At the Special Meeting of that committee, which approved the sending of the letter to Mr Bell, the committee also called for accounts of any sums paid by the MRC with respect to laying down and repairing the siding to Mr Bell's wharf, and the costs of moving waggons to the wharf.[138] On the other hand, this might simply be prudent record-keeping. It could also be further information useful to bolster a position already reached against Mr Bell's wharf.

To the extent that one can interpret the motives from the records remaining, it is not obvious that the MRC engaged in any 'calculation', even in a loose

[133] See, eg, *Bell* (n 18) De G&J 686, ER 1434.
[134] *Bell* (n 4) LJCP 276; WR 613.
[135] *Bell* (n 2) CB (NS) 292, ER 464.
[136] *Bell* (n 4) WR 613.
[137] *Broome* (HL) 1079 (Lord Hailsham LC).
[138] Minute of Meeting of Chairman's Committee of Midland Railway Company, 17 June 1857, RAIL 491/226, The National Archives, Kew, London.

sense. It seems that Mr Bell attempted, at several points, to reach a resolution outside of the courts, including by selling the wharf and surrounding lands and buildings to the company: minutes of meetings of the MRC's Board of Directors demonstrate these attempts.[139] Mr Bell's failed attempts to negotiate might be said to suggest that the MRC was engaged in cool calculation that any damages payable were likely to be outweighed by the ability to shut down the rival wharf without having to purchase it for its full commercial value. If this were the thought process, the Board must have been aware that any 'shut down' could potentially be only temporary if reversed by a court. The MRC also spent a great deal of money engaging in litigation rather than attempting to negotiate. The company's Law Committee records, now held by the National Archives at Kew, suggest that the bill ran to thousands of pounds.[140] This strategy, if considered from a profit perspective, appears too risky to be attributed to detached and calculating commercial minds. If this had been a dispute about money, they would have concluded a deal at some point.

Further, it is not obvious that the defendant company considered the possibility of having to pay damages from the outset at all: if its arguments before the courts are believed, it did not consider that Mr Bell had any rights that could be violated by the company. It is not at all clear that the directors turned their mind to even a minimum level of calculation with respect to legal penalties and net gain.

The company's conduct is more reminiscent of the type of conduct Lord Denning had in mind, not caught by Lord Devlin's second category, which sees a defendant seek to 'smash' an opponent at all costs. Indeed, Mr Bell appears to have had such a suspicion because in one letter to the directors, he noted that there were over 150 private sidings along the line and was therefore questioning why his had been singled out.[141] As far as this author can tell from the existing company records, it was a few months *after* the letter to Mr Bell that the Board of Directors resolved to look into the costs and arrangements concerning private sidings more generally.[142] Mr Bell's wharf does appear to have received special treatment, considering there were more than 150 other sidings facilitating trade for external parties (and therefore potential commercial competition).

It is possible, however, that while the courts were concerned about the MRC directors' honesty and integrity, the same directors objected to Mr Bell's conduct

[139] See, eg, Minutes of Meeting of Board of Directors of Midland Railway Company, 5 August 1857, 5 May 1858, 1 December 1858, RAIL 491/18, The National Archives, Kew, London.

[140] See Minutes of Meeting of Law Committee of Midland Railway Company, 2 March 1859, 23 October 1860, 5 May 1863, RAIL 491/195, The National Archives, Kew, London.

[141] Minute of Meeting of Board of Directors of Midland Railway Company, 5 August 1857, RAIL 491/18, The National Archives, Kew, London.

[142] Minute of Meeting of Board of Directors of Midland Railway Company, 6 October 1857, RAIL 491/18, The National Archives, Kew, London.

on similar grounds. This looks very much like a dispute about the morality of trade and integrity of trade relationships.[143] Perhaps Mr Bell had not kept the other directors informed as to the profits generated by his wharf business – the Board was certainly not confident about the scale of the MRC's contributions to the upkeep of the siding, and something precipitated the MRC's sudden interest in sidings and wharf trade in 1857. It may be that Mr Ellis' Quaker principles found abhorrent Mr Bell's solo venture – inconsistent with ideas of community and creating a conflict of interest which could threaten Mr Bell's ability to carry out his responsibilities as director. It might, in fact, be a case in which all directors – on both sides – acted in breach of their duties. It is also curious (to say the least) that Mr Bell appears to have continued in his post as director during this dispute with the company until shortly before the hearing of the appeal on the injunction early in 1859. He is reported as being present at many meetings of the Board during 1858.[144]

One is left only able to speculate; the records do not reveal the true nature of the disagreement. There is just enough to render it an awkward fit with a category concerning calculated profit-chasing.

IV. CONCLUSION: BELL AS A LANDMARK CASE?

In *Rookes*, Lord Devlin seemed to treat *Bell* as the first in a line of authority concerning the award of exemplary damages for conduct calculated to result in net gain after any penalty had been applied. However, on a close reading of *Bell*, it is difficult to see any convincing novelty or strong principle to this effect. *Bell* appears based on similar concerns and principles to earlier cases. Profit-seeking was one of many features flagged by the court in suggesting that exemplary damages might be awarded; it was not the principal feature. Furthermore, the judges did not appear to consider that the defendant railway had acted cynically in pursuing that profit.

It is also not a model case, on the facts, for Lord Devlin's second category. When one considers the close relationship between the parties to this dispute, and the dogged determination of the company to undermine Mr Bell's wharf and to fight him in the courts, it is difficult to view this case as one of cynical and calculated profit-seeking. It is altogether more personal in nature.

The true significance of *Bell* is as a case concerned with commercial morality at a time where both the law and society were coming to terms with the nature and consequences of the (proliferating) commercial corporation.

[143] I am grateful to Paul Mitchell for discussing with me his thoughts as to the true nature of the dispute, which I find convincing.

[144] See Minutes of Meetings of Board of Directors of Midland Railway Company, RAIL 491/18, The National Archives, Kew, London.

The court in *Bell* signalled disapproval, in a new context, of ruthless elimination of business competition and the apparent boldness of directors acting in concert. It appeared keen to ensure that corporations were not perceived to be able, with impunity, to act in contempt of Parliament's express instructions and without respect for the legal rights of other commercial parties. The corporate body was also unable to rely on the technicality of separate legal personality to distance itself from the ill-chosen words of its chairman: the veil did not stretch so far.

4

Rookes v Barnard (1964) 'Going Off the Lines'

IAIN FIELD*

I. INTRODUCTION

When Douglas Edwin Rookes was dismissed from his position as a draughtsman with the British Overseas Air Corporation (BOAC) in the spring of 1961, following threats by union officials that a strike would otherwise be ordered, it could scarcely have been predicted that the event would result in one of the most consequential judicial pronouncements on punitive (or exemplary) damages in legal history. But that is precisely how history would unfold and, nearly 60 years after *Rookes v Barnard* ('*Rookes*') reached the House of Lords,[1] Lord Devlin's (in)famous 'exegesis'[2] on punitive damages in that case remains the leading authority on the matter in English law. Writing for the Court, his Lordship declared that exemplary damages were an 'anomaly', which 'confuses the civil and criminal functions of the law',[3] but that, 'not wishing to show a complete disregard for precedent, and indeed of statute',[4] exemplary damages should not be excised entirely from the law.

*I am greatly indebted to Alan Paterson, who generously shared with me materials from his interviews with Lord Reid and Lord Devlin, unpublished in either of his well-known books on the Law Lords (and from which the subtitle to this chapter is extracted, see n 113 for the full quotation), and to Paul Smith, editor of *Historical Studies in Industrial Relations*, who was most gracious with his time and whose meticulous accounts of the *Rookes* litigation were invaluable. I refer liberally to the work of both authors. I am also grateful to Joachim Dietrich for reviewing an early draft of this chapter and to the editors of this book and the other participants at the workshop for their helpful comments.

[1] *Rookes v Barnard* [1964] AC 1129 (HL).

[2] A Paterson, *Final Judgment: The Last Law Lords and the Supreme Court* (Oxford, Bloomsbury, 2013) 264.

[3] ibid 1221. The judgment did not affect the law of Scotland, where punitive damages were (and remain) unavailable.

[4] ibid 1226.

Rather, his Lordship allowed that they would be available in three exceptional categories of case (the 'categories'):

1. those involving 'oppressive, arbitrary or unconstitutional action by the servants of the government';
2. 'those in which the defendant's conduct has been calculated by him to make a profit for himself which may well exceed the compensation payable to the plaintiff'; and
3. 'any category in which exemplary damages are expressly authorised by statute'.[5]

Lord Devlin further held that, whereas exemplary damages seek to 'punish and deter', aggravated damages afford compensation for injury to 'the plaintiff's proper feelings of dignity and pride' and are therefore consistent with the underlying principle of *restitutio in integrum*.[6]

Despite some initial hesitation by other judges,[7] and a recommendation by the Law Commission to implement a principled statutory expansion of punitive damages,[8] the idea that punitive damages are anomalous remains pervasive in England.[9] Corrective justice theorists, in particular, celebrate Lord Devlin's judgment as returning English law, as closely as possible, to a position consistent with their ideology.[10] In contrast, some judges in other common law jurisdictions have questioned the assertion that punitive damages are anomalous,[11] and many more have challenged the historical and normative bases of his Lordship's exceptional categories.[12] On appeal from one of those cases, *Uren v John Fairfax & Sons Pty Ltd*, the Privy Council declared that it was 'not prepared to say that the High Court was wrong in being unconvinced that a changed approach in

[5] ibid 1226–27.

[6] ibid 1221.

[7] *Cassell & Co Ltd v Broome* [1972] 2 QB 354 (CA) 382 (Lord Denning MR); *Cassell & Co Ltd v Broome* [1972] AC 1027 (HL) 1114 (Lord Wilberforce).

[8] Law Commission, *Aggravated, Exemplary and Restitutionary Damages* (Law Com No 247, 1997). The Commission reported that 72% of those consulted favoured either retaining the status quo or expanding the availability of punitive damages. Only 285 favoured abolition: 4–5.

[9] Some judges have nevertheless questioned the idea that private law does not punish, including Lord Reed in *One Step (Support) Ltd* v *Morris-Garner* [2018] UKSC 20, [2019] AC 649 [25], and various commentators have doubted it. See, in particular, N McBride, 'Punitive Damages' in P Birks (ed), *Wrongs and Remedies in the Twenty-First Century* (Oxford, OUP, 1996); P Cane, *The Anatomy of Tort Law* (Oxford, Hart Publishing, 1997) 116–19; A Burrows, *Remedies for Torts, Breach of Contract and Equitable Wrongs*, 4th edn (Oxford, OUP, 2019); J Goudkamp and E Katsampouka, 'Punitive Damages and the Place of Punishment in Private Law' (2021) 84 *MLR* 1257, 1258.

[10] See, eg, EJ Weinrib, 'The Gains and Losses of Corrective Justice' (1994) 44 *Duke Law Journal* 277, 294; A Beever, 'The Structure of Aggravated and Exemplary Damages' (2003) 23 *OJLS* 87, 110.

[11] See, eg, *Uren v John Fairfax & Sons Pty Ltd* (1966) 117 CLR 118 (HCA) 131–32 (Taylor J) ('*Uren*').

[12] ibid 132–38 (Taylor J), 145–47 (Menzies J), 152–53 (Windeyer J), 160 (Owen J); *Fogg v McKnight* [1968] NZLR 330 (SC) 333 (McGregor J). In Canada, Lord Devlin's judgment was rejected without any detailed analysis: *Vorvis v Insurance Corporation of British Colombia* [1989] 1 SCR 1085 (SCC) 1104–05 (McIntyre J), 1128 (Wilson J).

Australia was desirable',[13] and for the first time conceded to a divergence in the common law between England and Australia.

No book on landmark cases in the law of punitive damages would therefore be complete without a chapter devoted to *Rookes*. Yet there is an obvious challenge to writing such a chapter because the legacy of the case will invariably be tracked and critiqued across other chapters, as it has in prior works.[14] Two recent pieces also explore Lord Devlin's treatment of punitive damages in some detail,[15] and much has been written about the case from labour law and industrial relations perspectives.[16] With these points squarely in mind, my first aim in this chapter is to paint as complete a picture as possible of the factual, social and political context in which *Rookes* was decided. I do so partly for the sake of posterity, since that broader context is seldom explored in studies on punitive damages, but also because a closer look at the facts reveals issues of ongoing and contemporary relevance to the availability and function of punitive damages – specifically indemnities and crowdfunding arrangements. The 1960s was also a period of great social change in Britain, and it is well known that the Law Lords of the time played an unusually active role in the development of the law.[17] Judicial lawmaking was at its zenith and considerations of policy – though seldom articulated – weighed heavily in the House of Lords' judgments.[18] Certainly they did so in *Rookes*.[19] My second aim is to explore the implications of indemnities and crowdfunding arrangements in a contemporary context, and to consider whether those implications might yet afford some support for Lord Devlin's general rejection of punitive damages.

[13] *Australian Consolidated Press Ltd v Uren* [1969] 1 AC 590 (PC) 644.

[14] See the sources listed in n 9. Another challenge is posed by the recent and disturbing allegations made against Lord Devlin by his daughter, Clare: <https://www.theguardian.com/uk-news/2021/jul/25/our-silence-permits-perpetrators-to-continue-one-womans-fight-to-expose-a-fathers-abuse> accessed 7 May 2023. It is impossible to know whether these alleged events coloured Lord Devlin's views on punitive damages, and so I have not pursued the matter further in this chapter. It is nevertheless important to acknowledge that Lord Devlin's judgment has denied countless victims of sexual abuse the opportunity to sue their abusers for punitive damages.

[15] N Sinanis, 'Punishment in Tort: The Context of Ideas in *Rookes v Barnard*' (2022) 15 *Journal of Tort Law* 29; E Katsampouka, *Rethinking Punitive Damages* (Oxford, Hart Publishing) (forthcoming).

[16] The sources are numerous but see, in particular, Lord Wedderburn, 'Introduction: From *Rookes v. Barnard* to Social Charter' in Lord Wederburn, *Employment Rights in Britain and Europe* (London Lawrence and Wishart, 1991); P Smith, 'The Law Behind the Law: *Rookes v Barnard* [1964], the Common law and the Right to Strike' (2017) 38 *Historical Studies in Industrial Relations* 37 ('Law Behind the Law'); P Smith, 'Rookes v Barnard and the Trade Union Question in British Politics' (2019) 50 *Industrial Relations Journal* 431 ('The Trade Union Question'); R Bagshaw, 'Rookes' Tale' in J Adams-Prassl, A Bogg and ACL Davies (eds), *Landmark Cases in Labour Law* (Oxford, Hart Publishing, 2022).

[17] Paterson (n 2) 264–68. Shortly thereafter Lord Reid famously dismissed the idea that judges do not make law as a 'fairy tale': 'The Judge as Law Maker' (1972) (July) *Journal of the Society of Public Teachers of Law* 22, 22. See also J Skelly Wright, 'Law and the Logic of Experience: Reflections on Denning, Devlin, and Judicial Innovation in the British Context' (1980) 33 *Stanford Law Review* 179.

[18] Paterson (n 2) 264–68.

[19] ibid 264.

II. BACKGROUND

A. The Dispute in Context

By the mid-1950s trade unionism had come to occupy a central position in the social and political life of the United Kingdom[20] – far beyond that which it occupies today, recent increases in union membership notwithstanding.[21] In a very practical way, the unions were critical to the 'post-war consensus' that shaped British politics until the 1970s. The Trade Disputes Act 1906, passed in the wake of the hugely unpopular House of Lords' decision in *Taff Vale Railway Co v Amalgamated Society of Railway Servants*,[22] afforded unions near absolute liability from civil suit, creating what was colloquially referred to as the 'right to strike'. Strike action was nevertheless a polarising issue, reflecting deep political divisions in a country still grappling with its identity in the wake of a bruising world war, and there was a growing wariness of trade unionism in certain quarters. As Smith explains:

> Criticism of trade unions came in the *Daily Mirror Spotlight on Trade Unions* (Jacobson and Connor 1957), a purported friendly source. Its underlying theme, by now commonplace, was that in the context of full employment and the absence of 'dire want' unions were losing public support on account of 'bullying', unofficial strikes, abuse of the closed shop, demarcation and inter-union disputes, and restrictive practices (which inhibited economic productivity and economic growth). Moreover, union democracy was in a parlous condition; two chapters were devoted to the 'Communist Challenge' and 'the Battle School for Strikers' – a case study of the ETU under communist leadership.[23]

Whether these criticisms were all well founded, it is certainly true that some union officials enjoyed considerable power as the 'voices, eyes, and hands' of their unions, and that the line between official and unofficial ('wildcat') union activity, and thus between the actions of the collective and the individual, was seldom a bright one. Such was the case in *Rookes*.

Rookes was employed at the BOAC design office at Heathrow, where he had worked for some time alongside the first two defendants, Alfred James Barnard and Trevor John Fistal. All three were office members of the Association of

[20] Smith, Law Behind the Law (n 16) 40.

[21] L Elliot, 'Membership of UK Trade Unions Rises for Fourth Year in a Row', *The Guardian*, 27 May 2021) <www.theguardian.com/politics/2021/may/27/membership-of-uk-trade-unions-rises-for-fourth-year-in-a-row> accessed 7 May 2023. According to that article, roughly 6.6 million Brits are union members today, or 10% of the population. In contrast, 9.8 million Brits were union members in 1956, or 44.1% of the population (Smith, Law Behind the Law (n 16) 40).

[22] *Taff Vale Railway Co v Amalgamated Society of Railway Servants* [1901] 1 QB 170 (CA). In that case, the House of Lords unanimously held that unions are legal corporations and that, as such, may be liable in tort to pay damages from union funds.

[23] Smith, The Trade Union Question (n 16) 441.

Engineering and Shipbuilding Draughtsmen (the AESD or 'Union'),[24] which had achieved a 'closed shop' in the design office – that is to say, all workers in the office were Union members and, pursuant to an informal agreement with BOAC, only union members were to be employed in the future.[25] Rookes attempted to resign from the Union in November 1955.[26] His initial quarrel was not that he felt pressured into membership – indeed, he had been actively involved in achieving the closed shop in his office[27] – or that he had qualms about some or other Union activity. On the contrary, Rookes' resignation flowed from a failure by the Union to force the BOAC into action over sub-standard working conditions in the new drawing office. In Rookes' words:

> The office was excessively noisy and the ventilation and temperature control systems did not function properly so that during an unusually hot summer, the place, with its opaque glass double ceiling, became a veritable hot house, suitable perhaps for forcing tomatoes but far too uncomfortable for the delicate plants we in the Design Office thought ourselves to be. Minor incidents, such as the one where a tubular steel scaffolding pole had come crashing through the roof to smash a stool vacated only seconds before, did little to improve the temper of anyone.[28]

According to Sir Miles Thomas, Chairman of the BOAC at the time, the final straw for Rookes came when Union officials, having tried and failed (together with Rookes) to resolve the issue on prior occasions, refused to 'dance to his tune' and take further action.[29] Fistal stated that he and other Union members suspected Rookes' resignation to be a stunt aimed at garnering support for more 'direct' action over the issue,[30] and the third defendant – Reginald John Silverthorne, the Divisional Organiser of the AESD – claimed that Rookes resigned because he was 'fed up with the Union's lack of action' over the drawing office.[31] Rookes strongly disputed these versions of events, claiming that it was he who had proposed an end to agitation for new accommodation,[32] and that he had resigned from the Union simply because it had proved to be ineffectual and, on balance, 'was no longer selling the goods that I particularly

[24] The AESD became the Draughtsmen and Allied Technicians' Association (DATA) in 1960 before a series of amalgamations with other unions. It is now amalgamated with Unite (the UK's second largest union).

[25] Smith, Law Behind the Law (n 16) 49.

[26] *Rookes* (n 1) 1133; D Rookes, *Conspiracy* (London, Johnson Publications 1966) 11 ('*Conspiracy*').

[27] Smith, Law Behind the Law (n 16) 49.

[28] Rookes, *Conspiracy* (n 26) 7.

[29] J Mortimer, 'After the Rookes Case' *Tribune* 28(6) (Blackpool, 7 February 1964) 6. See also Rookes, *Conspiracy* (n 26) 8.

[30] According to Fistal, Rookes described other Union members as 'white livered' in their response to the affair: Law Report – May 1, *The Times* 55070, 2 May 1961, 5; Smith 'The Law Behind the Law' (n 16) 48.

[31] Law Report – April 28, *The Times* 55068, 29 April 1961, 12. See also Smith, The Trade Union Question (n 16) 443–44.

[32] Rookes, *Conspiracy* (n 26) 9.

wanted to buy.'[33] However, if it was indeed Rookes's strategy to force the Union into action through resignation it was a poor one: since he had contracted out of Union membership, the Union insisted that he had also 'denied himself the facility of Union meetings', and so he was unable to share his views with other members in an open forum.[34]

Determined to maintain the closed shop, Barnard, Fistal and Silverthorne tried on numerous occasions to talk Rookes around and to prevent him from encouraging others to follow his example.[35] All attempts failed and, in January 1956, the defendants issued a demand to the BOAC Board that Rookes be 'removed from the Design office … or a withdrawal of labour … will take place.'[36] Whether the defendants intended for Rookes to be fired, or simply relocated, was a matter of dispute,[37] although since the jury ultimately awarded punitive damages it appears that they doubted the defendants' accounts. BOAC acceded to the demand and Rookes was suspended from work for two months, before being dismissed in accordance with terms of his contract.[38]

No doubt the defendants felt confident that, as appears to have been widely assumed, the Trade Disputes Act afforded them an immunity from suit. But the difficulty for the defendants was that a 'no-strike' agreement had been reached between the AESD and BOAC, which now formed part of their employment contracts.[39] Any threat to strike, lawful or otherwise, was therefore a breach of contract, and Rookes claimed that this was sufficient to establish the tort of intimidation. No immunity existed, he argued, because although the Union itself could not be sued, in the circumstances of the case the Act afforded no protection to the defendants as individuals. These were the primary issues in the case, but they need not distract us further here. It suffices to say that – much to the horror of the unions – the House of Lords held unanimously that the tort of intimidation was made out and that no statutory immunity existed.[40] Rookes's victory was soured somewhat, however, by Lord Devlin's ruling on punitive damages. Since the jury had awarded Rookes a single sum of £7,500, covering all heads of damage, a new trial was necessary.[41] The parties settled out of court, however, before that trial commenced.

[33] ibid 13. Rookes claims to have used this phrase simply as a means of summing up his incomplete feelings on the matter, but the defendants may have viewed it as an intentionally provocative statement reflecting a neoliberal, capitalist ideology: Smith, Law Behind the Law (n 16) 48–49.

[34] Law Report – May 1, *The Times* 55070, 2 May 1961, 5.

[35] It is unclear whether he did encourage others, although he certainly discussed his negative view of the Union with at least one colleague: Rookes, *Conspiracy* (n 26) 10.

[36] *Rookes* (n 1) 1166 (Lord Reid).

[37] Law Report – April 28, *The Times*, 29 April 1961, 12.

[38] ibid 1164 (Lord Reid).

[39] ibid 1166 (Lord Reid); 1181 (Lord Evershed).

[40] ibid 1169, 1178 (Lord Reid); 1188, 1196 (Lord Evershed); 1201, 1203 (Lord Hodson); 1209, 1218 (Lord Devlin); 1235, 1238 (Lord Pearce).

[41] ibid 1179 (Lord Reid), 1233 (Lord Devlin).

B. The Parties

It is difficult to know quite what to make of Mr Rookes. Right-leaning commentators of the time championed him as a 'courageous' employee who 'dared to resign from his union'.[42] He also received ongoing political support from the right-wing press and other 'neoliberal organisations',[43] although he himself was of a socialist persuasion and he 'never allied' with those supporters.[44] In contrast, trade unionists and others on the left considered Rookes to be a turncoat and a 'blackleg',[45] and felt betrayed by a man they had once considered an ally.[46] Clive Jenkins, a leading (if contentious) voice of trade unionism at the time, declared the 'smug and oracular complacency' of an article written by Rookes to be 'repellent'.[47] For his part, Rookes claimed his victory over the Union to be one for the rights of the individual,[48] and he would go on to pen an autobiography in which he cast himself the victim of callous trade unionism and a self-serving British justice system.[49] He was a conscientious 'Trotsky' to the Union's ruthless 'Stalin', and the more he stood on his rights and fought for principle, the more the Union 'muscled-up' and fought back.

Of one thing we may be certain, though: Rookes was no 'company man'. Prior to the events giving rise to his dismissal, he was, as noted earlier, an active member and elected representative of the Union,[50] and his former employers were just as irritated by his recalcitrance as were the defendants.[51] Sir Miles Thomas commented:

> If Mr Rookes thinks that in a democratic industrial system a whole organisation serving the public can be brought to its knees at the initiative of one dissatisfied lone wolf he is entitled to his opinion, but must accept any consequences.[52]

There may be shades of truth to each of these accounts. The defendants were also diligently tight-lipped throughout the proceedings and declined

[42] RA Cline, 'Ganging Up', *The Spectator* 6944, 28 July 1961, 132.

[43] Smith, Law Behind the Law (n 16) 77 fn 192. Smith notes that Rookes was assisted both by Donald McLachlan, the editor of the *Sunday Telegraph*, and Geoffrey Howe MP.

[44] ibid. Rookes claimed to be a 'radical brought up in the British empirical tradition, eschewing Marx and finding greater community of outlook with Spencer, Morris and the early Fabians': Rookes, *Conspiracy* (n 26) 6.

[45] Or so Neville Faulks QC stated in his opening address, speaking specifically of comments allegedly made by Silverthorn: Law Report – 24 April, *The Times*, 25 April 1962, 21.

[46] Smith, Law Behind the Law (n 16) 48.

[47] C Jenkins, 'Trend', *Tribune* 28(5), Blackpool, 31 January 1964, 4.

[48] D Rookes, 'One Man's Fight for a Right', *The Sunday Telegraph*, 26 January 1964, 17 ('One Man's Fight').

[49] Rookes despised the legal profession. See Rookes, *Conspiracy* (n 26) 112, 121–23.

[50] Mortimer (n 29).

[51] Rookes believed that the board was in effect subservient to the Union: Rookes, *Conspiracy* (n 26) 28; Rookes, One Man's Fight (n 48).

[52] Rookes, *Conspiracy* (n 26) 108, citing letter to the editor, M Thomas, *The Daily Telegraph* (no date provided).

subsequent approaches by the media[53] – no doubt at the insistence of the Union – and so we are left with a rather uneven picture of events. Nevertheless, the overall impression one gleans from the available materials is that, bumptious though he was,[54] Rookes probably did receive a bit of a 'raw deal'.[55] Sachs J and the jury certainly thought so, as we will see shortly. Despite his ultimate victory against the Union, Rookes also felt let down by his solicitor, whom he assessed as having little interest in retrying the damages issue.[56] In the event, Rookes reluctantly settled out of court for £4,000,[57] gave up his trade, and worked for the remainder of his life as an English teacher,[58] a profession at which, if his colourful autobiography is any guide, he will have excelled.

Far less is known about the defendants, beyond Rookes' own accounts of them, which we must naturally treat with some caution. Perhaps surprisingly, Rookes seems to have been quite fond of Silverthorne, whom he believed to be a basically good-hearted but 'tempestuous and tormented soul',[59] deeply conflicted about his involvement in the whole affair. Silverthorne died of coronary thrombosis shortly after the trial, his personal and professional life in disarray.[60] Rookes also appears to have held some reluctant respect for Barnard, whom he saw as rough and moody, 'but much wider read and better informed than the two whose names were soon to be linked with his'.[61] Of Fistal, though, Rookes was far less complimentary, and his derisory descriptions of the man make for darkly entertaining reading.[62] Fistal may have got the last laugh, however: he was seemingly promoted by BOAC shortly afterwards.

III. THE PROCEEDINGS

A. Representation and Funding

It is a notable if unsurprising feature of the proceedings that the parties' representatives were drawn largely from the left. Rookes secured the services of Lewis Silkin and Partners in February 1951, well-known affiliates of the Labour

[53] Rookes, *Conspiracy* (n 26) 145.
[54] Rookes conceded to possessing an 'innate stubbornness': ibid 16.
[55] ibid 144, citing Letter from Samuel Silkin to Douglas Rookes (undated).
[56] Smith, Law Behind the Law (n 16) 76.
[57] Editorial, 'Mr. Rookes Accepts 4,000 Damages', *The Times* 56242, 10 February 1965; Rookes, *Conspiracy* (n 26) 150.
[58] Smith, The Law Behind the Law (n 16) 77.
[59] Rookes, *Conspiracy* (n 26) 125.
[60] ibid.
[61] ibid 19.
[62] See, eg, ibid 26–27.

Party, who in turn sought advice from Samuel Silkin.[63] Then at the bar, Silkin would later serve as Attorney-General under two Labour prime ministers before accepting a life peerage in 1985.[64] Silkin represented Rookes throughout the proceedings,[65] first as junior to Neville Faulks QC at trial and in the Court of Appeal and subsequently, then a QC himself, as leading counsel in the House of Lords (with Alan de Piro his junior). Faulks had to return his brief because he was appointed to the High Court bench in 1962.[66]

The defendants were supported throughout the proceedings by the Union – since renamed the Draughtsmen and Allied Technicians' Association (DATA) – and it was the Union, not the defendants themselves, who hired Williams Thompson Partners, a firm well known for its expertise in labour law and 'notable for its Communist Party heritage'.[67] The defendants were represented at trial by Colin Duncan and John Thompson QC, the latter of whom became a judge prior to the first appeal. Duncan represented the defendants in both appeals, where he was joined by J Previt and one of the great legal titans of the time, Gerald Gardiner QC. Gardiner's submissions clearly struck a chord with Lord Devlin, and he deserves at least some of the credit (or opprobrium) for his Lordship's judgment. Certainly, Lord Devlin's private correspondence suggests that he held Gardiner in (grudgingly) high regard, and his Lordship rightly predicted that Gardiner would be appointed Lord Chancellor in Wilson's Labour Government shortly after the proceedings.[68]

Rookes was granted legal aid at some point in 1956–57,[69] although, to his understandable frustration,[70] it would be another four years or so before his claim reached trial in April 1961. Interestingly, and importantly for reasons that we will come to later, the Union paid the defendants' costs but appears to have been unable to pay the damages from Union funds.[71] This was presumably due either to a lack of funds (which seems unlikely), or to some restriction in the terms of the Union's own rules, since to my knowledge there was then (and

[63] Smith, Law Behind the Law (n 16) 50. Rookes claims that he actually approached Gerald Gardiner to represent him, but Gardiner declined 'as he did not take legal aid cases': Rookes, *Conspiracy* (n 26) 122.

[64] L Silkin, The Peerage <www.thepeerage.com/p65937.htm> accessed 7 May 2023.

[65] He resigned before the matter was finalised, however, having been elected to Parliament and embarrassed that he would now be compelled to vote in favour of legislation overturning his own victory in the case: Rookes, *Conspiracy* (n 26) 144.

[66] N Faulks, *A Law unto Myself* (London, Kimber, 1978).

[67] Smith, Law Behind the Law (n 16) 50, citing S Allen, *Thompsons: A Personal History of the Firm and its Founders* (London, Merlin, 2012).

[68] J Sackar, *Lord Devlin* (Oxford, Hart Publishing, 2022) 198, quoting a letter from Lord Devlin to Dean Acheson, 2 May 1964 (Yale University Library, Dean Acheson Papers, folder 98).

[69] Smith, Law Behind the Law (n 16) 51.

[70] Rookes, *Conspiracy* (n 26) 121–23.

[71] Or so Rookes believed: ibid 131. Certainly, a country-wide appeal was established for this purpose.

is now) no general law preventing a Union from indemnifying its members. Indeed, this appears to occur not infrequently,[72] and the very basis of the House of Lords' decision in *Taff Vale* – undisturbed by the Trade Disputes Act 1906 – was that union officials have 'unlimited power of disposition over the funds of the union, except so far as it may be interfered with by the annual general meeting, or restricted by the operation of the society's rules.'[73] But whatever the reason, the Union established a national fund to pay for the damages and, at some stage following the trial but prior to the first appeal, most of the money was in place.[74]

B. The Trial

One of the most striking things about the *Rookes* litigation is that the question of whether punitive damages were available (the 'punitive damages issue') did not arise at all at trial or in the Court of Appeal, and was not even considered in the House of Lords until after the first judicial conference.[75] It would be wrong to dismiss this as an oversight, however. Politically and in the public mind, although not legally,[76] this was a case about the 'right to strike', the maintenance of the 'closed shop' and, more generally, the balance of power between the working class and the industrial complex. It was not, at the outset, a case about the finer points of remedial law. It was also generally accepted at the time that the availability of punitive damages was, if not entirely pellucid, tolerably clear as a matter of practice, and so counsel on both sides might be forgiven if they gave the matter comparatively little thought until it came to a head in the House of Lords.

The trial proceedings are nevertheless of some significance because Sachs J's summing up to the jury formed the basis of the defendants appeal to the House of Lords on the punitive damages issue. Sachs J was clearly unimpressed by the defendants' testimony and the tone of his directions can have left the jury in no doubt that he held the defendants' conduct in low regard, or that – entreaties that jury members must decide for themselves notwithstanding – he interpreted the facts almost entirely in Rookes's favour. Employing a rich

[72] See, eg, *Australian Building and Construction Commissioner v Construction, Forestry, Mining and Energy Union* [2018] HCA 3, (2018) 262 CLR 157 ('*CFMEU*').

[73] *Taff Vale* (n 22) (Lord MacNaughten) 437.

[74] Rookes, *Conspiracy* (n 26) 131.

[75] ibid 139–40.

[76] Sachs J was at pains to make this point to the jury in his summing-up: 'Do not concern yourselves with what the policy should be. Do not get entangled with arguments as to whether the Defendant's Union should have powers to insist on what is known as the 'closed shop' in an individual case … and do not get entangled into arguments whether they should not have the power.': ibid 164–65.

if unsubtle metaphor – which he may, ironically, have adapted from a letter written by Barnard[77] – Sachs J stated that the defendants had been holding the BOAC at 'pistol point',[78] suggested that the Union (ergo the defendants) were using the Union's resolution to strike as a 'negotiating weapon',[79] and remarked that the BOAC had 'been given a beating' by the defendants.[80] Finally, he implored the jury to 'have in mind: "Why use a pistol if you can achieve your object by peaceful means?"',[81] and asked them: 'Does it not look, on the balance of probabilities, as if they were simply willing to say "take any weapon to hand to beat this man"'.[82] The clear insinuation was that the defendants had viciously attacked the plaintiff with everything they had, and that their behaviour was wholly deserving of punishment. Indeed, it may be that Sachs J's summing up to the jury encouraged its members to award the relatively high amount that it did, which, in an ill twist of fate, was probably Rookes's downfall on the punitive damages issue, since this was the 'hook' upon which that aspect of the appeal to the House of Lords was hung.

At no point, however, can Sachs J fairly be said to have blurred the line between the defendants and the Union. Whereas the Union might have been standing behind the defendants, his Honour was clear that it was 'these three Gentlemen … who are the Defendants …'.[83] They were joint tortfeasors, he explained, and so 'entitled amongst each other … to dispute as to who should pay how much according to their blameworthiness'.[84] He also intimated to the jury that the strike was probably unauthorised.[85] Thus, in his summing up, Sachs J stated:

> There it is. You have to consider, in relation to exemplary damages, whether there was a deliberately engineered unofficial 'wild cat' strike, forced by these three to use, at all costs, an illegal pressure, and whether on the other hand there was provocation, which could reasonably be regarded as provocation for that line of conduct.[86]

Whether the jury expected any damages to be paid by the defendants themselves, or whether some or all of the members assumed (or were told during the trial) that the Union would in one way or another finance the defendants' liabilities in the case of a verdict against them, is a slightly different matter to which we will return.

[77] ibid 169.
[78] ibid 185.
[79] ibid 172.
[80] ibid 177.
[81] ibid 194–95.
[82] ibid 195.
[83] ibid 188.
[84] ibid 188.
[85] ibid 194.
[86] ibid 195–96.

C. The Court of Appeal

One might be forgiven for concluding that the punitive damages issue was entirely overlooked in the Court of Appeal,[87] but it was not. Indeed, it seems likely that Gardiner and Duncan presented a line of argument similar to that which they would later present later in the House of Lords.[88] However, it is difficult to know what, exactly, was argued since both of the official case reports omit the pleadings on this issue. In any event, since the Court of Appeal determined that there was no liability, the damages issue was moot and none of the judges considered it.[89]

D. The House of Lords

At Lord Reid's instruction, no arguments were heard on the punitive damages issue in the House of Lords during the first judicial conference,[90] and at that stage their Lordships appeared to be leaning in the respondents' favour on liability.[91] Neville Faulks, no longer acting for Rookes, recalled that one of the Law Lords, 'without committing himself, prepared me for disaster, and Colin Duncan and Gerald Gardiner looked uncommonly pleased with themselves. But then the great Lord Reid reconvened the tribunal.'[92] According to Paterson, 'after the initial hearing Lord Devlin was in a minority of one (or possibly two) favouring the appellant', but 'after a second conference and a reconvened hearing, he won them all round'.[93] When the House reconvened, the mood had changed and the importance of the punitive damages issue became apparent. Gardiner argued that Sachs J had misdirected the jury in various respects on damages, and that the only viable course was to order a retrial:

> As the jury were directed to fix one sum for damages, it is not known whether they took into account the special damages alleged, or awarded £7,500 entirely as exemplary damages. In any event the sum awarded was excessive. The following criticisms are made of the summing-up: (1) Exemplary damages cannot be awarded in a case such as the present. (2) Even if they can, the jury should not have been directed that they were bound to award exemplary damages. (3) The respondents' case on exemplary damages was not put to the jury. (4) The judge mistakenly led the jury to think that the action was in fact, although not in form, against the trade

[87] *Rookes v Barnard* [1963] 1 QB 623 (CA).

[88] Sellers J noted in his judgment that 'the defendants further appeal against the summing-up in respect of damages and against the amount of the jury's award': ibid 659. Gardiner simply stated that 'there is no complaint of misdirection on the facts excepts as to damages': ibid 639, and Duncan's submissions on this point are omitted: ibid 647.

[89] ibid 659 (Sellers J), 685 (Donovan LJ).

[90] Rookes, *Conspiracy* (n 26) 139–40.

[91] A Paterson, *The Law Lords* (London, MacMillan, 1982) 119.

[92] Faulks (n 66) 103.

[93] Paterson (n 91) 119.

union which would pay the damages, whereas in fact a trade union may not pay damages. That is of importance because in considering exemplary damages all the surrounding circumstances, including the means of a defendant, are to be taken into account. (5) The judge wrongly directed the jury that the respondents had acted in a way which they knew to be illegal and that the damages should be increased on that account.[94]

The appellant objected that the respondents should not be permitted to raise new arguments on punitive damages, having failed to do so earlier,[95] but Lord Reid disagreed.[96] Since the House essentially agreed with Gardiner's first criticism (that punitive damages could not be awarded in a case such as this) the remainder were not examined in any detail, which was perhaps just as well for the respondents since some of them are difficult to square with what Sachs J said. With respect, there was no direction at all that the jury 'was bound' to award punitive damages. At most, as Lord Reid accepted, the 'summing up as a whole' might have led the jury to believe that, unless they accepted the case on provocation, they should award exemplary damages.[97] Nor, if we are to give due credit to the jury, was there anything in Sachs J's summing up that could reasonably be said to conflate the respondents with the Union. Moreover, although the House might not have been aware of it, and Sachs J might still have been in error if he led the jury to think otherwise, the Union *had* by this time arranged a fund from which the damages would ultimately be paid.

In any event, the door was now open on the punitive damages issue and Gardiner went on to lay much of the groundwork for Lord Devlin's judgment, citing liberally from Street's *Principles on the Law of Damages*. He summarised his arguments as follows:

> (1) There is something called exemplary damages, which has been awarded for some 200 years, particularly in defamation cases, and has been recognised by the legislature ... (2) It has two distinguishing features, (a) unlike any other damages, it is not compensatory but punitive and (b) the means of the defendant are relevant. (3) There is no tort in which exemplary damages must always be awarded; they can only be awarded in exceptional cases. (4) Either (a) exemplary damages can be awarded in all torts or (b) they can be awarded in some torts and not others, not as a matter of principle but because the law has grown up in that way ...[98]

Silkin urged the House to accept an entirely different conception of exemplary and aggravated damages, which reflected a common understanding at the time but also, and perhaps fatally, resisted clear classification. On Silkin's account, (1) aggravated damages are both punitive and compensatory (for hurt feelings),

[94] *Rookes* (n 1) 1158–59.
[95] ibid 1161.
[96] ibid 1178 (Lord Reid).
[97] ibid.
[98] ibid 1163–64, citing H Street, *Principles of the Law of Damages* (London, Sweet and Maxwell, 1962).

and (2) exemplary damages may be awarded at the discretion of the jury in the majority of cases and in the light of all the circumstances, including whether the wrongdoer's conduct was 'wilful, contumacious, malicious, unscrupulous, etc'.[99] On this basis, he urged, it 'was open to the jury to find that the respondents' conduct was a malevolent attempt in the nature of a personal vendetta to get rid of a man who had defied them',[100] and that this was a sufficient basis for an award of exemplary damages. However, Silkin offered no view at all as to the purpose(s) of exemplary damages,[101] and his account clearly failed to impress Lord Devlin, who we now know was sympathetic to the views of some academic writers hostile to punitive damages, and intent on rationalising the law to curtail the availability of punitive damages.

IV. LORD DEVLIN'S JUDGMENT

A. *Per Curium* and *Per Incurium*

The first (obvious) point to make about Lord Devlin's judgment is that it was not his judgment alone. While he was clearly the driving force behind the House's decision to clarify the law on punitive damages, his judgment 'was actually the product of various suggestions from others on top of his basic framework'.[102] As Lord Devlin later recalled:

> Lord Reid had quite strong views about it but because it was purely an English point of law he didn't wish to write on it. I think he said to me, … well you put something down and I'll see if I agree with it, and I did and the others made a number of suggestions so that it became rather a judgment of the court in that sense. I modified it a good bit to fit in with other people's views.[103]

Lord Reid later viewed the same events with some regret:

> [W]e made a great mistake leaving it to Lord Devlin to give the only judgment because as it turned out people misunderstood it. It would have been much better if somebody else on this had given his own views in his own words and we wouldn't have had this bother.[104]

Most likely, the 'bother' to which his Lordship refers was the Court of Appeal's judgment in *Cassell & Co Ltd v Broome*,[105] in which Lord Denning

[99] ibid 1160.
[100] ibid 1161.
[101] It seems likely, though, given his choice of terminology and the fact that he viewed aggravated damages as partly punitive, that he saw exemplary damages as affording some sort of general deterrence.
[102] Paterson (n 2) 91 fn 115.
[103] Paterson (n 91) 99.
[104] Email from Alan Paterson to author (1 September 2022).
[105] ibid.

famously declared that, if 'ever there was a decision of the House of Lords given *per incurium* this was it.'[106] The gist of Lord Denning's criticism was that Lord Devlin disregarded earlier House of Lords' authority on the issue, in particular *Ley v Hamilton* ('*Ley*').[107] It is debatable whether this is correct, since there is a strong argument that *Ley* actually involved aggravated as opposed to punitive damages, despite Lord Salmon's use of the latter epithet.[108] In a more recent addition to the literature, however, Katsampouka offers a more thorough review of the earlier authorities.[109] She concludes, among other things, that Lord Devlin's categories are based on a series of misconceptions and misclassifications of that authority, and that a number of cases falling outside those categories were either ignored or 'wrongly interpreted as having awarded aggravated rather than punitive damages.'[110] If Katsampouka is correct in her analysis, and I am content to accept that she is, then this clearly removes some of the justificatory force behind Lord Devlin's judgment.

This is far from the end of the matter, however, since *any* attempt to clarify the law on punitive damages was likely to go against the grain of one or other line of authority – a point supported by the conflicting arguments run by the parties. Certainly, this seems to have been the view taken by Lord Devlin, who later claimed that, when 'House of Lord in *Rookes v Barnard* sought to tidy up the law of punitive damages, it was because they considered the law to be in a mess …'.[111] It is also apparent that the Law Lords were simply more concerned with 'the demands of the present' than they were with a 'comprehensive review of the historical cases'.[112] In an interview with Paterson, Lord Devlin openly acknowledged that he was 'really going off the lines' in *Rookes*,[113] and that his decision was grounded in considerations of policy.[114] Speaking more generally of this period in history, Paterson concludes:

> The 'period in the house 1962–66 was one marked by numerous instances of judicial law-making – albeit under the guise or dissimulation … Overt references to policy-considerations in these cases were unusual even where – as in Lord Devlin's exegesis on exemplary damages in *Rookes v Barnard* – the judgment was a purely policy

[106] *Cassell & Co Ltd v Broome* [1972] 2 QB 354 (CA) 382. Lord Devlin and Lord Denning nevertheless appear to have been 'firm friends': Sackar (n 68) 58–59.
[107] RWM Dias, 'The House of Lords and *per Incuriam*' (1971) 29 *CLJ* 188.
[108] ibid 187–89, 188; Sinanis (n 15) 20.
[109] Katsampouka (n 15).
[110] ibid 271.
[111] P Devlin, *The Judge* (Oxford, OUP, 1979) 95.
[112] Sinanis (n 15) 24.
[113] Email from Alan Paterson to author (1 September 2022). The full quote is as follows: 'I think there's something to be said by way of exception to the general rule that when you're really going off the lines then it's quite a good thing to start things off with one judgment because if you get a larger number then nobody will have any line to follow at all.'
[114] Later, in *Uren* (n 13) 641, the Privy Council supported this approach, concluding that the question of whether punitive damages are available is to be answered 'not so much by asserting that reasoning can lead to only one conclusion but rather by coming to a decision as to what the policy of the law should be'.

> based one. It was, however, an era which was marked by a less reverential attitude to precedent culminating in the celebrated adoption of the 1966 Practice Statement on Precedent in the House of Lords … which freed the House from following its own precedents.[115]

For Lord Devlin, the seeds of this less reverential attitude may have been sown while he was a pupil of Goodhart,[116] in whose view the *ratio decidendi* of a case is no more than the sum of the material facts of the case and its outcome,[117] and for whom the constraints of precedent might therefore be vanishingly narrow (depending on which facts are deemed material). Even if Lord Devlin had some sympathy for this view, however, he was no maverick. He was, as Kirby puts it, 'the conservative's radical',[118] and strongly opposed to what he described as 'judicial dynamism' (that is, 'judicial operations in advance of the consensus').[119] In contrast with judicial dynamism, Lord Devlin believed 'judicial activism' to be a legitimate if sub-optimal means of law reform:

> There is a limit to what counsel can do in time that is paid for by their clients, litigants are interested in the decision of their case and not in the development of the law. The persons who may be interested in that are not represented. Yet there are many people who would like to be heard on such questions as liability for careless misstatement or for punitive damages and who could speak adequately through professional bodies. New law ought not to be made until after consultation with the representatives of those who will be concerned with it …
>
> This is in my opinion the best way of lawmaking and I hope to see it greatly extended. But until it is in general use we cannot dispense with the second-best. The strongest argument for judicial activism is not that it is the best method of law reform but that, as things stand, it is in a large area of the law the only method.[120]

In Lord Devlin's view, the law on punitive damages was an area in which the public had impliedly consented to judicial lawmaking, providing it occurred 'in the traditional way, ie in accordance with precedent, and second, that parliamentary interference should be regarded as unobjectionable.'[121] Of course, we hit a snag here if we believe that *Rookes* was decided contrary to precedent, but as I have said, I doubt that any meaningful reform of the law in this area would have been possible that was not, in one way or another, inconsistent with precedent. Unless the law was to be left in a jumble some action was needed.

[115] Paterson (n 2) 264–65.

[116] Sinanis (n 15) 26.

[117] A Goodhart, 'The Ratio Decidendi of a Case' (1959) 22 *MLR* 117.

[118] M Kirby, 'A Conservative's Recipe for Legal Change: Lord Devlin and Reform of the English Trial' *The Australian* (January 1980).

[119] Devlin (n 111) 9.

[120] ibid 13. Ironically, the Law Commission's consultation process and recommendations on punitive damages were at odds with Lord Devlin's account and highly critical of his 'categories' formulation.

[121] ibid 9.

Whether the action taken was justifiable is a different matter, to which we now (briefly) turn.

B. Policy Considerations

Two immediate and interrelated problems arise when attempting to unpack Lord Devlin's judgment in *Rookes*. The first is that the term 'policy' is notoriously equivocal and ambulatory, and might refer to anything from broad social policy concerns employed in an instrumentalist fashion, through considerations of legal policy (such as coherence, consistency, and so forth), to what might better be described as underlying legal principles (such as *restitutio in integrum*). These various conceptions of policy might also seep into one another, and judges rarely specify which one they are invoking. The word 'policy' might also, of course, be used in a looser sense to describe the positions held by political groups. Whatever else the House of Lords might have had in mind in *Rookes*, though, we may be sure that party politics was not one of them. In a letter to Thompson, Gardiner conceded that, on the question of liability, he could 'see no reason whatever to suppose that … [their Lordships] were influenced by any party-political considerations, or were doing other than deciding the case according to law to the best of their ability'.[122] If party politics played no role in deciding the Trade Dispute Act issues in *Rookes*, it almost certainly played no role in the punitive damages issue, which was of technical interest to lawyers but 'left the public cold'.[123]

The second problem is that Lord Devlin does not clearly articulate the policy concerns that guided his judgment. However, we now know that his Lordship saw his judgment as a 'pure policy decision on how to rationalise the law (an assessment shared by Lord Wilberforce and Diplock)',[124] and, although he did not explicitly say so, his basic position on punitive damages appears to have drawn on – and was at any rate markedly consistent with – prominent academics work of the time, in particular *Salmond's Law of Torts*[125] and Street's *Principles of the Law of Damages*.[126] As Lord Devlin put it:

> Exemplary damages are essentially different from ordinary damages. The object of damages in the usual sense of the term is to compensate. The object of exemplary damages is to punish and deter. It may well be thought that this confuses the civil and

[122] Letter from Gerald Gardiner to John Thompson (4 March 1964), cited in Smith, Law Behind the Law (n 16) 77.

[123] Devlin (n 111) 11.

[124] Paterson (n 2) 205 fn 105.

[125] WTS Stallybrass, *Salmonds Law of Torts*, 10th edn (London, Sweet & Maxwell, 1945) 127. For the possible influence of this text on Lord Devlin, see Katsampouka, ch 10 of this volume, p 211.

[126] Street (n 98). A detailed account of Street's potential influence on Lord Devlin is provided by Sinanis (n 15).

> criminal functions of the law; and indeed, so far as I know, the idea of exemplary damages is peculiar to English law. … [Your] Lordships therefore have to consider whether it is open to the House to remove an anomaly from the law of England.[127]

Whereas the essential distinction between aggravated and exemplary damages has been broadly accepted, the idea that punishment has no role to play in civil cases, and that punitive damages are therefore anomalous, remains contentious. The basic arguments are well trodden and will not be explored in detail here. It suffices to say that, for correctivists, the assertion that punitive damages are anomalous marks a welcome return to principle,[128] whereas others argue that there was (and is) no reason in logic or history to insist that punishment is the sole function of the criminal law:[129] the proposition that the private law does not punish is founded on no more than an assertion,[130] critics say, and an ahistoric one at that. There are also practical problems. For example, compensatory and restitutionary remedies are said to provide insufficient protection for wrongs: aggravated (compensatory) damages require an aggravation of the loss on the claimant's part and restitutionary damages require a profit on the defendant's part, whereas punitive damages require neither.[131] The criminal law is also incapable of fully realising its own purpose (the punishment of wrongdoing), because, unless and until conduct is deemed 'criminal', the police cannot investigate that conduct and prosecution services cannot prosecute it,[132] and even if conduct is in fact criminal, the criminal justice system is imperfect and that conduct might go unpunished. In contrast, private individuals may choose to initiate civil action in respect of the same conduct, and punitive damages can provide a mechanism by which to develop the law and increase the likelihood of wrongdoers being punished.

The general rejection of punitive damages might also result in some practical benefits, however, one of which is illuminated by the facts of *Rookes*. It will be recalled that Rookes's damages were paid from a fund established by the Union and that, despite Gardiner's protestations that the jury had been misled into thinking that the Union would pay the punitive element of the award, the defendants were probably never in serious jeopardy of having to pay any damages personally. Indeed, in most cases unions will directly indemnify officials from personal liabilities arising in connection with industrial activity, even when it is unauthorised. Lord Devlin's judgment in *Rookes* limited the circumstances in which courts might be forced to reckon with the difficult question of whether punitive damages are appropriate when the defendant is indemnified,

[127] *Rookes* (n 1) 1221.
[128] See, eg, Weinrib (n 10) 294; Beever (n 10) 110.
[129] Burrows (n 9) 376; Goudkamp and Katsampouka (n 9).
[130] McBride (n 9) 195.
[131] Burrows (n 9) 376.
[132] McBride (n 9) 192–93.

but other jurisdictions must do so and, if the availability of punitive damages were ever to be expanded in England, it would be as well to do so in full view of the challenges that indemnities pose.[133]

C. Indemnities and 'Crowdfunding'

Whether indemnities (or other similar arrangements) create a problem for punitive damages depends, in part, on what we believe the purpose of those damages to be. The standard answer, provided by Lord Devlin in *Rookes*, is that punitive damages seek to 'punish and deter'. This is not immediately helpful, since punishment and deterrence are broad and slippery concepts, which might mean different things to different people and across different legal contexts.[134] However, if the goal is to punish and deter the individual wrongdoer (specific deterrence), then this is clearly not achieved if the defendant is indemnified. If the goal is to deter future would-be wrongdoers (general deterrence), then this goal might be achieved if the defendant is indemnified, insofar as the indemnifier and others in the same position are incentivised to limit the risk of similar conduct occurring in the future.[135] However, if the indemnifier and others in the same position choose not to take steps to manage the risk – and some unions, at least, are unlikely to do so[136] – then general deterrence is not achieved.

Punitive damages might also be explained on slightly different grounds, one of which Lord Devlin may have hinted at in his judgment. In his contribution to this book, Barker observes that, on one view,

[133] And a challenge it may well be. At the time of writing, strike actions over stagnant wages and cost-of-living concerns are rife across the industrialised world, and only the most optimistic observer would predict an end to this situation any time soon. In many instances, industrial relations statutes have now made the issue a statutory one, as *CFMEU* (n 72) demonstrates, but outlier cases will remain. Indemnities are also afforded to public servants in some instances, albeit more frequently in Australia than in the UK. See generally I Field, 'Good Faith Protections and Public Sector Liability' (2016) 23 *Torts Law Journal* 210.

[134] See, in particular, K Barker, 'Punishment in Private Law: No Such Thing (Any More)' in E Bant et al (eds), *Punishment and Private Law* (Oxford, Hart Publishing, 2021) 35. Punishment and deterrence might also be incompatible goals. See B Feldthusen, 'Punitive Damages in Canada: Can the Coffee Be Too Hot' (1995) 17 *Loyola of Los Angeles International and Comparative Law Review* 793, 799–800.

[135] Either way, there is reason to doubt that the civil law is, generally speaking, very good at deterring wrongdoing, although it might have a greater impact on the behaviours of institutions and corporations (which typically operate risk management practices) than it does on the conduct of individuals (who are unlikely to consider civil consequences at all). See, eg, B van Rooij and M Brownlee, 'Does Tort Deter? Inconclusive Empirical Evidence about the Effect of Liability in Preventing Harmful Behaviour' in B Van Rooij and DD Sokol (eds), *Cambridge Handbook on Compliance* (Cambridge, CUP, 2020). See also WJ Cardi, RD Penfield and AH Yoon, 'Does Tort Law Deter Individuals? A Behavioural Science Study' (2012) 9 *Journal of Empirical Legal Studies* 567.

[136] *CFMEU* (n 72) [86] (Keane, Nettle and Gordon JJ).

> the purpose of condemnation is not to rectify private injury, but to meet a public end in expressing society's commitment to the rule of law and the values embedded in it. Lord Devlin was close to this idea, I think, in *Rookes v Barnard*, when he said that exemplary awards 'vindicate the strength of the law.'[137]

We simply do not know whether punitive damages are effective in inculcating general respect for the law and legal institutions.[138] For my money, it is a more plausible goal than deterrence (general or specific), although since punitive damages are typically awarded in far smaller sums than compensatory damages,[139] any message that they send is likely to be muted. But whether punitive damages achieve this purpose, there is surely a risk that awarding punitive damages against an indemnified defendant might send entirely the *wrong* message. Far from vindicating the strength of the law, a punitive award that the defendant does not have to pay is liable to undermine legal institutions in the public consciousness, especially when the defendant occupies a position of power or authority.

One possible solution to these problems is to issue a court order alongside the award of punitive damages, which requires the defendant to pay those damages personally. This solution was recently considered by the Australian High Court in *Australian Building and Construction Commissioner v Construction, Forestry, Mining and Energy Union* (*CFMEU*),[140] albeit in the context of statutory pecuniary penalties. Myles, the second defendant and a vice president of the CFMEU, the first defendant, initiated a blockade at a work site operated by the claimants, preventing concrete trucks from entering the site and resulting in the spoilage of concrete that had already been poured.[141] The defendants conceded that the blockade was intended to coerce the claimant into allowing a CFMEU delegate onto the site, and that this contravened section 348 of the Fair Work Act 2009 (Cth).[142] That contravention gave rise to civil remedies under the Act, including punitive penalties, pursuant to which the CFMEU was fined A$60,000 and Myles was fined A$18,000.[143] Both defendants had engaged in similar conduct on numerous prior occasions,

> in the belief that any penalties that were imposed would be satisfied from funds which the CFMEU received from members and, to an extent of $8 million for the financial year ending 31 December 2014, from 'operating grant receipts' paid from public funds.[144]

[137] Barker, ch 6 of this volume, p 125 citing *Rookes* (n 1) 1226 and *Lewis v ACT* [2020] HCA 26, (2020) 271 CLR 192 [172] (Edelman J).
[138] See generally Barker, ch 6 of this volume.
[139] It may be different in the US, where punitive awards are often far higher than compensatory awards. In the UK, however, punitive damages awards are seldom excessive. See J Goudkamp and E Katsampouka, 'An Empirical Study of Punitive Damages' (2018) 38 *OJLS* 90, 92.
[140] *CFMEU* (n 72).
[141] ibid [80] (Keane, Nettle and Gordon JJ).
[142] ibid [3].
[143] ibid [4].
[144] ibid [86] (Keane, Nettle and Gordon JJ).

In order to ensure that Myles felt the sting of the punitive award, the trial judge issued a 'non-indemnification order' against the CFMEU, preventing it from affording Myles any financial assistance. As she put it, the 'effectiveness of an exercise of judicial power to impose penalties is significantly impaired where the reality is that the contravener is likely to be entirely indemnified from the consequences of the order'.[145] The first issue on appeal was whether this order was valid. A second issue was whether, if the order was not valid, a 'personal payment order' might instead be issued against Myles, preventing him from seeking or accepting indemnification from the CFMEU.

Although the case turned on complex and context-specific questions of statutory construction, many of the issues raised are of more general import. First, can a court make an order against one party, which is not the subject of a punitive penalty, preventing it from indemnifying the person against whom the penalty is made? In the specific context, the High Court unanimously agreed that such an order was not incidental to the statutory power afforded by the Act to impose a pecuniary penalty, and was thus invalid.[146]

In contrast, a majority of the Court concluded that a personal payment order against the defendant would fall naturally within the statutory power.[147] But on what basis might such an order be made in the absence of a specific statutory power? A prohibitory injunction may only be made in rare cases when a specific right has been infringed, such as a validly stated restraint of trade clause, or where there is an ongoing wrong, such as trespass to land or goods. There is no primary right to demand that a secondary obligation to pay compensation be satisfied by a wrongdoer, and thus no wrong to enjoin. Were a personal payment order to be made in support of a punitive damages claim at common law, therefore, the power to do so would first need to be granted by statute.[148]

There are also obvious difficulties in enforcing any order that is made. As Keane, Nettle and Gordon JJ for the majority observed,

> such orders have sometimes been criticised as creating special problems of enforcement, including by exposing vexed questions of identifying the source of funds used for payment. These are legitimate concerns. There is no point in a court making orders that cannot be enforced, and, if orders do go unenforced, the lack of enforcement is likely to detract from the prestige of the court and, ultimately, the efficacy of its processes. Even so, it should not be thought that difficulties of enforcement

[145] *Director of the Fair Work Building Industry Inspectorate v Construction, Forestry, Mining and Energy Union (No 2)* [2016] FCA 436 [190].

[146] ibid [28]–[33] (Kiefel CJ), [58] Gagler J, [110] (Keane, Nettle and Gordon JJ).

[147] ibid [49] (Kiefel CJ), [115] (Keane, Nettle and Gordon JJ). Gagler J dissented: [58].

[148] Nor does any general power exist in a criminal context to force an offender to personally pay a fine, although if the court is concerned that an offender will not be punished by a fine (because, say, a wealthy family member will meet the cost) then an alternative sentence such as community service order might be made, in which case the goals of the criminal justice system are still achieved. Civil courts, in contrast, have no alternative means of imposing punishment.

> are necessarily determinative. Ordinarily, it is to be assumed that a contravener who is ordered not to seek or accept indemnity or contribution from a co-contravener in relation to a pecuniary penalty will abide by the order rather than risk detection and punishment for contempt. It is also to be remembered that union officials who aid, abet, counsel or procure one of their number to contravene such an order may themselves be found guilty of contempt. And, as will be explained, this process may be facilitated by use of a penal notice. Consequently, it is not a precondition of the making of … [such] orders that the court be positively satisfied of their practical enforceability.[149]

Whether difficulties of enforcement might undermine the purpose of awarding punitive damages at common law damages depends, again, on what we believe that purpose to be.[150] In *CFMEU*, the trial judge sought both to deter the defendant (specific deterrence) and to deter future wrongdoing (general deterrence),[151] but neither of these purposes is served if a non-indemnity or personal payment order is contravened and not enforced. As Keane, Nettle and Gordon JJ observed, issuing a non-indemnification order or personal payment order that cannot be enforced is also more likely to undermine the strength of the law than it is to vindicate it. The possibility of contempt proceedings might have some deterrent effect. In my view, however, holding a party in contempt would do little to vindicate the efficacy of the court's processes or the institution of punitive damages. If anything, the need to resort to contempt proceedings seems indicative of a weakness in those processes.

The prospect of a claimant benefiting from an indemnity, or some other form of external funding to which the claimant has a right, raises further issues. In *Rookes*, Lord Devlin accepted (and both of the parties agreed) that the means of the parties are relevant to the calculation of punitive damages.[152] If the defendant is to be indemnified by a third party, should this be considered in assessing the defendant's means? In my view it should. If it is appropriate to take account of a defendant's income or assets in determining the quantum of punitive damages, then there is no obvious reason why an indemnity should be disregarded, albeit that the defendant and indemnifier cannot be treated as one and the same (so that the indemnifier is, in effect, treated as the defendant). Whereas the defendant's relative means might be enlarged by an indemnity, however, it is hard to see how increasing the amount of an award on that basis might further the stated goals of punitive damages, unless the award surpasses the level of the indemnity provided (and the defendant must personally pay the difference). Indemnities are comparable in this respect with insurance policies.[153]

[149] ibid [131] (Keane, Nettle and Gordon JJ). See also [47] (Kiefel CJ).

[150] In *CFMEU* (n 72), the question was one of statutory construction, and so concerns as to enforcement could not be determinative because the goal was to give effect to parliament's intention: ibid [47] (Kiefel CJ).

[151] ibid [87] (Keane, Nettle and Gordon JJ).

[152] *Rookes* (n 1) 1127–28.

[153] On which, see generally Barker, ch 6 of this volume.

More generally, should the mere fact that a defendant is indemnified bear upon the decision to award punitive damages in the first place? It might be argued that, since any indemnity arrangement between a defendant and a third party is external to the moral relationship between the parties to the dispute, it is irrelevant to the question of damages.[154] As Barker demonstrates in his contribution to this book, however, the judicially stated purpose of punitive damages is not to correct an interpersonal wrong but to punish and deter wrongdoing.[155] Punitive damages operate outside the framework of corrective justice and so it simply makes no sense to ignore external factors such as insurance coverage or, indeed, an indemnity, in deciding whether to make a punitive award.[156] It does not follow that the existence of an indemnity ought necessarily to preclude a punitive award. The critical question, as when a defendant is insured, is whether the goals of punitive damages can be achieved in the circumstances, notwithstanding the existence of an indemnity. Thus, specific deterrence might be achieved, as noted, if the quantum of the damages exceeds the indemnity, and the defendant must pay the difference. In some instances, punitive damages might also achieve a measure of general deterrence if they discourage certain parties (such as unions) from granting indemnities in respect of similarly wrongful conduct in the future, in turn exposing putative wrongdoers to the prospect of paying in full any punitive damages awarded against them.

It would plainly be wrong in principle, however, to increase a punitive award against a defendant as a means of surreptitiously punishing an indemnifier. It is true that (in contrast with an insurer) an indemnifier might in some instances be morally responsible in some way for the defendant's wrong,[157] and if the purported goals of punitive damages are to be achieved then it might seem appropriate in such a case to increase the award made against the defendant so that the indemnifier feels its sting. But unless the indemnifier's own conduct renders it a joint tortfeasor, or, as in *CFMEU*, some statutory basis exists upon which to hold the indemnifying party independently to account for its role in the wrongdoing, the culpability of the indemnifier can have no bearing on the quantum of the award made against the defendant. In such a scenario, the force of any message sent by the award might fall flat and, if the damages are modest relative to the means of the indemnifier, neither punishment nor deterrence are likely to be achieved.

[154] In this respect, indemnifying parties differ importantly from defendants who are vicariously liable, since the latter are (ordinarily) jointly and severally liable for the wrong and all of the damages awarded in respect of that wrong, including any punitive award. See, eg, *Rowlands v Chief Constable of the Merseyside Police* [2006] EWCA Civ 1773, [2007] 1 WLR 1065. The proportion of each defendant's contribution is also (again ordinarily) of no concern to the claimant or the world at large.

[155] See Barker, ch 6 of this volume, p 111.

[156] ibid.

[157] As was the case in *CFMEU* (n 72). In a non-union context, the most obvious type of situation in which this might occur is when the defendant is a member of, and has acted to further the agenda of, some special interest group.

Of course, the Union did not directly indemnify the defendants in *Rookes* – the damages were paid from a national fund established specifically for that purpose – but such funding practices have the potential to be just as damaging as indemnities, if not more so, since they send a very public message of support for conduct that a court has deemed worthy of punishment. Of particular note here is an increase in the use of crowdfunding platforms (such as GoFundMe), which may be established for the benefit of defendants and provide access to funds on a scale unimaginable prior to the advent of the internet.[158] One recent high-profile example is a GoFundMe campaign established to help Amber Heard pay US$5 million in punitive damages to Johnny Depp for defamation[159] (albeit that this fund was shut down because the organisers did not actually have any connection with Heard or her counsel).[160] Would, could or should a court concern itself with the source of funding in a case such as this? Should such funds be taken into account in assessing the defendant's means? The view might well be taken that it would better to avoid these difficult questions in the first place (or at least as far as possible).

V. CONCLUSION

Rookes was in many ways a tragedy, more so than a conspiracy. The defendants clearly abused the Union's (not inconsiderable) power to achieve their ends, and in my view Rookes deserved his punitive damages. The fact that the power in question was not governmental seems neither here nor there. But the defendants were also small cogs in a large and powerful machine, which demanded unflinching commitment to its cause, and one gets the sense that none of the parties (except, perhaps, Fistal) really wanted matters to escalate as they did. Silverthorne, in particular, appears to have been a victim of circumstance, even if those circumstances were partly of his own making. The statutory framework in place at the time ruled out the possibility of a civil suit against the Union itself, but in the particular circumstances of the case it was probably the more appropriate target. In this respect, modern industrial relations statutes strike a more appropriate balance, by allowing civil suits to be brought against all parties in appropriate circumstances.[161]

[158] On the sheer scale of GoFundMe campaigns generally, see R Monroe, 'When GoFundMe Gets Ugly' *The Atlantic*, November 2019 <www.theatlantic.com/magazine/archive/2019/11/gofundme-nation/598369> accessed 7 May 2023.

[159] *John C Depp II v Amber Laura Heard* (Fairfax County Circuit Court, 11 June 2022).

[160] H Hamilton, 'GoFundMe Removes Fundraiser Claiming to Help Amber Heard Pay Damages' *Washington Examiner*, 5 June 2022 <www.washingtonexaminer.com/news/gofundme-removes-fundraiser-claiming-to-help-amber-heard-pay-damages-report> accessed 7 May 2023.

[161] See, eg, Trade Union and Labour Relations (Consolidation) Act 1992 (UK), ss 20–22.

It was not my purpose in this chapter to reach a firm position on the merits of Lord Devlin's judgment, although it is to be hoped that, taken collectively, the case studies in this edited collection will help others to do so. My more modest aim, aside from providing a more complete account of the context in which *Rookes* was decided, was to explore the practical difficulties presented by indemnities and other similar funding arrangements. On balance, I do not think that these difficulties, though far from trivial, singularly justify the general rejection of punitive damages. They ought, however, to be taken into account in any future attempts to reform the English law on punitive damages.

5

Cassell & Co Ltd v Broome (1972) Maritime, Generational and Judicial Clashes

JAMES GOUDKAMP*

I. THE ARCTIC CONVOYS OF WORLD WAR II

When the Soviet Union entered World War II, the only way in which Britain and the United States could provide it with support in the near term was by sending it war materials. The most direct route by which these could be transported to Russia was by convoy passing through the Artic waters. But this journey was fraught with danger. This was because, as Churchill recounted in *The Hinge of Fate*, 'Hitler had directed the German Navy to concentrate its strength in Norway ... not only to prevent a British descent, but also to obstruct the flow of supplies and munitions to Russia'.[1] Despite the risks to which the convoys were exposed, which were greatly magnified during the summer months due to perpetual daylight, both Roosevelt and Stalin pressured Churchill to do whatever he could to transport resources until a second front could be opened.

The convoy, known as PQ17 and consisting of 34 merchant ships, represented the climax of the Anglo-American endeavours in this regard. On 27 June 1942, it sailed from Iceland bound for Russia. Its escort comprised six destroyers as

* This chapter has benefited immeasurably from documents held by the Churchill Archives Centre (specifically, the 'Papers of Jackie Broome GBR/0014/BRME 14' and 'Papers of Stephen Roskill GBR/0014/ROSK 19'). These materials are on such a staggering scale that it has been impossible to take account of more than a small fraction of them within the very limited space available. I refer to the documents held by the Centre by the markers '[BRME box/file/page]' and '[ROSK box/file/page]'. I am grateful to the Oxford Law Faculty for providing funding that allowed me to access these materials. I would like to thank the Bodleian Law Library, which provided me with electronic copies of many sources. Finally, I acknowledge the constructive comments of participants in the workshop at which a draft of this chapter was delivered. I am especially grateful to Mark Leeming and John Sackar who alerted me to certain sources that would have otherwise escaped my attention.

[1] W Churchill, *The Second World War Volume IV: The Hinge of Fate* (London, Penguin Classics, 2005) 235.

well as anti-aircraft ships, submarines and various smaller vessels. The closest support was that provided by several American and British cruisers and destroyers under the command of Rear-Admiral Sir Louis Hamilton. On 1 July, Hitler's forces identified the convoy and thereafter shadowed it and attacked it from the air. A new danger was then perceived. According to Churchill, by 4 July, there 'were strong reasons'[2] for the Admiralty to consider that the German battleship the *TIRPITZ* – then the most powerful warship in the world – and its supporting vessels were about to intercept the convoy. Because the cruisers commanded by Rear-Admiral Hamilton were no match for these German forces, it was thought 'that the only hope of saving a proportion of the convoy lay in scattering as widely as possible before the enemy arrived'.[3]

Accordingly, late on 4 July, the Admiralty issued three signals to Hamilton on the direct personal orders of the First Sea Lord, Admiral Sir Dudley Pound. The first, sent at 9.11 pm, was a direction to the cruiser force to withdraw to the westward. The second, sent at 9.23 pm, instructed the convoy to disperse and proceed to Russian ports. Finally, at 9.36 pm, a signal was given for the convoy to scatter.[4] In deciding to give the order to scatter, it appears that Pound was influenced by intelligence that had come to his attention via Commander Rodger Winn (later Lord Justice Winn)[5] as well as discussions with his chief advisor, Lieutenant-Commander Norman Denning (a younger brother of Lord Denning).[6] The signal to scatter was interpreted by those at sea, and could only have been interpreted, as indicating that the German surface fleet was about to attack with overwhelming force. Upon its being relayed, the merchant ships duly fanned out.

In charge of the escort was Commander John Egerton Broome, who was generally known as 'Jack' or 'Jackie'. The signals placed him on the horns of a dilemma. He had received no orders from either the Admiralty or from Hamilton. His instructions were to protect the convoy but, upon its having scattered, it could no longer be protected. In these circumstances, he proposed to Hamilton that his destroyers should join the latter's cruisers in the hope that they could keep the *TIRPITZ* occupied for long enough to give the scattering convoy a chance to escape. Hamilton acquiesced and Broome signalled to the escort accordingly.

However, the feared attack never came. It transpired that the German surface forces were still at anchor when the order to scatter was given due to Hitler, in one of his many strategic blunders, having prohibited the *TIRPITZ* from being used unless Britain's aircraft carriers had been located. Giving the order to

[2] ibid 229.

[3] ibid 235.

[4] ibid 235.

[5] Letter from Sir John Langford-Holt to Theodore Goddard & Co (25 July 1968) [BRME 1/1/51–52].

[6] R Brodhurst, *Churchill's Anchor: Admiral of the Fleet Sir Dudley Pound* (Barnsley, Leo Cooper, 2000) 244.

scatter was thus a mistake. The decision as to how to proceed should have been left to the naval officers who were at the scene. But because this was not done, the convoy ended up defenceless and hence vulnerable to U-boat and air attack. Most of the merchant vessels were gradually picked off. Out of the 34 ships that had left Iceland, 23 were sunk. To put this into context, more than 150 lives were lost together with huge quantities of *matérial*, including more than 200 aircraft and 400 tanks. Churchill remarked that 'This was one of the most melancholy naval episodes in the whole of the war'.[7]

A great deal has been written about the Arctic convoys and, in particular, Convoy PQ17.[8] These writings include a book authored by Mr David Irving entitled *The Destruction of PQ 17*, which was published in 1968 by Cassell & Co Limited. One of its distinctive features is that it attributed all or most of the responsibility for the withdrawal of the destroyers to Broome. It accused him of cowardice and indifference to the convoy's fate. It also alleged that he had disobeyed orders by proceeding closer to German air bases in Norway than had been directed. The publication of Irving's book triggered the proceedings – *Cassell & Co Ltd v Broome* – that are the subject of this chapter.

The case involved an extraordinary clash between the Court of Appeal and the House of Lords. The former dramatically held that it was not bound by a speech that Lord Devlin had given in *Rookes v Barnard*,[9] with which all other members of the Appellate Committee had concurred, on the basis that it had been decided *per incuriam*. It also advised lower courts to disregard it. Any attempt to follow *Rookes* was said to be 'bound to lead to confusion'.[10] Predictably, on an appeal against the Court of Appeal's decision, the House of Lords reprimanded the former for having had the temerity to suggest that judges were free to proceed other than according to its pronouncements. It also affirmed the correctness of the decision in *Rookes* and, accordingly, the infamous 'categories test', which restricts the power to award punitive damages to just three situations (ie, (1) cases involving oppressive, arbitrary or unconstitutional conduct by servants of the Government; (2) cases in which the defendant was motivated by a desire to make a profit; and (3) cases in which statute authorised their award).

II. THE PROTAGONISTS

Before delving into the details of the proceedings, it is convenient to add some colour regarding the protagonists. Broome was born in 1901 in Seattle, Washington, but

[7] Churchill (n 1) 237.

[8] See, eg, SW Roskill, '*The War at Sea 1939–1945*, vol 2 (Uckfield, Naval and Military Press, 1956) ch 5; P Lund and H Lundlan, *PQ 17: Convoy to Hell – The Survivor's Story* (London, Foulsham, 1968); J Broome, *Convoy is to Scatter: The Story of PQ17* (London, Futura Publications, 1972).

[9] *Rookes v Barnard* [1964] AC 1129 (HL). Regarding *Rookes*, see Field, ch 4 of this volume.

[10] *Cassell & Co Ltd v Broome* [1971] 2 QB 354 (CA) 384 (Lord Denning MR).

was raised in England. He served in the Royal Navy during both world wars. In 1942, he was promoted to the rank of Captain. In 1943, he was awarded the Distinguished Service Medal. A skilled cartoonist and caricaturist, Broome enjoyed drawing during his spare time (his drawings include a roundabout in Oxford adorned with several signposts all of which read 'Pub'). In 1947, he transitioned to civilian life and worked primarily as a writer on naval subjects. He was apparently well off. For many years, he maintained homes in both Chelsea and Oxford and was a member of, and frequent visitor to, the Garrick Club. Voluminous papers that he deposited with the Churchill Archives Centre and the books that he wrote reveal him to have been a highly intelligent and articulate man with a good sense of humour.

As regards convoy PQ17, Broome explained that it would 'always be my gloomiest nightmare'.[11] He attributed responsibility for the disaster to Pound and his advisors. He described the catastrophe as 'an epic in back-seat driving by a senile maniac'[12] and referred to the First Sea Lord as 'the first chap in naval history to have scattered a convoy by remote control'.[13] He was deeply offended by Irving's account of the relevant events. Thus, in correspondence with his friends he referred to Irving's 'malicious ignorance' and described his book in question as 'nasty'[14] and 'trash'.[15] He also wrote that 'Seldom has anyone shown such ill-mannered, conceited arrogance as this young author. If the BBC awarded a four-letter Oscar, it was his, outright'.[16]

Irving could hardly have contrasted more sharply with Broome.[17] He was born in Essex on 24 March 1938, which was not long before the events involving Convoy PQ17 unfolded. His father had served in the Royal Navy, which is ironic given that many of Irving's works were anti-British. His mother had been a professional writer and illustrator. In 1957, Irving started but never completed a degree in physics at Imperial College, London. Declared medically unfit for national service, in 1960 he took employment as a steelworker. In 1961, he started reading for a degree in economics at University College, London. While studying for that degree, he worked as a night-watchman at a building

[11] Letter from Captain John Broome to Admiral Sir Angus Graham (19 November 1968) [BRME 1/3/10]. In his official report to the Admiralty, Broome wrote that leaving the convoy 'was the most unpleasant decision I have ever had to make' (quoted in *Broome* (n 10) 377 (Lord Denning MR)).

[12] Letter from Captain John Broome to Admiral Sir Angus Graham (19 November 1968) [BRME 1/3/10].

[13] ibid.

[14] Letter from Captain John Broome to Vice Admiral Sir John Hayes (8 December 1968) [BRME 1/2/20].

[15] Letter from Captain John Broome to Admiral Sir Angus Cunningham (19 November 1968) [BRME 1/3/10].

[16] Letter from Captain John Broome to Vice Admiral Sir John Hayes (3 January 1969) [BRME 1/2/24–25].

[17] The text in this paragraph and the next draws on a letter that Irving wrote to his counsel by way of background dated 22 January 1970, which is available on Irving's website: <www.fpp.co.uk/Legal/PQ17Libel/Background220170.html> accessed 7 May 2023.

in Kensington. In order to keep himself occupied while at work, Irving started writing about World War II. The pay for this moonlighting was lucrative and he resolved to pursue a career as a professional writer. Irving's technique for securing interviews with public figures was unconventional. He would turn up unannounced in the evenings at their front door and ask if time could be made available for an interview a few days later. He apparently employed this 'personal approach technique' with Mr Justice Winn (as he then was) in connection with the research for *The Destruction of PQ 17*. Irving reports that the discussions that ensued were cordial, although this sits awkwardly with his acknowledging that the judge subsequently 'circulated a very hostile account of [his] having gate-crashed his house'.[18]

As for the publisher of the book, Cassell & Co, it was a large and experienced publishing house. It had earned a significant reputation as regards books on military history, having published Churchill's multi-volume classic, *The Second World War*. Cassell & Co apparently paid Irving a £2,000 (the equivalent of around £40,000 today) advance royalty for *The Destruction of PQ 17*.[19] Irving apparently hoped that the work would sell half-a-million copies, which would have resulted in both he and Cassell & Co making a vast profit.[20]

III. THE BOOK IS PUBLISHED

Irving had originally intended to call the book *The Knight's Move*. That title had been based on the name that the Germans had given to their operation to intercept the Arctic convoys. While carrying out research for the book, Irving wrote a letter to a German writer in which he said that he was 'all for attacking [Broome] because he will undoubtedly launch a Press counter-attack'.[21] Also as part of his research, Irving visited Broome at his home in Chelsea in order to speak with him about the convoy.[22] During this meeting he seemingly asked Broome if he had shot German pilots who he had plucked out of the water.[23] On 6 November 1966, Irving gave Broome a copy of the manuscript. The next day, Broome telephoned him angrily and complained that it was 'full of inaccuracies'.[24]

[18] 'Two Notes on my Techniques' (23 January 1970) <www.fpp.co.uk/Legal/PQ17Libel/Methods230170.html> accessed 7 May 2023. See also Irving's remarks quoted in an issue of *The Sunday Times* (the date of which is unknown) [ROSK 19/1/15].

[19] Letter from Captain John Broome to Vice Admiral Sir John Hayes (3 January 1969) [BRME 1/2/24–25].

[20] ibid 392.

[21] *Broome* (n 10) 375 (Lord Denning MR).

[22] ibid.

[23] Letter from Captain John Broome to Vice Admiral Sir William O'Brien (29 September 1968) [BRME 1/2/76].

[24] *Broome* (n 10) 375 (Lord Denning MR).

Irving initially offered the book to his regular publisher, William Kimber & Co. It declined to publish it on the recommendation of Captain Stephen Roskill,[25] who was the official naval historian (and the brother of Lord Roskill). Captain Roskill presciently wrote in his review, which the publisher showed to Irving, that[26]

> in general this book reeks of defamation and any publisher should be very cautious before issuing it. … I am no legal expert, but I'd be surprised if the publisher of this book, as it is written, does not end up in the law courts.

William Kimber & Co told Irving that the book was[27]

> a continuous witch hunt of Captain Broome, filled with exaggerated criticisms of what he did or did not do. … We could not possibly publish the book as it is unless you took out insurance against any writs for libel …

These and other exchanges demonstrated, as Lord Denning would later put it, 'that Mr. Irving deliberately set out to attack Commander Broome and in spite of the most explicit warnings persisted in his attack, because it would help sell the book'.[28]

In the event, Cassell & Co agreed to publish the book. Like Irving, it was well aware that it was defamatory and had been repeatedly warned of the possible consequences of publishing it.[29] For instance, on 27 December 1967 Broome wrote to Cassell & Co complaining that the intended book was defamatory. Cassell & Co responded stating that 'drastic revisions'[30] had been made to the text in view of his comments. In fact, and as Cassell & Co knew, none of the revisions affected the relevant paragraphs. On 16 February 1968, a director of Cassell & Co circulated an internal memorandum that stipulated that 'absolutely and positively not one single copy, on any pretext whatsoever, [was] to be removed from the house without reference to [him]'.[31]

However, Cassell & Co then changed its mind for reasons unknown, but presumably because it considered that the upside to publishing the work outweighed the downside. On 22 February 1968, it distributed 60 proof copies of the book. Insofar as the allegations against Broome were concerned, they fell into two main categories. The first accused him of disobedience. It was said that he had ignored the orders of Hamilton by taking the convoy within striking distance of the German airbases in Norway and thus exposed it to being attacked. The second group of allegations imputed cowardice.

[25] Letter from Captain Stephen Roskill to Captain John Broome (12 August 1968) [BRME 1/2/91].
[26] *Broome* (n 10) 375 (Lord Denning MR).
[27] ibid.
[28] ibid 376 (Lord Denning MR).
[29] ibid 376–78.
[30] ibid 377.
[31] ibid 378.

They insinuated that Broome had deserted the convoy and left it to be destroyed. The final sentence of the proof copies read that 'In short, the point of error was in Commander J. E. Broome's withdrawal of his escort destroyers, on his own initiative …'.[32]

IV. PROCEEDINGS ARE ISSUED

Broome instructed a prominent London law firm, Theodore Goddard & Co. The solicitor with carriage of the proceedings was initially Mr Michael Best and, later, the senior partner, Mr Derek Clogg, who was apparently one of Broome's former shipmates.[33] On 5 March 1968, Broome issued proceedings against both Cassell & Co and Irving. The letter giving notice of the claim stated that:[34]

> The book makes the most serious and utterly unfounded allegations … of such gravity as, disobedience of orders, … inadequate interpretation of signals, … grave errors of judgment, if not incompetence … [and] unjustifiable desertion of the convoy leaving it to its fate.

A few days later, Cassell & Co's solicitors, Oswald Kickson, Collier & Co, responded saying that their client had decided to 'defer publication of the book pending further research by the author'.[35] Additional correspondence, regarded as delaying tactics by Broome's solicitors, ensued leading to the writ being served on 21 May 1968. Broome strongly encouraged Captain David Lawford, who had been in command of one of the escort ships and criticised in the book, to join him in suing.[36] Lawford, however, was by this stage an elderly and frail man, and he declined to do so. He did, however, give evidence at the trial on behalf of Broome.

On 14 June 1968, the defendants served their defences. They took a similar line. They both disputed the meaning that Broome attributed to the words in issue and alleged that their natural and ordinary meaning was true. The defence of honest opinion was also pleaded. On 7 August 1968, Cassell & Co published a hardback edition of the book, which was in substance the same as the proof copies, to the public. Its dustjacket presented the work as being based on five years of intensive research. It is unclear why Cassell & Co took this step given that it was already facing proceedings in respect of the proof copies. Presumably, however, it considered that the profits that it could make would exceed any

[32] ibid 374.

[33] Letter from Captain John Broome to Vice Admiral Sir John Hayes (9 August 1969) [BRME 1-2/35].

[34] Letter from Theodore Goddard & Co to Cassell & Co Ltd (5 March 1968) [BRME 1-1/5].

[35] Letter from Oswald Kickson, Collier & Co to Theodore Goddard & Co (11 March 1968) [BRME 1-1/10–11].

[36] Letter from Captain John Broome to Captain David Lawford (10 November 1968) [BRME 1/2/114].

liability. In any event, the decision prompted Broome to issue a second claim on 23 August 1968. Pursuant to an order that was made on 18 December 1968, the two sets of proceedings were consolidated.

Broome was heavily involved in virtually all aspects of the litigation. He responded promptly and in an organised fashion to queries that his solicitors raised. He also reviewed the many documents in the case carefully and was instrumental in identifying both lay and expert witnesses. It is obvious that Broome was highly popular with many of the men with whom he served. Numerous colleagues of his, including some with whom he had evidently lost contact decades prior to the litigation, volunteered to do whatever they could to assist him and wrote to him in the warmest of terms. The Ministry of Defence was staunchly supportive of Broome's claim and permitted various officers to give evidence and to provide documents.[37] Broome's solicitors told him that 'for practical purposes, we only have to ask for anything and it will be given to us'.[38]

Broome found aspects of the case frustrating. He referred sarcastically to the 'super-sonic speed'[39] of the litigation and evidently hoped that a settlement could be achieved. Thus, he wrote to a colleague that 'Naturally, I would much prefer [it if the claim] never reached court, but as you doubtless know, Plaintiffs have to prove unflinching determination right up to the doors of the courts – so to speak – before "settlements" are contemplated'.[40] Although Broome liked his own lawyers, he disliked the legal profession, which he referred to as being 'scruple-free'.[41] On occasion, he had to 'bend [his own legal representatives] straight'.[42] He was aghast at the inefficiency of the judicial system. He referred to 'carefree legal extravagance'[43] and to its being 'apparently conventional to waste costly effort'.[44]

While the case was working its way towards trial, reviews of the book were published. One of these, which appeared in *The Guardian*,[45] led to a writ being issued against both the newspaper and the reviewer. On 15 April 1969, those defendants served a defence settled by (no less than) one TH Bingham.[46] It is unclear what happened to this litigation. On 23 January 1970, a paperback edition of the book was published (not by Cassell & Co, but under a licence

[37] See, eg, letter from Captain John Broome to Vice Admiral Sir John Hayes (3 February 1969) [BRME 1-2/24–25].

[38] Letter from Theodore Goddard & Co to Captain John Broome (4 October 1968) [BRME 1-1/72].

[39] Letter from Captain John Broome to Vice Admiral Sir John Hayes (5 March 1969) [BRME 1/2/30].

[40] ibid.

[41] Letter from Captain John Broome to Vice Admiral Sir John Hayes (9 August 1969) [BRME 1/2/35].

[42] ibid.

[43] Broome (n 8) 17.

[44] ibid.

[45] G Moorhouse, 'Abandon Convoy!', *The Guardian*, 12 September 1968.

[46] Defence [BRME 1-1/93–97].

given to another publisher[47]). By this stage, Broome, Irving and Cassell & Co were on the doorstep of the court. The publication was evidently timed to coincide with the trial.

V. THE TRIAL

The trial lasted for 17 days and took place between 26 January and 13 February 1970 before Lawton J sitting with a jury.[48] Broome was represented by Mr David Hirst QC and Mr Andrew Bateson. Irving's counsel were Mr Colin Duncan QC and Mr AC Pugh while Cassell & Co instructed Mr Michael Kempster QC and Mr Edward Adeane. Both Irving and Cassell & Co persisted in their defence of truth. It was not until the start of the trial that the issue of punitive damages arose. It apparently did so as a result of further disclosure that Irving had given[49] in relation to, presumably, the publication of the paperback edition of the book. In the course of his opening submissions, Broome's counsel told Lawton J that Broome wished to seek punitive damages under the second category in *Rookes*.

The defendants objected on the basis that no claim for punitive damages had been pleaded. This prompted Broome to apply for permission to amend. In his judgment on that application, Lawton J held that any claim in this regard needed to be pleaded. He wrote that:[50]

> The House of Lords in *Rookes v Barnard* has clarified the law and has decreed that exemplary damages are an exceptional form of award. In these circumstances anyone who wishes to say that he is making an exceptional kind of claim for damages and not a normal one should say so in his pleading.

He gave, however, permission to amend. Broome duly pleaded that the defendants had calculated that the money that the book would make if it contained the offending passages would probably exceed any damages for which they were adjudged liable with the result that punitive damages should be awarded.[51]

It is worth pausing here to draw attention to three points. First, the fact that *Broome* was even a case about punitive damages was due to the accidents of litigation. Broome's lawyers might easily have decided not to advance a claim in this regard so late in the day, or Lawton J could have rejected Broome's amendment application in circumstances where it had been made after the trial had

[47] *Cassell & Co Ltd v Broome* [1972] AC 1027 (HL) 1058.

[48] The trial is impressively analysed in F Houghton, 'The trial of Convoy PQ17 and the Royal Navy in Post-War British Cultural Memory' (2020) 31 *Twentieth Century British History* 197. Houghton convincingly argues that the trial was part of a 'wider social "clash of generations"' with the antagonists 'represented in reductive terms of degenerate modern "youth" versus honourable "duty and sacrifice" of an older generation' (at 200).

[49] *Broome v Cassell & Co Ltd* [1971] 1 All ER 262 (QBD) 263.

[50] ibid (footnote omitted).

[51] The amendment is quoted in the judgment of the House of Lords: see *Broome* (n 47) 1057.

already begun. Further, if the paperback edition had not been published, punitive damages would presumably not have been sought. Secondly, it is rather surprising that Lawton J gave Broome permission to amend his pleadings. Although Broome's application had seemingly been triggered by late disclosure and the publication of the paperback edition, the trial had already begun and the question of prejudice to the defendants at being confronted with a new case at this stage of the litigation seems not to have been considered. The third point concerns the rationale for the pleading requirement. Lawton J, as observed above, asserted that the pleading requirement was justified by the 'exceptional'[52] nature of the remedy. This, however, is not quite to the point. A claim for punitive damages should be pleaded because a person who is said to have engaged in serious wrongdoing is entitled to know precisely that which they are accused of having done in order that they are in a position to meet the allegations.[53]

Broome gave evidence for five days.[54] He also called numerous witnesses. Indeed, he called so many that it is impractical to say more than a few words in this regard. One of his witnesses was Vice Admiral Sir John Eaton, who had been the commanding officer of one of the three destroyers that were screening the cruiser force.[55] After giving evidence, he sent Broome a letter in which he wrote: 'The best of luck Jackie and dont [*sic*] forget that all men worth drinking with will be rooting for you'.[56] Another witness was Mr Basil Elliot, who had hoisted the signal to scatter. Broome recounts that Mr Elliot had contacted him out of the blue during the trial and 'went into the witness box the next day'. His evidence, Broome said, 'was outstandingly impressive'.[57] Yet another witness was Captain John Litchfield, who had been the Executive Officer of one of the covering cruisers. Broome described him as 'a great support throughout and an excellent witness'.[58] Litchfield believed in the litigation so strongly that he offered to contribute 200 guineas towards Broome's legal costs 'if things went wrong'.[59] Captain Roskill, the Official Naval Historian, was also called. Broome wrote that he 'was very helpful throughout my case, and gave excellent evidence'.[60] Roskill had agreed to pay £1,000 towards Broome's costs.[61]

[52] See the text to n 50.

[53] For a recent articulation of the principle, see *Kasem v University College London Hospitals NHS Foundation Trust* [2021] EWHC 136 (QB) [36]–[39]. The particular allegation in this case was one of fraud, but the principle applies to all forms of serious wrongdoing.

[54] Letter from Captain John Litchfield to Captain Broome (19 February 1970) [BRME 1-2/72–73].

[55] Note by Captain Broome regarding Vice Admiral Sir John Eaton [BRME 1-2/3].

[56] Letter from Vice Admiral Sir John Eaton to Captain Broome (9 February 1970) [BRME 1-2/8–9].

[57] Note by Captain Broome regarding Mr Elliot [BRME 1-2/11].

[58] Notes by Captain Broome [BRME 1-2/46].

[59] Letter from Captain John Litchfield to Captain Broome (22 August 1968) [BRME 1-2/52].

[60] Notes by Captain Broome [BRME 1-2/90].

[61] Letter from Captain Stephen Roskill to Captain John Broome (21 August 1968) [BRME 1/2/93]. See also the letter from Mr Derek Clogg to Captain Stephen Roskill (28 November 1969) [ROSK 19/1/95].

After Broome had closed his case, the defendants invited Lawton J to rule that there was no evidence from which the jury could infer that the claim for punitive damages fell within the second category in *Rookes*. That invitation was rejected. Neither Irving nor Cassell & Co called any witnesses, and Irving himself did not go into the witness box. Lawton J's summing up took place on 16 and 17 February 1970. As regards punitive damages, he directed the jury in accordance with what Lord Devlin had said in *Rookes*. *Private Eye*, apparently considering that Lawton J's summing up was slanted in Broome's favour, parodied it.[62] It appears that Irving sought to leave the courtroom during the summing up only to be told by one of his lawyers 'You sit here and sweat it out'.[63]

On 17 February 1970, the jury, having deliberated for nearly five hours,[64] returned a verdict against both defendants. They awarded Broome £1,000 in compensatory damages in respect of the 60 proof copies of the book (the equivalent today of around £11,000). Counsel for Broome had apparently waived any right to punitive damages in respect of this publication. As regards the hardback edition, £14,000 in compensatory damages were awarded and £25,000 by way of punitive damages (the combined sum is the equivalent of around £443,000 today). Strikingly, therefore, the punitive element was almost double the compensatory component insofar as the hardback edition was concerned. It is also one of the largest awards of punitive damages ever made in England both at the time and today.[65]

As they left the court, Broome and Irving shook hands.[66] The verdict attracted significant media attention with the BBC covering it during prime-time television.[67] Broome received around 500 letters of congratulation.[68] Irving also received a good number of letters which were, it seems, more mixed.[69] It appears that Broome, after buying a new car and an annuity, donated the damages to charity, apparently to the Churchill Archives Centre at Captain Roskill's request.[70] As for Irving, he wrote promptly to his leading counsel,

[62] 'Mr Justice Lawandorder Sums Up', *Private Eye*, 27 February 1970. The same view was formed by Houghton (n 48) 211.

[63] Quoted in an unknown issue of *The Sunday Times* [ROSK 19/1/15].

[64] *Broome* (n 47) 1096.

[65] Empirical data regarding the quantum of punitive damages in the twenty-first century is given in J Goudkamp and E Katsampouka, 'An Empirical Study of Punitive Damages' (2018) 38 *OJLS* 90.

[66] An image of their shaking hands is available at <www.gettyimages.co.uk/detail/news-photo/day-lawsuit-ends-with-a-handshake-captain-john-broome-and-news-photo/830353578> accessed 7 May 2023.

[67] Letter from Vice Admiral Sir John Eaton to Captain John Broome (18 February 1970) [BRME 1/2/10].

[68] ibid.

[69] Several are published on Irving's website: <www.fpp.co.uk/Legal/PQ17Libel/Mail1970.html> accessed 7 May 2023.

[70] Letter from Captain Stephen Roskill to Captain John Broome (28 September 1972) [BRME 1/2/105–106]; letter from Captain John Broome to Captain Stephen Roskill (8 October 1972) [BRME 1/2/107–108].

thanking him for defending him and adding that 'unlike a wartime leader, [he was] not going to blame [his] "generals" for the defeat'.[71] It is unclear whether Captain Broome was able (or sought) to enforce the judgment against Irving. The latter's solicitors apparently told the former that he had no assets.[72] Cassell & Co belatedly paid the compensatory damages under threat of winding-up proceedings.[73]

VI. THE COURT OF APPEAL

In the wake of the trial, Cassell & Co was purchased by an American publishing house and instructed new solicitors.[74] It appealed on seven grounds and sought orders for a retrial.[75] The grounds of appeal are wide-ranging and hence do not lend themselves to being summarised. However, and relevantly for current purposes, three of the grounds concentrated on punitive damages.[76] In this regard, it was contended that there was insufficient evidence to justify leaving the claim to the jury, that the jury had been misdirected as to both the law and facts and that the award was excessive. Irving also appealed. Although his grounds of appeal differed from those of Cassell & Co in important respects, his arguments as concerns punitive damages were ultimately along similar lines. While the appeal was pending, settlement discussions ensued,[77] but these ultimately came to nothing. Irving was ordered to pay security of £1,500 as a condition for appealing.

On 4 March 1971, Lord Denning MR[78] and Salmon and Phillimore LJJ dismissed both appeals, which were, incredibly, heard over the course of nine

[71] Letter from Mr David Irving to Mr Duncan QC (22 February 1970) <www.fpp.co.uk/Legal/PQ17Libel/Duncan220270.html> accessed 7 May 2023.

[72] Letter from Mr Derek Clogg to Captain Stephen Roskill (18 March 1970) [ROSK 19/1/50].

[73] ibid.

[74] FA Mann, *Life and Cases: Manuscript of an Autobiography* (Göttingen, Bonn University Press, 2021) 180.

[75] Notice of Appeal [BRME 1/1/118]. While the appeal was pending, Broome issued yet further writs in respect of subsequent publications of Irving's book: letter from Mr Derek Clogg to Captain Stephen Roskill (27 October 1970) [ROSK 19/1/4].

[76] FA Mann was Cassell & Co's solicitor on the appeal to the Court of Appeal and House of Lords. In his autobiography, he wrote that he 'never understood how the three passages in question [in Mr Irving's book] could be so read as to be capable of bearing the meaning alleged' (Mann (n 74) 180) and considered that 'there had never been any defamation' (ibid 182). He explained that many people with whom he had consulted agreed with him but that counsel who he instructed took a different view. Cassell & Co ultimately pursued only those grounds of appeal that were related to punitive damages (letter from Mr Derek Clogg to Captain Stephen Roskill (20 October 1970) [ROSK 19/1/5]).

[77] Letter from Mr Derek Clogg to Captain John Broome (10 September 1970) [ROSK 19/1/9].

[78] Broome's solicitors were concerned that they might draw Lord Denning. It was felt that he might reduce the damages 'as that is rather than way his mind goes'. However, they also remarked that 'As against this, he is a man who is much concerned about his public image and would be reluctant to disturb what was so obviously a very popular win' (letter from Mr Derek Clogg to Captain John Broome (10 September 1970) [ROSK 19/1/10]).

days. They ultimately did so on the basis that the directions of Lawton J had been adequate and because the sums awarded were not excessive in the circumstances. But the real significance of their decision lies in what they said about *Rookes*. This is addressed further below, but, in summary, they held that *Rookes* had been wrongly decided by the House of Lords and that it was not binding on them or any other court as a result. The speech of Lord Devlin (who had since retired as had all of the other members of the panel in *Rookes* save for Lord Reid) was said to have been delivered *per incuriam*. It was claimed that Lord Devlin had ignored two decisions of the House of Lords, *Ley v Hamilton*[79] and *E Hulton & Co v Jones*,[80] which were regarded as approving the jurisdiction to award punitive damages absent the shackles that Lord Devlin had placed upon them by the categories test. Juries, it was said, should be henceforward directed in accordance with the law as it had been understood prior to *Rookes*. The decision must have surprised everyone, not least Broome's solicitors, who had written to Captain Roskill in the period leading up to the appeal assuring him that 'the Court of Appeal cannot disagree with Devlin's judgment in Rookes v. Barnard'.[81]

The main reasons were given by Lord Denning and they exemplify his style. He painted a striking contrast between the litigants. He extolled the virtues of Broome (and his witnesses) and even likened him to Nelson. He referred in this regard to an instruction that Hamilton had given to Broome to keep his distance from the German airbase in Norway and wrote that the latter, by keeping the convoy moving to the east and hence shortening the voyage, 'was bolder'.[82] Broome 'did as Nelson did'.[83] Conversely, Lord Denning was intensely critical of the defendants. As regards Irving, he wrote:[84]

> Many persons afterwards wrote about the disaster. The official historian of the war wrote about it. He did not condemn Commander Broome. Nor did Mr. Winston Churchill. The condemnation was made 20 years later by an author who knew nothing about the war because he was a small boy at the time. David Irving was determined to write 'an authentic account.' His regular publishers – William Kimber & Co. Ltd.—refused to publish it. They thought it was too dangerous. So he got Cassell & Co. Ltd. to publish it.

Lord Denning also remarked:[85]

> It is plain that Mr. Irving was warned from most responsible quarters that his book contained libels on Commander Broome, and yet he determined to go on with it. In order to make it a success, he was ready to risk libel actions. In the apt French phrase, he was looking for a *succès de scandale*.

[79] *Ley v Hamilton* (1935) 153 LT 384 (HL).
[80] *E Hulton & Co v Jones* [1910] AC 20 (HL).
[81] Letter from Mr Derek Clogg to Captain Stephen Roskill (29 July 1970) [ROSK 19/1/27].
[82] *Broome* (n 10) 371.
[83] ibid.
[84] ibid 373.
[85] ibid 374.

He added that the defendants' conduct was, and was obviously regarded by the jury, as being 'absolutely outrageous'[86] and 'completely shocking'.[87] He thought Cassell & Co had behaved just as badly as Irving. There is not, he said, 'much to choose between them'.[88]

Turning to Lord Denning's analysis as regards the status of *Rookes*, it can be understood as having four main strands to it. First, he suggested that Lord Devlin had acted on a whim and had plucked the categories test out of thin air. He pointed out that the House of Lords in *Rookes* had not heard argument as regards the test and referred to it throughout his reasons as 'the new doctrine'. Secondly, he observed that *Rookes* had been subjected to 'devastating criticism'[89] and 'wholesale condemnation'[90] by distinguished appellate courts overseas. Thirdly, he considered that the House of Lords had awarded punitive damages in cases that fell outside Lord Devlin's categories and, since *Rookes* had been decided prior to the 1966 Practice Statement, that it had not been open to it to depart from its decisions concerned.[91] Fourthly, he assessed the categories test as being 'hopelessly illogical and inconsistent'.[92] He pointed out that it was nonsensical for punitive damages to be restricted, as per the first category, to public servants. He argued that punitive damages should be available as against a bully who acts oppressively regardless of whether they were a public servant. Analogous criticisms were made of the second category, that is to say, no reason was seen to limit it to conduct motivated by a desire to make a profit. Although Lord Denning considered that the appeal should be dismissed because the jurisdiction to award punitive damages was not restricted by the categories test, he went on to hold that, even if he had been bound by *Rookes*, the case fell squarely within the second category. There was, he observed, 'ample evidence' that the defendants had hoped to profit from their wrongdoing.[93]

Salmon LJ's reasons were broadly similar to those of Lord Denning. He too was offended by the defendants' behaviour. They had, he said, engaged in 'outrageous conduct of an altogether exceptionally high order'.[94] He argued that the first category in *Rookes* was 'unsupported by authority' and 'difficult to reconcile … with justice or common sense'.[95] He expressed similar sentiments as regards the second category. Salmon LJ said that he could 'find no sensible reason for putting the power to award [punitive] damages into the strait

[86] ibid 378.
[87] ibid 380.
[88] ibid 383.
[89] ibid 380.
[90] ibid.
[91] *Practice Statement (Judicial Precedent)* [1966] 1 WLR 1234.
[92] *Broome* (n 10) 381.
[93] ibid 382.
[94] ibid 394.
[95] ibid 386.

jacket which the second category in *Rookes v. Barnard* imposes'.[96] His ultimate conclusion was that 'Lord Devlin's whole approach in *Rookes* v. *Barnard* was based on a fundamental fallacy'.[97] He added that 'Far from punitive damages not having been approved in the House of Lords, they and the principles upon which they could form an element of an award of general damages had been explicitly approved by the House …'.[98] As with Lord Denning, Salmon LJ considered that the facts of the case in any event fell within the second category.[99] Phillimore LJ's brief reasons similarly largely tracked those of Lord Denning, albeit they were expressed more cautiously.

On any view, the Court of Appeal's decision was incendiary.[100] It was a direct challenge to the authority of the House of Lords and capable of being read as being offensive and condescending. Further, it was an unnecessary challenge since all members of the Court of Appeal agreed that the case fell squarely within Lord Devlin's second category. Julius Stone observed that 'in terms of judicial tactics, this approached disastrous comedy'.[101] Lord Devlin was reportedly left 'furious'[102] by the Court of Appeal's decision. He demanded that Lord Hailsham, who had recently become the Lord Chancellor, immediately rebuke Lord Denning, to whom he apparently attributed principal responsibility for the Court of Appeal's judgment. Much to Lord Devlin's annoyance, Lord Hailsham refused publicly to criticise the Court of Appeal then and there, but made it clear to Lord Devlin that since an appeal to the House of Lords was pending, 'things could be put right'[103] in due course.

VII. THE HOUSE OF LORDS

Cassell & Co (but not Mr Irving) appealed to the House of Lords. It did so solely regarding punitive damages. The appeal was atypical in at least four respects. First, the Appellate Committee sat as a panel of seven instead of the usual five.[104] Secondly, the appeal was heard over the course of 13 days, which one suspects was and still is unprecedented. Thirdly, and as Lord Hailsham made plain,[105] the House gave permission to appeal only because of the mutinous nature of the Court of Appeal's decision. The Law Lords were clearly

[96] ibid 387.
[97] ibid 390.
[98] ibid.
[99] ibid 392–93.
[100] Lord Devlin wrote extra-judicially that the Court of Appeal's decision 'in less exalted circles would have caused a "demo"': P Devlin, 'Judges and Lawmakers' (1976) 39 *MLR* 1, 10.
[101] J Stone, 'On the Liberation of Appellate Judges: How Not to Do It!' (1972) 35 *MLR* 449, 469.
[102] J Sackar, *Lord Devlin* (Oxford, Hart Publishing, 2020) 216.
[103] G Lewis, *Lord Hailsham: A Life* (London, Jonathan Cape, 1998) 279. See also Sackar (n 102) 216.
[104] Consider the discussion in A Burrows, 'Numbers Sitting in the Supreme Court' (2013) 129 *LQR* 305, 306.
[105] *Broome* (n 47) 1052.

aghast at the conduct of the Court of Appeal and were concerned that future constitutions thereof might be emboldened to defy them. Fourthly, all of the Law Lords gave separate speeches. They (or at least some of them) apparently did so because it was thought that it was problematic that only a single speech had been given in *Rookes* as regards the issue of punitive damages. For example, Lord Hailsham said that 'Whatever the advantages of a judgment of an undivided court delivered by a single voice, the result may be an unduly fundamentalist approach to the actual language employed'.[106]

In the end, a majority of the House of Lords constituted by Lord Hailsham, Lord Reid, Lord Morris and Lord Kilbrandon dismissed the appeal on the basis that Lawton J's directions to the jury had not been so defective as to warrant the verdict being set aside and because the punitive damages award was not excessive. However, in doing so they affirmed the decision in *Rookes* and criticised the Court of Appeal for refusing to follow it. Stone astutely remarked that the House of Lords' judgment 'may well be the most hostile *affirmation* of a Court of Appeal decision in our history'.[107] A minority comprising Viscount Dilhorne, Lord Wilberforce and Lord Diplock would have allowed the appeal. They thought that Lawton J had failed to make it sufficiently clear to the jury that they should not award punitive damages unless the compensatory damages were insufficient to achieve the goals of punishment and deterrence. The minority also considered that the award of punitive damages was excessive. Cassell & Co regarded 'the defeat [as being] an honorouable one'.[108] Broome's solicitor, for his part, described 'Hailsham's as one of the greatest, and most astute, Judgments I think I have ever read …'.[109]

The House of Lords engaged with various points of considerable interest regarding punitive damages. Certain of these are addressed below. However, the significance of the House of Lords' decision lies mainly not in what it says regarding punitive damages but concerning the doctrine of precedent. As Lord Hailsham observed, 'What began as a single proceeding between a plaintiff and two defendants … assumed, at the expense of two of the litigants, the dimensions of a constitutional question …'.[110] He then rebuked the Court of Appeal, remarking that it was not open to it 'to give gratuitous advice to judges of first instance to ignore decisions of the House of Lords'.[111] He added that 'it is necessary for each lower tier, including the Court of Appeal, to accept loyally the decisions of the higher tiers'.[112] Lord Hailsham, in a tit-for-tat, even suggested that Lord Denning had perhaps made *per incuriam* remarks himself insofar as he wrongly thought that the paperback edition of

[106] ibid 1068; see also at 1084–85. Lord Reid expressed similar views in an interview conducted by Alan Paterson.

[107] Stone (n 101) 451 (emphasis in original) (footnote omitted).

[108] Mann (n 74) 181. Several interesting procedural developments ensued in the wake of judgment being delivered: see ibid 181–82.

[109] Letter from Mr Derek Clogg to Captain Stephen Roskill (24 February 1972) [ROSK 19/1/32].

[110] *Broome* (n 47) 1053.

[111] ibid 1054.

[112] ibid.

the book had been published by Cassell & Co.[113] The rest of the House of Lords substantially aligned themselves with Lord Hailsham's views on these matters.

It is difficult to resist the conclusion that at least some of the Law Lords were not wholly successful in bringing a completely independent mind to all aspects of the appeal. Lord Hailsham had apparently already told Lord Devlin privately that he would put matters right.[114] He then hurried to heap praise on the latter's judgment in *Rookes*. He remarked that it contained 'a most valuable and important contribution to the law of exemplary damages …'.[115] He also denied that Lord Devlin's speech was inconsistent with either *Ley v Hamilton* or *E Hulton & Co v Jones*.[116] Although Lord Hailsham's reasons were elegantly crafted, expressed with great rhetorical effect and are compelling in many respects, they might be thought, insofar as they sought to support the categories test, to constitute an attempt to defend the indefensible. Lord Hailsham's biographer thought that there was 'doubtless … some partisanship'[117] in his speech.[118]

VIII. SUBSEQUENT EVENTS

After the House of Lords had handed down its judgment, Lord Devlin wrote to Lord Hailsham to say that he was:[119]

> Heartily glad that you put down with such a firm hand (albeit with 'studied moderation') the antics of the C.A. and that you had the unanimous support of the House in doing so. There is enough permissiveness in the world today without its penetration into the doctrine of precedent. I feel that your decision which we discussed in our chat, to deal with the situation in this way has been proved entirely right. I am also of course very glad that our efforts in Rookes v Barnard have not in the end been relegated to the perincurial limbo; and I appreciate in particular the kind things that you said about my speech.

For his part, Lord Denning candidly admitted that he had erred. In *The Discipline of Law*, he wrote 'Yes – I had been guilty – of lese-majesty. I had impugned the authority of the House. That must never be done by anyone save the House itself. Least of all by the turbulent Master of the Rolls'.[120] One unhappy consequence of the dressing down that the House of Lords gave to

[113] ibid 1058.
[114] See the text to n 102.
[115] *Broome* (n 47) 1060. See also at 1074 ('a careful and valuable decision').
[116] ibid 1075–76.
[117] Lewis (n 103) 317.
[118] Mann expressed similar sentiments: see Mann (n 74) 182 writing that the 'case … was characterised at every stage by an enormous amount of prejudice in favour of a gallant Captain of the Royal Navy …'.
[119] Sackar (n 102) 217.
[120] A Denning, *The Discipline of Law* (London, Butterworth, 1979) 313.

the Court of Appeal concerns the decision in *AB v South West Water Services Ltd*.[121] In that case, the Court of Appeal was evidently so concerned to adhere to every phrase in Lord Devlin's speech in *Rookes* and the speeches in *Broome* that they managed to eke from them the 'cause of action' test. That test blighted the law for almost a decade until it was abolished by *Kuddus v Chief Constable of Leicestershire*.[122]

As for the individual litigants, in 1972, Broome published his own account of the convoy and the litigation.[123] He went on to write several further books and died in 1985. *Cassell & Co Ltd v Broome* was just the beginning of Irving's involvement with the law. He was ultimately exposed as a Holocaust denier and was imprisoned in Austria for highly offensive and obviously false views that he expressed in speeches delivered in 1989. In 2000, Gray J found against Irving in another libel case. A US academic, Professor Deborah Lipstadt, had written a book entitled *Denying the Holocaust: The Growing Assault on Trust and Memory*,[124] in which she branded Irving as an apologist and partisan of Hitler and accused him of distorting evidence to suit his own agenda. Irving sued. Following a lengthy trial, Professor Lipstadt and her publisher, Penguin, succeeded in the defence of truth in respect of the principal defamatory statements.[125] Penguin published Gray J's judgment as a book.[126] Sedley LJ refused Irving permission to appeal on paper. Pill, Mantell and Buxton LJJ rejected a renewed application following a hearing.[127] The case was dramatised in the movie *Denial*, which starred Rachel Weisz.

IX. REFLECTION

This section of the chapter engages with selected issues that arise as regards punitive damages in light of *Broome*.

A. The Future of the Categories Test

Critics of *Rookes* generally argue that there is little or no logical reason to limit the award of punitive damages to specific categories of case, least of

[121] *AB v South West Water Services Ltd* [1993] QB 507 (CA).

[122] *Kuddus v Chief Constable of Leicestershire* [2001] UKHL 29, [2002] 2 AC 122. Regarding *Kuddus*, see Katsampouka, ch 10 of this volume.

[123] Broome (n 8).

[124] D Lipstadt, *Denying the Holocaust: The Growing Assault on Trust and Memory* (London, Penguin Books, 1994).

[125] *Irving v Penguin Books Ltd* 2000 WL 362478 (QBD).

[126] *The Irving Judgment: David Irving v Penguin Books and Professor Deborah Lipstadt* (London, Penguin, 2000).

[127] *Irving v Penguin Books Ltd* 2001 WL 825074 (CA).

all those which Lord Devlin distilled.[128] However, this criticism is somewhat unfair. Lord Devlin made it clear that his preferred course was to abolish the jurisdiction to award punitive damages but that he felt unable to do so without ignoring precedent.[129] He did what he thought was the next best thing, which was to limit the power to award punitive damages to categories of case in which they had previously been awarded. He did not maintain that the categories were supportable independently of precedent. One question that arises in this regard is whether Lord Devlin was right in his reading of the authorities and whether he overlooked any of significance. A great deal of intellectual energy has been invested into answering it including,[130] of course, by the judges of the Court of Appeal and House of Lords in *Broome*. In a sense, however, this issue, while interesting, is today a somewhat sterile one. That is because there cannot be any doubt that the Supreme Court would be justified in looking at the law governing the award of punitive damages afresh. That is perhaps especially so given that the Law Commission considered that the whole area cries out for reform.[131] None of this bodes well for the categories test, which is supportable, if at all, only by reference to (very dated) precedent.

B. Terminology

The labels 'punitive damages' and 'exemplary damages' are interchangeable.[132] The Law Commission preferred the former[133] whereas Lord Hailsham in *Broome* endorsed the latter although he was ultimately rather non-committal.[134] The term 'exemplary damages' has since tended to prevail in England.[135] Which is preferable? In considering this question, it is important to observe that the two labels emphasise different aspects of the jurisdiction. The language of 'punitive damages' stresses its retributive purpose whereas that of 'exemplary damages' emphasises that an example is being made of the defendant against whom they are awarded. The fact that both are used is a manifestation of the fact that the award discharges (at least) the twin purposes of retribution and deterrence. Since the former goal is the dominant one

[128] 'Lord Devlin's categories in *Rookes v Barnard* lack satisfactory rationale in principle or policy': A Burrows, *Remedies for Torts, Breach of Contract, and Equitable Wrongs* (Oxford, OUP, 2019) 374 (footnote omitted).

[129] *Rookes* (n 9) 1125–26.

[130] See, eg, Stone (n 101) 457–59; H McGregor, 'In Defence of Lord Devlin' (1971) 34 *MLR* 520.

[131] Law Commission, *Aggravated, Exemplary and Restitutionary Damages* (Law Com No 247, 1997) 92.

[132] '[T]he terms are synonymous': *Kuddus* (n 122) [51] (Lord Nicholls).

[133] Law Commission (n 131) 104.

[134] *Broome* (n 47) 1073.

[135] See, eg, Crime and Courts Act 2013 (UK), s 34.

(if it were not, the award would not be nearly as controversial as it is), the language of 'punitive damages' is preferable.

C. The Functions of Punitive Damages

A closely related issue is whether it is satisfactory that punitive damages are awarded with a view to achieving multiple purposes. The multiplicity of functions makes the law governing the award more complex than it would otherwise be, but a more significant concern is that the various functions sometimes pull in different directions from each other. Consider, for example, the fact that if a tortfeasor dies before judgment is entered against them, the claimant can recover punitive damages from their estate.[136] This is consistent with the goal of deterrence but incompatible with that of retribution. Efforts to achieve one objective undermine the other. Arguably, the remedy should have a single purpose. This would prevent the pursuit of more than one goal resulting in the other being undercut and, conceivably, neither from being realised. Conversely, it might be pointed out that sentences in the criminal law are typically awarded with several ends in mind.

D. Reservations regarding Punitive Damages

In *Broome*, the House of Lords expressed considerable antipathy regarding punitive damages. Lord Hailsham queried whether granting them was 'ever permissible'.[137] Lord Reid, echoing remarks that Lord Devlin had made in *Rookes*,[138] asserted that punitive damages were anomalous[139] and that the jurisdiction to award them involved a 'form of palm tree justice'.[140] These and cognate remarks may well have encouraged at least some judges to be particularly cautious in both awarding and assessing punitive damages. However, excessive caution in this regard animated by doubts as to whether the remedy ought to be recognised is inappropriate. The jurisdiction's existence has been confirmed, and it is quite wrong in these circumstances that it be hobbled on account of reservations about whether punitive damages should be a part of private law. If the remedy is considered undesirable, the logical course is for it to be abolished rather than restricted. Whether or not this step should be taken is, of course, intensely controversial.

[136] Law Commission (n 131) 90.
[137] *Broome* (n 47) 1060.
[138] *Rookes* (n 9) 1221, 1227.
[139] *Broome* (n 47) 1086–87, 1090. For doubts regarding this claim, see Lord Wilberforce's comments at 1114 and J Goudkamp and E Katsampouka, 'Punitive Damages and the Place of Punishment in Private Law' (2021) 84 *MLR* 1257.
[140] *Broome* (n 47) 1087.

E. The Pleading Requirement

In *Broome*, Lord Denning considered that a claim for punitive damages did not need to be pleaded and that it was hence unnecessary for Broome to have amended his pleadings to assert an entitlement in this regard.[141] Phillimore LJ agreed and described the suggestion that a claim for punitive damages had to be pleaded as 'ridiculous'.[142] Although the necessity to plead a claim for punitive damages might not have been established at the time, this approach is directly contrary to basic requirements of fairness. A person against whom serious allegations are made is entitled to know precisely what it is they are said to have done so that they are aware of the case that they have to meet. In the House of Lords, Lord Hailsham disagreed with the Court of Appeal. He rightly said that 'There is much to be said for the view that a defendant against whom a claim of this kind is made ought not to be taken by surprise'.[143]

It is true that evidence might emerge, or the defendant might otherwise engage in conduct, during the course of a trial which justifies or adds to a claim for punitive damages. It is clearly impractical, as Lord Denning and Phillimore LJ evidently considered, to amend the pleadings every time some relevant new fact emerges, especially at the end of the proceedings. But this is a world away from suggesting that there should be no pleading requirement as regards punitive damages at all. Although this controversy has been overtaken by the fact that the pleading requirement is now enshrined in the Civil Procedure Rules,[144] the reason for the requirement are worth bearing in mind.

F. Relationship with Compensatory Damages

In *Broome*, the House of Lords emphasised the importance of the 'if but only if' test that Lord Devlin had articulated in *Rookes*. Pursuant to that test, punitive damages can be awarded only if the compensatory damages are insufficient to punish and deter. Note that the test assumes, therefore, that compensatory damages serve a punitive function. Indeed, in *Broome* Lord Reid remarked that 'compensatory damages are always part of the total punishment'.[145] This claim appears to be significantly overstated. Although some rules that govern the award of compensatory damages might well be animated by retributive impulses,[146] the proposition that such damages are 'always' granted in order to punish is incorrect. Many if not most compensatory awards have no retributive edge to them

[141] *Broome* (n 10) 378.
[142] ibid 399.
[143] *Broome* (n 47) 1083.
[144] CPR 16.4(1)(c).
[145] *Broome* (n 47) 1089. See also Lord Morris's remarks at 1096 to like effect.
[146] See Goudkamp and Katsampouka (n 139).

and are made merely with restoration in mind. There is, ordinarily, no punitive component to damages granted in respect of lost wages, the cost of repairing damaged property, medical expenses that have been incurred and so on.

Further, observe that the House of Lords' endorsement of the 'if but only if' test is fundamentally incompatible with its claim that punitive damages are anomalous. As has just been observed, the assumption that is baked into the 'if but only if' test is that compensatory damages have a punitive element to them. But if that is right, it cannot be the case that punitive damages, because of their retributive agenda, are aberrant and pollute the purity of the civil law. This frank inconsistency between the 'if but only if' test and the assertion that punitive damages are anomalous, which appears to have gone unnoticed by all of the judges in *Rookes* and *Broome*, suggests significant instability in the intellectual foundations of, at least, punitive damages.

G. Joint Tortfeasors

It has long been clear that, in the case of a joint tort where the defendants are sued together, only a single sum can be awarded. In other words, it is impermissible to award different amounts against the various defendants. In *Broome*, the House of Lords held that this rule applied to punitive damages. This raised an issue as to how the punitive damages should be assessed. The Court of Appeal considered that the award should be fixed by reference to the more blameworthy defendant. Lord Denning pointed out that the scope for unfairness in this regard is minimised since the least blameworthy defendant, if he or she is called on to pay the award, can recover contribution.[147] Salmon LJ seemed to prefer the same rule on the basis that it is fair to impose the risk of suffering excessive punishment on joint tortfeasors. He memorably remarked that 'The moral may be that you must be as careful in choosing your companions in tort as you are in choosing your companions when you go out shooting'.[148] In the House of Lords, Lord Hailsham saw things differently. He held that the damages must be the lowest sum that would be appropriate to award against the least culpable defendant.[149] On the one hand, this makes sense given that it is unjust to impose on a given defendant more punishment than they deserve. On the other hand, it ensures that the goals of awarding punitive damages will not be discharged since the more culpable tortfeasor (or tortfeasors) will receive less punishment than they merit. They will receive none where one of the joint tortfeasors is undeserving of punishment. Neither the approach of the Court of Appeal nor that of the House of Lords is satisfactory. The *only* way of ensuring that the goals of awarding

[147] *Broome* (n 10) 383.
[148] ibid 393.
[149] *Broome* (n 47) 1063. See also Viscount Dilhorne's remarks at 1105, those of Lord Wilberforce at 1118 and Lord Diplock's comments at 1131.

punitive damages are not frustrated is for joint tortfeasors to be held severally liable for the remedy. Where there are joint tortfeasors, there is no good reason why each defendant should not be held separately liable for punitive damages and for the award to be tailored so that it is proportionate to their individual circumstances.

X. CONCLUSION

It is no overstatement to say that the *Broome* saga represents one of the most extraordinary episodes in the history of the common law. The litigation pitted a gallant member of the establishment against a younger, brazen agitator. The sensational trial resulted in a momentous event of World War II being relived. Most strikingly of all, however, the proceedings involved a clash between the appellate courts that was and remains unprecedented. One cannot help but feel that the House of Lords ended up retaining the categories test at least partly because of the extraordinarily undiplomatic way in which the Court of Appeal sought to remove it. Despite being subjected to devastating criticism from almost every other quarter, that rule remains part of English law to the present day.

6

Lamb v Cotogno (1987) Insured Punishment

KIT BARKER*

I. SETTING THE SCENE

IF SUNDAY EVENING is an ill-judged time to make a marketing call, it is a still worse one to deliver a court summons. At some time between 7.00pm and 7.30pm on 11 March 1979, this is nonetheless what Gary Lamb set out to do. It was the first time he had served court documents. The debtor and intended target of the summons, Guiseppe Cotogno (known to friends and family as Joe), was a 39-year-old, self-employed housepainter who also ran a dog kennelling business with his wife on a one- or two-acre plot in the semi-rural suburb of Bringelly, Western Sydney. At least part of the kennels business seems to have involved breeding and racing greyhounds, because records can be found of a brindle breeding bitch called Lovely Reporter that was at one time registered in his name.[1] The property proved frustratingly hard for Lamb to find. To boot, Cotogno turned out to be a large and volatile man. It is possible that he was a member of the Italian cycling squad that swept the medals table at the 1960 Rome Olympics,[2] but in any event, he was a serious physical presence.

* My thanks are due to James Goudkamp, Mark Lunney, Rob Merkin, Iain Field and Eleni Katsampouka for their comments and assistance in tracking down sources; and to Anna Kretowicz for her able research assistance. I also owe a special debt of thanks to Jim McIntyre RFD SC and Dr Andrew Morrison RFD SC, who acted as counsel for Cotogno and Lamb respectively in the Court of Appeal and then as junior counsel (led by PJ Newman QC and RJ Elliot QC respectively) on appeal to the High Court. They were kind enough to share their recollections of the case. All errors are my own.

[1] The records can be found on the Greyhound Racing Victoria website: <https://fasttrack.grv.org.au?Breeding/Details/-112333> accessed 5 February 2023.

[2] This is what he told his counsel, Jim McIntyre SC ('Correspondence', 4 December 2021) (on file with the author), although I have not been able to firmly establish the accuracy of that account. His name does not appear in the official list of Italian medal-winners at Rome in 1960, but this does not mean that he was not part of the squad. Evidence was presented at trial of the fact that he was a 'cyclist of some note in his earlier days' who had 'retired from the sport': *Lamb v Cotogno* NSW SC, No 14501/80, 14 December 1983, 12.

By comparison, Lamb was small in stature and walked with a limp. He had recently had the sixth in a long line of surgeries on his leg for osteomyelitis (a nasty type of bone infection) and had only been able to move around without the assistance of crutches for some three weeks prior. The wound was still unhealed, and he was no doubt in pain and acutely conscious of his physical vulnerability on the evening in question. He clearly neither expected, nor wanted trouble, but on this occasion trouble awaited him keenly nonetheless.

Cotogno flared up with all the incandescence of a Roman candle. It is not entirely clear why. In his later testimony at trial, he claimed that the name on the summons was that of his son, not his own. An alternative account provided by his counsel, Jim McIntyre SC, is that the name was good, but the address was incorrect and Joe took strong objection to the error, mistakenly thinking that it rendered the whole process of service invalid.[3] It is also possible that he simply resented being served by a creditor. He had only recently re-emerged from six years of bankruptcy and the experience was no doubt still raw. Whatever the precise source of his objection, there was a verbal confrontation, following which Lamb retreated swiftly to the safety of his car, dropping the summons onto the ground as he went, then motioning at it, and telling Cotogno bluntly that it was business he needed to deal with. Lamb got into the car, locked the doors and started to back out of the driveway with the clear intention of leaving. His desire to flee the scene was probably intensified by the presence of his girlfriend (later wife) in the vehicle's passenger seat. Unfortunately, the retreat seems only to have enraged Cotogno further. Now shouting death threats, he advanced upon the car and threw himself across its bonnet and windscreen in a crude attempt to prevent the escape. Lamb panicked and accelerated down the road at 30–40km/h, with Cotogno hanging on 'for dear life',[4] veering from side to side in an attempt to dislodge his unwanted passenger. He succeeded in this about 400 metres further on by slamming on the brakes, propelling Cotogno onto the road, crushing and fracturing his right ankle, damaging the bones in his left foot, and causing him several other, lesser injuries. Lamb then fled the scene, leaving his victim lying on the darkened road, where he was discovered by a neighbour half an hour later, bloodied and screaming in pain.

Unlikely and inglorious as these facts are, they gave rise to what remains perhaps Australia's most famous High Court case on exemplary damages[5] and to a particular conundrum that has never satisfactorily been solved. The puzzle lies not so much in the existence of exemplary awards in modern Australian law – these continue to have an active life, particularly in cases against the police[6] – but

[3] *Correspondence* (n 2). The address on the summons appears to have referred to Bringelli Kennels, but the correct name of kennels, which were situated in Bringelly, was said by Cotogno to be 'Jubilee' kennels.

[4] *Lamb* (n 2) 10.

[5] *Lamb v Cotogno* (1987) 164 CLR 1 (HCA).

[6] F Maher, 'An Empirical Study of Exemplary Damages in Australia' (2019) 43 *Melbourne University Law Review* 694, 730 (citing police cases as constituting 30.83% of the sample). For a

rather in the High Court's decision to uphold a A$5,000 exemplary award made against Lamb in respect of the described incident, despite its acceptance that he would never personally pay a cent of it, because he was fully indemnified under the terms of his compulsory motor liability insurance policy.

One might wonder, of course, why Lamb's motor insurer would cover a punitive liability in this way. That story has a twist, to which we shall come. More fundamentally, however, if the purpose of an exemplary award is to punish a tortfeasor, then how can it be justified where the tortfeasor is fully insulated against its financial effects? The making of such awards, Lord Nicholls pointed out in *A v Bottrill*,[7] must align with their intended purposes, but what purpose does financially 'punishing' a fully insured person serve? How does it even make sense to talk of punishment in such a case? In the end, the High Court provided three answers to this question, which we shall unpick later in this chapter. None of them, I shall suggest, appears satisfactory to modern eyes and the conclusion to which I shall ultimately come is that, if the case had been pleaded a little differently, the same A$5,000 award could – and probably should – have been justified in a different way.

A superficially similar question to the one posed by *Lamb* is raised in cases in which exemplary awards are paid not by a tortfeasor's insurer, but by a third-party employer who is vicariously liable for his or her misconduct; and the two scenarios are closely connected in recent judicial discussion. In fact, cases involving vicarious liability for exemplary awards have proven far more frequent in Australian law than those involving insurance, albeit that *Lamb* is regularly cited as supporting their positive results.[8] The only other Australian case involving an insured wrongdoer that I have been able to trace is the leading authority of *Gray v Motor Accidents Commission*,[9] decided in 1998, which is the subject of separate analysis by Felicity Maher elsewhere in this book. There, the High Court was invited to reconsider *Lamb*, but declined a (belated) application to do

similar picture of the health of exemplary awards in the UK, see J Goudkamp and E Katsampouka, 'An Empirical Study of Punitive Damages' (2018) 38 *OJLS* 90.

[7] *A v Bottrill* [2002] UKPC 44, [2003] 1 AC 449, 455.

[8] Recent cases in which the issue of vicarious liability (or the analogous statutory liability of the state) for an exemplary award has been raised include: *Burgess v Commonwealth of Australia* [2020] FCA 670, (2020) 378 ALR 501 (award upheld); *New South Wales v Cuthbertson* [2018] NSWCA 320, (2018) 99 NSWLR 120 (award in principle available but insufficient contumelious conduct); *New South Wales v Smith* [2017] NSWCA 194, (2017) 95 NSWLR 662 (award in principle available but insufficient contumelious conduct); *New South Wales v Randall* [2017] NSWCA 88 (award upheld); *New South Wales v Zreika* [2012] NSWCA 37 (award upheld, but reduced); *Whitbread v Rail Corporation NSW* [2011] NSWCA 130 (award available in principle, but not on facts); *New South Wales v Delly* [2007] NSWCA 303, (2007) 70 NSWLR 125 (award upheld, but reduced); *Zorom Enterprises Pty Ltd v Zabow* [2007] NSWCA 106, (2007) 71 NSWLR 354; *New South Wales v Ibbett* [2006] HCA 57, (2006) 229 CLR 638 (award upheld); *State of New South Wales v Bryant* [2005] NSWCA 393, (2005) 64 NSWLR 281 ('*Bryant*') (award upheld, Special Leave refused [2006] HCA Trans 319, 16 June 2006). The decisions in *Burgess* (at [222]) and *Bryant* (at [23]–[26]) make particularly clear reference to *Lamb* in support of their reasoning.

[9] *Gray v Motor Accident Commission* (1998) 196 CLR 1 (HCA) ('*Gray*').

so on the basis that the decision was at that stage little more than a decade old and unanimous; and also because the Court felt that any application to reopen *Lamb* would need first to reconsider all of the more fundamental questions about exemplary awards answered in *Uren*[10] and other, previous cases.[11] One gets the sense that the High Court in *Gray* felt that, if this particular stitch in the fabric of exemplary awards were to be unpicked, the whole garment might come embarrassingly loose. Leave to reconsider *Lamb* was hence flatly refused and the High Court has not had a subsequent opportunity to revisit the case, which is simply assumed in later authorities to be correct.[12]

There are two obvious reasons why the phenomenon of 'insured punishment' has featured so little in Australian (and English) law since *Lamb*. The first is that the terms of most liability insurance policies in these jurisdictions simply do not cover exemplary damages, or the type of behaviour that is likely to give rise to them.[13] This follows from the basic premise of all insurance contracts, which is that an assured is protected against chance, not intended events – and it is intended, or at least conscious or cynical wrongdoing, that is the main focus of the doctrine in both jurisdictions.[14] The assumption that there was insurance cover for the award in *Lamb* was a questionable oddity in this regard, as we shall see in the next section. The position is more complicated in the United States because the sort of behaviour that can prompt punitive awards in that country falls closer to the line that the industry considers commercially insurable. It potentially includes cases of recklessness, or grossly culpable negligence, not just intentional or malicious harm;[15] and insurers are reportedly reluctant explicitly to exclude cover for punitive liability from their products on marketing grounds, being concerned that this will make them commercially unattractive to businesses.[16]

[10] *Uren v John Fairfax & Sons Pty Ltd* (1966) 117 CLR 118 (HCA).

[11] *Gray* (n 9) [32]–[34].

[12] In *Gray* (n 9) [82]–[83], Kirby J suggested that the decision might need to be reconsidered in the future, but his has been a lone judicial voice in the wilderness.

[13] See section III.B below.

[14] In *Gray* (n 9) [14] Gleeson CJ, McHugh, Gummow and Hayne JJ accepted that 'conscious wrongdoing in contumelious disregard of P's rights' accurately 'describes at least the greater part of the relevant field'. For discussion of recent variations on the theme and their implications, see A Doecke, 'Exemplary Damages: Retribution and Condemnation – The Purpose Controlling the Scope of the Exemplary Damages Award' (2017) 38 *Adelaide Law Review* 87. In England, save where statute otherwise prescribes, courts may make awards only in cases of deliberate profiteering or government wrongdoing (*Rookes v Barnard* (1964) AC 1129 (HL) ('*Rookes*')), and in either case the wrongdoing needs to be highly reprehensible, contumelious or outrageous, which almost always involves conscious wrongdoing. See further J Goudkamp and E Katsampouka, 'Punitive Damages: Ten Misconceptions' in E Bant et al (eds), *Punishment and Private Law* (Oxford, Hart Publishing, 2021) 191. For a seminal statement of the normal limits of the insurance contract, see *Beresford v Royal Insurance Co Ltd* [1938] AC 586 (HL) 595 (Lord Atkin).

[15] *Smith v Wade* 461 US 30, 44–48, 52 (1983); C Sharkey, 'Revisiting the Noninsurable Costs of Accidents' (2005) 64 *Maryland Law Review* 409, 438–50.

[16] A Widiss, 'Liability Insurance Coverage for Punitive Damages – Discerning Answers to the Conundrum Created by Disputes Involving Conflicting Public Policies, Pragmatic Considerations and Political Actions' (1994) 39 *Villanova Law Review* 455, 488.

The second explanation lies in a tranche of statutory restrictions that now apply in Australia, both to the availability of exemplary damages awards themselves[17] and, in some cases, to the obligation of compulsory insurers to indemnify wrongdoers against liability for them.[18] Many of the former restrictions came about as a result of insurance industry lobbying in the early years of the new millennium, whilst the latter were introduced earlier on, as an immediate, visceral response to *Lamb* itself.[19] The combined effect of these developments is that, even if an insurer were, as matter of contractual construction, to expose itself in principle to liability for an exemplary award in Australia, the incidence of such awards is low, the amounts payable are standardly moderate, and some insurers are statutorily exempted from any obligation to indemnify the wrongdoer anyway, so that the latter is forced to bear the burden of the award himself.

The result is that the exact question asked in *Lamb* – 'should a court make an exemplary award against a fully insured wrongdoer who will never pay?' – is rarely asked in Australia these days and the High Court's positive answer to the question in 1987 is more often cited, as I suggested above, as implying support for exemplary awards in cases of vicarious liability. Despite the analogy, cases of the latter type actually pose a different question to the one posed in *Lamb*. They ask whether *a third party* should be punished for a wrongdoer's conduct, not whether one is justified in punishing the *wrongdoer* where he or she is likely to escape the personal consequences of the award. It is nonetheless easy to see how the two questions have become entangled and confused in courts' reasoning

[17] For a useful overview, see Maher (n 6) 700–03 and Appendix. Awards are now barred in QLD, the NT and NSW in personal injury cases, save where the injury is intentionally caused (or, in NSW, where the conduct causing it is not 'negligence'): Civil Liability Act 2003 (Qld), s 52(1); Personal Injuries (Liabilities and Damages) Act 2003 (NT), s 19; Civil Liability Act 2002 (NSW), s 21. They have also been abolished in all jurisdictions in defamation cases since 2005 under Uniform Legislation: see, eg, Defamation Act 2005 (NSW), s 37. Limitations of older origin preclude claims where the plaintiff dies before the proceeding (now in all jurisdictions, see, eg, Succession Act 1981 (Qld), s 66(2)(b)); in specific personal injury contexts such as motor vehicle accidents (Motor Accidents Compensation Act 1999 (NSW), s 144; Motor Accidents Injuries Act 2017 (NSW), s 4.20; Transport Accident Act 1986 (Vic), s 93); or injuries at work (Workers Compensation Act 1987 (NSW), s 151R, Accident Compensation Act 1985 (Vic), s 135A(7)(c)). Some jurisdictions have also, for some time, had either specific restrictions on the state's liability for exemplary damages in cases involving the police (Australian Federal Police Act 1979 (Cth), s 64B(3), Police Act 1892 (WA), s 137(6), 138(2), Weapons Act 1990 (Qld), s 165(3)), or total ousters of all liability for officers' conduct in the types of case ('serious and wilful misconduct') most likely to give rise to awards (Victoria Police Act 2013) (Vic), s 74(2). Such exclusions are especially significant because of the high proportion of cases in which exemplary awards are sought against the police: Maher (n 6); A Kildea, 'Power and Punishment: A Closer Look at Exemplary Damages as a Response to Tortious Conduct of Police Officers in Western Australia' (2021) *University of Western Australia Law Review* 10.

[18] Such provisions apply in respect of compulsory motor and workplace accident insurers: Motor Accident Insurance Act 1994 (Qld), s 55; Motor Vehicles Act 1959 (SA), s 113A; Workers Compensation and Rehabilitation Act 2003 (Qld), s 306B (the statutory insurer, WorkCover, is exempt from liability to indemnify employers in respect of injuries at work, where the employer's conduct justifies an exemplary award).

[19] *Gray* (n 9) [80] (Kirby J).

because in both instances a positive answer to the question results in a 'punitive' liability being born by a blameless third party.

Despite its limited practical impact, *Lamb* is still important today. It has implications for other jurisdictions, like the United States, where exemplary awards and liability insurance more regularly coincide. But it also plays a continuing role in the development of exemplary damages in Australia, precisely because it exposes in such a glaring way the justifications thought by the High Court to underpin such awards in this country. In endorsing these justifications so pertinaciously in circumstances in which their application was, to say the least, controversial, the judgment has wider ramifications than the isolated decision itself. It exercises a gravitational force upon the types of case in which lower courts are likely to be prepared to grant awards – and the justifications they are prepared to use in doing so – even when insurance is nowhere in the picture.

The following analysis divides into three sections. Section II examines the way in which the proceedings in *Lamb* were argued, highlighting some subtleties that help to explain the curious way in which the case was decided. Section III then examines the role of insurance in punitive damages cases more generally, considering both the question whether courts should in principle be influenced in their decisions in civil cases by a defendant's insurance position; and the pragmatic question whether such awards are actually insurable as a matter of fact, or public policy. Section IV then turns to the central mystery concerning the justification for making an exemplary award against a fully insured defendant, unpicking in the process the reasons given for doing so in *Lamb* itself and subjecting them to more critical scrutiny.

II. PROCEEDINGS, PLEADINGS AND SUBTLETIES

Cotogno's claim was framed as one for trespass to the person and initially succeeded at trial before Master Greenwood in December 1983.[20] The exemplary award of A$5,000 which he received formed part of a larger, total judgment of A$203,570, the bulk of which comprised compensatory damages for his injuries, pain and suffering, loss of earnings and medical expenses. He later successfully appealed the compensatory component of this award, getting it raised by the New South Wales Court of Appeal in June 1986.[21] A majority of that Court (Kirby P dissenting) upheld the original exemplary award at the same time. That exemplary award then formed the sole object of Lamb's appeal to the High Court, which unanimously affirmed it in October 1987.[22]

[20] *Lamb* (n 2).
[21] *Cotogno v Lamb No 3* (1986) 5 NSWLR 559 (CA).
[22] *Lamb* (n 5).

The action was subject to much procedural complication, delay and confusion from the start.[23] The pleading of the case as one of battery apparently took Lamb's counsel by surprise, since it was initially defended as if it were a straightforward case of negligence, carelessness on Lamb's part being denied and contributory negligence on the part of Cotogno being alleged. There was no prior case in Australia in which exemplary damages had been sought for battering someone with a motor vehicle, so the scenario was entirely new. Senior counsel for Cotogno at first instance, the late Barry Mahoney QC, had apparently always been keen to claim exemplary damages in exactly such a case,[24] but the novelty of the plea seems initially to have wrongfooted his opponents. Another confusing feature was that, whilst both compensatory and exemplary damages were sought, no separate claim was initially made for aggravated damages, despite the fact that the humiliation of being assaulted publicly and then left abandoned on a roadway would almost certainly have justified granting Cotogno an aggravated compensatory sum. It is not entirely clear why aggravated damages were not sought before Master Greenwood. The way in which the exemplary damages claim was particularised in the statement of claim suggested their appropriateness[25] and there was at one stage a pointed exchange between the Bench of the New South Wales Court of Appeal and Cotogno's counsel on appeal about the distinction between aggravated and exemplary damages, following which counsel rapidly sought to add a claim for an aggravated award.[26] By that stage, however, it was too late – a proper assessment of this component of damage would have required a retrial of the evidence, and whilst Kirby P was prepared to countenance this, a majority of the Court of Appeal was unconvinced and refused leave for the claim to be added.[27] Perhaps the Court thought that justice had already been delayed too long. In any event, the result was that the possibility of claiming an additional compensatory sum

[23] It took four years even to come to trial. For an account of the procedural history and delays, see *Cotogno v Lamb* (1985) 3 NSWLR 221 (CA) 222–23 (which interlocutory hearing itself addressed a further potential source of delay resulting from a member of the Court of Appeal, Mahoney JA, taking judicial leave from late 1985 until February 1986. The case continued with a reconstituted court).

[24] *Correspondence* (n 2).

[25] In *Lamb No 3* (n 21) 563, Kirby P noted that one of the particulars pleaded was that the events in question took place in the plain view of friends, neighbours and acquaintances – precisely the sorts of facts that would increase harm to the plaintiff's dignity. On further appeal, the High Court further noted that, on the facts found at first instance, Lamb's conduct was found to be 'an insult to the plaintiff' and that it was this that prompted the exemplary award: *Lamb* (n 5) 12–13 (Mason CJ, Brennan, Deane, Dawson, Gaudron JJ). One suggestion provided to me by Jim McIntrye (*Correspondence* (n 2)) as to why Mr Mahoney may not have initially made a claim for an aggravated compensatory sum was that his instructions led him to believe that he was dealing with a much clearer case for punitive damages than the facts at the trial ultimately revealed. Hindsight has 20/20 vision, but if he had known that his client would prove to be less innocent than he claimed, it is possible that he might have moderated the claim accordingly from a punitive one to an aggravated compensatory one.

[26] *Lamb No 3* (n 21) 563 (Kirby P).

[27] *Cotogno v Lamb* (NSWCA, 9 August 1985).

for the dignitary harm suffered by Cotogno over and above his physical injury was foreclosed by the time the case came before the High Court and the sole issue considered there was the appropriateness of the exemplary component. Had counsel pleaded aggravated compensatory damages from the outset, one may speculate that the exemplary claim might never have become the object of contention that it did. Indeed, it is even possible that the award would never have been made at all.

At first instance, proceedings were brief and the evidence conflicting. Master Greenwood ultimately accepted that Lamb's actions in driving away had initially been motivated by fear, but decided that there nonetheless came a point in time at which it should have been obvious to him that Cotogno no longer posed any physical threat, so that he had committed a battery by continuing to drive and then propelling Joe on to the road.[28] In respect of these actions, there could be no defence of *volenti non fit injuria* and Lamb had made no attempt to plead self-defence. Crucially for our purposes, the A$5,000 exemplary award was not made in respect of any of this conduct, precisely because it was found by his Honour to have been the product firstly of fear and then imprudence on Lamb's part, not malice. Rather, the award was justified as a mark of opprobrium for Lamb's 'callousness' in abandoning Cotogno at the scene of the accident – for his omission to stop and assist Joe after the event, at the scene of his injury.[29] That act of abandonment, the Court of Appeal later found, could not be justified as having been reasonably provoked by Cotogno's earlier aggression.[30] According to Jim McIntyre SC, the push to seek an exemplary award in respect of this, final aspect of Lamb's conduct was very much a last-ditch bid to salvage something from the original exemplary claim, it having become increasingly evident during the course of the trial, as the evidence unfolded and the true course of events emerged, that an exemplary award in respect of the initial battery itself was unsustainable.[31]

An immediate potential difficulty arising from this rationalisation of the award, identified on appeal by counsel for Lamb, is that, whilst failing to stop and assist was a criminal offence in New South Wales at the time,[32] it was not the conduct that constituted the battery forming Cotogno's civil cause of action

[28] *Lamb* (n 2) 10.

[29] ibid (n 2) 15. In the Court of Appeal, Kirby P admitted that this was not 'entirely clear' but nonetheless a 'fair reading' of Master Greenwood's reasons: *Lamb No 3* (n 21), 565. The passage is admittedly very brief.

[30] *Lamb No 3* (n 21) 576 (Kirby P); 579–80 (Glass JA). Provocation was raised only on appeal to the New South Wales Court of Appeal and Lamb was taken to have conceded that the defence could not apply in respect of the actionable acts of battery for the same reason that self-defence had not been pleaded, namely because they were disproportionate to the provoking conduct: ibid. The High Court stated only that it had to 'be supposed' that Master Greenwood had taken into account 'any provocation' in making the exemplary award: *Lamb* (n 5) 13.

[31] *Correspondence* (n 2).

[32] It remains so, now carrying a maximum sentence of 18 months' imprisonment for a first offence: Road Transport Act 2013 (NSW), s 146.

against Lamb in tort. The award seems therefore, on its face, to have been directed at punishing Lamb's criminal misconduct in abandoning the scene of the accident within a civil mode of trial, when that behaviour had never itself been alleged to be tortious. The objection was considered briefly but rejected by the High Court, either on the basis that the award could be seen as punishing the breach of a secondary (remedial) duty that Lamb had to address the consequences of his initial wrong,[33] or that there was sufficient continuity between the battery and the omission, such that the latter could be regarded as part and parcel of the same tortious course of behaviour.[34]

I personally find neither of these technical justifications very convincing. Damages are not granted in tort law for the breach of secondary, remedial duties; and it is hard to see, with respect, how driving away from an injured party without helping him constitutes or continues a positive battery upon him, although it obviously made Cotogno's consequent suffering and humiliation worse.[35] A more realistic view, to which we alluded in the preceding paragraph, is that Master Greenwood was not punishing the initial, imprudent tortious acts of battery at all, but the criminal offence of failing to stop and assist, but his reasoning is admittedly very brief and there is no clear recognition on its face that this is what he was doing. That explanation would also give rise to the awkward possibility that Lamb was ultimately punished twice for the same offence, because he had previously pleaded guilty to a 'serious criminal charge' of causing bodily harm by 'furious driving' in respect of the same incident.[36] It is hard to be sure about this, because I have not been able to track down the precise details of the sentence ultimately imposed upon him in respect of that offence and because the focus of that charge is on the initial causing of injury, not on subsequently failing to stop and assist. If there was indeed a risk of double punishment, it might seem surprising that the objection was not raised on appeal, since that risk is clearly accepted in Australian law as militating

[33] *Lamb* (n 5) 12 (a 'duty to take reasonable steps to alleviate the effects of his wrongdoing').

[34] ibid (the abandonment 'coloured the whole conduct of the defendant, including the [prior] assault'). This approach was preferred by the Court of Appeal: *Lamb No 3* (n 21) 588 (McHugh JA), 578 (Kirby P). Kirby P suggested that the problem of disjuncture might have been solved by a separate pleading of trespass in respect of the act of propelling Cotogno onto the road but this does, not, with respect, seem to have been the conduct of 'abandonment' that Master Greenwood had in mind when making the award either, although his Honour's statement was very brief (see n 29). There are some cases – especially cases of defamation – where behaviour subsequent to a tort (for example, repetition of the defamatory assertion, or poor behaviour during the course of trial) can increase a punitive award, but such cases are different in so far as the tortious act of defamation is effectively repeated).

[35] The case is clearly distinguishable in this respect from cases like *Fagan v Commissioner of Police of the Metropolis* [1969] 1 QB 439, in which an omission to break contact with a person's body results in a continuing battery to it.

[36] *Lamb No 3* (n 21) 573 (Kirby J) (he was 'presumably dealt with in accordance with law upon that plea'). This offence, which is described in very arcane terms by s 53 of the Crimes Act 1900 (NSW) carried a maximum sentence of two years' imprisonment.

strongly against an exemplary award.[37] A brief reference to Lamb's prior criminal punishment was made by Andrew Morrison SC in the application for special leave to appeal to the High Court,[38] but did not feature thereafter in argument. The probable reason why double-punishment was never seriously run as an argument, Andrew has since suggested to me in private discussion, is because it was always assumed by the defence (indeed, in the later stages, it became crucial to the line of that defence) that it would be the insurer and not Lamb himself who would pay the civil award.

A final peculiarity of the proceedings that is necessary for understanding the way argument progressed relates precisely to this key, unquestioned assumption that Lamb's liability for the A$5,000 award would be met by his compulsory insurer, the Government Insurance Office (GIO). This was not formally disputed by the parties (which did not include the GIO itself, although it was the real interest represented[39]) and was therefore never tested. The relevant legislation undoubtedly required Lamb to be insured against 'all liability' incurred in respect of personal injury 'arising out of the use of his car' and required the authorised insurer (of which the GIO was the only one in 1979) to indemnify him against 'all such liability'.[40] There was therefore no suggestion before any court at any level of the proceeding that the insurer would not meet the claim, or that judgment would have to be entered against it under the legislation if Lamb himself did not pay up.[41] Counsel for Lamb before the Court of Appeal and Junior Counsel in the High Court, Andrew Morrison SC, nonetheless tells an illuminating tale that casts the assumption into some doubt.[42] At the time, a large part of Andrew's practice was doing defence work for the GIO and it was in this way that he came to represent Lamb, since it was the GIO that was in reality running the defence. After judgment had been entered at first instance – and long after he had committed to defending Lamb's case in the Court of Appeal on the basis that the punitive award would be paid by the GIO and therefore had no point – the GIO, he recalls, communicated a fresh desire to challenge that assumption. Morrison quite rightly refused to change his argument, because this would have prejudiced the interests of

[37] The relevant law on this aspect is now stated in *Gray* (n 9). For an example, see *Whitbread v Rail Corporation NSW* [2011] NSWCA 130.

[38] *Lamb v Cotogno* (Transcript, Special Leave Application No 93/1986, 4 December 1986) 2.

[39] *Lamb No 3* (n 21), 569 (Kirby J). The acknowledgment was also made by RJ Ellicott QC, senior counsel for Lamb before the High Court: 'my client is really the Government Insurance Office' (Transcript, 6 May 1987, p 4).

[40] Motor Vehicles (Third Party Insurance) Act 1942 (NSW), ss 7(1), 10(1), 10(7).

[41] *Lamb* (n 5) 7. Before the High Court, Mr Ellicott QC, senior counsel for Lamb, indicated that he did not know whether cover was contested but that he understood that it was not, and that proceedings had been conducted throughout on this basis. He also addressed the terms of the policy and argued that the terms were broad enough to cover the acts in question: Transcript 6 May 1987, pp 11–20.

[42] Oral Interview with Dr Andrew Morrison SC, 8 December 2021 (transcript on file with the author).

his client.[43] What the anecdote nonetheless reveals is that the liability of an Australian insurer for exemplary damages – even a compulsory one that is required to indemnify a driver against 'all liability' – is far more controversial than it was assumed by the parties, or the High Court, to be. In fact, it seems that there was a precedent, which Brennan J referenced obliquely in the High Court proceeding, to the effect that equivalent policies issued under (slightly different) legislation in Queensland definitely did *not* cover punitive damages for acts of assault.[44] We return to this point in the next section, where the insurance position is considered more closely.

As it turned out, the High Court was itself ultimately 'far from clear' that an exemplary award was appropriate on the facts,[45] but it was simply not prepared to interfere in Master Greenwood's decision, given his opportunity to hear the full evidence at trial.[46] The identified 'callousness' of Lamb's conduct was limited in that decision to his act of abandonment and was very much on the borderline of the level of seriousness sufficient to justify an award.[47] The award itself was ultimately paid by New South Wales motorists – a result which Justice Kirby and Professor Luntz have independently described as 'absurd'[48] and against which Australian legislatures have unsurprisingly reacted.[49] Cotogno also never obtained any personal satisfaction from the award, tragically dying shortly before the High Court decision was handed down, at the age of only 46.[50] The right to claim exemplary damages has died with the victim in New South Wales since 1944, so it was, in a sense, another quirk of fate that the High Court came to hear the appeal at all.[51] In monetary terms, the award was a pittance from

[43] The potential conflict of interest between insurer and insured that occurs in such instances has resulted in restrictions in the US on the right of an insurer to select and direct the lawyer defending an insured: Widiss (n 16) 499–500.

[44] *Burton v Davies & General Accident Fire and Life Assurance Corporation Ltd* [1953] St R Q 26 (SC) (Townley J) ('*Burton*'). Brennan J could not remember the name of the case, but named the judge and the legislation (Transcript, 6 May 1987, p 14), so I think it is a fair bet that this was it. The only assault in respect of which (punitive) damages were awarded in this case, it should be noted, was one that took place *in* the car, not an assault *using* the car, so it is not 100% clear that it covered the instant case.

[45] *Lamb* (n 5) 13.

[46] Such deference is customary and appropriate. See recently, *Thorne v Kennedy* [2017] HCA 49, (2017) 263 CLR 85.

[47] It would now be insufficient for an exemplary award in Queensland, where an intention to cause the relevant personal injury is required in cases other than those involving sexual assault: Civil Liability Act 2003 (Qld), s 52(2)(a). By contrast, the equivalent New South Wales provision restricts exemplary awards only in respect of negligent conduct: Civil Liability Act 2002 (NSW), s 21.

[48] *Lamb No 3* (n 21), 570 (Kirby P, citing Luntz).

[49] See nn 17–18.

[50] My inquiries, which I have not been able to fully fact-check, indicate that he probably died on the 7 January 1987. The following website suggests that he may be buried at Kemps Creek Cemetery and Crematorium, not far from Bringelly: Find a Grave, Giuseppe 'Joe' Cotogno, <www.findagrave.com/memorial/148832671/giuseppe-cotogno> accessed 7 May 2023.

[51] Law Reform (Miscellaneous Provisions) Act 1944 (NSW), s 2(2)(a). Cotogno died after the application for special leave was heard (4 December 1986), but before the appeal itself was heard on 6 May 1987 (by which time his administratrix, Carol Doy Cotogno, had been permitted to step in).

the point of view of the insurer and must count amongst the smallest sums ever to form the object of a High Court appeal, but it would have been a significant amount for Lamb, had he personally been required to pay it. A$5,000 in 1979 translates to about A$25,000 today, which is poetically about the cost of a new Toyota Corolla – the make and model of the car which Lamb was driving when he battered Joe on the fateful evening in question.

III. THE ROLE OF INSURANCE

Lamb raises two questions of general importance about the role of insurance in cases involving punitive damages. The first is whether courts should in principle take account of a defendant's insurance position in deciding whether to make an award against him. The second is whether, if a court chooses to make an award, it is actually possible in practice for a defendant to insure against it.

A. Is Insurance Relevant to the Making of Exemplary Awards?

The traditional judicial view in both England and Australia, which accords with that of corrective justice theorists,[52] is that insurance is a factor external to the moral relationship between the two parties to a tort dispute and is therefore irrelevant to the determination of either their primary rights, or remedies.[53] Such rights and remedies are determined first in accordance with principles of justice; and insurance is a mechanism via which the parties may then adjust their positions in light of the determined legal rules, so as to avail themselves of a degree of financial protection when they are triggered. On this view, whether a defendant is insured or insurable is no more relevant to a civil court's decision than whether a defendant is rich or poor. But that position assumes, of course, that the function performed by an exemplary award in a tort case heard by a civil court is indeed corrective justice, a proposition that corrective justice theorists themselves reject.[54] Historically, there may have been an element of truth to the idea, owing to the fact that the purposes of damages awards were in days of yore combined without clear distinction in juries' minds. Exemplary awards also sometimes filled gaps in compensation for emotional distress and

[52] E Weinrib, 'The Insurance Justification and Private Law' (1985) 14 *Journal of Legal Studies* 681.

[53] For a classic exposition of this position (but not considering exemplary awards), see J Stapleton, 'Tort, Insurance and Ideology' (1995) 58 *MLR* 820. For important challenges, which describe a background role for insurance in shaping agreed legal relationships between parties about risk and thereby contributing to the creation of liabilities, not just their distribution, see R Merkin, 'Tort, Insurance and Ideology: Further Thoughts' (2012) 75 *MLR* 301; R Merkin and J Steele, *Insurance and the Law of Obligations* (Oxford, OUP, 2013).

[54] E Weinrib, *The Idea of Private Law*, 2nd edn (Oxford, OUP, 1995) 135 fn 25; 'Punishment and Disgorgement as Contract Remedies' (2003) 78 *Chicago-Kent Law Review* 55, 86.

harm to dignity.[55] Nonetheless, modern Australian courts are very clear that the purpose of awards is not to compensate, but to punish and deter wrongdoers, and to express judicial disapproval of their conduct;[56] and the fact that a defendant is insured clearly affects the extent to which he or she is personally likely to be punished or deterred. From this point of view, once courts accept, as they do, that exemplary awards have purposes of this sort and that the decision whether or not to make an award is governed by these purposes, insurance can no longer be regarded as an external factor to be ignored. Indeed, the fact that the High Court in *Lamb* expressly considered whether Lamb's insurance undermined the purpose of making the award – and concluded, for reasons that we examine section IV, that it didn't – clearly demonstrates that insurance considerations were intrinsic, not extrinsic to its thinking.

Whilst the fact of insurance is therefore generally disregarded by courts in determining primary legal rights or secondary rights to *compensation* in tort law, they must, as an inescapable matter of rational logic, have regard to it when considering whether to make an exemplary award, at least as long as they endorse their current line of thinking about the purposes of such awards. They are also logically required to take into account the precise extent of any cover when determining the award's quantum.[57] The fact that the High Court was prepared to uphold the award against Lamb despite the assumption that he was fully insured does not therefore mean that it considered the insurance *irrelevant* to its decision. It simply thought that the award was able to achieve its intended purposes *despite* it. That is a conclusion with which other courts have disagreed[58] and which we examine more critically in the next section, but the point is that the disagreement is not about the *relevance* of insurance, merely about the extent to which its presence weakens the case for making an award on the facts of any particular case.

B. Are Exemplary Awards Insurable?

The second general question, which was not at point in *Lamb* itself for reasons already explained but which is logically raised by it, is whether insurance is actually available in respect of an exemplary award. This is partly an empirical matter determined by the economics of the insurance market and partly a question of policy for determination by courts and (increasingly) by legislatures.

[55] For the full story, see A Sebok, 'What Did Punitive Damages Do? Why Misunderstanding the History of Punitive Damages Matters Today' (2003) 78 *Chicago-Kent Law Review* 101.

[56] See, eg, *NSW v Cuthbertson* (n 8) [87]–[88] (Beazley P); *Lule v New South Wales* [2018] NSWCA 125 [98] (MacFerlan JA).

[57] Law Commission, *Aggravated, Exemplary and Restitutionary Damages* (Law Com No 247, 1997), Rec 27, Draft Bill, cl 6(4).

[58] See, most famously, *Northwestern National Casualty Co v McNulty* 307 F 2d 432, 435 (5th Cir 1962) (although the case technically concerned the insurability of the award, not the question whether it should be made).

i. In Fact

On the empirical point, it is pretty clear that voluntary liability insurance contracts do not cover exemplary liabilities in England or Australia where the liability is personal for reasons earlier canvased,[59] and there are serious doubts as to whether compulsory policies do so either. The GIO clearly didn't think so and there was a precedent in Queensland from 1952 suggesting as much.[60] The English Law Commission, reporting in 1997, observed that, whilst liability insurance is now compulsory in a good number of instances outside the motor accidents scenario, none of the relevant statutory schemes requires cover for a punitive award, because their purpose is to ensure compensation for a plaintiff's loss, not his or her capacity to obtain the benefit of a windfall, punitive sum.[61] Compulsory third-party motor insurance policies in Australia typically exclude all liability where the injury or the accident was intentionally caused, or where the driver was involved in illegal activity, or later convicted of an offence.[62] In the United States, however, where awards are larger and available in respect of a broader range of conduct, the voluntary insurance market is much bigger and offers significant protection.[63] In some sectors of

[59] See text to nn 13–14 above. The terms of a policy were found to be wide enough to cover punitive liability that is vicarious in *Lancashire County Council v Municipal Mutual Insurance Ltd* [1997] QB 897 (CA) ('*Lancashire CC*'), but the CA was clear that the personal liability of individual police officers involved in an assault would not have been covered: 902, 907–08. An exception in respect of personal liability was noted in that case to exist in defamation actions in the UK, where liability is strict and newspapers widely rely on commercial indemnification (ibid 908). That market no longer exists in Australia since exemplary damages awards were abolished in defamation cases: see n 17 above.

[60] *Burton* (n 44).

[61] Law Commission (n 57) paras 1.270–1.273. By contrast, compulsory motor liability policies in the UK are required to cover compensatory liabilities in respect of personal injury or death, even in cases of deliberate running-down: R Merkin, *Colinvaux's Law of Insurance*, 12th edn (London, Sweet and Maxwell, 2019) para 23.131. On the role and limits of compulsory liability insurance generally, see Merkin and Steele (n 53) ch 9.

[62] In Queensland, see, eg, Suncorp Insurance, 'Driver Protection Cover Policy', <www.suncorp.com.au/content/dam/suncorp/insurance/suncorp-insurance/documents/car-and-vehicle/ctp/driver-protection-cover-policy-010716.pdf> accessed 7 May 2023. Alternatively, they contain warranties that entitle the insurer to recover from the insured in respect of liability resulting from behaviour of this type. For typical terms of this type under the standard policy issued by the Insurance Regulator under the Motor Vehicles Act 1959 (SA), s 104, see Insurance Regulator, 'Policy of Insurance' <www.ctp.sa.gov.au/for-vehicle-owners/policy-of-insurance> accessed 7 May 2023.

[63] E Meyers and J Hersch, 'Employment Practices Liability Insurance and Ex Post Moral Hazard' (2021) 106 *Cornell Law Review* 947, 966–68 (demand and supply are both strong in respect of cover for employers in respect of discrimination, harassment, retaliation and wrongful termination at work); A Davis, 'Insurance Coverage For Punitive Damages – Time for a Uniform Rule under General Maritime Law' (2013) 12 *Loyola Maritime Law Journal* 156 (attesting to the demand in respect of maritime risks); C French, 'Debunking the Myth that Insurance Coverage is Not Available or Allowed for Intentional Torts or Damages' (2012) 8 *Hastings Business Law Journal* 65, 67–69 (pointing to cover in respect of trademark and copyright infringement, invasion of privacy, defamation, disparagement, false imprisonment, malicious prosecution, improper employment practices and more); P Seyferth, 'The Construction and Admissibility of Insurance Policies that Provide Coverage for Punitive Damage Awards' (1990) 7 *Alaska Law Review* 71. For an early

activity, the practical demand for cover from businesses is apparently so strong that insurers have created work-arounds in order to provide it even in states in which it is officially banned.[64] If left to its own devices, it therefore seems likely that the market would provide exemplary damages cover at least in respect of non-intentional or accidental harm (where this is a legal possibility), as well as for businesses and governmental agencies whose exposure is vicarious, with such exceptions, limitations, deductions and other devices as are required to offset the normal commercial risks from the insurer's point of view.

ii. In Law

The policy question concerning the permissibility of insurance is more difficult and has divided the various American jurisdictions in which it has been raised.[65] The trend amongst both courts and legislatures is increasingly in favour of allowing it.[66] Of the 48 jurisdictions in which punitive awards were available in 2018,[67] only half a dozen or so appeared to rule it out completely,[68] with at least 26 allowing it in all instances,[69] and the rest permitting it where the liability

piece that considers and favours the construction of 'all sums' policies to cover punitive awards in the US, see RH Brin Jr, 'Punitive Damages and Liability Insurance' (1964) 31 *Insurance Counsel Journal* 265.

[64] Meyers and Hersch (n 63) 967, citing the use of offshore Bermuda 'wrap-around' policies and 'most favoured jurisdiction' clauses in EPLI contracts.

[65] The question is thought to be one on which 'reasonable minds differ': *St Paul Mercury Ins Co v Duke Univ* 849 F 2d 133, 137 (4th Cir 1988). See generally, C Yetka, 'Insurance Coverage for Punitive Damage' (2014) 44 *Brief* 1; Davis (n 63); T Baker, 'Reconsidering Insurance for Punitive Damages' (1998)(1) *Wisconsin Law Review* 101; Widiss (n 16); M DeMent-Donarski, 'Punitive Damages and Insurance: Are Punitive Damages Insurable – The North Dakota Supreme Court Says Yes, Despite North Dakota's Public Policy to the Contrary' (1994) 70 *North Dakota Law Review* 637; G Priest, 'Insurability and Punitive Damages' (1989) *Alaska Law Review* 1009, 1033–35 (1989); S Neal, 'Punitive Damages: Suggested Reform for an Insurance Problem' (1987) 18 *St Mary's Law Journal* 1019; A Walden, 'The Publicly Held Corporation and the Insurability of Punitive Damages' (1985) 53 *Fordham Law Review* 1383; JD Long, 'Should Punitive Damages Be Insured?' (1977) 44 *The Journal of Risk and Insurance* 1; W Zuger, 'Insurance Coverage of Punitive Damages' (1976) 53 *North Dakota Law Review* 239; R Anderson Jr, 'Indemnity Against Punitive Damages: An Examination of Punitive Damages, their Purpose, Public Policy, and the Coverage Provisions of the Texas Standard Automobile Liability Insurance Policy' (1973) 27 *Southwestern Law Journal* 593; G Moates, 'Exemplary Damages – An Insurable Risk for Texas Drivers' (1972) 10 *Houston Law Review* 192; K Lasson 'Punitive Damages: Punishment of an Insured Defendant' (1965) 25 *Maryland Law Review* 326; TD Fischer 'Insurance Coverage and the Punitive Award in the Automobile Accident Suit' (1957) 19 *University of Pittsburgh Law Review* 144.

[66] For a useful 2005 analysis tracking the change and advocating more insurance (on the hypothesis that the purpose of awards is to engage in social compensation), see Sharkey (n 15). For a more recent, detailed jurisdictional analysis, see Wilson Elser, 'Punitive Damages Review' <https://digital.wilsonelser.com/punitive-damages-review> accessed 5 February 2023.

[67] Only Michigan, Nebraska, Puerto Rico and Washington prohibited punitive awards entirely: 'Punitive Damages Review' (n 66) 2.

[68] ibid Utah, New York, Ohio (probably), California (probably), Colorado (probably, but the position is unclear where the liability is vicarious), Massachusetts (probably, but unclear where liability is vicarious). Columbia had similarly made no specific decision in 2018.

[69] ibid.

is vicarious,[70] or the conduct is unintentional.[71] This progressive shift in favour of allowing insurance can be seen as a response to the weight of exemplary awards upon commercial parties, which can still be heavy despite the Supreme Court's more recent moves to lighten it.[72] It is also a function of the power of free markets, and of differences in the purposes that punitive awards are thought to serve in some American jurisdictions. The late persistence in some states of the view that awards serve a compensatory function (a view shared by some modernising commentators such as Catherine Sharkey),[73] and the fact that they universally help to cover a plaintiff's otherwise irrecoverable litigation costs, means that the logical objections to allowing insurance are softened. Permitting protection against compensatory liabilities and costs is, after all, consistent with the objectives of such awards (indeed, some would argue that the workability of the whole tort system depends upon it) whereas permitting the insurance of punitive liabilities is, by contrast, prone to frustrate their aims, as we shall see. Free market libertarians (of which America obviously has its fair share) press the view that a party's freedom to bargain for protection against legal liability is paramount, even in respect of his or her own punishment, and that any policy ban on protection would constitute unacceptable state overreach into a private domain of contractual liberty. Some writers of a less libertarian ilk also suggest that insurance ironically advances the general deterrent and condemnatory functions of punitive awards because, although it insulates defendants against their personal impact, it nonetheless incentivises plaintiffs to bring claims when they otherwise would not, thereby making public examples of wrongdoers who would otherwise escape visible censure.[74]

In England and Australia, the demand for insurance is less than in the United States for reasons already canvased, but the policy settings are also a little different. Costs rules already favour successful plaintiffs and courts have long since abandoned the fiction that exemplary awards compensate loss, so that those particular justifications for permitting insurance are not available.

[70] ibid Florida, Illinois, Kansas, Missouri, Oklahoma, Pennsylvania, Indiana (probably), Maine (uncertain), Minnesota (probably), New Jersey (probably).

[71] ibid see, eg, Arkansas, Connecticut, Georgia, Kentucky, Texas, Virginia.

[72] *Exxon Shipping Co v Baker*, 554 US 471 (2008); *Philip Morris USA v Williams*, 549 US 346 (2007), 556 US 178 (2009); *State Farm Mutual Automobile Insurance Co v Campbell*, 538 US 408 (2003); *BMW of North America, Inc v Gore*, 517 US 559 (1996). On *Campbell*, see further Sharkey, ch 13 of this volume.

[73] Connecticut, Michigan, New Hampshire and Texas are (or were until recently) reportedly examples: Anderson (n 65) 595–96, 614. Radically modernising the old train of thought, Sharkey suggests that the purpose of punitive damages is to compensate 'social loss' so that insurance should be widely available: C Sharkey, 'Punitive Damages Transformed into Societal Damages' in E Bant et al (eds), *Punishment and Private Law* (Oxford, Hart Publishing, 2021) 185.

[74] D Markel, 'How Should Punitive Damages Work' (2009) 157 *University of Pennsylvania Law Review* 1383, 1468. It is sometimes also suggested that insurance promotes general deterrence in particular sectors, such as maritime commerce, where the rise in premiums resulting from a successful claim will be felt by a discrete group of 'similarly situated' premium-payers (shipowners) constituting a closely interconnected trading community: Davis (n 63) 183.

The commercial pressure to allow insurance is also less, because where exemplary awards are available, they are required by law to be moderate, and generally are so because they are determined by judges, not juries. The moral case for allowing a wrongdoer to insure him or herself is weaker too, because exemplary awards are only usually available where conduct is egregious, cynical, or the harm has been deliberately caused. Nonetheless, some of the arguments that have proven influential in the United States – in particular, the free market call not paternalistically to interfere in private contractual arrangements, and the suggestion that allowing insurance encourages important public interest claims – persuaded the English Law Commission that exemplary awards should be insurable in all cases, even where the liability in question is personal to a defendant, intentional, and the conduct criminal.[75] In justifying this approach, the Commission drew a sharp distinction between criminal punishment in public law, where insurance is impermissible on public policy grounds; and exemplary damages awards in civil cases, where it should be freely permitted and left to the market.[76]

This distinction is stark and only defensible if the purposes of criminal punishment and exemplary awards are themselves identifiably different. That is a credible, if not wholly watertight view, because criminal punishment is still partly (predominantly, in fact) a matter of retributive justice, whereas retribution has a diminishing role in the modern civil law for good reasons.[77] Retribution in the criminal law absolutely requires a penalty to be born personally by the wrongdoer,[78] whereas the justifications for exemplary awards in the civil law are overwhelmingly non-retributive and do not therefore necessarily require the same thing. You cannot be allowed to serve my prison sentence for me, even if you are willing, because retributive justice requires me to hurt personally for what I have done in proportion to my wrong, so that I receive my just desert. But you might – perhaps – be allowed to pay my exemplary damages award, because in such a case retribution is not the main end in view.

Interestingly, the same sort of distinction as was drawn by the Law Commission in England between criminal punishment and exemplary awards has recently been drawn by the High Court of Australia between

[75] Law Commission (n 57) paras 1.236–48. The same arguments persuaded Simon Brown LJ in *Lancashire CC* (n 59) 907–09, at least in cases in which the liability insured is vicarious (or attaches to the State under an equivalent statutory provision), not personal.

[76] Law Commission (n 57) para 1.258.

[77] K Barker, 'Punishment in Private Law: No Such Thing (Any More)' in E Bant et al (eds), *Punishment and Private Law* (Oxford, Hart Publishing, 2021) esp 44–47 (identifying punishment with retribution).

[78] This follows from the nature of retribution itself (ibid 45 – retributive justice 'takes [metaphorical] flesh from the wrongdoer'), but also explains the use by courts of the illegality doctrine to prevent persons convicted of a crime recovering compensatory damages from others who are alleged to be responsible for their behaviour: *Gray v Thames Trains Ltd* [2009] UKHL 33, [2009] 1 AC 1339. I am grateful to James Goudkamp for this point. *cf* J Goudkamp, 'Can Tort Law be Used to Deflect the Impact of Criminal Sanctions? The Role of the Illegality Defence' (2006) 14 *Torts Law Journal* 20.

exemplary awards (presumed insurable) and civil penalties (which should be born in person). In *Australian Building and Construction Commissioner v Construction, Forestry, Mining and Energy Union and Another*,[79] the High Court hence held that courts have the power to make an order requiring a defendant to bear the burden of a civil penalty under the Fair Work Act 2009 (Cth) personally, thereby barring him from seeking indemnity or support in respect of its payment from a third party. In doing so, it expressly rejected an argument that the contrary conclusion was impliedly mandated by *Lamb*.[80] The purpose of civil penalties, it said, is to deter a wrongdoer and others from engaging in the wrong and this purpose is likely to be defeated if the wrongdoer is permitted third-party indemnification. He must feel the penalty's sting upon his person and the court consequently has the power to ensure that the sting is felt. By contrast, the purposes of exemplary awards extend beyond deterrence and include the expression of disapproval for a wrongdoer's conduct. This, the court thought, explains why insurance was no obstacle to the making of the award against Lamb, whereas it was essential in *CFMEU* that the wrongdoer himself be made to pay the penalty in question.[81] Retribution and deterrence require personal payment, but disavowal and public censure of the wrongdoer's behaviour do not.

The reasoning of the High Court in *CFMEU* does not, as we shall see in the next section, fully gel with the High Court's thoughts in *Lamb*, because there the Court said that making an award against an insured person can still achieve the goal of general deterrence. On that logic, it would still be permissible to impose a civil penalty on a defendant where the penalty is going to be paid by a third party, because the penalty might still deter others from engaging in the 'same type of conduct', even though it leaves the wrongdoer himself personally unaffected. According to *Lamb*, arguments of general deterrence definitely do *not* require the sting of an award to be felt personally in the way that the Court in *CFMEU* suggests, but that is a disagreement to which we shall come in the next section and need not detain us further for now.

The above discussion does not, unfortunately, resolve the policy debate as to whether exemplary awards should be insurable as matter of policy, but what it does establish is that the answer to this question depends entirely on the purposes that awards are meant to serve. If the function of the award is retributive, then insurance should simply not be allowed, but if its purpose is other than this – for example to achieve general deterrence, some form of symbolic disavowal, or perhaps some hidden compensation for a plaintiff in respect of a loss that has otherwise been missed – then the case is not as clear. Unfortunately, as things stand, the purposes that awards are thought to serve

[79] *Australian Building and Construction Commissioner v CFMEU* [2018] HCA 3, (2018) 262 CLR 157.

[80] ibid 196.

[81] ibid 195–96.

differ between different jurisdictions, and even sometimes between different judges. This confusing picture squares with the broader disagreements about the continued contemporary relevance of exemplary damages. All one can safely conclude is that the further away from retribution the purposes of exemplary awards move in the modern age, the more the arguments are thought to favour their insurability.

The summary conclusions of this section are therefore threefold. Firstly, the High Court in *Lamb* was logically quite right to consider Lamb's insurance position in determining whether or not to award exemplary damages against him, even if it was wrong to uphold the award Master Greenwood had made on the facts. Secondly, the insurance market for punitive damages cover is complex, but the market is likely to supply such cover – at least in respect of vicarious liability and unintentional harm – if there is sufficient demand for it. In Australia, exemplary liability in tort lies in the main for conscious wrongdoing and there are other, significant statutory limits on awards, so that it is questionable whether there will, in the short term, be either significant insurance supply on the one hand, or demand, on the other. Thirdly, the question whether such insurance should actually be permitted as a matter of policy is entirely dictated by the purposes that awards are designed to serve. This, final policy question again only very rarely requires an answer in Australia and the United Kingdom, but it does sometimes surface. The current sense that one gets from the recent *CFMEU* case is that courts think that criminal sanctions and civil penalties should be grouped together as uninsurable on the basis that their retributive and deterrent purposes require the effects of an award to be felt by a wrongdoer, but that the purposes of exemplary awards are sufficiently different (in particular in respect of their 'condemnatory' function) to make such insurance in principle generally permissible, should the market for it ever really grow. There are, however, acknowledged statutory exceptions to this position in some Australian jurisdictions and contexts, where compulsory insurance against punitive awards has effectively been nullified, on the basis that it is wrong that the costs of awards be transferred to the premium-paying public, rather than being born by the wrongdoer himself.[82]

IV. CAN INSURED PUNISHMENT BE JUSTIFIED?

This brings us to the key puzzle in *Lamb* and perhaps the main point of the case's ongoing significance in reasoning terms. Assuming that a wrongdoer is indeed able to obtain (and has obtained) an enforceable indemnity against any exemplary liability, should a court nonetheless go ahead and make the award? What is the purpose of doing so?

[82] See n 18 above.

The argument against the award was put in two ways by counsel for Lamb. One suggestion was that the introduction of the statutory system of compulsory third-party motor insurance in New South Wales had impliedly limited plaintiffs' rights to claim exemplary damages at common law in cases covered by the Act. This suggestion was rejected by the High Court on the basis that there was nothing in the legislation from which any intention to disturb the existing common law could be inferred.[83] I say no more about it here. The other argument, which is central to the current inquiry, was that the presence of insurance stripped away any justification for the award on the facts, by undermining the extent to which it would fulfil its stipulated purposes of punishment and/or deterrence. The High Court conceded that there was 'strength' in this second line or reasoning, but rejected it on the basis that, whilst Lamb might indeed escape 'punishment', punishment is not the 'whole' objective of an exemplary award and there were three other potential justifications which survived.[84] These included the potential of the award to discourage private vigilantism, the thought that it might still deter others; and the idea that it would serve in any event to mark the court's condemnation of the wrong.

A. Personal Retribution

In accepting that Lamb would not be 'punished', the High Court must have meant that he would escape personal retribution. This is clearly correct. Even if retribution were the aim of exemplary awards in the modern law (which I have suggested elsewhere it is most probably not)[85] it could not justify an award against a party who is fully[86] insured against the award's effects, because retributive justice logically requires a wrongdoer to be harmed in proportion to the wrong that he or she has done.[87] Whilst it is possible that exemplary awards impose a social penalty (stigma, reputational harm, shame) upon a wrongdoer even when he or she is fully financially indemnified,[88] such harm is very unlikely to fully represent his or her 'just deserts' when there is no other price to pay.

[83] *Lamb* (n 5) 12. The argument was accepted by Kirby P (dissenting) in the Court of Appeal: *Lamb No 3* (n 21) 570–72.

[84] *Lamb* (n 5) 9–10.

[85] Barker (n 77). For the contrary view that awards rightly reflect a private party's liberty to be 'punitive' or 'vengeful', this being part of a private citizen's right to 'civil recourse' for a wrong going beyond the right to have the wrong corrected through compensation, see B Zipursky, 'A Theory of Punitive Damages' (2005) 84 *Texas Law Review* 105.

[86] Retributive justice will also not be effected – or properly effected – against a party who is only partly insured, unless the award is quantified in such a way as to exceed the level of cover by a margin that is fully proportionate to the wrong done. For this reason, arguments that awards against the insured still punish defendants who are only partly covered are flawed.

[87] For the idea of proportion in retributive justice and the distinction in respect of corrective and distributive justice, see Barker (n 77) 44–51.

[88] *de Montigny v Brossard (Succession)* 2010 SCC 51, [2010] 3 SCR 64 [52].

On the facts, Lamb would also have already been stigmatised by his criminal conviction, so that shaming him again through an exemplary award would have violated the injunction against double-punishment. If there is a justification for the award in *Lamb* itself, retributive justice was therefore clearly not it. Nor can it easily feature as a justification in any other case of insured punishment.

B. Avoidance of Vigilantism

One justification which the High Court did give for the award was that it might nonetheless serve to 'assuage any urge for revenge' felt by Cotogno and 'discourage' him from engaging in self-help likely to 'endanger the peace'.[89] There are at least three problems with this line of justification too. Firstly, if an award is meant to appease a plaintiff's personal sense of grievance and desire for revenge, it is unlikely to do so where he knows that his offender will pay not a cent of it. The receipt of money from a third-party insurer may mollify a victim to some degree, but her resentment will probably continue to fester where she knows that her offender has not been made to pay for his wrong.[90] If you purposely hit me, but your friend pays the bill, there will still – I am sorry to say it – be friction between us the next time we meet. It is only an acceptance of *personal* responsibility by the wrongdoer, or the clear imposition of that responsibility upon him by a court of law, that really appeases the wronged.

Secondly, the suggestion that the function of exemplary awards is to keep the public peace looks very odd to the modern eye. The authorities supporting it are ancient, harking back to a time when public enforcement systems were underdeveloped and the risk of private violence therefore more real. One of these cases, *Merest v Harvey*,[91] to which the High Court refers in its very brief reasoning on this point, was famously set against the background of the duelling practices of the landed English aristocracy and has an unreal feel in the twenty-first century.[92] The High Court accepted that appeasement is predominantly a historical function of exemplary awards, but insisted nonetheless that it remains an 'aspect' of them in the modern day.[93] That is hard to believe in the standard case. If a victim receives full compensation for his mental, physical and dignitary harm and knows that his offender is subject to criminal punishment through the now standard processes of public law, this will be more than enough to suppress his violent instincts and keep the peace in most instances, not least because taking the law violently into one's own hands is itself likely to result in a serious criminal sanction.

[89] *Lamb* (n 5) 9.

[90] But *cf Lamb No 3* (n 21) 587 (McHugh JA).

[91] *Merest v Harvey* (1814) 5 Taunt 442, 128 ER 761. See also *Grey v Grant* (1764) 2 Wils KB 2 52, 95 ER 794.

[92] See S Banks, *Duels* and Duelling (Oxford, Shire Publications, 2012).

[93] *Lamb* (n 5) 9.

Thirdly, even if there are still some, exceptional cases in which exemplary awards do help to prevent vigilantism because the normal criminal law processes have failed,[94] this was not one of them. Lamb – to repeat a now familiar refrain – had been charged with, and convicted, of a serious criminal offence in relation to the incident in question, as well as being obliged to pay substantial compensation for Cotogno's losses. The idea that in such circumstances, an exemplary award was needed to sate the latter's urge for revenge is nothing short of fanciful.

C. Specific Deterrence

Where a tortfeasor is fully insured, the proposition that an exemplary award serves the end of specific deterrence is very weak. The High Court in Lamb did not suggest otherwise. It is admittedly sometimes argued that the award could still have an indirect effect in cases in which the insurance arrangement is voluntary, because it could lead to the denial of future cover, the loss of the insured's no-claims bonus, or higher premiums.[95] If the insured is a commercial party, the insurer might also step in to take a more active role in managing the way in which the insured approaches risks in the future,[96] or even, in some instances, try to recoup its liability in an independent subrogation claim against the insured, thereby bringing legal consequences to bear upon the latter personally. These consequences are very unlikely where the cover is compulsory, as it was in Lamb.[97] In any instance, however, they are so speculative and contingent on unknown third-party behaviour that they cannot provide decent justifications for an award. They are therefore more likely to constitute an award's possible, hypothetical consequences, that a court's actual reasons for making it.[98] Perhaps

[94] This may be the case in some instances: *Lamb No 3* (n 21) 586 (McHugh JA). Historic failures on the part of police forces to give sufficient attention to the prosecution of domestic violence provide an example.

[95] Law Commission (n 57) para 1.240; *Lancashire CC* (n 59) 909 (Simon Brown LJ); *Lamb No 3* (n 21) 570 (Kirby P). The assertion is especially common in the academic literature supporting insurance: eg, Davis (n 62) 182–84; Baker (n 65) 112.

[96] Widiss (n 16) 501. For the full range of measures that insurers use to manage risk and which can therefore potentially count as deterrence mechanisms, see T Baker and P Siegelman, 'The Law and Economics of Liability Insurance: A Theoretical and Empirical Review' in J Arlen (ed), *Research Handbook on the Economics of Torts* (Cheltenham, Edward Elgar Publishing, 2013) esp 178–81.

[97] *Lamb No* 3 (n 21) 570 (Kirby P) (no indirect sanctions could be imposed by the insurer upon Lamb consistently with the language of the relevant legislation and the insurer's duties under it). In the UK, there is no known case in which an exemplary award has been claimed against a driver in a deliberate running-down case. If such an award were to be made, there is a residual possibility that the Motor Insurer's Bureau, which is required to cover 'any liability' where there is no other insurance cover in place (Road Traffic Act 1988 (UK), s 145) would in turn bring a subrogation claim against the driver, but this is all highly speculative. I am grateful to Rob Merkin for this point.

[98] In questioning before the High Court, Dawson J thought the arguments 'artificial' (Transcript, 5 May 1987, p 62). They have also been construed as apologetic in the sense that they do not justify awards against insured parties, but merely soften the arguments against them: D Ellis,

for this reason, Australian judges have tended to eschew any distinction between compulsory and voluntary insurance:[99] in neither case do they suggest with any conviction that the purpose of making the award is to change the wrongdoer's future behaviour. Their scepticism is endorsed to a degree by the recognition in some US courts that there is no empirical evidence to suggest that a party's insurance position in respect of punitive damages has any effect on his or her behaviour.[100] It also contrasts interestingly with their approach in making awards against vicariously liable parties, where judges are more clearly prepared to accept that the award will result in an employer (usually the state) taking measures to prevent or deter future wrongdoing on the part of its wayward employees, and that this is a legitimate part of the award's justification.[101]

D. General Deterrence

A further justification that the High Court did provide for the award was that, even if it did little to punish or deter Lamb personally, it might still deter others, because the deterrence objective underlying awards 'extends beyond the actual wrongdoer and the exact nature of his wrongdoing' and includes the deterrence of other 'like-minded persons' tempted to engage in 'conduct of the same reprehensible kind.'[102] Precisely who might be deterred by the award in

'Fairness and Efficiency in the Law of Punitive Damages' (1982) 56 *Southern California Law Review* 1, 75.

[99] *Lamb No 3* (n 21) 585 (McHugh JA); *Lamb* (n 5) 193 ('not an adequate distinction').

[100] *Harrell v Travelers Indem Co*, 567 P 2d 1013, 1016–17 (Or 1977) cited in Davis (n 63) 175.

[101] See, eg, *New South Wales v Zreika* [2012] NSWCA 37 [62], [75] (Sackville AJA); *New South Wales v Ibbett* [2006] HCA 57, (2006) 229 CLR 638 [38], [56]–[57]; *Bryant* (n 8) [23]–[24] (special leave refused [2006] HCA Trans 319 (16 June 2006)); *Kuddus v Chief Constable of Leicestershire Constabulary* [2002] 2 AC 122 (HL) 149 (Lord Hutton); *Goddard v Grand Trunk Ry*, 57 Me 202, 223–24 (1869). This contrast might at first appear to be a contradiction, but the readiness of courts to consider these consequences in cases of vicarious liability is actually supported by one line of thinking about the (admittedly confused) logic of vicarious liability itself: an employer is made responsible on behalf of the wrongdoer at least in part because of the incentive effects this is likely to have on the employer's safety practices and readiness to monitor and control the activities of its staff. The potential positive effect on these practices of making the employer liable for an exemplary award is therefore logically relevant to the decision whether or not to make it. The argument is stronger still where, as in cases like *Ibbett*, the liability of the state under statute for an officer's misconduct is not simply additional to that of the officer, but substitutes for it, for here the clear intention is that the conduct is the state's own, personal responsibility. Whether or not the imposition of liability will in fact lead to the intended deterrent consequences, or do so efficiently, still remains a matter of speculation, of course, as it does in the standard insurance case, and this is sometimes doubted: see, eg, Ellis (n 98) 67–71. There is nonetheless a better reason for thinking that such consequences, if real, should play an intrinsic part in courts' reasoning in cases of vicarious liability, rather than constituting merely the indirect, extrinsic consequences of an award. For a fuller examination of the justifications for vicarious punishment (concluding that it is justified only exceptionally, in cases against the state), see P Morgan, 'Vicarious Punishment: Vicarious Liability for Exemplary Damages' in E Bant et al (eds), *Punishment and Private Law* (Oxford, Hart Publishing, 2021) 287.

[102] *Lamb* (n 5) 10.

Lamb itself, and why, was left unstated. The Court accepted that the award was unlikely to deter other motorists (presumably because they would all also have compulsory insurance) but suggested that it would nonetheless have an 'undiminished' effect on others 'minded to engage in conduct of a similar nature which does not involve the use of a motor vehicle',[103] which might be taken to imply that the Court thought the award might deter other people, in other contexts, who are bent on committing assault. Although this fits the Court's stated view that the award was a response to Lamb's act of battery, it does not square, I have suggested, with Master Greenwood's original view that it was directed at his failure to stop and assist at the scene, unless, that is, one takes the rather unlikely view to which I have referred above, that the two behaviours were in fact one and the same. Furthermore, if, contrary to Master Greenwood's view, it really was acts of battery that the award was designed to deter, one might wonder why this was not already achieved by Lamb's criminal conviction for furious driving.

In the Court of Appeal, McHugh JA had suggested that the deterrent aim of the award might be even broader, so that it would serve to deter 'all those in the community who might engage in wrongdoing involving a conscious and contumelious disregard of another person's rights,'[104] which is tantamount to saying that it would deter anyone engaged in any behaviour that might, at the discretion of a judge, be considered appropriate for an award. A line of questioning put to counsel for Lamb by Deane J in the High Court seems to suggest that his Honour took a similar approach to deterrence to be at the heart of *Uren*.[105] By contrast, Kirby P was dismissive of the extent to which punishing the insured would achieve either specific, or general deterrence.[106] Certainly, for an award to have any effect on the behaviour of the public generally, or that of particular groups contemplating 'similar conduct', the relevant target group must be able to identify itself as engaging in conduct that is sufficiently 'similar' to the wrong committed, so that it can avoid behaving in that way. Since the target category of wrongdoer – and the precise feature of the conduct being sanctioned – were both left unclear in *Lamb*, it seems very unlikely that any particular section of the public would change its behaviour as a result of the award made, even assuming that the latter was sufficiently broadly publicised to make the public aware of it, which is a further issue in its own right.

There is also, surely, a very real question as to whether the making of a A$5,000 award against a party that is known to have been permitted to pass the burden on to an insurance company would have any significant impact on the behaviour of a member of the public, even if she were able to identify herself as engaged in conduct that is similar to that upon which the court had passed its

[103] ibid.
[104] *Lamb No 3* (n 21) 586; see also 580 (Glass JA).
[105] Transcript 6 May 1987 p 47.
[106] *Lamb No 3* (n 21) 571.

punitive judgment. Would the dominant impression of such an observer be that Lamb was punished for what he did (so that the observer should diligently avoid similar conduct), or that he escaped his punishment (so that he really need not worry too much)? The recent reasoning of the High Court in the *CFMEU* case, considered above, suggests that the aim of general deterrence probably *cannot* be achieved where a wrongdoer is allowed to rely on a third party to pay out his wrong,[107] which is consistent with the latter, more sceptical view. The general deterrence of others seems most unlikely where a defendant has been personally let off the legal hook.

Whilst virtually all modern courts endorsing exemplary awards refer to general deterrence as a justification for making them,[108] there is a well-known deficit in the empirical evidence relating to the deterrent effects of punitive awards. Without empirical evidence, justifications that themselves depend on empirical arguments have little credence, even on their own terms.[109] The honest answer is that we just don't know. On the facts of Lamb itself, there are particularly strong reasons for doubting whether the making of a A$5,000 award against a fully insured defendant would have had any significant impact upon the public consciousness. If it had any deterrent effect at all, that effect would be vanishingly small in comparison to the incentive provided by the compensatory component of the award against Lamb, which, as we indicated above, was ultimately fixed at some A$230,000 by the Court of Appeal.[110] In truth, it is highly implausible to suggest that an uplift of about two per cent in a liability that would in practice be paid by the general motoring public would have any broader impact on public behaviour at all.

E. Expressive Condemnation

This leaves just one, final arrow in the quiver. It consists in the popular idea that exemplary awards perform an expressive function in voicing a court's condemnation of egregious conduct. This seems to have been the sole justification offered by Master Greenwood for his award at first instance. The High Court indicated

[107] *CFMEU* (n 79) 195–96 (a penalty devoid of sting 'may not have much, if any, specific or general deterrent effect').

[108] R Sommers, 'The Psychology of Punishment and the Puzzle of Why Tortfeasor Death Defeats Liability for Punitive Damages' (2015) 124 *Yale Law Journal* 1295, 1295, fn 1 cites J Kircher and C Wiseman, *Punitive Damages: Law and Practice*, 2nd edn (St Paul, West Group, 2014) §4:12 as listing 41 US states in which general deterrence is recognised as at least one justification for exemplary awards. That view also prevails in both England and Australia.

[109] For a summary account of the limited information available and the wry observation that the answer has 'eluded empiricists', see C Sharkey, 'Economic Analysis of Punitive Damages: Theory, Empirics, and Doctrine' in J Arlen (ed), *Research Handbook on the Economics of Torts* (Cheltenham, Edward Elgar Publishing, 2013) 486, 501–02. There is a good case for the research to be done: C Morris, 'Punitive Damages in Tort Cases' (1931) 44 *Harvard Law Review* 1173.

[110] *Lamb No 3* (n 21).

that he had 'not exceeded the boundaries of his function'[111] in taking that line, but otherwise referred to the admonitory function of exemplary awards on only one other, brief occasion in its judgment, affording it much less space than the arguments about appeasement and general deterrence.[112] One might infer from this that it thought the justification too weak to be credible on its own.

This is unsurprising, as there are very good reasons to be sceptical of it. One issue is that it is difficult to find an aim underpinning condemnation that does not either concertina back into one of the other purposes of exemplary awards that we have already considered, or which is not already met by the law in other ways. If it is meant to vilify the wrongdoer hurtfully so as to fix upon him his just deserts, then the aim is retribution, and this is clearly not achieved where a defendant is insured. If it is meant to appease the victim, then it avoids vigilantism and keeps the peace, but those functions have also already been considered, and seriously doubted. If it is designed to change the wrongdoer's behaviour, or that of others, then the aim is deterrence. To gain any independent traction as a justification, condemnation must therefore have a different logic with its own, normative force. The High Court clearly thought this to be the case (otherwise it would not have referred to the idea separately), but it did not identify the distinct role that condemnation plays, or explain how a monetary award expressively condemns someone who will never be obliged to pay it.

i. Expression as Private Rectification

One possibility, which can be derived from the seminal work of Jean Hampton,[113] is that condemning a wrong sets right a moral injury that the wrongdoer has caused his or her victim, by publicly reaffirming the latter's moral worth as a human being. The idea of 'moral' injury lying at the heart of Hampton's account extends beyond reputational or subjective psychological harm suffered by the victim, and encompasses the objective 'diminishment' of his or her human 'worth,' or 'value' as a free agent deserving of respect in the Kantian sense.[114] Several modern writers endorse this understanding of the purpose of punitive awards.[115] A popular, shorthand way of stating the idea is to say that

[111] *Lamb* (n 5) 13.

[112] ibid 10.

[113] J Hampton, 'Correcting Harms Versus Righting Wrongs: The Goal of Retribution' (1992) 39 *University of California Los Angeles Law Review* 1659, 1685–98.

[114] ibid 1666–71, 1673–74, 1679 (moral injury is 'damage to the realization of a victim's value, or damage to the acknowledgement of the victim's value, accomplished through behavior whose meaning is such that the victim is diminished in value').

[115] A Sebok, 'Punitive Damages: From Myth to Theory' (2007) 92 *Iowa Law Review* 957, 961 (awards 'vindicate an interest in social dignity held by private citizens' and redress 'dignitary or moral injury'); M Galanter and D Luban, 'Poetic Justice: Punitive Damages and Legal Pluralism' (1993) 42 *American University Law Review* 1393, 1432–33 (awards 'express defeat' of the wrongdoer in a way that standard compensatory awards do not, articulating a commitment to human dignity); P-W Lee 'Contract Damages, Corrective Justice and Punishment' (2007) 70 *MLR* 887; Baker (n 65) 110–12.

condemnation 'vindicates the plaintiff', although this language should be used with caution because it is so slippery.[116]

If condemnation had this end, insurance would arguably be consistent with it, since the rectification of injury, as we observed above, is promoted by a liability insurance fund, not undermined by it. The problem, however, is that if condemnation is meant to rectify harm to human worth, dignity and entitlements, then this is something that is already done (or which could easily be done) by declaring the wrong and making the defendant liable to pay an aggravated compensatory award. We are back in the business of corrective or interpersonal justice (although the harm corrected is more subtly defined in terms of injury to moral rights) and the law already has a practical device for achieving this end. In the same way that a compensatory damages award in defamation law already serves in part to 'vindicate' a plaintiff and make good the impact on her dignity for the future,[117] so a declaration and an aggravated compensatory award can suffice to restore and reassert for the future the truth about a victim's equal moral worth.

ii. Public Ends – Enhancing Respect for the Legal System, Social Culture and Public Education

A second, more likely possibility is that the purpose of condemnation at the heart of punitive damages is not to rectify private injury at all, but to meet a public end in expressing society's commitment to the rule of law and the values embedded in it. Lord Devlin was close to this idea, I think, in *Rookes v Barnard*, when he said that exemplary awards 'vindicate the strength of the law.'[118] Similar statements are to be found about the purposes of criminal punishment, and 'vindicatory' damages awards, the latter of which have no place as a distinct category in English and Australian tort law,[119] but which are sometimes thought to play a similar, expressive role in cases involving the violation of constitutional legal rights.[120] Some of the clearest examples of cases attracting exemplary awards certainly seem to involve defendants who deliberately flout the law – the Roman noble who takes cynical pleasure in assaulting peasants in the market because he knows he can afford the required penalty and is willing to pay it, is cited as a classic case.[121] He is not just sticking his finger up at the victim, but at the system

[116] For a full deconstruction of the various ways in which the language of 'vindication' has been used in the modern law, see K Barker, 'Private and Public: The Mixed Meaning of Vindication in Torts and Private Law' in S Pitel et al (eds), *Tort Law: Challenging Orthodoxy* (Oxford, Hart Publishing, 2013).

[117] ibid 76.

[118] *Rookes* (n 14). See similarly, *Lewis v ACT* [2020] HCA 26, (2020) 381 ALR 375, [172] (Edelman J).

[119] *Lewis* (n 118); *R (Lumba) v Secretary of State for the Home Department* [2011] UKSC 12, [2012] 1 AC 245.

[120] See, eg, *Attorney-General of Trinidad and Tobago v Ramanoop* [2005] UKPC 15, [2006] 1 AC 328 [19].

[121] Aulus Gellius, *Noctes Atticae* 20.1.13, cited by J Edelman, 'In Defence of Exemplary Damages' in C Rickett (ed), *Justifying Private Law Remedies* (Oxford, Hart Publishing, 2008) 225.

itself. On this view, perpetrators are condemned not because this restores victims, but because it reinforces respect for the legal system as a whole and the legal rights, duties and values that it instantiates. Plaintiffs like Joe Cotogno are then private attorneys-general, who are rewarded for policing the public system of rules and bringing legal censure to those who abuse it. The act of condemnation, whilst not necessarily specifically deterring the wrongdoer himself, or directly changing the behaviour of others engaged in similar activity through threats of adverse consequence, can indirectly have valuable social consequences in maintaining and promoting a culture of respect for the law;[122] or it can be valuable in its own right in educating the wrongdoer or the public about the importance of the rights violated.[123] All of these arguments focus on the educational power of awards and their public benefits in terms of projecting norms and shaping public attitudes, drawing analogies with the criminal law and popular, expressive theories of punishment.[124] Whilst the criminal law remains the primary mechanism for attaining these ends, it has gaps. It may also be desirable from the constitutional point of view to give private citizens a fuller, independent, participatory role in enforcing respect for the rule of law from time to time.[125]

Although the expressive justification of exemplary awards is frequently voiced by courts, it is hard to be sure in any given case whether it is a court's driving aim in making an order, or merely a perceived and welcome secondary effect. If public messaging about the value of legal rights is really an *independent aim* of awards, sufficient *in its own right* to justify them in civil cases, there are then also several, key questions that need to be answered before we embrace it.

Firstly, does a 'punitive' monetary award provide a sufficiently *articulate* message about the value of rights, or one that is notably more so than a compensatory award, or a court's public declaration in its written reasons of its disapproval of the wrong? Bear in mind that for the exemplary award to speak more loudly than a compensatory one, it would need to be considerably bigger,[126] not as in *Lamb*, less than two per cent of the latter's overall size. But even then, would the intended message be meaningful, or clear? A dollar sum may speak loudly in a motivational sense to some, but what does it actually *say*? Meaning translates very poorly into money and is generally much better communicated in other ways.[127]

[122] Galanter and Luban (n 115) 1429 ('punishment prevents offences by norm projection and norm reinforcement').

[123] D Partlett, 'Punitive Damages: Legal Hot Zones' (1996) 56 *Louisiana Law Review* 781, 783–84.

[124] J Feinberg, 'The Expressive Function of Punishment' (1965) 49 *The Monist* 397–423.

[125] This is a popular view amongst those who celebrate a republican model of government, such as Partlett (n 123). But it may also explain the large number of awards made against government, for it is here that the 'prosecutorial' independence of a private enforcer can be important in order to avoid enforcement capture.

[126] Galanter and Luban (n 115) 1430.

[127] Barker (n 77) 59. The translation problem lies at the heart of the radical inconsistency in jury awards in the US: C Sunstein et al, 'Assessing Punitive Damages (with Notes on Cognition and Valuation in Law) (1998) 107 *Yale Law Journal* 2071.

Secondly, would the intended message actually be conveyed, where the entire award was paid by an insurer? One can see why the reassurance of insurance might incentivise plaintiffs to bring matters to court by guaranteeing their punitive reward, but what message would the consequent award send, where a wrongdoer bears no responsibility for paying it? One perception might be that the court was indeed condemning the wrong,[128] but was simply powerless in practice to prevent a wrongdoer escaping the award's consequences. Another, however, might be that the court was doing nothing to make its condemnation meaningful and was therefore simply not serious about it. The same problem of mixed or muted messaging that we encountered in the context of the general deterrence argument above therefore resurfaces here. That problem is not encountered in the criminal law, remember, because in that sphere the condemned are required by public policy to bear the consequences of their punishment personally. The irony, then, is that making awards against insured parties might indeed encourage the bringing of 'public interest' claims that 'speak', but at the very same time confuse the message delivered to such a degree as to entirely undermine their alleged justification.

Finally, even if we supposed that a clear public message about the importance of respect for legal rights was sent by an insured monetary award, would the civil justice system be the best way to send this message? Would it be the most efficient means of achieving our expressive and educational ends? Given the vanishingly small number of people who are ever likely to become aware of the content of court orders in civil cases, the vast expense of private proceedings and the virtually unlimited power of parties to settle their disputes out of court, this seems very unlikely. If these were indeed the ends that punitive awards were meant to serve, rather than simply their collateral consequences, one would at the very least expect courts approving punitive settlements to require wide publicity to be given to them in media outlets.

Whatever else one may say about all of this, Lamb is a most unlikely case for the pursuit of public messaging aims. The award was tiny in proportion to the compensatory sum that accompanied it; the value of Cotogno's rights had already been publicly declared through a sizeable compensatory award; Lamb's behaviour in battering him had already been publicly condemned through the criminal process; and any condemnatory message flowing from the award itself would be confused, if not entirely muted, I have suggested, by the 'mark' of the wrong being born not by Lamb's own financial person, but by the New South Wales public – the very social group that was supposed to be protected against his conduct.

[128] Baker (n 65) 112 hence appears to take the view that the message is not significantly affected: whether or not a punitive damages award is insured, it 'makes a public statement about the value of the victim'. The High Court in *Lamb* (n 5) at 10 stated that it did not think insurance 'entirely discount[ed]' the effect of the award, but it is not clear whether in saying this it was referring to the award's condemnatory effect, or its personal 'sting' upon a wrongdoer.

V. CONCLUSIONS

In the above discussion, I have not tried to answer the question whether exemplary damages have a rightful place in the modern law, but have simply accepted them as a fact. Pragmatically, it seems likely that they will continue to play a role in a small number of cases, for as long as our public enforcement mechanisms remain incomplete, or are perceptibly deficient in the pursuit of their regulatory aims. As a decision on its facts, *Lamb* is a peculiar precedent, to say the least, and the three justifications provided by the High Court for upholding the award appear brief, self-conscious and strained when isolated. They are no stronger in combination. It is hard to accept that a A$5,000 award against an insured party would have a significant role in terms of victim pacification or general deterrence and the 'messaging value' of any award is at best morally ambiguous in circumstances in which it is accepted that it will not be paid by the person against whom it has been made. The expressive lessons needing to be taught in respect of the unlikely events of that December day in 1979 had already been made public by the time of the High Court's decision in an unambiguous way through Lamb's criminal conviction for furious driving, the consequences of which were, by contrast and justifiably, both uninsured and uninsurable. Questions of punishment, appeasement, public condemnation and deterrence might so easily and fruitfully have been left to that process, given that it had already been engaged.

In seeking explanations for the result in *Lamb*, it is therefore worth paying close attention, I have suggested, to the processes of pleading in the case, which are so often the clandestine sculptors of our common law artefacts. Had a decent sum been sought and awarded at first instance for the humiliation and affront to human dignity which Joe Cotogno suffered in consequence of the more contemptible aspects of his treatment on Loftus Road (A$5,000 would seem to me to be a not unreasonable sum), he might have been properly compensated from the start and the exemplary claim – the case for which diminished rapidly in strength as the true, exculpatory facts about Lamb's flight from his aggressor came out at trial – might never have been pressed by counsel, or might have been dismissed by Master Greenwood. The precedential monument that Lamb represents in respect of the issue of insured personal punishment in Australia might then never have been constructed and answers to the questions of principle it raised postponed to a later date. In the current legal climate, the prospects of that question being asked again in this country are very slim, but this does not prevent the answers which the High Court provided to it in 1987 continuing to have their own, independent reverberations upon judicial reasoning well beyond their immediate point of impact. In this respect, the decision in *Lamb* is no different to the rest of us. Our reasons, good or bad, have a life that extends well beyond us.

7

German Federal Court of Justice, Judgment of 4 June 1992, Case IX ZR 149/91 (BGHZ 118, 312) (1992)

German Law's Dilemma with Punitive Damages

JOHANNES UNGERER

I. INTRODUCTION

GERMAN LAW FACES a dilemma when it comes to punitive damages, which potentially exposes it to the criticism of hypocrisy. On the one hand, doctrinally, the German law of damages is intended to be strictly compensatory and free from punitive damages. In order to protect its domestic system, the German Federal Court of Justice (*Bundesgerichtshof*) held in its 1992 landmark decision that German law does not recognise and enforce foreign judgments awarding punitive damages.[1] Yet, on the other hand, developments in German law both before and after this landmark decision have possibly watered down the doctrinal insistence on damages being solely compensatory. These domestic developments might have made it difficult for German law to maintain the refusal to recognise and enforce foreign judgments in which punitive damages have been awarded. Thus, the question to be answered is: can German law confidently claim that punitive damages are still sufficiently foreign to the domestic system and that punitive damages awarded by foreign courts can thus be rejected without self-contradiction?

To respond, the chapter will, after a short explanation of the doctrinal situation in German law, analyse the landmark case. The discussion will afterwards

[1] BGH (*Bundesgerichtshof*), 4 June 1992, case IX ZR 149/91, BGHZ (*Entscheidungen des Bundesgerichtshofs in Zivilsachen*) 118, 312. The case is sometimes referred to in English as *John Doe* (a pseudonym for the claimant) *v Eckhard Schmitz*, although this is not an official German citation due to anonymity of German court reports.

address the caveats that have been made by German courts for dealing with punitive damages. Finally, and changing the perspective slightly from the issue of recognition to applicable law, consideration will be given to how German courts handle claims that are governed by foreign law which allows awarding the remedy of punitive damages.

II. THE STATUTORY FRAMEWORK OF THE GERMAN LAW OF DAMAGES IN A NUTSHELL

Before diving into the case law and discussing the landmark case, it is necessary to address the doctrinal framework for damages in German statutory law. In the German Civil Code, the general provisions on the law of damages, which apply to both contract and tort, set out a strict compensatory principle. According to that principle, the person who is liable in damages must restore the position that would have existed if no harm had been done.[2] As has been refined by further principles, this means that there must be full compensation, that overcompensation/enrichment is impermissible, and that only actual losses can be the subject of compensation.[3] Pecuniary compensation can also be claimed for intangible losses, but only in expressly enumerated cases, such as bodily harm or the violation of the right to sexual self-determination.[4]

These general provisions on damages in the Civil Code do not include the award of punitive or exemplary damages. At the time of enactment at the end of the nineteenth century, it was clear that there should be no punitive aspect to damages.[5] The Civil Code only deals with punishment in the context of damages in a few specific provisions which allow private parties to agree on contractual penalty clauses. An interesting contrast can be drawn in this regard with the position in English law, which is a point to which this chapter returns below.[6] Apart from where contractually agreed, though, damages of penal character are unavailable under German law, especially for torts.

III. THE NON-RECOGNITION OF US PUNITIVE DAMAGES JUDGMENTS IN GERMANY

In its 1992 landmark decision, the German Federal Court of Justice established the general position in German law that US judgments are not to be recognised

[2] s 249 of the Civil Code (*Bürgerliches Gesetzbuch/BGB*) and subsequent provisions.

[3] O Brand, *Schadensersatzrecht*, 3rd edn (Munich, CH Beck, 2021) sec 2 paras 32ff.

[4] s 253 of the Civil Code. 'Intangible' seems the more appropriate translation than 'immaterial' as suggested by U Magnus, 'Sec 254' in G Dannemann and R Schulze (eds), *German Civil Code: Bürgerliches Gesetzbuch (BGB)*, vol 1 (Munich, CH Beck, 2020).

[5] B Mugdan, *Die gesammelten Materialien zum Bürgerlichen Gesetzbuch für das Deutsche Reich*, vol 2 (Heidelberg, R v Decker's Verlag, 1899) 'Motive' 10ff.

[6] See section IV.D.

insofar as those judgments award punitive damages. The following discussion summarises the facts of the case and engages with the Court's reasoning. Light will also be shed on subsequent case law.

A. The Facts and Development of the Case

As restated by the German Federal Court of Justice, the claimant sought recognition and enforcement in Germany of a Californian judgment according to which he was entitled to damages of US$750,260 from the defendant. Although the facts of the original case had not been reported in the Californian judgment,[7] it was apparent from the German Court's record that the damages had been granted because of sexual abuse committed by the defendant against the claimant in California. The total amount comprised, in addition to US$150,260 for costs of medical treatment and placement and US$200,000 for pain and suffering, the sum of US$400,000 for exemplary and punitive damages.

In Germany, the Court of First Instance (*Landgericht*) in Düsseldorf initially approved the recognition and enforcement in full.[8] On appeal by the defendant, the Higher Regional Court (*Oberlandesgericht*) of Düsseldorf modified the recognition and enforcement decision insofar as it only permitted it up to the total amount of US$275,325, which included an amount for punitive damages of US$55,065, ie roughly an eighth of the original judgment's punitive damages amount.[9] Both the claimant and the defendant appealed, and they both partly succeeded. The Federal Court of Justice held that only the amount of US$350,260 for the medical treatment and placement as well as pain and suffering can be recognised and enforced in Germany, whereas recognition and enforcement of the US$400,000 of punitive damages must be rejected completely.

B. The Reasoning of the Federal Court of Justice

In its reasoning,[10] the Federal Court of Justice appreciated that the amount of punitive damages awarded by US courts is discretionary and usually many times higher than the actual damage suffered because punitive damages aim to fulfil four main purposes. Firstly, punitive damages are intended to punish the defendant and to assuage a desire for revenge by the claimant. Secondly, they are also awarded in order to deter the defendant as well as the general public from engaging in the behaviour concerned in the future. Thirdly, the claimant is to be

[7] It was handed down by the Superior Court of California at Stockton for the County of San Joaquin, 24 April 1985, case 168-588, which is a first-instance trial court. It has remained unpublished and has apparently not been appealed.

[8] LG Düsseldorf, 12 April 1990, case 13 O 456/89, unpublished.

[9] OLG Düsseldorf, 28 May 1991, case 4 U 119/90, published in [1991] *Versicherungsrecht* 1161.

[10] BGH (n 1) 334ff.

rewarded for enforcing the law and for thereby strengthening the legal system in general. Fourthly, punitive damages are to supplement the compensation of the claimant where it is inadequate otherwise, for instance due to the lack of social security. This depiction of punitive damages can largely be considered to be fair and accurate.

What has however been criticised about the understanding by the Federal Court of Justice is the element and degree of discretion which the US courts are said to have over the amount of punitive damages to be awarded. Since the Federal Court of Justice only referred to the 'free' discretion of the US court, it has been contended that this neglects the fact that the discretion is limited to some extent by statutes and case law in the US.[11] Most notably the US Supreme Court later held in *BMW of North America Inc v Gore* that 'grossly excessive' punitive damages 'transcend the constitutional limit' of the Due Process Clause of the Fourteenth Amendment.[12] Although the discretion over awarding punitive damages is indeed (increasingly) limited,[13] these limitations still leave considerable leeway to the individual court. In any case, punitive damages are awarded *above and beyond* the actual damage suffered at the (albeit somewhat limited) discretion of the court in order to punish the defendant, which is the relevant aspect for explaining Germany's refusal to recognise the Californian judgment.

The central point for the rejection of recognition in the reasoning of the Federal Court of Justice was the declared violation of German public policy.[14] According to German civil procedure rules, recognition and enforcement of a foreign judgment is to be rejected if the recognition would yield a result which is incompatible with the fundamental principles of German law (public policy), especially if incompatible with the fundamental rights of the German constitution.[15]

Restating the relevant fundamental principles of the German law of damages in its decision, the Federal Court of Justice confirmed that the German law of damages is governed by the principle of compensation outlined above.[16] This, in turn, is based on the proportionality principle, which also applies in private law and is said to be rooted ultimately in the rule of law. Any enrichment on the part of the claimant would be incompatible with this principle, which also precludes any private prosecution.

[11] AR Fiebig, 'The Recognition and Enforcement of Punitive Damage Awards in Germany: Recent Developments' (1992) 22 *Georgia Journal of International and Comparative Law* 635, 650–51.

[12] *BMW of North America Inc v Gore*, 517 US 559 (1996), 585–86. Also see the further restrictions in *State Farm Mutual Automobile Insurance Co v Campbell*, 538 US 408 (2003) discussed in Sharkey, ch 13 of this volume.

[13] See further C Vanleenhove, *Punitive Damages in Private International Law* (Cambridge, Intersentia, 2016) 29ff.

[14] BGH (n 1) 338ff.

[15] s 328(1)(4), 723(2) sentence 2 of the Code of Civil Procedure (*Zivilprozessordnung*/*ZPO*).

[16] See section II.

Punishment of the defendant was considered to be the exclusive domain of criminal law, where notably any fine is payable to the state instead of to an individual. In civil proceedings, by contrast, claimants must not receive any rewards for acting like a private attorney general, which would be incompatible with the state's monopoly over prosecution, for which special constitutional protection is in place.[17] Although German law recognises contractual penalty clauses, it does not accept punitive damages for torts. With regard to the compensation for intangible losses, German law only permits damages which are adequate in the light of the degree of the suffering and impairment, whilst wider aims of punishment and deterrence are not pursued.

In the case at hand, the Californian court had awarded a distinct amount for intangible damages for the sexual abuse, which was recognisable under German law pursuant to the equivalent rule on damages for intangible harm due to violation of sexual self-determination. Yet this meant that the separate amount for punitive damages going above and beyond the compensatory amount could not be recognised.

Ultimately, the Federal Court of Justice reasoned that if foreign judgments awarding extra-compensatory punitive damages were to be recognised and enforced in Germany, this could lead to instances of liability which would be unimaginable in the domestic legal system. Such liability would not only be incalculable and non-insurable, it could lead to inequality and undermine the domestic liability framework. The reason given for this was that claimants from abroad ought not be permitted to enforce much higher judgments against assets in Germany than claimants from Germany ever could, who might however have suffered much greater losses but are restrained by the German domestic limitations.

C. Subsequent Case Law

Since 1992, the Federal Court of Justice has not amended or changed its view on the recognition of punitive damages. Several decisions by the Federal Constitutional Court on the issue of the service of foreign claims for punitive damages in Germany will be discussed below separately.[18] It is worth mentioning that the Federal Court of Justice clarified in a subsequent decision that German courts must not easily assume that high foreign damages awards are punitive.[19] In a case concerning the law of Panama, a Higher Regional Court

[17] See, eg, Art 103(2)–(3) of the German Federal Constitution (*Grundgesetz*/*GG*), which stipulates that 'an act may be punished only if it was defined by a law as a criminal offence before the act was committed' and 'no person may be punished for the same act more than once under the general criminal laws' (translation by C Tomuschat et al for the German Federal Ministry of Justice, <www.gesetze-im-internet.de/englisch_gg/englisch_gg.html> accessed 7 May 2023).

[18] See section V.B.

[19] BGH, 8 May 2000, case II ZR 182/98, [2000] *Neue Juristische Wochenschrift Rechtsprechungs-Report Zivilrecht* 1372, 1373.

distinguished the Spanish and French origins of that law from US legal traditions. The damages were eventually not considered punitive and, thus, there was no reason to reject recognition due to a public policy violation.[20] The same was found in a subsequent case concerning damages under Dutch law.[21]

It is understandable that the lower German courts and, therefore, ultimately the Federal Court of Justice have not had to deal more often with requests for the recognition of foreign punitive damages judgments given the determination and forcefulness of the 1992 decision. What can be observed as a consequence of this situation is that claimants have rather adjusted their behaviour and strategy when it comes to recognition requests in Germany.[22] An example is the case of a claimant who was awarded punitive damages of US$1 million in addition to compensatory damages in Wisconsin. When applying for recognition of the US judgment in Germany, she confined her request to the compensatory part, so that the Federal Court of Justice did not have to address the issue of punitive damages at all.[23]

On a related note, it should be said that there does not seem to be any German case law published on a situation where recognition of an English judgment awarding exemplary damages was sought in Germany.[24] This is understandable given the narrow categories of cases in which exemplary damages are available in English law after *Rookes v Barnard*.[25] Also, the first category in *Rookes* concerns cases of abuse of executive power by state officials (eg, malicious prosecution by the police), which makes it unlikely that enforcement of resulting judgments would be sought abroad since this would only be desirable if the UK had assets abroad into which enforcement could be sought.

IV. REVIEWING AND CONTEXTUALISING THE PUBLIC POLICY REASONING

The reasoning of the Federal Court of Justice in its 1992 decision is, in itself, consistent and convincing because it explains why punitive damages are seen as inconsistent with ideas in the German law of damages.[26] Shielding the German system from foreign punitive damages awards by holding them to contradict German public policy also shows that this inconsistency is perceived as a serious matter.

[20] OLG Hamburg, 25 January 2008, case 1 U 176/95, para 103 (available in the juris database).

[21] OLG Düsseldorf, 4 April 2011, case I-3 W 292/10, [2013] *Praxis des Internationalen Privat- und Verfahrensrechts* 349, 350–51.

[22] M Lendermann, *Strafschadensersatz im internationalen Rechtsverkehr* (Tübingen, Mohr Siebeck, 2019) 157.

[23] BGH, 29 April 1999, case IX ZR 263/97, BGHZ 141, 286.

[24] Search conducted by the author in the German comprehensive database 'juris', September 2022.

[25] *Rookes v Barnard* [1964] AC 1129 (HL).

[26] Similarly, U Magnus, 'Punitive Damages and German Law' in L Meurkens and E Nordin (eds), *The Power of Punitive Damages: Is Europe Missing Out?* (Cambridge, Intersentia, 2012) 248ff.

Yet the rejection of recognition on public policy grounds can only remain tenable and avoid the criticism of hypocrisy if, considering wider domestic developments, German law has not permitted any significant inroads into its supposedly firm fundamental principle of solely compensatory damages. Several potential deviations from the fundamental principle will be explored in the following sections in order to ascertain whether their domestic acceptance in fact undermines the refusal to recognise foreign judgments awarding punitive damages.

A. Penance and Satisfaction as Relevant Factors for Awarding Damages for Pain and Suffering

In German law, as already mentioned, damages can be claimed for intangible losses in cases of, for instance, bodily harm or violation of the right to sexual self-determination that are enumerated in the Civil Code.[27] Given this domestic approval of damages for pain and suffering, the question is whether they fulfil the sole purpose of compensation or whether their purpose goes above and beyond compensation, which might suggest that German law endorses further purposes of damages in such cases of intangible losses, possibly including the purpose of punishment.

Prior to the enactment of the Civil Code and its entry into force in 1900, awarding damages for pain and suffering was explicitly considered to be a form of private punishment.[28] The logic was that, although not always consistently followed in practice,[29] pain and suffering were then believed to be incommensurable with compensation in money.[30] It was not until the end of nineteenth century, and hence close to the enactment of the Civil Code, that this view changed and it was accepted that money can be an adequate compensation for pain and suffering,[31] which meant that these damages were no longer considered to be punitive.

Under the newly enacted Civil Code and during the early period of the Federal Court of Justice after the Second World War, damages for pain and

[27] s 253 of the Civil Code.

[28] See, eg, GF Puchta, *Pandekten*, 8th edn (Munich, Barth, 1856) 559 (sec 388); B Windscheid, *Lehrbuch des Pandektenrechts*, vol II/2 (Düsseldorf, Buddeus, 1866) 302–03 (sec 455).

[29] Court of Justice of the German Reich (*Reichsgericht*), 17 November 1882, case III 321/82, RGZ (*Entscheidungen des Reichsgerichts in Zivilsachen*) 8, 117.

[30] Degenkolb, 'Der spezifische Inhalt des Schadenersatzes' (1890) 76 *Archiv für die civilistische Praxis* 1, 22ff, esp 24; F Mommsen, *Beiträge zum Obligationenrecht*, vol 2 (Halle, Schwetschke, 1855) 122.

[31] C von Wächter, *Die Busse bei Beleidigungen und Körperverletzungen* (Leipzig, Edelmann, 1874) 72ff with criticism of Windscheid. In consequence, B Windscheid, *Lehrbuch des Pandektenrechts*, vol II, 5th edn (Stuttgart, Ebner & Suebert, 1879) 715–16 changed his view (see esp fn 31).

suffering were awarded on a strictly compensatory basis,[32] hence without, for instance, taking account of the degree of fault or the financial situation of the tortfeasor when assessing the amount of damages.[33] However, by 1955 the Federal Court of Justice changed its view on the matter drastically and found in a remarkable decision by the Court's Joint Senates for Civil Matters that the notion of penance was intrinsic to damages for pain and suffering. In order to be able to take account of the degree of fault and the financial situation of the tortfeasor, the Court established that damages for pain and suffering fulfilled two functions: compensation and satisfaction for the victim.[34] The award of damages for pain and suffering is in principle compensatory, but the amount cannot simply be arithmetically calculated; the award may be larger because, in short, the tortfeasor made life difficult for the victim and the award is meant to make the situation more bearable by also providing some sort of satisfaction.[35] The amount of money therefore depends primarily on the extent of the pain and suffering;[36] yet, since the Civil Code provision entitles the claimant to what can be translated as fair, equitable or reasonable damages (*billige Entschädigung*),[37] an additional element of penance or, in Swiss German terminology, satisfaction is necessary.[38] This remains the position of German law in this regard to the present day.[39] Yet it has remained difficult to say whether the notion of penance on the part of the tortfeasor and the function of providing satisfaction for the victim suggest that damages for pain and suffering are punitive after all.

Against this background, the Federal Court of Justice struggled to distinguish US punitive damages from the German developments regarding punishment in the law of damages in its 1992 decision when making two related arguments. First, the Court suggested that damages for pain and suffering are to be awarded in relation to the degree of impairment caused by the tortfeasor in order that they are not awarded out of proportion to it. Secondly, the Court argued that the function of satisfaction is inseparably connected with the compensatory function. These arguments are not entirely convincing: they try to explain that making the tortfeasor do penance and seeking satisfaction are not comparable to ideas underlying punishment because penance and satisfaction are not ordered and awarded in a manner disproportionate to the compensation due.

[32] J Köndgen, *Haftpflichtfunktionen und Immaterialschaden am Beispiel von Schmerzensgeld bei Gefährdungshaftung* (Berlin, Duncker & Humblot, 1976) 49ff.

[33] eg, BGH, 29 September 1952, case III ZR 340/51, BGHZ 7, 223.

[34] BGH (Joint Senates for Civil Matters), 6 July 1955, case GSZ 1/55, BGHZ 18, 149. This differed from the earlier use of the word *Satisfaktion* at the end of the 19th century when it had rather denoted compensation: H Dernburg, *Pandekten*, vol 2 (Berlin, H W Müller, 1886) 119 (sec 45).

[35] BGH (n 34) 154.

[36] BGH (n 33) 226–27.

[37] See, eg, the translation as 'reasonable' by Magnus (n 4).

[38] BGH (n 34) 155.

[39] In particular, the most recent major statutory law reform of the law of damages acknowledged and did not intend to change this position, *Entwurf eines Zweiten Gesetzes zur Änderung schadensersatzrechtlicher Vorschriften*, 7 December 2001, BT-Drs 14/7752, 14–15.

Yet punishment does not have to be, and in fact ought not to be, disproportionate either. Thus, these two arguments may represent necessary conditions of justice, but they are not sufficient conditions for distinguishing the domestic position concerning damages for pain and suffering from the rejection of recognition of foreign punitive damages judgments.

The Federal Court of Justice continued its reasoning with another attempt at explaining the difference in approach. The argument is based on the understanding that any overlap between German damages, which aim for penance and satisfaction for intangible losses, and US punitive damages can only matter insofar as the comparison with punitive damages equally concerns intangible losses. Since the Californian court had however awarded a separate amount for intangible losses, the Federal Court of Justice deduced that the amount for punitive damages did not cover any intangible losses and hence ruled out that any overlap between the German law of damages for pain and suffering could be established with the US punitive damages awarded in this case. This was true in the case at hand, and might work well, too, in many other cases, but it is not completely convincing. Just because punitive damages are explicitly punitive does not guarantee that damages for pain and suffering – on their own (under German law) or as a separate amount (under US law) – are completely free from notions of punishment. Therefore, this additional argument put forward by the Federal Court of Justice does not succeed, either in explaining the significant difference between the domestic law concerning damages for pain and suffering, and the approach taken with regard to the recognition of foreign judgments in which punitive damages are awarded.

Ultimately, though, it would be equally difficult to find that the existence of some elements of penance and satisfaction in the German law concerning damages for pain and suffering means that it is untenable for German law to maintain that its own domestic law does not provide for punishment through damages awards. When put in perspective, especially quantitatively, German awards of damages for pain and suffering are not comparable with awards of punitive damages under US law.[40] In consequence, it can be regarded as justifiably consistent that German law provides domestically for very moderate amounts of damages giving satisfaction in addition to compensation for intangible losses while at the same time rejecting recognition of foreign judgments awarding punitive damages which greatly exceed any compensatory amount and even exceed any amount necessary for the victim's own satisfaction. Indeed, in contrast to the German law of damages, punitive damages fulfil

[40] eg, comparing damages for pain and suffering due to sexual abuse in the 1980s, German courts awarded the equivalent of up to €5,000 (eg, OLG Düsseldorf, 12 October 1989, case 8 U 10/88), which is far lower than the amount of US$200,000 plus US$400,000 awarded by the Californian judgment in 1985 whose recognition was sought in Germany. In recent years, the Federal Court of Justice sanctioned a settlement of €70,000 (judgment of 29 April 2021, case 5 StR 498/20), but this was in an ancillary proceeding to the criminal prosecution of the defendant.

additional purposes regarding the public at large by strengthening the enforcement of the legal system generally, by creating a deterrent from future socially harmful behaviour generally, and by supplementing the lack of social security generally. These additional purposes in US law require, and equally justify, that punitive damages awards are significantly and distinctly higher than any amount of damages available under German law, where damages only fulfil the two functions of compensation and satisfaction for the individual victim in response to the specific past behaviour of the individual tortfeasor and where additionally an extensive social security system is available. Therefore, domestic damages for pain and suffering are not inconsistent with the rejection of foreign punitive damages awards.

B. Damages for the Infringement of Personality Rights

The dilemma of whether satisfaction might amount to punishment becomes even more critical when one considers the position of German law on damages for the infringement of personality rights. Initially, in the absence of statutory law providing for damages in such cases, the Federal Court of Justice awarded damages by analogy to damages for pain and suffering. The Court emphasised that, in cases of infringed personality rights, satisfaction for the victim,[41] and also sanctioning the tortfeasor,[42] was of greater relevance than actual compensation. This case law development was approved by the Federal Constitutional Court (*Bundesverfassungsgericht*) in view of the importance of the victims' underlying fundamental rights protected by the constitution.[43] Yet approving satisfaction and especially sanctioning as primary purposes of damages in cases of infringed personality rights might have made it untenable for German law to sustain its doctrinal insistence that damages awarded domestically are primarily compensatory.

Particularly remarkable are the amounts which damages for infringement of personality rights have reached for claims brought by prominent figures of public life against tabloid newspapers.[44] The awards first peaked at DM180,000 in 1996, which corresponds to roughly €150,000 today.[45] This amount was awarded to Princess Caroline of Monaco against tabloid journals that had published untrue stories and photographs of her without her consent.[46] When upholding a previous appeal, the Federal Court of Justice had established that satisfaction for the

[41] BGH, 14 February 1958, case I ZR 151/56, BGHZ 26, 349 (case pseudonym 'Herrenreiter').
[42] BGH, 19 September 1961, case VI ZR 259/60, BGHZ 35, 363 ('Ginseng').
[43] BVerfG (*Bundesverfassungsgericht*), 14 February 1973, case 1 BvR 112/65, BVerfGE (*Entscheidungen des Bundesverfassungsgerichts*) 34, 269 ('Soraya').
[44] For an overview in English, see B Markesinis, J Bell and A Janssen, *Markesinis's German Law of Torts: A Comparative Treatise*, 5th edn (Oxford, Hart Publishing, 2019) 43ff.
[45] Allowing for currency conversion and index developments.
[46] OLG Hamburg, 25 July 1996, case 3 U 60/93, [1996] *Neue Juristische Wochenschrift* 2870.

victim had to be the paramount consideration and required that the publisher's intention to profit from intentionally infringing personality rights had to be counteracted by assessing damages on a basis similar to the disgorgement of profits.[47] This latter consideration resembles the statement by Lord Devlin in the House of Lords in the English exemplary damages case of *Rookes v Barnard* that, in the context of damages for libel, 'one man should not be allowed to sell another man's reputation for profit',[48] and it demonstrates that German case law bears a concerning similarity to this English authority on exemplary damages.

Strikingly, the Federal Court of Justice made no reference to the 1992 decision on the non-recognition of the Californian punitive damages judgment in the case of Princess Caroline of Monaco, which was decided only a few years after, and did not even attempt to distinguish the domestic award of extremely high damages from the rejection of foreign punitive damages. Struggling to distinguish punitive damages in a later case, which concerned several unauthorised tabloid publications of photos of the baby daughter of Princess Caroline and Prince Ernst August of Hanover, for which €150,000 of damages were awarded, the Federal Court of Justice stated tersely that the non-recognition of the Californian punitive damages award had concerned a 'completely different set of facts without any parallels to the case at hand'.[49]

German courts have continued awarding high(er) amounts within German law, and the probably highest amount of damages for infringement of personality rights so far was €400,000 in 2009, which was awarded after numerous photograph montages of the Swedish Princess Madeleine had been illegitimately published by tabloids.[50] Very close to this was the total amount of €395,000 awarded in 2016 to the TV weather presenter Jörg Kachelmann for the unauthorised publication of photos of him that were taken when he was charged with rape but eventually acquitted.[51] Given the comparability of these amounts with the US$400,000 of punitive damages in the Californian judgment, and also the comparability to some extent of the underlying reasons for awarding the respective damages, it is not easy to convincingly distinguish the German damages for personality rights infringement from foreign punitive damages awards.

The only justification for treating punitive damages differently might be seen in the conceptual consideration that punitive damages in foreign jurisdictions are awarded *in addition* to damages for intangible losses. This means in turn that, although totalling very high amounts, the German domestic awards for pain and suffering and particularly for infringements of personality rights still observe a compensatory relation and limitation to the actual suffering of the victim and the actual profit of the tortfeasor, above and beyond which *no further*

[47] BGH, 15 November 1994, case VI ZR 56/94, BGHZ 128, 1 ('Caroline I').
[48] *Rookes* (n 25) 1227.
[49] BGH, 5 October 2004, case VI ZR 255/03, BGHZ 160, 298, 303 (translation by author).
[50] OLG Hamburg, 30 July 2009, case 7 U 4/08, [2009] *Archiv für Presserecht* 509.
[51] OLG Cologne, 12 July 2016, cases 15 U 175/15 and 15 U 176/15.

damages are awarded. This can be confirmed, for instance, by comparison with the English law on exemplary damages in libel cases against newspapers: the Court of Appeal held in *John v MGN Ltd* that compensatory damages were insufficient to punish the newspaper and deter it and others, and that therefore – in addition – exemplary damages were necessary to adequately reflect the gravity of the newspaper's conduct and to create an effective deterrent for the future.[52] In German law, in turn, the dilemma can thus be resolved by emphasising the compensatory intention of the amounts awarded as damages for intangible losses, in addition to which no punitive damage are awarded.

C. Damages for Infringement of Rights in Other Areas of Statutory Law

Besides these developments in German case law, there are a few statutory rules worth reviewing because they are sometimes said to be coming close to punitive damages. However, this allegation does not hold up on closer examination.

First, the German General Equality Act (*Allgemeines Gleichbehandlungsgesetz*) provides for damages for both tangible and intangible losses in cases of unjustified discrimination due to race, ethnicity, gender, sex, religion, disability or age in the employment context, or in any mass transaction in private law, such as grocery shopping in a supermarket or taking out insurance.[53] This is a special statutory rule for compensation outside the Civil Code,[54] but it shares the conceptional basis and method for the calculation of damages in all regards. Following jurisprudence of the Court of Justice of the European Union on the underlying Antidiscrimination Directives in the employment context, the damages must be effective and not fault-based in order to achieve both compensation and deterrence.[55] It has to be noted that, insofar as EU law as a supranational legal order requires deterrence, it does not provoke a contradiction within German law where damages are not awarded in order to punish. Indeed, the EU Directives neither require nor result in punitive damages,[56] in contrast to US law where punitive damages are available in employment discrimination cases according to the specific statutes.[57]

Secondly, moving on to the very different area of infringement of intellectual property rights, several statutes permit three methods for calculating

[52] *John v MGN Ltd* [1997] QB 586 (CA) 626. Nowadays, statute provides in England for exemplary damages against certain news providers who have committed libel or misuse of private information, s 34 of the Crime and Courts Act 2013.

[53] ss 15(1)–(2) and 21(2) of the General Equality Act (*Allgemeines Gleichbehandlungsgesetz*).

[54] Some of the provisions were previously enacted in s 611a of the Civil Code.

[55] CJEU, Case C-180/95 *Draehmpaehl v Urania Immobilienservice* [1997] ECR I-2195. See also more recently BAG (German Federal Labour Law Court/*Bundesarbeitsgericht*), 28 May 2020, case 8 AZR 170/19 [2020] *Neue Zeitschrift für Arbeitsrecht* 1392.

[56] CJEU, Case C-407/14 *Arjona Camacho v Securitas Seguridad España* ECLI:EU:C:2015:831.

[57] See, eg, 42 USC, s 1981a(a)(1), (b)(1) and Title VII of the Civil Rights Act 1964, as amended.

damages, which codify prior case law.[58] This does however not result in 'threefold' over-compensatory damages; the methods are just three different ways to make the calculation and proof easier for the claimant. One of these methods is, for instance, to claim damages equivalent to the hypothetical licencing costs, which confirms that the damages are very much of compensatory and not punitive nature. The idea is comparable to English 'negotiating damages'[59] (formerly '*Wrotham Park* damages'[60]), which are hypothetical bargain damages because they are assessed at the amount that the claimant might reasonably have demanded as a fee for permitting the behaviour in question, such as an agreement for using intellectual property.[61] Suggestions for introducing US-like treble damages into German law have not borne fruit.[62]

Thirdly, in cartel cases, German competition law clarifies that judges are permitted to estimate the loss of the claimant and that they may, in doing so, take account of the profit made by the defendant.[63] While estimations are by definition not always accurate, they are the most practicable way of at least getting close to the actual loss which is to be compensated. Not overcompensating the claimant in German law also corresponds with the unavailability of exemplary damages under English competition law,[64] because it is believed that courts can award sufficiently effective compensatory damages.[65]

Fourthly, in the German Civil Code itself,[66] but due to the EU influence of the Late Payment Directives, the rules on legislatively liquidated damages for late payment are considered by some to be of punitive nature, especially regarding the lump sum of €40 for enforcement costs in certain commercial cases.[67] This can however be rebutted because the amount of damages is a default rule

[58] s 97(2) of the Copyright Act (*Urheberrechtsgesetz*); s 42(2) of the Design Act (*Geschmacksmustergesetz*); s 24(2) of the Inventions Act (*Gebrauchsmustergesetz*); s 139(2) of the Patent Act (*Patentgesetz*); s 14(6) of the Trademark Act (*Markengesetz*). *cf* K Ernicke, *Die dreifache Schadensberechnung* (Tübingen, Mohr Siebeck, 2020).

[59] *Lunn Poly Ltd v Liverpool & Lancashire Properties Ltd* [2006] EWCA Civ 430, [2006] 2 EGLR 29 [22] (Neuberger LJ).

[60] *Wrotham Park Estate Co Ltd v Parkside Homes Ltd* [1974] 1 WLR 798 (Ch).

[61] *One Step (Support) Ltd v Morris Garner* [2018] UKSC 20, [2019] AC 649.

[62] See, eg, suggestions by HD Assmann, 'Schadensersatz in mehrfacher Höhe des Schadens' [1985] *Betriebs-Berater* 15.

[63] s 33a(3) of the Competition Act (*Gesetz gegen Wettbewerbsbeschränkungen*) with reference to s 287 of the Code of Civil Procedure.

[64] Sch 8A, para 36 of the Competition Act 1998, as introduced by Sch 1, para 4 of the Claims in respect of Loss or Damage arising from Competition Infringements (Competition Act 1998 and Other Enactments (Amendment)) Regulations (SI 2017/385). In the past, exemplary damages were awarded in competition law cases in England (see, eg, *2 Travel Group plc (in liq) v Cardiff City Transport Services Ltd* [2012] CAT 19, [2012] Comp AR 211 [448]–[598]).

[65] *Devenish Nutrition Ltd v Sanofi-Aventis SA* [2007] EWHC 2394 (Ch), [2008] 2 WLR 637 [56]–[74]. The issue of exemplary damages was not appealed in [2008] EWCA Civ 1086, [2009] Ch 390 [21].

[66] s 288 of the Civil Code.

[67] W Ernst, 'Section 288 BGB' in W Krüger (ed), *Münchener Kommentar zum BGB*, vol 2, 9th edn (Munich, CH Beck, 2022) para 32.

only which the parties may adjust and because it is intended to compensate the typical pre-estimated loss.[68] The same is true for the equivalent rules in English law.[69] Also with regard to another instance of legislatively liquidated damages, although outside the national realm of German statutes, the EU's Air Passenger Regulation provides for lump sum compensation in cases of denied boarding, etc.[70] The amounts of €250, €400 and €600 are certainly higher, but they are not punitive damages because they compensate the typical loss of valuable time of the air passengers.[71] The Air Passenger Regulation has likewise been retained in the UK post-Brexit.[72]

Lastly, the EU's General Data Protection Regulation (GDPR) provides for a claim to compensation for tangible and intangible losses in cases of data protection violations. The Regulation only stipulates in its Recitals that claimants 'should receive full and effective compensation for the damage they have suffered',[73] but it does not contain any further detail on the calculation of damages, which means that this is largely left to national law. It has yet to be clarified whether the Regulation requires that the amount of damages ought to have a distinctly deterrent effect,[74] given the CJEU's jurisprudence on the Antidiscrimination Directives referenced above. Insofar as German law applies, damages for data protection violations would however not come anywhere near punitive damages.

D. Penalty Clauses in Contract Law

While German law does not recognise punitive damages in contrast to Anglo-American tort law, German law but not Anglo-American law recognises penalty clauses in contracts, which might be perceived as illogical and yet another potential dilemma. Looking at English law, the rule against penalty clauses originated in equity[75] and has been adopted in the common law based on the disapproval of contracting parties agreeing on unconscionable and extravagant

[68] J Ungerer, *Gesetzlich pauschalierter Schadensersatz* (Berlin, Duncker & Humblot, 2022) 56ff, 89ff, 205ff.

[69] Late Payment of Commercial Debts (Interest) Act 1998.

[70] Art 7 of Regulation (EC) No 261/2004 of the European Parliament and of the Council of 11 February 2004 establishing common rules on compensation and assistance to passengers in the event of denied boarding and of cancellation or long delay of flights [2004] OJ L46/1.

[71] Ungerer (n 68) 124, 155ff, 205ff.

[72] s 3 of the European Union (Withdrawal) Act 2018. See also reg 8 of The Air Passenger Rights and Air Travel Organisers' Licensing (Amendment) (EU Exit) Regulations 2019 (SI 2019/278).

[73] Recital 146 GDPR.

[74] A preliminary ruling request has been made by BAG, reference of 26 August 2021, case 8 AZR 253/20 (A) (available in the juris database), which is pending as CJEU, Case C-667/21 *ZQ v Krankenversicherung Nordrhein*. Case C-300/21 *UI v Österreichische Post AG* ECLI:EU:C:2023:370 did not resolve the question.

[75] DJ Ibbetson, *A Historical Introduction to the Law of Obligations* (Oxford, OUP, 1999) 213–14, 255–56.

sums as remedies.[76] It essentially intends to limit the parties' ability to agree on overcompensation. According to the most recent modification of the test for distinguishing impermissible penalty clauses from permissible liquidated damages,[77] genuine pre-estimation of loss is no longer the most decisive factor. Rather, permissibility depends on whether a legitimate interest of the claimant in the performance of the contract is being protected and whether the protection is proportionate to that end. It is impermissible to impose a secondary obligation as a detriment out of proportion to any interest of the innocent party.

These factors used in English law to identify permissible liquidated damages clauses correspond perfectly well to the German statutory criteria for the enforceability of penalty clauses. If a penalty clause requires a disproportionately high payment,[78] the obligor can request from a German court to lower the amount to what is proportionate; when deciding on the proportionality, the court ought to take account of all legitimate interests of the innocent party.[79] Therefore, there is little difference in substance between English and German contract law on the matter, and the supposedly inconsistent positions mainly pertain to the labels used for the different clauses. This means that it is not (any more) illogical for German law, in comparison with English law, to permit that contractual parties can agree on proportionate amounts as remedies whilst rejecting punitive and exemplary damages in tort law; if anything, it is (more) illogical for English law to permit exemplary damages in tort law whilst being very strict on contractual agreements of overcompensatory remedies.

E. Interim Conclusions

To sum up, refusing to recognise foreign punitive damages awards in Germany is not undermined by the domestic situation of German damages law, which in all critical instances can be seen to sufficiently observe the compensatory principle. German law has developed towards accepting damages for pain and suffering because the courts have approved of the functions of penance and satisfaction in the law of damages domestically, but this does not make these damages punitive, especially with regard to the amounts usually awarded. Particularly high amounts are only awarded for the infringement of personality rights, yet

[76] *Dunlop Pneumatic Tyre Co Ltd v New Garage & Motor Co Ltd* [1915] AC 79 (HL).

[77] *Cavendish Square Holding BV v Makdessi* [2015] UKSC 67, [2016] AC 1172.

[78] All circumstances of the individual case have to be considered with regard to the performance interest of the innocent party as well as deterrence, the severity and extent of the breach, and the degree of fault of the party breaching the clause; see further C Chasapis, *Die Herabsetzung der unverhältnismäßig hohen Vertragsstrafe* (Berlin, Duncker & Humblot, 2014) 161ff.

[79] s 343(1) of the Civil Code. In the commercial context see s 348 of the Commercial Code (*Handelsgesetzbuch/HGB*).

those damages are still compensatory in nature because they primarily reflect the actual suffering of the victim, even if account is also taken of the profit of the tortfeasor. Where German statutory law provides for damages in special circumstances, such as for discrimination, the prima facie impression that they could be punitive has been equally rebutted. Also, whilst German law enforces contractual penalty clauses, this is limited to proportionate amounts. Therefore, the public policy reasoning of the Federal Court of Justice in its 1992 decision is consistent with the domestic position of the law, and it is not hypocritical of German law to refuse to recognise foreign punitive damages awards.

V. PUBLIC POLICY CAVEATS

Both in the 1992 decision of the Federal Court of Justice about the recognition of the Californian punitive damages judgment and in several subsequent decisions of the Federal Constitutional Court, these highest German courts have created certain public policy caveats for dealing with foreign punitive damages. These are important qualifications to the restrictiveness of the German legal position on the matter, and limit the rejection of punitive damages both in material and procedural terms as will be elucidated in the following two subsections.

A. Recognition of Damages Compensating Actual Losses

The Federal Court of Justice acknowledged in its 1992 decision[80] that foreign punitive damages awards could be recognised in Germany *insofar as* they were awarded to compensate for actual losses, especially for intangible losses. The same would be true for the victim's litigation costs or losses caused by default of the tortfeasor. There is indeed no need for German law to refuse recognition of foreign judgments *to the extent* that the awarded amounts correspond with compensatory damages permissible under German domestic law, even if the foreign damages are in fact termed 'punitive' and in total exceed amounts that would be awarded in similar cases governed by German law.

In the case at hand of the recognition of the Californian judgment, however, the Californian court had – in addition to the punitive damages of US$400,000 – awarded US$200,000 as compensation for pain and suffering. This meant in turn that the punitive damages were not intended to cover such losses. Moreover, the Californian court had ordered that the claimant's attorney in the US was entitled to 40 per cent of all monies awarded to the claimant as a contingent fee, so that the claimant's litigation costs were also covered.

[80] BGH (n 1) 340.

In a different but related regard, the Federal Court of Justice held further that, if a foreign judgment contains both punitive and compensatory damages *detailed separately* in the foreign judgment, recognition of the compensatory part without the punitive part is permissible. As explained above, the Californian judgment had indeed listed the individual amounts for the various compensatory damages separate from the amount of punitive damages. In contrast to the French position,[81] German law separates the individually detailed claims awarded in the foreign judgment because it is not believed to be necessary to decide about recognition holistically. The Federal Court of Justice found that partial recognition, as far as permissible for compensatory damages, ought to be granted as a limited fallback solution instead of the impermissible full recognition.[82] This can be understood to mean that complete rejection of recognition of the entire foreign judgment would, in the eyes of German law, violate the principle of proportionality; in other words, complete rejection is unnecessary when partial rejection suffices in order to achieve the public policy aims regarding punitive damages. Interestingly, this also shows that the French position of completely rejecting the recognition of foreign judgments containing punitive damages due to the disproportionality of the amount awarded as punishment is in itself disproportionate because it ignores the option to act proportionately and recognise the part of the foreign judgment which does not violate the French public order.[83]

B. Service of Foreign Claims for Punitive Damages in Germany

Although the Federal Court of Justice declared in its 1992 decision that foreign punitive damages judgments can in principle not be recognised and enforced in Germany, German courts have nonetheless complied with requests by foreign courts for the service of foreign claim forms which contained punitive damages claims against defendants in Germany. Following appeals against the decisions permitting service of punitive damages claims, the Federal Constitutional Court had to decide only a couple of years later, in 1994, on an alleged violation of fundamental rights and of the rule of law. It was argued in the Federal Constitutional Court that there would equally be a public policy violation when claims for punitive damages would be served onto German defendants.

[81] *cf* Rowan, ch 16 of this volume, p 314.

[82] BGH (n 1) 345–46.

[83] BW Janke and FX Licari, 'Enforcing Punitive Damage Awards in France after Fountaine Pajot' (2012) 60 *American Journal of Comparative Law* 775, 803 suggest that, in the French case, the claimants did not request partial recognition and therefore the court was prevented from granting it. However, this is not a problem of prohibited *révision au fond*. The relevant limitation is *ne ultra petita*, but this would not be infringed when less would be awarded than requested (ie, *infra petita*). *cf* H Gaudemet-Tallon, 'Cour de Cassation (1re Ch Civ) 1er Décembre 2010' [2011] *Revue critique de droit international privé* 93, 101–02.

Service of claim forms issued by US courts in Germany is governed by the 1965 Hague Convention,[84] which contains a public policy provision which differs somewhat from the national rule outlined above because the Hague Convention stipulates that a request for service may only be denied if service would be deemed to infringe the requested state's sovereignty or security.[85] The German lower courts had not found that there would be such a public policy violation. They had argued that, even if the claim succeeded in the US court after permitting service in Germany, the US judgment would only be enforced against the assets of the defendant in the US, ie outside Germany; it would be a separate issue then whether the US judgment would be enforceable in Germany against assets located in Germany, and a request for recognition and enforcement of the US judgment would most likely be denied in Germany in line with the 1992 decision of the Federal Court of Justice. German courts had, on the one hand, found it unnecessary and impossible at the stage of service of claim forms to protect German defendants from punitive damages enforcement actions that might or might not take place in the US. On the other hand, at the stage of service of claim forms, it was equally unnecessary and impossible to decide already whether the US judgment yet to be rendered would later be recognised in Germany. Since service and recognition concerned different procedural stages of a lawsuit, they could be decided independently and in different ways.

The Federal Constitutional Court affirmed the lower courts' practice permitting service of foreign claims for punitive damages in the absence of a public policy violation under the 1965 Hague Convention, and it denied violations of fundamental rights and the rule of law. It drew on the reasoning of the Federal Court of Justice that punitive damages can, to some extent, cover intangible losses and litigation costs, which can be recognised in Germany, too.[86] Additionally, the Federal Constitutional Court argued that service as the initial procedural step had at best the sole potential of endangering the defendant's financial position, but the defendant was still well protected from any real financial harm due to the national public policy defence against any subsequent request for recognition of the foreign judgment.[87] This decision by the Federal Constitutional Court, which was handed down by its First Senate, was also reaffirmed by the Second Senate more recently in 2013, when a similar issue about service of a punitive damages claim had to be decided.[88]

This demonstrates that punitive damages are not rejected by German law under all circumstances and at all times, which mitigates the harshness of the

[84] Convention of 15 November 1965 on the Service Abroad of Judicial and Extrajudicial Documents in Civil or Commercial Matters.

[85] Art 13(1) of the 1965 Hague Convention.

[86] BVerfG, 7 December 1994, case 1 BvR 1279/94, BVerfGE 91, 335, 344.

[87] ibid 344–45.

[88] BVerfG, 9 January 2013, case 2 BvR 2805/12 [2013] *Neue Juristische Wochenschrift* 990. The Second Senate thereby gave up its previously deviating position that originated from temporary injunctions which it had granted in the years 2003–2005, case 2 BvR 1198/03.

1992 decision of the Federal Court of Justice. Equally, the decisions by the Constitutional Court do not undermine the findings of the Federal Court of Justice since both concern different procedural stages. It also matters that, insofar as slightly different public policy criteria apply in national law and international conventions, German courts come to different conclusions about the various issues pertaining to punitive damages. Thus, the different treatment is justified due to factual and legal differences.

VI. THE COHERENT PROTECTION OF THE GERMAN DOMESTIC LIABILITY SYSTEM AGAINST PUNITIVE DAMAGES: FOREIGN PUNITIVE DAMAGES LAWS IN GERMAN COURTS

Finally, looking beyond the issues of service of foreign claims and recognition of foreign judgments in Germany, a coherent domestic protection against punitive damages has to deal as well with the issue of the potential applicability of foreign tort law, which provides for punitive damages, to a claim heard in a German court. To illustrate this with a scenario, instead of suing and winning in a foreign court and subsequently seeking recognition of the foreign judgment in Germany, a tort victim might sue a German tortfeasor in a German court and might try to argue that, for instance, Californian tort law applies to the case because the damage occurred in California. This is not a purely hypothetical scenario because, in the case of the sexual abuse committed by the defendant against the claimant in California, the claimant might have been able to sue in Germany.

Applicability of Californian or any other foreign tort law in a German court depends on the conflict of laws rules of Germany. Insofar as the claim could result in an award of punitive damages, this would undermine the ultimate argument made by the Federal Court of Justice in its 1992 decision against the recognition of foreign punitive damages judgments, as mentioned above, that giving effect to foreign punitive damages awards in Germany must not disrupt the German domestic liability system.[89] In other words, it would throw the domestic system off balance if, by applying foreign law in German courts, German debtors could be exposed to liability which was unavailable to German creditors. It shows that fending off foreign judgments which award punitive damages to foreign creditors against German debtors does help protect the German liability system, but it would – as a procedural measure – be insufficient on its own. As a logical corollary, non-recognition of foreign punitive damages judgments has to be complemented by equal measures in the conflict of laws regarding the applicability of foreign law and the availability of foreign remedies in German courts.

[89] BGH (n 1) 344–45.

The relevant rules for German courts on the conflict of laws for torts have been harmonised by the EU in the Rome II Regulation.[90] The application of the foreign governing law may be refused 'if such application is manifestly incompatible with the public policy *(ordre public)* of the forum'.[91] The wording of this public policy exception is, on the one hand, much closer to the rule in German civil procedural law for the rejection of recognition of a foreign judgment.[92] In this regard, it differs from the 1965 Hague Convention's phrase of 'sovereignty or security'.[93] On the other hand, the Rome II Regulation requires that the incompatibility with the forum's public policy is 'manifest'. In the legislative process leading to the Regulation's enactment, it had been proposed by the European Commission to illustrate the manifest incompatibility with a reference to punitive damages.[94] Upon objection by the UK, fearing for the availability of English exemplary damages when English law is applied in other European courts, this illustration, however, was not adopted in the end.[95] Only in the non-operative Recitals of the Rome II Regulation it is stated somewhat cryptically that:[96]

> In particular, the application of a provision of the law designated by this Regulation which would have the effect of causing non-compensatory exemplary or punitive damages of an excessive nature to be awarded may, depending on the circumstances of the case and the legal order of the Member State of the court seised, be regarded as being contrary to the public policy *(ordre public)* of the forum.

In the absence of a European harmonised standard for the public policy exception, especially with regard to punitive damages, it is thus left to the national legal perceptions of the forum states to decide about the incompatibility.[97] This enables German courts to draw on their national public policy conceptions in the conflict of laws for torts as expressed in the German rules.[98] These national rules are also applied directly to cases outside the scope of the European harmonisation, especially in cases of 'violations of privacy and rights relating to personality', which are excluded from the Regulation.[99]

[90] Regulation (EC) No 864/2007 of the European Parliament and of the Council of 11 July 2007 on the law applicable to non-contractual obligations (Rome II) [2007] OJ L199/40.

[91] Art 26 of the Rome II Regulation.

[92] See the text to n 15.

[93] See the text to n 85.

[94] Art 24 of the Proposal for a Regulation of the European Parliament and the Council on the law applicable to non-contractual obligations ('Rome II'), COM (2003) 427 final.

[95] T Petch, 'The Rome II Regulation: An Update (Part 2)' (2006) 21 *Journal of International Banking Law and Regulation* 509, 516.

[96] Recital 32 of the Rome II Regulation.

[97] A Fuchs, 'Art. 26 Rome II' in P Huber (ed), *Rome II Regulation* (Munich, Sellier, 2011) para 18.

[98] Art 40(3) of the Introductory Act to the Civil Code (*Einführungsgesetz zum Bürgerlichen Gesetzbuche/EGBGB*). In the 1992 decision, BGH (n 1) 328ff addressed Art 38 at length, which was the predecessor of Art 40(3) until a reform in 1999 but differed in substance. Art 40(3) is more specific than the general public policy rule in Art 6 and therefore takes precedence.

[99] Art 1(2)(g) of the Rome II Regulation.

According to the German rules, as far as relevant here, claims governed by foreign law will not be granted in a German court insofar as they significantly exceed the necessary amounts for adequate compensation or obviously serve other purposes than adequate compensation. This makes it perfectly clear that, insofar as punitive damages exceed and pursue non-compensatory objectives, German courts do not apply foreign law to that extent. It is interesting to note that this is not an absolute rejection of punitive damages but a limitation of the amount to the necessary compensation. The public policy caveat in the Federal Court of Justice's 1992 decision reflects this notion that recognition of a foreign punitive damages judgment can be permissible to the extent that the amount covers intangible losses or litigation costs insofar as they would be recoverable, too, under German law. Excessive punitive damages claims can however not be pursued successfully against German debtors in German courts.

The coherence with which punitive damages are fended off by German courts is also supported on additional grounds when considering who, ultimately, picks up punitive damages awards. For instance, in the English legal system, it is likely that punitive damages are awarded in cases of vicarious liability or where the defendant is indemnified by other means, for instance by the Crown, depending on the case category. By contrast, similar indemnity is not available in the German legal system to a comparable extent because, although insurance is also widely available, German law does not ordinarily provide for amounts of damages which cannot possibly be paid by an individual, and thus does not need to provide for legal structures which can channel and absorb such amounts instead of an individual. German law is not prepared for punitive damages in any regard, and it is thus necessary and coherent in all regards that they are excluded insofar as they exceed compensatory damages.

VII. CONCLUSION AND OUTLOOK

Contrary to the fear of being exposed to criticism for hypocrisy, German law has been able to resolve the dilemma of how to handle punitive damages without self-contradiction. It has proved tenable to differentiate sufficiently clearly between damages available domestically and foreign punitive damages. Although domestic legal developments have led to damages awards which are not strictly limited anymore to purely compensatory purposes and amounts, compensation is still the guiding principle. It is therefore consistent to reject recognition of foreign judgments insofar as they award punitive damages which go above and beyond what is necessary for compensation, as it was established in the 1992 landmark decision by the Federal Court of Justice. Yet, as much as the rigidity of strict compensation has worn off domestically, caveats have been made to mitigate the rigidity of the rejection of foreign punitive damages in material and procedural terms. Consistency regarding punitive damages is nonetheless ensured between how foreign judgments are treated and how foreign law is applied in Germany.

Looking ahead, the German position regarding the recognition of punitive damages judgments is unlikely to change under the 2019 Hague Judgments Convention,[100] which will enter into force for Germany and almost all other EU Member States in September 2023. The US have signed but not yet ratified the Convention, and the UK has not even signed it, so that it will not have any effect for the recognition of Anglo-American judgments in the EU.[101] In any case, the Convention provides that 'recognition or enforcement of a judgment may be refused if, and to the extent that, the judgment awards damages, including exemplary or punitive damages, that do not compensate a party for actual loss or harm suffered'.[102] This would allow German courts to keep rejecting punitive damages judgments insofar as they go above and beyond compensatory awards.

[100] Convention of 2 July 2019 on the Recognition and Enforcement of Foreign Judgments in Civil or Commercial Matters.

[101] On a related note, the 2005 Hague Convention on Choice of Court Agreements has been ratified by both the EU and the UK, but it will rarely apply in the tort context. The US has signed but not ratified it.

[102] Art 10(1) of the 2019 Hague Convention; and similarly Art 11(1) of the 2005 Hague Convention.

8

John v MGN Ltd (1995) Enclosing the Jury Paddock?

MARK LUNNEY*

IN SOME RESPECTS, the decision of the Court of Appeal in *John v MGN Ltd*[1] is an unusual choice for a collection dealing with leading cases on exemplary damages. True, the question of exemplary damages was an important issue in the case, and some clarification was given over the culpability and standard of proof requirements for such an award to be made.[2] However, as is indicated by the dearth of later cases discussing these aspects of the decision, this is not why the case is well- known. Rather, it is the approach of the Court of Appeal to calculation and review of jury awards of damages that gave the case its notoriety. Paradoxically, in the specific context of the case – jury awards in defamation actions – the decision has become largely obsolete in light of the effective abolition of jury trial in defamation actions by section 11 of the Defamation Act 2013. Nonetheless, the approach taken in *John* has proved influential in other contexts so it remains relevant beyond defamation. More broadly, it also represents an important turning point in how appellate courts viewed the sanctity of jury verdicts. Exemplary damages, with their lack of any meaningful comparator, were an especially good testing ground for the change in approach adopted by the Court of Appeal.

I. ELTON'S DIET OF DEATH

The Court of Appeal decision arose out of an appeal against a jury verdict in a libel action brought by Elton John against MGN Ltd. Just after Christmas in December 1992, the *Sunday Mirror* published a story about a new diet John was

* I would like to thank the participants in the workshop on which this collection is based for helpful comments and observations and, in particular, Dr Eleni Katsampouka for feedback on an earlier draft of the chapter.

[1] *John v MGN Ltd* [1997] QB 586 (CA).

[2] ibid 616–19.

supposedly practising to keep his weight in check. On the left-hand corner of the first page, there were headings 'World Exclusive' and 'Elton's "diet of death"'. The headline referred the reader to pages 4–5 of the paper where the story was recited in full. Apparently, at a Christmas party in Los Angeles hosted by his manager, John Reid, and for which John had flown in from London, John was both boasting of and practising a new diet. This involved him chewing food but not swallowing it; he would spit the food out after chewing. As Professor Hubert Lacey, a specialist in eating disorders at St George's Medical School London observed (the paper having sought out his opinion on the general practice described), this was very dangerous. It was likely to trigger a later binge and then self-induced vomiting. Another expert noted that this behaviour was one form of bulimia. As John had suffered from this affliction in the past, there was a clear suggestion that he had regressed. While a spokesman for John was reported as saying he knew nothing about it, the article published the views of one guest at the party who stated John was behaving in this way and actually advocating its benefits for his weight and overall mental health.

The article was not the result of one of the *Mirror's* own journalists. The source of the article was a freelance journalist in California, Tony Brenna, who over a period had provided the *Mirror* with content and was clearly a trusted partner. Brenna himself was relying on the evidence of two other people who alleged they had seen John at the party and had observed and spoken to him about his behaviour. Brenna's draft article was submitted to a *Mirror* employee, Paul Scott, and the final version was published under both their names. Although the precise details were vague, it seems that both Brenna and Scott had taken some steps to ascertain the accuracy of the story: Brenna took recordings of interviews with his sources and provided a transcript – albeit the recordings and transcripts of the original versions conducted before the trial were lost – and Scott said he tried to get in touch with Reid or members of his organisation to verify the story. The only confirmed attempt that Scott made was a phone call to Frank Presland of Frere Cholmley Bischoff, John's solicitors. Presland told Scott he did not know where Reid was, that the story sounded unbelievable, and that no doubt Scott would be 'very careful'. When Scott affirmed his faith in the reliability of the sources, Presland rather ominously replied that he had successfully sued many papers who had first told him that and wished Scott a Merry Christmas!

A letter before action was sent by John's solicitors before the end of the year and the writ was issued in January 1993. The *Mirror* sought time to investigate the claim and in March 1993 accepted that their sources had made a mistake – in that Elton John was not at the event in question – and also that they had good reason to believe the veracity of the sources. An apology was proposed based on the 'mistaken identity' theory, but this was rejected, and no apology was ultimately published. As negotiations continued, the parties' positions hardened: John wanted MGN to recognise that 'the article was a wholly invented piece of fiction which was irresponsibly published'[3] while MGN thought that John's 17-year history of drug abuse weakened his claim that he had been defamed. Perhaps as part of this deterioration, John amended the action to add a claim for exemplary damages.[4] The gist of this claim was that the defendant had taken no or insufficient steps to ascertain the accuracy of the story with the result that the defendant published the words recklessly, not caring whether they were true or false. Further, by publicising the story in sensationalist terms on the front page to attract members of the public to purchase the *Sunday Mirror*, an inference could be drawn that the publication had been made on the calculated basis that the newspaper would be likely to gain more financially from such publication than it would have to pay in damages if it was sued (the second of the *Rookes v Barnard* categories where exemplary damages could be awarded).

The trial took place in November 1993. The plaintiff's allegation was that, effectively, the article alleged he was a hypocrite: having made public statements that he had overcome his many addictions, he had not. As his counsel, the irrepressible George Carman QC, asked the jury how they would feel if they had overcome an addiction that was destroying their lives, and held themselves up as an example, only to be 'knocked by an article that was saying you are a hypocrite, failure, sham and on the road to death.'[5] John's evidence primarily consisted of the extensive efforts he had made in his attempts to overcome addiction and to live a more healthy life. This included between 1,300 and 1,400 visits to various addiction clinics,[6] attending up to three sessions a day.[7] It gave him back his self-respect and was the most important thing he had ever done in his life. For the article to 'nonchalantly toss that away without substantiation after all the work I have put in is most disgraceful and extremely hurtful.'[8]

More interesting legally, perhaps, is the framing of John's case by Carman, especially John's plea for exemplary damages. Even when not specifically addressing this issue, Carman took every opportunity to stress the culpability of MGN's behaviour. The *Sunday Mirror* article was a 'wicked invention' made by people who had gate-crashed Reid's party and were thrown out within an hour.'[9] Moreover, it was an invention 'for money which should have been checked out

[3] ibid 601. See also R Duce, 'Elton Story Was "Work of Fiction"', *The Times*, 3 November 1993, 7, where John's solicitor said he (John) thought the *Mirror*'s explanation was 'an insult to his intelligence'.

[4] The decision to allow the amendment was appealed to the Court of Appeal but the appeal was dismissed: *John v MGN Limited*, Official Transcripts (1990–97) [1993] Lexis Citation 2520.

[5] R Duce, 'Elton John Pursues Damages for Report of "Bizarre" Diet', *The Times*, 2 November 1993, 5.

[6] B Mouland, 'I Survived Life as Addict Says Elton', *Daily Mail*, 2 November 1993, 18; D Leigh, '"I Needed to Be Cured – I Was Living in Hell"', *Daily Mirror*, 2 November 1993, 3.

[7] E Oxford, 'Elton John Sues Paper Over Report of Bizarre Diet' *The Independent*, 2 November 1993, 3.

[8] Mouland (n 6) 18.

[9] ibid.

by Mr Brenna and Mirror Group Newspapers. And that is the extraordinarily flimsy basis on which the Sunday Mirror decided in a World Exclusive to assassinate Elton John's reputation.'[10] But Carman kept his most powerful rhetoric and imagery to deal specifically with the question of exemplary damages. He began with arguments suitable to make the case for an award of aggravated damages:[11]

> MGN, while writing pretty words in letters, haven't had the decency, courage or candour to offer you, the jury, any evidence for their conduct of publishing this disgraceful article. Worse than that, they haven't even admitted that what they published was a libel.

But Carman's renowned mastery in defamation cases is evidenced in his address to the jury on exemplary damages which bears repeating at length:[12]

> Mr Carman asked the jury to imagine the MGN directors sitting round a boardroom table. The Chairman says 'How much did libel cost us last year?' and the accountant gives the precise figure from the balance sheet. A look of gloom passes across the faces of the board of directors. Then the Chairman says 'But by how much did our circulation and advertising revenue increase last year?' and the figure is duly trotted out by the accountant. A smile spreads across the board's faces. Mr Carman told the seven-man, five-woman jury: 'When you come to award exemplary damages, to punish the newspaper, as I say you should, you are entitled to wipe the smile off the faces of the board of directors of Mirror Group Newspapers.'

Although MGN Ltd led no evidence at the trial, documents exchanged just before trial showed that the *Sunday Mirror's* sales figures for the period October 1992 to March 1993 varied between 2.4 million to 2.9 million per issue, with the issue in question standing at the bottom of the table.[13]

It is not necessary for present purposes to analyse the summing up of the trial judge, Drake J, except to note, as the *Daily Mirror* did, that the trial judge warned the jury about awarding a very large amount in damages.[14] Despite the warning, the jury, by a majority of 10–2 and after five hours of deliberation, made what were very large awards for the times: compensatory damages (which must under *Rookes v Barnard*[15] have included any award of aggravated damages) of £75,000 and an award of £275,000 for exemplary damages. A contemporary newspaper stated it was the eighth highest award in a libel claim, but as at least one of the higher awards (to John in a previous action) was through a settlement

[10] C Randall, 'Elton John Sues Paper Over "Diet of Death" Lies', *Daily Telegraph*, 2 November 1993, 3.

[11] R Spencer, 'Jury Asked to Wipe Smile from Face of Newspaper Board', *Daily Telegraph*, 4 November 1993, 3.

[12] ibid.

[13] *John* (n 1) 602–03.

[14] Understandably, the *Daily Mirror* put it more evocatively as a warning against 'massive' damages: 'Elton judge in warning', *Daily Mirror*, 4 November 1993, 5. For an interdisciplinary critique of the summing up, see P Robertson, 'The Catalyst of Libel Reform: The Risks of Puncture Repair at Speed' (1997) 10 *International Journal for the Semiotics of Law* 79.

[15] *Rookes v Barnard* [1964] AC 1129 (HL).

it was actually higher in terms of jury awards. All of the top 10 awards had been made in the previous six years.[16] Accordingly, the award in *John v MGN Ltd* added to growing public concerns about an increase in awards made in defamation cases. While there were obvious legal differences between awards of compensatory and exemplary awards, the criticisms of the awards were not so refined. Concerns over awards in libel cases spilled over into both types of damages and focused on what was perceived to be the main shortcoming: they were made by juries.

II. THE CONSTITUTIONAL POSITION OF THE JURY

Trial by jury, including civil jury, was an integral part of the administration of civil justice in England for almost 800 years. Historically, they were lauded as a bastion of liberty under the English constitution. Blackstone, quoting *Magna Carta*, described them as the 'bulwark of our liberties'[17] and Lord Camden stated: 'Trial by jury is indeed the foundation of our free constitution; take that away and the whole fabric will soon moulder into dust.'[18] These words are hardly surprising from the man who was as responsible as any for cementing the constitutional status of the jury by defending the exemplary awards made by the jury in *Huckle v Money* and *Wilkes v Wood*. These were not libel actions, but the constitutional status for the jury in this context was reinforced by Fox's Libel Act that determined the question of libel/no libel was for the jury, and not the judge, in criminal libel cases.[19] While the plaudits were primarily for the use of the jury in the protection of civil liberties against infringement by over-reaching criminal law, civil juries benefitted by association. Blackstone, for example, makes no distinction in his laudatory comments on juries between civil and criminal juries.

The general plaudits for the jury extended to giving jury verdicts on quantum an almost unimpugnable standing. For non-pecuniary components of awards, this may have resulted from a piece of historical serendipity rather than a considered view of the status such awards should have. In recent work, Sinanis has traced the development of appellate control of jury awards where aggravating factors had been pleaded by the plaintiff.[20] This possibility was facilitated by the rise of the post-trial motion for a new trial, one basis for which could be an excessive damages award. Sinanis finds the first reported case of a new

[16] R Duce, 'Jury Awards £350,000 Damages to Elton John', *The Times*, 5 November 1993, 3.

[17] W Blackstone, *Commentaries on the Laws of England*, Book 3 (Oxford, Clarendon Press, 1765–1769) 350.

[18] JL Campbell, *Lives of the Lord Chancellors*, vol 7, 5th edn, 35, cited in RM Jackson, 'Jury Trial Today' (1938) 6 *CLJ* 367.

[19] P Mitchell, 'Shepherding Juries: John v MGN' (1997–98) 8 *King's College Law Journal* 107, 109.

[20] N Sinanis, 'Aggravation in Tort Before 1763' (2022) 43 *Journal of Legal History* 24.

trial being ordered for an excessive damages award, in the absence of procedural irregularity, to be *Wood v Gunston* in 1655.[21] However, while there were cases ordering new trials for excessive awards over the next century, it is unclear whether the order was made solely because of the size of the award or because of some procedural irregularity such as the failure of the jury to act in accord with a direction of the trial judge. As Sinanis notes, it was not until a century later, in *Wilford v Berkeley* in 1758,[22] that the practice was subject to substantial appellate scrutiny. In *Wilford*, a criminal conversation case, Lord Mansfield's Court of King's Bench held that there was 'no doubt' that the court had a proper discretion to set aside verdicts because of the size of the award.[23] But where a claim in tort was involved, this could only be done where there was some measure against which the court could judge whether the award was excessive:[24]

> [T]he quantum of the damage really suffered by the plaintiff could be apparent, or they were of such a nature that the Court could properly judge the degree of the injury, and could see manifestly that the jury had been outrageous in giving such damages as greatly exceeded the injury.

The Court also recognised that, in many cases, tort awards depended on the circumstances of the case which also made appellate review a difficult exercise. This was especially so in criminal conversation cases such that the Court was not 'competent to say that £500 was too much [the jury award]; or that £50 was too little'.[25] Sinanis argues that the reluctance to interfere with awards allowed for punitive elements in awards to stand but what is important for present purposes is that the reluctance was justified by the inability to find a yardstick by which judges could gauge the accuracy of the award rather than a recognition that the jury award had any constitutional status. There was no overt public interest in *Wilford* either; the defendant was 'a clerk in the Exchequer, during pleasure, at a salary of 50 l a year, only: which was his whole substance.'[26] The note to the Burroughs report refers to the case of *Chem v Brigg*, decided by Lord Chief Justice Pratt, which was said to be exactly the same as this in that the same amount was awarded and the Court refused to order a new trial 'upon the very same principles' as in *Wilford v Berkeley*. I have not been able to locate the reference provided to the case,[27] but Pratt was Lord Chief Justice between 1718 and 1725, which suggests that the Mansfield Court was drawing on established law in detailing the boundaries of appellate review of jury verdicts.

It was Lord Chief Justice Pratt's third son by his second marriage, Charles Pratt, who more than anyone was responsible for the transformation of the

[21] *Wood v Gunston* (1655) Style 462, 82 ER 864.
[22] *Wilford v Berkeley* (1758) 1 Burr 609, 97 ER 472.
[23] ibid.
[24] ibid.
[25] ibid.
[26] ibid.
[27] The reference given by Burroughs is 'M 6 G 1, B R'.

status of jury verdicts. In 1763, in a motion for a new trial before the Common Pleas, Pratt CJ, on one level, largely followed the approach in *Wilford v Berkeley*. The facts in *Leeman v Allen*[28] involved the unlawful entry onto the plaintiff's premises, the Rummer Tavern in Chancery Lane, by what were described in the report as 'Reforming Constables' who had secured a warrant to enter and arrest the plaintiff. This appears to have been a misguided attempt by groups trying to eradicate prostitution in the area but about 20 witnesses testified that the Rummer Tavern was a 'house of good repute'. In her various actions for trespass, the jury awarded the plaintiff £300. Pratt CJ refused to order a new trial. On the excessive damages ground, he accepted that there was a power for courts to review awards but said that 'Courts should be very cautious how they overthrow verdicts that have been given by twelve men upon their oaths.'[29] For the reasons identified in *Wilford*, tort claims presented particular difficulties with the result that, for Pratt CJ, the threshold for review was high: 'whether the damages are beyond all measure unreasonable, though they cannot say exactly what damages ought to be given.'[30] But in setting out the factors that might explain such a large award, it is Pratt CJ's focus on the illegal nature of the defendant's activity – as opposed to the measure of the plaintiff's harm – that is striking:[31]

> I do not think the damages excessive in the present case; here are a number of persons like a new sort of grand jury, who meet once or twice in a week, and take upon themselves to present, correct, reform, and commence prosecutions ... I think the King's Bench would grant an information against these persons for setting themselves up as a kind of grand jury; an informer is a most odious character: and I am glad of an opportunity of declaring my dislike towards these reformers ...

Upholding the jury's verdict in part because of disapproval of vigilante justice is not quite the same as recognising a constitutional role for the jury but Pratt CJ's hostility to the improper use of legal processes in palpable. The events taking place in Chancery Lane may too have been a factor: as Boorman has argued, Chancery Lane itself was a highly politicised space.[32] The same hostility underpins Pratt's famous judgments in the 'North British' cases, *Huckle v Money*[33] and *Wilkes v Woods*.[34] It is only in the former case that the Court in banc had to consider whether the jury award of £300 should be allowed to stand. Although the case generally is famous for being the first to use the term 'exemplary

[28] *Leeman v Allen* (1763) 2 Wils KB 160, (1763) 95 ER 742.

[29] ibid 161, 743.

[30] ibid.

[31] ibid.

[32] FC Boorman, 'The Political Space of Chancery Lane, c1760–1815' (Institute of Historical Research, School of Advanced Studies, University of London), available at sas-space.sas.ac.uk/5797/1/Francis_Boorman_-_The_Political_space_of_Chancery_Lane_c._1760-1815.pdf.

[33] *Huckle v Money* (1763) 2 Wils KB 206, (1799) 95 ER 768.

[34] *Wilkes v Wood* (1763) Lofft 1, (1763) 98 ER 489.

damages', on the motion for a new trial little was said expressly on this point. A lot, though, was said about the latitude given to the jury to determine damages in tort cases, the starting point of which was to reiterate that circumstances were all in trying to assess whether a jury award was manifestly excessive.

It is striking that Pratt CJ said almost nothing about the constitutional role of the jury. The only reference was to what damages the jury might be restricted in awarding by virtue of their oath ('to consider mere personal injury only'), a proposition he rejected. But what did have constitutional implications were the 'circumstances' of the case – something which fell within the remit of the jury. It is in describing the circumstances that the jury might consider that Pratt CJ produced his constitutional arguments: the

> great point of law touching the liberty of the subject appeared to them at the trial; they saw a magistrate over all the King's subjects, exercising arbitrary power, violating Magna Charta, and attempting to destroy the liberty of the kingdom, by insisting upon the legality of this general warrant before them …[34a]

At the end of his judgment, however, Pratt CJ restated that it was

> very dangerous for the Judges to intermeddle in damages for torts; it must be a glaring case indeed of outrageous damages in a tort, and which all mankind at first blush must think so, to induce a Court to grant a new trial for excessive damages.[34b]

Given the power of his description of the circumstances, it is hard to resist the inference that what he was really saying was that since the jury had been given these important constitutional questions – including what damages should be awarded for constitutional breaches – appellate intervention had to be highly circumscribed. In doing so, the process of a civil jury making an award of damages – including, in whatever sense he meant it, exemplary damages – was transformed from an adjudicative into a constitutional one. It is not surprising that Pratt CJ would be the one to make the connection. As Sinanis notes, in 1752 Pratt had represented William Owen in his seditious libel trial where he had advocated for a greater role for the jury in determining whether the elements of the offence had been committed. Describing his judgment in *Leeman*, but even more applicable perhaps to *Huckle*, Sinanis observes: 'It is perhaps reasonable to suppose that in *Leeman* Pratt CJ looked to assert the constitutional importance of civil trial by jury as a buttress of English liberties.'[35]

Whatever the rhetorical commitment to the civil jury encompassed in these views, from the middle of the nineteenth century, civil juries as a mode of trial went into decline. The reduction in the use of civil juries should not be overstated but neither should it be underestimated. In particular, the reforms of the early 1930s – which largely reintroduced World War One reforms that allowed trial by judge alone in a wide variety of situations – made a significant inroad

[34a] *Huckle* (n 33) 207, 769.
[34b] ibid.
[35] Sinanis (n 20) 42.

into the prevalence of jury trials.[36] In the King's Bench Division, apart from a selected number of causes of action, trial by jury was not mandated. Rather, the Court was given power to order a trial by jury. Even in the cases for which trial by jury was mandated, this was subject to the limitation that trial by jury could be dispensed with where the trial required any prolonged examination of documents or accounts or any scientific or local investigation which could not be conveniently made with a jury.[37] While early commentators on the legislative change noted that the right to grant a jury trial was unfettered and did not require a plaintiff to show a special reason why a jury was required,[38] as time went on trial by jury in civil cases became less common. In his Hamlyn Lectures, 'The Jury', in 1956, Patrick Devlin noted that 'the popularity of trial by judge alone is now decisively established; the proportion of jury trials is now 2 per cent, or 3 per cent, of the whole.'[39] According to Devlin, the reason for the decline was not because requests for jury trial were being declined – the number of refusals was quite negligible – but was 'due to the fact that juries are not being asked for.'[40]

The same point was made by Denning MR 10 years later in *Ward v James* in the context of jury trials in personal injury actions:[41]

> But in personal injury cases trial by jury has given place of late to trial by judge alone, the reason being simply this, that in these cases trial by judge alone is more acceptable to the great majority of people. Rarely does a party ask in these cases for a jury.

However, *Ward v James* did not simply report the demise of civil jury trial in personal injury actions: it cemented it. A five-member Court of Appeal declared that, in cases where the assessment of non-pecuniary loss was concerned, attention needed to be paid to awards made in other comparable cases. Viewed globally, three factors were important in giving credibility to such awards: accessibility, uniformity and predictability.[42] But no measure of guidance to the jury, such as advising the jury of awards in comparable cases or by advising the jury of the conventional amount awarded for the injury in question, was satisfactory. For the former, the prospect of possibly dubious or tangentially analogous awards being raised only to be challenged in cross-examination did not seem to their Lordships to provide assistance to the jury. Conversely, given that any reference to conventional figures needed to be reasonably related to the award the

[36] RM Jackson, 'The Incidence of Jury Trial During the Last Century' (1937) 1 *MLR* 132, 141.

[37] Administration of Justice (Miscellaneous Provisions) Act 1933, s 6.

[38] Jackson, 'The Incidence of Jury Trial During the Last Century' (n 36) 142, citing *Hope v GWR* (1937) 53 TLR 399 (CA).

[39] P Devlin, *The Jury* (London, Stevens & Sons, 1956) 132.

[40] ibid 133. Devlin put the decline down to the prevalence of employer's liability and motor vehicle accidents where recognised standards already existed and what plaintiffs wanted was the certainty that those standards would be applied in determining the case so that 'an informed mind was needed rather than a fresh one': ibid 142–43.

[41] *Ward v James* [1966] 1 QB 273 (CA) 295.

[42] ibid 299–300.

judge thought appropriate, this made the need for the jury redundant: 'But if he can give them narrow limits of that kind, there is little point in having a jury at all. You might as well let the judge assess the figure himself.'[43]

Far from jury awards in defamation cases being immune from the criticisms highlighted in *Ward v James*, there was actually a long record of complaint and suggestions for reform. Writing in 1937, the Cambridge academic RM Jackson opined that the amount of damages awarded in libel cases 'is becoming a grim joke.'[44] The Porter Committee on the Law of Defamation in 1948 recognised that judge-only trial during World War II had not eliminated the wide discrepancies between verdicts, but that judge-made awards were generally lower than that made by juries in respect of the same libel.[45] Irrespective of mode of trial, it also thought that some awards made in defamation cases on any basis of assessment were excessive.[46] Almost 30 years later, the Faulks Committee on the Law of Defamation in 1975 considered jury trial in some detail. Going considerably further than the Porter Committee, it recommended that where jury trial did take place, the jury's role on damages should be limited to stating whether the damages should be substantial, moderate, nominal or contemptuous. The judge would assess the actual amount of the award within the limits of the jury's finding on the appropriate category.[47] The problem of excessive punitive awards in defamation cases was to be solved more drastically by legislatively abolishing them.[48] More generally, one thing that was common to both the Porter and Faulks Reviews was the recommendation to liberalise the power of the Court of Appeal to set aside jury verdicts for being excessive. Given the Faulks recommendation on formally curtailing the jury's role was never implemented, it was to the control of the amount of jury verdicts, including verdicts for exemplary damages, to which efforts at restraint had to be directed.

It was one thing to recognise that control over the amount of jury verdicts was one, admittedly blunt, way to deal with the perceived problem of excessive awards of damages made by juries, including exemplary damages. It was quite another for judges to do something about it. This was because the constitutional role of the jury clearly included the right to set damages and any interference with this right by appellate judges risked the charge of usurping that constitutional role. Among the bodies recommending reform, such sentiments carried increasingly little weight. One need only compare the short but relatively unequivocal support for jury trial in defamation actions in the Porter Committee with the

[43] ibid 303.

[44] Jackson, 'Jury Trial Today' (n 18) 378.

[45] *Report of the Committee on the Law of Defamation* (Cmd 7536, 1948) ('Porter Committee') para 157.

[46] ibid para 158.

[47] *Report of the Committee on Defamation* (Cmnd 5909, 1975) ('Faulks Committee') para 516.

[48] ibid para 360. The Committee referred to the abolition of exemplary damages in defamation action in New South Wales (Defamation Act 1974 (NSW), s 46(3)(a), New South Wales Law Reform Commission, *Defamation* (No 11, 1971) paras 42–55.

more resigned position of the Faulks Committee. The latter clearly thought the constitutional argument largely misconceived:[49]

> We believe that much of the support for jury trials is emotional, and derives from the undoubted value of juries in serious *criminal* cases, where they stand between the prosecuting authority and the citizen. But the true function of the civil jury is to weigh the facts impersonally and recompense the claimant for an injury that he may have sustained – tasks for which the judge is trained by many years of experience and for which jurors have no training at all.

Whatever judges thought privately, sitting in their judicial capacity the constitutional role of the jury in setting awards was frequently referred to in judgments before and after the decision in *John v MGN*. But the jury had a place in popular imagination well beyond the judges.[50] As noted above, the Administration of Justice Act (Miscellaneous Provisions) Act 1933 provided the cases where trial by jury was to be at the choice of the parties. The Supreme Court Bill 1981, as introduced into the House of Lords, largely retained that selection as well as retaining a discretionary right for a court to order trial by jury in other cases. When the Bill was in the House of Lords, several judicial members successfully sought an amendment allowing an additional exception for the as-of-right jury trials where the length of the trial (as opposed to any prolonged examination of documents or accounts or any scientific or local investigation) made it unsuitable for jury trial.[51] But when the Bill came to the Commons with this amendment, the attack on what seems, in hindsight, a relatively minor amendment was based on the infringement of the constitutional 'right' of jury trial. The member for Warley West, Peter Archer, commented that the Bill removed 'almost by a side wind, what has been considered an important constitutional right, and one which has proved itself in practice to be an effective institution worthy of the confidence that it has won from the community.'[52] The member for Abertillery, Jeffrey Thomas, noted that the amendment deprived citizens of their rights and liberties.[53] And Frank Dobson, Member for Holborn and Saint Pancras South, was particularly critical. After expressing his lack of trust in lawyers in protecting the judicial system, he said they would 'do their job only if they are properly restrained by statute law and by the effectiveness of the jury's intervention in most forms of trial on important matters.' In a vituperative finale, he contrasted the worth of the jury with the worth of lawyers: 'Jury service is more important to the preservation of individual liberty and

[49] Faulks Committee (n 47) para 496. See also Devlin (n 39) ch 6. The possibility that jury awards of punitive damages might be justified in the same way as for criminal cases was not raised by the Committee.

[50] JW Cairns, '"The Dearest Birthright of the People of England": the Civil Jury in Modern Scottish Legal History' in JW Cairns and G McLeod (eds), *'The Dearest Birthright of the People of England': The Jury in the History of the Common Law* (Oxford, Hart Publishing, 2002) 1–2.

[51] HL Deb 2 March 1981, vol 417, cols 1253–54 (2 March 1981) (Lords Roskill, Denning and Lane).

[52] HC Deb 6 May 1981, vol 4, col 204.

[53] ibid col 227.

the preservation of our judicial system than all the scurvy race of lawyers put together.'[54] Even discounting for political opportunism – all three were members of the Labour Party opposition – it is evident they thought the appeal to the sanctity of the jury was something that transcended party politics.

As discussed above, there is no doubt that the use of trial by civil jury diminished from the middle of the nineteenth century.[55] But what is important is that the cases where trial by jury was retained as the default option – in both the 1933 and 1981 legislation – were cases where the kinds of constitutional circumstances that enlivened Pratt CJ's judgment in *Huckle* could reappear, albeit in microcosm. In particular, Lord Devlin's first category where exemplary damages could be awarded in *Rookes v Barnard* – oppressive, arbitrary, or unlawful actions by servants or agents of the Government – was created out of the constitutionally-important cases of which *Huckle* formed part. For Lord Devlin, what was significant was the subject matter constraints that these cases could create for exemplary awards, but he effectively left the constitutional argument for the civil jury intact. But Lord Devlin's second category, which in practice covered defamation cases, was a much more difficult sell in terms of a constitutional argument. The use of criminal libel that may have prompted Pratt CJ to extoll the virtue of civil jury awards of damages seemed out of place when litigants were private parties and defendants largely newspapers increasingly protesting that large awards of damages by juries, including exemplary awards, were infringing their right of freedom of expression. Together with the wider disquiet over civil juries in cases where exemplary damages were not in issue – particularly in personal injury cases – by the late 1980s, the historical dogma about the constitutional role of the jury in awarding damages was coming under pressure. *John v MGN Ltd* was part of the story of how the courts confronted this challenge.

III. CHALLENGES TO THE OLD ORDER

It is striking how little the judicial descriptions of the threshold needed for appellate review of jury awards changed between the middle of the eighteenth century and the end of the twentieth. The open-ended nature of the threshold meant that there was also the possibility of a lower standard of appellate review being adopted in practice, but formally the position remained that only in exceptional cases could an appellate court interfere with an award by a jury. In *Sutcliffe v Pressdram Ltd*,[56] Lord Donaldson provided a summary of the various

[54] ibid col 226.

[55] M Lobban, 'The Strange Life of the English Civil Jury' in JW Cairns and G McLeod (eds), *'The Dearest Birthright of the People of England': The Jury in the History of the Common Law* (Oxford, Hart Publishing, 2002) ch 10.

[56] *Sutcliffe v Pressdram Ltd* [1991] 1 QB 153 (CA).

expressions that had been used: 'the damages are so excessive that no 12 men could reasonably have given them';[57] 'There must be some reasonable relation between the wrong done and the solatium applied';[58] 'The damages are "out of all proportion to the circumstances of the case"';[59] 'It is out of all proportion to the facts or such that 12 reasonable men could not have made such an award';[60] 'The jury's award was "divorced from reality"'.[61] As late as 1984, Stephenson LJ went as far as to say the power of the Court of Appeal to overturn a jury award of damages was 'apparently obsolescent'.[62] While Lord Donaldson thought this overstated the case, it is evident that it would be difficult to impose any significant control over jury awards with any of the standards that had been suggested. The constitutional significance of jury awards continued to exert its influence even if judges, as they increasingly did, thought that such awards needed to be subjected to greater control.

If the amount of the verdict itself was difficult to challenge on appellate review, the other way of trying to bring some control over jury awards was to shepherd them in making the award. But attempts to do this suffered from the same difficulties that attached to doing this for jury awards in personal injury cases: as noted above, in *Ward v James*, the Court of Appeal rejected the idea that juries could be told about awards in comparable cases or that figures within conventional bands should be disclosed to the jury by either counsel or the trial judge.[63] In *Ward v James* the Court of Appeal solved these problems by effectively abolishing civil juries in these cases,[64] but for causes of action where trial by jury remained as of right, this was not an option.

The question of guidance was expressly raised in *Sutcliffe v Pressdram Ltd*. The plaintiff, the former wife of the Yorkshire Ripper, Peter Sutcliffe, sued the magazine *Private Eye* in libel over allegations she had used her position as Sutcliffe's wife to sell her story. A jury awarded her compensatory damages of £600,000. One ground of appeal was that the award was excessive, and this was upheld by the Court of Appeal, finding that the award was so manifestly excessive as to meet the various threshold tests for interference with an award. Damages were ultimately agreed at £60,000. As the plaintiff's counsel had asked the Court to consider what guidance could be given to juries to ensure awards were not excessive, the Court canvassed a number of options presented to them. While both Donaldson MR and Russell LJ affirmed for libel cases the

[57] *Praed v Graham* (1889) 24 QBD 53 (CA) 55 (Lord Esher MR).

[58] *Greenlands Ltd v Wilmshurst and the London Association for Protection of Trade* [1913] 3 KB 507 (CA) 532–33 (Hamilton LJ); *Tolley v JS Fry and Sons Ltd* [1930] 1 KB 467 (HL) 476 (Scrutton LJ).

[59] *Scott v Musial* [1959] 2 QB 429 (CA) 437 (Morris LJ).

[60] *Lewis v Daily Telegraph Ltd* [1963] 1 QB 340 (CA) 380 (Holroyd Pearce LJ).

[61] *McCarey v Associated Newspapers Ltd (No 2)* [1965] 2 QB 86 (CA) 111 (Willmer LJ).

[62] *Blackshaw v Lord* [1984] QB 1 (CA) 28.

[63] *Ward* (n 41) 301–03.

[64] The description used by the Privy Council in *The Gleaner Co Ltd v Abrahams* [2003] UKPC 55, [2004] 1 AC 628 [43]–[46].

approach the Court of Appeal had adopted in *Ward v James* for personal injury actions – that no comparable cases or suggested figures should be given to the jury – one piece of guidance was to be allowed. Following an approach used by Pearson LJ in *McCarey v Associated Newspapers Ltd*,[65] Donaldson MR suggested that juries could be reminded about the value of money when asking them to assess an award:[66]

> [T]he judge could, I think, properly invite them to consider what the result would be in terms of weekly, monthly or annual income if the money were invested in a building society deposit account without touching the capital sum awarded or, if they have in mind smaller sums, to consider what they could buy with it.

While some of the reasoning was slightly patronising,[67] the thinking was clear. Whatever remained of the constitutional reasons for jury trial in libel cases – and Nourse LJ thought they remained strong[68] – the untrammelled discretion of the jury to consider the circumstances of the case needed to be reined in with some more practical guidance. At least two reasons were identified in *Sutcliffe*. The first was that excessively high awards had endangered the freedom of the press to investigate and report fearlessly on matters of public interest. Nourse LJ recognised the potential difficulty, but noted that not all press that attracted defamation proceedings deserved protection.[69] The second issue was more concrete. Since *Rookes v Barnard*, awards for damages could not have a punitive component in the absence of being specifically pleaded and falling within one of Lord Devlin's two categories where exemplary damages were allowed. Very large awards suggested, however, that this separation had not happened; both Russell LJ and Nourse LJ thought the jury must in practice have included a large punitive element in the award.[70] To allow de facto awards of exemplary damages was to defeat the logic of *Rookes v Barnard*. However, part of the problem lay in *Rookes* itself:[71]

> I cannot help thinking that the occasions on which exemplary damages are now claimed in defamation cases are rarer than the framers of the rule would have expected. More significantly, it is possible that they did not well appreciate the difficulties which its application would cause to juries, and perhaps to judges also.

The particular problem to which Nourse LJ was referring was the categorical distinction *Rookes* had drawn between aggravated (compensatory) and exemplary

[65] *McCarey* (n 61) 106.

[66] *Sutcliffe* (n 56) 178. See also the similar comments of Nourse LJ (185–86) and Russell LJ (190).

[67] eg, 'Despite the inflation which has occurred in the post-war years, sums of money of £100,000 or more, and in many cases less, still lack the reality of the £1 coin or the £5 note. In the lives of ordinary people they are unlikely ever to intrude except in the form of the nominal sale or purchase price of a house': *Sutcliffe* (n 56) 178.

[68] ibid 181–83.

[69] ibid 183.

[70] ibid 185 (Nourse LJ), 191 (Russell LJ).

[71] ibid 183 (Nourse LJ).

damages. Whatever the merits of the distinction post-*Rookes*, it is very doubtful that the pre-1964 cases lend themselves to the ex-post division into aggravated and exemplary awards that Lord Devin undertook. Prior to 1964, appellate review of jury awards under the high threshold set in the eighteenth-century cases took place with the possibility that the jury had taken aggravating factors into account in determining its award, either through an enhanced compensatory award for non-pecuniary loss or as a genuinely punitive measure. This greater latitude given to the jury made it even more difficult for appellate courts to find them excessive; Nourse LJ recognised as much in *Sutcliffe*. But in the post-*Rookes* world, exemplary components had to be dismissed from compensatory awards and, even if aggravated elements were present, the award could not stray beyond compensation.[72] Further, if, as Nourse LJ implicitly suggests, *Rookes* had been too successful in narrowing exemplary damages claims, the risk was that – wittingly or unwittingly – juries would nonetheless add a punitive element to the award. As long as the conditions for an award of aggravated damages existed through some discreditable conduct of the defendant, there might actually be a tactical advantage for a plaintiff in putting all the eggs in the aggravated damages basket even if an exemplary award might have been available because aggravated awards were not subject to the strictures *Rookes v Barnard* had imposed on the award of punitive damages. To avoid this result, the compensatory award, including any aggravated damages, needed to have some objective basis for review. This would then allow the court to say, as Nourse LJ did in *Sutcliffe*:[73]

> It is enough to say that we cannot, in a case where there is no claim for exemplary damages, uphold an award which, if it could have been upheld at all, could only have been upheld if there had been such a claim.

IV. GENERAL DAMAGES FOR PERSONAL INJURY AS A GUIDE FOR DAMAGES FOR NON-PECUNIARY LOSS?

One possibility for a standard for determining whether awards for exemplary damages, and other non-pecuniary loss more generally, were excessive was to compare the awards given by judges (almost exclusively since 1966) for non-pecuniary loss in personal injury cases. As is already evident, much of the impetus for reform came from defamation cases, and it was in that context that Diplock LJ suggested as far back as the mid-1960s that it was permissible for an appellate court to compare awards of non-pecuniary loss in personal injury

[72] N Sinanis, 'Punishment in Tort: The Context of Ideas in *Rookes v Barnard*' (2022) 15 *Journal of Tort Law* 29.

[73] *Sutcliffe* (n 56) 186.

cases with compensatory awards in defamation cases to determine whether a jury award in the latter case was excessive:[74]

> I do not believe that the law today is more jealous of a man's reputation than of his life or limb. That is the scale of values of the duel. Of course, the injuries in the two kinds of case are very different, but each has as its main consequences pain or grief, annoyance or unhappiness, to the plaintiff.

The other members of the Court of Appeal did not address the issue, finding the award excessive even under the restricted rules applying to review of jury verdicts, so Diplock LJ's approach was obiter. It suffered from the difficulty that compensatory awards in defamation actions were not simply about providing compensation for non-pecuniary loss; they had a vindicatory component that made direct comparisons with awards in personal injury actions difficult[75] and it also raised the question of whether there was any validity between comparing interferences with bodily integrity and reputation given the different interests at stake. Even though the Law Commission, in its 1993 Consultation Paper on Aggravated and Exemplary Damages, thought that punitive damages might, historically, have had some compensatory component, there is no reference to Diplock LJ's suggestions as a means of assisting in the calculation of the award. This is unsurprising as the Commission's preferred view was that exemplary damages were justified not just as a means of punishment but also as a vindication of certain rights and interests protected by certain torts.[76] This rationale was different from compensation so a tool devised for assisting in the calculation of compensatory damages would not obviously be useful in assessing punitive awards. But it is striking how little of the Consultation Paper dealt with the question of the assessment of awards of exemplary damages and the Commission's view seems primarily to have been that there were really no obvious comparators to assist in determining a 'correct' figure and that fixed awards created more difficulties than they solved. Yet the Commission noted at the commencement of the Consultation Paper the concerns over the 'discretion according to indeterminate principles' which determined the amount of an exemplary award.[77] Why did the Commission say so little on this point? The answer may lie in a decision of the Court of Appeal handed down just before the Consultation Paper was released, *Rantzen v Mirror Group Newspapers Ltd*,[78] which indicated that new powers given to the Court of Appeal to interfere with jury awards of damages could assist in providing consistency and moderation among awards. The case is mentioned a number of times in the

[74] *McCarey* (n 61) 109.
[75] *Cassell & Co Ltd v Broome* [1972] AC 1027 (HL) 1071 (Lord Hailsham).
[76] Law Commission, *Aggravated, Exemplary and Restitutionary Damages: A Consultation Paper* (Law Com CP No 132, 1993) paras 2.20–2.28.
[77] ibid para 1.6.
[78] *Rantzen v Mirror Group Newspapers Ltd* [1994] QB 670 (CA).

Consultation Paper and suggests the Commission saw this development as providing as good a mechanism as any for dealing with the criticisms directed at the quantum of exemplary awards.[79]

Rantzen involved a claim by the well-known television personality, Esther Rantzen, for libel in respect of allegations that she had protected a sexual abuser at a school who had helped her to expose other abuse at the school. The details are not important except to note that there was no claim for exemplary damages. The plaintiff was awarded £250,000 by the jury and the defendant appealed on the primary basis that the award was excessive. However, since the *Sutcliffe* case, an important statutory development had taken place. Section 8(2) of the Courts and Legal Services Act 1990 allowed for rules of court to provide for the Court of Appeal, in such classes of case as may be specified in Rules of Court, to have power, in place of ordering a new trial, to substitute for the sum awarded by the jury such sum as appeared to the court to be proper. The relevant Rule of Court was Order 59 Rule 11(4), which stated that in any case where the Court of Appeal had power to order a new trial on the ground that damages awarded by a jury were excessive or inadequate, the court could, instead of ordering a new trial, substitute for the sum awarded by the jury such sum as appeared to the court to be proper. In *Rantzen*, using this power, the Court of Appeal substituted an award of £110,000 for the jury's original verdict.

However, section 8(1) limited the powers in section 8(2) to situations where the Court of Appeal had power to order a new trial on the ground that the damages awarded by the jury were excessive or inadequate. It was for this reason that the Lord Chancellor, Lord Mackay, when introducing the provision at the Report State of the Courts and Legal Services Bill in the House of Lords, described it as a 'useful although not a major change in the law.'[80] In particular, Lord Mackay made it clear that the proposed clause did not change the grounds on which the Court of Appeal could interfere with jury awards of damages. This view of the language of section 8 was, unsurprisingly, adopted in *Rantzen*. But what made the Law Commission more confident about the effect of section 8 was the Court of Appeal's view in *Rantzen* that developments in the law outside of the reform made by section 8 required a re-evaluation of the threshold for when the Court of Appeal could interfere with jury awards of damages.

The driver for the reassessment of the threshold for interference was the risk that English law might not be compliant with Article 10 of the European Convention on Human Rights (the right to freedom of expression). While restrictions on the right were allowed, they had to be prescribed by law, and the Court of Appeal was concerned that the limited guidance given to juries, as well as the limited power of an appellate court to correct the award, would not meet this requirement.[81] As a consequence, the Court of Appeal held that

[79] Law Commission (n 76) paras 3.45, 3.59, 3.103, 5.36, 6.30.
[80] HL Deb 20 February 1990, vol 516, col 170.
[81] *Rantzen* (n 78) 689.

the meaning of 'excessive' in section 8 needed to be interpreted so as to ensure compliance of English law with Article 10:[82]

> We consider therefore that the common law if properly understood requires the courts to subject large awards of damages to a more searching scrutiny than has been customary in the past. It follows that what has been regarded as the barrier against intervention should be lowered. The question becomes: 'Could a reasonable jury have thought that this award was necessary to compensate the plaintiff and to re-establish his reputation?'

This dealt with the second concern that had been expressed – limited appellate review – but the Court of Appeal also took the opportunity of determining whether further guidance needed to be given to the jury before they calculated the award to be made. Like previous courts, the *Rantzen* Court thought that the jury should not be told about comparable awards in similar cases because those awards themselves might be unsound as they had been made without any or sufficient guidance of the kind the Court of Appeal was about to suggest. But awards made by the Court of Appeal exercising its powers under section 8 of the Courts and Legal Services Act 1990 stood on a different footing. It was permissible for these to be cited to the jury, especially when over time a sufficient corpus of awards would accumulate so as to provide meaningful guidance. However, as Hopkins noted, this 'sensible suggestion would carry more weight if the Court of Appeal had devoted more than one brief paragraph to explaining why it felt £110,000 to be a more appropriate figure'.[83]

The most difficult issue for the Court of Appeal was whether the jury should be referred to awards of general damages in personal injury actions, but ultimately the Court decided they should not. The component of compensatory awards in defamation cases, aimed at vindication of the plaintiff's reputation, was not replicated in general damages awards in personal injury cases so there was 'no satisfactory way in which the conventional awards in actions for damages for personal injuries can be used to provide guidance for an award in an action for defamation.'[84]

As noted, *Rantzen* was not a case about exemplary damages, but the approach to the interpretation of section 8 had, as the Law Commission recognised, ramifications for exemplary as well as compensatory awards. But there is something slightly odd about the Law Commission's thinking here. If the power given to the Court of Appeal under section 8 and the associated Rule of Court was the way that English law was to comply with ECHR requirements, this arguably required attention to both *ex ante* instructions to the jury from the trial judge and ex post appellate review. Moreover, in the context of compensatory awards, it made sense to see section 8 as having an ameliorative effect because juries were being told to consider the purchasing power of

[82] ibid 693.
[83] CA Hopkins, 'A Terrible (But Transient) Ordeal' [1994] *CLJ* 9, 11.
[84] *Rantzen* (n 78) 695.

money (and in the future previous awards approved by the Court of Appeal). In substituting awards, the Court of Appeal would be guided by the same considerations that guided (or ought to have guided) the jury in determining the award. But in the absence of any meaningful *ex ante* criteria for juries to consider in awarding exemplary damages, interference by the Court of Appeal with a jury award (in practice, by reducing it) could only be based on intuition. As the Commission noted, the measure of an exemplary award should reflect its purposes of punishment, deterrence, condemnation or symbolic indemnification, but recognised these were extremely difficult to value.[85] The only guidance it located from the cases was of limited value. The presence of a compensatory award and its possible punitive effect was clearly relevant to whether an exemplary award should be made at all – as was clear from *Rookes v Barnard* – but this gave little guidance as to what the amount of an exemplary award should be if one could be made. And exhortations by judges to juries that exemplary awards should be moderate provided no effective guidance in the absence of giving any standard for determining moderation. Almost as an afterthought, the Commission noted the effect of *Sutcliffe* and *Rantzen*:[86]

> In the context of compensatory awards, it was said that juries should not only be invited to consider the purchasing power of any award they made, but should also be asked to ensure that it was proportionate to the damage which the plaintiff had suffered. It should be possible to give similar guidance in the case of exemplary awards.

Thus, even though the purpose of compensatory and exemplary awards was categorically different, the means through which jury awards were to be controlled could be same.

V. THE REACTION TO THE JURY VERDICT IN *JOHN v MGN LTD*

Rantzen was decided only a few months before the jury verdict at the trial of *John v MGN Ltd.* Immediately the decision came out, there was considerable press criticism of the amount of the award. In an editorial, the *Daily Mail* questioned 'the amount of the damages as wholly disproportionate to the wrong committed'[87] and Auberon Waugh in *The Telegraph* thought that 'all precedent seems to go out of the window as soon as you give modern jurors freedom to award any sum they like'.[88] The *Sunday Times*, while recognising the judge had

[85] Law Commission (n 76) para 3.87.

[86] ibid para 3.103. In *Riches v News Group Newspapers Ltd* [1986] QB 256 (CA) 282, Parker LJ thought the fact that the exemplary award was eighty-three times compensatory damages 'suggest strongly that something must have gone seriously wrong, for the punishment must bear some reasonable relation to the gravity of the "crime"'.

[87] 'Overcompensation – Daily Mail Comment', *Daily Mail*, 5 November 1993, 8.

[88] A Waugh, 'Way of the World – Unpopularity Explained', *The Telegraph*, 8 November 1993, 21.

done his best to keep the jury award moderate, thought the award 'nonsense' and that juries were encouraged to think hurt feelings alone deserve big cash handouts.[89] Matthew Bond in *The Times* portrayed John as a serial litigator milking the system:[90]

> The jury, though, was sympathetic, very sympathetic, and awarded him a comforting £350,000 in damages. Having picked up a distinctly addictive £1.4 million in legal settlements in five years, John has taken swift action – he's just joined Litigants Anonymous. (No, I know that's not true either, Elton, it's a joke).

The criticism by the *Daily Mirror* itself was more pointed. In three pieces shortly after the verdict, it expressly drew a contrast between awards made to victims of personal injury and the John award. In a provocative headline, with an accompanying picture, the paper detailed the story of a young mother who had lost her arm and who, after six years, recovered £54,000. The paper noted that in personal injury cases there were guidelines for amounts to be awarded for injury but that judges 'cannot direct juries on the amount of damages' in libel claims. In the editorial included in the article, the paper concluded 'Most reasonable people will ask why there should be such a difference between an ordinary person and a pop star.'[91] The same theme was contained in a published letter a few days later, comparing the low amount for a personal injury claim (£3,250), and the seven years it took to get, with the John award, and concluding 'There's no justice in these things.'[92] And the final piece noted the contrast between payments under the Criminal Injuries Compensation Scheme (here to the parents of a 12-year-old child killed in the IRA bombing in Warrington) and John's award. Even though it was unrelated, the article also included a list of conventional awards in personal injury actions in civil courts. The conclusion was familiar: '*It just doesn't seem right, does it?*'[93]

It is impossible to see this campaign as anything other than an attack on the Court of Appeal's decision in *Rantzen* to prevent judges from telling libel juries about the value of conventional awards in personal injury actions. The pressure was building and support came from another source. In July 1995, in *Tolstoy v UK*, the European Court of Human Rights held that an award of £1.5 million in a libel action was not proportionate to any damage suffered by the plaintiff resulting in a breach of Article 10.[94] The Court affirmed the criticisms that the Court of Appeal in *Rantzen* had made of the limited scope of appellate review of jury awards of damages. It noted, without endorsement,

[89] A Peter, 'Laughter Before Litigation', *Sunday Times*, 7 November 1993, 13.

[90] M Bond, 'Diary – On a Point of Disorder', *The Times*, 6 November 1993, 16. See also T Parsons, 'As Rockers Take to the Courts – The Real Scandal', *The Telegraph*, 11 November 1993, 14.

[91] P Wilson and T O'Hanlon, 'It Took Six Years to Get £54,000 for Losing my Arm. What Has Elton John Lost to Deserve £350,000?', *Daily Mirror*, 7 November 1993, 7.

[92] 'Justice is Out of Tune', *Daily Mirror*, 12 November 1993, 26.

[93] J Kerr, '£7,500: The Value of Bomb Victim Tim's Life', *Daily Mirror*, 28 November 1993, 5.

[94] *Tolstoy Miloslavsky v The United Kingdom* (1995) 20 EHRR 442 [51].

the approach advocated in *Rantzen*, holding simply that the law at the time of the award was non-compliant.[95] The Court did not accept the alternative argument of the applicant that the lack of guidance to juries meant that the potential liability of a libel defendant could not be calculated, so that any restriction on Article 10 consisting of libel damages was not prescribed by law.[96] But as *Tolstoy* did not involve a claim for exemplary damages, it was not clear whether the green light given to the approach to compensatory awards would extend to exemplary awards.

VI. *JOHN v MGN LTD* IN THE COURT OF APPEAL

MGN Ltd appealed on the quantum of both the compensatory and exemplary award. Lead counsel for MGN Ltd was Charles Gray QC, who had also appeared for the newspaper in *Rantzen*. While there were similarities in the arguments run in the two cases, there were also important differences. Even though the Court of Appeal in *Rantzen* considered whether the jury should be referred to amounts awarded in personal injury actions, if the report of counsel's argument in the *Law Reports* is to be believed, this was not canvassed by either counsel. In *John*, however, Gray expressly submitted that public policy required a rational relationship between such awards. Exemplary damages were subjected to a withering attack: they were not justified, large awards violated Article 10, and whatever the position for compensatory damages, the inability to provide any *ex ante* guidance for an exemplary award meant such damages were anomalous.[97]

When the Court of Appeal delivered its judgment, however, the lengthiest part concentrated on the question of compensatory damages (nine pages of the judgment compared to three on exemplary damages). Evocatively, the jury was described as being 'in the position of sheep loosed on an unfenced common, with no shepherd'.[98] As a result, and even though the Court of Appeal in *Rantzen* had rejected references to personal injury awards being given to the jury less than three years earlier, the question could be reconsidered because:[99]

> [T]here is continuing evidence of libel awards in sums which appear so large as to bear no relation to the ordinary values of life. This is most obviously unjust to defendants. But it serves no public purpose to encourage plaintiffs to regard a successful libel action, risky though the process undoubtedly is, as a road to untaxed riches. Nor is it healthy if any legal process fails to command the respect of lawyer and layman alike, as is regrettably true of the assessment of damages by libel juries.

[95] ibid [50].
[96] ibid [44].
[97] *John* (n 1) 592.
[98] ibid 608.
[99] ibid 611.

Despite the apparent affirmation of the *ex ante* guidance given to defamation juries, almost everything *Rantzen* rejected was allowed in *John*. Apart from references to previous awards – which had been reached without the now appropriate guidance – the jury should now be told about awards in personal injury actions:[100]

> The conventional compensatory scales in personal injury cases must be taken to represent fair compensation in such cases unless and until those scales are amended by the courts or by Parliament. It is in our view offensive to public opinion, and rightly so, that a defamation plaintiff should recover damages for injury to reputation greater, perhaps by a significant factor, than if that same plaintiff had been rendered a helpless cripple or an insensate vegetable.

This was, of course, the argument that had been run by the *Mirror* in the aftermath of the jury award. The Court of Appeal also accepted that brackets within which the award might fall could be suggested to the jury by counsel and the trial judge,[101] and, like in *Rantzen*, that Court of Appeal awards made in the exercise of powers under section 8 of the Courts and Legal Services Act 1990 could also be mentioned.[102] Even though the European Court of Human Rights had been more sanguine about the adequacy of the jury instructions, the Court of Appeal expressly decried any reliance on Convention jurisprudence in reaching its conclusions even if it thought they were consistent with such jurisprudence.[103]

When the Court came to consider exemplary damages, a different approach was taken. Even though both the discussion of compensatory and exemplary damages is contained in a section entitled 'The principles of law relating to damages in defamation', the section on compensatory damages is almost exclusively on the calculation of the award. Conversely, most of the discussion on exemplary damages is about the circumstances in which an award can be made (in this case, focusing on the elements of Lord Devlin's second category). When it came to quantum, the Court of Appeal simply noted that the authorities 'give judges no help in directing juries on the quantum of exemplary damages'.[104] The only guidance formally offered was that the award should never exceed the minimum sum necessary to meet the public purpose underlying such damages – that of punishing the defendant – showing that tort does not pay and deterring others. The same result was reached under Article 10. Yet the Court's final statement – 'Freedom of speech should not be restricted by awards of exemplary damages save to the extent shown to be strictly necessary for the protection of reputations' – does little to add clarity.[105] Although the language used is that of Article 10, the protection of reputations might largely be seen as being covered

[100] ibid 614.
[101] ibid 615–16.
[102] ibid 612.
[103] ibid 619.
[104] ibid.
[105] ibid.

by compensatory damages. And when the Court of Appeal went to analyse the amount of the exemplary award of £275,000, it did so in one paragraph, simply asserting that an amount of £50,000 would fully meet the requirements of punishment and deterrence.[106] The contrast between the lengthy exposition and application of the law on compensatory awards, and the brief review of the exemplary award, is striking.[107]

In hindsight, *John* is important for the calculation of exemplary damages for at least two reasons. The first, and more patent, is that the Court of Appeal simply decided that there was no *ex ante* guidance that could meaningfully be given to the jury. Unlike compensatory damages, exemplary damages would have to be kept under control by post-trial review and, if necessary, substitution by the Court of Appeal under section 8 of the 1990 Act. But the second reason *John* is important is that, in a different way, *John* revealed this to perhaps be only superficially correct. In truth, many of the wider reasons that supported greater control of compensatory awards in defamation actions applied equally to exemplary awards. It is no surprise that the *Mirror* in its campaign after the jury verdict in *John* drew no distinction between the compensatory and exemplary components of the award. If awards as a whole were too large, then something needed to be done to keep awards as a whole under control. Outside appellate review, there were only two possibilities for the exemplary component of the award.

The first was to rethink the role of the jury in awarding damages. In a penetrating analysis of *John*, Paul Mitchell noted the 'inadequate basis' for the constitutional place of civil juries in libel claims.[108] But the immediate post-*John* cases, like the contributions to the debate on the Supreme Court Bill, show just how difficult this change was in practice. In *Kiam v Neil (No 2)*,[109] Beldam LJ, after citing Bingham MR's comments on giving brackets to the jury, noted:[110]

> It is, I think, necessary to bear in mind that Parliament has repeatedly declined to attenuate the right of a plaintiff who claims trial by jury in a libel action. Unless the complexity of the documents or the issues involved make it unsuitable, the plaintiff is entitled to trial by jury. Whilst it is tempting to think that the greater the guidance given by judges, the more rational the jury's conclusion is likely to be, it seems to me that if the failure of the jury to keep its award within bounds indicated by a judge gives rise merely to the possibility that their judgment is to be preferred to that of the judge, the court may appear to preserve only the semblance of a right which Parliament has repeatedly affirmed … At present it remains the plaintiff's constitutional right …

[106] ibid 626.

[107] I Loveland, 'Reforming Libel Law: The Public Law Dimension' (1997) 46 *International and Comparative Law Quarterly* 561, 570–71.

[108] Mitchell (n 19).

[109] *Kiam v Neil (No 2)* [1996] EMLR 493 (CA).

[110] ibid 507.

The constitutional position of the jury was also fiercely defended by Henry LJ in *Clark v Chief Constable of Cleveland Police*.[111] Unlike the cases discussed above, this was not a defamation case but involved trespass to the person. Henry LJ did not accept that the standard of review for appellate courts of jury awards of damages had been lowered by section 8 other than in defamation cases (where Article 10 was relevant). In his view, these were arguments on the constitutional position of the jury.[112] Less directly, the increased guidance to the juries, ostensibly for compensatory awards, also did not attract universal approval. While the High Court of Australia had by the time of *John* come round to recommending comparison with personal injury awards be given to libel juries,[113] the New Zealand Court of Appeal took a different view in *Television NZ Ltd v Quinn*.[114] More broadly, the Privy Council in 2004 refused to find that the Court of Appeal of Jamaica was in error in declining to allow the jury to be told this information.[115] This was a matter of policy for the courts in Jamaica.[116] The hope too that the 'corpus' of Court of Appeal mandated awards might provide guidance was also proving somewhat illusory: by 2002 that corpus amounted to six cases.[117] As Simon Brown LJ noted in *Kiam v MGN Ltd*, there was a tension in the authorities: on the one hand, stressing the limits on jury awards by increasing guidance whilst on the other continuing to place emphasis on the importance of the jury's role in assessing damages.[118] The end result of this tension, as Lloyd-Bostock and Thomas observe more generally about jury reform, was that changes to the jury system tended to be piecemeal and incremental rather than sweeping,[119] and depriving the jury of its power to assess damages could be seen as going too far towards abolition rather than mere reform.

If juries could not be prevented from assessing damages, the only other option was to be more prescriptive in the amounts that the jury could award. While *John* had allowed for bands to be cited to the jury, Bingham MR was

[111] *Clark v Chief Constable of Cleveland Police* (CA, 7 May 1999).

[112] ibid (sections 1 and 2 of the judgment of Henry LJ).

[113] *Coyne v Citizen Finance Ltd* (1991) 172 CLR 211 (HCA); *Carson v John Fairfax & Sons Ltd* (1993) 178 CLR 44 (HCA). On the international position, see J Gotanda, 'Punitive Damages: A Comparative Analysis' (2004) 42 *Columbia Journal of Transnational Law* 391.

[114] *Television NZ Ltd v Quinn* [1996] 3 NZLR 24 (CA).

[115] *The Gleaner Co Ltd v Abrahams* [2003] UKPC 55, [2004] 1 AC 628.

[116] ibid 649. Although a detailed comparative analysis is beyond the scope of this chapter, the civil jury retains its advocates in the old Dominion jurisdictions: R Brown and M Yahya, 'Respecting Civil Juries' (2005) 30 *Advocates Quarterly* 110; J Horan, 'Perceptions of the Civil Jury System' (2005) 31 *Monash University Law Review* 120. Conversely, for an argument that the *John* guidance could usefully be incorporated into guidance for US juries, see C Cole, 'Charging the Jury on Damages in Personal-Injury Cases: How New York Can Benefit from the English Practice' (2004) 31 *Syracuse Journal of International Law and Commerce* 1.

[117] *Kiam v MGN Ltd* [2002] EWCA Civ 43, [2003] QB 281, 293.

[118] ibid.

[119] S Lloyd-Bostock and C Thomas, 'Decline of the "Little Parliament": Juries and Jury Reform in England and Wales, (1999) 62 *Law and Contemporary Problems* 7, 11.

careful to stress that these remained guidelines and that 'real weight' had to be given the possibility that a jury award outside the recommended band was to be preferred to that of the judge.[120] But this was taken further, in the context of both compensatory and exemplary damages, in *Thompson v Commissioner of the Police for the Metropolis*.[121] Spurred by some of the same factors that had influenced the Court of Appeal in *John* (largely an increase in the level of jury awards in trespass to the person and malicious prosecution actions against the police),[122] the Court of Appeal set out specific bands, including caps, for awards in false imprisonment and malicious prosecution actions against the police. Recognising that there may be good reasons for keeping juries in these types of case, it was counterproductive to give juries an 'impossible task'.[123] Thus concrete figures were provided for compensatory, aggravated and exemplary components of awards in these cases: for exemplary awards, these would start at £5,000 (anything lower would mean the case was not one for which an exemplary award was justified at all), £25,000 could only be justified for conduct particularly deserving of condemnation, and £50,000 regarded as the absolute maximum involving conduct of senior police officers.

There is nothing explicit in *Thompson* linking the setting of the guideline figures to amounts of general damages in personal injury cases, but the amounts set were below what would be awarded for the most serious personal injuries. Given the different purpose of exemplary awards, the reasonable relationship with personal injury awards was not required as a matter of legal logic. But legal coherence was not the only factor at play here. The fact remained (and remains) that punitive awards are received by the claimant in exactly the same way as a purely compensatory award. The practical reality is that a claimant in receipt of an exemplary award receives a higher award as a consequence of the tort committed against her than one who receives only compensatory damages. It was to this dissonance that the *Daily Mirror's* campaign against the *John* award was implicitly targeted: John's total package of 'compensation' – the total damages he received as a result of the tort – was disproportionate to what other, seemingly more seriously injured plaintiffs, were receiving for their injuries. The dissatisfaction with this discrepancy was at the heart of the challenge to jury verdicts: whatever once was the constitutional significance of jury awards, they needed now to conform to broad notions of distributive justice where compensation for serious physical or emotional harms attracted the most compensation. That could only be done by linking both compensatory and exemplary awards to conventional awards of non-pecuniary loss in some notional way. It is striking that this trend extended beyond defamation and

[120] *John* (n 1) 616.
[121] *Thompson v Commissioner of the Police for the Metropolis* [1998] QB 498 (CA).
[122] S Tendler, 'Yard wants court to set limits on damages payouts', *The Times*, 7 May 1996, 3.
[123] *Thompson* (n 121) 513.

trespass to the person cases and beyond jury trials: in 2002 the Court of Appeal set three bands (with caps) for injury to feelings in discrimination cases.[124] By 2013, in *Cairns v Modi*, the Court of Appeal could note that it was 'conventional' to recognise a ceiling for compensatory damages in defamation actions 'corresponding to the current maximum level of damages for pain and suffering and loss of amenity in personal injury cases'.[125]

Tariffs also received the approval of the Law Commission when it released its final report on Aggravated, Exemplary and Restitutionary Damages in 1997. But this formed part of the Commission's wider recommendation that the availability and assessment of punitive damages should always be for the judge and not a jury.[126] Paradoxically, the Commission saw the creation of tariffs through judicial development as analogous to that for compensatory damages, and that once a tariff had emerged, the assessment of punitive damages might be no more unpredictable 'than the assessment of damages for, say, personal injury.'[127] There the similarities ended: the tariff that was to be judicially created had its own value scale. The Commission was far less clear on how those value scales were converted into concrete figures. The state of mind of the defendant, the nature of the right or rights infringed by the defendant, the nature and extent of the harm the defendant intended to cause the plaintiff, any benefit the defendant derived or intended to derive from the plaintiff, and – tellingly – any other matter which the judge in his or her discretion considers to be relevant.[128] The overarching factors, however, that should inform awards were moderation and proportionality.[129] For moderation, Bingham MR's short statement in *John*, discussed above, was cited but only for the (very) general proposition that the award had to balance the need for the award to punish and deter against the threatened or actual interference with the defendant's civil liberties due to the award. Little wonder the Commission argued in favour of tariffs to give some substance to this approach. But tariffs have to start from some base. Whether intended or not, the association of conventional awards in personal injury action with compensatory awards in *John* also provided a de facto comparator for exemplary damages awards, even where judges rather than juries were involved. The analogy was crude but not meaningless. And even if the connection was only implicit, can it be doubted that the fact that the exemplary award in *John* went beyond the maximum non-pecuniary award to a person rendered a helpless cripple or an insensate vegetable contributed to the finding that the award was excessive?

[124] *Vento v Chief Constable of West Yorkshire Police* [2002] EWCA Civ 1871, [2003] ICR 318.
[125] *Cairns v Modi* [2012] EWCA Civ 1382, [2013] 1 WLR 1015 [25].
[126] Law Commission, *Aggravated, Exemplary and Restitutionary Damages* (Law Com No 247, 1997) para 5.90.
[127] ibid para 5.92.
[128] ibid paras 5.125–28.
[129] ibid para 5.120.

VII. CONCLUSION

Perhaps this chapter has taken a very long time to make a simple point. When we are dealing with incommensurables, there are choices that have to be made in determining what price we are going to put on them, if put a price on them we must. Historically, the choice made in the common law when it came to damages claims for aggravated harm was to leave it to the jury to value. Appellate review when it became possible was understandably hesitant: how could judges decide any better than the jury? This position was reinforced when the civil jury was endowed with constitutional status. But by the late twentieth century, civil juries no longer held the rhetorical sway they once did. Judges replaced juries in personal injury actions, and with judges came greater emphasis on comparability. Where juries held on, their verdicts, once sacrosanct, could now be said generally to compare unfavourably to assessment by judge alone.[130]

It might have been best if at this point civil juries did the honourable thing and quietly died out as assessors of quantum but, as they did not, the next best thing that could be done was for juries to behave as if they were judges. *John v MGN Ltd* was the culmination of that approach in the context of awards of compensatory and exemplary damages in defamation actions.[131] While detailed guidance to the jury was approved for compensatory damages, my argument is that the same logic seeped into appellate review of the award of exemplary damages. It is worth remembering that the reduction in the exemplary award in *John* was higher than for the compensatory award. 'Moderation' needed to have some content, and there is no reason to think that the purchasing power of money, or conventional awards in personal injury actions – now allowed by *John* – did not inform the assessment of exemplary awards for juries as much as for judges. The path-breaking study of Goudkamp and Katsampouka of awards of exemplary damages in the first 16 years of the twenty-first century – after *John* had been decided – reveals that awards were relatively modest.[132] They are certainly modest by reference to awards of general damages in personal injury actions.

[130] Devlin (n 39) ch 6.

[131] And as a result, allow their constitutional position to be reinforced: A Kenyon, 'Problems with Defamation Damages' (1998) 24 *Monash University Law Review* 70, 93.

[132] J Goudkamp and E Katsampouka, 'An Empirical Study of Punitive Damages' (2018) 38 *OJLS* 90, 91–92.

9

Gray v Motor Accident Commission (1998)

Does the Criminal Punishment of the Defendant Bar Exemplary Damages? Questions Answered and Unanswered

FELICITY MAHER

I. INTRODUCTION

THE DECISION OF the High Court of Australia in *Gray v Motor Accident Commission*[1] was the fifth decision of that apex court on exemplary damages in 33 years. *Gray* is a landmark case, not only for the questions it answers, but also for those which were left for another day. Although the High Court declined to opine definitively on several issues which were raised by the parties, but unnecessary to decide on the facts, the Court sent some important signals about how those issues might be decided. *Gray* is also a long case, at some 52 pages. Most of those pages are dedicated to discussion of the issues which were not decided.

Of the questions which the High Court did answer in *Gray*, some were old, and some were new. The old questions, which had been considered by Australian courts before, concerned the availability of exemplary damages in negligence cases and in cases where the wrongdoer is insured against liability for exemplary damages, and the distinction between exemplary damages and aggravated damages. The new questions, which had not previously been judicially considered in detail in Australia, concerned the significance of the defendant's punishment by the criminal law for the conduct said to give rise to exemplary

[1] *Gray v Motor Accident Commission* (1998) 196 CLR 1 (HCA).

damages, and the role of discretion in the award of exemplary damages, both where there has been criminal punishment, and generally.

The unanswered questions arose out of these issues and are inseparable from them. But they also concern broader, more fundamental issues, including the purposes and proper place of exemplary damages in the civil law: what *are* the purposes of exemplary damages? Is there any *hierarchy* of purposes, some being primary and others secondary? *Should* exemplary damages have any place in the civil law? In turn, what are the functions of the civil law and the criminal law? Is the civil law concerned *only* with compensation, not punishment? And is the criminal law the *exclusive* home for punishment? As we will see, the strong signal sent by the High Court in *Gray* is that, although exemplary damages may be anomalous, in Australia, they are here to stay.

The decision in *Gray* is, accordingly, a prime example of the exercise of judicial caution. Such restraint was a guiding philosophy of the High Court or, at least, several of its members at the time and in the years that followed.[2] As a landmark decision of the final appellate court in Australia, it has attracted surprisingly little commentary. It has been lightly criticised by some, for its tentative, non-committal and unconvincing answers given to even the questions which were decided. It has also been suggested that the decision represents an *excess* of judicial caution; that the Court deferred all the difficult questions and would have been better to defer everything, or nothing.[3] The decision does indicate the need for further discussion about the proper role of the highest court in the land, and the merits of restraint.

Notwithstanding these doubts, the High Court's answers to the questions it did give have had a real-world impact, even beyond the parties. For example, the confirmation of the availability of exemplary damages in negligence cases, where the wrongdoer is insured against such liability, prompted some legislative responses.[4] But perhaps the most important observation which can be made of *Gray* is that it demonstrates that the resolution of most issues in relation to exemplary damages depends on the view taken of the *purposes* of the remedy. This is a theme emerging across this collection.

[2] Most notably, Heydon J (who joined the High Court five years after *Gray* was decided, in 2003): JD Heydon, 'Judicial Activism and the Death of the Rule of Law' (2003) 47 *Quadrant* 9.

[3] See, eg, A Gray, 'Punitive Damages: Time for Re-examination' (2018) 26 *Tort Law Review* 18, 36; J Manning, '*Daniels v Thompson*: Double Punishment or Double Trouble?' [1998] *New Zealand Law Review* 721, 740.

[4] Various State and Territory and Commonwealth statutes limit or preclude exemplary damages in negligence cases. See the summary of statutory interventions in F Maher, 'An Empirical Study of Exemplary Damages in Australia' (2019) 43 *Melbourne University Law Review* 694, 700–03. Also see BW Collis, '"Tort and Punishment" – Exemplary Damages: the Australian Experience' (1996) 70 *Australian Law Journal* 47, 52; M Tilbury, 'Exemplary Negligence in Negligence Claims' (1997) 5 *Tort Law Review* 85, 87; Gray (n 3) 25; R Mulheron, 'The Availability of Exemplary Damages in Negligence' (2000) 4 *Macquarie Law Review* 61, 85; *Review of the Law of Negligence: Final Report* (Canberra, Canprint Communications Pty Ltd, 2002) para 13.165. Under this legislation, the remedy is unavailable in many negligence cases, involving personal injury, workplace injury, motor vehicle accidents, and generally. The remedy is also excluded where the wrongdoer is insured. Some of this

The purposes of exemplary damages have been identified in various cases, and by commentators, and are also discussed in other contributions to the collection.[5] They include, principally, punishment and deterrence. In particular, the punitive rationale of the remedy is concerned with retribution, or 'just desserts'. It is backwards-looking. The deterrent rational has two aspects. The first, so-called specific deterrence, relates to the defendant. The second, so-called general deterrence, relates to the conduct. Together, the remedy seeks to deter the defendant and the public at large, from repeating the conduct, or conduct like it. Seen through the lens of this purpose, exemplary damages seek to influence behaviour. Deterrence, unlike punishment, is forward-looking. Punishment and deterrence are often described as the 'primary' purposes of exemplary damages. Either separately or together, they are usually treated as sufficient to justify the remedy. Further purposes of exemplary damages have also been identified. These include vindication – or appeasement – and denunciation.[6] The former is concerned with the interests and attitude of the plaintiff. The remedy has been said to 'assuage any urge for revenge felt by victims' and to 'discourage any temptation to engage in self-help likely to endanger the peace'.[7] The latter is concerned with disapproving the conduct of the defendant.[8] Exemplary damages are viewed as a vehicle to express the condemnation of the court, and society generally, and to permit 'just censure' of the defendant. These purposes of the remedy are usually seen as secondary, and not sufficient – either separately or together – to justify an award of exemplary damages.

It is self-evident that the resolution of most issues depends on one's starting point. In this context, the starting point is an understanding of the purposes – the functions and rationale – of exemplary damages. The answer to that question – *What is (are) the purpose(s) of the remedy?* – will largely determine the answers to more specific questions, including those considered by the High Court in

legislation pre-dated *Gray*. But at least one statutory intervention appears to have come about as a direct response to the *Gray* litigation. s 113A of the Motor Vehicle Act 1959 (SA) was introduced when the High Court's decision, on appeal from the South Australian Supreme Court, was awaited: see Statutes Amendment (Motor Accident) Act 1998 (SA), s 6. *Gray* was heard by the High Court on 28 May 1998 and the decision was handed down on 17 November 1998.

[5] See the discussion in, eg, B Feldthusen, 'Punitive Damages: Hard Choices and High Stakes' [1998] *New Zealand Law Review* 741, 750; J Manning, 'Reflections on Exemplary Damages and Personal Injury Liability in New Zealand' [2002] *New Zealand Law Review* 143, 148–52; P Walker, 'Vicarious Liability for Exemplary Damages: a Matter of Strict Liability?' (2009) 83 *Australian Law Journal* 548, 549–51; R Mulheron, 'Exemplary Damages and Tort: An International Comparison' (2000) 2 *University of Notre Dame Australia Law Review* 17, 27–28; C Sharkey 'Punitive Damages Transformed into Societal Damages' in E Bant et al (eds), *Punishment and Private Law* (Oxford, Hart Publishing, 2021) 157–61; K Barnett, 'Exemplary Damages in Contract Law' in E Bant et al (eds), *Punishment and Private Law* (Oxford, Hart Publishing, 2021) 228–35.

[6] N Witzleb and R Carroll, 'The Role of Vindication in Torts Damages' (2009) 17 *Tort Law Review* 16, 27–28.

[7] *Lamb v Cotogno* (1987) 164 CLR 1 (HCA) 9.

[8] *Australian Building and Construction Commissioner v Construction, Forestry, Mining and Energy Union* [2018] HCA 3, (2018) 262 CLR 157 [117].

Gray. If one takes the view, for example, that the only or main purpose of exemplary damages is the deterrence of others, irrespective of the punishment or deterrence of the defendant, then there is less objection to the availability of exemplary damages where the wrongdoer is insured. It will matter less that, because of the insurance, the wrongdoer personally may not suffer any – or at least, any pecuniary – detriment as a result of the remedy. Likewise, on this view, there may be no need to restrict exemplary damages to cases involving intentional conduct, which could be said to be most deserving of punishment, or to exclude the remedy where the defendant has already been punished by the criminal law.

The thesis of this chapter is that, in the analysis of the questions which arose in *Gray*, and in relation to exemplary damages generally, we must start with the purposes of the remedy. In every case, the question should be: will the award of exemplary damages serve the identified purpose or purposes of the remedy? Have they already been achieved, or will they fail to be achieved, if an award is made? Accepting that the court has a *discretion* in all cases may best facilitate this approach. In *Gray*, the High Court rejected a discretion to award exemplary damages in all cases and appeared to recognise the legitimacy of each of the purposes of exemplary damages identified earlier.[9] The insight – that the resolution of the issues before the Court turned on its understanding of the purposes of the remedy – will also expose that the Court may not always have been consistent in its analysis.

With this insight in mind, this chapter focuses on the first main question answered by the High Court in *Gray*, namely, the significance of criminal punishment of the defendant for the conduct in relation to which exemplary damages are sought. It places that question in the context of the broader questions to which the decision gives rise, as well as leading cases and influential commentary in Australia and other jurisdictions. Space does not permit a detailed analysis of the other main question answered by the High Court, namely the availability of exemplary damages for negligence. This issue is considered, by reference to the decision of the Supreme Court of New Zealand in *Couch v Attorney-General (No 2)*,[10] in another contribution to this collection.[11] Nor does space permit consideration of three further questions answered by the High Court, regarding insurance,[12] aggravated damages and discretion. Section II of the chapter summarises the facts and conclusions in *Gray*. And section III considers the question of the significance of criminal punishment of the defendant for the conduct in relation to which exemplary damages are sought.

[9] As noted by J Edelman, 'Exemplary Damages Revisited' (1999) 7 *Tort Law Review* 87, 89–90.
[10] *Couch v Attorney-General (No 2)* [2010] NZSC 27, [2010] 3 NZLR 149.
[11] Todd, ch 15 of this volume.
[12] Also considered in another contribution to this collection: see Barker, ch 6 of this volume.

II. THE DECISION IN *GRAY*

A. Facts and History of the Proceedings

Donald Gray was an Aboriginal Australian. On 9 September 1988, aged just 16 years old, he was badly injured when he was struck by a car driven by Darren Bransden.[13] At the relevant time, Mr Gray was one of a group of young pedestrians near the junction of Grange Terrace and Gawler Street in Salisbury, Adelaide. Mr Bransden was near his car. The car was stationary. He was not occupying it. The group went past and away from Mr Bransden. He then got in his car and pursued the group driving his vehicle towards them. He drove directly at two of them on the left-hand side of the road. They jumped clear. Mr Gray was on Mr Bransden's right. Mr Bransden changed course and drove his vehicle directly towards Mr Gray. He did so with the intention of running him down and really hurting him. He succeeded.[14]

Mr Bransden was charged with the criminal offence of intentionally causing grievous bodily harm to Mr Gray. He was tried, convicted and sentenced to seven years' imprisonment. In his sentencing remarks, the trial judge described the attack as 'brutal and cowardly' and one for which there was 'no mitigating factor at all'.[15]

Subsequently, Mr Gray brought civil proceedings against Mr Bransden in the District Court of South Australia, claiming damages for negligence. The claim was not framed in terms of trespass to the person, but the relief claimed included exemplary damages.

Mr Bransden was insured, pursuant to the compulsory third-party insurance provisions of the Motor Vehicles Act 1959 (SA). The insurer was the Motor Accident Commission. Under that legislation, the Commission was substituted as defendant in the District Court proceedings. Section 125A(3)(a) of the 1959 Act provided that the Commission was taken to have

[13] It appears that Bransden was something of a hardened criminal. At around the same time as the attack on Gray, he was charged with (and later convicted of) two separate counts of armed robbery in company. Both concerned bank hold-ups in which he and his associates made away with, in the first case, A$22,109 and, in the second, A$36,689. Several years earlier, Bransden had also been convicted of inflicting grievous bodily harm on a three-month-old baby girl he had violently shaken in anger. An issue in that case was whether, at trial, he had been improperly cross-examined on further prior convictions: *R v Bransden* [1981] 27 SASR 474 (SC). In a later appeal in relation to his convictions for armed robbery, the Court observed that Bransden had a 'long string of prior convictions' and a 'bad record of previous offending, a record which indicates that he has not learnt by his encounters with the law in the past': *R v Bransden* (Supreme Court of South Australia, Court of Criminal Appeal, 18 June 1990, King CJ, Legoe and Olsson JJ). See also *Gray v Motor Accident Commission* [1998] HCATrans 199 ('Gray Transcript') 25 (Gleeson CJ) ('the trial judge here was not dealing with a person who was likely to be responsive to deterrence by way of economic imposition: he was a man with convictions for armed robbery; his life was a life of crime, although he was only a relatively young man').

[14] Gray Transcript (n 13) 10.

[15] *Gray* (n 1) 3.

> directly assumed the liability (if any) of the insured person upon the claim in respect of ... bodily injury and, where such a liability is found to exist, judgment upon that claim will be given not against the insured person but against the insurer...

The District Court trial was presided over by Judge Pirone. Instead of proving the facts by witness testimony and other evidence, the parties, by consent, tendered the record of the criminal proceedings (including the sentencing remarks) against Mr Bransden.[16] It was not disputed at trial that Mr Bransden had been negligent. Indeed, it was not contested that his conduct had been deliberate. The judge found that Mr Bransden had the intention of running down Mr Gray, and seriously hurting him.[17] The judge opined that exemplary damages were available in a case like this, despite its not having been framed in trespass, and notwithstanding that the defendant was the insurer, rather than the tortfeasor.[18] Further, he assessed those damages at A$10,000.[19] However, the judge ultimately declined to award exemplary damages on the basis of the decision of the Tasmanian Supreme Court in *Watts v Leitch*.[20] In that case it had been held that exemplary damages are a discretionary remedy and, where the defendant has already been punished by the criminal law, the discretion should be exercised to refuse an award. Following *Watts v Leitch*, Judge Pirone refused to award exemplary damages because Mr Bransden had been sentenced to a substantial period of imprisonment for the same conduct.[21]

Mr Gray appealed to the South Australian Supreme Court. Justices Millhouse, Bollen and Williams dismissed the appeal.[22] Their Honours agreed with the trial judge that the Court had a discretion to award exemplary damages and, following *Watts v Leitch*, where the defendant had already been punished by the criminal law, the Court should exercise that discretion to refuse the remedy. Accordingly, the judge had properly exercised his discretion and the Supreme Court would not interfere.[23]

B. The Conclusions of the High Court

Mr Gray then appealed to the High Court.[24] There were three judgments: the plurality, consisting of Gleeson CJ, McHugh, Gummow and Hayne JJ; and

[16] Gray Transcript (n 13) 11–13. It appears that this course was adopted, in part, because, as a result of the attack, Mr Gray suffered from amnesia in relation to the events of that day: ibid 11, 36.

[17] *Gray* (n 1) 20.

[18] ibid.

[19] ibid.

[20] *Watts v Leitch* [1973] Tas SR 16 (SC) 20.

[21] *Gray* (n 1) 20–21.

[22] *Gray v State Government Insurance Commission* (Supreme Court of South Australia, 10 September 1996).

[23] ibid 4.

[24] In the High Court, counsel for Mr Gray was Sydney Tilmouth QC and counsel for the Motor Accident Commission was Stephen Walsh QC. Interestingly, Mr Tilmouth had appeared for

separate judgments from each of Kirby and Callinan JJ. The Court was, however, unanimous in its decision: no exemplary damages should be awarded.

As foreshadowed, the main questions for the High Court were the significance of the defendant's punishment by the criminal law for the conduct said to give rise to exemplary damages, and the availability of exemplary damages in negligence cases. There was also an issue about the propriety of the remedy where the wrongdoer is insured against liability for exemplary damages. What follows is a brief summary of the conclusions of the Court in respect of each of these issues.

As to the significance of criminal punishment, the plurality concluded that there could be no award of exemplary damages where 'the criminal law has been brought to bear upon the wrongdoer and substantial punishment inflicted … for what is substantially the same conduct'.[25] Moreover, this was not just a matter of discretion. In these circumstances, exemplary damages were barred.[26] On the facts here, given Mr Bransden's seven-year term of imprisonment, there had been substantial punishment, and exemplary damages were not available. Kirby J reached the same conclusion, noting the rule that a person shall not be tried or punished again for an offence for which he or she has already been finally convicted or acquitted.[27] However, his Honour viewed this as a matter of discretion rather than an absolute bar.[28] Callinan J took the same view, concluding that the punishment of the defendant by the criminal law was a relevant consideration in the exercise of a discretion to award exemplary damages, and it would not always be conclusive.[29] A more fulsome discussion of the Court's reasoning in relation to this question, and its implications, occurs in section III of this chapter.

As to negligence, the plurality held, consistent with longstanding authority,[30] that there could be no award of exemplary damages if there had been no 'conscious wrongdoing' by the defendant. Further, they observed that, in most negligence cases, there would be *no* conscious wrongdoing by the defendant. However, the plurality recognised that there may be cases, framed in negligence, which nonetheless involve conscious wrongdoing. The present was such a case. Although Mr Gray had framed his case in negligence, the case had been conducted at trial as one in trespass.[31] Along similar lines, Kirby J held that what matters is the conduct of the defendant, not the nature of the tort. However, his Honour also opined that the punishment of deliberate wrongdoing is not the

Mr Bransden in earlier criminal proceedings in relation to separate charges: *R v Bransden* (Supreme Court of South Australia, Court of Criminal Appeal, 3 April 1990).

[25] *Gray* (n 1) 14.

[26] ibid.

[27] ibid 31.

[28] ibid 33–34.

[29] ibid 50.

[30] *Whitfeld v de Lauret & Co Ltd* (1920) 29 CLR 71 (HCA) 77; Gray (n 1) 7, 9–10.

[31] *Gray* (n 1) 10.

sole reason for exemplary damages. In several recent cases, exemplary damages had been awarded if the conduct of the defendant had, objectively, 'called for disapprobation'.[32] Callinan J noted, like the plurality and Kirby J, that the pleaded cause of action does not matter. However, his Honour considered that awards of exemplary damages for negligence would be 'extremely rare'.[33]

So, the High Court confirmed that exemplary damages are available in negligence cases. What matters is the quality of the defendant's conduct, rather than the legal category into which it falls. It is substance rather than form – the way the case is formally pleaded – that is determinative. In so holding, the High Court also confirmed the primacy of the test for exemplary damages in *Whitfeld v de Lauret*:[34] the defendant must engage in *conscious* wrongdoing in contumelious disregard of the plaintiff's rights. The application of this test will necessarily render the award of exemplary damages in negligence cases a rare occurrence. The broader question, not grappled with by the High Court, is whether the *Whitfeld* test is the proper test: *should* subjective wrongdoing – a guilty mind – be an essential condition for exemplary damages?

As to insurance, the plurality decided that this question had been conclusively determined by the High Court in *Lamb v Cotogno*[35] and that case should not be reopened. *Lamb* held that exemplary damages are available notwithstanding that the defendant was not the tortfeasor but an insurer.[36] Kirby and Callinan JJ agreed but the former suggested that this question would someday require reconsideration.[37] Accordingly, the Court's reasons for refusing to reopen *Lamb* were essentially procedural and did not consider the competing policy considerations. These arguments will have to be rerun on another day.

The High Court also decided that Mr Gray was not entitled to aggravated damages. However, this decision was reached on the purely procedural ground that he had not pleaded a claim for such damages.[38] At the hearing of the appeal, a belated application for aggravated damages was made by counsel for Mr Gray but this was rejected as having been made far too late.[39] In their judgments, the plurality and, especially, Kirby J, nonetheless made some helpful observations about the distinction between aggravated and exemplary damages.[40]

Mr Gray also appealed to the High Court on the ground that the compensatory damages he had been awarded at trial (which were confirmed on appeal to the Full Court of the South Australian Supreme Court) were manifestly inadequate. The High Court agreed. In the event, the High Court ordered that there

[32] ibid 29.
[33] *Gray* (n 1) 51.
[34] *Whitfeld* (n 30).
[35] *Lamb* (n 7).
[36] *Gray* (n 1) 12–13.
[37] ibid 25–27, 46–47.
[38] ibid 4–5, 34–36, 52.
[39] Gray Transcript (n 13) 28–31, 35–36; *Gray* (n 1) 4–5, 34–36, 52.
[40] *Gray* (n 1) 7, 34–35.

be a new trial on the issue of damages, other than exemplary and aggravated damages.[41] It appears, however, that the new trial did not proceed, the parties instead reaching a settlement.[42]

The next section of this chapter considers and critiques the reasoning of the High Court in support of its conclusion in relation to the significance of criminal punishment of the defendant and, more generally, the Court's treatment of the questions it did not decide.

III. THE SIGNIFICANCE OF CRIMINAL PUNISHMENT OF THE DEFENDANT

A. Questions Answered

We have just seen the principle enunciated by the plurality in *Gray*, and supported by Kirby and Callinan JJ, in relation to the significance, in the award of exemplary damages, of the criminal punishment of the defendant. But by what reasoning did the Court reach this conclusion? As a matter of principle and policy, the reasoning essentially boils down to the *purposes* of exemplary damages – namely, the punishment of 'the offender' and the deterrence of 'others' – being 'wholly met' in such cases, and the need to avoid double-punishment.[43] Further, as a matter of precedent, the Court considered that the weight of authority, in Australia and other jurisdictions – including New Zealand, Canada and the United States – favoured this conclusion.[44]

In *Gray*, the plurality in the High Court engaged in a partial and cautious application of the approach of the majority of the New Zealand Court of Appeal in in *Daniels v Thompson*.[45] It is not the purpose of this chapter to engage in a lengthy analysis of that decision. However, a brief description of the reasoning of the Court is necessary, as it provides important context to the decision of the High Court in *Gray*.

The majority in *Daniels* held that there can be no exemplary damages in respect of conduct that is, or is likely to be, subject to criminal punishment.

[41] *Gray* (n 1) 52.

[42] A Buti, *A Stolen Life: The Bruce Trevorrow Case* (Fremantle, Fremantle Press, 2019) 77–38.

[43] *Gray* (n 1) 14. See also: Gray Transcript (n 13) 13, 17, 19 (Kirby J), 18–19 (Gleeson CJ).

[44] *Gray* (n 1) 15. The Australian authority on this question was limited, essentially confined to *Watts v Leitch* (n 20). In *Lamb* (n 7) it appears that Mr Lamb had pleaded guilty to a 'serious criminal charge' in respect of the incident the subject of the civil suit. However, it is not clear with what precise offence he was convicted, nor what sentence was ultimately imposed upon him. In any event, no point was made of the fact of prior punishment by the criminal law on the appeal to the High Court: *Gray* (n 1) 15 fn 71. See also Barker, ch 6 of this volume.

[45] *Daniels v Thompson* [1998] 3 NZLR 22 (CA). See discussion of this case in, eg, J Smillie, 'Exemplary Damages and the Criminal Law' (1998) 6 *Torts Law Journal* 113; Manning (n 3); Feldthusen (n 5); K Wilshire, 'Double Jeopardy: Exemplary Damages and Criminal Proceedings' (2000) 9 *Auckland Law Review* 177; S Todd, 'Accident Compensation in New Zealand and Exemplary Damages' (1999) 7 *Tort Law Review* 194.

In particular, a prior conviction for the same conduct constitutes an absolute bar to exemplary damages. Where there has been a prior acquittal for the same conduct, civil proceedings seeking exemplary damages will be struck out as an abuse of process. And where criminal prosecution is likely, albeit not yet commenced when exemplary damages are sought in civil proceedings, the latter will be stayed to prevent an abuse of process.[46] Why? The majority reasoned that, if a defendant has received a criminal punishment, the purposes of exemplary damages – namely, punishment and deterrence – will have been met. Further, if exemplary damages are awarded nonetheless, the defendant will be subjected to double punishment, contrary to constitutional norms. And even in the case of acquittal, although there is no risk of double punishment, the award of exemplary damages would be an attempt to relitigate the criminal proceedings, so would offend the finality principle.[47]

The minority in *Daniels* took a different view, holding that the defendant's prior criminal punishment was not an absolute bar. Rather, in such cases, the civil court retained a discretion to award exemplary damages.[48]

Daniels was appealed to the Privy Council. In *W v W*, the Judicial Committee upheld the majority decision.[49] Their Lordships opined that a claim for exemplary damages cannot be maintained against a defendant in respect of conduct which is also a criminal offence, when the subject of a criminal prosecution is convicted or acquitted, whatever the ground.[50] This is an absolute bar. Why? Again, the Privy Council was concerned about offending fundamental protections against double punishment and double jeopardy. Their Lordships also, quite overtly, engaged in judicial abstention, noting that the decision of the New Zealand Court of Appeal involved a policy choice, not the application of legal principle. The proper approach of the Privy Council on appeal was to leave untouched the policy decisions of the national court.[51]

New Zealand is not the only other jurisdiction to have considered this issue. In England and Wales, the Law Commission, in a 1997 report[52] recommended that, 'usually' there should be no award of exemplary damages where the defendant had already been convicted of an offence involving the conduct which

[46] *Daniels* (n 45) 45–53.

[47] ibid.

[48] ibid 77–78.

[49] [1999] 2 NZLR 1 (PC). See the discussion of this case in J Manning, 'Exemplary Damages and Criminal Punishment in the Privy Council' (1999) 7 *Torts Law Journal* 129; Todd (n 45).

[50] *W v W* (n 49) [12]–[14].

[51] ibid.

[52] Law Commission, *Aggravated, Exemplary and Restitutionary Damages* (Law Com No 247, 1997). The High Court in *Gray* was familiar with this report. See Gray Transcript (n 13) 28 (Gleeson CJ). *cf* a number of recent cases in England and Wales in which it has been held that prior criminal punishment does not preclude exemplary damages: see, eg, *AT v Dulghieru* [2009] EWHC 225 [68]; *Axa Insurance UK plc v Financial Claims Solutions Ltd* [2018] EWCA Civ 1330, [2019] RTR 1 [25]. For criticism of these cases, on the ground that they fundamentally misunderstand the authority on which they are based, *Borders (UK) Ltd v Commissioner of Police of the Metropolis* [2005]

founded the claim for exemplary damages. But this was a matter of discretion, not an absolute bar. The Court should take into account any other sanctions already imposed, in the exercise of that discretion. And conviction was the key. Acquittal of a crime involving the same conduct should not preclude exemplary damages. Further, the conduct might be the same, or 'substantially the same'.[53] The Law Commission's view reflects that of Kirby and Callinan JJ in *Gray*. Likewise, in Canada, the Ontario Law Commission preferred the view that a civil court asked to award exemplary damages in a case where the defendant had already been punished by a criminal court for the same conduct, had a discretion still to make an award. The prior criminal punishment was 'a factor' in the exercise of the discretion, not a bar.[54] In some US states, the same view prevails.[55]

It is clear that what separates the majority and minority approaches in New Zealand, and what drove the plurality decision in *Gray*, is the decision-maker's understanding of the *purposes* of exemplary damages. The majority in *Daniels* worked from a narrow view of those purposes. They regarded the *sole* purposes of exemplary damages as punishment of the defendant, which was primary, and deterrence – understood as specific, rather than general deterrence – which was consequential on punishment. And they regarded other alleged purposes of exemplary damages, including vindication and appeasement – so-called 'therapeutic' functions – as well as condemnation and education, as having *no role*. In contrast, the minority recognised that exemplary damages could perform a range of socially useful functions, including therapeutic functions.

Commentators have argued that the majority approach in *Daniels* was 'extreme', 'radical' and 'extraordinary', and that the minority approach was more cautious.[56] Evidently, both approaches involve value judgments and policy choices. The unique statutory context in New Zealand at the time *Daniels* was decided is also highly relevant. Under the *Accident Compensation* legislation,[57] plaintiffs had no common law right to compensatory damages for losses suffered as a result of accidents (as defined by the legislation). Their exclusive remedy was provided by the legislation. However, that remedy was widely regarded as inadequate. Accordingly, when *Daniels* was decided, there was concern about plaintiffs seeking exemplary damages as a way to 'top up' their statutory compensation. In Australia, this context is absent. And yet, the plurality in *Gray* took much the same view as the majority in *Daniels*.

EWCA Civ 197, [2005] Po LR 1, see J Goudkamp and E Katsampouka, 'Ten Misconceptions about Punitive Damages' in E Bant et al (eds), *Punishment and Private Law* (Oxford, Hart Publishing, 2021) 210–13.

[53] Law Commission (n 52) Part V, paras 1.44(21), 1.103–1.115.

[54] Ontario Law Commission, *Report on Exemplary Damages* (1991). See discussion in Feldthusen (n 5) 756; Wilshire (n 45) 185–86.

[55] Wilshire (n 45) 189. See also in Singapore *ACB v Thomson Medical Pte Ltd* [2017] SGCA 20, [2017] 1 SLR 918 [180], [182], [187].

[56] Smillie (n 45) 121–22; Manning (n 3) 722; Feldthusen (n 5) 743.

[57] Accident Rehabilitation and Compensation Insurance Act 1992 (NZ), s 14. See also Accident Insurance Act 1998 (NZ); Accidents Insurance Act 2001 (NZ).

The decision of the plurality in *Gray* implicitly identifies punishment and deterrence as the primary purposes of exemplary damages. That starting point dictates that, where these purposes have already been achieved – by the imposition of a criminal punishment on the defendant – there is no need, nor justification for, exemplary damages. It is also implicit in the plurality decision that an award of exemplary damages is not justified by the secondary purposes of vindication and denunciation (etc) alone.

This raises a question about whether the view of the High Court in *Gray* as to the purposes of exemplary damages is inconsistent with the view of the Court in *Lamb v Cotogno*. As noted earlier, in *Gray*, the High Court declined to overrule *Lamb*, instead holding that, in relation to the question of the availability of exemplary damages where the defendant is an insurer, it was still good law. In *Lamb*, which is considered in detail in a separate contribution to this collection by Kit Barker,[58] the tortfeasor was insured against liability for exemplary damages. The High Court held, unanimously, that this was not a bar to the remedy. The Court reasoned that, although the purposes of punishment and deterrence of the tortfeasor would be foiled, as the insurer, rather than the tortfeasor, would pay, the remedy should be available as its other purposes could still be achieved – including the deterrence of others, vindication and denunciation. The Court said: 'It is an aspect of exemplary damages that they serve to assuage any urge for revenge felt by victims and to discourage any temptation to engage in self-help likely to endanger the peace'.[59] So, in *Lamb*, exemplary damages were available notwithstanding the absence of any punishment or deterrence of the tortfeasor. But in *Gray*, there could be no exemplary damages because there had already been punishment and deterrence of the tortfeasor. At first glance at least, the cases appear to be inconsistent.

It is possible, however, to reconcile the two decisions. Clearly, the High Court in *Gray* was concerned not only with specific deterrence – of the defendant – but also with general deterrence – of others, and like conduct. This emerges from the plurality's reference to punishment 'of the offender' and deterrence 'of others'.[60] And in *Lamb*, the High Court identified general deterrence as one of the purposes of exemplary damages, beyond the punishment of the defendant and specific deterrence, which can, of itself, justify an award. In *Gray*, the Court refused exemplary damages because, by the imposition of a criminal punishment on Mr Bransden, the purposes of punishment, specific *and general* deterrence were achieved. Accordingly, both cases hold that there must be *some deterrence*, specific or general, to justify exemplary damages.[61]

[58] Barker, ch 6 of this volume.

[59] *Lamb* (n 7) 9.

[60] *Gray* (n 1) 14.

[61] It may, however, be arguable that in *Lamb*, the Court contemplated that exemplary damages are justified even where there is no deterrence, specific or general, so long as the purposes of vindication and/or denunciation are achieved by the award.

The effect of the approach of the plurality of the High Court in *Gray*, like that of the majority of the New Zealand Court of Appeal and the Privy Council in *Daniels*, is largely to reserve the role of punishment of criminal conduct to the criminal law. The approach protects the criminal law as the near-exclusive vehicle for the punishment of conduct which is a crime.[62] It therefore creates a fairly strict demarcation between the criminal and civil law.

This approach is said to have various advantages. Several of these reflect arguments against exemplary damages generally. It is said that it is anomalous for the civil law to exact punishment: this is the province of the criminal law, not the civil law, as the former is properly set up to punish.[63] The criminal process provides various procedural and evidential safeguards to the defendant which are absent in the civil law.[64] It is also said that confining punishment to the criminal law avoids windfall gains to the plaintiff. Why should the price of the defendant's crime be paid to the plaintiff, rather than the state? Further, it is argued that this approach avoids a civil court having to 'mark the exam paper' of a criminal court. Civil courts asked to award exemplary damages, in cases where a punishment has already been imposed by a criminal court, are saved from having to decide whether the criminal sentence was adequate. It is far from clear how a civil court might do this, especially if it assumes, as it must, that the criminal court took into account all relevant factors when imposing the sentence. There may be no principled basis for the assessment. And for a civil court to undertake it risks undermining the criminal process, usurping the credibility and autonomy of the criminal court, and compromising the role of the criminal justice system.[65]

There are, however, responses to these arguments, some of them powerful:

(1) The criminal law may be inadequate to punish appropriately all conduct which is criminal. The criminal justice system, in any jurisdiction, is inevitably far from perfect; it will not always 'get it right'.[66]
(2) Criminal punishment and civil punishment are different. The former arguably has greater stigma than the latter; and the former can be far more serious, potentially involving a threat to the defendant's liberty.[67]
(3) The process from commencement of a criminal prosecution through to the imposition of a sentence is different from the process from commencement of civil proceedings through to the award of exemplary damages. The standard of proof is different, and different rules of evidence apply.

[62] Manning (n 3) 730.
[63] J Smillie, 'Exemplary Damages and Accident Compensation: a Response to Joanna Manning' [1997] *New Zealand Law Review* 314, 315.
[64] Law Commission (n 52) Part V, para 1.21.
[65] Wilshire (n 45) 195; S Todd 'Exemplary Damages' (1998) 18 *New Zealand Universities Law Review* 145, 174–75; Todd (n 45) 196.
[66] Manning (n 3) 732.
[67] Law Commission (n 52) Part V, para 1.23.

Accordingly, the decisions as to the sentence, and award, may be based on different proven facts. When this is borne in mind, it is far less clear that the civil court is second-guessing the criminal court.[68]

(4) The majority approach may rob a plaintiff of the choice to cooperate in criminal proceedings or pursue civil proceedings for exemplary damages. If the plaintiff, as the victim of a crime, and without legal advice, does the former, they may inadvertently exclude the possibility of the latter.[69]

(5) If it is enough to exclude exemplary damages that a criminal prosecution is 'likely' (as the majority approach in *Daniels* suggests) then a defendant in civil proceedings might incongruously argue: 'I should be criminally prosecuted for this conduct'. The civil court would then be placed in the invidious position of having to assess whether the defendant's conduct is a crime before the determination of the same question by the criminal court.[70]

(6) There are advantages for a plaintiff as a participant in the civil justice system, as compared with the criminal justice system. The plaintiff is a party to the proceedings, so has control over their case and can be legally represented. There is far greater formal equality between the plaintiff and the defendant in civil proceedings, than between accused and victim in criminal proceedings. Further, the civil standard of proof is less demanding than the criminal standard. In short, the opportunities for vindication and satisfaction are far greater for the plaintiff in the civil system.[71]

(7) The criminal law and the civil law serve different interests. Arguably, the criminal law serves *society's* interest in inflicting punishment for the crime against the state. It redresses public wrongs. The civil law serves the plaintiff's interest in exacting punishment for the wrong done to them. It redresses private wrongs.[72] So the two are not mutually exclusive, and it is not obvious that either must always prevail.[73]

(8) In relation to the objection that a civil court should not 'mark the exam paper' of the criminal court – in other words, *assess the adequacy* of the criminal sentence – we need to ask: adequate *for what?* For serving society's interests and redressing the crime against the state, or for serving the victim's interests, and redressing the wrong done to them (or both)? The criminal sentence will have considered only – or mainly – the former, not the latter.

[68] Feldthusen (n 5) 759; Wilshire (n 45) 195; Todd (n 65) 174–75; Todd (n 45) 198; Manning (n 3) 731.

[69] Manning (n 3) 735; Wilshire (n 45) 198.

[70] Smillie (n 45) 120; Manning (n 3) 735.

[71] Manning (n 3) 731; B Feldthusen, 'The Civil Action for Sexual Battery: Therapeutic Jurisprudence?' (1993) 25 *Ottawa Law Review* 203, 213–17; *ACB* (n 55) [186].

[72] Wilshire (n 45) 184; Manning (n 49) 134; *ACB* (n 55) [186].

[73] *cf* Smillie (n 45); Todd (n 45) 196; Manning (n 5) 165.

(9) In *Gray*, the plurality in the High Court recognised that there is no strict demarcation between the civil and the criminal law.[74] Their roots are intermingled, and, in modern times, the existence of criminal injuries compensation and civil penalty regimes indicate that the tension between the two systems may be more apparent than real.[75]

(10) The civil law, by the award of exemplary damages, can serve a valid and valuable corrective role. It can provide, in exceptional cases, a safety valve against the failure of the criminal law. By serving a residual, and supplementary rather than supplanting function, it may even increase the respect for the law as a whole.[76]

Thus there are strong arguments *for and against* the availability of exemplary damages for conduct which has been (or will be) punished by the criminal law. The arguments are finely balanced. Determining where the balance lies is difficult. This is why courts, commentators and law reform bodies across the common law world continue to grapple with the question. The critical insight is that the resolution of the question is, and must be, driven by the *purposes* of exemplary damages. If the plurality in the High Court in *Gray* had taken a different view of those purposes – for example, if they had accepted that the remedy was principally concerned not with the punishment of the defendant, but with general deterrence, or vindication of the plaintiff and denunciation – the rule enunciated by the Court would have been different. In particular, the objections to double punishment, and double jeopardy, might have fallen away.

So, again, in the analysis of the appropriateness of exemplary damages in cases where the conduct in question is a crime, we must start with the purposes of the remedy. There must, in the first instance, be a policy choice – a value judgment – in order to weigh the competing arguments. In every case, the question should be: will the award of exemplary damages serve the identified purpose or purposes of the remedy? Have they already been achieved, or will they fail to be achieved, if an award is made? These are the fundamental questions which a court must ask itself when deciding whether a defendant who has already been, or may be, punished by a criminal court for the same conduct should be made liable for exemplary damages. The answer to these questions will depend on the purposes identified. Further, accepting that the court has a *discretion* in all cases may best facilitate this approach.[77] At the least, there should be a discretion for the hard cases.

It is apparent that, at the hearing of the appeal in *Gray*, the High Court was willing to be persuaded that the best approach to this issue was to recognise

[74] *Gray* (n 1) 7–8, citing *Uren v John Fairfax & Sons Pty Ltd* (1966) 117 CLR 118 (HCA) 149.

[75] *Gray* (n 1) 7–8; Edelman (n 9) 89.

[76] Manning (n 3) 733; Todd (n 65) 175; Wilshire (n 45) 197.

[77] To like effect, see Goudkamp and Katsampouka (n 52) 213. This approach was recently adopted by the Singapore Court of Appeal: *ACB* (n 55) [180]–[187].

a discretion to award exemplary damages where the defendant had already been punished by the criminal law – albeit a discretion that would rarely be exercised – rather than an absolute bar.[78] However, the concern with this approach, expressed repeatedly during argument, was that there was insufficient clarity around the considerations informing the exercise of the discretion.[79] Respectfully, counsel for Mr Gray did not provide an adequate response to this concern. Asked the same question, counsel for the Motor Accident Commission suggested that the Court must look to the purposes of exemplary damages, as identified in *Lamb v Cotogno*.[80] Gleeson CJ saw the merit in this, saying that 'what it is that informs the exercise of the discretion is the purpose of awarding exemplary damages in the first place' and further: 'punishment for the same conduct by the criminal justice system would ordinarily satisfy the purposes which would otherwise be served by an award of exemplary damages and would therefore produce the result that this is not a proper case for such an award'.[81] However, on reflection, and after conferral, his Honour (together with the other members of the plurality) evidently preferred the absolute bar approach.

B. Questions Unanswered

The High Court in *Gray* also identified, but left open, many questions as, on the facts, it was not necessary to decide them. Among these questions are: what if there has been some plea bargaining?[82] What if the criminal punishment is merely a nominal penalty?[83] What if the criminal offence is one of strict liability?[84] Should it ever be open to a civil court to judge the adequacy of a criminal sentence? What is the meaning of 'substantial'? What if criminal proceedings have not yet been commenced or, if commenced, completed, when exemplary damages are sought? How close a connection must there be between the criminal proceedings, in which punishment was imposed, and the civil proceedings, in which exemplary damages are sought? What if the defendant was acquitted?[85]

[78] This was the primary submission of counsel for Mr Gray at the hearing. See Gray Transcript (n 13) 13, 16, 20–21.

[79] Gray Transcript (n 13) 14, 27 (Hayne J) 21, 78 (Gummow J) 71 (Kirby J).

[80] *Lamb* (n 7) 9. See Gray Transcript (n 13) 70, 78.

[81] Gray Transcript (n 13) 70 (Gleeson CJ).

[82] This question was raised at the hearing of the appeal by Gummow J: Gray Transcript (n 13) 35.

[83] At the hearing of the appeal, McHugh J suggested the example of a landlord who cuts off the electricity to drive out a tenant and receives only a summary fine under the governing legislation: 'In such a case it may be appropriate to award exemplary damages' (Gray Transcript (n 13) 26). Hayne J suggested a similar example: 'the employer who acts in flagrant disregard of occupational health and safety requirements to earn a profit and is convicted and fined A$100 in the local court for breach of the regulation, and a plaintiff worker is cruelly injured' (Gray Transcript (n 13) 27).

[84] This question was also raised at the hearing of the appeal by Gummow J: Gray Transcript (n 13) 69.

[85] *Gray* (n 1) 14–16. This question was raised at the hearing of the appeal by McHugh J: Gray Transcript (n 13) 37.

And does the bar on exemplary damages apply only where the criminal punishment of the defendant is 'substantial'?

In relation to several of these questions, however, the Court gave some signals about the answers. In relation to the important question of whether it should ever be open to a civil court to judge the adequacy of a criminal sentence, the Court opined that there was much to be said for the approach of the majority of the New Zealand Court of Appeal in *Daniels v Thompson*.[86] In that case the majority held that a civil court should never be called upon to revisit a criminal sentence. With that in mind, the High Court in *Gray* suggested that it would be a 'most unusual case' in which a civil court could conclude that the outcome of criminal proceedings did not take sufficient account of the need to punish the defendant and deter others.[87] At the hearing of the appeal, several members of the Court expressed the concern that there should be no review by the civil court of the criminal court's assessment of the proper sentence.[88]

The Court also provided some guidance in relation to an adjacent controversy: the meaning of 'substantial punishment'. All members of the Court indicated that a term of imprisonment would always be a substantial punishment.[89] But what about a non-custodial sentence, or a financial imposition? This was left to be decided on a case-by-case basis. Subsequent cases have taken a broad approach. For example, *Cheng v Farjudi* held that the recording of a conviction, and the imposition of a good behaviour bond, is not an *in*substantial punishment.[90] This suggests that most criminal sentences will be substantial.

However, the meaning of 'substantial' gives rise to difficult questions. In the writer's view, by 'substantial', the High Court in *Gray* did *not* mean *adequate*, in the sense just discussed. The Court did not intend that, in deciding whether a sentence imposed by a criminal court was substantial, the civil court should revisit the sentence – 'mark the exam paper' – of the criminal court. As just seen, it was plainly not intended that the civil court should decide afresh what sentence *should* have been imposed and therefore whether that actually imposed was appropriate in all the circumstances. Instead, by 'substantial' the High Court intended an objective inquiry, of a general nature, not a judgment on the particular facts of the case: generally, in the eyes of reasonable members of society, is a sentence of *x* a 'substantial' punishment? This is to be distinguished from an inquiry into the adequacy of a criminal punishment, which is tied to the specific facts of the case: given the conduct in question, and in all the circumstances, was the punishment imposed by the criminal court a proper one? This must follow, given the strong signals sent by the Court that it is not appropriate for a civil court to ask this question.[91]

[86] *Daniels* (n 45).
[87] *Gray* (n 1) 15.
[88] Gray Transcript (n 13) 17 (Kirby J) 27 (Hayne J) 28, 34–35 (Gummow J).
[89] *Gray* (n 1) 16.
[90] *Cheng v Farjudi* [2016] NSWCA 316, (2016) 93 NSWLR 95 [105].
[91] *Gray* (n 1) 16.

Gray also left unanswered the question: what if criminal proceedings have not been commenced or, if commenced, completed, when the plaintiff seeks exemplary damages in civil proceedings? Here, the plurality signalled that the *mere possibility* of criminal proceedings is probably insufficient to bar exemplary damages.[92] This is not unlike the position in New Zealand where civil proceedings will be stayed to prevent an abuse of process if criminal prosecution is 'likely'. But in England and Wales, the Law Commission has recommended that there should be no bar to exemplary damages unless the defendant has actually been convicted in criminal proceedings. And in Canada, and some jurisdictions in the United States, the prospect of criminal prosecution is but a factor to be taken into account in the exercise of a discretion to award exemplary damages. Subsequent Australian cases have also considered this question. In *Niven v SS*, the potential – which became a reality – of later criminal proceedings did not prevent an award of exemplary damages and that award was upheld on appeal, after the prosecution resulted in an acquittal.[93] However, in practice, a stay of civil proceedings is likely to be imposed until concurrent criminal proceedings have concluded. The difficult cases will be those in which criminal proceedings have not yet even commenced. The question will be: *how likely* must it be that they will be commenced? This is a question which remains to be answered in subsequent decisions, on a case-by-case basis.

In relation to other questions left open by the High Court in *Gray*, however, their Honours gave no guidance. Much remains unanswered in relation to the meaning of 'substantially the same conduct'. The plurality expressly regarded it as unnecessary to decide *how close* the conduct the subject of the criminal and civil proceedings must be. The English Law Commission has grappled with this issue, but its proposal adds little to the High Court's statement.[94] It seems that whether the conduct is sufficiently similar must be worked out on a case-by-case basis. As a body of subsequent decisions is formed, it may then be possible to distil some general principles. But in the 24 years since *Gray* was decided, this is still a work in progress.

An important unanswered question is: what if the defendant is *acquitted* in criminal proceedings? Again, the High Court gave no clear signals here. Other jurisdictions have settled on a range of answers. In New Zealand, the Court of Appeal, by majority, in *Daniels*, and the Privy Council in *W v W*, held that the bar to exemplary damages applies where the defendant has been acquitted, because civil proceedings seeking this remedy would be struck out as an abuse of process. In contrast, in England and Wales, the Law Commission has recommended that there should be no bar to exemplary damages unless the defendant has been *convicted* by a criminal court. In Canada and some jurisdictions in the

[92] ibid 15. This was debated at the hearing of the appeal. See Gray Transcript (n 13) 71 (Kirby J), 72 (Gleeson CJ).

[93] *Niven v SS* [2006] NSWCA 338.

[94] Law Commission (n 52) Part V, para 1.105.

United States, an acquittal in prior criminal proceedings – like a conviction – is not a bar to the remedy but a relevant factor in the exercise of discretion.

The New Zealand position is justified on the basis that, although there is no risk of double punishment where the defendant is acquitted – acquittal not resulting in any punishment – the award of exemplary damages in such circumstances would still offend the finality principle, being an attempt by the plaintiff to relitigate issues which have already been decided by a court. This argument is not without response. The relitigation objection is not made where what the plaintiff seeks in the civil proceedings is *compensation*. Further, in Australia (as well as New Zealand and possibly England) exemplary damages are a *parasitic* remedy. The remedy does not stand alone but must be sought in addition to compensatory damages – or at least, it must be established that the plaintiff has the *right* to compensatory damages in order to claim exemplary damages.[95] So, this objection is really an objection to relitigating *the issue of punishment*, rather than relitigating per se. But when the defendant has been acquitted by the criminal court, there has been *no criminal punishment*, so the issue of punishment has (on one view) not already been decided. (What will have been decided, perhaps, is that the defendant should *not* be punished, rather than, if some punishment is appropriate, what that punishment should be.) On this view, the objection falls away.[96]

Subsequent cases in Australia have not treated the defendant's acquittal as a bar to exemplary damages. In *Niven*, for example, the civil proceedings in which exemplary damages were sought came first. An award was made. Then came the criminal proceedings, in which the defendant was acquitted. The defendant then appealed against the award of exemplary damages. The New South Wales Court of Appeal allowed the award to stand. The defendant's acquittal was not a bar to exemplary damages.[97] In *Whitbread v Rail Corporation NSW*, McColl JA concluded that the High Court needed to determine this question.[98] But Whealy JA was prepared to decide that exemplary damages are not barred by the defendant's acquittal for the same or similar conduct, because an acquittal is not a 'substantial punishment'. In such a case, the Court had a discretion to award the remedy, and would consider the criminal proceedings as a relevant factor.[99]

Finally, another unanswered question is whether the bar to exemplary damages applies *only* when a criminal court has imposed a substantial punishment for substantially the same conduct. Is there any bar outside these conditions, or does the court have a discretion to award exemplary damages

[95] *XL Petroleum (NSW) Pty Ltd v Caltex Oil (Australia) Pty Ltd* (1985) 155 CLR 448 (HCA) 468–69; *Fatimi Pty Ltd v Bryant* [2004] NSWCA 140, (2004) 59 NSWLR 678 [71]–[76].

[96] Todd (n 45) 197–98.

[97] *Niven* (n 93).

[98] *Whitbread v Rail Corporation NSW* [2011] NSWCA 130.

[99] ibid [239].

in those circumstances? The plurality in *Gray* expressly regarded this as not necessary to decide, and gave no hints as to how it might be decided.[100] But commentators have suggested that the Court left open the possibility that the bar would *only* apply where the punishment is substantial, and the conduct is substantially the same, such that the general discretion to award exemplary damages would revive where either of those conditions was not met.[101] Subsequent cases have proceeded on this basis.[102] For example, in *Whitbread*, Whealy JA said that where there is no substantial criminal punishment – for example, where the defendant is acquitted – exemplary damages are not barred and the court has a discretion, in the exercise of which the criminal proceedings are a relevant factor.[103] Similarly, in *Cheng*, Beazley JA said that *Gray* does not preclude exemplary damages where something other than substantial criminal punishment has been imposed.[104]

IV. CONCLUSION

Gray is a landmark case, not only for the questions it answered, but also for those which were left for another day. This chapter has considered the first main question answered by the High Court in *Gray*, regarding the significance of criminal punishment of the defendant, and sought to place it in the context of the broader questions to which the decision gives rise.

The High Court laid down a new rule regarding the availability of exemplary damages where the defendant has been punished by the criminal law for the same conduct. The bar on the remedy where the criminal punishment is 'substantial', and the conduct 'substantially the same', provided a clear answer on the facts of *Gray*. However, as the chapter has identified, the bar gives rise to – and the Court left unresolved – various complex issues which still need to be worked out.

The undercurrent to the Court's consideration of this, and the other issues to which the case gave rise, as well as their Honours' comments regarding the nature of the discretion to award exemplary damages, was that this remedy is a part of Australian law and is likely to remain so. But perhaps the most important observation which can be made of *Gray* is that it demonstrates that the resolution of most issues in relation to exemplary damages depends on the view taken of the *purposes* of the remedy. The answer to that question – *What are the purposes of exemplary damages?* – will largely determine the answers to more specific questions, including those considered in *Gray*. If one takes the view,

[100] *Gray* (n 1) 14.
[101] Manning (n 3) 739.
[102] See, eg, *Niven* (n 93) [64]; *Whitbread* (n 98).
[103] *Whitbread* (n 98) [242].
[104] *Cheng* (n 90) [87].

for example, that the only, or main purpose of exemplary damages is the deterrence of *others*, irrespective of the punishment or deterrence of the defendant, then there is less objection to the availability of exemplary damages where the wrongdoer is insured. Likewise, on this view, there is no need to restrict exemplary damages to cases involving intentional conduct, which could be said to be most deserving of punishment, or to exclude the remedy where the defendant has already been punished by the criminal law.

The thesis of this chapter has been that, in the analysis of the questions considered in *Gray*, and in relation to exemplary damages generally, we must start with the purposes of the remedy. In every case the question should be: will the award of exemplary damages serve the identified purpose or purposes of the remedy? Have they already been achieved, or will they fail to be achieved, if an award is made? Accepting that the court has a *discretion* in all cases may best facilitate this approach.

In *Gray*, the High Court appeared to recognise the legitimacy of all the purposes of exemplary damages identified in this chapter. But tacitly, it gave undoubted primacy to the punitive and deterrent (specific *and general*) purposes. This emphasis has shaped the development of the remedy in Australian law since and will continue to do so in years to come.

10

Kuddus v Chief Constable of Leicestershire Constabulary (2001)

A Milestone in the Expansion of Punitive Damages

ELENI KATSAMPOUKA*

I. INTRODUCTION

A LANDMARK CASE can be defined as a decision which is regarded as a milestone in the development of law in a particular area. *Kuddus v Chief Constable of Leicestershire Constabulary*[1] deserves this label in the English law of punitive damages. The landmark ruling in *Kuddus* was that punitive damages can be awarded for *any* tort provided the defendant's conduct is 'so outrageous'[2] that it merits punishment (and the facts fall within one of the three categories of *Rookes v Barnard*).[3] In *Kuddus* the House of Lords deviated for the first time from a decades-long trend of restricting the availability of the remedy.[4] This shift steered English law closer towards the position adopted in other common law jurisdictions.

Perhaps more importantly, *Kuddus* brought the English law on punitive damages closer to the remedy's theoretical underpinnings. According to the case law, punitive damages are primarily aimed at punishment and deterrence.[5]

* I am indebted to Omar Kuddus (the claimant in *Kuddus*), Lord Mackay (one of the judges who decided *Kuddus*) and HHJ Simon Freeland KC, HH David Harris KC and Guy Mansfield KC (counsel for the parties in *Kuddus*) for discussing their recollections from the litigation. I am especially grateful to HH David Harris KC for sharing the bundles submitted to the House of Lords and to Peter Cane, James Goudkamp, Yanni Goutzamanis, Mark Lunney and Nick McBride for generously providing comments on an early draft. All errors are mine.

[1] *Kuddus v Chief Constable of Leicestershire Constabulary* [2001] UKHL 29, [2002] 2 AC 122.

[2] ibid [63] (Lord Nicholls).

[3] *Rookes v Barnard* [1964] AC 1129 (HL).

[4] ibid; *Cassell & Co Ltd v Broome* [1972] AC 1027 (HL); *AB v South West Water Services Ltd* [1993] QB 507 (CA).

[5] See, eg, *Rookes* (n 3) 1221 (Lord Devlin): 'The object of exemplary damages is to punish and deter'. The term 'punishment' as a goal of punitive damages is synonymous with 'retribution'.

The courts have, at times, invoked three additional rationales to justify such awards: (1) appeasement of the victim;[6] (2) vindication of the claimant's rights;[7] and (3) condemnation of the defendant's conduct.[8] A common feature in these justifications is their focus on 'the outrage which a defendant's conduct sometimes evokes'.[9] By holding that the touchstone for an award of punitive damages is the character of the defendant's conduct rather than the cause of action in which a claim is pleaded, *Kuddus* was a much anticipated step towards aligning the remedy's availability with its rationales.

Kuddus also set the scene for a potential further expansion of punitive damages to non-tortious causes of action. In its wake, a debate has arisen as to whether punitive damages are, and should be, available in claims in equity, contract and under the Human Rights Act 1998 (HRA 1998). Fundamentally, *Kuddus* laid the foundations for reconsidering the place of punitive damages in English private law, a question which will hopefully soon be resolved by the Supreme Court.

The chapter unfolds in six sections. Section II provides an outline of the law as it stood when *Kuddus* came to be decided. Section III examines the factual and legal background to the case. Section IV attempts to explain the shifting attitudes that English law has exhibited towards punitive damages over time (with *Kuddus* being the first milestone towards expanding the remedy's scope). Section V explores the aftermath of *Kuddus* with a focus on two questions which the House of Lords left open. First, whether punitive damages are available in claims under the HRA 1998 and second, whether English law should abolish the 'categories test' or the remedy in its entirety. Section VI concludes.

II. PUNITIVE DAMAGES BEFORE *KUDDUS*

A. A Restricted Jurisdiction

i. The 'Categories Test'

Punitive (or 'exemplary')[10] damages have been part of English law since at least 1763.[11] The earliest reported cases in which the label 'exemplary damages' was

[6] See, eg, *W v W* [1999] 2 NZLR 1 (PC) (Lord Hoffmann): 'The prosecution of an action for exemplary damages enables the victim … to inflict punishment, even revenge, in ways which a criminal prosecution may not satisfy'.

[7] See, eg, *Kuddus* (n 1) [29] (Lord Nicholls): Punitive damages serve as 'an emphatic vindication of the claimant's rights'.

[8] See, eg, *Rookes* (n 3) 1228 (Lord Devlin): Punitive damages are awarded 'to mark the [court's] disapproval of [the defendant's] conduct'.

[9] *Kuddus* (n 1) [65] (Lord Nicholls).

[10] The terms can be used interchangeably: see *Kuddus* (n 1) [51]. In this chapter, I have opted for the term 'punitive damages' because it is more general and encompasses the various functions of the remedy (*cf* the term 'exemplary damages' which emphasises the remedy's deterrent function).

[11] T Sedgwick, AG Sedgwick and JH Beale, *A Treatise on the Measure of Damages*, 8th edn (New York, Baker, Voorhis, 1891) 502 suggest an even earlier start: 'The term "exemplary damages"

used are *Huckle v Money*[12] and *Wilkes v Wood*.[13] Since then, and for over two centuries, punitive damages could be granted whenever the defendant's conduct 'merit[ed] punishment, which [wa]s only considered to be so where his conduct [wa]s wanton, as where it disclose[d] fraud, malice, violence, cruelty, insolence or the like, or … where he act[ed] in contumelious disregard of the plaintiff's rights'.[14]

Although punitive damages were a standard feature of the law for over 200 years, by the second half of the twentieth century they came to be regarded as an 'anomaly [which] confuses the civil and criminal functions of the law'.[15] In *Rookes v Barnard*, the House of Lords took the first step towards restricting the scope of the remedy. Because it would have been too radical to abolish a doctrine of such long lineage, Lord Devlin instead sought to confine punitive damages awards to three categories of case. These are: (1) cases of oppressive behaviour by government officers; (2) cases where the defendant aimed to extract a profit from their wrong; and (3) cases in which Parliament sanctions the award. This restriction is known as the 'categories test'.

ii. The 'Cause of Action Test'

In 1970, in *Cassell & Co Ltd v Broome*,[16] a unanimous Court of Appeal declared the 'categories test' to be unworkable and boldly advised lower courts to disregard it. However, the House of Lords, dissatisfied with the Court of Appeal's 'aberration',[17] quickly overturned its decision. The scope of punitive damages in English law thus got ensnared in a quest to teach the Court of Appeal a lesson about the power of precedent. In addition to affirming the *Rookes* categories, the House of Lords' decision in *Cassell & Co Ltd v Broome* gave birth to a second limitation on the availability of punitive damages. According to Lord Diplock '*Rookes v Barnard* was not intended to extend the power to award exemplary … damages to particular torts for which they had not previously been awarded'.[18] In subsequent decades, this statement was interpreted as limiting punitive damages

seems to have owed its origin to Lord Camden, the first reported case in which it occurs being that of *Huckle v Money* [1763] … It can hardly be said that the decisions in this case and those which are cited as following it established a new rule of damages. They were, on the contrary, cases where the court held to old precedent in the face of hard pressure to establish a novel doctrine'.

[12] *Huckle v Money* (1763) 2 Wils KB 205, 95 ER 768.

[13] *Wilkes v Wood* (1763) Lofft 1, 98 ER 489.

[14] H McGregor, *Mayne and McGregor on Damages*, 12th edn (London, Sweet & Maxwell, 1961) [207]. See also FO Arnold, *The Law of Damages* (London, Butterworth, 1913) 6: '[Punitive] damages are awarded in cases where the court is entitled and sees fit to mulct the defendant in respect of the heinousness of his conduct'.

[15] *Rookes* (n 3) 1221 (Lord Devlin). It is unclear where this animus towards punitive damages originated. Section IV of this chapter explores possible hypotheses for this phenomenon.

[16] *Cassell & Co Ltd v Broome* [1971] 2 QB 354 (CA).

[17] *Broome* (n 4) 1084 (Lord Reid).

[18] ibid 1130–31. See similar statements by Lord Hailsham LC (at 1076), Lord Wilberforce (at 1114) and Lord Reid (at 1086).

to causes of action for which they had been awarded prior to 1964, the year when *Rookes* was decided (the 'cause of action test' or 'pre-1964 test').

For example, in 1983 Falconer J refused to award punitive damages in a patent infringement action on the basis that such a claim was 'not open to the plaintiffs in the absence of any authority that exemplary damages had been awarded for infringement of patent prior to the decision in *Rookes v Barnard*'.[19] In 1990, a punitive damages claim for inducing breach of contract was also rejected on the same basis.[20] The 'cause of action test' was formally adopted as a limitation on the power of a court to award punitive damages in 1992 in *AB v South West Water Services Ltd*.[21] Stuart-Smith LJ, with whom Simon Brown LJ and Sir Thomas Bingham MR agreed, held that 'before an award of exemplary damages c[ould] be made by any court or tribunal the tort must be one in respect of which such an award was made prior to 1964'.[22]

B. English Law as an Outlier

The 'categories test' is, and the 'cause of action test' was, a distinctive feature of English law. The suggestion that punitive damages should be confined to particular categories of case and causes of action proved highly unpopular overseas. Appellate courts in Australia,[23] Canada,[24] New Zealand,[25] Ireland[26] and Singapore[27] refused to adopt the 'categories test'. Having rejected the *Rookes* categories, courts in these jurisdictions were never faced with the question of whether they should also adopt the 'pre-1964 test'. As Palmer J noted in *Digital Pulse Pty Ltd v Harris*, 'the controversies as to … what was decided in *Rookes* and in *Broome* have bypassed Australia [due to the High Court's rejection of the *Rookes* categories]'.[28] Rather than freezing the law on punitive damages by reference to decisions handed down prior to *Rookes v Barnard*, courts elsewhere in the Commonwealth have tended towards a position in which punitive damages are available for virtually any civil wrong. English law is thus an outlier with respect to the stringency of the limitations it has placed on the scope of punitive damages. That most of the common law world has

[19] *Catnic Components Ltd v Hill & Smith Ltd* [1983] FSR 512 (Ch) 541 citing obiter dicta from *Broome* (n 4).

[20] *Datasolve Ltd v Butterworth (Eurolex) Ltd* (QBD, 19 March 1990) 13. Note however, that punitive damages had been awarded for inducing breach of contract prior to that case, see *Warner v Clark* (CA, 29 July 1983).

[21] (n 4).

[22] ibid 523.

[23] *Uren v John Fairfax & Sons Pty Ltd* (1966) 117 CLR 118 (HCA).

[24] *Vorvis v Insurance Corp of British Columbia* [1989] 1 SCR 1085.

[25] *Taylor v Beere* [1982] 1 NZLR 81 (CA).

[26] *Conway v Irish National Teachers Organisation* [1991] 2 IR 305 (SC) [324].

[27] *ACB v Thomson Medical Pte Ltd* [2017] SGCA 20, [2017] 1 SLR 918 [174].

[28] *Digital Pulse Pty Ltd v Harris* [2002] NSWSC 33, (2002) 166 FLR 421 [159].

unequivocally accepted punitive damages while English law has tergiversated is an interesting phenomenon. One might wonder why Lord Devlin's speech in *Rookes* has been so influential in English law when the position that he reached has rightly been characterised as arbitrary[29] (in the sense that his formulation divorces the law of punitive damages from the remedy's rationales). The answer, as the analysis in section IV suggests, may lie in the power of precedent in English law.[30]

C. Towards a More Permissive Approach

Shortly after the decision in *AB*, the Law Commission published a consultation paper on the reform of punitive damages.[31] The divergence of English law from the position adopted overseas was noted as 'reinforc[ing] the need to reassess the availability of [the remedy]'.[32] In 1997, the Law Commission published its final report in which Lord Devlin's categories were criticised as being 'overly restrictive'.[33] The 'cause of action test' was said to add a further peculiar requirement which made punitive damages awards dependent on 'the accidents of precedent'[34] and the state of authorities in 1964. It was thus recommended that both limitations should be abandoned and that the availability of punitive damages should instead depend on a general test focusing on the character of the defendant's conduct.[35]

Unfortunately, two years after the Law Commission Report was published, the Government announced that it did not intend to implement the relevant recommendations. David Lock, the then minister in the Lord Chancellor's Department, commented: 'the Government have decided not to take forward the Law Commission's proposals for legislation on exemplary damages. It may be that some further judicial development of the law in this area might help clarify the issues'.[36]

[29] See, eg, Law Commission, *Aggravated, Exemplary and Restitutionary Damages* (Law Com No 247, 1997) 107ff.

[30] An analogy might be drawn here with damages for nervous shock. A similar uneasiness exists with such claims but, instead of adopting a clear stance, the courts have opted for a series of artificial qualifications and restrictions: see *Alcock v Chief Constable of South Yorkshire* [1992] 1 AC 310 (HL). I am grateful to Peter Cane for this point.

[31] Law Commission, *Aggravated Exemplary and Restitutionary Damages: A Consultation Paper* (Law Com CP No 132, 1993).

[32] ibid 6.

[33] Law Commission, *Aggravated, Exemplary and Restitutionary Damages* (n 29) 107.

[34] ibid 93. See also the criticism in WVH Rogers, *Winfield and Jolowicz on Tort*, 15th edn (London, Sweet & Maxwell, 1998) 746: 'Whatever one's views on exemplary damages this is an unfortunate state of affairs because it commits the law to an irrational position in which the result depends not on principle but upon the accidents of litigation (or even law reporting) before 1964'.

[35] Law Commission, *Aggravated, Exemplary and Restitutionary Damages* (n 29) 6, 107–08.

[36] HC Deb 9 November 1999, vol 337, col 502. J Morgan, 'Reflections on Reforming Punitive Damages in English Law' in L Meurkens and E Nordin (eds), *The Power of Punitive Damages:*

Although the Law Commission's proposals were not taken up by the Government, the Report signalled a shift towards liberalising the jurisdiction to award punitive damages. It was against this background that the House of Lords was called upon to decide the case of *Kuddus*, approximately four years after publication of the Law Commission's Report.

III. *KUDDUS*

A. Background

On 14 June 1996 Omar Kuddus discovered that a theft had taken place in his flat in Leicester. He promptly reported the incident to PC Adrian Cavendish (an officer serving with the Leicestershire Constabulary). PC Cavendish assured Kuddus that the matter would be investigated, but two months later, he forged Kuddus's signature on a written statement withdrawing the complaint of theft. Why PC Cavendish did this remains a mystery and his reasons are not revealed in any of the public documents concerning this case. The forgery resulted in the police investigation into the complaint of theft ceasing, a fact that Kuddus only discovered several months later.

After obtaining a legal aid certificate to fund the litigation costs,[37] Kuddus was able to bring a claim in misfeasance in public office against PC Cavendish and, on the basis of vicarious liability, the Chief Constable of Leicestershire Constabulary. Despite the admitted forgery by PC Cavendish, the CPS did not pursue criminal charges against him. He was, however, removed from the police force after an internal enquiry.[38]

B. The County Court Decision

Kuddus brought his action in the Leicester County Court. The value of the claim was just under £7,000 at the time (about £16,000 in today's terms). In addition to the claim for the value of the stolen goods, Kuddus sought aggravated and punitive damages.[39]

Is Europe Missing Out (Cambridge, Intersentia, 2012) 196 criticised this development as 'a failure of leadership when the Commission had proposed a rationalisation preferable, surely, to the prevailing law in *Rookes v Barnard* and … *AB v South West Water Services*'.

[37] Obtaining a legal aid certificate in this type of litigation was more common in the late 1990s. Although legal aid is still available for claims against public authorities, the Legal Aid, Sentencing and Punishment of Offenders Act 2012 (LASPO 2012) reforms have restricted eligibility criteria and limited access to representation for litigants without substantial means. For criticism of these reforms, see The Bar Council, 'Report on the LASPO 2012: One Year On' (2014), available at www.familylaw.co.uk/docs/pdf-files/LASPO_One_Year_On_-_Final_Report__September_2014_.pdf.

[38] *Kuddus v Chief Constable of Leicestershire Constabulary* (26 November 1998, Leicester County Court) 18.

[39] Claimant's Particulars of Claim, 9 (on file with the author).

Both parties accepted the fact of forgery and that PC Cavendish's conduct amounted to the tort of misfeasance in public office. As regards remedies, the defendant applied for an order to strike out Kuddus's claim for punitive damages on the basis that such damages were irrecoverable for the tort of misfeasance in public office. The parties explored settlement but the defendant considered that settling would be impossible unless the claim for punitive damages was withdrawn or struck out first.[40] Mr Recorder Waine, applying *Rookes v Barnard* and *AB*, held that punitive damages were only available in English law if a claim (1) fell within one of the categories established by Lord Devlin in *Rookes* (the 'categories test') and (2) was pleaded in a cause of action for which such damages had been awarded before 1964 (the 'cause of action test'). Although the 'categories test' was satisfied on the facts, because the defendant was a public servant whose conduct could be characterised as oppressive, Kuddus could not point to a case in which punitive damages had been awarded for misfeasance in public office before 1964.[41] Accordingly, an order striking out the claim for punitive damages was made.

C. The Court of Appeal Decision

The sole issue for determination on Kuddus's appeal was whether punitive damages were, in principle, available for the tort of misfeasance in public office. The appeal was heard by Auld and Beldam LJJ and Sir Christopher Staughton.

Beldam LJ and Sir Christopher Staughton noted that the Court of Appeal was bound by its earlier decision in *AB*, and that because misfeasance in public office had not attracted an award of punitive damages before 1964 the claim was doomed to fail. They thus dismissed Kuddus's appeal.[42]

In his powerful dissent, Auld LJ said that the 'cause of action test' was not justified on the basis of precedent,[43] principle[44] or policy considerations.[45] He remarked that the rule produced 'two arbitrary groups of torts',[46] one in respect of which punitive damages were available and another in which they were not. This resulted in the preclusion of punitive awards from actions for misfeasance in public office, a tort which lay at the heart of Lord Devlin's first category. Auld LJ further observed that the rule required a search through

[40] I am grateful to HHJ Simon Freeland KC for this point.

[41] The claimant relied on *Ashby v White* (1703) 2 Ld Raym 938 in support of the proposition that punitive damages had been awarded for misfeasance in public office prior to *Rookes*, but the court was not convinced that a case dating from the early eighteenth century provided clear evidence on this point.

[42] *Kuddus v Chief Constable of Leicestershire Constabulary* (CA, 10 February 2000) 16, 20.

[43] ibid 3 and 9.

[44] ibid 9.

[45] ibid 10.

[46] ibid 9.

nearly three centuries of law reports including early cases which may have been reported inadequately or imprecisely[47] and in which it could not be readily ascertained whether punitive damages had been awarded.[48] He therefore concluded that the Court of Appeal should depart from its decision in *AB*[49] and allowed the appeal.

Accordingly, a majority of the Court of Appeal dismissed Kuddus's appeal. However, he was granted leave to appeal to the House of Lords.

D. The House of Lords Decision

Kuddus's appeal was heard by a panel of five judges and was again confined to the issue of the availability of punitive damages in the tort of misfeasance in public office. Relying on the Law Commission's report, the House of Lords unanimously held that punitive damages were available for the tort of misfeasance in public office and that the 'cause of action test' should be abandoned.

In particular, Lord Slynn agreed with Auld LJ that the 'cause of action test' was unprincipled and inefficient in that it required courts to undertake the difficult task of examining pre-1964 authorities to decipher whether punitive damages could be awarded in a particular cause of action.[50]

Lord Mackay observed that the 'cause of action test' conflicted with the traditional common law method of incremental development.[51] Concurring with Lord Slynn, he also held that precedent did not dictate the adoption of the 'cause of action test' in *AB*.[52]

According to Lord Nicholls, the 'cause of action test' represented 'an arbitrary and irrational restriction'[53] on the scope of punitive damages. His view was that punitive damages 'as a remedy of last resort, fill what otherwise would be a regrettable lacuna'.[54] He thus also concluded that the House should depart from the 'cause of action test'.

[47] ibid 10.

[48] This difficulty arose for two main reasons. First, because juries commonly made a global assessment of damages without always identifying if their awards included a punitive component and second, because in the pre-1964 case law, there was confusion between 'punitive' and 'aggravated' damages both conceptually and semantically, see ibid 10.

[49] Although Auld LJ considered *Young v Bristol Aeroplane Co Ltd* [1944] KB 718 (CA) which specifies three exceptions to the rule that the Court of Appeal is bound by its previous decisions he decided (at 12) that it was 'a mistake to treat [*Young v Bristol*] as a rigid rule of law, circumscribing the Court of Appeal's ability to prevent it from correcting what it regards as its own manifest errors, especially where, as in this instance, its earlier resultant rulings prove to be unworkable'.

[50] *Kuddus* (n 1) [22].

[51] ibid [33].

[52] ibid [44].

[53] ibid [55].

[54] ibid [63].

Lord Hutton emphasised the value in maintaining punitive damages as a remedy with a deterrent effect which 'serves to uphold and vindicate the rule of law'.[55] He ruled that the Court of Appeal in *AB* had been wrong to establish the 'cause of action test' on the basis of obiter dicta from *Broome*[56] and that the nature of the defendant's conduct should be the touchstone for a punitive damages award.[57]

Finally, Lord Scott expressed doubts about the general propriety of punitive damages in private law.[58] Although his Lordship clearly viewed any expansion of the jurisdiction to award punitive damages with regret, he nevertheless held that the 'cause of action test' should be abandoned because it 'encourage[d] a tedious trawl through ancient history' and 'commit[ed] the law to an irrational position'.[59]

Accordingly, the House of Lords unanimously held that punitive damages awards should no longer be restricted based on the identity of the wrong pleaded. The decision of the House of Lords to abolish the 'cause of action test' meant that Kuddus's claim for punitive damages could proceed to a substantive trial. However, the case eventually settled for an amount which is not publicly available.

IV. EXPLANATION

The story so far reveals that English law has been moving back and forth with regards to punitive damages. The development of the relevant law can be divided into three time periods, each of which reflects a different attitude towards punitive damages:

(1) 1763[60]–1964: Over this 200-year period, punitive awards were fairly standard. The idea that damages can be awarded with a view to punishing a wrongdoer appeared to be taken for granted by the courts.

(2) 1964–2001: In 1964, Lord Devlin singled out punitive damages as 'anomalous' and expressed a desire to expunge them from English law. A highly restrictive attitude dominates this period. Punitive damages are sealed off behind two artificial limitations (the 'categories test' and 'the cause of action test'), which produce significant technicality and complexity. Both tests appear to be driven by a hostile attitude to civil punishment.

[55] ibid [79].
[56] ibid [89].
[57] ibid [91].
[58] ibid [108]–[111].
[59] ibid [117].
[60] The term 'exemplary damages' was used in the case law for the first time in that year, see the text to n 11.

(3) 2001–today: The final period covers the last two decades. It starts in 2001 with the abolition of the 'cause of action test'. As Lord Nicholls observed in *Kuddus* the departure from the 'cause of action test' 'revolutionise[d] the law's approach to exemplary damages. It … mean[t] that, far from being an undesirable anomaly whose use is to be restricted, exemplary damages are now regarded as a convenient tool which the law should seize and be able to use more widely'.[61] This attitude was reinforced by the enactment of four statutes[62] authorising punitive damages awards in certain (limited) contexts in recent years.

What factors could have driven these changes in the law's approach? Why were punitive damages restricted in 1964? And what were the possible factors leading to a more permissive approach in 2001 in *Kuddus*?

A. Explaining the Shift Towards a Restrictive Approach

It is unclear where the animus towards punitive damages, which was reflected in the positive law by 1964, came from. The four possible explanations explored are: the impact of scholarly work; the power of precedent; influence from foreign jurisdictions; and procedural developments which may have affected the substantive law.

One possibility is that the hostility towards punitive damages arose from scholarly work. Two early tort treatises (ie, *Clerk & Lindsell on Torts*,[63] and *Salmond's Law of Torts*[64]) contain traces of an antipathy towards the notion of civil punishment. In the view of these scholars (which can be contrasted to that of other contemporary textbook writers),[65] 'exemplary damages' were, despite their misleading name, better understood as serving a consolatory rather

[61] *Kuddus* (n 1) [60].

[62] Crime and Courts Act 2013, ss 34–39 (claims against media defendants); High Speed Rail (London-West Midlands) Act 2017, s 51(10)–(11); High Speed Rail (West Midlands-Crew Act) 2021, s 48(10); Environment Act 2021, s 125(4) (claims in respect of breach of certain environmental covenants).

[63] JF Clerk and WHB Lindsell, *The Law of Torts* (London, Sweet & Maxwell, 1889) 94: Courts speak of 'exemplary [damages], as if the object of allowing them were punitive, and to deter … But it is doubtful whether the better view is not that they are consolatory rather than penal'. The statement is repeated in later editions until 1954 (11th edn).

[64] J Salmond, *The Law of Torts: A Treatise on the English Law of Liability for Civil Injuries* (London, Stevens and Haynes, 1907) 102: 'vindictive damages (otherwise called exemplary) … are often said [to be] awarded not by way of compensation for the plaintiff, but by way of punishment for the defendant. It seems more accurate, however, to regard them as a solatium for wounded dignity and feelings'.

[65] See, eg, JD Mayne and L Smith, *Mayne's Treatise on Damages*, 3rd edn (London, Stevens and Haynes, 1877) 37–38; CG Addison, *Wrongs and Their Remedies: A Treatise on the Law of Torts*, 4th edn (New York, Banks and Brothers, 1876) 1184 fn (a); FT Piggott, *Principles of the Law of Torts* (London, W Clowes, 1885) 148.

than penal purpose.[66] By the mid-twentieth century, these traces had matured into clear criticisms. In 1945, in the tenth edition of *Salmond's Law of Torts*, WTS Stallybrass, the Principal of Brasenose College Oxford and an Honorary Bencher of Lincoln's Inn, voiced his distaste towards civil punishment and articulated for the first time a distinction between aggravated and punitive damages (which was later adopted in *Rookes v Barnard*):[67]

> It seems that the punitive element in [exemplary] damages cannot be entirely excluded, but to take it into account in the law of torts is *an anomaly*, for the principle underlying that branch of the law in general is compensation, not punishment. No distinction has been taken in the authorities between *'aggravated' and 'exemplary' damages. The former expression seems more apt for compensation where the damages are at large, the latter where the damages are awarded to mark the Court's disapproval of the defendant's conduct.*

The text by Salmond and Stallybrass presents similarities to Lord Devlin's speech in *Rookes*.[68] Nevertheless it remains unclear if his decision to reshape the law as he did was, in fact, influenced by scholarly work.[69] And there are some reasons to doubt this academic influence theory. First, as Alan Paterson observed, in the 1960s (when *Rookes* was decided) 'the Law Lords were not ... likely to be influenced by academic comment ... It thus might appear that academics, unless they [we]re Benchers ha[d] very little influence as a reference group for the Law Lords'.[70] Second, Lord Devlin has been described as a judge who was 'inclined to

[66] A debate about the nature of punitive damages had occurred in the mid-nineteenth century in the US, see S Greenleaf, 'The Rule on Damages Ex Delicto' (1848) 5 *Western Law Journal* 289, 290–96 (arguing that punitive damages were additional compensation for wounded feelings and insult); *cf* T Sedgwick, 'The Rule of Damages in Actions Ex Delicto' (1848) 5 *Western Law Journal* 193, 194 (arguing that punitive damages are awarded to punish the offender).

[67] WTS Stallybrass, *Salmond's Law of Torts*, 10th edn (London, Sweet & Maxwell, 1945) 127 (emphasis added). The statement is repeated in later editions until 1961 (ie, the 13th edition, which is the closest chronologically to the date when *Rookes* was decided). The distinction between aggravated and punitive damages was explored in more detail a few years later by H Street, *The Law of Torts* (London, Butterworth & Co, 1955) 460–61; *Principles of the Law of Damages* (London, Sweet & Maxwell, 1962) 28–33.

[68] One similarity lies in the distinction between aggravated and punitive damages. To the best of my knowledge, this distinction, which Lord Devlin formally introduced into the law in *Rookes*, first appeared in the tenth edition of Salmond's tort treatise (see Stallybrass (ibid) 127). A second similarity lies in the description of the function of aggravated damages. According to Lord Devlin, aggravated damages are awarded when the defendant injures the claimant's 'proper feelings of dignity and pride' (see *Rookes* (n 3) 1221). Salmond, and then Stallybrass had spoken of 'damages as a solatium for wounded dignity and feelings' (see Stallybrass (ibid) 126). A third similarity lies in the interpretation of the decision of the House of Lords in *Ley v Hamilton*. Both Lord Devlin and Stallybrass explained the case in terms of compensation rather than punishment (see *Rookes* (n 3) 1230–31; Stallybrass (ibid) 126–27). Finally, both Lord Devlin in *Rookes* (n 3) 1221 and Stallybrass (ibid) 126 referred to the absence of punitive damages from Scottish law.

[69] For an argument that Lord Devlin was influenced by the work of Harry Street, see N Sinanis, 'Punishment in Tort: The Context of Ideas in *Rookes v Barnard*' (2022) 15 *Journal of Tort Law* 1, 8–17.

[70] A Paterson, *The Law Lords* (London, Macmillan, 1982) 15.

look down on university lawyers'.[71] Of course, it is possible that, notwithstanding his supposed anti-academic sentiments, Lord Devlin consulted the leading tort textbooks of the time (such as *Salmond's Law of Torts*) while preparing his speech in *Rookes v Barnard*.[72] If so, he may well have stumbled across a thesis he agreed with. Third, if Lord Devlin's hostility towards punitive damages was a product of academic influence then a follow-up question is why this academic work did not influence appellate judges in other jurisdictions which never restricted the availability of punitive damages.[73] Ultimately, although it is unclear if scholarly work actually played a role in the way *Rookes* was decided, it is possible that certain academics contributed to a general ambience of hostility towards punitive damages from the 1880s onwards.

Given that the common law develops incrementally and by reference to past cases, a seemingly more obvious hypothesis is that the antipathy towards punitive damages came from the judges. If this hypothesis were correct, one would expect to find negative dicta regarding punitive damages in various cases leading up to the decision in *Rookes v Barnard*. However, the state of the case law before *Rookes* does not reveal any such scepticism towards punitive damages (in the sense that no other judge had complained about the fact that punishment was a function of damages). Instead, such awards were taken for granted.[74] Lord Devlin appears to be the first judge in the UK to characterise punitive damages as 'anomalous'. As such, we can reject the hypothesis that the decision in *Rookes* was the product of incremental common law development.[75] It seems more likely that it was the product of Lord Devlin's personal position on the desirability of punitive damages. Although it appears that Lord Devlin was clearly committed to his view, what is more curious is why the other members of the House of Lords supported his reform.[76] Whatever their reasons, this antipathy could not rationally be based on precedent. That said, the power of precedent kept Lord Devlin from abolishing punitive damages

[71] N Duxbury, *Jurists and Judges: An Essay on Influence* (Oxford, Hart Publishing, 2001) 89 (see further at 74 and 104).

[72] Lord Devlin cited the 13th edition of *Salmond's Law of Torts* in his discussion of the tort of intimidation (see *Rookes* (n 3) 1205) and Street's *Principles of the Law of Damages* in his discussion of punitive damages (see *Rookes* (n 3) 1221).

[73] See the text to nn 23–27.

[74] Thus, Lord Denning remarked in *Broome* (n 16) 381 that 'the common law of England on this subject was so well settled before 1964, and on such sound and secure foundations'.

[75] This is despite the fact that Lord Devlin saw what he was doing as incremental development. Somewhat ironically, in *Rookes* Lord Devlin overruled his own decision in *Loudon v Ryder* [1953] 2 QB 202 (CA) 209 in which he had directed a jury to award punitive damages outside the *Rookes* categories.

[76] Although there is little information on this point, Lord Devlin, when asked about the punitive damages aspect of *Rookes* in an interview in the 1980s, said: 'Lord Reid had quite strong views about it but because it was purely an English point of law he did not wish to write on it. I think he said to me, … well you put something down and I'll see if I agree with it, and I did and the others made a number of suggestions so that it became rather a judgement of the court in that sense. I modified it a good bit to fit in with other people's views': see Paterson, *The Law Lords* (1982) 99.

altogether.[77] Indeed, Lord Devlin couched his reasoning for the 'categories test' in the language of precedent.

Although it is difficult to explain the first turn towards a restrictive approach that was taken in *Rookes v Barnard* on the basis of adherence to precedent, the persistence of the 'categories test', and the introduction of the 'cause of action test' in *AB*, are illustrative of the power of an apex court in a common law system. The 'categories test' introduced in *Rookes* was affirmed by the House of Lords in *Broome*. This was despite the fact that several judges recognised it as an illogical rule.[78] Why then was it affirmed? The answer to this question may have a lot to do with institutional politics. Lord Denning, who gave the main judgment of the Court of Appeal, was highly critical of Lord Devlin's speech in *Rookes*. He audaciously ruled that the decision in *Rookes* was decided *per incuriam* and, as such, was not binding on the Court of Appeal. As Julius Stone observed, if Lord Denning and his colleagues considered that this would bring about a revision of the 'categories test', they were 'over-sanguine'.[79] On the contrary, this move probably motivated the House to assert its power and reinforce the duty of lower courts to follow its decisions. Lord Reid's observations in *Broome* are revealing in this respect:[80]

> [S]uppose [a defendant] commits the tort not for gain but simply out of malice, why should he not also be punished? … I freely admit there is no logical reason. … *If logic is to be preferred … then this category must be widened. But … I would, logic or no logic, refuse to extend the right to inflict exemplary damages to any class of case which is not already clearly covered by authority.* On that basis I support this category.

Adherence to precedent in an already hostile climate towards punitive damages was also the primary motivation for establishing the 'cause of action test'. The Court of Appeal in *AB* justified its decision on the basis that it was following obiter dicta from *Broome*.[81]

Another possibility is that the antipathy towards punitive damages is attributable to foreign influence. The problem with this hypothesis is that other common law jurisdictions always recognised punitive damages. On the other hand, as was noted in the tenth edition of Salmond, the remedy never featured

[77] *Rookes* (n 3) 1226 (Lord Devlin): 'your Lordships could not, without a complete disregard for precedent, and indeed of statute, now arrive at a determination that refused altogether to recognise the exemplary principle'.

[78] *Broome* (n 4) Lord Reid (at 1088), Viscount Dilhorne (at 1108–11), Lord Wilberforce (at 1119).

[79] J Stone, 'On the Liberation of Appellate Judges: How Not to Do It!' (1972) 55 *MLR* 451, 467–68.

[80] *Broome* (n 4) 1088 (emphasis added). See also his remarks at 1084: 'I would have expected the [Court of Appeal] to know that they had no power to … direct [lower judges] to disregard a decision of this House'.

[81] *AB* (n 4) 523: 'there is no binding authority on this court which compels us to disregard the dicta of the House of Lords in *Broome* and accordingly' the 'cause of action test' was established. For criticism see P Cane, 'The Scope and Justification for Exemplary Damages' (1993) 5 *Journal of Environmental Law* 149, 169–70.

in Scotland or civilian systems.[82] Whilst it is generally not the habit of English judges to consult civil law when deciding cases,[83] Scottish law may have had some influence here. Lord Devlin's observation in *Rookes* that punitive damages are 'peculiar to English law'[84] implies that he considered the position in other jurisdictions. A counterargument here may be that it is relatively unusual for an English court to use Scottish law as a guide, particularly in a case that did not originate from Scotland.

A final possibility is that the animosity towards punitive damages has procedural origins. It may be linked with the procedural reforms of the Judicature Acts 1873–75, in particular the creation of a civil division in the Court of Appeal. In 1902, Kenny wrote:[85]

> In recent years, the question as to the dividing line between civil and criminal proceedings has assumed in England great practical importance, and has occupied the attention of the courts with unusual frequency. … in considering whether a cause is appealable or not, it becomes highly important to have the dividing line between causes civil and criminal sharply defined.

This procedural division may have had a knock-on effect on the way in which judges thought about civil punishment. Another procedural feature which may have motivated the hostility towards punitive damages was the dissatisfaction with civil juries.[86] The thought here is that by restricting a head of damages which would be typically assessed by juries, one would indirectly restrict the power of civil juries. Indeed, others have postulated that a desire to reduce the role of civil juries was a factor motivating Lord Devlin's decision in *Rookes*.[87] What is clear is that Lord Devlin held concerns about the ability of juries to produce consistent damages awards in similar cases.[88] It is not implausible, therefore, that punitive damages were collateral damage in a quest to restrict the role of civil juries.[89] A dampener to this jury dissatisfaction theory, however, is that by the 1960s it had become increasingly common for judges to assess damages. As such, the amount of cases in which punitive damages were awarded and juries were involved in their assessment would have been

[82] Stallybrass, *Salmond* (1945) 126: 'exemplary damages … are unknown in the Roman civil law and in Scotch law'. The statement is repeated in the 1961 edition (which was the most recent edition when *Rookes* was decided).

[83] For criticism of this 'insular habit' see P Birks, 'The Academic and the Practitioner' (1998) 18 *Legal Studies* 397, 408.

[84] *Rookes* (n 3) 1221.

[85] C Kenny, *Outlines of Criminal Law* (Cambridge, CUP, 1902) 15.

[86] Sinanis (n 69) 32–35.

[87] ibid.

[88] *Rookes* (n 3) 1227–28. See further Lord Devlin's extrajudicial writings on civil juries: P Devlin, *Trial by Jury* (London, Stevens, 1956).

[89] The effect of procedural features (including the availability of jury trials) on substantive law can also be observed elsewhere. For example, the concept of duty of care in the law of negligence became more generalised because of the decline of civil juries, which happened between the 1880s and 1930s, see M Dyson, *Explaining Tort and Crime* (Cambridge, CUP, 2022) 166–67.

relatively small.[90] That said, it would not have been negligible and civil juries were still commonly used in defamation actions. *Rookes* itself (an intimidation case) involved a jury award so it is plausible that the role of civil juries featured in Lord Devlin's thinking.

B. Explaining the Shift Towards an Expansive Approach

Although the period between 1964 and 2001 was dominated by severe limitations on punitive damages, since 2001, when *Kuddus* was decided, English law has gradually expanded the scope of the remedy. A reversal in many of the factors that may have contributed to the hostility towards punitive damages in the mid-twentieth century can be observed in the years leading up to *Kuddus*.

First, as the second half of the twentieth century progressed, academic work became increasingly influential on judges. According to Duxbury, 'There is evidence that, as compared with the courts of th[e] earlier period, the English appeal courts of the late twentieth century became generally more receptive to, and more willing to acknowledge the influence of, academic opinion'.[91] Those favouring retention and expansion of punitive damages in recent years include Peter Birks,[92] Andrew Burrows[93] and Nick McBride.[94] That said, there remain academics who are opposed to any expansion of the punitive damages jurisdiction.[95] Perhaps a more important development in the second half of the twentieth century was the founding of the Law Commission, which 'entailed acknowledgement that academic lawyers have an important role to play in law reform'.[96] Indeed, in the 1990s, the Law Commission, under the leadership of Jack Beatson[97] and Andrew Burrows,[98] scrutinised the restrictive approach on punitive damages and made a powerful case in favour of expansion. The Law

[90] Punitive damages were awarded in a 'judge only' trial in eg, *Rook v Fairrie* [1941] 1 KB 507 (CA) (defamation); *Perera v Vandiyar* [1953] 1 WLR 672 (CA) (unlawful eviction).

[91] Duxbury, *Jurists and Judges* (2001) 77.

[92] P Birks, 'Harassment and Hubris: The Right to Equality of Respect' (1997) 32 *Irish Jurist* 1, 25–26.

[93] A Burrows, 'Right Way to Deter Civil Wrongdoers', *The Times*, 23 December 1997, 31.

[94] N McBride, 'Punitive Damages' in P Birks (ed), *Wrongs and Remedies in the Twenty-First Century* (Oxford, Clarendon Press, 1996).

[95] See, eg, E Weinrib, *Corrective Justice* (Oxford, OUP, 2012) 97; A Beever, 'The Structure of Aggravated and Exemplary Damages' (2003) 23 *OJLS* 87. A common feature of the scholars who have remained hostile to punitive damages is perhaps that they have a theoretical commitment to the idea that private law should be all about one thing: corrective justice or the vindication of primary rights. For a recent criticism of 'grand theorists', see J Stapleton, *Three Essays on Torts* (Oxford, OUP, 2021) ch 1.

[96] Duxbury, *Jurists and Judges* (2001) 101.

[97] Law Commissioner when the Consultation Paper on *Aggravated, Exemplary and Restitutionary Damages* was published in 1993.

[98] Law Commissioner when the Report on *Aggravated, Exemplary and Restitutionary Damages* was published in 1997.

Commission's work had a major influence on the *Kuddus* litigation. It was heavily relied on to support the claimant's argument[99] and even influenced the drafting of the defendant's pleadings.[100] The Law Commission's recommendations were also referred to by all five Law Lords deciding *Kuddus*.[101] Further evidence of the impact of the Law Commission's work is supplied by the fact that its core recommendations on punitive damages were implemented, albeit in the narrow context of outrageous wrongdoing by media defendants, in sections 34–43 of the Crime and Courts Act 2013.

A second influential force for the change of direction in 2001 could be past cases. Although the case law in the years before *Kuddus* reflects animosity towards punitive damages[102] there also existed influential critiques of the prevailing restrictive approach, and those critiques may have contributed to the expansive shift taken in *Kuddus*.[103] This can be contrasted with Lord Devlin, who could not point to any judicial dicta in support of his view that punitive damages were an anomaly in 1964.

It is perhaps even more important that *Kuddus* (unlike *Broome*) found its way to the House of Lords in the orthodox way (ie, without the drama of a disobedient Court of Appeal disregarding the authority of the UK's highest court). The lower courts in *Kuddus* followed precedent and faithfully applied the 'cause of action test'. The absence of any controversy regarding respect for the court hierarchy allowed the House of Lords to examine the issue of punitive damages with fresh eyes, and without a perceived need to blindly prioritise precedent over logic. The judges in *Kuddus* could thus focus solely on the force of the parties' arguments in deciding the case.[104] Of the two sides, the claimant's argument was stronger. There was no principled reason for putting the courts through the trouble of examining pre-1964 cases to decide whether a punitive award could be granted in a specific action. It is equally significant that *Kuddus* was a case involving a tort of bad faith and facts which did not make good reading for the police. The House of Lords determined that it would be completely irrational

[99] Appellant's skeleton argument, paras A.4, B.4.2.–B.4.5, B.5, C.2.3, C.2.8 (on file with the author).

[100] In particular, it influenced the defendant's decision to abandon their initial design of challenging punitive damages in their entirety, see the text to n 145 below.

[101] *Kuddus* (n 1) [23] (Lord Slynn), [35] (Lord Mackay), [65] (Lord Nicholls), [71] (Lord Hutton), [132] (Lord Scott). Most Law Lords also referred to Professor Rogers's criticisms of the 'cause of action test' in the 15th edition of *Winfield and Jolowicz on Tort*, see *Kuddus* (n 1) [22] (Lord Slynn), [33] (Lord Mackay), [117] (Lord Scott).

[102] This sentiment is echoed in Lord Scott's speech, see *Kuddus* (n 1) [111].

[103] See, eg, Lord Nicholls, *Let Equity Prevail* (Huddersfield, D&M Heritage Press, 2015) 207 where he singled out 'two lawyers, both judges, whose work [he] ha[d] mostly admire[d]'. These were Lord Denning and Lord Wilberforce. Both were involved in deciding *Cassell & Co Ltd v Broome* and gave powerful speeches in favour of punitive damages. In fact, Lord Nicholls in *Kuddus* (n 1) [63], virtually repeated Lord Wilberforce's words from *Broome* when he said that he found 'most striking … the extent to which the principle of exemplary damages continue[d] to have vitality'. See also *Broome* (n 4) 1114 (Lord Wilberforce): 'I am impressed … with the fact that the principle [of exemplary damages] has shown, and continues to show, its vitality …'.

[104] I am grateful to Lord Mackay for this point.

for punitive damages to be available for torts such as false imprisonment and malicious prosecution but not for misfeasance in public office. By contrast, in *AB* the Court of Appeal set its face against punitive damages in circumstances where the claimants had suffered ill effects for a few days and there was no admitted bad faith breach of duty by the defendant.[105] There is a world of difference between the facts of *AB* and a forgery committed by a police officer in the course of his duties against a member of the public that he was supposed to serve and protect.

A third influential factor for this change may be the now solidified tendency in other common law jurisdictions to award punitive damages more freely. English law was, for many years (and insofar as the *Rookes* categories are concerned is still), swimming against that tide. This trend became even clearer after a succession of cases criticising and refusing to adopt the English position.[106] This did not pass unnoticed in *Kuddus*. The claimant's counsel relied extensively on the position in other common law jurisdictions in the skeleton argument and the authorities bundle submitted to the House of Lords.[107] Further, Lord Nicholls referred to the 'negative reception' of the English position overseas.[108]

As for procedural features that may have contributed to this shift in attitude, two points are relevant. First, although the procedural division between criminal and private law survives, in 1972 Parliament introduced the general power for criminal courts to make compensation orders.[109] Such orders require the offender to pay compensation for any personal injury, loss or damage resulting from an offence. Compensation orders are intended to be a simple measure of corrective justice which is conventionally perceived as belonging to private law.[110] This development arguably reduces the force of the argument for maintaining a bright line between the function(s) of private law and criminal law. Second, insofar as restrictions on punitive damages developed as a means to control civil juries, there is no longer any such need. If civil juries were already restricted in the mid-twentieth century, they have almost vanished in recent years. Today, jury trials are very rarely available in claims which may involve punitive damages awards.[111]

[105] The torts involved in *AB* were public nuisance, negligence and breach of statutory duty. Unlike misfeasance in public office these are not torts of bad faith.

[106] See nn 23–27.

[107] Appellant's skeleton argument, section B.4 (on file with the author).

[108] *Kuddus* (n 1) [64].

[109] Powers of Criminal Courts Act 1973, ss 35–38 (see now Sentencing Act 2020, ss 133–146). Under ss 147–151 of the Sentencing Act 2020, criminal courts also have the power to make restitution orders in certain circumstances.

[110] For discussion see A Ashworth, 'Punishment and Compensation: Victims, Offenders and the State' (1986) 6 *OJLS* 86, 108ff.

[111] These are primarily claims for false imprisonment and malicious prosecution: Senior Courts Act 1981, s 69(1); County Courts Act 1984, s 66(3).

V. AFTERMATH

Bearing in mind the fierce criticisms of the decision in *AB* it was no surprise that the departure from the 'cause of action test' in *Kuddus* was welcomed as a step in the right direction. In a note published shortly after the decision was handed down, Bagshaw commented: 'The House of Lords's rejection of the "[cause of action] test" certainly has the merit of allowing future cases to turn on … principle … rather than on arbitrary accidents of legal history'.[112] Jonathan Morgan similarly remarked in 2003 that the decision in *Kuddus* meant that 'some coherence … [had] returned to the law on exemplary damages'.[113] And more recently, Pey-Woan Lee wrote that the 'cause of action test' was 'rightly … rejected' in *Kuddus*.[114]

While few would disagree that the 'cause of action test' was an irrational and inefficient rule, there remain two contentious questions that *Kuddus* left unanswered. First, although it is relatively uncontroversial that *Kuddus* extended punitive damages awards to all torts,[115] it remains unclear whether the abolition of the 'cause of action test' also applies outside of tort (for example in claims in equity, contract and under the HRA 1998). Second, the merits of the 'categories test' and the general desirability of punitive damages are yet to be considered by the Supreme Court. It is to these two questions that the chapter now turns.

A. Punitive Damages for Non-Tortious Causes of Action

This section discusses the availability of punitive damages in claims under the HRA 1998. The reason for this choice is twofold. First, this question was explicitly raised, albeit not answered, in *Kuddus*.[116] By contrast, the House of Lords did not contemplate the potential effects of the abolition of the 'cause of action test' in the fields of contract or equity. Second, the availability of punitive damages under the HRA 1998 has not been discussed extensively in the literature.[117]

[112] R Bagshaw, 'Exemplary Damages – Misfeasance in Public Office' (2002) 35 *Student Law Review* 63, 64.

[113] J Morgan, 'Privacy, Confidence and Horizontal Effect: "Hello" Trouble' (2003) 62 *CLJ* 444, 469 fn 155. See also A Burrows, 'We Do This At Common Law But That In Equity' (2002) 22 *OJLS* 1, 13: the cause of action test 'was, thankfully, removed … by the House of Lords in *Kuddus*'.

[114] P-W Lee, 'Contract Damages, Corrective Justice and Punishment' (2007) 70 *MLR* 887, 887 fn 3.

[115] It has been doubted whether punitive damages can be awarded in the tort of negligence, see *Inglis v Ministry of Defence* [2019] EWHC 1153 (QB), [2020] PIQR P2 [228].

[116] *Kuddus* (n 1) [92] (Lord Hutton): 'I wish to reserve my opinion on the point [of whether punitive damages could be awarded where a plaintiff is entitled to damages under the HRA 1998] until the matter arises directly for decision' (see also Lord Mackay at [46]).

[117] *cf* discussions about the availability of punitive damages in contract and in equity in, eg, A Burrows, *Remedies for Torts, Breach of Contract and Equitable Wrongs*, 4th edn (Oxford, OUP, 2019) 360–61, 377–78 (breach of contract), 536–37 (equitable wrongs); E Katsampouka, 'Punitive

i. Are Punitive Damages Recoverable under the HRA 1998?

The HRA 1998 was enacted to guarantee in domestic law the rights provided in the European Convention on Human Rights.[118] Under section 8 of the HRA, a court may award damages when a public authority acts, or proposes to act, unlawfully. This has been classified by the House of Lords as a non-tortious statutory wrong.[119]

The relevant provisions do not expressly address whether punitive damages are recoverable in actions under section 8. Nevertheless, the provisions themselves, as well as the relevant legislative history, leave open multiple interpretative arguments for or against the availability of punitive damages under the HRA 1998.

First is section 8(3), which provides that (emphasis added): 'No award of damages is to be made unless … the court is satisfied that the award is necessary to afford *just satisfaction* to the person in whose favour it is made'. It is arguably difficult to accommodate punitive damages (which are traditionally linked with punishment and deterrence) within the language of 'just satisfaction'.[120] That said, it is notable that section 8 does not contain an explicit restriction on non-compensatory awards. By contrast, section 9(3) provides that, in proceedings related to a judicial act, 'damages may not be awarded otherwise than to compensate a person …'. Although the term 'just satisfaction' in section 8(3) could be said to cover similar ground, it is clearly vaguer than the restriction in section 9(3). If the legislature intended to preclude non-compensatory awards under section 8(3) it could have used the same clear language employed in section 9(3).[121] Further, the wording of section 8(3) can, at least, be reconciled with the appeasement rationale of punitive damages according to which the award may 'serve as a satisfaction, and … assuage any urge for revenge felt by victims'.[122]

Damages and "Cause of Action Restrictions"' [2024] *Lloyd's Maritime and Commercial Law Quarterly* (forthcoming).

[118] At the time of writing the Government is considering repealing and replacing the HRA 1998 with a Bill of Rights Bill. The Bill includes the same rights as the HRA 1998 but will change the way in which British courts interpret and apply those rights. For discussion see M Elliott, 'The UK's (New) Bill of Rights' (2022), available at publiclawforeveryone.com/2022/06/22/the-uks-new-bill-of-rights.

[119] *R (Greenfield) v Secretary of State for the Home Department* [2005] UKHL 14, [2005] 1 WLR 673 [19]; *R (Sturnham) v Parole Board for England and Wales* [2013] UKSC 23, [2013] 2 AC 254 [29].

[120] A Burrows, 'Damages and Rights' in A Robertson and D Nolan (eds), *Rights and Private Law* (Oxford, Hart Publishing, 2011) 293.

[121] There has been some controversy in recent years as to whether references to 'legislative intent' are appropriate and/or useful in statutory interpretation, see, eg, A Burrows, *Thinking About Statutes: Interpretation, Interaction, Improvement* (The Hamlyn Lectures, Cambridge, CUP, 2018) 30. *cf* P Sales, 'In Defence of Legislative Intention' (2019) 48 *Australian Bar Review* 6. Nevertheless, the concept is still used in practice to mount construction arguments and is therefore employed here to demonstrate how a potential argument regarding the interpretation of s 8(3) might be framed.

[122] Law Commission, *Aggravated, Exemplary and Restitutionary Damages* (n 29) 53. J Varuhas, *Damages and Human Rights* (Oxford, Hart Publishing, 2016) 122 argues that this language is also consistent with the idea that punitive damages vindicate the claimant's rights. See also the text to nn 6–7.

Second, section 8(4) provides that:

> In determining—
>
> whether to award damages, or
>
> the amount of an award,
>
> the court must take into account the principles applied by the European Court of Human Rights in relation to the award of compensation under Article 41 of the Convention.[123]

This arguably suggests that the nature of damages under section 8 is compensatory. Why else would the court be directed to take into account principles regarding an award of compensation? Such an interpretation is reinforced by the fact that the Strasbourg Court 'has … considered it inappropriate to accept claims for damages with labels such as "punitive"'.[124] However, despite the Strasbourg Court's practice of only awarding compensatory damages, it has never held the domestic availability of punitive damages to be inconsistent with the Convention. Member States are able to 'organise their system of remedies consistently with their own domestic traditions'.[125] Additionally, one might argue that the direction given to UK courts by section 8(4) to 'take into account' compensatory principles applied by the European Court when determining the award of damages does not mean that punitive considerations are never relevant.

Third, during parliamentary debates regarding the bill that became the HRA 1998 Lord Lester opined that 'It would be absurd, if … domestic law concepts such as that of exemplary damages in an appropriate case, which is not a concept that has been developed by the European court, were to be excluded.'[126] Although a comment by a single parliamentarian in parliamentary debates is not authoritative, it potentially indicates that the purpose of section 8(4) was not to exclude punitive damages from the range of remedies available under the HRA 1998.[127]

[123] One of the main differences between the HRA 1998 and the Bill of Rights Bill is that a British court will no longer be required or authorised to interpret UK legislation in line with the ECHR; see Elliott (n 118).

[124] European Court of Human Rights Practice Directions (19 September 2016) [9], available at www.echr.coe.int/Documents/PD_satisfaction_claims_ENG.pdf. See also *Watkins v Secretary of State for the Home Department* [2006] UKHL 17, [2006] 2 AC 395 [32]. *cf* D Fairgrieve, 'The Human Rights Act 1998, Damages and Tort Law' [2001] *PL* 695, 705; J Edelman, *McGregor on Damages*, 21st edn (London, Sweet & Maxwell, 2021) para 50-175.

[125] Edelman (ibid) para 50-115. See also HL Deb 29 January 1998, vol 585, col 383: Lord Mackay contended that in deciding damages issues 'the courts need not be limited by the principles applied [by the Strasbourg Court]'.

[126] HL Deb 29 January 1998, vol 585, col 386.

[127] Clause 17(1) of the Bill of Rights Bill does not preclude the possibility of awarding punitive damages: 'If a court finds that an act (or proposed act) of a public authority is (or would be) unlawful … , the court may, … grant such remedy as it considers just and appropriate'.

Finally, it might be argued that if it was intended for HRA damages to be solely compensatory, the legislature could have simply used the term 'compensation' (rather than the more ambiguous 'damages') as it does in other statutes.[128]

Despite the availability of various statutory interpretation arguments, no reported cases contain a detailed analysis of whether punitive damages are available under the HRA 1998. As mentioned above, the issue was first raised, but left open, in *Kuddus*.[129] The first attempt at providing an answer came in the Court of Appeal judgment in *Anufrijeva v Southwark LBC*.[130] Lord Woolf CJ stated in obiter dictum that 'exemplary damages are not awarded' under the HRA 1998.[131] No substantive reasoning was given for this conclusion, however. Instead, it appeared that Lord Woolf CJ treated it as an obvious inference based on the text of sections 6–8. In *Watkins*, Lords Hope and Rodger indicated that punitive damages were unavailable in a claim under the HRA on the basis of the section 8(4) argument set out above.[132]

ii. De Facto Punitive Awards?

Notwithstanding the above judicial statements indicating that an action under the HRA 1998 cannot yield punitive damages, punishment and deterrence have underpinned 'ordinary' damages awards in such actions. An illustration is *R (Faulkner) v Secretary of State for Justice*.[133] There, the Court of Appeal assessed damages for unlawful detention under the HRA 1998 based on the need to disapprove the executive's actions and prevent public officials from repeating their errors. These goals are irrelevant to compensation and an award which was quantified in light of them cannot, in turn, be regarded as purely compensatory. In his discussion on damages, Sedley LJ said:[134]

> We are entitled ... to place weight ... on the courts' ... disapproval of executive action which unlawfully restricts or interferes with [liberty]. We are also entitled to take into account the fact that damages not only compensate the wronged party but will – or ought to – concentrate the mind of the wrongdoer, especially where the latter is a public authority which is capable, unless it changes its ways, of repeating its error. ... None of these considerations trespasses on the separate role of exemplary damages, which are not claimed here.

With respect, Sedley LJ's suggestion that consideration of these factors did not trespass on the separate role of punitive damages is questionable. It was not

[128] See, eg, Data Protection Act 1998, s 13; Data Protection Act 2018, ss 168–69.
[129] See text to n 116.
[130] *Anufrijeva v Southwark LBC* [2003] EWCA Civ 1406, [2004] QB 1124.
[131] ibid [55].
[132] *Watkins* (n 124) [32] (Lord Hope), [64] (Lord Rodger).
[133] *R (Faulkner) v Secretary of State for Justice* [2011] EWCA Civ 349, [2011] HRLR 23.
[134] ibid [12].

explained how the role of punitive damages is 'separate' from these considerations. Expressing disapproval of the defendant's conduct and ensuring that the wrong will not be repeated are commonly accepted goals of punitive damages.[135] Although ordinary damages may have an incidental deterrent effect, the quantification of an award based on these goals is inconsistent with a compensatory account which focuses on the claimant's loss.

DSD v Commissioner of Police of the Metropolis[136] is another example. There, in determining the amount of damages to be awarded to two rape victims in respect of the police's failure to conduct an effective investigation, Green J considered, among other factors, the nature of the police's failing as 'systemic'[137] and the 'need to impose a sum … to encourage compliance in the future or to mark the "moral" opprobrium of the court'.[138] The court also referred to the 'need to include a deterrent element in the award'.[139] Although Green J mentioned these factors in quantifying 'ordinary' damages, surprisingly he did not think this was a case in which it would have been proper to award punitive damages.[140] However, as Edelman notes, encouraging compliance or reprimanding systemic failures 'could only be relevant to a punitive award'[141] which was effectively made in disguise in this case. It is arguable that, for reasons of fairness and transparency, it would be preferable if the courts were explicit about awarding punitive damages instead of doing so surreptitiously. However, this strays into a broader normative debate on whether punitive damages should be available in proceedings under the HRA 1998. This question is beyond the scope of this chapter and the answer to it will, very likely, turn on one's pre-existing view as to the desirability of punitive damages.[142]

B. The 'Categories Test' and the General Desirability of Punitive Damages in English Law

Another question that *Kuddus* left unanswered is that of the general desirability of punitive damages. Should English law fully embrace them, as the rest of the common law world has done, or should it abolish them entirely? The parties in *Kuddus* were not prepared to raise this question. On the claimant's side, it was deemed unnecessary to take the risk of challenging the *Rookes* categories in circumstances where the claim satisfied the 'categories test'. It was

[135] See the text to nn 5–8.

[136] *DSD v Commissioner of Police of the Metropolis* [2014] EWHC 2493 (QB), [2015] 1 WLR 1833. For further illustrations, see *R (Greenfield)* (n 119) [19]; *Re CZ (A Child) (Human Rights Claim: Costs)* [2017] EWFC 11, [2017] 1 WLR 2467 [58].

[137] *DSD* (n 136) [138].

[138] ibid [127].

[139] ibid [40].

[140] ibid [28] (relying on *Anufrijeva* (n 130)).

[141] Edelman, *McGregor on Damages* (2021) para 50-178.

[142] For a summary of arguments in favour and against punitive damages, see Law Commission, *Aggravated, Exemplary and Restitutionary Damages* (n 29) 94–104.

thought safer to plead the narrower point of abolishing the 'cause of action test' on which the claimant had a strong principled case.[143] On the other hand, the defendant had originally 'indicated an intention to raise this issue but on mature consideration … decided not to do so'.[144] The defendant's counsel took the view that the likelihood of the House of Lords abolishing punitive damages altogether was low. They believed that if they had argued this point they would have lost because punitive damages were too entrenched in the law and the Law Commission's report had recommended an expansion of the remedy.[145]

If the wider question of whether punitive damages should be retained had been raised in *Kuddus* one might suspect that it would have been answered in the affirmative. Lords Hutton and Nicholls made explicit statements in favour of punitive damages in *Kuddus*. Lord Hutton noted the existence of ample authority supporting the proposition that 'in certain cases the awarding of exemplary damages serves a valuable purpose … in vindicating the strength of the law'.[146] Lord Nicholls also valued the retention of punitive damages and even indicated a willingness to expand their scope by jettisoning the 'categories test'.[147] The tenor of Lord Slynn's speech suggests that he too supported punitive damages.[148] By contrast, Lord Scott expressed doubts about the general propriety of the remedy.[149] Acknowledging that he held a 'minority view' on the matter,[150] his Lordship opined that 'there [wa]s no longer any need for punitive damages in the civil law'.[151] Finally, Lord Mackay's speech suggests that he may also have been against punitive damages,[152] subject to a detailed examination of the 'law in action' in that area. By way of obiter dicta, his Lordship noted that changes in the legal landscape since *Rookes v Barnard* may 'affect the propriety of and the necessity for a power to award exemplary damages to continue to be recognised in the law of England'.[153] He acknowledged at the same time the fact that the Law Commission, 'after a very full and thorough consultation, ha[d] reached the view that exemplary damages should continue to be part of the law … on a more extended basis'.[154]

[143] Discussion of the author with HH David Harris KC, who acted for the claimant.

[144] *Kuddus* (n 1) [35] (Lord Mackay).

[145] Discussion of the author with HHJ Simon Freeland KC, who acted for the defendant.

[146] *Kuddus* (n 1) [75].

[147] ibid [66]–[67]. See also ibid [63]: 'Exemplary damages, as a remedy of last resort, fill what otherwise would be a regrettable lacuna.'

[148] ibid [25]–[26] emphasising that the House of Lords had refused to abolish punitive damages in *Rookes* and *Broome*. My interpretation of Lord Slynn's speech is speculative but it is shared by counsel for both parties in *Kuddus*.

[149] ibid [110].

[150] ibid [111]: 'I would be receptive to a submission that exemplary damages awards should no longer be available in civil proceedings. However, … having had the advantage of reading the texts of my noble and learned friends' speeches on this appeal, it is apparent that mine is a minority view'.

[151] ibid.

[152] ibid [36]–[37].

[153] ibid [36].

[154] ibid [35]. In my discussion with Lord Mackay, he mentioned that today he is 'in favour of punitive damages but not in vicarious liability actions'.

English law is yet to take a clear stance regarding the place of punitive damages in private law. Although the debate continues, as of 2001 when *Kuddus* was decided, the tide has begun to turn. Consistently with the traditional common law method, sooner or later another case will have to pick up where *Kuddus* left off and address the wider question of the desirability of punitive damages. The High Court was recently faced with the question of whether it should award punitive damages in a scenario which fell outside the *Rookes* categories.[155] The defendant had been responsible for the death of the claimant's father as a result of a bomb detonated in Hyde Park in 1982. The claimant sought damages under the Fatal Accidents Act 1976. The defendant's criminal trial had collapsed because he had erroneously been given assurance under the post-Troubles 'on-the-runs' scheme that he was not under any investigation when he travelled to England. The claim for punitive damages failed because the killing of someone in a terrorist attack did not satisfy the 'categories test'. Being bound by *Rookes v Barnard*, the High Court rejected the claim, declaring at the same time its sympathy with the claimant.[156] Spencer J said that if this was 'an appropriate case to extend the categories of recovery of exemplary damages, such an extension would be for either Parliament or the higher courts, and probably the Supreme Court'.[157] At the time of writing, the case has been appealed and will be heard by the Court of Appeal.[158] It is hoped that this (or another suitable case) will reach the Supreme Court and provide an opportunity for England to take the final step towards liberalising punitive damages awards and achieving alignment with their rationale.

VI. CONCLUSION

This chapter argued that *Kuddus* deserves the label of a 'landmark case' in the English law of punitive damages because it constitutes a milestone in the liberalisation of the remedy's scope. In attempting to explain how the House of Lords was driven to this expansive shift after decades of restrictions, the possibilities explored were the impact of scholarly work, the impact of past cases, influence from foreign jurisdictions and procedural developments. Of course, the task of explaining trends in the law, or factors underlying judicial decisions, is always difficult. For this reason, these explanations were presented as mere hypotheses. The chapter also considered two questions which *Kuddus* left unanswered, namely the availability of punitive damages for claims under the HRA 1998 and the merits of the 'categories test'. Although there are scant

[155] *Young v Downey* [2020] EWHC 3457 (QB).
[156] ibid [37]–[38].
[157] ibid [38].
[158] See the online Case Tracker for Civil Appeals, available at casetracker.justice.gov.uk/getDetail.do;jsessionid=82E198B242A145A393690106EB27E405?case_id=CA-2021-000475.

dicta suggesting that punitive damages are unavailable under the HRA 1998, it was argued that courts are making de facto punitive awards under the guise of ordinary damages. As for the general desirability of punitive damages, this will probably fall to be determined in a future case. This is especially so given the low likelihood of legislative reform in this area in the foreseeable future.[159] The story continues.

[159] Burrows, *Remedies* (2019) 377: '[T]here seems little chance in the foreseeable future of legislative reform dealing generally with punitive damages'.

11

Whiten v Pilot Insurance Co (2002)

How Can Something So Wrong Feel So Right?

ZOË SINEL*

I. INTRODUCTION

CANADIANS ARE GENERALLY considered reserved, pleasant, and maybe just a little dull. With its one-million-dollar punitive damages award for breach of contract, the Supreme Court of Canada's 2002 decision in *Whiten v Pilot Insurance Co*[1] challenges our mild-mannered reputation. Considered alone, punitive damages are controversial, but when they respond to a pure breach of contract, they are just about unprecedented.[2] Indeed, in its recognition of punitive damages for pure breach of contract, Canada stands alone in the Commonwealth.[3] What I have found to be the most puzzling aspect

* Thank you to participants at the Landmark Cases in Punitive Damages Workshop and to Joanna Langille and Ryan Liss. I am especially grateful to Eleni Katsampouka and Jason Neyers for their valuable input.

1 *Whiten v Pilot Insurance Co* 2002 SCC 18, [2002] 1 SCR 595.

2 The usual story about the non-availability of punitive damages for breach of contract relies on the House of Lords' decision in *Addis v Gramophone Co Ltd* [1909] 1 AC 488 (HL) as the authority for their exclusion. As James Goudkamp notes, however, in 'Exemplary Damages' in G Virgo and S Worthington (eds), *Commercial Remedies: Resolving Controversies* (Cambridge, CUP, 2017) 321–22, *Addis* is a weak authority for the exclusion of punitive damages for breach of contract since only two of the Law Lords (Lord Atkinson and Lord Gorell) explicitly discussed punitive damages and even they split on their availability, while the other Law Lords could be interpreted as talking about the non-availability of non-pecuniary damages for breach of an implied term with respect to manner of dismissal rather than about punitive damages. For similar doubts, see R Cunnington, 'Should Punitive Damages be Part of the Judicial Arsenal in Contract Cases?' (2006) 26 *Legal Studies* 369, 373. A notable exception to the exclusion of punitive damages for breach of contract is the historical and now obsolete cause of action of breach of promise to marry. See D Venour, 'Punitive Damages in Contract' (1988) 1 *Canadian Journal of Law and Jurisprudence* 87.

3 The Singapore Court of Appeal, however, in *PH Hydraulics & Engineering Pte Ltd v Airtrust (Hong Kong) Ltd* [2017] SGCA 26, [2017] 2 SLR 129 [136]–[137] refused to foreclose entirely on the availability of punitive damages for breach of contract. Nonetheless, the Court noted that such an award would 'hardly ever be available'. For further commentary on this landmark case, see Lee, ch 17

of *Whiten* is not the Supreme Court of Canada's break from contract doctrine orthodoxy, but how the decision nonetheless feels so right. Thus, one objective of this chapter is to explain and resolve my own ambivalence about *Whiten*. This ambivalence is not merely my own; rather, it is likely to be shared by anyone who takes seriously the distinction between criminal and civil responses to wrongs. Ultimately, I argue that the award in *Whiten* is justified, although not for the reasons given by Canada's highest court. Indeed, my argument is that, insofar as the award is understood as *punitive*, it cannot be justified.

I begin with the principal reason that *Whiten* is intuitively compelling: its facts disclose a plaintiff for whom we feel great sympathy and a defendant for which we feel great disgust. I next explain why most legal scholars nonetheless think it is a deeply flawed decision. Here, I present the core specific criticisms of *Whiten* as well as the more generally acknowledged difficulties that punitive responses pose for private law, especially the law of contract. In the final substantive portion of the chapter, I look to explain the felt rightness of the award in *Whiten*. First, I attempt to offer a way to justify the award as a punitive award. Here, I suggest potential responses to the core problems punitive awards raise for private law's coherence. These responses prove ultimately unsatisfactory; yet, through their exploration, two better and novel ways to justify the award in *Whiten* are revealed. According to my understanding of *Whiten*, the award should not be characterised as punitive, but rather as either vindicatory or compensatory. The million-dollar sum either vindicates the integrity of the court as a public institution vested with the authority and responsibility to secure the system of private law rights or it compensates the plaintiff for a violation of her right to an unimpeded civil avenue of redress. Either of these alternatives can resolve the ambivalent feelings *Whiten* generates.

II. WHY *WHITEN* FEELS SO RIGHT …

It was a frigid winter night in Ontario's cottage country when Daphne Whiten and her husband discovered a fire in their home. Wearing only their pajamas, Ms Whiten, her husband, and their daughter fled the house, leaving their belongings and three cats to be engulfed by flames. Fortunately, Daphne Whiten was insured. Initially her insurer, Pilot Insurance, provided C$5,000 for living expenses and covered the Whitens' rental of a nearby winterised cottage. After a couple of months, however, Pilot abruptly discontinued its rent payments

of this volume. In jurisdictions in the US in which punitive damages have been permitted for breach of contract, bad faith breaches of insurance contracts are now usually determined on the basis of the *tort* of bad faith breach of contract. See C Bridgeman, 'Corrective Justice in Contract Law: Is There a Case for Punitive Damages?' (2003) *Vanderbilt Law Review* 237, 268.

and began pursuing an aggressive and adversarial approach to Ms Whiten's insurance claim. In essence, Pilot and its agents alleged that the Whitens had set fire to their own home and, on this basis, refused to pay the C$345,000 due under the insurance contract. Pilot's allegation was not supported by any evidence and was indeed contradicted by evidence from its own expert investigator.[4] It appears that the suspicion of arson – a suspicion generated and relentlessly pursued by one of Pilot's lawyers – arose solely from the Whitens' socioeconomic status.[5] The insulting and stigmatising implication was that the Whitens had set fire to their own home for the insurance proceeds.

Daphne Whiten was an affecting plaintiff. She and her family had lost their home, their belongings, their cats, and now, due to Pilot's unsubstantiated allegations of arson, even their good names in the small community in which they lived.[6] The Whitens were forced to undergo an eight-week trial on Pilot's allegation of arson, for which they incurred C$320,000 in legal costs – money which the Whitens did not have and which could only be paid for through Ms Whiten's sole asset: her insurance claim. At trial for Pilot's breach of contract, the jury was evidently of the view that the arson charge was wholly unsubstantiated, and, moreover, that Pilot's motive for pursuing this charge was to force Ms Whiten to settle for a sum less than what she was owed under her contract. The jury awarded Ms Whiten the C$345,000 due under the contract, her legal costs, and C$1m in punitive damages.[7] Pilot appealed to the Ontario Court of Appeal, where a majority of the court reduced the punitive damages award to C$100,000.[8] The Supreme Court of Canada (SCC), with one justice dissenting,[9] restored the trial court's C$1m punitive damages award.

Pilot Insurance's conduct was reprehensible. For no good reason, and in fact for a very bad reason, Pilot Insurance – a company that held itself out as the protector of those rendered vulnerable due to life's vicissitudes – pursued a course of conduct for the sole purpose of denying Ms Whiten the benefit of her

[4] Among other poignant details, Pilot's investigator noted that, following her return to the site of the fire, Ms Whiten vainly attempted to salvage various fire-destroyed items. As well, Mr Whiten suffered serious frostbite to his feet (an injury that required hospitalisation and later required him to be in a wheelchair for some time) when he gave his slippers to his daughter so that she could walk to the road to get help. If the fire were premeditated arson, as Pilot implied, would the Whitens not have thought to dress more sensibly for the sub-zero temperatures? Would they not have arranged to save some of their more precious belongings, in particular, their three cats?

[5] 'The problem here is that Pilot embarked on a "train of thought" … that led to the arson trial, with nothing to go on except the fact that its policy holder had money problems': *Whiten* (n 1) [102] (Binnie J).

[6] It is worth noting that the Whitens' community, Haliburton County, is small. In 2016, the entire population was under 20,000. Thus, when Pilot discontinued its financial support of the Whitens, the clear implication of arson spread throughout the community.

[7] *Whiten v Pilot Insurance Co* (1996) 132 DLR (4th) 568 (ONSC).

[8] *Whiten v Pilot Insurance Co* (1999) 42 OR (3d) 641 (CA). Justice Laskin dissented. He would not have altered the jury's award.

[9] Justice Lebel would have denied the appeal to alter the Ontario Court of Appeal's reduction in punitive damages from C$1m to C$100,000. Despite this position, Justice Lebel had some of the harshest words for Pilot's behaviour: 'The insured had the misfortune to run across what might be characterized as the insurer from hell' (*Whiten* (n 1) [159]).

insurance contract. Ms Whiten, a person of relatively few means who, through no fault of her own, had just lost her house, her belongings, and her cats, had to endure not only the uncertainty regarding the resolution of her claim, but also the indignity of Pilot's demeaning treatment of her and her family. If ever there was a breach of contract case that cried out for something more than an award of compensation, this was it.

Evidently, the SCC agreed. In a landmark ruling, Justice Binnie, penning the majority decision, upheld the jury's C$1m punitive award. In doing so, he relied on two earlier SCC decisions, *Hill v Church of Scientology of Toronto*[10] and *Vorvis v Insurance Company of British Columbia*.[11] *Hill* established the 'if but only if' test for the availability of punitive damages. The purpose of punitive damages is to deter, denounce, and punish. Therefore, they are only rationally required if the compensatory award is insufficient to achieve these objectives. As Justice Corey explained in *Hill*, 'It is important to emphasize that punitive damages should only be awarded in those circumstances where the combined award of general and aggravated damages would be insufficient to achieve the goal of punishment and deterrence.'[12] In *Vorvis*, the SCC recognised, although somewhat reluctantly, that a breach of contract claim could merit a punitive response.[13] With respect to what it is that can be punished, Justice McIntyre emphasised that:[14]

> It surely cannot be merely conduct of which the Court disapproves, however strongly the judge may feel. Punishment may not be imposed in a civilized community without a justification in law. The only basis for the imposition of such punishment must be a finding of the commission of an actionable wrong which caused the injury complained of by the plaintiff.

This passage has subsequently been interpreted as setting out the so-called 'independently actionable wrong' requirement for the availability of punitive damages for breach of contract.[15] In addition to a breach of contract, the plaintiff must show an independently actionable wrong that would merit a punitive response.

In *Whiten*, the SCC found that the compensatory damages awarded to Ms Whiten – damages that amounted merely to the paying out of her contractual entitlement – were insufficient to achieve the goals of punishment, deterrence and denunciation. Further, the Court held that Pilot's insurance breach of its contractual obligation of good faith was sufficient to satisfy *Vorvis*'s independently actionable wrong requirement.

[10] *Hill v Church of Scientology* [1995] 2 SCR 1130 (SCC).
[11] *Vorvis v Insurance Company of British Columbia* [1989] 1 SCR 1085.
[12] *Hill* (n 10) [196].
[13] *Vorvis* (n 11) 1107.
[14] ibid 1105–06.
[15] *Whiten* (n 1) [31].

III. ... BUT IS SO WRONG

Notwithstanding the effect *Whiten*'s emotionally compelling facts have on my natural sympathies, when I teach the case to my more tender-hearted students, I remind myself and them that the decision is deeply and irredeemably flawed. What is my problem? Am I heartless? Why can't I just let what feels right be right? My problem is the usual one people have with punitive damages: they are not apt responses to private wrongs *qua* private wrongs.

The usual story about the inappropriateness of punitive damages for civil wrongs concerns the institutional limits of the civil court to mete out punishment. For several rule-of-law-type arguments, a civil court should not be in the business of punishment. For one, defendants in a civil suit lack the procedural protections enjoyed by those accused of criminal wrongdoing. The state must show beyond a reasonable doubt that the criminal accused committed the crime. By contrast, in a civil suit, the evidentiary standard is the balance of probabilities. As well, the substantive criteria for punitive damages are sufficiently vague that they might be considered void for vagueness if they were a matter of criminal law. What sort of conduct is 'so malicious, oppressive and high-handed that it offends the court's sense of decency'?[16] Finally, since criminal punishment does not exclude the possibility of a punitive award,[17] the possibility looms of double jeopardy for the civil defendant. When it comes to awarding punitive damages for breach of contract, additional practical arguments against them have been levied, primarily focusing on the disruptive and destabilising effects punitive awards would have on commercial dealings.[18]

These practical concerns can and do have practical rejoinders.[19] My problem with punitive damages echoes some of these practical concerns – in particular, the noted difficulty of imposing a punitive response to a voluntarily assumed obligation.[20] It is, however, not only for practical reasons that civil courts

[16] *Hill* (n 10) [196] (Cory J).

[17] *Whiten* (n 1) [123].

[18] For a survey of these practical concerns, see S Rowan, 'Reflections on the Introduction of Punitive Damages for Breach of Contract' (2010) 30 *OJLS* 495, 497. Rowan argues that for the coherence of the doctrine, punitive damages should not be awarded for breach of contract. See also Goudkamp, 'Exemplary Damages' (2017) 325–27 for a similar list of concerns. Goudkamp argues that none of the five common arguments against punitive damages in fact hold up under close scrutiny.

[19] See Goudkamp, 'Exemplary Damages' (n 2). Due to the perceived over-statement of the practical concerns with punitive damages for breach of contract, many authors have argued in favour of their availability: N McBride, 'A Case for Awarding Punitive Damages in Response to Deliberate Breaches of Contract' (1995) 24 *Anglo-American Law Review* 369; N McBride, 'Punitive Damages' in P Birks (ed), *Wrongs and Remedies in the Twenty-First Century* (Oxford, Clarendon Press, 1996); W Dodge, 'The Case for Punitive Damages in Contracts' (1999) 48 *Duke Law Journal* 629; J Edelman, 'Exemplary Damages for Breach of Contract' (2001) 117 *LQR* 539; Cunnington (n 2).

[20] As the Law Commission expresses this concern, 'a contract is a private arrangement in which parties negotiate rights and duties, whereas the duties which obtain under the law of tort are imposed by law; it can accordingly be argued that the notion of state punishment is more readily applicable to the latter than to the former' (Law Commission, *Aggravated, Exemplary and Restitutionary*

should not respond to civil wrongdoing with punishment, but for conceptual reasons as well. Specifically, the nature of private law's entitlements and their relationship to their remedies excludes punishment from the ambit of appropriate remedial responses. If remedies are determined by the rights they respond to, and the rights themselves do not contain a right of punishment, then problems arise when a court orders a punitive response for the violation of a private law right.

Punitive responses are not appropriate, in this view, because they exceed the authority of the private law right-holder (the plaintiff) and, by virtue of this over-reach, the authority of the civil court tasked to recognise, determine, and secure the plaintiff's entitlements. One way to understand the nature of a private law entitlement is as a right to coerce another.[21] If I am the owner of Blackacre, I can order you not to step foot on it, can shove you off of it if you do step a foot on it (provided of course that I give you fair warning and reasonable time to remove yourself), and take you to court for stepping foot on it and request compensation for whatever material damage your foot might have caused. The remedial responses available to me are limited by the circumference of my right. My right is to the exclusive use and possession of Blackacre and the profits that might flow from this use and possession, and so my remedy can only preserve my entitlement to exclusive use and possession and its effects. The remedy does so through excluding you (by an order of ejectment, for example) and by ordering you to pay compensation for any unauthorised use or damage you cause or any profits you make (or expenses you save) through your unauthorised use and possession. Moreover, anyone acting on my behalf or at my behest is equally

Damages (Law Com No 247, 1997) para 1.72). This point is further supported by the rule against penalty clauses in contracts. If we could privately punish one another, why are we prevented from enforcing these penalising clauses? See Rowan (n 18) 508–09 for a lucid account of the inconsistency punitive damages awards present for rules concerning penalty clauses.

[21] This story is often told through the lens and language of corrective justice. In this account, punitive damages are inappropriate for private law because they are awarded on the basis of a unilateral consideration, a consideration that affects only one party to the transaction. They are awarded to deter *this defendant*, to denounce *his blameworthiness*, and to punish *his wrong*. The defendant's moral turpitude and amenability to deterrence are not, in other words, appropriately relational and so cannot ground a private law coercive obligation. Private law, so this story goes, is constituted by reasons that apply equally to the defendant and plaintiff because the form of these reasons is relational. Only reasons that apply equally to the plaintiff and the defendant can be the basis of normative considerations of liability and remedy. For this account, see EJ Weinrib, 'Punishment and Disgorgement as Contract Remedies' (2003) 78 *Chicago-Kent Law Review* 55. For attempts to justify punitive damages by reference to corrective justice, see Bridgeman (n 3) and P-W Lee, 'Contract Damages, Corrective Justice and Punishment' (2007) 70 *MLR* 887. Notably, some commenters (in particular, civil recourse theorists) have taken a different standpoint. Rather than argue that punitive damages are inapt because they do not fit corrective justice, these scholars argue that corrective justice is inapt as an expository theory of tort law because it cannot explain punitive damages, an obvious feature of tort law for centuries. See B Zipursky, 'Rights, Wrongs, and Recourse in the Law of Torts' (1998) 51 *Vanderbilt Law Review* 1, 95–96. At the descriptive level, this criticism has some bite; however, at a normative level, it fails to provide a satisfactory explanation, that is, a justification, for the legitimacy of tort law.

so limited. This means that, unless my private entitlement also contains within it a private right of punishment,[22] when you violate my right, I do not have the authority (and nor does anyone else who is acting to secure and preserve my rights) to punish you for this violation.

On my take, the right to punish is found not in responses to private but to public wrongs. Public wrongs are violations of rights that everyone is under an obligation to respect – rights with respect to persons and property. Moreover, the wrong is only public if the actor who commits the wrong does so while in possession of a particular mental state with respect to that wrong – what the criminal law labels *mens rea*.[23] Because of the kinds of rights they are directed at and the kind of mental state that accompanies them, public wrongs represent threats to the authority of law and the system of rights as such. They are threats to the system of law that protects each of us in the security and possession of rights we already happen to have. Thus, these wrongs are wrongs to *all of us*, not just wrongs to the person who has experienced it directly. The crime of murder is wrong not by virtue of the victim's life that was taken, but by virtue of its contravention of the law of the land against homicide, a law which purports to keep us all safe from violations of our right not to be killed.[24] For the personal valence of the wrong of homicide, we must look to the law of torts.[25] Only wrongs that are public in this sense can be legally punished, and, further, the authorisation for the execution of this punishment can only be a wrong against the state. The right to punish public wrongs (criminal violations of the law) arises out of society's duty to secure rights as well as the institutions that constitute these rights. To preserve the system of rights as such and itself, society can punish violations of its law that are committed in a way that expresses a disregard for the system of rights and thereby threatens this system. Legal punishment, to put the point bluntly, should be a response to the wrongs of criminal law, not to the wrongs of tort.

[22] Which is something along the lines of what Benjamin Zipursky believes, see 'A Theory of Punitive Damages' (2005) 84 *Texas Law Review* 105. Zipursky argues that punitive damages have a civil aspect in that they relate to the plaintiff's 'right to be punitive'. I find this right to be punitive hard to square with civil recourse theory's central tenet that private persons give up their private rights to seek redress in exchange for the state's provision of an avenue of civil recourse. Zipursky, however, appears to see this right to punish as analogous to our right to self-defence, a right we do not give up when we exit the state of nature (ibid 151–52).

[23] Notably, mental states that fall below subjective intent or recklessness or even advertent negligence can satisfy criminal law's 'guilty mind' requirement. I am of the view that to hold someone criminally responsible absent their willed violation of the law is unprincipled and incoherent; however, this chapter is not the place to fully engage with this argument. For a helpful analysis of the kinds of mental states that are coherently thought to attract criminal attention, see A Beever, 'The Structure of Aggravated and Exemplary Damages' (2003) 23 *OJLS* 87, 88–89.

[24] My gratitude to Ryan Liss for helping me work through this point.

[25] Notably, the common law of torts was on its own impotent in this regard until statutory intervention that permitted the circumvention of the common law *actio personalis* rule according to which private rights of action died with the rights-holder.

Moreover, while it is true that the conduct that attracts tort liability, if committed intentionally,[26] also attracts criminal attention, this is not the case for the law of contract. Battery, assault, false imprisonment, and defamation all have criminal analogues, but pure breach of a commercial contract does not.[27] Although most often committed with the requisite criminal intention – the subjective intention to breach a legal norm – breaching an ordinary commercial contract is never thought to be a matter meriting the attention of criminal law. Why not? Since it is not the mental element that is lacking, it must be that a contractual entitlement is not the kind of right the violation of which amounts to a public wrong. Its breach is not a wrong to all of us. If A breaches his contract with B, he only interferes with B's rights, not the rights of all of us. We all don't have contractual rights against A; only B does. By contrast, if A steals B's cow, his action signals that the law against cattle-thieving is not one that applies to him. We all have the same right against A not to steal our personal property. And A's theft threatens the security of all of our rights to private property, not just B's. By the lights of his own reason for his action and the action itself, A puts himself outside the operation of the norm that we all accept regarding private property. He sets himself apart from us in his willful violation of a law and a duty that he owes to all of us. By contrast, when A breaches his contract with B, he puts himself merely outside the bilateral norm of contractual performance that exists between him and B.[28]

It has been suggested to me that there is no need of a criminal law analogue to justify the imposition of punitive damages for breach of contract since the latter are not *criminal* punishment, but *civil* punishment, and that because civil punitive damages are monetary only, they do not carry the stigma that criminal punishment does. My thought, however, is that *only* the criminal law can mete out punishment. Civil punitive damages aim to denounce, deter, and punish (in the sense of retribution). These goals are identical to the aims of criminal punishment.

[26] I use here the criminal understanding of intention, not the tort conception.

[27] But see s 422(1) of the Criminal Code of Canada, RSC, 1985, c C-46, which prohibits criminal breach of contract in certain circumstances. This chapter is not the place to explain this provision in the Canadian criminal code, nor am I the person to attempt such an explanation. One plausible interpretation is that the contract breacher is using the breach of contract as a means to violate the bodily integrity or physical property of another (sub-ss (a)–(c)) or as constituting the crime of public nuisance set out in s 180 (sub-ss (d) and (e)). We could argue that the breaches outlined in ss 422 and 180 of the Criminal Code would threaten the security of all of us and hence attract the punitive power of the state.

[28] Of course, by breaching his contract with B, A makes it predictively more likely that he will breach his contract, perhaps even similar contracts, with C, D, E, and anyone else who is unlucky enough to contract with A. Moreover, if we punish this kind of breach, it might very well make it less likely that A will breach these kinds of contracts in the future. But the issue here not about the predictive likelihood of rights violations or their deterrence, but about the nature of the norm that is violated and what violation of that norm publicly expresses. This is part of the reason that willed violations of contract are (usually, but see n 27) not criminalised, while intentional interferences with property and persons are. More needs to be said on this topic and it is not strictly necessary for the point I make here, which is that, even those who accept punitive damages for torts, often balk at their availability for breach of contract.

Thus, the core question is whether a civil court, the authority of which is limited by the rights of the parties before it, can punish. My answer is that it cannot.

From these criticisms of punitive damages for private law actions, two related problems come into focus. First, there is the problem of the limitations on remedial responses set by the nature of the private law right in issue. Here, the question is whether the violation of a contractual entitlement, understood as an obligation that binds only the parties to the contract, merits a punitive response. The second concerns the authority of a civil court to dispense extra-compensatory awards – that is, awards that exceed the ambit of the plaintiff's entitlement against the defendant. We are here concerned with the legitimate authority of the court – whether it can go beyond the authority to coerce that is provided to it by the defendant's violation of the plaintiff's entitlement. It is for these conceptual reasons regarding the limits of a contract party's entitlement following the breach of her contract and how these limits affect the court's remedial powers that I have for years thought *Whiten* to be wrongly decided.

Even those who do not perceive as strict a line as I do between private and public wrongs have decried *Whiten* for its incoherence. *Whiten* is no darling of Canadian jurisprudence. Two core criticisms stand out: (1) the non-necessity of punitive damages on its facts; and (2) the court's interpretation of the independent actionable wrong requirement. These criticisms, we will see, are intimately related.

One of the most damning of the doctrinal criticisms is that the Supreme Court of Canada failed to apply the 'if but only if' test correctly. Punitive damages may only be awarded if they serve a rational purpose. Only if the compensatory damages awarded are insufficient to punish, denounce, and deter the defendant's conduct is there a rational need for punitive damages. Thus, it is a problem for those defending *Whiten*'s punitive damages award that the Supreme Court of Canada (as well as the courts below) overlooked the availability of the full gamut of compensatory damages.[29] In explaining how the jury came to the C$1m award, Justice Binnie opines:[30]

[29] The full array of compensatory damages available was not pleaded by counsel. One likely reason for this was that, at the time, most lawyers would not have considered mental distress damages as obviously available damages for breach of contract. It was not until *Fidler v Sun Life Assurance Co of Canada* 2006 SCC 30, [2006] 2 SCR 3 that the Supreme Court of Canada clearly established that these damages were available pursuant to the general principle of remoteness in contract as set out in *Hadley v Baxendale* (1854) 9 Exch 341 for contracts for which peace of mind was an object. Therefore, it might not be fair to say that these damages were overlooked. Further, if they weren't pleaded, this could mean that it was not open to the court to award them, thus satisfying the 'if but only if' test since the essence of that test is that other remedies that *are available* are inadequate for punishment, denunciation, or deterrence. Here, so this response goes, they were simply not available. However, the plaintiff in *Whiten* did plead compensatory damages for the breach of her contract and aggravated damages and mental distress damages are compensatory damages. As such, one could say that, unlike punitive damages, which would need to be specifically pleaded in the plaintiff's statement of claim lest their judicial consideration catch the defendant unawares, aggravated damages might not.

[30] *Whiten* (n 1) [103].

> The jury was obviously incensed at the idea that the respondent would get away with paying no more than it ought to have paid after its initial investigation in 1994 (plus costs). It obviously felt that something more was required to demonstrate to Pilot that its bad faith dealing with this loss claim was not a wise or profitable course of action. The award answered a perceived need for retribution, denunciation, and deterrence.

In other words, the jury felt that a successful claim by Daphne Whiten would only have yielded the sum she was due under the contract as well as her lawyer's costs. To award her only what she was owed in the first place – that is, to put her in the position she would have been in had the contract been performed – fails to respond to Pilot's reprehensible behaviour. Pilot, the jury surmised, had weaponised the non-performance of its contractual obligation – an obligation it had no good reason to dispute being under – in an effort to force Ms Whiten to give up her contractual entitlement. If the judicial response to this behaviour is simply to order Pilot to perform its contract, then the essence of Pilot's wrongful behaviour, which was not merely non-performance but rather non-performance for the purpose of exploitation, goes unaddressed.

But the award of her promised indemnity[31] plus her lawyer's fees, as critics have noted, are not the only compensatory damages available on *Whiten*'s facts.[32] The contract between Ms Whiten and Pilot Insurance was a peace-of-mind contract – that is, a contract in which one of the very things bargained for is mental tranquility. When these kinds of contracts are breached, plaintiffs can recover non-pecuniary losses – also known as mental distress damages. Canadian case law[33] after *Whiten* has affirmed that these non-pecuniary damages are governed by the general principle of remoteness in contract damages as set out by *Hadley v Baxendale*.[34] But case law prior to *Whiten* also established their availability.[35] If part of what the plaintiff bargained for was peace of mind, then breach of the contract can bring mental distress within the ambit of reasonable foreseeability. A personal contract of insurance, especially home insurance from an insurer that markets itself as 'guiding people like you into safe harbours',[36] clearly falls within the class of contract for which non-pecuniary damages would be available.

[31] Swan posits that the nature of the damages was never really properly expressed. In reality, Swan argues, Ms Whiten's claim was not a claim for damages to compensate her for loss, 'but for the indemnity she had been promised in the policy she had purchased from the defendant.' This is just the value of her contractual right – the right she possessed under her policy. See J Swan, 'Punitive Damages for Breach of Contract: A Remedy in Search of a Justification' (2004) 29 *Queen's Law Journal* 596, 607.

[32] Weinrib (n 21) 97–98; JD McCamus, 'Prometheus Bound or Loose Cannon – Punitive Damages for Pure Breach of Contract in Canada' (2004) 41 *San Diego Law Review* 149, 1515; Swan (n 31) 607–08.

[33] *Fidler* (n 29).

[34] *Hadley* (n 29).

[35] *Jarvis v Swan Tours* [1973] QB 233 (CA); *Newell v Canadian Pacific Airlines Ltd* (1977) 14 OR (2d) 752 (Co Ct); *Pilon v Peugeot Canada Ltd* (1980) 29 OR (2d) 711 (HC); *Vorvis* (n 11); *Farley v Skinner* [2001] UKHL 49, [2002] 2 AC 732.

[36] *Whiten* (n 1) 129 (Binnie J).

In addition to mental distress damages owed as compensation for the breach of the contractual obligation to provide mental peace, aggravated damages should have been available to compensate Ms Whiten for the high-handed manner in which the contract was breached. While non-pecuniary damages for breach of contract compensate the plaintiff for a benefit she was deprived of under the contract or for a loss that is a reasonably foreseeable and thus a contemplated consequence flowing from the breach, aggravated damages respond to and compensate for the diminution of a plaintiff's dignity or feelings of self-worth brought about by the way in which the defendant wronged her. Whether you see aggravated damages as compensating for the additional hurt feelings a plaintiff suffers as a result of particularly nasty breach or as compensating the plaintiff for the assault to her dignity,[37] the facts of *Whiten* support the award of these damages.[38] Pilot treated Daphne Whiten's economic vulnerability as a means to coerce her into settling for less than what it knew she was entitled to. Through this exploitation, Pilot treated her not as a person entitled to equal treatment and respect, but rather as an object of disdain and disrespect.

Finally, consider that, according to the court in *Vorvis*, punitive damages for breach of contract require the defendant to have committed an independently actionable wrong. In *Whiten*, the court found that this wrong is the breach of the implied contractual obligation of good faith. If this really is an independently actionable contractual violation,[39] shouldn't Ms Whiten receive compensation for it? Once compensatory damages are awarded for this separate breach of the duty of good faith, we then must ask whether the total compensatory damages she is entitled to is sufficient to deter, denounce, and punish the defendant – that is, we must apply the 'if but only if' test. Only if it is not do we consider punitive damages to be rationally required. And now it seems we are in a potential situation of infinite regress, since we need an additional independently actionable wrong over and above the breaches of contract to ground punitive awards. Once this additional wrong is identified, we would have to compensate it and then ask again if the compensatory award achieved the necessary punitive objectives. And so on.[40] In sum, since the full extent of the compensatory damages that Ms Whiten was entitled to were not awarded, it is difficult to know if punitive

[37] For the former view, see A Burrows, *Remedies for Torts, Breach of Contract, and Equitable Wrongs*, 4th edn (Oxford, OUP, 2019) 287–88. For the latter view, see P Birks, 'Harassment and Hubris: The Right to An Equality of Respect' (1997) 32 *Irish Jurist* (ns) 1; B Chapman, 'Punitive Damages as Aggravated Damages: The Case of Contract' (1990) 16 *Canadian Business Law Journal* 269; Beever (n 23).

[38] See *Fidler* (n 29) [52].

[39] Although I must admit I struggle to see how it could be absent an actual breach of a contractual term of the contract. I can act in bad faith but still satisfy the terms of the contract (say my malicious motives fail to pan out). I doubt that my counterparty could sue me for breach of contract just because I acted in bad faith.

[40] For the same critique of infinite regress generated by the independent actionable wrong requirement, see Weinrib (n 21) 100: 'the requirement of a further actionable wrong, in combination with the notion that punitive damages are given only if compensatory damages are insufficient renders impossible the very award that the requirement is supposed to condition.'

damages were needed at all and, if they were, whether C$1m was the amount rationally required.

The infinite regress entailed by the interaction between *Hill*'s 'if but only if' test and *Vorvis*'s independently actionable wrong requirement leads us to the second core criticism of *Whiten*, namely that the Court misinterpreted the latter requirement. According to one commentator, all Justice McIntyre was after when he gave voice to this requirement was that the wrong in question be one for which punitive damages would be an appropriate response.[41] On the facts of *Vorvis*, a wrongful dismissal case, no such wrong was available. The Court in *Whiten* interpreted Justice McIntyre's decision to use the word 'wrong' rather than the American Restatement's preferred word 'tort' as an indication that not only torts but possibly separate breaches of contract could satisfy this requirement. A more likely explanation, however, was that Justice McIntyre chose the term 'wrong' rather than 'tort' in order to include such things as equitable wrongs.[42] Contrary to the *Whiten* court's expansive interpretation of the independently actionable wrong requirement, punitive damages probably should not be awarded for pure breaches of contract that are not accompanied by an independent wrong that is not also a breach of contract. As another commentator has recently written, 'As it stands now, the *Whiten* test for an "independent wrong" is clearly erroneous because it essentially makes every breach of contract case open to a claim for punitive damages.'[43] In the wake of *Whiten*, to award punitive damages for breach of contract, a court can simply carve up the contract into a number of separate obligations and pin the punitive damages on the breach of just one of these.[44]

Immediately following *Whiten*, we could have addressed this concern by explaining that most contracts would not fall within *Whiten*'s ambit since the contractual obligation breached has to be one to which punitive damages could attach such as the breach of the obligation of good faith. Yet, in 2014, the Supreme Court of Canada announced in *Bhasin v Hrynew* that the principle of good faith is an 'organizing principle' of Canadian contract law.[45] This recognition led at least one commentator to fret that, in doing so, 'the Court appears to have opened the way for an expanded use of the doctrine of good faith in punitive damages cases.'[46] This concern, however, has been tempered somewhat by the Supreme Court of Canada's 2020 decision in *Atlantic Lottery Corporation Inc v Babstock*.[47] Striking out the plaintiffs' claim for punitive

[41] McCamus (n 32) 1498 and 1504.

[42] ibid.

[43] M Harrington, 'A Lawless Science: Punitive Damages for Breach of Contract in Canada' (2015) 69 *Supreme Court Law Review* (2d) 185, 212.

[44] For a similar criticism, see Swan (n 31).

[45] *Bhasin v Hrynew* 2014 SCC 71, [2014] 3 SCR 494 [33].

[46] Harrington (n 43) 222; see also E Andrews '*Lex Punit Mendacium*: Punitive Damages and *Bhasin v Hrynew*' (2017) 7 *Western Journal of Legal Studies* 1 for a similar worry.

[47] *Atlantic Lottery Corp Inc v Babstock* 2020 SCC 19, 447 DLR (4th) 543.

damages for breach of contract, Justice Brown, writing for a majority of the Court, explained that, according to *Bhasin*, 'not every contract imposes actionable good faith obligations on contracting parties' and that '[w]hile good faith is an organizing principle of Canadian contract law, it manifests itself in specific circumstances.'[48] Caution is still warranted, however, since the majority in *Atlantic Lottery* is a slim one, with four justices dissenting on this precise point. According to Justice Karakatsanis's dissenting opinion, the plaintiffs in *Atlantic Lottery Corporation* pleaded a breach of the duty of honest performance, a duty recognised in *Bhasin* as applying to all contracts, and that breach of this implied duty could justify an award of punitive damages.[49]

IV. SOLUTIONS TO MY AMBIVALENCE

The above criticisms are trenchant and yet I cannot help feeling that the C$1m award in *Whiten* was deserved. In the past, I have written off these feelings as vestiges of sentimentality that somehow resisted expunction during my legal training. Here, however, I take these intuitions seriously, using them to motivate my search for a justification for the jury's extraordinary award, a justification that responds to the conceptual and doctrinal criticisms outlined above.

One way to resolve my ambivalence would be if we could characterise the wrong in *Whiten* in such a way that it no longer gives rise to the two related problems awards of punitive damages pose for private law: the kind-of-right problem and the institutional competence problem. Recall, according to the first problem, a contractual right is just not the kind of right the violation of which can attract something like punishment. To solve this problem, we might want to recharacterise the nature of the private law right at issue in *Whiten*. According to the second problem, civil courts do not have the right kind of authority to mete out a sanction that extends beyond the authority granted to them by the reach of the plaintiff's right. To solve this problem, we must look to when and how this apparent over-reach can be justified.

To recharacterise the contractual right in *Whiten*, we might look to the language of exploitation used throughout the *Whiten* decision coupled with the feature of the contract that it was one in which the insurer had an obligation of good faith.[50] Recall that the historical exception to the rule against punitive

[48] ibid [65] (Brown J). In this case, Justice Brown found that the 'contract between ALC and the plaintiffs does not fit within any of the established good faith categories. Nor did the plaintiffs advance any argument for expanding those recognized categories' (ibid).

[49] ibid [129]–[134].

[50] A few examples of this language from the judgment: 'The jury obviously concluded that people who sell peace of mind should not try to exploit a family in crisis' *Whiten* (n 1) [4] (Binnie J); 'The financial or other vulnerability of the plaintiff, and the consequent abuse of power by a defendant, is highly relevant where there is a power imbalance' *Whiten* (n 1) [114] (Binnie J); 'The obligation of good faith dealing means that the appellant's peace of mind should have been Pilot's objective, and

responses for breach of contract lay in the obsolete action of breach of promise to marry. If we understand the insurance contract as something more than just a contract between two formally equal parties, but rather as an agreement by a relatively more powerful party (the insurer) to act in the best interests (or at least not to exploit the interests) of the more vulnerable party (the insured), then the right involved looks less contractual and more fiduciary in nature. The fiduciary flavour of the right might solve the kind of right problem since we are now dealing with an *in rem* right of sorts. The idea here is that the right in cases like *Whiten* is more than merely contractual. The language in *Whiten* of exploitation supports this interpretation. I doubt, however, whether this means it should support a claim for punitive damages. When you behave in a particularly reprehensible way, aggravated damages, not punitive damages, are the appropriate response. One could also say that characterising the right in this way could support a remedy like disgorgement;[51] however, notably, the defendant in *Whiten* did not profit from its wrongdoing.[52]

To style the wrong committed as one that affects all of us in the security of our entitlements, we need to do more than call the breach a breach of trust that could attract fiduciary-like remedies. One way in which we can do this is by recharacterising the wrong in *Whiten* not as a mere breach of contract, but rather as a crime, specifically the crime of fraud. According to section 380 of the Criminal Code of Canada, 'Everyone who, by deceit, falsehood or other fraudulent means … defrauds the public or any person … of any property, money or valuable security or any service, is guilty of an indictable offence.'[53] Because Ms Whiten did not rely on Pilot's dishonesty, she was neither deprived of money or property, nor was she exposed to the risk of this deprivation, and thus the crime is probably better characterised as the crime of *attempted* fraud than fraud.[54] But the difficulty with this explanation, although it goes a long way in explaining our intuitions regarding the wrongfulness of Pilot's behaviour, is that it cannot explain the result in *Whiten* itself. *Whiten* is a civil, not a criminal case. As such, our proposed justification must also be civil.

A promising place to look for such a justification is in the jurisdiction with the most restrictive approach to the award of punitive damages: England. Despite the removal of the cause of action limitation on punitive damages in

her vulnerability ought not to have been aggravated as a negotiating tactic. It is this relationship of reliance and vulnerability that was outrageously exploited by Pilot in this case' *Whiten* (n 1) [129] (Binnie J).

[51] See *Attorney-General v Blake* [2000] UKHL 45, [2001] 1 AC 268.

[52] Although perhaps if it had been successful in its attempts to disentitle Ms Whiten, we could say it profited by saving the expense of paying out on her contract of indemnity.

[53] *Criminal Code of Canada*, RSC, 1985, c C-46.

[54] See *R v Theroux* [1993] 2 SCR 5 (SCC). Note, however, that the court in *R v Olan* [1978] 2 SCR 1175 (SCC) made it clear that the victim does not need to show economic loss to prove the offence; that the imperilling of an economic loss is sufficient. It is an open question whether Ms Whiten's insurance proceeds were imperilled by Pilot's deceitful behaviour.

Kuddus v Chief Constable of Leicestershire Constabulary[55] and despite the extraordinary award of restitutionary (disgorgement) damages for breach of contract in *Attorney-General v Blake*,[56] punitive damages remain unavailable for breach of contract in England and are only permitted in tort in three situations: (1) oppressive or arbitrary conduct by the servants of government; (2) where the defendant's conduct was calculated to make a profit; and (3) where a statute expressly authorises them.[57] At first blush, it seems that the second category is the most promising category for situations like *Whiten*, in which we have the cynical exploitation of one party by the other in order to save an expense.

But it cannot be just the intention to make a profit that would justify the imposition of punitive damages. A malicious intention cannot turn an otherwise non-wrongful act into a wrong,[58] so how could it be relevant for a grounding of extra-compensatory damages? What is happening in these situations, I suggest, is that the only objective interpretation of the defendant's behaviour is that he is treating the plaintiff's civil remedy as a *price* that he can pay in order to wrong her. That is, he is using the civil remedial system as a licensing scheme to permit his wrong. If the court were to award compensatory damages only, the court would be legitimating this conduct. In doing so, it is as if the court licenses the defendant's wrong. Imagine that the usual and known damage award for a slap across the face was C$500. Imagine further that I am incredibly wealthy and that I despise you. I calculate that expressing my hatred of you with a well-delivered slap is well worth the C$500 I will no doubt subsequently be ordered to pay you.[59] If a court ordered me to pay you just the C$500 and no more, it would be treating the reason for which I acted as if it were legitimate; it would be legally recognising my cynical disregard for your rights by my treatment of them as things that can be bought for a price. The court thus abdicates its role and obligations as the securer of private rights by turning itself into an agent of wrongdoing. Extra-compensatory damages appear justified in tort when the situation is such that a court's award of compensatory damages only amounts to the court's public legitimation of the defendant's malicious intent.

But I think we can clearly see how this rationale, while persuasive for tort, fails to do the trick for contract. Famously – some might say infamously – contract law countenances the possibility of efficient breach. Here, the breacher calculates that it is in his or her financial interest to breach his or her contract

[55] *Kuddus v Chief Constable of Leicestershire Constabulary* [2001] UKHL 29, [2002] 2 AC 122.

[56] *Blake* (n 51).

[57] *Rookes v Barnard* [1964] AC 1129 (HL).

[58] For more on this, see Z Sinel, 'Malicious Means and Spiteful Ends' (unpublished). Also see *Bradford v Pickles* [1895] AC 587 (HL). But see *Tuttle v Buck*, 107 Minn 145, 119 NW 946 (1909).

[59] This illustration is drawn from the story of a wealthy citizen of Rome around the first century BCE, Lucius Veratius, who would walk through the Forum slapping citizens in the face. Veratius was followed by a slave whose job was to hand over 25 asses (the sum stipulated in the *XXII Tables*) to the victim. This behaviour did lead to changes in Roman private law with respect to damages for *iniuria*; see R Zimmermann, *The Law of Obligations: Roman Foundations of the Civilian Tradition* (Oxford, Clarendon Press, 1996) 1052.

with the plaintiff and pursue a more lucrative contract with another (or no one). It is better, in other words, for the defendant to breach and pay damages than to perform. The defendant in these situations clearly views the plaintiff's remedial entitlement as merely a price he or she has to pay to wrong the plaintiff. But this common situation is not one that anyone would say should attract punitive damages. We could even, somewhat controversially, say that the defendant, by paying contract damages, satisfies the contractual obligation, understood as an obligation to perform *or* to pay damages.[60] The nature of the wrong that attracts punitive damages in tort is precisely the defendant's treatment of the plaintiff's right to his or her person and property as a disjunctive obligation, as an obligation either to respect the right or pay for its violation. The law of contract is different in this regard.

The facts of *Whiten* could nonetheless reveal a potential avenue for this kind of justification. It is not the defendant's contemptuous disregard for the plaintiff's rights that grounds an award for the apparently punitive damages for breach of contract, but rather his disregard for the system of private law's rights and remedies as such. In the law of torts, this contemptuous (and punishable) disregard is expressed in the defendant's treatment of the plaintiff and her civil remedy as a means to his ends, as a price to pay for his wrongdoing. In contract, the contemptuous or malicious motivation is directed to the plaintiff's ability to exercise and have remedial rights at all. In some ways, this describes the situation in *Whiten* fairly well. Here, the defendant embarked on a course of conduct intending to deprive Ms Whiten of her contractual rights under the contract. As Peter Benson lucidly explains, extra-compensatory damages for breach of contract may be appropriate[61]

> where a defendant's breach is not limited to mere nonperformance ... but involves conduct that specifically demonstrates a manifest malicious intent (evidenced often by fraud or conscious recklessness) that in effect denies the plaintiff's very capacity to have and to enjoy any contractual rights at all.

This last justification gets at the heart of the issue in *Whiten*: the wrong is to the system of rights as such, not to Ms Whiten personally. If the court were to allow wrongdoers like Pilot to exploit not just Ms Whiten but the whole system of contract law and its remedies, then it would be allowing the system to work an exploitative purpose on the vulnerable. We can maybe now see how the problem for punitive damages with respect to the kind of right can be addressed by recharacterising the right as a right to the capacity to exercise and enjoy one's rights. However, we still need to come to terms with the second problem faced by punitive awards, namely, whether a civil court has the authority to

[60] J Nadler, 'Freedom from Things: A Defense of the Disjunctive Obligation in Contract Law' (2021) 27 *Legal Theory* 177.

[61] P Benson, *Justice in Transactions: A Theory of Contract Law* (Cambridge, Harvard University Press, 2019) 556. Benson identifies *Whiten* as a clear example of this kind of breach.

dispense them. To make this argument I suggest that the situation in *Whiten* is analogous to a different sort of wrong, a wrong for which civil courts have historically been permitted to mete out punishment: the wrong of contempt of court. When a party acts in contempt of court, this means he or she is acting in a way that disrespects the court's authority – for example, failing to do as the court orders – or is behaving in a way that obstructs or hinders the system of justice.[62] Civil courts can find parties before them in contempt and can issue punishment, even imprisonment, as a remedy.

The facts not only of *Whiten* but also of a key case that preceded it, *Royal Bank of Canada v W Got & Associates Electric Ltd*,[63] can fit within the description of contempt of court. *Got* involved the Royal Bank of Canada's breach of contract in its failure to give notice for its decision to cut off the plaintiff's line of credit. *Got* looks like a case in which punitive damages were awarded for breach of contract. Indeed, both Edelman and Goudkamp refer to *Got* as the first case where punitive damages were awarded for breach of contract.[64] It makes sense that they would think this; by the time the case came before the Supreme Court of Canada, the matter was being resolved on the grounds of breach of contract alone with no other cause of action doing any of the work.[65] But what is really going on in this case, I suggest, is a different kind of a wrong. It is to this wrong that so-called 'punitive' damages are a response. While the relevant breach of contract was the failure to give notice, the trial judge 'found that the bank's wrongful conduct in securing the receivership order was not limited to insufficient notice; he concluded that the bank had misled Master Funduk in obtaining the receivership order by tendering a misleading affidavit.'[66] To mislead a Master strikes me as a clear instance of abuse of process for which a court can respond in a potentially punitive fashion. If the defendant's action impugns the proper administration of the court's own processes, then the court should be able to address this violation.

A similar issue occurs in *Whiten*. Here, however, it was the defendant's lawyer, a Mr. Crabbe, who embarked on a 'train of thought' with no evidential basis and convinced his client to pursue an exploitative strategy of denying Ms Whiten's claim solely for the purpose of forcing her to make an unfair settlement. The implication of abuse of process or contempt of court can be found in the judicial reaction to the 9 June 1994 letter of Mr Crabbe to his client:[67]

> Pilot also conceded at the Court of Appeal that these inculpatory opinions were influenced by Crabbe.

[62] See M Shapiro, 'Procedural Wrongdoing' (2022) 48 *BYU Law Review* 197 for a similar perspective.

[63] *Royal Bank of Canada v W Got & Associates Electric Ltd* [1999] 3 SCR 408 (SCC) ('*Got*').

[64] Goudkamp (n 2) 324; Edelman (n 19) 539.

[65] In the courts below, the cause of action of conversion was still in play.

[66] *Got* (n 63) [12].

[67] *Whiten* (n 1) [22].

> The trial judge commented unfavourably about Crabbe's role in this litigation. He felt that his 'enthusiasm for his client's case appears to have caused him to exceed the permissible limits which ought to confine a lawyer in the preparation of witnesses'.

While in *Got*, the defendant misled an officer of the court (a Master), in *Whiten*, an officer of the court (a lawyer) works the procedural injustice. In both cases, the actions of the defendant threaten the just operation of the judicial process. Both involve the weaponising of just procedures and tactics to achieve a known injustice. In *Got*, the defendant knew that it was producing false evidence to obtain its order of receivership. In *Whiten*, Pilot's counsel (and, by implication, Pilot as well) knew that there was no legitimate reason to fight Ms Whiten's insurance claim. If the court permits defendants to act in these abusive ways – ways which are abusive not just of the plaintiff, but of the court itself – with impunity, it allows itself to be used as a tool of injustice.[68]

I am not sure, however, that just because the defendant is using the court as an accomplice to achieve his spiteful ends, to abstract himself from the system of rights, that we must necessarily characterise the response to this kind of wrong as punitive. These damages do not stem from the court's authority as limited by the circumference of the plaintiff's right. Rather they come from the authority of the court as a public institution, vested with the authority to preserve and secure the system of rights. The court awards these extra-compensatory damages in defence of this system of private rights. In this sense, it is a response to a public wrong. However, it is a mistake to think that all responses to public wrongs are punitive. Every exercise of public authority is not punishment. If these awards are not punitive, we can avoid some of the concerns about double jeopardy and other procedural issues raised by the specter of non-criminal punishment. The authority to dispense extra-compensatory damages comes from the court's inherent jurisdiction to protect its own integrity. On this understanding, they are truly not punitive damages, but rather damages that vindicate the court's status as a public institution.

I find this a plausible explanation of the award in *Whiten*. It provides a justification to extend the civil court's authority beyond the ambit of the plaintiff's right. However, it has one major disadvantage in that it cannot explain why the *plaintiff* should be the beneficiary of this award, of this exercise of the court's authority. If the wrong is a wrong to the court, why does the plaintiff pocket the financial proceeds of the wrong's sanction? In closing, therefore, I would like to offer one final alternative explanation for the kind of award that was given in *Whiten*. Here, the idea is that the award is not punitive, but rather compensatory. The award compensates for a wrong done to the plaintiff's right to a right of action. The money reflects the distinct wrong of the defendant in trying to

[68] We might now think that the kind of wrong involved in these cases is in fact most akin to the first category of where punitive damages are permitted as outlined in *Rookes* (n 57): the oppressive and arbitrary behaviour of a state official. If the court ignored the misconduct of the defendants in *Got* and in *Whiten*, it would be turning itself into an agent of the defendant's malicious maxim.

dispossess the plaintiff of her right of action through his abuse of process. The gist of this wrong is that the defendant has a legal obligation to the plaintiff, knows that it does, but is doing everything in its power to frustrate the plaintiff's legitimate attempts to get it to perform its legal obligation. The advantage of this explanation is that it offers a good explanation for why the plaintiff gets the money. The award under this understanding is actually compensatory, not extra-compensatory, as the alternative above sees it, as it compensates the plaintiff for a violation of her civil right of redress.[69] Problems for this explanation, however, arise on a practical level in that it is very difficult to tell the difference between a defendant who litigates hard and one who is litigating dirty.

V. CONCLUSION

To summarise, the violation of the right that grounds a claim for punitive damages is not the contractual right that the plaintiff has against the defendant, but rather the right the court has against the defendant not to undermine its very ability to be the protector of rights. A noted difficulty with this argument is that if we characterise the wrong as a wrong to the court, as I am suggesting, then it does not make sense to have the award go to the plaintiff. If the wrong is a wrong to another, receipt of damages for that wrong is a clear windfall. If we consider again the facts of *Whiten*, one of the things that feels so right about it is that poor Ms Whiten receives the C$1m for her suffering. But that's just it: the punitive damages should not have been awarded for her *suffering*; that is what aggravated damages should have been used for. The reason that *Whiten* feels so right is that the reprehensible behaviour of the defendant merited a response. Ms Whiten deserved compensation for the high-handed way in which she was treated, but she should not have been compensated through an award of *punitive* damages. This analysis, I hope, goes some way to explaining the reasons for our ambivalence about Canada's leading case on the availability of punitive damages.

[69] Thank you to Robert Stevens for helping me see this alternative solution to the problem posed by *Whiten*'s award and for the following apposite movie recommendations which exemplify this solution: *The Verdict* (1982); *The Rainmaker* (1997); and *Dark Waters* (2019).

12

Harris v Digital Pulse Pty Ltd (2003) Equity, Penalties, Controversy and Costs

MARK LEEMING*

I. INTRODUCTION

NO OTHER DECISION of an Australian intermediate appellate court has generated such intense commentary and controversy, locally and internationally, as that of the New South Wales Court of Appeal, delivered in 2003 in *Harris v Digital Pulse Pty Ltd*.[1] Prominent critics include Andrew Burrows,[2] James Edelman[3] and Michael Kirby;[4] prominent defenders include Patrick Keane[5] and Charles Rickett.[6] The judgment coincided with two publications which contributed to the controversy. The Law Commission had recently published its report *Aggravated, Exemplary and Restitutionary Damages*, which 'consider[ed] it unsatisfactory to perpetuate the historical divide between common law and equity, unless there is very good reason to do so'.[7] Conversely,

* I acknowledge the participation of Damien Allen, Andrew Bulley, the Honourable Keith Mason and the Honourable George Palmer, each of whom kindly consented to my interviewing them about the case and reviewed earlier drafts of this chapter. I also acknowledge the helpful response from Ramenka Kako and the research assistance of Beata Szabo.

[1] *Harris v Digital Pulse Pty Ltd* [2003] NSWCA 10, (2003) 56 NSWLR 298 ('*Harris Appeal Judgement*'), allowing an appeal from [2002] NSWSC 33, (2002) 166 FLR 421 ('*Harris First Instance Judgement*').

[2] A Burrows, 'We Do This At Common Law But That in Equity' (2002) 22 *OJLS* 51; A Burrows, 'Remedial Coherence and Punitive Damages in Equity' in S Degeling and J Edelman (eds), *Equity in Commercial Law* (Sydney, Lawbook Co, 2005) 381.

[3] J Edelman, 'A "fusion fallacy" fallacy?' (2003) 119 *LQR* 375.

[4] M Kirby, 'Equity's Australian Isolationism' (2008) 8 *Queensland University of Technology Law Journal* 446.

[5] P Keane, 'The 2009 W A Lee Lecture in Equity; The Conscience of Equity' (2010) 84 *Australian Law Journal* 92.

[6] CEF Rickett, 'Punitive Damages: The Pulse of Equity' (2003) 77 *Australian Law Journal* 496.

[7] Law Commission, *Aggravated, Exemplary and Restitutionary Damages* (Law Com No 247, 1997), chaired by (then) Dame Mary Arden, including Andrew Burrows as a member, Part V, para 1.55. The Commission recommended enacting legislation to authorise exemplary damages for breach of fiduciary duty (which is of course quite different from legal innovation by a court).

the fourth edition of *Meagher, Gummow and Lehane's: Equity: Doctrines and Remedies* (of which I was a co-author) was published while the appeal was pending.[8] It was roundly critical of the reasoning at first instance,[9] and included an unwarranted *ad hominem* attack upon the judge which was not repeated in the following edition.[10] These were years which have been labelled the 'equity wars':[11] 'an unedifying feud of Lilliputian proportions between Little-endian commercial-equity practitioners and judges in New South Wales and Big-endian adherents to the academic neo-roman law philosophy of Peter Birks at Oxford University', as one commentator recently put it.[12]

The broad issue is familiar; indeed it is entrenched in undergraduate curricula as a standard example of the nature of equity and its contrast with common law.[13] Can equity, when an egregious breach of fiduciary duty is established, order pecuniary relief going beyond compensation for loss caused by the fiduciary, taking away assets gained in breach of duty and stripping profits, so as to amount to a penalty? In jurisdictions where the counterparts of Lord Cairns' Act are traditionally worded and the statute is understood to be confined to cases of contracts or torts,[14] the issue presents as one of principle, not directly affected by statute.

There is a threshold difficulty with terminology. 'Equitable compensation' hardly connotes an order which is penal rather than compensatory. 'Damages' suggests a common law remedy for a breach of an equitable duty, and thus the view that such remedies are freely available for breach of any duty, whatever its juristic nature. Evidently conscious of this, Spigelman CJ referred to 'punitive monetary awards', and this chapter will follow the same course. I do not deprecate the significance of the language used to describe legal concepts,[15] but my

[8] The preface is dated 10 September 2002, after the appeal was heard, but with publication occurring before the appeal was determined (see *Harris Appeal Judgement* [60] and [108]).

[9] RP Meagher et al, *Meagher, Gummow and Lehane's Equity: Doctrines and Remedies*, 4th edn (Sydney, LexisNexis Butterworths, 2002) para 2.310.

[10] ibid para 23.020; *cf* JD Heydon et al, *Meagher, Gummow and Lehane's Equity: Doctrines and Remedies*, 5th edn (Sydney, LexisNexis Butterworths, 2015) paras 2.355, 23.595 and 42.190.

[11] See K Mason, *Lawyers Then and Now* (Sydney, Federation Press, 2012) 174–82. See also K Barker's review of S Degeling and J Edelman (eds), *Equity in Commercial Law* (Sydney, Lawbook Co, 2005) in (2007) 70 *MLR* 163 referring to the 'dramatic exothermic effects' associated with the topic of fusion.

[12] S Gageler, 'The Coming of Age of Australian Law' in B McDonald et al (eds), *Dynamic and Principled: The Influence of Sir Anthony Mason* (Sydney, Federation Press, 2022) 26.

[13] See (without attempting to be exhaustive) M Bryan et al, *A Sourcebook on Equity & Trusts in Australia*, 2nd edn (Cambridge, CUP, 2019); A See et al, *Property and Trust Law in Singapore* (The Netherlands, Wolters Kluwer, 2019); G Virgo, *The Principles of Equity & Trusts* (Oxford, OUP, 2012).

[14] See *Force India Formula One Team Ltd v 1 Malaysia Racing Team SDN BHD* [2012] EWHC 616 (Ch), [2012] RPC 757 [389]–[93]; contrast the broadly drafted Victorian provision considered in *Giller v Procopets* [2008] VSCA 236, (2008) 24 VR 1.

[15] 'The label carries with it connotations which cannot but help shape the listener's or reader's understanding. Much of the success of what Richard Dawkins would call the "meme" that is a "fusion fallacy" is its evocative, alliterative and catchy name': M Leeming, *The Statutory Foundations of Negligence* (Sydney, Federation Press, 2019) 62; see also 6–7 and 167.

point is merely that the issue determined by *Harris v Digital Pulse* turned on substance rather than form. No one contended that the order sought by Digital Pulse was unavailable merely because it might be called 'exemplary damages' and 'damages' (whether exemplary or compensatory) were not available for breach of an equitable duty.

The trial judge (Palmer J) and the dissentient on appeal (Mason P) held that punitive monetary awards were available for breach of fiduciary duty. The majority of the Court of Appeal divided. Heydon JA said they were not available. Spigelman CJ held that where a breach of fiduciary duty is based on a contract (such as an employment contract), punitive monetary awards are not available in equity, just as they are unavailable for the breach of contract (Spigelman CJ explicitly left open the more general question of punitive monetary awards in equity).[16] The decision is only authority for the narrower proposition.[17] At the level of authority, *Digital Pulse* leaves unresolved whether a punitive monetary award is available for a breach of an equitable confidence or breach of trust by the trustee of a resulting trust. More generally, *Harris v Digital Pulse* revealed a deep methodological division on the approach to be taken when courts are asked to decide a novel proposition of law. This was picked up almost immediately by the editor of the Australian Law Journal, whose note focused 'on the remarks by the majority to the effect that single judges in equity should no longer consider themselves as able to advance the law',[18] a point returned to below. It is difficult to imagine special leave for a further appeal to the High Court of Australia being refused, but it was not sought. The decision was partly a product of its time, when the way in which equity was to be developed was a highly contested issue, with antagonists on both sides (including, to my regret, me) resorting to rhetoric and invective, and before a reconciliation was worked out, rejecting any notion of automatic fusion but accommodating the possibility of equity and common law drawing upon one another by analogy in appropriate cases.

This chapter attempts to place the Digital Pulse litigation in context, by reference to the primary documents and recollections of the participants at trial, albeit two decades after the event.

II. SOURCES

In addition to the judgments themselves, which are substantial,[19] this chapter draws upon interviews with the trial judge the Hon George Palmer, and with

[16] *Harris Appeal Judgement* (n 1) [4]–[5].

[17] Spigelman CJ's reasons are meaningfully regarded as 'narrower' than those of Heydon JA: see P Herzfeld and T Prince, *Interpretation*, 2nd edn (Sydney, Lawbook Co, 2020) 729 citing *King v Palmer* 950 F 2d 771, 781 (1991).

[18] P Young, 'Perhaps Equity is Beyond Childbearing' (2003) 77 *Australian Law Journal* 221.

[19] They are 176 and 478 paragraphs long, respectively.

the counsel who ran the trial, Andrew Bulley and Damien Allen. Andrew Bulley appeared for Digital Pulse at trial and on appeal (where he was led by Martin Einfeld QC); Damien Allen appeared for Messrs Harris and Eden and the company Juice-D Media Pty Ltd at trial and on appeal (where he was led by Peter Walsh).[20] Those interviews took place after I had reviewed what remains of the original files at first instance and on appeal, extracted from a file archived in a warehouse in western Sydney.[21] The Court of Appeal file includes, fortuitously, the transcript of the appeal, even though ordinarily that would not have been 'filed'. Unfortunately, while the written submissions served in advance of the appeal would have been filed, they are not preserved on the file. However, the generous assistance of one of the counsel, Andrew Bulley, extended to extracting a penultimate draft of the respondent's submissions from his personal back-up storage, so that only the appellants' written submissions are missing.[22] While I spoke to Keith Mason about the formation of the bench and the aftermath of the appeal, I did not seek his recollections, or the recollections of the other members of the Court of Appeal, of the hearing; the transcript is the best evidence of that. In the first instance file, most of the affidavits have survived (with the trial judge's record of objections marked on the original affidavits in hand).[23] Unfortunately, no transcript of the trial appears to be available.[24]

III. THE DISPUTE

Digital Pulse was established in 1996. Its controlling director was Mr Brett Heil. In 1998 it had only one other employee, but it expanded very rapidly, including by employing Mr Christopher Harris and Mr Anthony Eden to work in marketing and web design. Both men's contracts expressly provided that they not compete with Digital Pulse while employed. By mid-1999, Digital Pulse had some 10 employees. Messrs Harris and Eden fell out with Mr Heil towards the end of 1999. They incorporated Juice-D Media Pty Ltd in January 2000, and their employment with Digital Pulse ceased on 4 and 5 February 2000, shortly

[20] Interviews with the Hon George Palmer (7 April 2021), Damien Allen (21 October 2021) and Andrew Bulley (27 October 2021). The lockdown following the outbreak of the delta variant of the COVID-19 virus delayed my interviewing counsel. Each counsel very kindly supplemented their recollection by additional notes.

[21] What remains of the Equity Division and Court of Appeal files, together with two other completely unrelated proceedings from 1996 and 2004, is found in box SC126599, indexed by reference to the Equity Division file 50032/00.

[22] The 'appeal' was, strictly, a concurrent hearing of an application for leave to appeal from a decision from which no appeal lay as of right because the only substantive challenge was to the orders of A$20,000 and exemplary damages, and hence required leave by reason of s 101(2)(r) of the Supreme Court Act 1970 (NSW) because it did not involve a matter in issue exceeding A$100,000.

[23] One of Brett Heil's affidavits is missing from the file.

[24] It seems likely a daily transcript would have been obtained, but it is absent from the file.

after Mr Heil discovered their dealings with Digital Pulse's clients on behalf of Juice (according to him, he was surprised when one client asked him about a meeting at the Cammeray office (which did not exist), and then whether Juice was affiliated with Digital Pulse).[25] Digital Pulse sued them for equitable compensation or an account of profits derived from 10 projects, mostly for the development of websites for clients ranging from various professional firms, a jazz festival, and certain divisions of Coles Myer (a large retail business). Digital Pulse advanced a wide range of claims, notably damages for breach of contract and equitable remedies for breach of fiduciary duty.[26]

IV. THE TRIAL

Lengthy affidavits of Messrs Heil and Harris (each exceeding 200 paragraphs) were read and they were cross-examined, as was Mr Eden. The defendants also prepared affidavits from five lay witnesses[27] explaining why they preferred to deal with Harris and Eden or why there was no profit from the work obtained by Juice, and there was a very lively dispute between expert accountants as to the money made by Juice and the loss suffered by Digital Pulse. Digital Pulse's expert said that the company had suffered losses in excess of A$587,000 from the 10 projects, and also that Juice had made profits of some A$153,000. As will be seen, the trial judge took a very different view of both those opinions.

The evidence concluded on the afternoon of the fourth day (a Thursday). Both counsel had clear recollections of aspects of the trial, two decades later. Both were in their very early years at the Bar.[28] Bulley had a clearer recollection of the trial (where he won) and Allen had a clearer recollection of the successful appeal (memory is often selective). Both recalled that they were very green, and that the trial commenced badly, with too many objections from Allen, irritating the judge, and a failure to prepare the court book by the plaintiff, leading to Bulley's solicitor being called to explain the deficiencies. Bulley's clearest memory was that, after the evidence closed around 3.15pm on the Thursday, he proposed an early adjournment so that he could provide written submissions.

[25] Affidavit of Brett Heil sworn 18 May 2001, para 80. In response, Mr Harris said that Mr Heil was probably making that up: Affidavit of Christopher Harris sworn 1 August 2001, para 186. Mr Harris' evidence was not accepted by the trial judge, although no finding was made on this particular issue.

[26] A claim for copyright infringement was dismissed and no appeal was brought from that decision. Had it been accepted, 'additional damages' under s 115(4) of the Copyright Act 1968 (Cth) (the equivalent of s 97(2) of the Copyright, Designs and Patents Act 1988 (UK)) would have been available on a conventional basis, and with the further consequence that an appeal lay to a Full Court of the Federal Court rather than the Court of Appeal: Jurisdiction of Courts (Cross-vesting) Act 1987 (Cth), s 7.

[27] Ms Tracey Conlan, Ms Ruth Buchanan, Ms Christine Champion, Ms Catherine Gardner and Mr Stephen Rayleigh.

[28] Bulley was admitted in 1997, Allen in 1998. Both had previously worked as solicitors in litigation.

The judge responded that court time was precious and only grudgingly granted him one, on terms that there be written submissions by 8am on Friday. At that stage, the clients (who were in court) told him they were certain they were going to lose. Bulley told me that he worked most of the night drafting submissions, but it was not until 9.30am that they were typed and given to the judge. On the Friday, in closing submissions, and for the first time that week, Palmer J invited counsel in for morning tea.[29] He said he had something to say. Bulley thought it would be a complaint that the submissions were late. Instead, it was an apology for the judge behaving intemperately the previous afternoon, which had been uncalled for. Bulley recalled it was a pity he hadn't said this in open court! The trial judge recollected the same morning tea:[30]

> I do recall feeling very sorry that I had expressed myself intemperately and that I apologised. Bulley may well have thought I should have done so in open court. If he had been brave enough to suggest that at the time – and what barrister of his seniority at the bar would have had such courage? – then I would like to think I would have acted upon his suggestion. Life is full of such regrets!

Allen also recalled that morning tea, but a different aspect. He said the judge said to him 'You must think I am an old [fart]' and he replied 'like a schoolboy'[31] that he did not think he was that old, illustrating a sound rule of advocacy that it is often best not to say the first thing that enters one's head in response to a judge.

Bulley recalled making submissions, based on *Bailey v Namol Pty Ltd*[32] and *Aquaculture Corporation v New Zealand Green Mussel Co Ltd*,[33] in support of the availability of exemplary damages. Allen believed the question of exemplary damages was not really addressed by either side, and that for his part he brushed away the possibility of their being ordered in equity. The trial judge recollected not being greatly helped by either side. To be fair, both counsel would have been preoccupied by the legion of factual disputes both on breach and on quantum emerging from four days of evidence.

V. THE JUDGMENT AT FIRST INSTANCE

The Honourable George Alfred Palmer QC came to the Bar in 1974 and developed a practice in equity and company law. He took silk in 1986 and was

[29] This custom was prevalent when appearing before many trial judges, and subject to the firm rule that nothing could be said about the hearing save for how it was progressing in terms of time. But in a case with two very junior counsel, which involved allegations of fraud, it would have been natural not to have morning tea until the evidence was closed.

[30] G Palmer, Personal communication, 21 June 2022.

[31] D Allen, Personal communication, 14 October 2021.

[32] *Bailey v Namol Pty Ltd* (1994) 53 FCR 102 (Full Ct).

[33] *Aquaculture Corporation v New Zealand Green Mussel Co Ltd* [1990] 3 NZLR 299 (CA).

appointed to the Equity Division of the Supreme Court of New South Wales in April 2001. When the trial took place, between 26 and 30 November 2001, he had recently ceased being the most junior judge in the Court.[34] He is one of the most famous judges the Supreme Court of New South Wales has produced. That is not so much because of his judgments, but rather because of his success as a composer of classical music. His more creative career was the subject of a well-received documentary,[35] and, by chance, a short, playful work he wrote, based on a restaurant in Paris near where he and Penny, his wife of some 51 years, had honeymooned, had been broadcast while I ate breakfast on the morning on which I interviewed him for the purpose of this chapter. The fact that he composed music was far from widely known in 2001, and I cannot help but think that Roddy Meagher, a generous supporter of the arts, might have been less ill-disposed to him had he known as much.[36]

The former judge recalled a trial at the end of the year, conducted by two very junior counsel (both in their first five years at the Bar) and a judgment written in the vacation when (as a very junior judge) he had been assigned as Duty Judge. He recalled acting for a client similar to the defendant when he had been a very junior counsel.[37] He recalled the energy and enthusiasm of the plaintiff's counsel, Andrew Bulley, but nonetheless very little assistance from either side when the question of exemplary damages arose. An entitlement to them had been pleaded, reflecting the egregious and contemptuous nature of the breaches of duty by Mr Harris found at trial, no aspect of which was disturbed on appeal. They assumed greater importance when the trial judge rejected most of the substantial claims for pecuniary relief, either by way of equitable compensation or account of profits.

The trial judge said that Mr Harris 'demonstrated a capacity for extravagant falsehood', including by fabricating three university degrees and five years' more experience in the IT industry than he in fact possessed.[38] Mr Eden was found to have given obviously false evidence concerning whether the clients whose work was diverted to Juice were Digital Pulse's customers.[39]

[34] The next appointment was that of the Hon JC Campbell. He was sworn in on 26 October 2001, serving in the Equity Division and then as a Judge of Appeal until an early retirement in 2012 whereupon he became an Adjunct Professor at the University of Sydney.

[35] 'Judgment Day', aired 5 April 2004 on 'Australian Story', described thus: 'Behind the robes, wig and formalities of life as a judge of the New South Wales Supreme Court, Justice George Palmer has been working for 40 years on his "other life" as a composer. But the music he wrote had never been performed or recorded – until now. Impending deafness prompted Justice Palmer to employ a group of musicians to record the music, and to his own amazement, the project snowballed into a live to air concert at the ABC's Eugene Goosens Hall in Sydney.' (ABC Library Sales <www.abccommercial.com/librarysales/program/australian-story-judgement-day> accessed 7 May 2023.

[36] Palmer told me their enmity dated from the Bar.

[37] The litigation was *Timber Engineering Co Pty Ltd v Anderson* (1980) 2 NSWLR 488 (SC), in which Palmer had been opposed, in a trial over some three weeks, to DE Horton QC.

[38] *Harris First Instance Judgement* (n 1) [34].

[39] ibid [35].

Even so, Digital Pulse failed to make out large parts of its case. Further, when it did establish a breach, the difficulty faced by Digital Pulse was that Juice received no fee for some of the work it had wrongly obtained from Digital Pulse, and had the work been done by Digital Pulse, it would have produced no fee nor any profit.[40] His Honour awarded equitable compensation of A$11,000 for the misuse of some confidential information plus at its election an accounting for profits or equitable compensation for six projects where breach had been found. Prior to the appeal being heard, Digital Pulse had elected to obtain an account of profits in the amount of A$13,119.51 (plus interest) and the loss shown to have been sustained by Digital Pulse was less than A$10,000.[41]

His Honour found that the wrongdoing of Harris and Eden was calculated to produce profit for themselves, and harm to a vulnerable employer, was consciously dishonest and carefully planned.[42] The judge added that the men exulted in their success in diverting work, demonstrating a contumelious disregard for Digital's rights, and that Digital Pulse had probably failed to uncover the full extent of their misconduct.[43] Palmer J was perfectly conscious of the novelty of the proposition that a punitive monetary order could be made, and in marked contrast to judgments which appear not even to have appreciated the novelty of the proposition,[44] explained why in his view it was available in principle.[45] That and the careful analysis of the individual breaches, and the accounting evidence bearing upon each, considerably added to the length of his judgment, to the horror of his new tipstaff for 2002, for whom proofing it was her first task and one which made a lasting impression.[46] Each of Messrs Harris and Eden was ordered to pay 'exemplary damages' of A$10,000. His Honour also ordered the defendants to pay Digital Pulse's costs.

Most accounts of *Digital Pulse* fail to explain how costs influenced the decisions in the litigation. One might readily infer that where the conventional remedies were a mere A$24,000, and even when the controversial exemplary damages of A$20,000 were added, they were trifling compared to the costs of the litigation. The primary documents enable that inference to be tested with some precision. By chance, located on the archived file is the certificate of a costs assessor.[47] The assessment was conducted by junior counsel,[48] who determined that the assessed[49] costs be A$176,474.54.[50] A prescribed fee of A$3,080 was

[40] eg, this was the case for the website design for the Australian Jazz Festival.

[41] See *Harris Appeal Judgement* (n 1) [229].

[42] *Harris First Instance Judgement* (n 1) [118]–[120].

[43] ibid [123]–[124].

[44] *cf Aquaculture* (n 33) 301 'a full range of remedies should be available as appropriate, no matter whether they originated in common law, equity or statute'.

[45] *Harris First Instance Judgement* (n 1) [141]–[173].

[46] Ramena Kako, Personal communication, 27 May 2022.

[47] Introduced by the Legal Profession Reform Act 1993 (NSW), and as described in *Attorney-General of New South Wales v Kennedy Miller Television Pty Ltd* (1998) 43 NSWLR 729 (CA) 731, a regime of assessment had replaced traditional taxation of costs before an officer of the court.

[48] Mr Mark Robinson.

[49] That is, the amount of costs recoverable against the defendants.

[50] See order entered on 7 April 2003 and affidavit of Ingrid Switzer sworn 29 July 2003.

payable for the assessment in accordance with section 203(1) of the Legal Profession Act 1987 (NSW), being one per cent of the amount of costs in dispute at the time the application for assessment was made.[51] This establishes that Digital Pulse's solicitor–client costs were some A$308,000. That is very high indeed for a five-day trial with junior counsel in 2001.

More importantly, the Supreme Court Rules at that time provided that where a plaintiff who had commenced proceedings in the Supreme Court recovered a sum not more than A$225,000, the plaintiff was not entitled to costs 'unless, it appearing to the Court that the plaintiff had sufficient reason for commencing or continuing proceedings in the Court, the Court makes an order for payment'.[52] The rule displaced the 'usual order' that costs followed the event in civil litigation, familiar in Australia and the United Kingdom, but foreign to the United States of America. The judge told me that he anticipated that the plaintiff's costs were enormous. He was right. However, when Digital Pulse succeeded on a novel and important point of principle, there was ample basis for departing from the usual rule as to costs for small claims; hence the costs order in Digital Pulse's favour.

VI. THE APPEAL

There was no challenge to any of the factual findings, or the adverse views of the primary judge on the credit of Messrs Harris and Eden. Nor, in the event that there was power to make a punitive monetary award, was there any challenge to the power being exercised, or to the A$10,000 amounts ordered. Digital Pulse did not for its part file a cross-appeal challenging the findings that its losses had been trifling and Juice's profits meagre. In short, the only challenge to any part of the reasons of the primary judge was as to power: was such an order available?

It is difficult to resist the conclusion that the appeal was driven largely by the objective of obtaining a less unfavourable costs order. An order setting aside the punitive orders of A$10,000 and leaving Digital Pulse to the ordinary position following a small judgment in the Supreme Court would have left Messrs Harris and Eden and Juice hundreds of thousands of dollars ahead. Further, it might be expected that in a 'one issue' appeal, Digital Pulse would be ordered to pay the costs of the appeal, in accordance with the usual rule.

[51] The transcript of the appeal makes it plain that the application for assessment was made before the appeal was heard (and a special order was made staying the execution of the result of the assessment to the extent of two thirds – it being clear that with unchallenged findings of breach and compensation, even if the appeal were allowed, Messrs Harris and Eden and Juice would have to pay at least some of the costs of trial): see transcript, 31 July 2002, 40–41. The fee prescribed by cl 26B(2)(c) of the Legal Profession Regulation 1994 (NSW) for applications for assessment made on or before 31 August 2002 was 1% (the same fee was prescribed for applications made later by cl 55(3)(c) of the Legal Profession Regulation 2000 (NSW)).

[52] Supreme Court Rules, Pt 52A r 33(2) (see now Uniform Civil Procedure Rules 2005 (NSW), r 42.34 to substantially the same effect for proceedings in the Supreme Court recovering amounts less than A$500,000).

The hearing of the appeal was expedited, because steps had been taken to execute the judgment and assess Digital Pulse's costs. Expedition and a stay of execution were granted by Heydon JA on 8 July 2002.[53]

The President of the Court of Appeal allocates judges to each appeal. The appeal obviously exposed an important point of principle, and Heydon JA had heard the application for a stay and an expedited hearing; it is usual in such cases for that judge, who has already been exposed to the issues, to sit on appeal. It was an appropriate case for a very senior bench, hence the Chief Justice and the President. Keith Mason told me that in addition, he thought it on the cards that he and Heydon would disagree, added to the desirability of allocating a very senior third judge to the appeal.

The oral submissions recorded on the transcript, and the respondent's written submissions, are of high quality. There is no reason to doubt that the same was true of the appellants' written submissions. The transcript records a careful, thorough grappling with each aspect of the reasons deployed by Palmer J to justify the existence of a power. Bulley's recollection of working late into the evening on submissions[54] is mirrored by the recollection of his leader Einfeld QC that their researches were 'vast and time-consuming'.[55]

The reasons of Mason P and Heydon JA appear to have been drafted independently and concurrently, which is not unusual when a divergence emerges at the conclusion of the hearing. Both were evidently circulated prior to those of Spigelman CJ.[56] The Chief Justice agreed with the orders proposed by Heydon JA allowing the appeal, setting aside the orders for exemplary damages, but leaving in place the costs orders at first instance. Highly unusually, despite the appellants' success on the only point argued, no order was made for the costs of the appeal, in recognition of the fact that only A$20,000 was at stake and their 'deplorable behaviour' had made the litigation necessary.[57] Further, although the discretion as to the costs of the trial had to be re-exercised on the basis that no order in the nature of exemplary damages should have been made, the Court did not interfere with the order that the defendants pay Digital Pulse's costs. Thus, while the appeal stands as an important landmark in the structure of private law in this country, for practical purposes, it was almost entirely unsuccessful. The appellants were required to pay all the amounts ordered by Palmer J, save for A$20,000, and in addition they were ordered to pay the costs

[53] A single Judge of Appeal may exercise the powers of the Court of Appeal for those purposes: Supreme Court Act 1970 (NSW), s 46. Neither the transcript of argument nor reasons (if any were given) is available.

[54] He told me that he recalled preparing submissions coincided with the birth of his second child.

[55] M Einfeld, *I Object!* (Sydney, Brio Books, 2022) 236.

[56] The Chief Justice introduced his judgment noting he had had the advantage of reading the other two judgments in draft. The explanation at [187] ('Since writing this portion of my reasons I have had the advantage of reading the judgment of the Chief Justice in draft') by Mason P makes it clear that [187] and perhaps some other paragraphs were added after receipt of the Chief Justice's reasons.

[57] *Harris Appeal Judgement* (n 1) [477].

of the appeal. Very occasionally, typically where 'the entire appeal process has been necessitated by the failure of an appellant to take a point in the court below', a successful appellant may be ordered to pay the unsuccessful respondent's costs.[58] The costs order in *Digital Pulse* is, with respect, difficult to justify and it is difficult to think of any comparable case. Indeed, despite their success on the question of law, the order that they pay Digital Pulse's costs in addition to their own must surely have seemed to Messrs Harris and Eden to be somewhat penal.[59]

A further appeal to the High Court of Australia lay only by way of special leave. No application for special leave to appeal was ever brought. The trial judge recalled being told that a group of silks had offered to run the special leave application on a speculative basis,[60] but that Brett Heil was sick of litigation and did not wish to take it any further.

VII. THE JUDGMENTS OF THE COURT OF APPEAL

Heydon JA observed that authority was scant and left the decision at large for the Court of Appeal.[61] His Honour turned to the unavailability of exemplary damages in contract, which was significant because it tended against the trial judge's argument from anomaly based on conduct which constituted both deceit at common law and breach of fiduciary duty in equity. He referred to the abolition of exemplary damages for defamation and for negligence,[62] and under the Trade Practices Act 1974 (Cth), in contrast to its predecessor the Australian Industries Preservation Act 1906 (Cth). He surveyed academic writing, which pointed in both directions, then turned to dicta in a range of decisions much of which amounted to high-level statements that equitable remedies do not punish. He addressed the more generous awards of interest awarded against defaulting trustees (including compound interest), upon which Palmer J had relied, in order to conclude that the purpose was not punitive, but to prevent the fiduciary from retaining any profit. Much the same exercise was conducted in relation to

[58] See *Rockcote Enterprises Pty Ltd v FS Architects Pty Ltd* [2008] NSWCA 39 [123], citing *Hampton Court Ltd v Crooks* (1957) 97 CLR 367 (HCA) 378 and *Miller v Miller* (1978) 141 CLR 269 (HCA) 276–77.

[59] I am grateful to Eleni Katsampouka for noticing that the costs order might reflect punishment for the appellants' deplorable behaviour.

[60] That is to say, on the basis that they would not charge a fee unless the appeal were allowed. Martin Einfeld QC has also written that he advised a further appeal: Einfeld (n 55) 236–37.

[61] Favouring the appellants there were only the dicta of a Full Court of the Federal Court in *Bailey v Namol Pty Ltd* favouring the dissent in *Aquaculture* ('But there is much to be said for the contrary view, put by Somers J in *Aquaculture* (n 33) 302, that 'equity and penalty are strangers') and the decision of the Supreme Court of Western Australia, constituted by Commissioner Pringle QC, in *Yamabuta v Tay (No 1)* (1995) 16 WAR 254 (SC) 261 on an amendment application, the only Australian judgment directly on point, which (as Heydon JA observed) had been far from fully argued.

[62] By s 46 of the Defamation Act 1974 (NSW) and s 21 of the Civil Liability Act 2002 (NSW).

accounting for profits and the making of just allowances. He considered that while there was an onus on the fiduciary to make out a case for just allowances, that was inconsistent with the order being punitive, for 'ordinarily a person subject to criminal punishment bears no burden'.[63] Heydon JA relied on more general arguments: that in substance the proposed change in the law amounted to the judicial creation of a new criminal sanction, and that the fusion effected by the Judicature legislation did not alter the systems of law and equity. He was strongly critical of the results reached in *Aquaculture* and some of the reasoning in Canadian decisions,[64] and regarded the early sixteenth- and seventeenth-century cases as not bearing upon the issue. On the more general topic of the circumstances in which courts below the High Court should develop the law, Heydon JA said:[65]

> As to Sir George Jessel MR's account of the development of equity in *Re Hallett's Estate*, it is true that the rules of equity have changed from time to time, and true that individual Chancellors – and Masters of the Rolls, Lord Keepers and Vice Chancellors – have effected these changes. It is also true that the rules can be changed in future. But those deeds of single judges were done when there was no appellate jurisdiction in the House of Lords, or very limited access to it, at a time before modern parliamentary democracy had developed, and members of parliaments consisted largely of wealthy men who in turn supported Cabinets composed largely of aristocratic oligarchs whom it was difficult to interest in the details of private law. What individual judges did in those constitutional and forensic conditions is not a sound guide to what modern Australian courts, at least at levels below the High Court, can do. A single equity judge in the time of Sir George Jessel MR had the power, the competence, the authority and the capacity to compel acceptance from other judges which only the High Court has now, at least where the change goes beyond the application of existing principles in a new way or marginal extensions of the law.
>
> ...
>
> Sir George Jessel MR's judicial life coincided with the time when democracy in a modern form was beginning and the responsiveness of Parliament to social or legal ills was starting to develop. It was a time when the judiciary was small, highly skilled and united. It is now large, less skilled, and far from entirely united. For courts below the High Court to act in the manner of the single judges sitting in Chancery who made modern equity is to invite the spread of a wilderness of single instances, a proliferation of discordant and idiosyncratic opinions, and ultimately an anarchic 'system' operating according to the forms, but not the realities, of law.

Mason P disagreed with most of this. Three matters warrant emphasis. The first is that the President rejected the close analogy with contract, considering rather that the conduct of Messrs Harris and Eden was better characterised as

[63] *Harris Appeal Judgement* (n 1) [336].
[64] Notably, *M(K) v M(H)* [1992] 3 SCR 6 (SCC).
[65] *Harris Appeal Judgement* (n 1) [456] and [458].

tortious than a breach of contract.[66] The second is that the President rejected the submission based on novelty in terms, saying that for decades Australian courts below the High Court had innovated, that it was open to have regard to the endorsement of the position by the Supreme Court of Canada and the New Zealand Court of Appeal. The third is that the President prayed in aid traditional equitable technique in its auxiliary jurisdiction, where novel remedies issued precisely because of the limitations at common law. 'Within its auxiliary jurisdiction, equity intervenes *because of* the deficiencies and inadequacies of the common law. Why should equity turn coy in its exclusive jurisdiction?'[67]

Spigelman CJ rightly said that this case 'raises fundamental issues about the principled development of the law'.[68] His judgment was evidently written in the knowledge that his views would be dispositive, and was well placed to identify the central issues emerging from the competing views of Mason P and Heydon JA. The Chief Justice said that 'the identification of a principle at a high level of abstraction, from which is derived a rule of particular application' was a mode of reasoning incompatible with the traditional common law judicial method. The Chief Justice regarded that an approach as lying at the heart of the reasoning of Palmer J and of the respondent's submissions, saying:[69]

> The general principle appears to be: Persons who go beyond merely breaching their obligations to others and act in contumelious disregard of those obligations should be subject to condign punishment. From that general principle there is to be deduced, with respect to each specific field of the law of civil obligations, a rule empowering the court to award 'exemplary damages' to the party to whom the obligations so breached were owed.

His Honour said that that did not reflect the Australian legal system, adding: 'Our legal tradition is much messier than that'.[70] He insisted upon the distinctiveness of common law and equity, aided by the late enactment of judicature legislation in New South Wales. He relied upon the fact that the egregious conduct of Messrs Harris and Eden was no different from that of other fiduciaries over centuries, and thus the absence of Australian and English decisions tended to confirm that it was a matter for legislative intervention if a change were to be made. The Chief Justice regarded the contractual analogy as more appropriate, because the source of the employees' fiduciary obligations lay in

[66] There is also a suggestion in ibid [189] that his Honour while recognising that exemplary damages for breach of contract were unavailable until the High Court changed its position, thought that that was a 'peculiar' position.

[67] ibid [224].

[68] ibid [6].

[69] ibid [12].

[70] ibid [14]; *cf* Professor Simpson's observations that 'We must start by recognizing what common sense suggests, which is that the common law is more like a muddle than a system, and that it would be difficult to conceive of a less systematic body of law': AWB Simpson, *Legal Theory and Legal History: Essays on the Common Law* (London, Hambledon Press, 1987) 381, and see *Fistar v Riverwood Legion and Community Club Ltd* [2016] NSWCA 81, (2016) 91 NSWLR 732 [50].

contract. Thus the unavailability of exemplary damages for the undoubted breach of contract pointed against the unavailability of a similar remedy for their undoubted breach of equitable obligation. Finally, he hypothesised a contract with an express provision that a payment of A$10,000 would be made if there was a breach in addition to damages or an account of profits. That would be struck down as a penalty. Considering that as an aspect of the common law of contract,[71] he said that there was no basis to think that equity would override that aspect of the common law. It followed that for equity to award exemplary damages would create an incompatibility.

VIII. CONSIDERATION

I return to the broad statements about the appropriateness of courts lower than the ultimate appellate court to make law. Undoubtedly times have changed since the day of Sir George Jessel: the judiciary is larger, not to mention much more prolix, and many bodies are now tasked with law reform. But if the approach in *Digital Pulse* were applied in terms, it would work a great change to the lawmaking function possessed and exercised by all courts, most notably in the construction of statutes, which constantly give rise to contestable points unlikely to have been foreseen by their drafters.

There seem to me to be three aspects which are underplayed by the majority. The first is to observe that all four judges 'made law' in a real sense. There was no fully reasoned Australian authority on the point before *Harris v Digital Pulse* was determined. The members of the majority who rejected the availability of punitive pecuniary remedies made law just as much as the trial judge or the dissentient who held to the contrary. The judges did not have a choice in the matter; the appeal had to be resolved, one way or another.

The second is that it is to be recalled that the High Court of Australia was an intermediate court of appeal for most of its existence. In appeals concerning private law, almost every decision was liable to further appeal to the Privy Council until the last few decades of the twentieth century. Much of the nuance in the work of Sir Owen Dixon and Sir Victor Windeyer reflects an appreciation of this. Yet it could not for a moment be said that there was a want of legal innovation in the Australian High Court at its apogee. More generally, and as any poet or composer is acutely aware, the welcoming of constraints may be the deepest secret of creativity.[72]

[71] The Chief Justice regarded this as a rule of common law in *Harris Appeal Judgement* (n 1) [60]; in Australia, it is now seen as an aspect of equity: *Andrews v Australia and New Zealand Banking Group Ltd* [2012] HCA 30, (2012) 247 CLR 205. The United Kingdom Supreme Court and the Singapore Court of Appeal have subsequently taken (different) divergent courses: *Cavendish Square Holding BV v Talal El Makdessi* [2015] UKSC 67, [2016] AC 1172 and *Denka Advantech Pte Ltd v Seraya Energy Pte Ltd* [2020] SGCA 119, [2021] 1 SLR 631.

[72] See, generally, D Hofstadter, *Le Ton beau de Marot: In Praise of the Music of Language* (New York, Basic Books, 1997) and at xix in particular.

The third point is empirical. McHugh JA wrote – shortly after his appointment to the Court of Appeal of New South Wales, and prior to his elevation to the High Court – that there were 'a significant number of cases where an intermediate court of appeal has a creative role open to it'.[73] My own experience over the last decade sitting in the same court is the same.[74] The principal reason emerges from practical realities of workflow. It is of course not uncommon for an ultimate appellate court to be asked to change the law: those courts tend to control their own workload through a filtering system, and often what could only ever be a formal challenge in a lower court may be fully argued in the ultimate appellate court. However, while such challenges form a greater *proportion* of appeals in ultimate appellate courts than in intermediate appellate courts, it must also be borne in mind that many more appeals are heard and determined in the latter. The New South Wales Court of Appeal and Court of Criminal Appeal determine some 600–700 appeals each year, which is an order of magnitude more than are determined by the High Court of Australia.[75] Most of those appeals involve no challenge to any proposition of law, but their sheer volume means that even though challenges are relatively rare, they may still be quite numerous. Moreover, those challenges which are made in the High Court tend to have been advanced in lower courts, sometimes by way of formal submission, but at other times substantively; after all, a good reason for refusing special leave to appeal is that the point was not taken in the lower courts.

Most contemporary lawmaking involves statute.[76] The Digital Pulse litigation presented a rare example of an unresolved question of law in an area largely unaffected by statute, and it was necessary for the courts to resolve it. There is force in the inertial proposition on which Spigelman CJ relied that where the conduct has recurred for centuries, the absence of authority for a particular order tells against its availability. But that cannot be determinative, otherwise manufacturers would still not be liable in negligence for harm to consumers caused by defects in their goods,[77] *Anton Piller* orders would never be made, and so on. Sometimes there is a place for innovation, and thus the status quo falls short of a compelling reason telling against innovation. Otherwise, the law would lose something of its suppleness and capacity to accommodate to changing conditions.

[73] M McHugh, 'Law Making in an Intermediate Appellate Court: The New South Wales Court of Appeal' (1987) 11 *Sydney Law Review* 183, 186.

[74] In 2020, I participated in 23 decisions which involved a determination of novel questions of law unconstrained by binding authority: the decisions, and the points determined, may be seen in M Leeming, 'The Modern Approach to Statutory Construction' in B McDonald et al (eds), *Dynamic and Principled: The Influence of Sir Anthony Mason* (Sydney, Federation Press, 2022) 46–47.

[75] The actual number of decisions (counted by media neutral citation) for the last three calendar years (2019–21) are: High Court: 50, 48, 44; New South Wales Court of Appeal and New South Wales Court of Criminal Appeal: 323 + 321 = 644; 361 + 356 = 717; 342 + 319 = 661.

[76] See Leeming (n 74) 45–48.

[77] *cf MacPherson v Buick Motor Co* 217 NY 382, 111 NE 1050 (1916); *Donoghue v Stevenson* [1932] AC 562 (HL).

The result of *Harris v Digital Pulse* was that there was divergence in the law of Australia and Canada and New Zealand[78] (for although the decision was merely that of an intermediate appellate court, it would be difficult for another intermediate appellate court to reach a different conclusion). This disunity in the common law recalls Sir Victor Windeyer's article, 'Unity, Disunity and Harmony in the Common Law',[79] which refers to the reference in *Tomlins' Law Dictionary* to 'the continual hesitation of lawyers' in the Privy Council in the time of William III. There is a long tradition of a suspicion of innovation. *The Book of Common Prayer* contrasted some that

> think it a great matter of conscience to depart from a peece of the least of their Ceremonies; they be so addicted to their old customs' from those 'on the other side, some be so newfangled, that they would innovate all things, and so despise the old, that nothing can like them but that is new.

Windeyer made the point that there was a middle way, based on discerning from history the flowing stream of the law, an approach which in turn rests on the fundamental observation that 'the greatest quality of our system of law is in its capacity for development in response to the developments of the society in which it rules'.[80]

Chief Justice Spigelman's reasons were distinctive in two respects. The first was their narrowness. The Chief Justice confined his decision to cases where fiduciary obligations were sourced in contract, and left open the position for breach of fiduciary duties not based on contracts. His Honour held that as a matter of coherence with the law of contract, it would be wrong to permit a remedy denied to cases which could also be run as actions for breach of contract. A difficulty with the second aspect of the reasoning is that most such cases would be capable of being run as an action in deceit, focusing upon the knowing lies told by Messrs Harris and Eden, that being the conduct going to the heart of what gives rise to the need for punishment. But Digital Pulse declined to advance any such case. For many years, plaintiffs have had choices in the causes of action they litigate, and the choice between contract, tort and breach of fiduciary duty (and indeed the availability of (statutory) contributory negligence as a partial defence to those claims)[81] is a prominent aspect of the legal system which has been erected ad hoc and with practicality rather than logicality in mind.[82]

[78] New Zealand courts have, unsurprisingly, noticed *Harris v Digital Pulse Pty Ltd* but continued that country's less circumscribed approach to remedies: see *Skids Programme Management Ltd v McNeill* [2012] NZCA 314, [2013] 1 NZLR 1 [120]–[24] and the decisions there mentioned.

[79] B Debelle (ed), *Victor Windeyer's Legacy: Legal and Military Papers* (Sydney, Federation Press, 2019) ch 10.

[80] ibid 123.

[81] Notably, see the reasoning in decisions roughly contemporaneous with *Harris v Digital Pulse* in *Astley v Austrust Ltd* [1999] HCA 6, (1999) 197 CLR 1 and *Pilmer v Duke Group Ltd (in liq)* [2001] HCA 31, (2001) 207 CLR 165.

[82] This theme is developed in M Leeming, 'Overlapping Claims at Common Law and in Equity – An Embarrassment of Riches?' (2017) 11 *Journal of Equity* 229.

For those reasons, the considerations of coherence may be less powerful than was indicated by the Chief Justice.

Parts of Spigelman CJ's judgment anticipate the powerful reaction in recent Australian law against so-called 'top-down' reasoning. Decisions in the following years such as *Roxborough v Rothmans of Pall Mall Australia Ltd*,[83] *Lumbers v W Cook Builders Pty Ltd (in liq)*[84] and *Bofinger v Kingsway Group Ltd*[85] rejected a methodology which would derive rules of decision in particular cases from general principles (notably, in unjust enrichment). His Honour's judgment recalled what Lord Radcliffe had said half a century earlier, to the effect that 'English common law' (including Equity) 'seems to me rather short on philosophy and rather uncertain in logic', and that 'Its virtue has lain in other things: in its copiousness, in a strong sense of the practical, in a readiness to keep its nose to the grindstone'.[86]

This chapter concludes with a personal note. I appeared as a junior counsel not much senior to Bulley and Allen before Palmer J only a few months after the publication of the fourth edition of *Equity: Doctrines and Remedies*.[87] I recall worrying whether I needed to tell my solicitor of the criticism in the book on the judge. I need not have worried. Palmer J was strict and even-handed and scrupulously fair. I think he well appreciated that the language was that of his old *bête-noire*, Roddy Meagher.

[83] *Roxborough v Rothmans of Pall Mall Australia Ltd* [2001] HCA 68, (2001) 208 CLR 516 [73]–[74].

[84] *Lumbers v W Cook Builders Pty Ltd (in liq)* [2008] HCA 27, (2008) 232 CLR 635 [84]–[85].

[85] *Bofinger v Kingsway Group Ltd* [2009] HCA 44, (2009) 239 CLR 269 [86]–[89].

[86] C Radcliffe, 'The Place of Law Courts in Society' in *Not in Feather Beds* (London, The Quality Book Club, 1968) 31. While conscious of a movement for 'a thorough-going rationalisation', Radcliffe found that much of the argument that it promoted seemed sterile.

[87] *Alfabs Engineering Group Pty Ltd v Regan* [2002] NSWSC 316.

13

State Farm Mutual Automobile Insurance Co v Campbell (2003)

The Misguided Legacy of Proportionality

CATHERINE M SHARKEY*

I. INTRODUCTION

STATE FARM V *Campbell* stands as the 'high water mark' of constitutional excessiveness review of punitive damages in the United States, where the US Supreme Court has held that the Due Process Clause of the Fourteenth Amendment prohibits the imposition of grossly excessive or arbitrary punitive damages on a tortfeasor based on the notion that:[1]

> Elementary notions of fairness enshrined in our constitutional jurisprudence dictate that a person receive fair notice not only of the conduct that will subject him to punishment, but also of the severity of the penalty that a State may impose.

In *Campbell*, the Court overturned a US$145m punitive damages verdict against an insurance company that was assessed US$1m in compensatory damages for bad-faith failure to settle an automobile tort claim of one of its insureds. In so doing, the Court reasoned that 'few awards exceeding a single-digit ratio between punitive and compensatory damages, to a significant degree, will satisfy [constitutional] due process'.[2] Moreover, according to the Court, 'an award of more than four times the amount of compensatory damages might be close to the line of constitutional impropriety'.[3]

* Abdullahi Abdi (NYU Law 2024) and Aster O'Leary (NYU Law 2025) provided helpful research assistance.

[1] *State Farm Mut Auto Ins Co v Campbell* 538 US 408, 425 (2003) (Justice Kennedy) ('*Campbell*').

[2] ibid 425 (Justice Kennedy).

[3] ibid (Justice Kennedy).

With these dicta in *Campbell*, the Court planted the seeds of a particular type of 'proportionality' jurisprudence of punitive damages, focused narrowly on the ratio of punitive-to-compensatory damages. The effect on lower state and federal courts can be seen in their tendencies to 'race to ratios' of punitive to compensatory damages in their analyses of the validity of punitive damages awards.[4] And the impact on legal scholarship is likewise evident in the rash of articles highlighting the quasi-criminal aspects of punitive damages excessiveness review.[5]

My central claim is that this particular brand of 'proportionality jurisprudence', which stems from an over-reading, if not misreading, of *Campbell*, has had a profound impact. It stands as *Campbell*'s misguided legacy. Regarding the proportionality-fueled ratio analysis, nowhere does the Court explain why the amount of compensatory damages should be an appropriate comparator for the excessiveness of the amount of punitive damages. Justice Kennedy (author of the *Campbell* majority opinion) himself evinced deep scepticism (in an earlier case): 'The Constitution identifies no particular multiplier of compensatory damages as an acceptable limit for punitive awards; it does not concern itself with dollar amounts, ratios, or the quirks of juries in specific jurisdictions'.[6]

The relationship that should matter is between size of the punitive damages award and the legitimate objectives of punitive damages (punishment and deterrence) – which do not relate in any systematic way to the amount of compensatory damages.[7] That critical point is obscured in the *Campbell* Court's pronouncement that 'Single-digit multipliers are more likely to comport with due process, while still achieving the State's goal of deterrence and retribution, than awards with ratios in [the] range of 500 to 1'.[8] The Supreme Court recognises here – as it has throughout its trilogy of punitive damages cases concerning constitutional excessiveness – that punitive damages is a state law remedy; and the Court is establishing 'guidelines' for reviewing excessiveness, not mandates to override legitimate state interests.[9]

This federalism principle – in this case, respect for the legitimate state law purposes of punitive damages – should mitigate the effects of the *Campbell*

[4] *Thornton v Am Interstate Ins Co* 940 NW2d 1, 41 (IA 2020). See below section II.B.

[5] See the text to n 37.

[6] *TXO Prod Corp v Alliance Res Corp* 509 US 443, 467 (1993) (Justice Kennedy, concurring in part and concurring in the judgment).

[7] See CM Sharkey, 'Economic Analysis of Punitive Damages: Theory, Empirics, and Doctrine' in J Arlen (ed), *Research Handbook on the Economics of Torts* (Cheltenham, Edward Elgar Publishing, 2015) 486, 500. Justice Breyer also recognised this in his concurrence in *BMW v Gore* 517 US 559, 586 ('*Gore*') (Justice Breyer, concurring).

[8] *Campbell* (n 1) 425 (Justice Kennedy) (emphasis added).

[9] See CM Sharkey, 'Federal Incursions and State Defiance: Punitive Damages in the Wake of *Philip Morris v Williams*' (2010) 46 *Willamette Law Review* 449. See also *Thornton* (n 4) 29 (Justice Appel): 'Even when the Supreme Court crossed the Rubicon and applied substantive due process review of the amount of punitive damages verdicts, the Court continued to repeatedly employ language of respect for state court processes'.

Court's dicta that might otherwise be read as establishing a presumption (if not a bright-line rule) in favour of punitive awards with single-digit punitive-to-compensatory ratios. But few courts pause to consider the threshold question of why (ie, the purposes for which) punitive damages have been awarded at all, before plunging into their ratio analyses.

To the extent courts and scholars do pause to engage the purposes of punitive damages, *Campbell*'s 'proportionality' message – drawn from the language of criminal law, where punishments are to be proportional to the crime – steers them towards the retributive punishment underpinnings of punitive damages, to the exclusion of the (non-retributive) deterrence purposes. Thus 'blinded by proportionality', courts and scholars – both in the United States and abroad – fail to recognise an alternative (but at least as crucial) non-retributive deterrence framework, centered on the internalisation of widespread harms.

II. PROPORTIONALITY AND PUNISHMENT

A. *Campbell* and the Punitive–Compensatory Ratio

State Farm v Campbell occupies a place in the torts canon. A featured case in leading US torts casebooks,[10] widely cited by lower state and federal courts,[11] its influence extends beyond that of the other two US Supreme Court punitive damages excessiveness cases that bookend it.[12] Given its showcase status, it is worth exploring not only what the case held but, perhaps even more significantly, what it has come to stand for.

Curtis Campbell was a defendant in an automobile accident lawsuit. He had driven his car negligently across the traffic line, to pass six vans ahead of him on a two-lane highway, into oncoming traffic, causing two approaching cars to collide, leading to the death of one of the drivers and serious permanent injury to the other.[13] The victims were willing to accept US$50,000 (US$25,000 each), which was the limit of the Campbells' State Farm insurance policy, but State Farm (which took over the defence of the action) refused to settle, all the while assuring the Campbells not to worry about their potential exposure in a subsequent lawsuit.[14] At trial, the jury awarded nearly US$200,000 (an amount well in excess

[10] RA Epstein and CM Sharkey, *Cases and Materials on Torts*, 12th edn (Boston, Aspen Publishing, 2020) 831; MA Franklin et al, *Tort Law and Alternatives: Cases and Materials*, 11th edn (New York, Foundation Press, 2021) 760; Prosser et al, *Torts: Cases and Materials*, 14th edn (New York, Foundation Press, 2020) 618.

[11] According to a Westlaw search (conducted in February 2023), 3,500 state and federal court opinions cite *Campbell*.

[12] *Gore* (n 7); *Philip Morris USA v Williams* 549 US 346 (2007).

[13] *Campbell* (n 1) 412–13.

[14] State Farm assured the Campbells that 'their assets were safe, that they had no liability for the accident, that [State Farm] would represent their interests, and that they did not need to procure separate counsel': ibid (Justice Kennedy).

of the US$50,000 policy limit). Ultimately, State Farm then suggested that the Campbells were on their own to satisfy the excess portion, ominously suggesting that the Campbells should put their house up for sale.[15] After State Farm lost its appeal of the initial judgment, it agreed to pay the nearly US$200,000 verdict in full. But, the die was already cast.

The Campbells had reached an agreement with the plaintiff victims of the car accident, in which the plaintiffs agreed not to enforce the judgment against the Campbells. In exchange, the plaintiffs' attorneys would represent the Campbells in a tort lawsuit against State Farm for bad faith failure to settle, and the car crash victims would receive 90 per cent of any proceeds from a subsequent verdict against State Farm.[16]

In hindsight, State Farm made a bad business decision not to settle the automobile claims for US$50,000 (the limits of the policy), while the crash victims' attorneys wisely chose to forgo enforcing the jury verdict against the Campbells in exchange for a 90 per cent stake in a bad faith action against State Farm. At trial, the jury heard evidence of how State Farm had altered company records, disregarded the overwhelming likelihood of the Campbells' liability, and disregarded the near certainty that, if brought to trial, the judgment against the Campbells would exceed policy limits.[17] The jury also heard of similar 'hardball business' tactics in which State Farm engaged over the years, which constituted a pattern and practice of company-wide corporate misconduct.[18] Consequently, the jury awarded compensatory damages of US$2.6m (which the trial court reduced to US$1m) for the emotional distress inflicted upon the Campbells for the 18 months in which they lived under the shadow of the outstanding judgment against them and feared they might lose their home. The jury then awarded a sizeable US$145m in punitive damages (which the trial judge reduced to US$25m). On appeal, the Utah Supreme Court reinstated the full punitive damages award, noting that an earlier US$100m judgment had gone unreported to State Farm's corporate headquarters, and that the regional vice president had no plans to report the judgment under review.[19] State Farm appealed to the US Supreme Court.

The *Campbell* Court reiterated the three 'guideposts' it had laid down in *BMW v Gore* for constitutional excessiveness review of punitive damages awards: (1) the reprehensibility of the actor's conduct;[20] (2) the ratio of the punitive damages to the actual (or potential) harm; and (3) comparable civil and criminal penalties.[21] It earned its place in the torts canon – and thus its

[15] ibid.
[16] ibid 413–14.
[17] ibid 419.
[18] ibid 420.
[19] *Campbell v State Farm Mut Auto Ins Co* 65 P3d 1134, 1153 (UT 2001) ('*Campbell UT*').
[20] The Court repeatedly states that 'reprehensibility is "the most important indicium of the reasonableness of a punitive damage award"': *Campbell* (n 1) 419 (quoting *Gore* (n 7) 575).
[21] For discussion of the relative lack of utility of this third guidepost, see NW Hines, 'Marching to a Different Drummer: Are Lower Courts Faithfully Implementing the Evolving Due Process

legacy status – not from echoing the *BMW v Gore* guideposts, but instead by highlighting the proportionality at the heart of the Court's due process analysis. The Court stated that 'courts must ensure that the measure of punishment is both reasonable and proportionate to the amount of harm' someone suffers.[22] The Court also signalled that it was serious about reducing punitive damages: 'When compensatory damages are substantial' – especially if they contain large non-economic damages, such as pain and suffering which themselves include a 'punitive' component – in which case, 'then a lesser ratio, perhaps only equal to compensatory damages, can reach the outermost limit of the due process guarantee'.[23]

Prior US Supreme Court cases had borrowed the criminal punishment analogy – namely that punitive damages should not be 'grossly out of proportion to the severity of the offense'.[24] But *Campbell* fixed this association between proportionality and retributive punishment in punitive damages jurisprudence. The *Campbell* Court, moreover, gave short shrift to the lower courts' findings with respect to the link between likelihood of under-detection and size of punitive damages.[25] The Court aimed to send marching orders to state and federal courts, more clearly than ever before, to rein in awards of punitive damages via the ratio analysis.[26]

Campbell ignited heightened attention to punitive–compensatory ratios as the linchpin of proportionality analysis, pointing to a 'long legislative history, dating back over 700 years and going forward to today, providing for sanctions of double, treble, or quadruple damages to deter and punish'.[27] By the time the

Guideposts to Catch and Correct Excessive Punitive Damages Awards?' (2013) 62 *Catholic University Law Review* 371, 394.

[22] *Campbell* (n 1) 426 (Justice Kennedy).

[23] ibid 425 (Justice Kennedy). See *In Re the Exxon Valdez*, 296 F Supp2d 1071 (D Alaska 2004) (District Judge Holland): 'Under this [ratio] guidepost, the court may also consider whether the compensatory damages award contained a punitive component'. See also CR Sunstein et al, 'Assessing Punitive Damages (With Notes on Cognition and Valuation in Law)' 107 (1998) *Yale Law Journal* 2071, 2133: 'Although pain-and-suffering awards are essentially compensatory, there can be little doubt that such awards sometimes reflect jury judgments about the egregiousness of the defendant's behavior. Hence, such judgments are likely to have a punitive component'.

[24] *Pac Mut Life Ins Co v Haslip* 499 US 1, 22 (1991) (Justice Blackmun).

[25] In reinstating the US$145m punitive award, the Utah Supreme Court relied (in part) on the trial court's finding that 'State Farm's actions, because of their clandestine nature, will be punished at most in one out of every 50,000 cases as a matter of statistical probability': *Campbell UT* (n 19) 415 (Justice Durham). The US Supreme Court rejected this line of reasoning on the ground that 'the argument that State Farm will be punished in only the rare case … had little to do with the actual harm sustained by the Campbells': *Campbell* (n 1) 427 (Justice Kennedy). Even more to the point, the Supreme Court worried that such an under-detection rationale would justify 'a departure from well-established constraints on punitive damages' (ibid) (Justice Kennedy).

[26] Justice Ginsburg, who also dissented in *BMW v Gore*, recognised that that Court was sending a stronger message in *Campbell*. See *Campbell* (n 1) 439 (Justice Ginsburg, dissenting): 'Even if I were prepared to accept the flexible guides prescribed [in *Gore*], I would not join the Court's swift conversion of those guides into instructions that begin to resemble marching orders'.

[27] *Campbell* (n 1) 425 (Justice Kennedy). See also *Gore* (n 7) 581 (Justice Stevens): 'Scholars have identified … early English statutes authorizing … multiple damages for particular wrongs. Some

Supreme Court decided *Exxon Shipping Co v Baker* it could proclaim: 'The potential relevance of the ratio between compensatory and punitive damages is indisputable, being a central feature in our due process analysis'.[28]

But the Supreme Court's repeated invocation of the ratio guidepost is not tantamount to an analytic justification. Indeed, the punitive–compensatory ratio – though undoubtedly providing a definitive metric by which to judge the size of punitive damages awards – is 'theoretically bankrupt'.[29] The Court has never even tried to relate the ratio factor to any underlying justification for punitive damages, be it retributive punishment or economic deterrence. With respect to the punishment goal, the absence of a correlation between the *mens rea* (culpable state of mind) of the wrongdoer and the measure of the actual harm inflicted should surprise no one. If, instead, the law-and-economics deterrence goal is considered, the relevant relationship between punitive and compensatory damages focuses on the likelihood of detection, not the relative size of the compensatory damages.[30] The ratio guidepost then would seem to distinguish itself as having attained supreme relevance in the constitutional due process review scheme, notwithstanding its complete lack of justifiability.

B. At Home in the United States

Campbell cast a long proportionality shadow. The Supreme Court remanded *Ford Motor Co v Romo* – a case in which the lower court, remarking that 'neither the Legislature nor the judiciary has established a fixed ratio between the compensatory and punitive damages that provides a standard for determining excessiveness', upheld a significant punitive award (US$290m) on deterrence grounds – for further consideration in light of *Campbell*.[31] Additionally, states

65 different enactments during the period between 1275 and 1753 provided for double, treble, or quadruple damages'.

[28] *Exxon Shipping Co v Baker* 554 US 471, 507 (2008) (Justice Souter). In *Exxon Shipping*, the US Supreme Court selected a 1:1 punitive-to-compensatory damages ratio as the 'fair upper limit' for federal maritime law purposes. Lower courts have tended to distinguish the federal maritime context from the *Campbell* constitutional excessiveness inquiry. See, eg, *Grosch v Tunica County Miss*, 2009 WL 161856, at *44 (ND Miss 2009) (District Judge Pepper): 'the holding in *Exxon* was confined to cases arising under federal admiralty law and has no application to the case at hand'; *Smith v Xerox Corp*, 584 F Supp 2d 905, 915 fn 18 (ND Tex 2008) (District Judge Godbey): '*Exxon Shipping* was a maritime common law case, inapplicable here'.

[29] CM Sharkey, 'The *Exxon Valdez* Litigation Marathon: A Window on Punitive Damages' (2009) 7 *University of St Thomas Law Journal* 25, 28.

[30] To the economist, the punitive damages 'multiplier' should be the inverse of the probability of detection. In other words, if a wrongdoer's activities would likely escape detection half of the time, compensatory damages alone would not sufficiently deter the actor's wrongdoing, and a multiplier of 2 (the inverse of ½) would have to be applied.

[31] *Romo v Ford Motor Co* 99 Cal App 4th 1115, 1147 (2002) (Justice Vartabedian): 'The key question before the reviewing court is whether the amount of damages exceeds the level necessary to properly punish and deter' (internal quotations omitted), cert granted, judgment vacated in *Ford Motor Co v Romo*, 538 US 1028 (2003) (remanding case for further consideration in light of *Campbell* (n 1)).

revised their pattern jury instructions to highlight the ratio analysis. Georgia, for example, instructs the jury: 'The measure of such damages is your enlightened conscience as an impartial jury … (but not more than (insert ratio range) to your compensatory award)'.[32]

Lower state and federal courts, eager for definitive guidance in assessing whether punitive damages awards were constitutionally excessive, glommed onto the second 'ratio guidepost' as a nearly iron-clad single-digit limitation,[33] especially where juries awarded so-called 'blockbuster' punitive damages awards.[34] Prior to *Campbell*, appellate courts sometimes acknowledged that strict adherence to a single-digit ratio would not effectively deter many defendants, particularly large corporations inflicting widespread, diffuse harms.[35] But post-*Campbell*, in their 'race to ratios', few reviewing courts pause to consider first the underlying objectives of punitive damages, other than to echo the US Supreme Court's cursory recitation of punishment and deterrence.[36]

Scholars too have been inspired by *Campbell* to explore the retributive punishment rationale for punitive damages. There is much good scholarship in this vein, with insights probing the civil–criminal boundary line as well as underlying philosophical justifications for a form of retributive punishment within civil tort law.[37]

But if *Campbell* 'has launched a thousand ships', what remains of concern is the deterrence fleet left behind moored to the docks. For retributive punishment is not the exclusive state law justification for punitive damages. Nor did *Campbell*, when read carefully, so hold. But the proportionality jurisprudence

[32] SB Scheuerman and AJ Franze, 'Instructing Juries on Punitive Damages: Due Process Revisited After *Philip Morris v Williams*' (2008) 10 *University of Pennsylvania Journal of Constitutional Law* 1147, 1191. Kentucky includes a similar instruction (ibid).

[33] See Sharkey, 'Economic Analysis of Punitive Damages: Theory, Empirics, and Doctrine' (n 7) 495: 'lower courts have taken [the punitive–compensatory ratio] to be a "rule of thumb" in favor of single digit ratios'.

[34] AF Del Rossi and WK Viscusi, 'The Changing Landscape of Blockbuster Punitive Damages Awards' (2010) 12 *American Law and Economics Review* 116, 138–46 tables 6, 7, 8; 151–53 table 11 (reporting a drop in the punitive–compensatory ratio in blockbuster punitive damages awards after *Campbell*).

[35] See, eg, *Johansen v Combustion Engineering, Inc* 170 F3d 1320, 1338, 1339 (11th Cir 1999) (Senior Circuit Judge Hill): 'The 100:1 ratio of the punitive to the actual damages is … justified by the need to deter this and other large organizations from a "pollute and pay" environmental policy'.

[36] But see *Mathias v Accor Economy Lodging Inc* 347 F3d 672, 676 (7th Cir 2003) (Judge Posner): 'We must consider why punitive damages are awarded and why the Court has decided that due process requires that such awards be limited'. *Mathias* is, in many ways, the exception that proves the rule, see Bublick, ch 14 of this volume.

[37] See MO DeGirolami, 'Reconstructing Malice in the Law of Punitive Damages' (2021) 14 *Journal of Tort Law* 193, 197 (compensating a victim for 'malice' is one of the key aims of punitive damages in state tort law); TB Colby, 'Beyond the Multiple Punishment Problem: Punitive Damages As Punishment for Individual, Private Wrongs' (2003) 87 *Minnesota Law Review* 583, 588–89 (arguing that the 'law limits each plaintiff's recovery to the amount necessary to punish the defendant only for the harm done to the individual plaintiff'); BC Zipursky, 'A Theory of Punitive Damages' (2005) 84 *Texas Law Review* 105 (characterising the 'double aspect' of punitive damages, namely the criminal aspect that focuses on imposing punishment and the civil aspect that focuses on the plaintiff's 'right to be punitive').

that it has spawned – developed in the lower state and federal courts and elaborated upon by scholars – has all but ruled out, and at a minimum stunted the growth of, a powerfully significant alternative deterrence, or internalisation of widespread harms, rationale for punitive damages.

C. Abroad

Campbell's 'proportionality message' has travelled abroad.[38] Several Argentinian decisions invoke the proportionality principle of *Campbell* in the course of identifying and applying constraints on punitive awards.[39] Argentina's consumer defence law provides for punitive damages for certain statutory violations.[40] When awarding punitive damages, courts are to consider[41]

> the damage resulting from the infringement for the consumer or user, the position in the market of the offender, the amount of the benefit obtained, the degree of intentionality, the seriousness of the risks or social damages derived from the infringement and its generalization, recidivism and other relevant circumstances of the act.

When considering the size of the punitive awards, courts have looked to *Campbell* for guidance and, at least in a few cases, have read the case to establish a single-digit ratio limit.[42] More generally, the courts have looked to *Campbell*'s proportionality principle to ensure prudential determination of punitive awards and thereby avoid arbitrary and excessive awards.[43]

[38] Here I focus specifically on *Campbell*'s influence. But in order to fully appreciate the baseline for comparison, one must acknowledge decisions that pre-date *Campbell* but nonetheless look to punitive to compensatory ratios as part of an excessiveness inquiry. Thus, in *Riches v News Group Newspapers Ltd* [1986] QB 256 (CA) 282, which deemed excessive a £250,000 punitive damages award – which amounted to 83 times the amount of compensatory damages – Parker LJ reasoned: 'Both the total amount of the award and its relationship to the damage suffered by the plaintiffs suggest strongly that something must have gone seriously wrong, for the punishment must bear some reasonable relation to the gravity of the "crime".'

[39] The source for the Argentinian decisions is La Ley Next, Thomson Reuters.

[40] Law No 24.240, 15 October 1993, BO (Arg).

[41] ibid Art 49.

[42] In a products liability case brought against General Motors Argentina, the complainant alleged that the vehicle they purchased contained irreparable defects, in violation of several provisions of Argentina's consumer protection statute. Here, the Argentinian Court relied on *Campbell* and the proportionality principle to justify the punitive damages award of 25,000 pesos. Dirección General de Defensa y Protección de Consumidores y Usuarios del Chubut [DGDPCyUChubut] [Consumer Protection and Defense Directorate of Chubut], 06/08/2010, 'Akar Automotores SA c General Motors Argentina SRL y/o quien resulte responsible', TR LALEY AR/JUR/85411/2010 (Arg). The court directed that the damages be paid to a government account.

[43] Consumers in the Mendoza province of Argentina challenged a gambling agency's advertising campaign directed at luring minors. The Third Chamber of Appeals awarded punitive damages in the amount of 20,000 pesos. The court relied on *Campbell*'s proportionality argument to ensure the prudential determination of punitive damages awards and to avoid arbitrary and excessive awards. Cámara 3a de Apelaciones en lo Civil, Comercial, Minas, de Paz y Tributaria de Mendoza [C 3A Civ Com Minas Paz y Trib Mendoza] [Third Court of Appeals in Civil, Commercial, Mining, Peace and Tax Matters of Mendoza], 6 June 2012, 'Protectora Asociación de Defensa al Consumidor y

In India, the Delhi High Court has likewise read *Campbell* as imposing a proportionality requirement. It is worth delving into the reasoning of the Court in the 2007 trademark infringement case, *Indian Performing Right Society Ltd v Debashis Patnaik*.[44] The plaintiff musical society sought to enforce its trademark against its unauthorised use by a hotel and requested punitive damages in light of evidence that the defendant continued its illegal practices even after the High Court of Delhi had issued an interim injunction prohibiting defendant from using plaintiff's work without paying royalties.[45]

What stands out about the Court's reasoning is the extent to which it discussed the threshold question of the purposes of punitive damages. As it elaborated:[46]

> The expression 'punitive' masks a variety of specific purposes that such damages are intended to actually serve apart from the punishing element and the deterrent cause of award of such damages. Such damages have various other useful purposes which include, inter alia, retribution, deterrence, compensation, education and law enforcement. Some authors have suggested that such damages have the effect of deterring not only the defendant from repeating the offence, but also deter others from committing the same; preserving peace; inducing private law enforcement; compensating victims for otherwise uncompensable loss and the payments of attorney's fees.

Specifically taking up the deterrence mantle, the Court signaled that:[47]

> The time has come when the Courts dealing actions for infringement of trademarks, copyrights, patents etc. should not only grant compensatory damages but award punitive damages also with a view to discourage and dishearten law breakers who indulge in violations with impunity out of lust for money so that they realise that in a case they are caught, they would be liable not only to reimburse the aggrieved party but would be liable to pay punitive damages also, which may spell financial disaster for them.

otros c Instituto Provincial de Juegos y Casinos s/ amparo', TR LALEY AR/JUR/41938/2012 9. In another consumer case, involving a plaintiff who sued a telephone service provider for statutory violations, the court invoked the role of punitive damages in vindicating public rights and sanctioning activities that infringe on those rights. But, notwithstanding the recognition of a role for punitive damages to vindicate public rights, the court invoked *Campbell*'s proportionality principle as a limitation. Cámara Nacional de Apelaciones en lo Civil y Comercial Federal [CNFed Civ y Com] [National Court of Appeals in Federal Commercial and Civil Litigation, sala III, 4 October 2017, 'Gagliardo, Jaime Luis c Telefónica Móviles SA s/ sumarísimo', TR LALEY AR/JUR/85557/2017 (Arg).

[44] *Indian Performing Right Society Ltd v Debashis Patnaik* (2007) 34 PTC 201 Del.

[45] ibid [6]–[8].

[46] ibid [27] (Gita Mittal J). Notwithstanding this seemingly protean embrace of myriad underlying rationales, the Court nonetheless reigns in the scope by restricting the underlying justification to moral-based corrective justice (ibid [34]) (Gita Mittal J): 'The punitive damages are founded on the philosophy of corrective justice and, as such, in appropriate cases these must be awarded to give a signal to the wrong-doers that law does not take a breach merely as a matter between rival parties but feels concerned about those who are not party to the *lis* but suffer on account of the breach'.

[47] ibid [34] (Gita Mittal J) (internal quotation omitted).

The Court even seemed to appreciate that punitive damages are called for where the defendant's actions have caused widespread societal harm extending beyond the specific plaintiff before it when the Court recognised that[48]

> it is not only the plaintiff, who has suffered on account of the infringement of its trademark and Magazine design but a large number of readers of the defendants' Magazine ... also have suffered by purchasing the defendants' Magazines under an impression that the same are from the reputed publishing house of the plaintiff company.

The Court explicitly cites *Mathias v Accor Economy Lodging Inc*, setting forth its under-detection rationale for punitive damages: 'If a tortfeasor is caught only half the time he commits torts, then when he is caught he should be punished twice as heavily'.[49]

But, just at the brink of an embrace of a non-retributive societal deterrence rationale for punitive damages, the Court blinked and reverted back to retributive punishment: 'The Court is of the view that the punitive damages should be really punitive and not flee bite and quantum thereof should defend upon the flagrancy of infringement'.[50] The pull of the proportionality principle from *Campbell* proved too strong; the Court concluded that 'The punitive damages also have to bear a fair ratio to the compensatory damages awarded to the plaintiff'.[51] The Court arrived at a punitive damages amount 'in the proximity of double the amount of compensatory damages' and is satisfied that it is significantly more than what would 'merely flee bite the defendant'.[52]

Goudkamp and Katsampouka similarly read the *Campbell* proportionality requirement as offering a potential constraint on punitive damages awards in England.[53] They read *Campbell* – and its interpretation by lower courts and scholars alike – as a response to the fear and anxiety surrounding excessive punitive awards.[54]

III. INTERNALISATION AND DETERRENCE

Given the multiple strands of language in *Campbell* (and the Court's other punitive damages cases), coupled with deference on federalism grounds to legitimate state interests, lower state and federal courts have considerable breathing room

[48] ibid.

[49] ibid (citing *Mathias* (n 36)).

[50] The court added a caveat (ibid [34]) (Gita Mittal J): 'In this case, the Court emphasised the intent of exemplary damages to punish the wrongdoer and also emphasised the deterrent effect of the damages'.

[51] ibid [43] (Gita Mittal J).

[52] ibid [48] (Gita Mittal J).

[53] J Goudkamp and E Katsampouka, 'An Empirical Study of Punitive Damages' (2018) 38 *Oxford Journal of Legal Studies* 90.

[54] ibid 114.

to recognise a non-retributive societal deterrence purpose for punitive damages. The first place to look for such recognition is in the set of cases that eschew *Campbell*'s call for single-digit punitive–compensatory ratios. But given that such larger ratios might be defended on various grounds, next one must probe courts' underlying rationales for evidence of this alternative rationale. While picked up in only a few reported cases, momentum for societal deterrence seems to be building in scholarship, both in the United States and abroad.

A. At Home in the United States

Lower state and federal courts uniformly adopt the framework established in *Campbell*; nonetheless, there remains wide variation in outcomes in terms of punitive damages awards. In the words of the Iowa Supreme Court, the US Supreme Court's punitive damages trilogy presents 'a tapestry of different colors'.[55]

i. Greater than Single-Digit Ratios

A slew of lower court cases recognise that the punitive–compensatory ratio is not the 'be-all and end-all' for constitutional excessiveness review.[56] Such cases tend first to remind that the US Supreme Court declined to impose a 'bright-line' ratio that a punitive award cannot exceed.[57] And then they proceed to defend awards that constitute a larger-than single-digit ratio.[58] A California state appellate court upheld a US$13.8m punitive award – approximately 16 times the compensatory damages – against a cigarette company 'In light of such extreme reprehensibility, including the vast scale and profitability of [defendant's] misconduct'.[59] The Oregon Supreme Court upheld a 22:1 punitive-to-compensatory ratio in an employment discrimination case in which the jury awarded US$6,000 in lost wages, reasoning that the US$175,000 punitive award was 'not so high that we can say that it exceeds, rather than serves, this state's interests in deterring and punishing'.[60] As the Iowa Supreme

[55] *Thornton* (n 4) 29 (Justice Appel).

[56] ibid 41 (Justice Appel): 'reprehensibility is clearly the most important factor, and the ratio of punitive damages to compensatory damages … is not a be-all and end-all'.

[57] *Campbell* (n 1) 424 (Justice Kennedy).

[58] See, eg, *Mathias* (n 36) 674 (37.2:1 ratio of punitive damages to compensatory damages upheld); *Phelps v Louisville Water Co* 103 SW3d 46, 55–56 (Ky 2003) (Justie Stumbo) (11:1 punitive–compensatory ratio upheld given the 'egregiousness' of defendant's actions and the minimal amount awarded to compensate victims' families for harm suffered and court's recognition that 'Clearly the jury did not feel the deterrent effect of punitive damages would be accomplished by awarding a lower amount').

[59] *Bullock v Philip Morris USA Inc* 198 Cal App 4th 543, 550 (2011) (Justice Croskey).

[60] *Hamlin v Hampton Lumber Mills Inc* 246 P3d 1121, 1123 (Or 2011) (Justice Walters).

Court remarked in a recent case, 'a ratio of 18 to 1 does appear in the cases and is not necessarily out of bounds'.[61]

ii. Internalisation/Deterrence Justification

Lower courts have found room for an internalisation of widespread harms approach within the US Supreme Court's existing doctrinal framework.

Given the pull of the Court's retributive punishment, and its proportionality 'marching orders', courts have been rather creative in terms of masking a societal deterrence perspective within strictures of the Court's framework. One tactic taken by some courts is to focus on the compensatory damages denominator, and argue that it is a poor proxy for the relevant harm (or potential harm) inflicted by the defendant.[62]

Another tactic is to find room for internalisation within the 'reprehensibility' prong. Notwithstanding its natural affinity with a retributive punishment approach, courts have looked to the sub-component of patterns of misconduct threatening widespread societal harm to defend a societal deterrence approach. Two of the Supreme Court's articulated reprehensibility factor sub-components map well onto a societal deterrence perspective: (1) whether tortious conduct showed an indifference to or reckless disregard of the health or safety of others; and (2) whether an isolated incident or repeated misconduct.[63] The Court has specifically stated that harm to others could be used as factor in determining reprehensibility of conduct.[64] Thus, lower courts have concluded that[65]

> where a party has engaged in a prolonged pattern of egregious and deceitful conduct that poses an extreme threat to the health and safety of a significant segment of the population of the state, the state's interest in punishing and/or deterring such conduct is heightened, and a punitive damages award that exceeds the single-digit ratio may be justified.

A few lower courts have been more emphatic, acknowledging that 'If the purpose of punitive damages is to punish a tortfeasor for outrageous conduct and to deter him or others from similar conduct, then *a requirement of proportionality defeats that purpose*'.[66] In a Pennsylvania state court case, the

[61] *Thornton* (n 4) 41 (Justice Appel).

[62] See, eg, *Willow Inn Inc v Pub Serv Mut Ins Co* 399 F3d 224, 236 (3d Cir 2005) (including awards of attorney fees and costs as part of compensatory damages for *Campbell* multiplier purposes).

[63] The other sub-components map rather exclusively to a retributive punishment perspective: whether harm was physical as opposed to economic; whether plaintiff was financially vulnerable; and whether conduct involved intentional malice, trickery or deceit.

[64] *Williams* (n 12) 355.

[65] *Goddard v Farmers Ins Co* 179 P3d 645, 661 fn 3 (Or 2008) (Justice Gillette). *cf Thornton* (n 4) 41 (Justice Appel): 'there was no evidence in this case … of a companywide pattern and practice of bad-faith conduct or widespread personal injuries caused by deceit'.

[66] *Kirkbride v Lisbon Contractors Inc* 555 A2d 800, 803 (Pa 1989) (Justice Zappala) (emphasis added).

jury was explicitly instructed: 'The amount you assess as punitive damages need not bear any relationship to the amount you choose to award as compensatory damages'.[67] Nonetheless, the jury awarded US$7,000 in compensatory damages and US$70,000 in punitive damages (a 10:1 punitive–compensatory ratio). The punitive award was reduced by the intermediate appellate court, but then reinstated by the Pennsylvania Supreme Court which recognised that 'In making its determination, the jury has the function of weighing the conduct of the tortfeasor against the amount of damages which would deter such future conduct'.[68]

Subsequent cases (including those post-dating *Campbell*) have reiterated that 'under Pennsylvania law, punitive damages need bear no proportional relationship to the compensatory damages awarded in a particular case'.[69] Pennsylvania courts emphasise that 'No mathematical equation has been developed for calculating punitive damages to require that they correlate proportionally with the compensatory awarded'.[70] The courts point instead to the proportionality that *should* matter – namely the relationship between the size of the punitive damages award and the legitimate objectives of punitive damages (punishment and deterrence).[71]

Finally, in a few cases, courts have directly recognised the need for punitive damages to force defendants to internalise widespread harms inflicted upon others or society more generally. Thus in *Sundquist v Bank of America*, a California federal bankruptcy judge highlighted the 'governmental and societal interests in punishing unlawful conduct and deterring its repetition'.[72] In that case, Bank of America was held to account not only for its mistreatment of a couple during foreclosure proceedings, but also for a wider pattern and practice of abuse and deceit directed at vulnerable victims. Given the need for punitive damages to 'vindicate the societal interests', the judge awarded the plaintiffs US$45m in punitive damages, with a remittitur to US$5m if Bank of America contributed US$30m to various nonprofit and educational entities.[73]

[67] ibid 801 (Justice Zappala).

[68] ibid 803 (Justice Zappala who, moreover, explicitly recognised the wealth of the defendant as relevant to the deterrence rationale (ibid): 'In performing this duty, the jury must weigh the intended harm against the tortfeasor's wealth').

[69] *Taha v Bucks County Pennsylvania* 172 FSupp3d 867, 873 (ED Pa 2016) (Judge Beetlestone). One federal court has noted the 'apparent conflict' between *Kirkbride* and the US Supreme Court's pronouncements on proportionality in punitive damage awards, but declined to resolve the 'thorny issue': *In re Remington Home for the Aged*, 777 F3d 620, 632 fn 3 (3d Cir 2015).

[70] *Tuski v Ivyland Café* 2004 WL 4962363, at *24 (Pa Com Pl Dec 22, 2004) (Judge Younge).

[71] *Sprague v Walter* 656 A2d 890, 925 (Pa Super 1995) (Judge Cercone): 'A reasonable relationship must exist between the amount of the punitive damage award and the twin goals of punishment and deterrence, the character of the tortious act, the nature and extent of the harm suffered by the plaintiff, and the wealth of the defendant'.

[72] See *Sundquist v Bank of Am NA* 566 BR 563, 614 fn 107 (Bankr ED Cal 2017) (Bankruptcy Judge Klein citing CM Sharkey, 'Punitive Damages as Societal Damages' (2003) 113 *Yale Law Journal* 347), vacated in part by *In re Sundquist*, 580 BR 536 (Bankr ED Cal 2018) (citing Sharkey ibid).

[73] ibid 618–19.

Several courts have carried the 'punitive damages as societal damages' mantle forward (although primarily in the bankruptcy realm). In the words of a Virginia federal bankruptcy judge, 'The amount of punitive damages required to redress the harm caused to the parties and serve the legitimate societal interests is greater than what principles of fairness would justify awarding solely to the Plaintiffs'.[74]

B. Abroad

Traces of the societal deterrence/internalisation of widespread harms approach for punitive damages can be found in oversees jurisdictions. Some of these cases, moreover, situate their holdings vis-à-vis *Campbell* and its 'proportionality' paradigm.

A consumer protection case in Argentina provides a vivid illustration.[75] The plaintiff purchased a glass bottle of Pepsi from a local kiosk. After opening the bottle, the plaintiff noticed a small used packet of aloe vera intimate gel floating within the Pepsi.[76] Plaintiff sued Cerveza Quilmes, the local manufacturer and producer of Pepsi, requesting 1,500 pesos in compensatory damages and two million pesos in punitive damages.[77] The Argentinian court upheld the sizeable punitive damages award, finding that it was justified in light of the potential health risks that such a manufacturing defect posed to consumers.[78] (The court also emphasised that punitive damages, unlike compensatory damages, are based on defendant's conduct, not harm suffered by the plaintiff.) The court invoked *Campbell* but maintained that in Argentina (unlike the United States), there is no 'proportionality' requirement for punitive damages.[79]

[74] *In re Charity*, No 16-31974-KLP, 2017 WL 3580173, at *22 (Bankr ED Va 2017) (Bankruptcy Judge Phillips). See also *In re Stefani*, No BR 18-00395-LT13, 2019 WL 762661 (Bankr SD Cal 2019); *In re Houck*, No 11-51513, 2020 WL 5941415, at *17 (Bankr WDNC Oct 6, 2020) (Bankruptcy Judge Beyer): 'Punitive damages serve legitimate governmental and societal interests in punishing unlawful conduct and deterring its repetition. Of the two goals, the court believes that deterrence … is the most important', affd sub nom *Houck v Lifestore Bank*, No 5:13-CV-00066-DSC, 2021 WL 970495 (WDNC 2021); *In re Brown*, No 20-00240-GS, 2020 WL 9602338, at *3 (Bankr D Alaska 2020) (Bankruptcy Judge Spraker imposing punitive damages 'in furtherance of deterring any future similar violations'); *In re LeGrand*, 612 BR 604 (Bankr ED Cal 2020). For more discussion of this line of cases invoking the societal purpose of punitive damages, see CM Sharkey, 'Punitive Damages Transformed into Societal Damages' in E Bant et al (eds), *Punishment and Private Law* (Oxford, Hart Publishing, 2021).

[75] Juzgado de 1a Instancia en lo Civil y Comercial de 5a Nominación de Córdoba [Juzg Civ y Com Córdoba] [Civil and Commercial Court of 1st Instance, 5th Nomination of Cordoba], 23 March 2011, 'Teijeiro o Teigeiro, Luis M c Cervecería y Maltería Quilmes SAICA', TR LALEY 70070864.

[76] ibid.

[77] ibid.

[78] ibid.

[79] ibid.

Thus freed from the constraints of proportionality, the court could pursue societal deterrence (among other aims for punitive damages).[80]

Another Argentinian consumer protection case likewise illustrates the court's impulse to look beyond the harm to the individual plaintiff before it to consider more widespread societal harm when evaluating a punitive damages award.[81] The plaintiff requested 250,000 pesos in statutorily authorised punitive damages against a travel agency that engaged in deceptive marketing practices that mislead the plaintiff as well as other consumers.[82] The court cited *Campbell* for support as it considered 'the generalized and indeterminate nature of the affected subjects' and noted that this was not a singular incident but an extensive marketing practice with wide-reaching impact.[83]

Scholars have picked up the mantle as well, with suggestions as to how to reorient courts and scholars abroad to an internalisation of harm/societal deterrence approach for punitive damages.[84] Australia may likewise provide fertile terrain for exploring the societal deterrence goal for punitive damages, especially with regard to corporate misconduct. France may be another jurisdiction where courts are receptive to the use of punitive damages to vindicate public rights, perhaps including via societal deterrence.[85]

IV. CONCLUSION

As I have explored in prior work, 'Whether termed civil penalties or statutory multiplied damages, "supra-compensatory" damages are of increasing theoretical and practical interest not only in the United States, but also abroad, notably in France and Australia'.[86] In this chapter, I have explored the unfortunate

[80] The court was intent on preventing future harm by imposing an award that would deter the introduction of harmful contaminants in products placed on the marketplace. In addition to the potential societal harm from the product defect, the court focused on the seriousness of defendant's actions, market position, degree of intentionality, and profits obtained from harmful conduct (ibid). The court, moreover, links the societal damages rationale with distribution of the award. At the conclusion of its decision, the court alludes to scholarly proposals to place some portion of punitive damages in a special fund.

[81] Cámara Nacional de Apelaciones en lo Comercial [CNCom] [National Commercial Court of Appeals], sala b, 5 November 2021, 'Balbi, María Lucía c almundo.com SRL s/ ordinario', TR LALEY AR/JUR/174575/2021 (Arg).

[82] ibid.

[83] ibid.

[84] See, eg, MJ Legg, 'Economic Guidelines for Awarding Exemplary Damages' (2004) 30 *Monash University Law Review* 303 (putting forward suggestions for Australian courts seeking to implement optimal deterrence); M Martínez Allez, 'Punitive Damages: Reorienting the Debate in Civil Law Systems' (2019) 10 *Journal of European Tort Law* 63. See also J Park, 'Searching for the Optimal Level of Punitive Damages' (2015) 15 *Asian Business Lawyer* 115.

[85] M Parker, 'Changing Tides: The Introduction of Punitive Damages into the French Legal System' (2012) 60 *American Journal of Comparative Law* 775 (suggesting vindication of public rights via punitive damages is compatible with France's tort goals).

[86] Sharkey, 'Punitive Damages as Societal Damages' (n 72) 1.

'proportionality' shadow cast by *Campbell*, which has unduly focused courts and scholars on the ratio of punitive-to-compensatory damages and corresponding retributive punishment rationales for punitive damages. But, at the same time, a few courts and scholars – both in the US and abroad – have broken free of this retributive punishment fixation to reconceive punitive damages as societal damages, based upon a non-retributive deterrence framework, centered on the internalisation of widespread harms.

14

Mathias v Accor Economy Lodging, Inc (2003)

Judge Richard A Posner's Message and Method on Punitive Damages

ELLEN M BUBLICK*

I. INTRODUCTION

SOMETIMES THE LOOMING threat of a potential danger is best illustrated through its tiny foils – the unwitting beings on whom these dangers will be unleashed. Such was the case in William Stafford's legendary poem, 'At the Bomb Testing Site'.[1] In Stafford's poem, a tiny lizard 'at the flute end of consequences' of atomic weapons, 'waited for history, its elbows tense'. The lizard watched the 'curve of a particular road', 'looking at something farther off than people could see ... ready for a change ... [Its] hands gripped hard on the desert'.[2]

Judge Richard Posner's decision in *Mathias v Accor Economy Lodging, Inc*[3] is US tort law's equivalent of the Stafford poem. Judge Posner, who viewed 'the power of Cardozo as of Holmes' as largely 'that of a rhetorician – a poet', unleashed his full poetic power in *Mathias*.[4] In *Mathias*, Posner deployed the tiny harms inflicted by bed bugs as a foil for the potentially law and life-changing

* For helpful comments on an earlier draft, thanks to Andy Coan, James Goudkamp, David Jacobs, Eleni Katsampouka, Gregory Keating, Brian Laird, Eric Posner, Carol Rose, Steven Shavell, the participants of the Oxford 'Landmark Cases on the Law of Punitive Damages' workshop and the Arizona Law Faculty workshop. I am especially grateful to Laura Carlson for her valuable research assistance.

[1] W Stafford, *West of Your City* (Harper & Row, New York 1960).

[2] ibid.

[3] *Mathias v Accor Economy Lodging, Inc* 347 F3d 672 (7th Cir 2003).

[4] RA Posner, *Cardozo: A Study in Reputation* (Chicago, University of Chicago Press, 1990) 56–57 (stating as his own 'most controversial claim – that rhetorical power may be a more important attribute of judicial excellence than analytical power').

punitive damage limits endorsed by the United States Supreme Court in *State Farm v Campbell*.[5]

Two notes of context are critical to understanding this American punitive damages story. First, most European cases in this volume view punitive damages awards themselves as a threat. *Mathias* reflects the American view that unprincipled *limits* on punitive damages awards can also be a threat. In part, this different perspective stems from the stronger role that civil litigation plays in the United States vis-à-vis other forms of regulation. As European authors wryly note,[6]

> Americans do not trust their business nor their regulators. In Europe, on the other hand, people tend to believe that most businesses, or at least the well-reputed ones, are ethical and that the state will offer protection against those that are not.

Second, many of the Commonwealth punitive damages cases in this volume focus on individual dignitary harms. By contrast, *Mathias* confronts profitable corporate misconduct that creates harms that aggregate but are difficult to redress – a frequent concern of Judge Posner's jurisprudence and the core concern of many important US punitive damages cases.[7] If, as many US scholars and judges believe, punitive damages awards 'can save lives in an efficient manner',[8] unprincipled limits on their availability could needlessly imperil lives and well-being.

Judge Posner's *Mathias* opinion, issued a mere two weeks after the Seventh Circuit's own oral argument in the case, and just six months after the US Supreme Court's decision in *State Farm*, was designed to take on the Supreme Court's ruling. Judge Posner sought to answer the gaping legal questions that *State Farm*'s punitive-to-compensatory damages award measure had opened for lower courts. In particular, after *State Farm*, could courts still impose meaningful punitive damages awards to serve deterrent and retributive purposes?[9] If they

[5] *State Farm Mutual Automobile Insurance Co v Campbell*, 538 US 408 (2003) (suggesting that few damage awards exceeding a single-digit ratio of punitive to compensatory damages would pass constitutional scrutiny).

[6] G Howells and T Wilhelmsson, *EC and US Approaches to Consumer Protection – Should the Gap Be Bridged?* (1997) 17 *Yearbook of European Law* 207, reprinted in JA Davies and PT Hayden, *Global Issues in Tort Law* (Eagan, West, 2008) 198.

[7] *cf* CM Sharkey, 'Punitive Damages Transformed into Societal Damages' (2003) 113 *Yale Law Journal* 347 (discussing a US study showing that punitive damages are awarded in a greater percentage of cases that plaintiffs win against businesses than in cases plaintiffs win against individuals) (hereinafter Sharkey, 'Punitive Damages Transformed') with J Goudkamp and E Katsampouka, 'An Empirical Study of Punitive Damages' (2018) 38 *OJLS* 90 (finding that the reverse may be true in the United Kingdom).

[8] J Hersch and W Viscusi, 'Saving Lives Through Punitive Damages' (2010) 83 *Southern California Law Review* 229, 230. For comprehensive criticism of the thesis that tort law should be understood as a price system, see GC Keating, *Reasonableness and Risk* (OUP, Oxford 2022) esp 185–228.

[9] See, eg, L Efting, 'Punitive Damages: Will the Courts Still Punish the Wrongdoer After *State Farm Mutual Automobile Insurance Co v Campbell*' (2003) 49 *South Dakota Law Review* 67; D Schechter, 2003 Comm Fin News 101 (examining a potential 'trend' of California cases in which

could not, as *State Farm*'s restrictions seemed to portend, would anyone mourn that loss?[10]

In *Mathias*, Judge Posner raised punitive damages doctrine from its seeming death and paid homage to its crucial protections. The *Mathias* opinion advocated proportional punishment and deterrence to guide judicial analysis, rather than mindless application of punitive-to-compensatory damages ratios.[11] Inferentially, *Mathias* also resisted *State Farm's* mandate to confine punitive damages awards to harm done to a specific claimant.

Judge Posner's opinion provides an erudite lesson on the need for punitive damages and the character of their limits. Indeed, the opinion, on its face, rightly commands judicial, academic and practitioner attention.

However, deeper exploration into the *Mathias* case reveals a surprising, if more important, story that has been obscured from view. I argue that once readers understand a fact that Judge Posner (deliberately?) misstated concerning the potential availability of other legal remedies in *Mathias*, the opinion becomes even more deeply telling and instructive. *Mathias* not only conveys Judge Posner's direct message about the proper proportionality standard to guide courts' punitive damages review, but also reveals his pragmatic method for reviewing punitive damages awards.

But before we turn to this hidden story, let's begin with an examination of the *Mathias* case on its own terms.

II. THE *MATHIAS* LITIGATION

The *Mathias* case began at a Motel 6 at 162 East Ontario Street, in Chicago's swanky Gold Coast neighbourhood. The motel rented its 191 rooms for about US$150 a night.[12] In 2000, the motel's total room-night rentals were placed at 48,000 for the year.[13]

'the court struggled to free itself of the shackles imposed by the United States Supreme Court' and its 'single-digit multipliers').

[10] MO DeGirolami, 'Reconstructing Malice in the Law of Punitive Damages' (2021) 14 *Journal of Tort Law* 193, 199 (suggesting that constitutional doctrines impair the deterrence objective of punitive damages by restricting 'the amount of punitive damages to what are often sub-optimally deterrent levels').

[11] CM Sharkey, 'Modern Tort Law: Preventing Harms, Not Recognizing Wrongs' (2021) 134 *Harvard Law Review* 1423, 1450. See also D Dobbs et al, *Torts and Compensation: Personal Accountability and Social Responsibility for Injury*, 9th edn (St Paul, West, 2023) 938: 'Suppose the defendant malevolently and repeatedly fires his rifle at the plaintiff, but has so far only chipped the plaintiff's US$10 sunglasses. If the jury awards US$10 compensatory damages, the ratio rule suggests that punitive awards should be some modest multiple of that sum. It is apparent that this cannot be right'.

[12] Transcript of Oral Argument, 2003 WL 25789315 (hereinafter 'Transcript of Oral Argument').

[13] Brief of the Defendants-Appellants, 2003 WL 22706484 12.

The facts of the case, extraordinarily well developed through plaintiffs' court filings, and expertly recounted by Judge Posner, suggest that for just US$500, management could have sprayed every room at the first sign of bed bugs – the course of action recommended by its expert pest-control service. Instead, the motel refused the bug company's recommendation. For the next two years the motel let its infestation spiral out of control to what Judge Posner termed 'farcical' proportions.[14] For example,[14a]

> a guest, after complaining of having been bitten repeatedly by insects while asleep in his room in the hotel, was moved to another room only to discover insects there; and within 18 minutes of being moved to a third room he discovered insects in that room as well and had to be moved still again.

Frequent refunds to guests who complained of bug bites were well documented in the record.[15] Call logs from motel management to the pest control company acknowledged 'that there was a "major problem with bed bugs" and that all that was being done about it was "chasing them from room to room"'.[16] As Judge Posner relayed, 'Rooms that the motel had placed on "Do not rent, bugs in room" status nevertheless were rented'.[17]

Into this maelstrom entered plaintiffs – brother and sister Burl and Desiree Mathias – who flew into Chicago from Ontario, Canada for a busy packaging conference at the McCormick Place convention centre. After being unwittingly placed in a room that had been internally listed on 'do not rent status', Desiree awoke after her first night's sleep to bumps on her skin that itched throughout the day. During the second night, when awoken from sleep, Burl turned on the lights to find bed bugs teeming all over himself, his sister and the room.[18]

Once home, the Mathiases hired Chicago attorney Peter Stamatis to file suit. Plaintiffs Burl and Desiree Mathias and defendants Motel 6 and Accor Economy Lodging (the company that owned and operated the motel) were citizens of different jurisdictions. Accordingly, Stamatis filed the plaintiffs' suit in federal court based on diversity jurisdiction. For each plaintiff, the complaint plead six causes of action – battery, intentional infliction of emotional harm, fraudulent concealment, consumer fraud under the Illinois Consumer Fraud and Deceptive Business Practices Act, gross negligence and negligent failure to maintain the hotel in a habitable condition.[19] As a remedy, the plaintiffs requested physical and psychological damages of more than US$75,000 (a necessary allegation for federal diversity jurisdiction); any other 'just and proper' damages; attorney fees and costs under the state consumer fraud statute; and

[14] ibid.
[14a] ibid.
[15] ibid.
[16] ibid.
[17] ibid.
[18] Combined Brief of Plaintiffs-Appellees, Cross-Appellants, 2003 WL 22706704, 26–28.
[19] Second Amended Complaint, 2002 WL 32966388, [73]–[95].

'An award of punitive damage … in an amount sufficient to deter [defendants] … from engaging in such a deceptive practice in the future'.[20]

The defendants filed a motion to dismiss all of the claims except for negligence. Judge Joan Lefkow, in an unpublished opinion available on Westlaw, rejected the defendants' motion on every count.[21] She further wrote that several of defendants' arguments were 'frivolous' or 'border on frivolous'.[22] Accordingly, discovery in the case was permitted to proceed.

Through that discovery, the plaintiffs' counsel uncovered ample evidence of the motel's infestation-related problems, knowledge of the problems, failures to address them and affirmative efforts to conceal the infestation.[23] Apparently unmoved by the evidence against it, the defendants reportedly offered little in the way of settlement. At one point, they offered a four-figure settlement to avoid trial – not enough to pay costs incurred in litigation let alone pay attorney fees or provide compensation to plaintiffs.[24]

Consequently, a full federal trial was held. The defendants filed at least nine motions *in limine*, of which the judge granted only two.[25] Evidence at trial included the plaintiffs' testimony, as well as the testimony of employees, another guest of the hotel who was bitten by bed bugs on the same day, the motel's pest control service and an independent pest control expert.[26] Notably, University of Illinois pest control expert Robert Novak, PhD, Senior Entomologist, described the blood feeding of the *Cimex lectularis* in detailed and graphic terms. Novak also opined that a hotel infested with bed bugs 'was not fit for human habitation'.[27]

Throughout the trial, the plaintiffs' counsel avoided quantifying the dollar value of their injuries. It was the defence counsel who suggested a compensatory damage award of US$5,000 per plaintiff – a request that the jury ultimately granted. However, the plaintiffs' counsel directly asked the jury to hold defendants to account for 'placing profits above the health and safety of their guests'.[28] The jury also granted that request. Although counsel did not suggest a specific punitive damages award amount, or method of calculation, the jury elected to award each plaintiff US$186,000 in punitive damages. The final award of US$191,000 per claimant was thought to reflect an assessment of US$1,000 damages per room for each of the motel's 191 rooms.[29]

[20] ibid [75], [78], [84], [88], [92], [95].
[21] Memorandum Decision on Defendant's Motion to Dismiss, 2002 WL 221523, 4.
[22] ibid 3.
[23] Combined Brief of Plaintiffs-Appellees, Cross-Appellants (n 18) 8–30.
[24] Telephone interview with plaintiffs' attorney, Peter Stamatis (9 December 2022).
[25] Rulings on Motions in Limine, 2002 WL 1611582.
[26] Combined Brief of Plaintiffs-Appellees, Cross-Appellants (n 18) 10.
[27] ibid 9.
[28] ibid 42–43.
[29] Transcript of Oral Argument (n 12).

The defendants' net worth, in billions, had also been admitted at trial.[30] Judge Lefkow upheld the jury's US$382,000 award.

Hoping that they would have better luck with the Seventh Circuit, a conservative court with a majority of Republican judicial appointees, the defendants appealed. Indeed, the three-judge panel assigned to hear *Mathias* well reflected the court's political make-up. However, from the very first question at oral argument, it seemed clear that defendants had failed to land a more sympathetic audience.

Judge Richard Posner began the oral argument with the questions: 'Why are you appealing? I'm puzzled by this. It's a very small amount of money'. '[Want] your bedbug experience to be discussed at length in a federal reporter?'[31] Defendants did not address the potential reputational costs of public litigation, but instead focused on the amount of the punitive damages award, which they characterised as 'unfairly imposed'.

Foremost in the minds of judges and counsel during the oral argument was a case that the United States Supreme Court had decided during the pendency of *Mathias*' Seventh Circuit appeal. After the defendants' opening brief and the plaintiffs' response had been filed, the Supreme Court had issued a new punitive damages decision in *State Farm v Campbell*.[32]

Ordinarily, a US Supreme Court opinion might not be particularly important to an Illinois torts case. In the United States, damage issues, like tort law issues more generally, are governed by *state* law as defined by state courts. Federal courts sitting in diversity jurisdiction, as the Seventh Circuit sat in *Mathias*, decide common law cases based on state substantive common law – here, Illinois' common law. However, in the mid-1990s the US Supreme Court held that the US Constitution itself spoke to the issue of punitive damages. Specifically, the Court held that the Due Process Clause of the 14th Amendment contains substantive due process protections that prohibit arbitrary or excessive punishments, including 'excessive' punitive damages.[33] The clause reads: 'No State shall … deprive any person of life, liberty, or property, without due process of law'.

With no explicit constitutional language about punitive or excessive damages, the *State Farm* Court invented its own test of excess. The Court counselled that under constitutional analysis, while there was not 'a bright-line ratio' requirement for valid punitive damages awards, 'in practice, few awards exceeding a single-digit ratio between punitive and compensatory damages, to

[30] Combined Brief of Plaintiffs-Appellees, Cross-Appellants (n 18) 8 (US$1.6b net worth of Motel 6, briefs varied concerning the net worth of defendant Accor).

[31] ibid.

[32] *State Farm* (n 5).

[33] *Honda Motor Co v Oberg*, 512 US 415, 420 (1994); *BMW of North America, Inc v Gore*, 517 US 559, 568 (1996). But see *BMW v Gore*, 517 US 559, 598–99 (1996) (Scalia J dissenting): 'I do not regard the Fourteenth Amendment's Due Process Clause as a secret repository of substantive guarantees against 'unfairness' – neither the unfairness of an excessive civil compensatory award, nor the unfairness of an 'unreasonable' punitive award'.

a significant degree, will satisfy due process'.[34] In line with those ratios, the *Mathias* defendants argued that *State Farm*'s new constitutional due process analysis required each of the jury's US$186,000 punitive damages awards (a 37.2 ratio of punitive to compensatory damages) to be reduced to US$20,000 – a 4:1 ratio.

In addition to the punitive-to-compensatory-damages ratio, the spectre of two individual plaintiffs' recovering for harm to other motel guests could also have threatened the *Mathias* award. According to *State Farm*, punitive damages could not be awarded 'to punish and deter conduct that bore no relation' to a particular claimant's harm. To prevent 'the possibility of multiple punitive damages awards for the same conduct', the Supreme Court had warned that when calculating punitive damages, courts should not 'adjudicate the merits of other parties' hypothetical claims against a defendant'.[35]

In light of *State Farm*'s articulated concern about multiple punitive damages awards, at oral argument in *Mathias*, Judge Posner asked the defence counsel about the possibility of multiple claims in the case: 'You worry about a lot of bed bug cases? Is this the first of thousands or what? Are there others?'[36] The defence counsel represented that 'There were no other suits that we are aware of across the country',[37] apparently obviating Judge Posner's concern about the potential for multiple awards.

Judge Posner also explored whether plaintiffs' punitive damages verdict had been based on the claims of other parties. At first, plaintiffs' attorney had suggested that 'what the jury did was give a total award of … a thousand dollars per room'. But Judge Posner pressed, 'How do you know that's what the jury did here?' 'What did you argue to the jury with regard to punitive damages?' The plaintiffs' counsel confirmed that he 'didn't suggest a number' for punitive damages to the jury, let alone one based on other rooms or claimants.[38]

III. JUDGE POSNER ARTICULATES REASONS FOR PUNITIVE DAMAGES AND THEIR LIMITS

Judge Posner's opinion in *Mathias* can only be described as a *tour de force*. The opinion deploys every judicial technique that he lauded with respect to Justice Cardozo's famed decision in *Palsgraf*. First, *Mathias* is written by a judge of 'enormous reputation'. Second, it contains a statement of facts that 'strips away extraneous detail'. Third, the opinion is 'eloquently pedagogical' and set up 'to teach some basic truths'. The opinion is brief and vivid and the author's

[34] *State Farm* (n 5) 410. See also D Dobbs et al, *The Law of Torts*, 2nd edn (Minneapolis, West, 2011) [485] (constitutional requirements governing the award of punitive damages).
[35] *State Farm* (n 5) 423.
[36] Transcript of Oral Argument (n 12).
[37] ibid.
[38] ibid.

'confidence sweeps the reader along'. And finally, as I will argue in section V, the opinion also 'misstates facts' to rhetorical effect, perhaps deliberately.[39] If you have not yet read the *Mathias* opinion verbatim, you will thank me for exhorting you to do so now.

The *Mathias* opinion shows why, despite Judge Posner's post on the federal bench, he is rightly classified as one of the great common law judges of our time. In just six pages of the federal reporter, Judge Posner explains the fundamental principles that should guide punitive damages awards and their limits – marshalling ample Illinois case law, examining the core concerns of due process protections, and elucidating the subject by reference to everything from Aristotelean notions of corrective justice to economic analysis of law, to news of the day (the comeback of bed bugs in the face of declining pesticide use).

Judge Posner begins the opinion by detailing facts that show sufficient evidence of willful and wanton conduct – a prerequisite to upholding any punitive damages award. After determining that punitive damages are warranted, Judge Posner's analysis focuses on the difficult question: 'But in what amount?' Rather than embrace a mindless ratio as his metric, Posner makes a beeline for key principles. First, he assures readers that the Supreme Court's *State Farm* opinion does not bind the lower courts to a single-digit ratio (contrary to what many observers thought the Supreme Court had done). Instead, Judge Posner proffers that *State Farm* 'said merely that 'there is a presumption against an award that has a 145-to-1 ratio'.[40] He then explains why it would be 'unreasonable' to lay down a mandatory compensatory-to-punitive damages ratio rule.

To explain that unreasonableness, Judge Posner concentrates on two important questions. First, 'why punitive damages are awarded'. And second, 'why the [Supreme] Court has decided that due process requires that such awards be limited'.[41]

Answering the second question first, Judge Posner writes that limits are imposed to assure that legal punishment fits the wrongfulness of defendants' acts. While the proportionality of the defendant's wrong to the legal response is central, punishment might nevertheless be modified upwards in cases in which either a) the probability of detection is low, or b) the defendant might profit from the crime. In addition, to make a rational determination about how to act, an actor like Holmes' bad man needs clear standards to provide 'reasonable notice of the sanction'. Moreover, 'sanctions must be based on the wrong done, rather than the status of the defendant'. But the defendant's status can be important for at least one purpose – to consider whether defendant's high net worth gives it an ability to make litigating against it very costly.[42]

[39] Posner (n 4) 43–45.

[40] *Mathias* (n 3) 676.

[41] ibid.

[42] See also AM Polinsky and S Shavell, 'Punitive Damages: An Economic Analysis' (1998) 111 *Harvard Law Review* 869.

In sum, limits ensure that punitive damages awards are proportionate to wrongfulness, need for deterrence, and disgorgement of unwarranted profits. And limits must be admeasured by standards rather than a defendant's ability to pay or ability to quash meritorious litigation.

After articulating good reasons for limits, Judge Posner outlines good reasons *for* punitive damages awards as well. Beginning with early punitive damages judgments from the eighteenth century, civil punitive damages played a role in 'relieving the pressures on an overloaded criminal justice system' in the case of minor crimes.[43] By way of illustration, Posner offers the crime of spitting in another's face. Such an offence need not be prosecuted under criminal law because it can be as easily deterred by levy of a civil fine through the tort of battery.

Compensatory damages alone would not provide sufficient deterrence. For one thing, the amount of actual damage can be difficult to determine. In addition, compensatory damage awards might be too slight to provide incentives for suit. Given these litigation difficulties, the defendant would be able to 'commit the offensive act with impunity provided he was willing to pay'. Moreover, without an avenue for legal relief, injured plaintiffs might seek retribution.[44]

The need for punitive damages awards to deter wrongful conduct and fund legal action is particularly acute in cases in which plaintiffs' compensatory damages would be slight. By contrast, Judge Posner opines that punitive damages serve a lesser role in cases that involve substantial compensatory damages. Judge Posner illustrates this latter category by reference to *State Farm* and the case of punitive damages 'sought for a billion-dollar oil spill' (presaging, or perhaps influencing, the Supreme Court's later judgment in the Exxon Valdez litigation).[45]

Applying these articulated standards to the facts of *Mathias*, Judge Posner affirms the role of punitive damages in this case. According to the opinion, the defendants' behaviour was outrageous, compensable harm was both slight and difficult to quantify because it was rooted in emotional harm. Furthermore, the defendants may have profited by their ability to rent rooms at an ordinary rate despite the infestation. In addition, the motel's concealment of the bed bugs (at times by referring to them as 'ticks' – ironically a more dangerous insect), may have helped the defendants' misconduct escape detection. 'If a tortfeasor is "caught" only half the time he commits torts, then when he is caught, he should be punished twice as heavily'.[46] Increasing damages to supra-compensatory levels when the probability of detection is low ensures

[43] ibid. See also WM Landes and RA Posner, 'New Light on Punitive Damages' (1986) 10 *Regulation* 33.

[44] *Mathias* (n 3) 677.

[45] *Exxon Shipping Co v Baker*, 554 US 471, 496 (2008).

[46] *Mathias* (n 3) 677.

that tortious conduct yields no expected benefit to the defendant, thus deterring the behaviour.[47]

In terms of damages amount, Judge Posner counsels that a cap on punitive damages of 4-to-1, in this case US$20,000 per plaintiff, might well have given the plaintiffs difficulty in financing their lawsuit. He notes that wealthy corporations' efforts to increase the costs of suit are often an effort to develop 'a reputation intended to deter plaintiffs'.[48] Indeed, Judge Posner suggests that such an interest likely explains 'the great stubbornness with which [Motel 6] has defended this case'.[49]

Finally, Judge Posner looks at regulatory and criminal penalties to which the defendant could have been subject. These include a US$2,500 fine per endangered person and the revocation of the hotel's licence. The court 'felt sure that defendant would prefer to pay the punitive damages assessed in this case than to lose its license'.[50]

Applying the court's proportionate, standard-based, deterrence principles to the case at hand, the Seventh Circuit could not say that 'the award of punitive damages was excessive'.[51] When reviewing jury damages awards, the judicial function 'is to police a range, not a point'.[52] Absent mandatory guidelines, 'it is inevitable that the specific amount of punitive damages awarded whether by a judge or by a jury will be arbitrary'.[53]

Thus, when it seemed to many courts and commentators that the Supreme Court had closed the door on significant punitive damages awards through ill-advised constraints in *State Farm*, Judge Posner guided courts, litigators and scholars to an open window.[54] He eschewed punitive-to-compensatory damages ratios, and instead refocused the inquiry on the need for extra-compensatory damages to deter reprehensible but profitable misconduct and to motivate suit.

[47] See Polinsky and Shavell (n 42).

[48] *Mathias* (n 3) 677.

[49] ibid.

[50] ibid 678. See also E Bublick, 'When Regulation Fails?: Public Nuisance Liability as Fallback Option or Policy Plan' *Jotwell Torts Blog* (12 August 2022) (a liability rule, even one that imposes significant financial liability, can be a desirable option for defendants).

[51] *Mathias* (n 3) 678.

[52] ibid.

[53] ibid.

[54] Dobbs et al, *The Law of Torts* (n 34) [485]: 'Although now seemingly entrenched, the emphasis on the actual compensatory award seems hard to square with the reprehensibility guidepost and hard to square as well with the deterrence function The risk of harm – meaning both the likelihood of harm and its potential magnitude – bears strongly on the reprehensibility issue, but the actual award to a particular plaintiff does not'; J Hersch and WK Viscusi, 'Saving Lives Through Punitive Damages' (2010) 83 *Southern California Law Review* 229, 233 (proposing a punitive damages approach that incorporates 'Value of a Statistical Life' into punitive damage formulation and 'shifts the focus from admissible punitive damages ratios to the total monetary amount needed for deterrence'); D Rendleman, 'Common Law Punitive Damages: Something for Everyone?' (2009) 7 *University of St Thomas Law Journal* 1, 23: 'An unyielding ratio is a crude and unsatisfactory technique to apply to measure the proportion between misconduct and injury'.

IV. THE INFLUENCE OF *MATHIAS*

Mathias has had a significant influence in US legal education, practice and scholarship. However, its impact has been dampened by the US Supreme Court's continued embrace of a constitutional substantive due process ratio requirement along the lines of its decision in *State Farm*.[55]

On the academic side, Judge Posner's opinion has joined the very small list of cases taught in all five leading US tort law casebooks.[56] In four of the five books, *Mathias* is printed as a main case.[57] The quality of Judge Posner's analysis makes *Mathias* an ideal classroom teaching text. In addition, *Mathias*'s lively and thoughtful prose provides welcome relief from the long trudge through densely worded concepts that is the *State Farm v Campbell* opinion.

In terms of the opinion's influence in practice, few US judges have the gravitas to steer courts away from mechanical application of rules thought to be required by Supreme Court precedent. Judge Posner's outsize reputation and knowledge, and his persuasive analysis, produced this effect.

Reaction to the *Mathias* opinion was swift and widespread. Within months, courts from New York to Tennessee to Oregon had already cited the case.[58] By the end of 2004, at least 31 articles had addressed it. In the decision's first year in print, at least 69 briefs invoked it. From the start, the case was rightly understood as a challenge to *State Farm*. As one noted scholar wrote, 'Since *Campbell* was decided, one respected federal appellate judge has distinguished it and affirmed a punitive damage award thirty-seven times greater than the compensatory damages'.[59]

Citations to the opinion were numerous as well as immediate. By the kind of citation metrics that Judge Posner used to measure *Palsgraf's* impact, *Mathias* has been cited in more than 140 cases, 200 articles, and 1,400 documents in the Westlaw database.

Yet while *Mathias* is well cited and widely taught, its impact is far overshadowed by *State Farm*. For example, 489 journals and articles addressed *State Farm* in the first year after it was handed down. The citation differentials between

[55] See also Sharkey, ch 13 of this volume.

[56] Dobbs et al, *Torts and Compensation* (n 11); R Epstein and C Sharkey, *Cases and Materials on Torts*, 12th edn (Boston, Aspen Publishing, 2020); MA Franklin et al, *Tort Law and Alternatives: Cases and Materials*, 11th edn (St Paul, West, 2021); J Goldberg et al, *Tort Law: Responsibilities and Redress*, 5th edn (Boston, Aspen Publishing, 2021); and V Schwartz et al, *Prosser, Wade, and Schwartz's Torts: Cases and Materials*, 14th edn (St Paul, West, 2020).

[57] The *Prosser, Wade and Schwartz* book (n 55) is the one exception.

[58] *Fresh v Entertainment USA of Tennessee, Inc*, 340 F Supp 2d 851, 859 (TN 2003); *Hitchcock Plaza, Inc v Clark*, 781 NYS2d 624 (NY 2003); *Planned Parenthood of Columbia/Willamette, Inc v Am Coal of Life Activists*, 300 F Supp 2d 1055, 1064 (OR 2004) (threats of violence); affirmed in part, reversed in part and remanded, 422 F3d 949 (9th Cir 2005).

[59] S Yeazell, 'Punitive Damages, Descriptive Statistics, and the Economy of Civil Litigation' (2004) 79 *Notre Dame Law Review* 2025, 2043–44.

State Farm and *Mathias* are easy to explain. Because *State Farm* purports to interpret the US Constitution, it is binding precedent for all federal and state courts. *Mathias*, by contrast, governs only the Seventh Circuit (and then, only to the extent the opinion is not in conflict with Supreme Court precedent).

While many parties and courts cite *Mathias*, its seeming conflict with *State Farm* makes courts' ability to fully follow the opinion unclear, in the Seventh Circuit as elsewhere.[60] One empirical study of punitive damages judgments shows that courts of appeal typically reduce damages ratios to about four times compensatory damages – suggesting that Judge Posner's embrace of greater ratios and different standards is still an exception rather than the rule.[61]

In practice, bureaucrats beat poets; positional power beats moral and intellectual authority. That Supreme Court opinions garner citations because of influence rather than quality is a truism that Judge Posner well understood.[62] If Judge Posner's view had changed Supreme Court doctrine, as it had on some prior occasions,[63] his opinion truly could have had widespread effects. But in the United States, as in any common law country, intermediate appellate court judges cannot override high court precedent.[64]

Even so, Judge Posner's opinion may yet influence future US Supreme Court judgments. The idea that the US Constitution proscribes high state punitive damages awards has been increasingly subject to challenge.[65] In addition, as courts and scholars in other countries liberalise punitive damages standards,[66] they may view Judge Posner's approach as an intellectually superior alternative to *State Farm*, as many US judges and scholars do.

[60] See, eg, *Saccameno v US Bank Nat'l Ass'n*, 943 F3d 1071 (7th Cir 2019).

[61] LJ Hines and NW Hines, 'Constitutional Constraints on Punitive Damages: Clarity, Consistency, and the Outlier Dilemma' (2015) 66 *Hastings Law Journal* 1257, 1288 (median punitive damages ratios in study sample were very close to 4-to-1).

[62] Posner (n 4) 72: 'A more serious problem is the judge's and lawyer's natural preference for citing a case of the highest court of the jurisdiction in preference to a better-reasoned or more eloquent case of a lower court, illustrating the fact that law has a more authoritarian cast than science does [so that in citation counts there is a] between influence and quality'.

[63] See, eg, *Khan v State Oil Co*, 93 F3d 1358 (7th Cir 1996) (Posner criticised a Supreme Court antitrust opinion as 'unsound when decided' and 'increasingly wobbly'). The Supreme Court subsequently overruled the doctrine in *State Oil Co v Khan*, 522 US 3 (1997).

[64] See also Goudkamp, ch 5 of this volume.

[65] See, eg, AB Spencer, 'Due Process and Punitive Damages: The Error of Federal Excessiveness Jurisprudence' (2006) 79 *Southern California Law Review* 1085 (challenging the Court's finding that the Due Process Clause imposes limits on punitive damages and arguing that the holding lacks precedential basis and is an unreconcilable departure from maxims of constitutional construction); ML Rustad, 'Happy No More: Federalism Derailed by the Court that Would be King of Punitive Damages' (2005) 64 *Maryland Law Review* 461 (criticising the constitutionalisation of punitive damages based on federalism); MH Redish and AL Mathews, 'Why Punitive Damages are Unconstitutional' (2004) 53 *Emory Law Journal* 1, 10: 'A federalised democratic system should not tolerate so blatant a usurpation of state legislative and judicial prerogatives by an unaccountable federal judicial body'.

[66] See Katsampouka, ch 10 of this volume.

V. REANALYSING PUNITIVE DAMAGES BASED ON THE FACTS OF *MATHIAS*

Having discussed *Mathias* on its face, let me add one new wrinkle to the analysis. Because of a nearly imperceptible factual misstatement at the start of the *Mathias* opinion, Judge Posner was able to dodge the very issue that *Mathias* purports to address – the need for *punitive damages* to deter wrongful conduct and provide incentives for suit. Ironically, it is that misstatement which may be most revealing about Judge Posner's pragmatic method for reviewing punitive damages awards.

A. Message and Misstatement

A full understanding of *Mathias* requires an appreciation of the extent to which the opinion served as a vehicle for Judge Posner's message on punitive damages. To Judge Posner, the timing of plaintiffs' exceptionally well developed and well argued *Mathias* case in the Seventh Circuit shortly after *State Farm* was decided must have been fortuitous. As Judge Posner once wrote of Cardozo's legendary opinion in *Palsgraf*, 'if Cardozo had drawn another tort case instead of *Palsgraf* he might have made of it a *Palsgraf*'.[67]

Because the punitive damages message was the motive for the opinion, the motive may have distorted its analysis. Judge Posner well understood the tension between the aesthetic function of a great opinion 'to state a rule clearly, memorably' and the need for a judge to state facts accurately.[68]

Though critical of Cardozo, 'who defended the right of a judge to deliberately misstate facts', Judge Posner's opinion appears slyly to misstate a key fact in the very first paragraph.[69] The opinion notes that plaintiffs cross-appeal the dismissal of their Illinois Consumer Fraud and Deceptive Business Practices Act claim. But Judge Posner then writes, 'they do not seek any additional damages, and so, provided we sustain the jury's verdict, we need not address the cross-appeal'.[70] This assurance simplifies the analysis and creates a singular focus on punitive damages – a move that magnifies the opinion's clarity and power.

However, the nearly imperceptible slight-of-hand that plaintiffs did not seek additional damages is not an accurate representation. On the state consumer fraud act claim, and that claim alone, plaintiffs' complaint clearly asked for 'prejudgment interest, costs *and reasonable attorney's fees incurred herein*'.[71] At no point in the litigation did plaintiffs' counsel waive or withdraw this

[67] Posner (n 4) 47.
[68] ibid 55.
[69] ibid 43.
[70] *Mathias* (n 3) 674.
[71] Second Amended Complaint (n 19) [19] (emphasis supplied).

claim. In fact, plaintiffs' Seventh Circuit brief asked the court to 'enter judgment' on plaintiffs' cross-appeal, 'or in the alternative, remand the matter to the district court for new trial on that count'.[72] Although Judge Posner often asked attorneys at oral argument if they would waive certain arguments, the oral argument in *Mathias* contained no such request for waiver and no waiver was proffered.

Once it is factually established that plaintiffs did not abandon their state consumer fraud act claim, the implications are straightforward. To anyone who has practised law in Illinois (as I once did, beginning with a clerkship for another Seventh Circuit judge in which my office was located within Judge Posner's chambers), the statement seems an obvious mistake.

It is difficult to imagine that Judge Posner, a brilliant jurist who frequently decided diversity cases based on Illinois law, missed the potential availability of attorney fees under the Illinois statute. Before *Mathias* was decided in 2003, the Seventh Circuit frequently determined attorney fees for prevailing parties by 'lodestar' calculations. Lodestar calculations compute attorney fees by multiplying the attorney's hours reasonably spent on litigation by a reasonable hourly rate, after which upward or downward adjustments can be made.

A few years before *Mathias*, Judge Posner had discussed, at length, when a prevailing plaintiff could seek attorney fees under the Illinois Consumer Fraud and Deceptive Business Practices Act.[73] In *Door v Pro-Line*, Judge Posner wrote that when a plaintiff prevails in a consumer fraud act case, the court should ask 'whether the defendant had lacked a solid justification for the defense or had put the plaintiff to an unreasonable expense in suing'.[74] A case like *Mathias*, in which Judge Posner called several of defendant's arguments 'frivolous' and 'pertinacious', seemed ripe for analysis under the statute's attorney-fee standard.

Neither does it seem that Judge Posner entertained any doubt about whether defendant's conduct sank to the level of consumer fraud. Judge Posner definitively stated that the motel's 'failure to warn guests or to take effective measures to eliminate the bedbugs amounted to fraud'.[75] When common law fraud had been shown, consumer fraud under Illinois law was akin to a lesser included offence. Illinois' Consumer Fraud and Deceptive Business Practices Act claims were widely understood to employ a broader and more plaintiff-forgiving test.

One easy solution to *this* case then, in which Judge Posner worried aloud about whether plaintiffs could finance suits for small compensatory damage claims,[76] was simply to decide plaintiffs' cross-appeal of the directed verdict on the consumer fraud count first. Under that state claim, plaintiffs could have obtained attorney fees and costs for the unreasonably protracted litigation

[72] Combined Brief of Plaintiffs-Appellees, Cross-Appellants (n 18) 52.
[73] *Door Sys, Inc v Pro-Line Door Sys, Inc*, 126 F3d 1028, 1031 (7th Cir 1997).
[74] ibid.
[75] *Mathias* (n 3) 675.
[76] ibid 677.

defendants caused on plaintiffs' meritorious but small claims. Such a result might have been easily reached because both trial and appellate courts had already chastised the defence. If the Seventh Circuit had awarded plaintiffs their fees and costs, the compensation would have been significant. The cost of litigating a full federal trial and federal appeal, might well have yielded a monetary award similar in size to the punitive damages award.[77]

But as with Justice Cardozo's renowned opinion in *Palsgraf* – a case that could have been resolved on the basis that there was 'little evidence of negligence of any sort' – deciding *Mathias* on the obvious ground of a state attorney-fee statute would have preserved the plaintiffs' recovery but spoiled the opinion.[78] A narrow holding based on state statute would have had little import or staying power.[79]

And in any case, the statement in *Mathias* could be defended. Judge Posner wrote only that plaintiffs 'do not seek additional *damages*'. He did not say that plaintiffs 'do not seek additional *relief*'. The Seventh Circuit subsequently held that 'an award of attorneys' fees' 'differs from "damages"' and is often counted as a 'cost'.[80] But even if attorney fees are classified as costs rather than damages, the opinion's statement is still a misstatement. Judge Posner himself counted half-truths known to be misleading as fraud under various causes of action.[81] Here, the representation about plaintiffs' claims was used to dispose of the court's need to respond to plaintiffs' well-pleaded cross-appeal. Judge Posner implied that the court did not need to consider plaintiffs' appeal because the plaintiffs themselves, not the judges, had dropped it. In fact, it was the judges, and not the plaintiffs, who had.

But as we shall soon see, Judge Posner was not required to uphold the jury's verdict through the least impactful route. The Court of Appeals must uphold a jury verdict 'if a reasonable basis exists in the record to support the verdict'.[82] There were multiple bases on which to affirm. Upholding the punitive damages award was one.

[77] Lodestar calculations of attorney fees at the time began with a calculation of hours reasonably expended by the attorney multiplied by the attorney's reasonable hourly market rate. See, eg, *Kitchen v TTX Co*, 284 F3d 688, 692 (7th Cir 2002) (upholding US$1.1m attorney fee award in a case in which plaintiffs accepted offers of judgment totalling US$610,000; hourly rates of US$240 per hour and US$185 per hour were reasonable rates for lawyers in the case, given their experience levels).

[78] Posner (n 4) 38 (citing Judge Friendly). But there may have been negligence in *Palsgraf*. The intermediate court's ruling suggests that rather than closing the door of the train before it the conductors left it open and assisted the passenger's attempt to board a moving train: 222 App Div 166 (1927).

[79] ibid 106–07.

[80] *Carolina Cas Ins Co v Merge Healthcare Sols Inc*, 728 F3d 615, 617 (7th Cir 2013) (Easterbrook CJ).

[81] eg, in *Emery v Am Gen Fin, Inc*, 71 F3d 1343, 1347 (7th Cir 1995) Judge Posner discussed a case in which 'a laboratory had omitted from a report on the toxicity of a drug an opinion by a consultant that the drug had some toxic effects'. The court held that 'the jury was entitled to find that this omission was fraudulent, given the impression, conveyed by the report, of the utter harmlessness of the drug'.

[82] *Kapelanski v Johnson*, 390 F3d 525, 530 (7th Cir 2004) (Williams CJ).

B. Overlapping Mechanisms for Deterrence

Reflecting on *Mathias* in light of the potential availability of *both* punitive damages and attorney fees presents an important question that Judge Posner did not directly address. What should be the relationship between these two forms of relief? The question is but one part of a broader dialogue concerning overlapping forms of deterrence. When should punitive damages be granted in circumstances in which their availability coexists with other legal, regulatory and non-legal incentives and sanctions?[83]

If we view Judge Posner's decision to ignore the availability of attorney fees in *Mathias* not simply as a misstatement designed to enhance the persuasive power of the court's opinion, but as a conscious substantive choice, the opinion's lack of analysis of intersectional overlap may actually aid that analysis. In the case of overlapping remedies, Judge Posner elected to focus on the suitability and function of the damages award rather than its particular form. This pragmatic focus placed legal efforts to promote fair dealing at the centre of the deterrence analysis, in contrast with another noted US law and economics approach.

C. Fair Dealing and Deterrence

The substantive outcome Judge Posner embraced was the judicial project of 'bringing the law into closer conformity with lay institutions of fair dealing'.[84] He wrote, 'the more law conforms to prevailing moral opinions ... the easier it is for lay people to understand and comply with law'.[85] Embracing rules of commercial fair dealing also tread a careful line between 'oracular and nihilist judging'.[86] In *Mathias*, fair dealing would not permit taking money under false pretences.

Judge Posner wrote that intentional harms '[are] inflicted for purposes of obtaining some specific gain that could be obtained through a voluntary market transaction'.[87] In *Mathias*, a bargain-forcing mechanism was needed. 'Motel 6 could not have rented any rooms at the prices it charged had it informed guests that the risk of being bitten by bedbugs was appreciable'.[88] Accordingly, fair dealing required that defendants not earn money, or at least not earn as much money, for rooms that they could not have rented in

[83] See, eg, Maher, ch 9 of this volume (addressing the overlap of civil punitive damages and criminal law sanctions); Sharkey, Punitive Damages Transformed (n 7) (civil punitive damage overlap with regulatory fines).

[84] Posner (n 4) x, 92.

[85] RA Posner, 'Professionalisms' (1998) 40 *Arizona Law Review* 1, 14. Posner (n 4) 18.

[86] Posner (n 4) 18.

[87] Landes and Posner (n 43) 33.

[88] *Mathias* (n 3) 675.

voluntarily market transactions had they disclosed the truth. As Judge Posner had written in a prior case, 'the loss of business from telling the truth is a social gain, not a social loss'.[89] Fair dealing supported mulcting the defendants of earnings that they could not have obtained in honest market transactions. The award of punitive damages in *Mathias* served the purpose of 'limiting the defendant's ability to profit from its fraud by escaping detection and (private) prosecution'.[90]

D. The Law and Economics Critique

Judge Posner's argument – that punitive damages were needed for deterrence of wrongful conduct in the *Mathias* case – is in tension with some theories of the economic approach he employs in the decision. Before *Mathias*, distinguished law and economics professors Mitchell Polinsky and Steven Shavell had argued that market mechanisms might provide effective deterrence in the case of customers rather than strangers – obviating or minimising the need for punitive damages in the customer context.[91] The authors asserted that with respect to customers, defendants will already have market-based incentives to attend to risks of harm. For example, harms to customers might impair sellers' reputation, make customers unwilling to purchase goods and services from the defendant, or pay as much for them.[92] In an article about the *Mathias* opinion, Professor Shavell argues that Judge Posner's analysis should have been guided by the customer/stranger distinction. 'Preserving its reputation' would seem 'to have been a powerful motivation for Motel 6 to cure its bedbug problem'.[93]

Though an enticing argument, Judge Posner's decision not to vitiate the plaintiffs' punitive damages awards based on the plaintiffs' status as customers makes good sense. In terms of law and economics rationales, the defendants were very likely to escape liability for wrongfully caused harm (and indeed had with all other potential plaintiffs over a long period of time), not only because of the difficulty of advance detection, but also because of the significant effort and expense of bringing suit to pursue such small claims.[94] In addition, the defendants did not face adequate reputational costs because of the lack of meaningful

[89] *Wassell v Adams*, 865 F2d 849, 853 (7th Cir 1989).

[90] *Mathias* (n 3) 677.

[91] See Polinsky and Shavell (n 42).

[92] ibid.

[93] S Shavell, 'On the Proper Magnitude of Punitive Damages: Mathias v Accor Economy Lodging, Inc' (2007) 120 *Harvard Law Review* 1223 (suggesting that Motel 6's non-legal reputational interest in attracting and retaining customers makes the need for punitive damages to accomplish deterrence 'a much lower order' than in cases in which victims are not customers).

[94] See AM Polinsky and S Shavell, 'Punitive Damages' in B Bouckaert and G De Geest (eds), *Encyclopedia of Law and Economics*, vol 2 (Cheltenham, Elgar, 2000) 764–81.

consumer information channels at the time. Even now, companies may have other means of avoiding deserved reputational hits – for example, by suppressing critical speech, renaming the business entity, and splintering off sub-entities. Tellingly, the motel was wholly capable of giving the plaintiffs full information about the bed bug problem prior to their arrival and injury at the hotel. They didn't. This deliberate choice to conceal information from motel guests deprived plaintiffs of *ex ante* opportunities to bargain and consigned them to the inferior position of post-injury refund negotiations. In cases in which *ex ante* injury negotiations are possible, the threat of punitive damages can induce bargaining.[95] 'Misinformation can only hurt, and can never help, the process of voluntary exchange.'[96]

More broadly, it would be odd for courts to curb customers' damage awards on the theory that arm's-length sellers, as a blanket category, have buyers' best interests at heart. From a legal viewpoint, even in jurisdictions in which the ancient rule of rule caveat emptor no longer holds full force, sellers are not legally required to act as buyers' fiduciaries.[97] Nor does it seem desirable, from an empirical view, for courts to assume that sellers across industries, regions and time will adequately protect customer interests.

To say that defendants typically have more interest in consumer welfare than they do in the welfare of others is not to say that defendants won't disregard both customers' and strangers' interests in favour of their own. Indeed, the motel's bed bug issue seems to aptly illustrate this problem – the defendants posed broad public health risks to guests and strangers alike to avoid their own costs of remediation. As Judge Posner noted,[98]

> the defendant may well have profited from its misconduct because by concealing the infestation it was able to keep renting rooms. Refunds were frequent but may have cost less than the cost of closing the hotel for a thorough fumigation.

The motel's greater interest in its immediate costs than in its customers' welfare might seem to be a one-off situation were it not for the legions of reported consumer fraud claims and the hundreds of general and specific state statutes enacted to combat the problem of consumer fraud.[99] The recent opioid cases on their own cast doubt on the efficacy of producers' 'market-based incentive to be attentive to the risk of harm to their customers'.[100]

[95] ibid 771.

[96] RA Epstein, *Torts* (Gaithersburg, Aspen, 1999) 548.

[97] See, eg, *Onita Pacific Corp v Bronson Trustees*, 843 P 2d 890 (Or 1992) (Justice Peterson): 'two adversarial parties negotiating at arm's length to further their own economic interests' owe no duty of care to each other for purposes of negligent misrepresentation.

[98] *Mathias* (n 3) 677.

[99] E Bublick et al, *Dobbs on Economic and Dignitary Torts*, 2nd edn (Minneapolis, West, 2011) [563]–[568].

[100] Polinsky and Shavell, 'Punitive Damages' (n 94) 935.

E. Merging Moral and Economic Perspectives

Some US scholars might view it as ironic that Judge Posner, a central figure in the law and economics movement in the United States, eschewed the theory that contracting customers could be adequately protected by market mechanisms and regulatory penalties. Further, it might seem that *Mathias* reflects the sort of moralistic reaction that Judge Posner himself disdained.

However, *Mathias* is a context in which 'moral and economic perspectives merge' – a situation that Judge Posner thought central to effectuating pragmatic jurisprudence.[101] In *Mathias*, Judge Posner's pragmatic jurisprudence made law 'facilitative' rather than 'constitutive'.[102] The law was enlisted to serve 'communities self-chosen ends rather than as a norm imposed on those communities in the service of a higher end'.[103] On that account, Judge Posner's use of moral language for the specific purpose of bringing the law into sync with commercial morality is no conflict. As Judge Posner has written, 'Commercial morality is perhaps the same thing as efficiency'.[104]

Judge Posner's view of the compatibility of market incentives and tort liability is well illustrated by his discussion of two of Justice Cardozo's famous common law opinions. The case of *Glanzer v Shepard*, involved negligent and inaccurate weighing of beans by a public weigher, in a market transaction in which the weight facilitated pricing in a private sale.[105] *Ultramares Corp v Touche* concerned a negligent audit on which a lender had relied.[106] In reference to each case, Judge Posner acknowledged the important market incentives that affected defendants. With regard to *Glanzer*, he wrote: 'weighers who develop a reputation for negligence will lose business'.[107] With respect to *Ultramares*, he said: 'even without the threat of legal liability hanging over their heads accountants will have market incentives to maintain a reputation for care'.[108] While acknowledging these market forces, Judge Posner also thought plaintiff protections 'deficient' in both cases absent a legal remedy for negligence.[109] They were deficient because denying a claim would not be in accord with commercial morality and because the consequences of non-liability were an inferior approach to loss avoidance (because victims were inferior loss avoiders). In *Mathias* too, a remedy was warranted based on the 'pragmatic goal of making the law an effective, fully rational instrument of social welfare', in part by 'bringing law closer to the (informed) non-lawyer's sense of justice'.[110]

[101] Posner (n 4) 102.
[102] ibid 94.
[103] ibid.
[104] ibid 101.
[105] *Glanzer v Shepard*, 135 NE 275 (NY 1922).
[106] *Ultramares Corp v Touche*, 174 NE 441 (NY 1931).
[107] Posner (n 4) 101.
[108] ibid 112.
[109] ibid 101.
[110] ibid 114, 126–27.

F. Function rather than Form

If an informed sense of justice warranted a remedy for wrongful conduct in *Mathias*, there was still the question of what that claim and remedy should be. *Mathias* concerned wrongful conduct directed at multiple consumers who had no rational economic interest in filing individual suits. This problem was a particular concern for Judge Posner. As he memorably described when permitting class status in a different case, 'The *realistic* alternative to a class action is not 17 million individual suits, but zero individual suits, as only a lunatic or a fanatic sues for $30'.[111]

Remedies for cases involving financial gain from wrongful conduct undertaken at multiple plaintiffs' expense, might be pursued through various legal causes of action and forms of relief. *Mathias* allowed a punitive damages award based on intentional torts. As mentioned earlier, attorney fees under state statute presented another viable option in the case. If the US$1,000 per room award was designed to reflect small harms inflicted on multiple guests, a possibility Judge Posner referred to as 'likely not a coincidence', a class action lawsuit might have been pursued.[112] Furthermore, widespread fraudulent schemes using mail or wire can be redressed under state and federal civil RICO statutes, for which treble damages may be available.[113] An infestation of bugs that spreads via hotel guests and their belongings might count as a public nuisance, for which private or public damages or an injunction could be sustained. Claims for restitution, disgorgement of profits and payment of civil penalties might also present practicable remedies.[114] These numerous forms of civil redress are supplemented by additional forms of deterrence outside the common law system. Regulatory sanctions are but one example. Across this expansive range of possibility, the Seventh Circuit affirmed the jury's compensatory and punitive damages award for intentional torts.

Judge Posner was open to varied forms of recovery, but also investigated the potential downside of a particular format before choosing to deploy it. For example, one potential problem of deterring wrongful conduct through an award of substantial punitive damages to the *Mathias* plaintiffs was the potential for overlapping judgments that could have been awarded to multiple injured

[111] See, eg, *Carnegie v Household Intern, Inc*, 376 F3d 656, 661 (7th Cir 2004) (emphasis added).

[112] EJ Cabraser, 'The Class Action Counterreformation' (2005) 57 *Stanford Law Review* 1475, 1520: 'An alternative approach would have been to join all victims of the bedbug plague as class members, and award both compensatory and punitive damages to the entire class. The total amount of punitive damages would likely have been the same but would have constituted a much lower multiplier of the compensatory damages, and would have been apportioned equitably among the victims, rather than being awarded to Mr and Mrs Mathias alone as bounty hunters'.

[113] Bublick (n 99) 593–609.

[114] In intentional torts cases, plaintiffs can recover either their damages or the defendants' profits, whichever is greater. See, eg, *Williams Elecs Games, Inc v Garrity*, 366 F3d 569, 577 (7th Cir 2004) (Circuit Judge Posner): 'if all that the plaintiff is seeking is a sum of money equal to the defendant's profit, an order of restitution will do fine'.

guests. Interrogating defence counsel about whether suits had been filed by other injured guests was important to assure that punitive damages would not result in duplicative judgments and thus provide a poor mechanism for recovery.

Presented with a damages award that was proportionate to defendants' wrongdoing, for conduct that breached notions of fair dealing, when systemic reasons for concern about the form of the award had been negated, Judge Posner was content to uphold the jury verdict.

The affirmance and reasoning in *Mathias* suggest that as long as the cause of action and damages awarded were proportionate to the wrongfulness of defendant's actions, the particular cause of action pursued or type of damages sought was of secondary interest. Implicitly, then, *Mathias* seems to endorse a functional approach to overlapping remedies – when punitive damages and attorney fees are both potentially available, courts may be appropriately agnostic about which form of recovery to permit. Such a stance seems to stand in contrast to England's 'if but only if' test for punitive damages awards.[115]

G. A Good Enough Result

Agnosticism between punitive damages and attorney fees may have been particularly easy in *Mathias* because the punitive damages award may have been similar in amount to the remedy for attorney fees and costs. In other cases, the two approaches can yield glaring differences. Even in *Mathias*, *both* forms of damages could have been awarded. Moreover, whether an award is labelled as punitive damages or attorney fees could result in different financial distributions between plaintiffs and their attorneys, depending on fee agreements.

One nagging question about the *Mathias* misstatement then is whether it compromised fairness to the plaintiffs themselves. A case can be made that if the court had analysed *Mathias* with only that case in mind, it might have upheld the punitive damages award *and* returned the case to trial on the separate issue of statutory consumer fraud, for which attorney fees could have been awarded.

What would have happened if the Seventh Circuit had found plaintiffs' consumer fraud act claims viable, as seems likely from its fraud analysis, is unclear. The court should then have reversed the directed verdict for defendants on the consumer fraud act claim and returned the claim to the lower court for trial. But whether the consumer fraud act claim alone should have been retried to a jury, or the court should then have returned the plaintiffs' successful intentional tort claims to the jury as well, to avoid duplicative remedies, is unclear. Thus, even a positive result on plaintiffs cross-appeal might have jeopardised plaintiffs' substantial recovery. Equally unclear is whether the court would have deemed the damages award excessive if the same punitive damages had been

[115] See Goudkamp, ch 5 of this volume. See also J Goudkamp and E Katsampouka, 'Punitive Damages and the Place of Punishment in Private Law' (2021) 84 *MLR* 1257, 1262.

awarded along with attorney fees.[116] Moreover, holding not one but two full federal trials on an issue too small for all other potential plaintiffs to litigate seems an unreasonable expense for parties and the court.

Because the plaintiffs' sizeable jury award was affirmed, and a more favourable monetary award was not assured even if plaintiffs had prevailed on the consumer fraud cross-appeal, the appeal seems to have yielded a favourable outcome for plaintiffs. With respect to the defendants, a retrial would have added guaranteed legal expense, and perhaps an additional judgment to pay. Taking a pragmatic focus, the practical consequences of upholding the judgment arguably made sense for both parties. And yet, whether the misstatement counts as 'harmless error' in these circumstances is ultimately for the reader to judge.

VI. CONCLUSION

Looking back, *Mathias* conveys an important message about punitive damages standards. The opinion forcefully and eloquently articulates the failings of the US Supreme Court's approach in *State Farm*. On that ground alone, the *Mathias* opinion provides great value to students of punitive damages jurisprudence across the globe.

When 'willful and wanton conduct' warrants punitive damages, *Mathias* accepts the US Supreme Court's admonition that proportionality review is constitutionally required. Per *Mathias*, however, the proportionality test should measure punitive damages awards against the wrongfulness of defendants' conduct, need to deter it, and need to disgorge profits, *not* against the compensatory damages awarded in the case.

The opinion's unseen misstatement about the availability of other remedies, when viewed as a substantive choice, reveals another important aspect of Judge Posner's approach – flexibility in addressing which of multiple overlapping remedies can be used to deter misconduct. In reviewing the jury's punitive damages award, Judge Posner focused less on the format of the award than on the need for commercial fair dealing to facilitate efficiency.

Looking at the issues in the *Mathias* opinion, both those that it discussed and those that it did not, the case well illustrates not one but two American views on punitive damages – that unprincipled *limits* on punitive damages raise concerns, and that courts can employ a pragmatic method of review to ensure that claims and awards function to promote fair commercial dealings, in whatever format they are presented.

[116] If the right level of punitive damages brings defendants' total liability up to the level it would have paid in compensatory damages if all victims had appropriately recovered, the recovery of both punitive damages and attorney fees could have been appropriate: *cf* Polinsky and Shavell (n 94) 888–96.

15

Couch v Attorney-General (No 2) (2010)
The Susan Couch Litigation

STEPHEN TODD

I. INTRODUCTION

THE DECISION OF the Court of Appeal in *Taylor v Beere*[1] in 1982 was the first decision in New Zealand to give close consideration to the general principles upon which an exemplary award should be made. Yet what precisely *Taylor* decided and how it ought to be understood later came to be called into question, first in the *Bottrill* saga in the Court of Appeal[2] and in the Judicial Committee of the Privy Council,[3] and then, after the right of appeal from the New Zealand Court of Appeal to the Privy Council was abolished, in New Zealand's Supreme Court in the second of two decisions in the *Couch* litigation.[4] *Couch (No 2)* is a highly significant decision, both in laying down in definitive terms the legal requirements for the making of an exemplary award in New Zealand and in resolving certain associated and disputed issues. For these reasons, it can fairly be described as a further landmark in the developing law and, accordingly, the *Couch* litigation has been chosen as the subject of this chapter.

Couch (No 1), the first of these two Supreme Court decisions, examined the question whether, in the circumstances, it was reasonably arguable that the

[1] *Taylor v Beere* [1982] 1 NZLR 81 (CA).

[2] *Bottrill v A* [2001] 3 NZLR 622 (CA); J Manning, 'Exemplary Damages in Negligence: The Story of a Screening Programme' (2001) 9 *Torts Law Journal* 1.

[3] *A v Bottrill* [2003] UKPC 44, [2003] 1 AC 449 (PC); J Manning, 'Never Say Never: Exemplary Damages in Negligence' (2003) 119 *LQR* 24; R Tobin, 'Exemplary Damages in New Zealand: The End of the Story' (2003) 11 *Torts Law Journal* 20; A Todd, 'Outrageous Negligence' (2004) 12 *Tort Law Review* 8.

[4] *Couch v Attorney-General (on appeal from Hobson v Attorney-General)* [2008] NZSC 45, [2008] 3 NZLR 725 ('*Couch (No 1)*'); *Couch v Attorney-General (No 2) (on appeal from Hobson v Attorney-General)* [2010] NZSC 27, [2010] 3 NZLR 149 ('*Couch (No 2)*').

defendant owed a duty of care to Ms Couch, and we will look at this decision first in order to explain the basis for the defendant's potential liability. We will then consider the particular reason why exemplary damages were in issue. Claims for compensation for personal injury covered by the Accident Compensation Act 2001 (NZ) are barred, and as Ms Couch had suffered covered personal injury she made no claim for compensatory damages. Accordingly, the question posed was whether the accident compensation bar extended to claims for exemplary damages standing alone. Next, we come to the heart of our inquiry – the basis for making an award of damages on an exemplary basis. This will involve an examination of the background to *Couch (No 2)*, and in particular the decision of the Privy Council in *Bottrill*. That background will take us to an analysis and an evaluation of the opinions of the Justices in the majority and of the opinion of the Chief Justice in her dissent. Finally, the claim alleged the vicarious liability of an employer for the wrongdoing of an employee, which raised the questions whether there could be a vicarious liability to pay exemplary damages, and if there could, whether such liability could be imposed in actions against the Crown.

II. THE DUTY ISSUE

Ms Couch was very seriously injured by a violent criminal called William Bell, who attacked her while he was robbing the Panmure premises of the Returned Services Association (RSA) where she worked. Three fellow employees were murdered by Bell, who was later sentenced to 33 years' imprisonment. Bell was on parole at the time, following his release after serving two-thirds of a five-year sentence for the aggravated robbery of a petrol station. Bell had been placed at the RSA with the knowledge of the probation service for work experience, and he returned there to commit his crimes. No one at the RSA knew that he was on parole.

Any claim that Ms Couch might make for compensatory damages was barred by the accident compensation legislation,[5] but she sued the Attorney-General seeking exemplary damages for what she alleged was grossly deficient supervision of Bell by the Probation Service of the Department of Corrections.[6] Heath J in the High Court struck out an identical claim brought by the estate of one of the deceased employees,[7] and this claim, together with that filed by Ms Couch,[8] were both struck out in the Court of Appeal.[9] Ms Couch alone

[5] See section III below.

[6] The Attorney-General thus was alleged to be vicariously liable for the conduct of employees of the Probation Service, as to which see section V below.

[7] *Hobson v Attorney-General* [2005] 2 NZLR 220 (HC).

[8] The High Court had removed the issue arising in Ms Couch's case to the Court of Appeal for concurrent determination.

[9] *Hobson v Attorney-General* [2007] 1 NZLR 374 (CA).

appealed to the Supreme Court,[10] which held unanimously in *Couch (No 1)* that her claim was arguable and that it should be allowed to proceed to trial. However, there was a difference of opinion as to the legal principles to be applied in coming to that conclusion.

Taking the majority view first, Blanchard, Tipping and McGrath JJ (in a judgment delivered by Tipping J) recognised that whether a duty of care was owed would be determined on the basis of whether it was fair, just and reasonable to impose it. Proximity and policy were the two headings under which the courts had determined that ultimate question. More particularly, the law had traditionally been cautious about imposing duties of care in cases of omission, in cases where a public authority was performing a role for the benefit of the community at large, and in cases where the actions of a third party were the immediate cause of loss. All three were present in the case before them, but it was the third which was the most significant on the issue of proximity.[11]

In third-party cases, there needed to be control over the wrongdoer. The question was whether the defendant had the power and ability to exercise the necessary control. And as regards the relationship between plaintiff and the defendant, this should be special in the sense that there was sufficient proximity between the parties to render it fair, just and reasonable, subject to policy, to impose a duty. The decisions showed that the more specific and obvious the risk, the stronger the case for holding that a defendant with power of control had a duty to the plaintiff.[12] Accordingly, Ms Couch had to show that as an individual or a member of an identifiable class, she was or should have been known to be the subject of a distinct and special risk of suffering harm of the kind she sustained at the hands of Bell – distinct as being clearly apparent; and special, in the sense that her individual circumstances or her membership of the necessary class rendered her particularly vulnerable to the harm. If there was no such proximity, there was no need to go on to examine the policy issues in the case at hand.[13]

On the pleaded facts, their Honours were satisfied that there was no arguable case. There was nothing in Bell's background to point to fellow workers being at special risk. It was not enough that fellow employees were in more frequent physical proximity to Bell than the general public. Bell had a greater opportunity to harm them, but this did not amount to a special risk. However, there was a possibility of amending the pleadings to make the claim arguable.

[10] The estate of the deceased employee did not appeal, this seemingly on account of s 3(2)(a) of the Law Reform Act 1936 (NZ) which bars a claim for exemplary damages by an estate against a wrongdoer. A claim *against* an estate for such damages is possible, so, as matters stand, a living tortfeasor causing death goes unpunished while the tortfeasor's innocent dependants may be penalised.

[11] *Couch (No 1)* (n 4) [78]–[80].

[12] Citing, inter alia, *Home Office v Dorset Yacht* [1970] AC 1004 (HL); *Hill v Chief Constable of West Yorkshire* [1989] AC 53 (HL) 62.

[13] *Couch (No 1)* (n 4) [81]–[85], [108]–[13].

The defendants knew that Bell was classified as at high risk of reoffending. His earlier service station robbery was marked by an attempt at gratuitous and random violence. Bell was also known to be in constant need of money to feed his alcohol addiction. He was allowed to work at premises where significant cash was likely to be present and where he could familiarise himself with the security system. This might make the RSA a predictable target, so anyone present would be at greater risk of injury, and these persons would be particularly vulnerable because of Bell's tendency to random violence. So the claim should not be struck out.[14]

Elias CJ and Anderson J, taking a broader approach, did not think that the authorities compelled the view that duties of care could be owed only to those who were members of a limited class. It was in the nature of public functions that, if statutory responsibilities were discharged negligently, those foreseeably at risk would be a wide class, perhaps as wide as the general public if the responsibilities were imposed for public protection (as the supervisory duties imposed on the Probation Service by the Criminal Justice Act 1985 (NZ) were) and if the risk warranted it.[15] This view seems to contemplate a common law duty arising simply through the exercise or existence of statutory powers, but it has little support elsewhere and has been condemned in the House of Lords and the UK Supreme Court. If a situation supports a common law duty of care on ordinary principles, then there may be liability, but the statutory duty itself does not give rise to the common law duty. This cannot grow parasitically out of a statutory duty not intended to be owed to individuals.[16] By limiting the duty in the way favoured by the majority, the burden of liability is reasonably manageable and reasonably proportionate to the defendant's wrongdoing. The implications of the minority views are startling. They might be applied to the police, the prison service, and indeed to many other public persons or bodies charged with functions aimed at benefiting or protecting the public at large. It is doubtful whether such wide-ranging liability founded upon other people's wrongdoing is desirable as a matter of policy.

III. EXEMPLARY DAMAGES IN PERSONAL INJURY CASES

A. Ambit of the Bar in Personal Injury Claims

At this preliminary point, before turning to consider the award of exemplary damages at common law, we will consider a question which is unique to

[14] ibid [117], [121]–[24], [128]–[31].
[15] ibid [67]–[72].
[16] *Gorringe v Calderdale MBC* [2004] UKHL 15, [2004] 1 WLR 1057 [71]; *Robinson v Chief Constable of West Yorkshire Police* [2018] UKSC 4, [2018] AC 736 [32]–[36]; *Poole BC v GN* [2019] UKSC 25, [2020] AC 780 [26]–[34], [70]–[75].

New Zealand and which needs to be explained. Any person in New Zealand who suffers personal injury in a way that is covered by the Accident Compensation Act 2001 (NZ) can make a claim to the Accident Compensation Corporation for payment of accident compensation.[17] Where cover for personal injury exists, a bar on common law actions applies. By section 317(1) of the 2001 Act, no person may bring proceedings independently of the Act, in any court in New Zealand, for damages arising directly or indirectly out of personal injury covered by the Act or a former Act.[18] The bar cannot be avoided by failure to make a claim, or a purported denial or surrender of rights under the Act or its predecessors, or a lack of entitlement to any particular benefit.[19] But where there is no cover, the right to sue remains.[20]

Ms Couch had suffered very serious personal injuries at the hands of the criminal, and was covered by the 2001 Act on the basis that she had suffered personal injury caused by an accident.[21] She had in fact made a claim and received minimal payments by way of compensation from the Accident Compensation Corporation.[22] Accordingly, she made no common law claim for compensatory damages in respect of her injuries, but sought only an award of exemplary damages. The Supreme Court in *Couch (No 2)* needed to examine whether, in these circumstances, she was able as a matter of law to make her claim.

Let us consider first certain existing authority relevant to this inquiry. Exemplary damages are intended not to compensate a plaintiff but to punish and deter a wrongdoer,[23] and in *Donselaar v Donselaar*[24] the Court of Appeal held that actions claiming damages of this kind could still be maintained. Allowing them would not undermine the policy of the legislation, for the statutory bar was aimed only at actions for compensation. Richardson J explained

[17] There are 12 specific categories of cover, which fall broadly into four categories – personal injury caused by an accident, by treatment, by employment-related disease or infection, and by way of mental or nervous shock in certain defined circumstances: Accident Compensation Act 2011 (NZ), s 20(2) (ACA 2001). The scheme covers everyone in New Zealand, including temporary visitors, but non-residents are not eligible for certain benefits provided by the scheme, in particular for earnings-related compensation. Cover extends to New Zealand residents who suffer injury while abroad for which there would be cover had the injury occurred within New Zealand: ACA 2001, s 22.

[18] The former Acts are the Accident Compensation Act 1972 (NZ), the Accident Compensation Act 1982 (NZ), the Accident Rehabilitation and Compensation Insurance Act 1992 (NZ) and the Accident Insurance Act 1998 (NZ).

[19] ACA 2001, s 317(7).

[20] *Queenstown Lakes District Council v Palmer* [1999] 1 NZLR 549 (CA) 555; and see *McGougan v DePuy International Ltd* [2018] NZCA 91, [2018] 2 NZLR 916 [25]–[40].

[21] ACA 2001, s 20(2)(a). 'Accident' means, inter alia, a specific event involving the application of a force or resistance external to the human body: s 25(1)(a)(i).

[22] The compensation which is recoverable by claimants covered by the accident compensation scheme extends to rehabilitation expenses, weekly compensation calculated by reference to past earnings up to a statutory maximum, lump sums for loss of amenity subject to a maximum, and dependency claims. The compensation sometimes may be inadequate, as it was in Ms Couch's circumstances. For further discussion see n 69 below.

[23] See generally *Taylor v Beere* (n 1). For further discussion, see n 41 below.

[24] *Donselaar v Donselaar* [1982] 1 NZLR 97 (CA).

that proceedings for exemplary damages were not 'proceedings for damages arising directly or indirectly out of' a person's injury or death, because exemplary damages did not arise out of the plaintiff's injury and were not directed to the plaintiff's loss. They were awarded against the defendant because of the outrageous manner in which he had conducted himself in the course of committing the tort. In a strict sense, such damages did not 'arise' at all, and in a looser sense, they could be said to arise out of the acts of the defendant.

In *Couch (No 2)*, the defendant contended that *Donselaar* was wrongly decided, on the grounds that the 'damages' referred to in section 317(1) included exemplary damages, and that without actionable compensatory damages the tort of negligence was incomplete, so there was no tort for which exemplary damages might be awarded. However, Tipping J was not convinced by either argument. His Honour accepted that *Donselaar* involved a narrow reading of the word 'damages' and may have been a debatable conclusion at the time, but thought that far too much water had gone under the bridge since then to contemplate taking a different view. Further, since *Donselaar* was decided, Parliament had had several opportunities to include exemplary damages expressly within the bar and had not done so. That had to represent an acceptance of the Court of Appeal's conclusion that the policy of the accident compensation legislation was not undermined by permitting exemplary damages to be claimed in circumstances defined by the courts. This proposition was underlined by the introduction of section 319(1) of the 2001 Act, providing that exemplary damages could be awarded despite the court's inability to award compensatory damages.[25] Tipping J recognised that the purpose of section 319 was to eliminate the double jeopardy bar created by *Daniels v Thompson*,[26] where there was a claim for exemplary damages in respect of conduct punishable by the criminal law, but pointed out that the general reach of subsection (1) was not cut down by the following subsections aimed at achieving that purpose. The effect was that Parliament had expressly recognised and reinforced the *Donselaar* principle whereby exemplary damages might be awarded in cases of personal injury covered by the Act. Accordingly, the ordinary need for there to be damage to complete the tort of negligence should for this purpose be seen as satisfied by there being a case for the award of exemplary damages.[27]

McGrath J similarly was satisfied that *Donselaar* was correctly decided. The preference for the view that the general language expressing the bar did not extend its application beyond proceedings for compensation reflected the statutory purpose. Futhermore, there was a continuing social need for what Cooke J had described as 'constitutional remedies for high-handed and illegal conduct,

[25] See section IIIB below.
[26] *Daniels v Thompson* [1998] 3 NZLR 22 (CA). For further discussion, see n 30 below.
[27] *Couch (No 2)* (n 4) [84]–[90].

public or private'.[28] In *Donselaar* the Court stated the law of exemplary damages in a way that enabled the statutory bar to operate consistently with its purpose while at the same time meeting the continuing need for the special remedy.[29]

B. Overlap with the Criminal Law

In approving *Donselaar*, the court in *Couch (No 2)* did not need to evaluate *Daniels v Thompson*[30] or its reversal in section 319. However, we will do both, for section 319 has a significant impact on the circumstances in which exemplary damages may be awarded. *Daniels* was a conjoined appeal with three further cases – *J v Bell*, *W v W* and *H v P* – where a majority of the Court of Appeal decided that either conviction or acquittal in a criminal proceeding prevented any subsequent recovery of exemplary damages in a civil action based on the same facts, and that where a prosecution was likely any civil action should be stayed until the prosecution either was concluded or it became clear it would not be brought. Allowing the civil action after a conviction was seen to carry the risk that the defendant might be punished twice for the same offence, and if the criminal proceedings resulted in an acquittal, the defendant would still be at risk of double jeopardy. *W v W* and *J v Bell* were taken on further appeal to the Privy Council,[31] which dismissed the appeals on the basis that the question was one of public policy and that their Lordships should not interfere with the views of the national court.[32] So the decision of the Court of Appeal stood. Its import for any action taking advantage of the *Donselaar* principle was clear. In cases where the personal injury was caused by criminal conduct, a civil action against the offender was likely to be barred, not by the statute but by the application of common law principle.

Daniels was criticised on the ground that it was unjust to victims of criminal misconduct, particularly in sexual abuse cases. While such persons could still make a claim for exemplary damages notwithstanding that they were covered for accident compensation, they would very likely be barred because the defendant had been or was likely to be prosecuted for the criminal offending. Parliament accepted this criticism and inserted a new section 396 into the Accident Insurance Act 1998 (NZ), which provision is now section 319 of the 2001 Act. It provides, in essence, that where the defendant's conduct has caused personal injury covered by the Act, a claim for exemplary damages can still be brought irrespective of

[28] *Donselaar* (n 24) 106.
[29] *Couch (No 2)* (n 4) [199]–[203]. Elias CJ [7], Blanchard J [71] and Wilson J [250] all agreed.
[30] *Daniels* (n 26). See further Maher, ch 9 of this volume.
[31] *W v W* [1999] 2 NZLR 1 (PC); J Manning, 'Exemplary Damages and Criminal Punishment in the Privy Council' (1999) 7 *Torts Law Journal* 129.
[32] Applying *Australian Consolidated Press Ltd v Uren* [1969] 1 AC 590 (PC) and *Invercargill City Council v Hamlin* [1996] 1 NZLR 513 (PC).

whether the defendant has been charged, not charged, convicted, acquitted or discharged of an offence involving the conduct concerned in the civil claim, but in deciding whether to make an award or the amount of the damages the court may have regard to any criminal penalty imposed in respect of that offence. So section 319 reverses *Daniels* in the case of claims which are covered for accident compensation. It also is of retrospective effect.[33]

Section 319 raises a number of difficulties. In particular, we should ask what a provision of this nature is doing in the 2001 Act. The issue is as to the relationship between the criminal and the civil law, which has nothing to do with accident compensation. Bizarrely, section 319 only applies in the case of personal injury covered by the Act, whereas *Daniels* seemingly applies in other cases. The ordinary rule is that the existence of cover for personal injury under the Act means that the victim cannot bring a private action for damages, yet in a claim for exemplary damages, that rule is reversed and the victim *can* sue. An offender who is convicted for breaking into a house and assaulting and injuring the occupier can still be held liable to pay exemplary damages, whereas an offender who is convicted for breaking into a house, threatening the occupier with a gun and burning down the house cannot. It is certainly hard to see section 319 as achieving a considered and well-thought-out conclusion of policy. If Parliament decided, after a serious analysis of the issues, that the view taken in *Daniels* ought to be rejected, one might have expected that it would have been rejected across the board.

Much of the criticism of the *Daniels* case in reality was about the bar on actions for *compensatory* damages and the low level of benefits obtainable under the Accident Compensation Act, not about issues of double jeopardy. In responding to this, section 319 does precisely what the courts have said should not be done. It encourages personal injury victims to bring actions for compensation in the guise of actions for exemplary damages. Indeed, in *Couch (No 2)* Blanchard J and Tipping J, reflecting views found in a number of earlier decisions, specifically warned against using exemplary damages to remedy perceived shortcomings in the statutory scheme.[34] Maybe the victims of criminal offending, and sex abuse victims in particular, were and possibly still are treated badly by the statutory scheme, but this has nothing to do with the award of exemplary damages. If there was or still is a problem in this respect, then the solution surely lies in changing the rules of entitlement or raising the level of benefits available under the statutory scheme.[35]

[33] *W v W* (2000) 14 PRNZ 157 (CA).

[34] *Couch (No 2)* (n 4) [67] and [135]. For earlier such warnings, see *Donselaar* (n 24) 107; *McLaren Transport Ltd v Somerville* [1996] 3 NZLR 424 (HC) 433; *Daniels* (n 26) 29; *Bottrill v A* (n 2) 637; *S v Attorney-General* [2003] 3 NZLR 450 (CA) [89]; *Wilding v Attorney-General* [2003] NZCA 205, [2003] 3 NZLR 787 [15].

[35] Lump sums to compensate for lost amenity due to physical or mental injury, not available at the time of the *Daniels* decision, were reintroduced in the ACA 2001.

IV. BASIS FOR AN EXEMPLARY AWARD

Having determined that Ms Couch's claim against the Attorney-General was arguable, the Court adjourned the hearing of the appeal to enable the parties to make submissions on various matters concerning the award of exemplary damages. The hearing was later resumed, arguments were heard and the Court delivered its judgment in *Couch (No 2)*. However, before turning to this decision, we need to consider the earlier cases providing the legal background to the issue which the Court was required to decide.

A. Background

At the outset, there is the fundamental question whether the civil courts in private law actions ought to make awards of exemplary damages at all. Finding the answer, of course, raises significant issues of policy. There are certain core, and related, objections that ultimately are founded upon the proposition that the role of civil proceedings should be to adjudicate upon disputes between private parties, not to punish offenders. They are that a form of civil punishment is inflicted without the evidential and procedural safeguards of the criminal law; the basis upon which this punishment is imposed lacks an objective foundation and is undesirably uncertain; and the damages can be described as a windfall in the plaintiff's hands, there being no particular connection between those damages and the plaintiff who is bringing the action. On the other hand, the award of exemplary damages may be justified by various competing arguments: civil punishment is different from criminal punishment and it is coherent to pursue the aims of punishment through the civil law; a criminal offence is a wrong against both the victim and against society at large, with punishment being sought by or on behalf of the state, whereas a civil wrong is a wrong against the individual victim, who seeks an exemplary award to punish an egregious wrongdoer on his or her own account; and the objectives of civil proceedings have various objectives apart from compensation, including punishment and deterrence, and exemplary damages can help to achieve these objectives.

In New Zealand, as in other common law countries, the latter arguments have prevailed. From the early days when the courts were developing the common law in the colony, they accepted that exemplary damages might, in principle, be awarded. A significant decision to this effect was that of Chapman J in *McComb v Low*.[36] His Honour observed that cases of personal torts might have an element of public scandal or public outrage which the law permitted

[36] *McComb v Low* (1873) 1 NZ Jur 49.

to be met by exemplary or punitory or vindictive damages. He recognised that there might be some anomaly in the rule in that it clearly looked beyond the parties to the action, and allowed that part of the damages to find its way along with the compensatory portion into the pocket of the plaintiff, but it was nevertheless well recognised law. This decision having laid the ground, the jurisdiction to make an exemplary award thereafter was affirmed on a number of occasions.[37] However, while these decisions all reiterated the punitive nature of the remedy, the approach to be adopted in deciding whether, in the circumstances of any particular case, a court should in fact make an award was not spelled out.

The context for an inquiry into this question came with the decision of the House of Lords in *Rookes v Barnard*,[38] restricting the award of exemplary damages, at least in the UK, to three categories of claim: where there was oppressive, arbitrary or unconstitutional action by servants of the Government, where the defendant's conduct had been calculated to make a profit, and where an award was authorised by statute. The authority of *Rookes* in English law was maintained in the House of Lords in *Cassell & Co Ltd v Broome*,[39] although in the meantime the Privy Council in *Australian Consolidated Press Ltd v Uren*[40] had held that *Rookes* did not oblige the Australian courts to change their settled approach to defamation damages. Then, in *Taylor v Beere*,[41] the question whether to follow *Rookes* came before the New Zealand Court of Appeal.

The defendant had published a perfectly innocent photograph of the plaintiff and her granddaughter in a book containing pornographic images and text. The plaintiff sued in defamation, alleging that it would appear that she had consented to the publication in that context, and sought both compensatory and exemplary damages. As regards the latter, the Court declined to limit the damages to the *Rookes* categories. Richardson J thought that setting arbitrary limitations of the kinds formulated by Lord Devlin would be wrong in principle and unsatisfactory in practice. It was the quality of the conduct which should count. The availability of the remedy should not hinge on the occupation of the defendant or any fine analysis of his or her motivation. So what should be the test? In Richardson J's words, by awarding exemplary damages the jury or judge registered condemnation of 'outrageous' or 'heinous' conduct by the defendant and marked the 'contumelious disregard' by the defendant of the plaintiff's rights.[42]

[37] eg, *Stapleton v Smith* (1888) 6 NZLR 663 (SC); *Norton v Stringer* (1909) 29 NZLR 249 (CA) 256; *Butler v Black* [1920] NZLR 17 (SC); *Matheson v Schneideman* [1930] NZLR 151 (SC) 160; *C W Wah Jang and Co Ltd v West* [1933] NZLR 235 (SC).

[38] *Rookes v Barnard* [1964] AC 1129 (HL). See Field, ch 4 of this volume.

[39] *Cassell & Co Ltd v Broome* [1972] AC 1027 (HL); Goudkamp, ch 5 of this volume.

[40] *Australian Consolidated Press Ltd v Uren* [1969] 1 AC 590 (PC).

[41] *Taylor* (n 1).

[42] ibid 90–91.

A test looking for outrageous misconduct arguably still needed further examination, in order so far as possible to lay down its parameters: and one question in particular was whether it could encompass tortious conduct that was merely careless, as opposed to conduct motivated by malice or an intention to harm. This issue lay at the heart of the difference in the view taken by the Court of Appeal and by the Privy Council in the *Bottrill* litigation.[43]

The defendant, a pathologist, misread and misreported the results of cervical smears taken from the plaintiff, causing serious delay before the plaintiff was diagnosed as suffering from cervical cancer. The plaintiff's treatment would have been far less severe and her prognosis better had the smears been correctly reported. The plaintiff successfully claimed accident compensation, on the basis that she had suffered medical misadventure, and then sought to recover exemplary damages from the defendant. Her claim initially failed, on the ground that sufficiently serious incompetence had not been shown, but, after the trial, an analysis and review of the defendant's reading of smears showed that his false negative reporting rate could not have been less than 50 per cent. The plaintiff applied for a new trial, alleging that there had been a miscarriage of justice because material evidence had been discovered since the trial which could not reasonably have been foreseen or known before the trial. The trial judge allowed the application, and the defendant appealed to the Court of Appeal. The majority of the court (Richardson P, Gault and Blanchard JJ, Tipping J concurring, Thomas J dissenting) held that the remedy of exemplary damages should be confined to cases where the defendant was subjectively aware of the risk to which his or her conduct exposed the plaintiff and acted deliberately or recklessly in taking that risk. Applying this principle, the new evidence about the defendant's error rate did not address or bear upon his awareness of his deficiencies. There was nothing from which it could plausibly be argued that he had a conscious disregard for his patient's welfare. Accordingly, the appeal was allowed and the plaintiff's claim dismissed.

The decision was thereafter taken to the Privy Council where, in a majority decision (Lord Nicholls, Lord Hope and Lord Rodger, Lord Hutton and Lord Millett dissenting), the plaintiff's appeal was allowed. Lord Nicholls thought that the court's discretionary jurisdiction could be expected to extend to all cases of tortious wrongdoing where the defendant's conduct satisfied the criterion of outrageousness. Any departure from this principle needed to be justified. In the nature of things cases satisfying the test would usually involve intentional wrongdoing with, additionally, an element of flagrancy or cynicism or oppression or the like. Or, at the very least, the defendant proceeded with reckless indifference such that the conduct evoked a sense of outrage. But, exceptionally, negligence might qualify. There might be rare cases where the defendant departed so far and so flagrantly from ordinary or professional precepts of

[43] *Bottrill v A* (n 2) and *A v Bottrill* (n 3).

prudence or standards of care that the conduct satisfied this test even though the defendant was not consciously reckless.[44]

The decision in *Bottrill* was one of the last cases to go on appeal from New Zealand to the Judicial Committee of the Privy Council. In 2003 that right of appeal was abandoned, and the New Zealand Supreme Court was created as a new court of final appeal, with the purpose, inter alia, to enable important legal matters to be resolved by New Zealand judges with an understanding of New Zealand conditions, history and traditions.[45] The question at issue in *Bottrill* then arose once again, this time before the new Supreme Court, in the resumed hearing in *Couch*.

B. The Decision in *Couch (No 2)*

If we put aside for a moment the arguments of principle and policy bearing upon the choice before the Court, the question whether or when the Supreme Court should depart from earlier decisions of the Privy Council needed to be taken into account. The members of the Court held unanimously that they were not bound by such decisions, but they would be slow to depart from Privy Council authority and would only do so for good reason, not merely because the Court would have decided differently. However, there was a difference of opinion as to how those principles should apply in *Couch*. In the view of the majority (Blanchard, Tipping, McGrath and Wilson JJ), it was proper in the circumstances for the Supreme Court to decline to follow the decision of the Privy Council in *Bottrill*. It was out of step with other decisions, the Privy Council itself was divided on the issue, it had overturned a decision of the Court of Appeal consistent with previous authority, and there had been no general reliance on the Privy Council's decision. The majority accordingly held that the decision of the Privy Council should be overruled and that exemplary damages should be awarded in accordance with the test laid down in *Bottrill* in the Court of Appeal. Elias CJ dissented on this issue, and would have accepted and applied the Privy Council decision. We will first consider her Honour's dissent, and then examine the reasoning of the majority.

Elias CJ noted that the arguments as to the test to be applied had been canvassed at length in *Bottrill*, and expressed her agreement with the reasoning of Thomas J in the Court of Appeal and Lord Nicholls in the Privy Council. She considered that their Lordships' decision was consistent with the general application of the exemplary principle recognised in New Zealand in *Taylor v Beere*, and was not shown to be inconsistent with Australian and Canadian

[44] *A v Bottrill* (n 3) [24]–[27].

[45] Supreme Court Act 2003 (NZ), s 3(1). The 2003 Act was repealed by the Senior Courts Act 2016 (NZ), s 182(3), and the Supreme Court as constituted is continued by Part 4 of that Act.

law. Rather, her Honour was satisfied that restriction of the principle was inconsistent with its continued vitality. She also strongly criticised the decision reached by the other members of the court. In her view, it reintroduced a 'cause of action' condition for exemplary damages despite earlier rejection in New Zealand, Australia and Canada of similar attempts in the United Kingdom at such restrictions as unprincipled and arbitrary. Furthermore, it required construction of a 'species of negligence' in which intention or conscious recklessness was an element, in order to exclude a remedy of otherwise general application once liability in tort was established. The restriction was said to be justified on the basis that exemplary damages were 'anomalous', yet such assessment rested in part on the erroneous but persistent view that making an example of the defendant was not a proper function of the law of torts. That view had been accurately characterised as question-begging, was unhistorical, and was rejected in New Zealand by all members of the Court of Appeal in *Taylor v Beere*. In that case, by rejecting confinement of exemplary damages to categories, the Court of Appeal affirmed that they were awarded under a principle of general application. Accordingly, her Honour would decline to impose a precondition on making an award restricting the general exemplary jurisdiction marking society's condemnation of outrageous behaviour by the defendant which was insufficiently addressed by other remedy. It would, she thought, sap the vitality of the exemplary principle in meeting the needs of modern New Zealand society.[46]

Blanchard J, by contrast, was satisfied that the Privy Council's decision was out of step with the way in which the law had developed both in New Zealand and in comparable jurisdictions. It appeared to be the only decision of a senior court, directly addressed to the issue, which expressly countenanced exemplary damages for an inadvertent act of negligence. Nor was *Bottrill* the better approach and suited to New Zealand conditions. The purpose of exemplary damages was to punish the defendant for outrageous conduct, to deter the defendant from any repetition and to deter others from similar behaviour. There was a real question whether a civil court should involve itself in punishing people, especially those who had genuinely not been conscious of doing any wrong. However, there was a proper moral role for exemplary damages as a deterrent to outrageous harmful behaviour, and in New Zealand such damages might provide a useful counterbalance to the absence of the sanction of compensatory awards for tortious infliction of personal injury. But if the defendant was not conscious of creating a hazard for others, the deterrent role of exemplary damages was much diminished.[47]

Tipping J, delivering a leading judgment, saw the purpose of exemplary damages as punishment for the commission of a civil wrong in a particularly

[46] *Couch (No 2)* (n 4) [3]–[6]. Her Honour's reasoning is developed at [12]–[44].
[47] ibid [52]–[68].

reprehensible way. Dicta in some recent cases suggested that the purpose of exemplary damages was substantially wider than to punish, and included vindication, education, appeasement of the victim, therapeutic effect and expressing general societal disapproval. However, these features were best regarded as consequences of a punitive award rather than as purposes of the award in their own right. It conduced to clarity and simplicity in the field of exemplary damages to concentrate on their punitive purpose and to let such other purposes as might be implicit do their work silently. This concentration reinforced the point that exemplary damages were not a surrogate way of awarding compensation, even though plaintiffs might view them as having an additional compensatory effect. Indeed, a plaintiff-focused approach was inconsistent with the whole concept of exemplary damages. The focus should be on the defendant, the question being what the defendant should pay, not what the plaintiff should receive. The plaintiff received vindication and appeasement only indirectly through the punishment of the defendant.[48]

What, then, should be the defendant's state of mind? Tipping J recognised that there was a distinction between objective and subjective recklessness. A person might be described as reckless who did not appreciate an obvious risk of causing harm and proceeded to cause the harm without appreciation of the risk. This was objective recklessness, and was the practical equivalent of a high level of negligence. On the other hand, a person might appreciate the risk of causing harm and proceed nonetheless deliberately to run that risk and end up causing the harm. That was subjective recklessness, which was generally seen as more culpable and deserving of punishment. In *Bottrill* the Court of Appeal adopted as the test for exemplary damages the standard of subjective recklessness of an outrageous kind, whereas the Privy Council adopted the lesser standard of objective recklessness of an outrageous kind. The question having arisen again, his Honour was satisfied that the Court should depart from their Lordships' decision and return to the approach taken by the Court of Appeal.[49]

Tipping J noted first that punishment was generally meted out only to those who had deliberately caused harm or deliberately run the risk of doing so. While certain statutory offences did not require a conventionally guilty mind, the anomalous nature of exemplary damages was such that they should be restricted to circumstances which were analogous to the conventional offences which required conscious appreciation of wrongdoing. This should be a necessary precondition to the infliction of punishment, or the distinction between crime and tort would become even more blurred. An allied point was that punishment should not be inflicted unless the person concerned was able to determine in advance with some certainty when his or her conduct was liable to

[48] ibid [92]–[96], [115].
[49] ibid [100]–[103].

punishment. Assessing whether the defendant consciously appreciated the risk inherent in the relevant conduct involved an objective and conceptually certain inquiry into the defendant's state of mind, and a test for exemplary damages which did not require this element would depend entirely on an after-the-event assessment of whether the relevant conduct should be viewed as outrageous. That was a subjective and inherently uncertain criterion on which minds might well differ.[50]

Turning to *Bottrill*, Tipping J noted that the assumption underlying their Lordships' decision – that the criterion of outrageousness was a principle of general application, departures from which had to be justified – begged the question of what the general principle should be. The general rule was said to spring from the rationale of exemplary damages, but the rationale for including high-level objective recklessness was not discussed. Exemplary damages were seen as appropriate where something more was required than compensatory damages to demonstrate that the conduct in question was 'altogether unacceptable to society', yet that allowed punishment on the basis of an inherently imprecise and undesirably uncertain test. Their Lordships had also observed that it was wrong to conclude that negligent conduct, in the absence of intentional wrongdoing or conscious recklessness, would never give rise to 'a justifiable feeling of outrage'. But that again begged the question whether a justified feeling of outrage should be the sole criterion.[51]

In Tipping J's view, the concept of outrageousness was unsatisfactory as the sole criterion. It was far better to have a test which focused objectively on the state of mind of the defendant as a precursor to any subjective assessment by the judge or jury of whether the defendant's conduct was outrageous. This focus on the state of the defendant's mind also helped to underline that the consequences of the defendant's conduct were not the primary question. The more important question was the level of risk to the plaintiff's safety which the defendant consciously ran and the level of harm which the defendant appreciated would eventuate if the risk he or she was consciously running became a reality. This was a more principled basis for deciding whether exemplary damages should be awarded than the uncertain and amorphous concept of the defendant's conduct being outrageous. Furthermore, this conclusion did not introduce a 'cause of action' condition for exemplary damages, involving subcategories of the tort of negligence in a way which created different 'species' of negligence. It was possible to describe the qualifying kind of negligence as a species or subcategory of the tort; but that description was no more than a facet of distinguishing between the kind of inadvertence that should qualify for exemplary damages and that which should not. The objection was the same as saying that outrageous negligence was a species of negligence or

[50] ibid [111]–[112].
[51] ibid [118]–[121].

a subcategory of the tort. That objection could just as well be levelled at the conclusion favoured by the majority of the Privy Council.[52]

McGrath J and Wilson J both delivered judgments preferring the approach taken by Blanchard J and Tipping J. For McGrath J, two points were of fundamental importance. The focus of an exemplary award was on punishment, so it was the culpability of the defendant that mattered. The test adopted by the Court of Appeal in *Bottrill* provided for the mental element that was appropriate for actions to be punished. That was not the case with a test based on perceptions of outrageousness. The other consideration of particular importance was the accident compensation scheme, for the likely impact of continuing the approach of the Privy Council was that it would be destructive of the exceptional nature of the exemplary remedy. A stand-alone outrageousness test posed a very uncertain standard, which was likely to mean that like cases would not be decided alike and to lead to many claims and multiple appeals.[53]

C. Evaluation

It is apparent from this summary of the arguments that the decision of the majority in *Couch* puts the focus squarely on the defendant's state of mind. The plaintiff should be required to show intentional or reckless misconduct. Elias CJ would leave open the possibility of outrageous negligence. Which is the better view? Authorities elsewhere provide no certain answer, but in any event we should direct our attention to the purpose or purposes of exemplary damages and consider the light they may throw on the different approaches. And these very arguably support the majority reasoning.

It has been recognised by the courts on many occasions that the primary purpose of exemplary damages is to punish a wrongdoer. Some would see punishment, in the sense of retribution, as just one of a number of purposes, these including deterrence, condemnation of wrongdoing, appeasement of victims and vindication of victims' rights. Yet there is a strong argument that such additional perceived purposes are simply purposes of tort law generally, and that they lack any particular or sufficiently clear connection with the award of exemplary damages.[54] However, if we accept at least that exemplary damages have a proper role in deterring wrongdoing, on the basis that punishment is inextricably bound up with deterrence, the test for their award should be calculated to promote that purpose. And deterrence is more likely to be achieved in relation to conduct that is intentional or reckless. As was emphasised in the

[52] ibid [150]–[153].
[53] ibid [238]–[243].
[54] A Beever, 'The Structure of Aggravated and Exemplary Damages' (2003) 23 *OJLS* 87. As we have seen, this point is considered in detail in Tipping J's judgment.

majority judgments in *Couch*, any deterrent role must be much diminished in a case where the defendant's wrong was unthinking or inadvertent.

Turning to punishment, the emphasis must be on the character of the defendant's conduct, not on the injury or damage suffered by the plaintiff. Yet outrage is very much a matter of individual impression. As pointed out by Lord Hutton and Lord Millett in their dissent in *Bottrill*, and by the majority in *Couch*, it is a subjective concept upon which minds can easily differ. Certainly, its focus is on the plaintiff's or a bystander's or the court's reaction – it is not clear which – to the defendant's conduct. By contrast, a test requiring advertence or recklessness as to consequences is based firmly on the quality of the relevant conduct rather than the reaction to it by others. It also sets a more precise and certain standard. Intention or subjective recklessness provides a test with conceptually certain criteria, whereas outrage does not. The latter at least creates a greater risk of like cases not being decided alike. Further, the test for exemplary damages should be co-extensive with its rationale of punishment and, accordingly, should require a guilty mind.[55] Intention or subjective recklessness achieves a degree of consistency with criminal law principles, which, in New Zealand, broadly require a state of mind based on subjective culpability, and in this way it provides for the mental element that is the appropriate test for actions to be punished. The question as to the test for exemplary damages has a good deal more in common with these ordinary principles than with the lesser standards that sometimes suffice in the case of regulatory offences.

We might also ask why the test of outrageousness should be regarded as having been set in stone. In *Rookes v Barnard*[56] Lord Devlin considered that none of the various adjectives that had been used in the cases could be regarded as definitive, and in *Cassell & Co Ltd v Broome*[57] Lord Diplock recognised that cases in which the manner in which the tort had been committed had attracted a whole gamut of dyslogistic judicial epithets. Therefore there is no magic in having outrageousness as the single touchstone; it is merely one of a large number of overlapping adjectives or phrases which have been used to justify an award. Lord Reid included conduct that was said to be wilful, wanton, high-handed, oppressive, malicious and outrageous. Others that can be found in the cases include vindictive, insolent, arrogant, cynical, reckless indifference, and contumelious disregard of the plaintiff's rights. Their underlying theme very arguably suggests that the defendant's misbehaviour needs at least to be advertent or reckless, and the decision in *Couch*, by spelling this out, has assisted in achieving greater clarity and certainty in the law. There is likely to be uncertainty in some or many cases whatever the test, but the problem is exacerbated if outrageousness is the sole criterion.

[55] C Harlow, 'A Punitive Role for Tort Law?' in L Pearson et al (eds), *Administrative Law in a Changing State*, (Oxford, Hart Publishing, 2008).

[56] *Rookes* (n 38) 1229.

[57] *Broome* (n 39) 1129.

In summary, and drawing upon Tipping J's words in *Couch*, a focus upon the defendant's state of mind is a more principled basis for deciding whether exemplary damages should be awarded than the uncertain and amorphous concept of the defendant's conduct being outrageous.

V. VICARIOUS LIABILITY FOR EXEMPLARY DAMAGES

There is one further matter deserving of attention. Ms Couch's claim was brought against the Attorney-General rather than the individual in the Probation Service who was alleged to be responsible for the failure to supervise the criminal, which raises the issue whether there can be a vicarious liability to pay exemplary damages. The Supreme Court did not decide this question, because the Attorney-General had agreed to indemnify the responsible officer and the case proceeded on the assumption that any vicarious liability of the probation service was admitted. However, Elias CJ and Tipping J ventured comment about it.

Looking first at decisions overseas, they are split on this issue. In the UK, in *Kuddus v Chief Constable of Leicestershire Constabulary*,[58] Lord Hutton thought that the power to make an exemplary award in respect of conduct amounting to misfeasance in public office served to uphold and vindicate the rule of law and to deter wrongdoing by public officers.[59] But Lord Scott saw an award of exemplary damages where the defendant was not a wrongdoer and the award would be met out of public funds as not adding anything at all to the deterrent effect of a finding in favour of an injured person. A defendant should not be liable to pay exemplary damages unless he had committed punishable behaviour, a principle that left no room for an award where liability was vicarious only.[60] The Court of Appeal in England later took the former view,[61] and this also may be the approach taken in Australia.[62] On the other hand, the Supreme Court of Canada has held that punitive damages could not be awarded in the absence of reprehensible conduct specifically referable to the employer.[63]

[58] *Kuddus v Chief Constable of Leicestershire Constabulary* [2001] UKHL 29, [2002] 2 AC 122; Katsampouka, ch 10 of this volume.

[59] *Kuddus* (n 58) [78]–[79].

[60] ibid [108], [131]. Lord McKay also saw difficulty with a vicarious award, saying at [47] that while the defendant's means might be important in considering an award of exemplary damages against the defendant personally, where the case was one of vicarious liability he found it somewhat difficult to accept that the relevant means were those of the defendant rather than those of the wrongdoer.

[61] *Rowlands v Chief Constable of the Merseyside Police* [2006] EWCA Civ 1773, [2007] 1 WLR 1065.

[62] *New South Wales v Ibbett* [2006] HCA 57, (2006) 229 CLR 638, although the decision in this case turned on the provisions of a New South Wales statute.

[63] *Blackwater v Plint* 2005 SCC 58, [2005] 3 SCR 3 [91]; and see *McCabe v Roman Catholic Episcopal Corp* [2015] ONCA 213.

In New Zealand, the decision of the Court of Appeal in *S v Attorney-General*[64] took the approach favoured by Lord Scott. Blanchard J said that it would be quite unfair to inflict a punishment upon someone who had been found not to have been complicit in the wrongdoing. The damages would not then be a reflection of the culpability of the defendant, and exemplary damages were not intended and should not be used to provide an additional monetary remedy. Furthermore, in the case of workplace injury, it was debatable whether an award against an employer whose agent or employee had behaved disgracefully would provide an additional incentive to take further and effective precautions going beyond those required by an ordinary duty of care. However, the balance might possibly be different in a case in which an official of the state had deliberately, recklessly, or in a grossly negligent manner, directly inflicted personal injury on the plaintiff, and whether the Crown might be held vicariously liable in such a case should be left open. On the facts, it was determined that the Department of Social Welfare was vicariously liable to the plaintiff to pay compensatory damages for his foster parents' sexual assaults and batteries, but was not liable to pay exemplary damages.

Coming back now to *Couch (No 2)*, Elias CJ remarked that to the extent that the Probation Service might be liable for the negligence of the probation officer on a vicarious basis, it might be an open question whether the outrageous conduct which could justify an award of exemplary damages was only that of the probation officer or might also extend to the conduct of the entity or persons vicariously responsible for her actions. The answer depended on legal policy, reflecting the public interests served by liability for exemplary damages and vicarious liability. Some cases and commentators had suggested that an employer vicariously liable for the tort of an employee, who had taken all reasonable steps to prevent harm should be liable only for compensatory damages. Others recognised a public interest in permitting such claims to promote higher standards. However, it would be wrong for the Court to express any view on this difficult point. Whether some fault on the part of the person vicariously responsible was required for an award of exemplary damages raised significant questions of policy which it would be inappropriate to enlarge upon in the absence of argument.[65]

Tipping J, by contrast, expressed an opinion on the matter. He thought that when one person acted on behalf of another, the wrong was seen for the purposes of compensation as having been committed both by that person and by the other. But the policy behind awarding compensatory damages against a person on the basis of vicarious liability did not mean that exemplary damages should be similarly awarded. There was no policy basis for punishing someone for the conduct of another unless the first person's conduct itself also qualified

[64] *S v Attorney-General* [2003] 3 NZLR 450 (CA) [88]–[94].
[65] *Couch (No 2)* (n 4) [40].

for punishment. People should not be vicariously liable for punishment on account of the conduct of someone else just because that conduct rendered them liable to compensate the plaintiff.[66]

The view rejecting vicarious liability is the better one.[67] The core objection is simple – the injustice involved in punishing innocent parties. In Lord Scott's words, 'silently and without any proper or principled justification for it, a system of vicarious punishment of public employers for the misfeasances of their employees has crept into our civil law'.[68] This suggests that it is very doubtful whether, as mooted in *S*, there is room for an exception for officials of the state either.

On this view, in the absence of the Attorney-General's agreement to accept vicarious responsibility, the claim by Ms Couch might have failed. However, putting that argument aside, there was a difficulty facing Ms Couch in relation to the special position of the Crown. The Court accepted that the Crown's liability, if any, had to be vicarious, by reason of section 6(1) of the Crown Proceedings Act 1950 (NZ) (which is identical in material respects with section 2 of the Crown Proceedings Act 1947 (UK)). Section 6(1) recognised Crown liability, but subject to the proviso that it was not liable unless its servant or agent was liable independently of the Act. The Solicitor-General argued that the claim should be struck out, because section 86 of the State Sector Act 1988 (NZ) protected a chief executive or employee from acts done in good faith in intended pursuance of their functions or powers, which removed the requisite liability of the servant or agent, and hence the Crown was not liable by virtue of the section 6(1) proviso. However, a majority (Elias CJ, Blanchard J and Tipping J) held that the purpose of section 86 was an internal one, namely that a department could not recover from its chief executive or employee provided that they had acted in good faith, notwithstanding that it was their conduct that had rendered the department liable. It did not remove the capacity of the chief executive or employee to be personally liable to the plaintiff.

VI. CONCLUSION

The decisions reached in *Couch (No 1)* and *Couch (No 2)* both identified the legal obstacles in the way of Ms Couch eventually succeeding in her action,

[66] ibid [158].

[67] The whole question is discussed in detail in S Todd, 'Vicarious Liability, Personal Liability and Exemplary Damages' in S Degeling et al (eds), *Torts in Commercial Law* (Thomson Reuters, Sydney, 2011) 409–48. For recent discussion, see P Morgan, 'Vicarious Punishment: Vicarious Liability for Exemplary Damages' in E Bant et al (eds), *Punishment and Private Law*, (Oxford, Hart Publishing, 2021).

[68] *Kuddus* (n 58) [136].

which was left to be determined. The duty issue was taken to the Supreme Court in an application for the action to be struck out on the ground that no duty of care was owed, and the decision on the damages issue determined only what the test for the award of exemplary damages should be. Accordingly, at the conclusion of the litigation, Ms Couch still needed to pursue her claim at the trial of the action, and establish both that a duty of care was in fact owed in the circumstances of the case and that the 'conscious wrongdoing' test for exemplary damages was satisfied. The former of these probably would be the more easily proven. The Court spelled out the basis for recognising a limited duty owed by the Probation Service to Ms Couch, founded upon the foreseeable risk to her as a member of a limited group of people, which very arguably would satisfy well-established criteria for the imposition of a duty to control tortious misconduct by third parties. However, as regards the latter, while the probation officer may have been objectively reckless or, in Tipping J's words, guilty of a high level of negligence, subjective recklessness as to the consequences of failing to control the criminal would very likely be hard to establish. The test certainly could have harsh consequences for Ms Couch, but it appropriately recognised the exceptional nature of a remedy which is aimed at punishing an offender, not compensating a victim. A better way of treating a victim such as Ms Couch would be to modify the accident compensation legislation, by expanding some of the criteria governing the entitlement to benefits and raising the level of payments made to persons who are covered by the scheme but who lack any or a substantial work record.[69]

Accordingly, at the conclusion of the litigation Ms Couch still faced a difficult and lengthy trial as well as the possibility thereafter of further appeals. However, the Attorney General entered into negotiations with Ms Couch's counsel, following which the defendant agreed to pay NZ$300,000 to Ms Couch in settlement of the action. This was a generous settlement, because there was a substantial risk that the claim ultimately would have failed and, even if it succeeded, it was very likely that the agreed sum was a good deal more than a court would have awarded. It appears to be, by a substantial margin, considerably higher than any sum awarded by way of exemplary damages by a court in New Zealand. The courts have often emphasised that the quantum of exemplary awards should not include any element of compensation for harm suffered by the plaintiff and that awards should be kept to moderate levels.[70] In this case, however, it appears that the Attorney-General chose to ignore these principles.

[69] By reason of her work history Ms Couch qualified only for minimal weekly compensation, potentially the most valuable benefit provided under the scheme. Various changes in the way weekly compensation is calculated which benefit applicants have been made since *Couch (No 2)* was decided.

[70] See *McDermott v Wallace* [2005] 3 NZLR 661 (CA) for detailed discussion of the considerations a court should take into account.

In view of the permanent and life-changing injuries suffered by Ms Couch, the failures of the Probation Service, the inadequacy of accident compensation payments in her particular case, and the extended and, from her point of view, inconclusive litigation that was involved in pursuing her claim, some generosity in bringing the matter to an end certainly was merited.

16

Schlenzka & Langhorne v Fountaine Pajot (2010)

The Recognition and Enforcement of Foreign Punitive Damages Awards in France

SOLÈNE ROWAN

I. INTRODUCTION

'WHEREAS AN ORDER to pay punitive damages is not, in itself, contrary to public policy, it will be otherwise when the amount awarded is disproportionate to the loss sustained and the breach of the contractual obligation'. So said the *Cour de cassation* in the landmark *Fountaine Pajot* ruling of 1 December 2010, the first occasion on which France's highest court considered whether a foreign judgment that contains an award of punitive damages can be recognised and enforced in France.[1] It held that recognition and enforcement are possible but only where the damages award is proportionate.

At the time, the decision was regarded as remarkable.[2] Punitive damages were (and continue to be) unavailable as a private law remedy in France. In both contract and tort, punishment is not, at least formally, an objective of damages,

[1] Civ (1) 1 December 2010, no 09-13.303, noted in *D* 2011.423; *JCP Ed G* 2011.I.139; *Revue critique de droit international privé* 2011.93; *Gazette Palais* 24 March 2011.83.13.

[2] V Wester-Ouisse and T Thiede, 'Punitive Damages in France: A New Deal?' (2012) 3 *Journal of European Tort Law* 115; BW Janke and F-X Licari, 'Enforcing Punitive Damage Awards in France after Fountaine Pajot' (2012) 60 *American Journal of Comparative Law* 775; F-X Licari, 'Exécution des jugements et actes' *D* 2011.423; D Sindres, 'Le contrôle par le juge de l'exequatur des condamnations étrangères prononcées par un juge étranger' *Revue critique de droit international privé* 2021.533 [1]; C Vanleenhove, *Punitive Damages in Private International Law, Lessons for the European Union* (Cambridge, Intersentia, 2016) 131.

which are awarded to compensate loss. The victim of a breach can expect to be returned, insofar as possible, to the position that he or she would have been in, if the breach had not been committed. This is assessed exclusively by reference to his loss. The seriousness of the breach and the extent of any profit accruing to the party in breach are irrelevant.[3]

This chapter analyses the decision. It begins with a summary of the underlying facts and the litigation that culminated in the foreign punitive award. This is followed by discussion of the principle established by the *Cour de cassation* and its implications. To conclude, the chapter surveys various developments since the decision. It will be shown that this readiness to recognise proportionate foreign punitive awards is part of a growing openness in France over the last 20 years both to punitive awards and to the use of a principle of proportionality in private law contexts. Several reform projects relating to the laws of contract and tort have recommended that punitive sanctions should be available where the existing array of civil remedies is too weak to deter reprehensible conduct.[4] Whilst these recommendations have not yet obtained legislative approval, there appears to be a clear desire amongst reformers for civil liability to go beyond mere compensation.

II. THE BACKGROUND TO THE 2010 *COUR DE CASSATION* RULING

A. The Facts of the *Fountaine Pajot* Case

The claimants were an American couple living in California. In July 1999, they purchased a catamaran to sail around the world from the French maritime construction company Fountaine Pajot. The purchase price was US$826,009. This covered both the vessel and delivery from France to the United States. It was a term of the agreement that the courts of California would have jurisdiction in respect of all disputes.

In December 1999, the catamaran, which was docked in the harbour of La Rochelle in France, was seriously damaged. A powerful storm broke the vessel from her mooring and caused her to collide with other boats. The purchasers were not made aware of these events before the vessel was delivered to them in the US in February 2000. Nor were they told that Fountaine Pajot had undertaken significant repair work on the vessel. However, they soon discovered that she was affected by important structural defects, which they claimed was due to the inadequate repairs and meant that she could not be used safely. After settlement negotiations failed, they sued Fountaine Pajot in California.

[3] Civ (2) 8 May 1964, *Semaine Juridique* 1965.II.14140, noted by P Esmein.

[4] S Rowan, *The New French Law of Contract* (Oxford, OUP, 2022) 243–48; S Rowan, 'Reflections on the Introduction of Punitive Damages for Breach of Contract' (2010) 30 *OJLS* 495; S Carval, *La responsabilité civile dans sa fonction de peine privée* (Paris, LGDJ, 1995).

B. The Judgment of the Superior Court of California

The Superior Court of California gave judgment in favour of the purchasers in 2003.[5] It found that serious damage had been caused to the vessel's hull during the storm; that prior to delivery, Fountaine Pajot had carried out hasty and defective repairs; that when the purchasers discovered the defects following delivery, the sellers refused to repair them in breach of warranty; and finally that the directors of Fountaine Pajot concealed these facts by making false declarations to the purchasers and to the court under oath.

The Californian court ordered Fountaine Pajot to pay damages to the purchasers in excess of US$3,250,000. This comprised US$1,391,650.12 in compensatory damages; US$402,084.33 for attorney's fees; and US$1,460,000 in punitive damages. The court justified the punitive award on the ground that the manufacturer had committed fraud. Its aim was to punish it for having concealed the damage to the vessel, and her subsequent repairs, from the purchasers. It also sought to deter it from engaging in similar future conduct.

The punitive award was calculated by reference to the US$7.3 million net worth of Fountaine Pajot. A sum representing 20 per cent of that amount was found to be appropriate. The court held that:[6]

> [T]he only way to ensure the defendants take responsibility, with the aim that they will be deterred from acting in this way again in the future, is to order them to pay significant financial penalties … Therefore, the question arises as to what is reasonable in view of the defendants' egregious conduct? It must not be an amount which is exceptionally high or which would result in the defendants' total financial ruin, but an amount which is exemplary and serves to deter the defendants from engaging in such behaviour in the future.

The purchasers commenced litigation in the French court in 2005 to have the Californian judgment recognised and enforced in France. This was the beginning of a process that lasted for over 10 years and was ultimately unsuccessful.

C. The Conditions for the Recognition and Enforcement of the Decision of the Superior Court of California

By deference to foreign courts, French courts do not review the merits of the underlying case when determining issues of recognition and enforcement.[7] Rather, and in the absence of a specific international convention between France

[5] *Schlenzka v Pajot*, TR 26 February 2003, no 837722-1 (California Superior Court).

[6] Translation of the original transcript of the Californian decision that is reproduced in CA Poitiers 26 February 2009, no 07/02404.

[7] Civ 7 January 1964, *arrêt Munzer*, noted by H Battifol in *Revue critique de droit international privé* 1964.344; P Mayer, V Heuzé and B Remy, *Droit international privé*, 12th edn (Paris, LGDJ, 2019) [377]–[379].

and the United States regulating the recognition of foreign judgments, three conditions must be satisfied for a decision to be recognised in France.[8] The first is that the foreign court must have jurisdiction to hear the dispute *(compétence du juge étranger)*,[9] which is established by proving a sufficient connection and 'points of contact' between the dispute and the country of the foreign court *(rattachement du litige au juge saisi)*.

The second is that the foreign decision must not be contrary to the French '*ordre public international*' ('international public policy').[10] *Ordre public international* comprises a core set of procedural and substantive principles that embody the fundamental cultural, political and social values of French society.[11] It has been defined by the *Cour de cassation* as 'the universal principles of justice which are considered in France as having absolute international value'.[12]

Foreign judgments can only be recognised and enforced where they are compatible with the principles of *ordre public international*. It is rare for recognition to be refused because of a perceived incompatibility. This only occurs in exceptional cases, for example where the judgment contravenes judicial impartiality or the right of a party to be represented.[13] Another example is one well-known case in which a foreign judgment allowed the unilateral repudiation of a wife by her husband.[14] It is not sufficient that a different solution would have been reached by a French court. There is an acceptance that French courts 'should be more tolerant of certain results in international cases, which involve a diversity of foreign legal cultures, than in domestic disputes'.[15]

The final condition is the absence of fraud in the choice of foreign law or jurisdiction (*fraude à la loi* or *fraude au jugement*).[16] There is a fraud in the choice of law (*fraude à la loi*) where the claimant obtains a foreign ruling with the intention of avoiding the application of the law that would have been applied by the competent court if it had heard the dispute. A fraud in the choice of jurisdiction (*fraude au jugement*) occurs where the claimant artificially creates 'points of contact', and therefore a connection, with a foreign court under the first condition of recognition, to avoid the competent court having jurisdiction over the dispute. An oft-cited example is where a party fraudulently changes nationality or domicile so that a court does not have competence to hear a case.[17]

[8] Civ 7 January 1964, *arrêt Munzer*, noted by H Battifol in *Revue critique de droit international privé* 1964.344; Civ 20 February 2007, *arrêt Cornelissen* noted by B Ancel and H Muir Watt in *Revue critique de droit international privé* 2007.420; Mayer, Heuzé and Remy (n 7) [377]–[379].

[9] Civ 9 May 1900, *arrêt De Wrède*, S 1901.1.185; Mayer, Heuzé and Remy (n 7) [380]–[392].

[10] Mayer, Heuzé and Remy (n 7) [393]–[404].

[11] Janke and Licari (n 2) 792.

[12] Civ 25 May 1948, *Rev crit* 1949. 89, noted by H Batiffol, *D* 1948. 35.

[13] Civ (1) 19 September 2007, no 06-17.096; Mayer, Heuzé and Remy (n 7) [393]–[404].

[14] Civ (1) 4 November 2009, no 08-20.574.

[15] Janke and Licari (n 2) 792.

[16] Civ 7 January 1964, *arrêt Munzer*, noted by H Battifol in *Revue critique de droit international privé* 1964.344; Civ 20 February 2007, *arrêt Cornelissen* noted by B Ancel and H Muir Watt in *Revue critique de droit international privé* 2007.420; Mayer, Heuzé and Remy (n 7) [405]–[413].

[17] Mayer, Heuzé and Remy (n 7) [405]–[413].

III. THE DECISION OF THE POITIERS COURT OF APPEAL

Whether the Californian judgment, and in particular the punitive award, could be recognised and enforced against Fountaine Pajot was considered on appeal by the Poitiers Court of Appeal in 2009.[18] It held that the first and third conditions for recognition of the Californian judgment were satisfied.[19] California was sufficiently connected to the litigation, therefore the Superior Court of California had jurisdiction to hear the dispute. As 'contact points' between California and the dispute, the Court of Appeal relied, amongst other things, on the facts that the purchase agreement expressly conferred jurisdiction on the courts of California, the purchasers were domiciled in California and were American citizens, and that the place of delivery of the catamaran was in the United States. On the question of fraud, it found 'no evidence to deduce that the choice of jurisdiction in California or the law of this state resulted from fraud'.

However, the second condition – compliance with *ordre public international* – was not satisfied. The punitive award contravened *ordre public international* in three ways. First, the award, which was 'very largely in excess of the purchase price of the catamaran and the amount of compensatory damages already awarded to repair the loss suffered by the purchasers' was 'manifestly disproportionate'. This offended the principle of proportionality of sanctions guaranteed by Article 8 of the Declaration of Human Rights of Man and of the Citizen. Article 8 states that 'the law shall provide for such punishments only as are strictly and obviously necessary, and no one shall suffer punishment except it be legally inflicted in virtue of a law passed and promulgated before the commission of the offence'.[20]

Second, the punitive award was contrary to the principle of full compensation (*principe de la réparation intégrale du préjudice*). It exceeded 'the loss suffered and the gain of which the claimants were deprived'. In the words of the Court of Appeal, full compensation is the 'essence of civil liability' and the aim is 'to restore as exactly as possible the balance destroyed by the wrong and to put the victim back in the situation in which they would have been had the wrongful act not occurred'. Damages awards should be commensurate with the loss suffered (*tout le préjudice mais rien que le préjudice*) and should 'not be determined by the extent of the breach nor the financial situation of the wrongdoer'.[21]

[18] The claimants' request for the recognition and enforcement of the Californian judgment was refused on an earlier occasion in 2005 on the ground (unrelated to the Californian award of punitive damages) that the French courts had exclusive jurisdiction over the dispute (CA Poitiers 28 June 2005 (not published)). Their request for recognition and enforcement was re-examined by the Poitiers Court of Appeal after the *Cour de cassation* relaxed the conditions under which foreign decisions can be recognised and enforced in France (Civ (1) 22 May 2007, no 05-20.473, Bull I no 196). It was at this point that the relevance of the Californian punitive damages award was considered. For reasons of space constraints, the focus of this paper is on the relevance of the punitive award on the enforcement request of the claimants. A summary of the earlier litigation can be found in Janke and Licari (n 2).

[19] CA Poitiers, 26 February 2009, no 07/02404.

[20] Translation of Janke and Licari (n 2) 794.

[21] CA Poitiers 26 February 2009, no 07/02404.

Full compensation in contract law is enshrined in the Civil Code at old Article 1149, now new Article 1231-2.[22] This provides that the victim of a breach of contract is entitled to damages in respect of 'the loss that they have incurred or the gain of which they have been deprived'. The Court of Appeal did not cite Article 1149. It cited Article 74 of the United Nations Convention on Contracts for the International Sale of Goods 1980 (the CISG or Vienna Convention) as the textual basis for the principle of full compensation. However, this appears to have been an error since the Convention does not apply to private sales and to sales of ships and vessels and was inapplicable on the facts of the case.[23] This was because the purchasers had bought the catamaran as consumers, for their private use.

The third ground on which the punitive award was found to contravene *ordre public international* was unjust enrichment (*enrichissement sans cause*). It was held that the award gave a windfall to the purchasers, which would unjustly enrich them. This led the Court of Appeal to refuse to recognise and enforce the Californian judgment in its entirety, including the compensatory element.

IV. THE DECISION OF THE *COUR DE CASSATION*

The purchasers appealed on several grounds, amongst which were that full compensation is a rule of domestic French contract law and not of *ordre public international*; that by applying the full compensation principle, the Court of Appeal effectively reviewed the decision on its merits, which is not permissible when determining whether a foreign judgment should be recognised and enforced; and that the amount of punitive damages was not disproportionate given, first, that the purchasers had paid a high price but were unable to use the vessel over a period of 10 years, and, second, the fraudulent behaviour of Fountaine Pajot, which concealed the damage, putting the lives of the purchasers and their children at risk.

A. Proportionate Foreign Punitive Awards are Capable of Recognition and Enforcement in France

The *Cour de cassation* dismissed their appeal and held that the Californian punitive award contravened *ordre public international* for want of proportionality.

[22] Rowan, *The New French Law of Contract* (n 4) 223–38. In tort law, the principle is found at Art 1240 of the Civil Code which provides that 'any human action whatsoever which causes harm to another creates an obligation in the person by whose fault it occurred to make reparation for it'.

[23] See Art 2 of the CISG: 'this Convention does not apply to sales: (a) of goods bought for personal, family or household use, unless the seller, at any time before or at the conclusion of the contract, neither knew nor ought to have known that the goods were bought for any such use … (e) of ships, vessels, hovercraft or aircraft.'

In affirming the decision of the Poitiers Court of Appeal, it laid down a new general principle that a foreign award of punitive damages is capable of recognition and enforcement in principle. Only where the punitive award is disproportionate in amount to the loss suffered and the breach of contract will it be contrary to *ordre public international* and incapable of recognition and unenforceable. In the words of the court, 'whilst an order for punitive damages is not, per se, contrary to public policy, it will be otherwise when the amount awarded is disproportionate to the loss sustained by the injured party and the breach of the contractual obligation'.

This was significant. It was the first time that the *Cour de cassation* had addressed head-on the question of whether a foreign judgment providing for punitive damages could be recognised and enforced in France. The only prior decision on the point was of a court of first instance, which had refused to recognise a punitive award made from a foreign court on the grounds that it offended the principle of full compensation and was penal in nature and therefore not capable of recognition and enforcement in French civil courts.[24] Previously the *Cour de cassation* had only ruled on the recognition and enforceability of punitive sanctions that have analogues in domestic French law. It had for example recognised foreign decisions upholding penalty clauses and imposing punitive monetary sanctions for non-compliance with court orders (for which the analogue in France is the *astreinte*), which are both available in French law.[25] The *Cour de cassation* went further in *Fountaine Pajot* by approving the recognition and enforcement of proportionate foreign punitive damages as a matter of principle, despite this form of relief not being part of the French arsenal of private law remedies.

The *Fountaine Pajot* decision is an *arrêt de principe*, that is, a decision that establishes a persuasive precedent. *Arrêts de principe* are exceptional in France, where decided cases are not formally a binding source of law. At least in theory, the role of the courts is merely to apply and give effect to the law. It is impermissible for a court to rely upon decided cases. The basis for a ruling must always be in statute. In practice, however, the judiciary plays an important role in shaping the law, interpreting and adapting statutory provisions. This is done partly through *arrêts de principe*.[26]

B. The Principle of Full Compensation does not Belong to *Ordre Public International*

In addition to laying down a general principle, *Fountaine Pajot* is significant in several other respects. First, it establishes that full compensation is not part

[24] Janke and Licari (n 2) 778.

[25] Rowan, *The New French Law of Contract* (n 4) 206–07 and 239–42.

[26] ibid 24–26; H Beale et al, *Cases, Materials and Text on Contract Law, Ius Commune Casebooks for the Common Law of Europe*, 3rd edn (Oxford, Hart Publishing, 2019) 80.

of *ordre public international* despite being a seminal rule in domestic law.[27] As Fages explained:[28]

[T]his forcefully confirms that the principle of full compensation, however rooted it may be in domestic law (*droit interne*), is not part of the *short list* of fundamental principles and values … which the mechanisms of private international law are intended to guarantee.

This illustrates that the rules of *ordre public international* do not necessarily coincide with, and can be narrower in scope than, those considered to be fundamental in French domestic law.[29] The Court of Appeal therefore 'went too far by applying a principle of domestic concern, which may otherwise violate *ordre public interne*, and calling it a matter of *ordre public international*.'[30]

That full compensation is not part of the fundamental values of the French legal order should not cause surprise. The principle is subject to exceptions in French law. Contracting parties can also derogate from it by agreement. They can for example agree exclusion or limitation clauses that reduce the quantum of damages payable upon breach. Similarly, since penalty clauses are valid in France, they can agree to increase the sum payable beyond compensation in order to deter breach and coerce performance.[31]

C. Ascertaining whether a Foreign Punitive Damages Award is Proportionate

The *Fountaine Pajot* decision is also significant for the use by the *Cour de cassation* of a proportionality test as a limiting mechanism. A punitive award, whilst capable of recognition and enforcement in principle, ceases to be so when disproportionate in comparison with the loss suffered by the injured party and the breach of contract. This serves to protect defendants with assets in France from excessive and potentially abusive foreign penal awards. The aim is to avoid extreme outcomes that subjugate the interests of the contract-breaker to those of the injured party. A balancing exercise is conducted between their competing interests.

Whilst proportionality had long been relied on as a limiting mechanism in areas such as administrative law, it was less common in the context of French private law, albeit not unknown. It was (and still is) relevant for example in the related context of penalty clauses.[32] Old Article 1152, para 2 of the Civil Code (that applied in 2010), which has since become Article 1231-5,[33] gives French

[27] F-X Licari, 'La compatibilité de principe de punitive damages avec l'ordre public international: une décision en trompe-l'œil de la Cour de cassation?' *D* 2011.423, 452; Vanleenhove (n 2) 123.

[28] B Fages, *Chroniques*, *RTD Civ* 2011.124.

[29] Vanleenhove (n 2) 123; Sindres (n 2) 538.

[30] Janke and Licari (n 2) 793.

[31] Art 1231-5 of the Civil Code; Rowan, *The New French Law of Contract* (n 4) 239–42.

[32] Fages (n 28) 125.

[33] On the recent reforms of French contract law, see Rowan, *The New French Law of Contract* (n 4).

courts the power to moderate an agreed penalty that is 'manifestly excessive'.[34] It provides that 'the court may, even on its own initiative, reduce or increase the agreed penalty if it is manifestly excessive or derisory'. In deciding whether the penalty clause is manifestly excessive, the court will consider whether there is disproportion between the loss suffered and the stipulated sum.[35] It will be manifestly excessive where the disproportion is extreme or there is an obvious abuse of the coercive function of penalty clauses.[36]

The degree of disproportion that will render a foreign punitive award incapable of recognition and unenforceable is unclear from the *Fountaine Pajot* decision. No detailed guidance was provided by the *Cour de cassation*. It merely adopted the factual finding of the Court of Appeal that the award of the Californian court 'greatly exceed[ed]' compensation and was 'manifestly disproportionate' in amount to the loss sustained by the injured party. The words 'greatly' and 'manifestly' suggest that courts can only refuse recognition and enforcement in extreme cases. It must be unequivocally excessive. That the sum is a little high is unlikely to suffice. The norm would appear to be the recognition and enforcement of punitive foreign awards.

This view has not been universal, however. There have been divergent opinions amongst commentators on the finding of disproportion in *Fountaine Pajot*. For Gaudemet-Tallon, for example, the US$1,460,000 punitive damages award was clearly excessive and disproportionate, since 'ultimately the damage sustained by the purchasers was only their inability to use the catamaran for pleasant leisure'.[37] Others questioned whether the punitive part of the award really did greatly exceed the compensatory part.[38] The difference between the two was only US$70,000, which was relatively minor in comparison with the sums in issue.[39]

Some commentators suggested that this minor difference between the punitive and compensatory awards indicates that the punitive part of the award must not be greater in amount than the compensatory part. Anything in excess of a 1:1 ratio will lead to a refusal to recognise and enforce the award. They observed that, if this approach is taken in all cases, 'many punitive damages awards [will] not be enforced in France'.[40] This would go against the wording of the Court of Appeal adopted by the *Cour de cassation* that the degree of disproportion must be great and excessive. It would also represent a departure from the approach of the courts in the context of penalty clauses, where it is not sufficient that the

[34] The courts also have the power to modify clauses upwards, but this power is rarely used: Rowan, *The New French Law of Contract* (n 4) 239–42.

[35] 11 February 1997, *RTD civ* 1997.654 noted by J Mestre.

[36] Rowan, *The New French Law of Contract* (n 4) 239–42; G Viney, P Jourdain and S Carval, *Traité de droit civil, Les effets de la responsabilité*, 4th edn (Paris, LGDJ, 2017) [256].

[37] *Revue critique de droit international privé* 2011.93 (n 1) [11], noted by H Gaudemet-Tallon.

[38] This has been severely criticised by Licari (n 2) 426.

[39] ibid 800.

[40] Janke and Licari (n 2) 795; Vanleenhove (n 2) [307]–[312]; see also Sindres (n 2) [27].

stipulated sum is no greater than the loss suffered by the injured party.[41] Even where there is no loss at all, it does not necessarily follow that the agreed sum should be regarded as 'manifestly excessive'.[42]

Commentators have also criticised the uncertainty that inheres in proportionality being assessed by reference to the breach of contract. What exactly does this involve? It has been suggested to relate to 'the seriousness of the fault'[43] and 'the degree of culpability or the blameworthiness of the fault'.[44] However, in related contexts such as penalty clauses, the *Cour de cassation* has ruled that the conduct of the contract-breaker is irrelevant.[45]

The absence of more precise guidance on the proportionality test from the *Cour de cassation* leaves these questions unanswered. Without greater clarity as to where the line between proportionate and disproportionate punitive awards is drawn, it falls to be determined in the complete discretion of lower courts (*pouvoir souverain des juges du fond*)[46] on the facts before them.

D. A Decision Reflecting the Mood of the Time

In line with the opaque and laconic style of French judgments, the decision of the *Cour de cassation* is brief and does not contain detailed analysis.[47] The rationale for embracing foreign punitive damages that are proportionate therefore does not emerge from the judgment, which simply lays down the principle. However, what can be said is that the openness of the *Cour de cassation* to penal awards was in keeping with the mood of the time.

Punitive damages were somewhat in vogue in France. Only a few years previously,[48] an important reform project had proposed their introduction in French contract and tort law as a means of preventing reprehensible conduct.[49]

[41] TGI Nice 19 July 1977, *Rev Jur Com* 1978.265 noted by E-M Bey; CA Douai 10 March 1976, *RTD* 1977.338 noted by G Cornu; CA Versailles 13 October 1989, *D* 1989.IR.301.

[42] Soc 21 March 1978, Bull civ V no 218.

[43] Sindres (n 2) 540.

[44] Vanleenhove (n 2) [310]–[312].

[45] Fages (n 28) 125.

[46] Vanleenhove (n 2) 133.

[47] Note that the *Cour de cassation* issued new guidelines on 1 October 2019 requiring its chambers to issue more detailed judgments. The new mode of drafting court decisions and their reasoning in expanded form: Cour de cassation <www.courdecassation.fr/acces-rapide-judilibre/comprendre-une-decision-de-la-cour/le-nouveau-mode-de-redaction-des> accessed 7 May 2023.

[48] S Rowan, 'Comparative Observations on the Introduction of Punitive Damages in French Law' in J Cartwright, S Vogenauer and S Whittaker (eds), *Reforming the French Law of Obligations, Comparative Reflections on the Avant-projet de réforme du droit des obligations et de la prescription ('the Avant-projet Catala')* (Oxford, Hart Publishing, 2009) 325.

[49] *Avant-Projet de Réforme du Droit des Obligations (Art 1101 à 1386 du Code civil) et du Droit de la Prescription (Art 2234 à 2281 du Code Civil)* under the direction of P Catala, 22 September 2005 (Documentation Française, 2006) translated into English by J Cartwright and S Whittaker, <www.justice.gouv.fr/art_pix/rapportcatatla0905-anglais.pdf> accessed 7 May 2023. See also generally J Cartwright, S Vogenauer and S Whittaker (eds), *Reforming the French Law of Obligations:*

The 'Proposals for Reform of the Law of Obligations and the Law of Prescription', commonly referred to as the 'Catala proposals', were published in 2005 to coincide with the bicentenary of the Civil Code. Aimed at revising the Articles of the Code relating to the law of contract, civil liability, unjust enrichment and limitation, they were considered by many to be the most ambitious attempt to reform the core areas of French private law since the creation of the Civil Code in 1804.[50]

Draft Article 1371 on punitive damages provided as follows:

> A person who commits a manifestly deliberate fault, and notably a fault with a view to gain, can be condemned in addition to compensatory damages to pay punitive damages, part of which the court may in its discretion allocate to the Public Treasury. A court's decision to order payment of damages of this kind must be supported with specific reasons and their amount distinguished from any other damages awarded to the victim. Punitive damages may not be the object of insurance.

The scope of the draft Article was wide, encompassing both contractual and extra-contractual liability. It would apply regardless of the motives of the wrongdoer. All 'manifestly deliberate faults', of which 'fault with a view to gain' was one example, would be caught and potentially subject to the remedy. The relief would also be available where the wrongdoer acted for profit or maliciously.

This was followed in July 2010 – only five months before the *Cour de cassation* decision in *Fountaine Pajot* – by another reform project. The Beteille Proposals advocated the introduction of punitive damages for deliberate faults with a view to gain in comparable terms to the Catala proposals.[51] One notable difference was that the punitive award would be subject to an upper limit of twice the amount of the compensatory damages awarded, which was intended to avoid disproportion.

Overall reactions to these projects were mixed and the proposals to introduce punitive damages generated much discussion. Several commentators agreed that punitive awards could assist in tackling wrongful conduct. It was also recognised that deterrence and punishment were already present in the French law of remedies, despite not being formally recognised as objectives.[52] The examples cited were the enforcement of penalty clauses, the disapplication of the remoteness

Comparative Reflections on the Avant-projet de réforme du droit des obligations et de la prescription ('the Avant-projet Catala') (Oxford, Hart Publishing, 2009).

[50] S Vogenauer, 'The *Avant-projet de réforme*: An Overview' in J Cartwright, S Vogenauer and S Whittaker (eds), *Reforming the French Law of Obligations: Comparative Reflections on the Avant-projet de réforme du droit des obligations et de la prescription ('the Avant-projet Catala')* (Oxford, Hart Publishing, 2009) 3.

[51] See Art 1386-25 of the Béteille proposals of 9 July 2010 (proposition de *loi* no 657 portant réforme de la responsabilité civile, <www.senat.fr/leg/ppl09-657.html> accessed 7 May 2023.

[52] S Rowan, *Remedies for Breach of Contract: A Comparative Analysis of the Protection of Performance* (Oxford, OUP, 2012) 44–45; J-S Borghetti, 'Punitive Damages in France' in H Koziol and V Wilcox (eds), *Punitive Damages: Common Law and Civil Law Perspectives* (New York, Springer, 2009) 55.

rule resulting in larger damages awards for deliberate wrongful conduct, and the imposition of the *astreinte* to sanction non-compliance with court orders.[53] Many saw the introduction of punitive damages as simply formalising and developing the role of deterrence and punishment in contexts where the existing array of civil remedies was too weak.[54]

Whilst neither reform project was enacted, the *Cour de cassation* was undoubtedly aware of their unanimous support for a remedy that goes beyond full compensation and its decision moves in the same direction.

E. The Rejection of the Enforcement of the Entire Judgment

The effect of the *Fountaine Pajot* ruling was to prevent the recognition and enforcement of the Californian judgment in its entirety, including the compensatory damages award. This was lamented by commentators who criticised that the purchasers, and claimants in other foreign proceedings who seek to enforce their awards in France, face a 'seemingly inescapable quandary'. In the words of Janke and Licari:[55]

> [T]he American plaintiff faces a dilemma if his French defendant has no significant U.S. assets. If he seeks punitive damages, the chances of enforcing the judgment in France are small. If he renounces punitive damages before the American court, he does not have as much to gain.

To circumvent this problem, some have argued for partial or selective recognition and enforcement. A compensatory award that does not contravene *ordre public international* would be recognised and enforced and only the punitive element disregarded. However, as Vanleenhove has noted, for this solution to be viable,[56]

> it is vital … that the U.S. judgment clearly identifies and singles out the punitive damages because the prohibition against reviewing the foreign judgment on its merits forbids a French court from reducing the global amount of damages that a foreign court has awarded.

There appears to have been consensus in academic literature at the time that if partial recognition and enforcement had been sought in *Fountaine Pajot*, it would have been granted by the *Cour de cassation*.[57] Perhaps prompted by these reactions, the purchasers made a fresh application to the Californian court in 2012 for a *nunc pro tunc* judgment, that is a judgment that would amend retroactively the earlier 2003 ruling by itemising the different heads of

[53] Carval (n 4) [36]–[41].
[54] ibid [18]–[19]; A Jault, *La notion de peine privée* (Paris, LGDJ, 2005).
[55] Janke and Licari (n 2) 802.
[56] ibid. This is something which US courts seem to do in practice.
[57] ibid 803; Gaudemet-Tallon (n 37) 96 and 101–02; Vanleenhove (n 2) 135–36.

damages more clearly. Having successfully obtained this judgment, they then returned to France to seek its partial recognition and enforcement, this time with their application confined to the compensatory part of the award and excluding the punitive part.

This was rejected at every judicial level in France.[58] The *Tribunal de Grande Instance* of La Rochelle found that the *nunc pro tunc* judgment did not constitute a new ruling. It therefore failed to overcome the *res judicata* effect (*l'autorité de la chose jugée*) of the original *Cour de cassation* decision. There was no substantive modification of the original Californian decision and the application of the purchasers was substantively similar to the request that had resulted in recognition and enforcement being refused in the preceding litigation.[59]

The appeal of the purchasers was rejected by the Poitiers Court of Appeal. It held that there was no essential difference between the 2003 and 2012 Californian rulings. The latter did not rectify or interpret the former, but simply 'presented … in a more formal manner the allocation of damages'. It did not

> change anything in relation to the nature, distribution or amount' of the damages awarded. The attempt to obtain a new ruling and enforce part of the award was an abuse of process. It was frivolous and 'based mainly on a procedural artifice … intended to circumvent the consequences of *res judicata*.[59a]

This conclusion was echoed by the *Cour de cassation*. It noted that the application for partial recognition and enforcement had 'the same parties' and 'an identical object and cause' as when enforcement was originally refused. Therefore, the Court of Appeal was 'correct to conclude that the request, which ran counter to the authority of *res judicata*, was not admissible'. It upheld the finding that the application was an abuse of process.

Although definitive that the purchasers could not use a *nunc pro tunc* judgment to obtain a second bite of the cherry, the ruling of the *Cour de cassation* does not resolve the question of whether the purchasers would have been granted partial recognition and enforcement, if that is what they had originally sought. Later cases have not provided guidance on this issue and it remains unclear whether partial recognition and enforcement, with the punitive part of an award excluded, is possible.

V. DEVELOPMENTS SINCE THE *FOUNTAINE PAJOT* DECISION

The principle established in *Fountaine Pajot* remains good law and has been applied in at least two subsequent reported cases. The possibility of punitive

[58] TGI La Rochelle 8 August 2014; CA Poitiers 24 June 2016, no 15/00523; Civ (1) 24 May 2018, no 16-26.012.

[59] CA Poitiers 24 June 2016, no 15/00523.

[59a] ibid.

sanctions being introduced into French private law has also continued to generate interest over the last 10 years. It has been a focus of two other reform projects, which consecutively proposed the introduction of gain-based damages and civil penalties to tackle 'profitable wrongs'. In parallel, the principle of proportionality has grown in significance, having been given a prominent role in the Civil Code in the recent overhaul of French contract law.[60]

A. The Application of the *Fountaine Pajot* Decision in Later Cases

Two reported cases appear to have directly applied the principle established by the *Cour de cassation* in *Fountaine Pajot*. The first concerned the design and construction of a house in the United States by an architect based in France. The house was built defectively and the claimants, a couple who lived in the United States, sued the architect before the court of first instance in Travis, Texas. The court ordered the payment of US$759,001.60 in respect of the cost of curing the defects, the inability of the claimants to use the house and its diminution in value; US$1.5m in punitive damages for deliberate breach of contract by the architect; US$47,750 in lawyers' fees; and US$170,016.26 in interest.

The application for recognition and enforcement of the Texan judgment in France was granted at first instance. This was overturned by the Poitiers Court of Appeal, which held that the Texan decision contravened *ordre public international* because the punitive part of the award was 'manifestly disproportionate'.[61] Quoting the *Fountaine Pajot* principle word-for-word and applying the proportionality test enunciated in that case, it found the punitive damages award to be disproportionate to the damage suffered. This was because the claimants would recover 'in addition to damages for the repair works, loss of enjoyment and the diminution in value of the building, an award which greatly exceeds these sums'.

As in *Fountaine Pajot*, the recognition and enforcement of the foreign judgment was refused in its entirety. This included the compensatory part of the award. However, in contrast with *Fountaine Pajot*, the claimants had sought the partial recognition and enforcement of the compensatory element only in the alternative, in case the court found that the punitive award contravened *ordre public international*. Unhelpfully, the Court of Appeal appeared to ignore the claim for partial recognition and enforcement without any explanation. Since it was not addressed, whether such requests will always be rejected in the future is to a large extent speculative.

The second case relates to the recognition and enforcement of several related judgments from California. One such judgment contained an award

[60] Rowan, *The New French Law of Contract* (n 4) 248–54.
[61] CA Poitiers 4 March 2011, no 09/02077.

of US$10,846,246 to reverse an unjust enrichment (*enrichissement sans cause*); another contained a punitive damages award in the same amount. The defendant alleged, amongst other things, that permitting the enforcement of the awards would violate *ordre public international*. In particular, the award in the second judgment did not 'compensate loss actually suffered' (*un préjudice réellement subi*) and was punitive in nature.

The Paris Court of Appeal allowed the recognition and enforcement of both judgments,[62] ruling that the defendant had failed to demonstrate how the awards violated *ordre public international*. Quashing this decision, the *Cour de cassation* found that the Court of Appeal had not considered whether 'the judgments were disproportionate in relation to the damage suffered'.[63] It remanded the matter to the Court of Appeal in Versailles,[64] which allowed the recognition and enforcement of the unjust enrichment award but not the second punitive award. This refusal was on the basis of a contravention of the procedural rules of *ordre public international*, in that the award was not supported by 'any reasoning that allowed an understanding of the facts and law that led to the punitive award'. The documents put before the court to explain the award did not shed light on the factual underpinnings of the punitive ruling. The insufficient reasoning of the foreign court therefore did not enable the French court to 'assess whether the punitive award [was] in proportion to the damage suffered'.

It is difficult to generalise and draw meaningful conclusions from these cases, which seem to turn on their own facts, and are frustratingly uninformative. They offer no guidance on the application of the proportionality test and shed little light on how French courts will deal with applications for partial enforcement. The only conclusion that can safely be drawn is that it is likely to be hard for litigants to obtain the recognition and enforcement of foreign judgments that award punitive damages.

B. The Continuing Debate on Punitive Awards as a Private Law Remedy in France

Whilst there remain many uncertainties as to the application of *Fountaine Pajot*, the debate regarding the possible introduction of punitive sanctions into French private law has gathered pace. The Catala and Beteille proposals to introduce punitive damages ultimately came to naught. They did however trigger wider discussion and analysis of how best to tackle wrongs against which the protection afforded by compensatory damages and the criminal law was thought by many to be inadequate.[65]

[62] CA Paris 30 June 2011, no 10/00293.
[63] Civ (1) 7 November 2012, no 11-23.871.
[64] CA Versailles 19 September 2013, no 13/02154.
[65] Rowan, *The New French Law of Contract* (n 4) 243–48.

i. Profitable Wrongs

The focus of further reform proposals has almost exclusively been on 'fault with a view to gain', often referred to in France as 'profitable wrongs', rather than all deliberate wrongs. A common denominator of profitable wrongs is that the 'beneficial consequences for the wrongdoer would not be undone by the simple reparation of any harm which it has caused'.[66] The wrongdoer must intend that, even taking into account any liability to compensate the losses that flow from the wrong, they will make a profit or save money.[67] Such wrongs have been characterised in France as 'morally condemnable',[68] 'morally shocking',[69] 'socially and economically harmful'[70] and 'unacceptable'.[71]

Two elements are thought to be particularly objectionable. The first is that one party can infringe the private rights of the other, simply by paying compensation. The second is that this is done intentionally with the calculation of making a gain.[72] What causes outrage is the deliberateness of the wrongdoing and the disregard of the law and the rights of the other. Both are violated with impunity and to exploit a deficiency in the available remedies. On this basis, commentators have argued[73] that any financial incentives to break the law should be neutered. These arguments have been met with general support from those tasked with reforming French contract and tort law but without any clear agreement on the most appropriate solution.

ii. Proposals for Gain-Based Damages and Civil Penalties

A frequently expressed concern in respect of the proposed introduction of punitive damages was that it would lead to undeserved windfalls.[74] There were also fears of litigation floodgates opening, as well as of arbitrariness and excess in

[66] G Viney, 'Exposé des motifs: Sous-titre III. De la responsabilité civile (Article 1340 à 1386)' in *Avant-projet de réforme du droit des obligations et de la prescription: Rapport remis au garde des Sceaux* (Paris, La Documentation française, 2006) 159, 168.

[67] D Fasquelle, 'L'existence de fautes lucratives en droit français' LPA 20 November 2002 no 232 27, 30; G Viney, 'Projet de réforme du droit des obligations: les Éléments clés en matière de droit de la responsabilité' *Revue Lamy Droit Civil* 2005 no 22.

[68] F Graziani, 'La généralisation de l'amende civile: entre progrès et confusions' D 2018.428; J Meadel, 'Faut-il introduire la faute lucrative en droit français?' *LPA* 17 April 2006 no 77, 6; Y-M Laithier, 'Le prononcé de dommages-intérêts punitifs en cas de faute lucrative' in N Ferrier and A Pélissier (eds), *L'entreprise face aux Évolutions de la responsabilité civile* (Paris, Economica, 2012) 117, 117–18.

[69] D Fasquelle, 'L'existence de fautes lucratives en droit français' *LPA* 20 November 2002 no 232 27, 28; M Chagny, 'La notion de dommages et intérêts punitifs et ses répercussions sur le droit de la concurrence – Lectures plurielles de l'article 1371 de l'avant-projet de réforme du droit des obligations' *JCP G* 2006.I.149.

[70] E Dreyer, 'La sanction de la faute lucrative par l'amende civile' D 2017.1136; B Javaux, 'L'amende civile, entre sanction pénale et punitive damages?' *JCP G* 2019.6.152.

[71] Graziani (n 68).

[72] Dreyer (n 70).

[73] See Carval (n 4); Graziani (n 68); J Prorok, 'L'amende civile dans la réforme de la responsabilité civile. Regard critique sur la consécration d'une fonction punitive Générale' *RTD civ* 2018.327.

[74] M Behar-Touchais, 'L'amende civile est-elle un substitut satisfaisant à l'absence de dommages et intérêts punitifs?' *LPA* 2002, no 232, 36; Prorok (n 73).

the quantum of damages awards.[75] These criticisms led to gain-based damages being proposed as an alternative to punitive damages by a competing reform project led by a group of academic lawyers. In its draft Article 120, the 'Terré project' proposed that 'in case of deliberate breach, the injured party may be awarded [instead of compensatory damages] all or some of the profit resulting from the breach'.[76]

This was met with broad approbation as a less drastic and more proportionate solution,[77] but there were also concerns that it would be too weak. Since it would be limited to gains accruing from the wrongful conduct, a party tempted to commit a profitable wrong might form the view that they have little to lose. With the punitive and deterrent effects removed, at worst they would be deprived of their ill-gotten gains.[78]

As a middle ground between punitive damages and gain-based damages, the sanction proposed in the most recent reform project on civil liability, which was published in 2017, is the civil penalty (*amende civile*).[79] The 2017 Reform Bill on Civil Liability seeks to reform Articles of the Civil Code relating to contractual liability and compensatory and agreed damages. Draft Article 1266-1 provides as follows:

> In extra-contractual matters, where the author of the harm has deliberately committed a fault with a view to gain or making a saving, a court may, at the request of the victim or the *ministère public* (the state) and by specially reasoned decision, order payment of a civil penalty.
>
> This penalty is proportionate to the seriousness of the fault, the financial means of the wrongdoer, and the profit gained from the wrongful conduct.
>
> The penalty cannot be more than tenfold the amount of the profit gained.
>
> If the wrongdoer is a corporation, the penalty can be up to 5% of the amount of the highest turnover before tax made in France in the tax years since the year preceding that when the fault was committed.
>
> This penalty is directed to the financing of a compensation fund related to the nature of the harm suffered or, failing this, to the public treasury.
>
> It is not insurable.

[75] S Carval, 'L'amende civile' in 'Avant-projet de loi portant réforme de la responsabilité civile, Observations et propositions de modifications' *JCP suppl* 25 July 2016 42 [7].

[76] Art 120, Terré Reform Project.

[77] R Mesa, 'L'opportune consécration d'un principe de restitution intégrale des profits illicites comme sanction des fautes lucratives' *D* 2012.2754; Carval, 'L'amende civile' (n 75). See also Z Jacquemin, 'Pour une reconnaissance de la spécificité contractuelle dans les effets de la responsabilité' *RDC* 2016.808; Laithier, 'Le prononcé de dommages-intérêts punitifs en cas de faute lucrative' (n 68) 117; Y-M Laithier, 'Clause pénale et dommages et intérêts incitatifs' in C Jamin (ed), *Droit et Économie des contrats* (Paris, LGDJ, 2008) 141.

[78] Prorok (n 73).

[79] Ministère de la Justice, 'Projet de réforme de la responsabilité civile' (13 March 2017), www.justice.gouv.fr/publication/Projet_de_reforme_de_la_responsabilite_civile_13032017.pdf; English translation by S Whittaker and J-S Borghetti, Reform Bill on Civil Liability (March 2017), <www.textes.justice.gouv.fr/art_pix/reform_bill_on_civil_liability_march_2017.pdf> accessed 7 May 2023.

Civil penalties are already made in various contexts in France.[80] The aim is to deter and punish conduct that is reprehensible but insufficiently serious for criminal liability. This includes the breach by state officials of certain public duties;[81] bringing court proceedings abusively;[82] and demolishing a building without the requisite permission.[83] Being more familiar with civil penalties, many French commentators perceive them as being less controversial than punitive damages.

Civil penalties can hurt the wrongdoer more than gain-based damages, partly through being calculated by reference to the gravity of the wrong. This may be much greater than the profit made from the wrong, as well as being significant in absolute terms.[84] Since payment of the penalties is made into a designated fund set up to counteract at a general level the negative consequences of the wrongful conduct, the victim is not benefited directly.[85] This is faithful to the cardinal principle that the victim should not be awarded any more than is necessary to compensate their loss[86] and also to the general principle of full compensation.[87]

Draft Article 1266-1 would only apply to extra-contractual liability and not to contractual liability. This was justified by the drafters on the basis that it is open to contracting parties to incorporate a penalty clause in their contract if they wish to deter and punish breach. There were also fears that to import civil penalties into a contractual setting was too radical and might deter international businesses from opting for French law as their governing law in cross-border contracts.[88] Only the pre-contractual period, which is governed by extra-contractual principles, is within the scope of draft Article 1266-1.

Whether draft Article 1266-1 will ever appear in the Civil Code remains a matter for speculation. At the time of writing (January 2023), the proposals of the 2017 Reform Bill are yet to be implemented. It is unclear whether this will happen and if so when and in what form.[89]

[80] Behar-Touchais (n 74); Jault (n 54) [402]; J-S Borghetti, 'Faut-il distinguer les dommages et intérêts compensatoires des dommages et intérêts en lieu et place de la prestation?' *RDC* 2016.787, [18]–[21].

[81] Art 50 of the Civil Code.

[82] Art 32-1 of the New Code of Civil Procedure.

[83] Arts L430-2 and L430-9 of the Urban Code.

[84] Dreyer (n 70); Prorok (n 74).

[85] Carval, 'L'amende civile' (n 75) 42; *Projet de réforme de la responsabilité civile* (n 79).

[86] Borghetti (n 80) [50]; Dreyer (n 70) [13]; Prorok (n 74); Graziani (n 68); M Cappelletti, 'Comparative Reflections on Punishment in Tort Law' in J-S Borghetti and S Whittaker (eds), *French Civil Liability in Comparative Perspective* (Oxford, Hart Publishing, 2019) 329.

[87] Borghetti (n 80) [47]; 'Projet de réforme de la responsabilité civile' (n 79).

[88] S Carval, 'Le projet de réforme de la responsabilité civile' *JCP* 2017.401; J-S Borghetti, 'Un pas de plus vers la réforme de la responsabilité civile: présentation du projet de réforme rendu public le 13 mars 2017' *D* 2017.770; T d'Alès and L Terdjman, 'L'introduction envisagée de mécanismes répressifs dans le droit de la responsabilité civile: le Rubicon sera-t-il franchi ?' *AJ Contrat* 2017.69.

[89] In July 2020, several senators who were impatient to see reforms enacted put forward proposals amending the 2017 reforms: '23 propositions pour simplifier la vie des Français en facilitant la

C. The Growing Use of Proportionality as a Limiting Mechanism in the Context of Contractual Remedies

In contrast with the hesitation in respect of the introduction of punitive sanctions, proportionality as a limiting mechanism has grown in significance in the context of contractual remedies. Proportionality has been given a central role in the Civil Code following the 2016 overhaul of the contract law section. Specific enforcement, price reduction, and termination[90] are all newly subject to this standard.[91] The objective is to balance the competing interests of the parties and avoid extreme outcomes.

In the context of specific performance, for example, the remedy is unavailable where there is a 'manifest disproportion' between the cost of performance and the interest of the injured party in obtaining it.[92] This exception, which can be found at Article 1221 of the Civil Code, is new and amongst the most notable changes made by the 2016 reforms of the code.[93] Previously, the courts did not have any discretion as to whether to grant specific enforcement. An order could not be resisted on the ground of disproportionality. Nor was there an undue hardship bar, meaning that the remedy could be obtained even at the financial ruin of the contract-breaker.[94]

Another example is the proportionality test that can now be found in the new remedy of price reduction. This was introduced as part of the 2016 reforms to the Civil Code in new Article 1223.[95] It confers on the injured party a right to accept performance that falls short of the contractually agreed standard but at a lower price. The reduction must be in proportion to the shortcomings in the performance. In practice, this is the difference in value between the promised performance and the performance that was actually rendered.

Comparable to the proportionality requirement of Articles 1221 and 1223 is the requirement of reasonableness at Article 1222 in the context of 'replacement' (*faculté de remplacement*), where the contract-breaker is required to indemnify the injured party in respect of the cost of employing a third party to perform the obligation that has been breached.[96] Replacement must occur 'within a reasonable time and at a reasonable cost'.

réparation des dommages' Sénat, 22 July 2020, <www.senat.fr/rap/r19-663/r19-6631.html> accessed 7 May 2023. This was followed by a 'proposition de loi': <www.senat.fr/leg/ppl19-678.html> accessed 7 May 2023. They recommend not to introduce '*amende civile*' to avoid further debate and delay in enacting the reforms.

[90] Through the requirement of a sufficiently serious breach at Art 1224: see Rowan, *The New French Law of Contract* (n 4) 213–23.

[91] Rowan, *The New French Law of Contract* (n 4) 248–54.

[92] Art 1221 of the Civil Code.

[93] Rowan, *The New French Law of Contract* (n 4) 198–208.

[94] Civ (3) 3 December 1969, Bull civ III no 2.

[95] Rowan, *The New French Law of Contract* (n 4) 210–13.

[96] ibid 208–10; S Whittaker, 'Performance of Another's Obligation: French and English Law Contrasted' in D Johnston and R Zimmerman (eds), *Unjustified Enrichment: Key Issues in Comparative Perspective* (Cambridge, CUP, 2002) 433, 450.

In all these contexts, as in relation to the enforcement of foreign judgments, proportionality remains an uncertain concept. No guidance is provided in the reformed Civil Code either as to its meaning or the factors that are relevant to assessing where to draw the line. In the context of specific performance, commentators have suggested that relevant factors are likely to include the seriousness of the breach, the extent of the injured party's loss, the level of difficulty obtaining the promised performance elsewhere, and the risk of under-compensation in the event that compensatory damages were awarded.[97] As for 'manifest disproportion', there is consensus that it must be blatant, in the sense of 'certain, evident and flagrant',[98] which serves to limit the scope of the exception.[99]

VI. CONCLUSION

In contrast with the approach of courts in other European jurisdictions such as Germany,[100] the French *Cour de cassation* showed an openness towards punitive damages in *Fountaine Pajot*. The *Cour* ultimately refused to recognise and enforce the punitive award and has since reached the same conclusion in other cases concerning US punitive awards, but importantly it accepted in principle that the recognition and enforcement of proportionate punitive awards are possible.

Whilst US punitive awards have to date proved too extreme for French courts, more moderate foreign awards, perhaps from other jurisdictions, could in the future be recognised and enforced. England is an example of a jurisdiction where relatively modest punitive damages awards can be made. English courts have warned against the 'danger of an excessive award'[101] and follow principles that ensure some degree of proportionality. These include that any penalty must be the minimum necessary to achieve the dual purposes underlying punitive damages, namely punishment and deterrence;[102] punitive damages orders should take into account the wrongdoer's means so as not to be impossible to bear;[103] only if the compensatory award is inadequate to punish the wrongdoer for his outrageous conduct and deter others will a court order that punitive damages be paid;[104] and any criminal penalties should be taken into account so

[97] O Deshayes, T Genicon and Y-M Laithier, *Réforme du droit des contrats, du régime général et de la preuve des obligations*, 2nd edn (Paris, LexisNexis, 2018) 555.
[98] G Chantepie and M Latina, *La réforme du droit des obligations, Commentaire théorique et pratique dans l'ordre du Code civil*, 2nd edn (Paris, Dalloz, 2018) [638].
[99] Deshayes, Genicon and Laithier (n 97) 555.
[100] See also Ungerer, ch 7 of this volume.
[101] *Cassell & Co Ltd v Broome* [1972] AC 1027 (HL) 1081 where Lord Hailsham said that juries should be 'fully aware of the danger of an excessive award'.
[102] ibid 1081.
[103] ibid 625.
[104] *Rookes v Barnard* [1964] 1 AC 1129 (HL) 1228.

as not to punish the same conduct twice.[105] Punitive awards are also generally itemised. Whether litigants who have been awarded moderate punitive damages would wish to seek their recognition and enforcement in France remains to be seen. Few are likely to bring a claim in the knowledge that they cannot thereby benefit substantially. There would also be a real risk of increased legal fees as a result of the uncertainty that currently surrounds the guidance provided by the *Cour de cassation*, which incentivises the defendant to oppose recognition and enforcement. Whilst this uncertainty remains, attempts to enforce punitive foreign awards in the French courts seem likely to be few.

APPENDIX

Translation of Cour De Cassation, First Civil Chamber, 1 December 2010, Case No 09-13.303[106]

THE COURT OF CASSATION, FIRST CIVIL CHAMBER, has issued the following judgment:

On the single ground of the main appeal, in five parts:

Whereas the spouses X …, of American nationality and living in the United States, applied for the recognition and enforcement (*exequatur*) in France of a decision rendered on 26 February 2003 by the Supreme Court of California (Alameda county) which ordered the French company Fountaine Pajot to pay them the sum of US$3,253,734.45, consisting of US$1,391,650.12 for the repair of the boat manufactured by the French company which they had purchased for US$826,009, US$402,084.33 for legal fees and US$1,460,000 for punitive damages;

Whereas the spouses X … object to the judgment under appeal (CA Poitiers 26 February 2009), rendered on dismissal after *cassation* (Civ 1, 22 May 2007, no 05-20.473), which stated that the decision contravened substantive international public policy and dismissed their application for recognition and enforcement (*exequatur*), therefore, according to the means:

1°/ that a foreign decision ordering a party to pay punitive damages is not, in principle, contrary to substantive international public policy; that by ruling to the contrary, the Court of Appeal violated articles 3 and 15 of the Civil Code, article 509 of the Code of Civil Procedure and the principles governing the procedures of recognition and enforcement (*exequatur*);

[105] *John v MGN Ltd* [1997] QB 586 (CA).
[106] Civ 1, 1 December 2010, 09-13.303 available in French: <www.legifrance.gouv.fr/juri/id/JURITEXT000023165365> accessed 7 May 2023.

2°/ that the Court of Appeal expressly noted that the choice of Californian law designated in the contract is not fraudulent and is binding on Mr and Mrs X … and the company Fountaine Pajot; that in ruling on the basis that the decision of the Superior Court of California (County of Alameda) of February 26, 2003 contravenes substantive international public policy, on the terms of article 74 of the Vienna Convention of 11 April 1980 on the International Sale of Goods, the Court of Appeal, which did not draw the legal consequences from its own findings, violated, by refusing to apply articles 3 and 15 of the Civil Code, article 509 of the Code of Civil Procedure and the principles governing the procedure of *exequatur*, and, by erroneous application, article 74 of the Vienna Convention;

3°/ that in any event, the Vienna Convention of 11 April 1980 on the International Sale of Goods is not applicable to sales of goods purchased for personal or family use or to the sale of boats; in the present case, it is not disputed that Mr and Mrs X … bought a catamaran for private and family use; that by relying on the Vienna Convention to state that the decision of the Superior Court of California (County of Alameda) of 26 February 2003 contravenes substantive international public policy, the Court of Appeal violated by erroneous application articles 25 and 74 of the Vienna Convention of 11 April 1980 on the International Sale of Goods;

4°/ that the control of the compliance of the foreign decision with international public order should not lead to its review on the merits; that by basing itself on the common French law of civil liability and contract law to rule that the decision of the Superior Court of California (County of Alameda) of 26 February 2003 contravenes substantive international public policy, the Court of Appeal violated articles 3 and 15 of the Civil Code, article 509 of the Code of Civil Procedure and the principles governing the procedures of recognition and enforcement (*exequatur*);

5°/ that by affirming that an indemnity, awarded by a foreign decision to the buyers of a boat, greatly exceeding its purchase price, is disproportionate in that it provides them with unjust enrichment without taking into account … the absolute impossibility for Mr and Mrs X … to use a boat acquired ten years earlier for a price paid in full of US$690,000, the fraudulent behaviour of the company Fountaine Pajot, seller and manufacturer of the boat, which concealed the damage affecting it, putting the lives of the buyers and their children at evident risk and without searching whether the order to pay compensation exceeding the price of the vessel was ultimately not justified and hence proportionate, the Court of Appeal's decision lacked any legal basis with regard to articles 3 and 15 of the Civil Code, article 509 of the Code of Civil Procedure and the principles governing the procedures of recognition and enforcement (*exequatur*);

But whereas an order to pay punitive damages is not, in itself, contrary to public policy, it will be otherwise when the amount awarded is disproportionate to the loss sustained and the contract-breaker's breach of their contractual obligation; that in the present case, the judgment notes that the foreign decision granted the purchasers, in addition to the reimbursement of the price of the boat and the cost of the repairs, compensation which greatly exceeds this sum; that the Court of Appeal was able to deduce that the damages award was manifestly disproportionate in view of the loss sustained and the breach of the contractual obligation so that the foreign judgment could not be recognised in France; that the plea cannot be accepted;

FOR THESE REASONS, and without there being any need to rule on the possible appeal:

DISMISSES the main appeal;

condemns spouses X … to costs;

With regard to article 700 of the Code of Civil Procedure, rejects the applications;

It is thus ordered and adjudged by the Court of Cassation, first civil chamber, and pronounced by the president in his public hearing of 1 December two thousand and ten.

17

PH Hydraulics & Engineering Pte Ltd v Airtrust (Hong Kong) Ltd (2017)

Orthodoxy Rules

PEY-WOAN LEE*

IF *PH HYDRAULICS & Engineering Pte Ltd v Airtrust (Hong Kong) Ltd*[1] ('*PH Hydraulics*') qualifies as a landmark decision, it would be because it is a rare attempt at challenging the deeply entrenched orthodoxy that punitive damages cannot be awarded for a breach of contract. In this case, the claimant sought punitive damages for (what it regarded as) an egregious breach of contract. The trial judge found the defendant's conduct sufficiently reprehensible as it had breached the contract fraudulently. On appeal, however, the Court of Appeal overruled the finding of fraud. It also ruled that punitive damages would not, *as a general rule*, be available for breach of contract but left open the possibility that such an award may be made in truly exceptional situations involving 'particularly outrageous' breaches. The different outcomes reached at trial and on appeal suggest that the case was not an open-and-shut one and hence particularly apropos for re-examining the rule.

In England, the standard authority for the ban on punitive damages in contract remains *Addis v Gramaphone Co Ltd*,[2] which has often been criticised as a weak authority because the law lords were not *ad idem* in their reasoning.[3]

* I would like to thank Eleni Katsampouka and James Goudkamp for their very helpful suggestions and comments. I am also deeply grateful to Mr Tan Chuan Thye SC, lead counsel for the claimant (Airtrust), for his invaluable insights on the practical and tactical factors that constrained the development and outcome of the case.

[1] *PH Hydraulics & Engineering Pte Ltd v Airtrust (Hong Kong) Ltd* [2017] SGCA 26, [2017] 2 SLR 129.

[2] *Addis v Gramaphone Co Ltd* [1909] 1 AC 488 (HL).

[3] Its discussion of punitive damages is strictly obiter since only two of the five judges discussed punitive damages. Lord Atkinson was of the view that 'damages for breach of contract were in the nature of compensation, not punishment' (ibid 494). On the other hand, Lord Collins, dissenting, thought that exemplary damages were available for breach of contract (ibid 497–500).

In Australia, the authority cited for disallowing PD for contracts is *Harris v Digital Pulse Pty Ltd*,[4] which is really more concerned with breach of equitable obligations. Canada, of course, is home to *Whiten v Pilot Insurance Co*,[5] the celebrated but much criticised decision that departed from orthodoxy. Against this backdrop, *PH Hydraulics* is an important addition to a small collection of final appellate decisions that have considered the debate at length.

This chapter considers the contributions of *PH Hydraulics* to the ongoing discourse on the role of punishment in private law. It begins by examining the practical concerns that shaped or constrained the legal arguments. It highlights the heavy evidential burden borne by the claimant in a highly technical dispute, which did not bode well for its attempt at overturning orthodoxy. Secondly, it considers the unequivocal distinction that the CA draws between compensatory and punitive damages even whilst it acknowledges that each category may incidentally achieve the purposes of another category. This confirms that the possibly 'substitutive' effects of compensatory for punitive damages are not a reason for expanding the availability of punitive damages for breach of contract. Thirdly, it observes that the legitimacy contract law accords to self-interested conduct is the key distinction between contractual breaches and torts. Importantly, this standard of conduct prevails in contracts not merely by reason of party autonomy but as a normative contracting behaviour. Drawing a sharp distinction between contracts and torts does not, however, necessarily lead to a 'remedial gap' in contracts because exceptionally oppressive conduct may still be redressed through actions in tort, particularly if the latter adopts a more expansive approach to the availability of punitive damages. Finally, it explores the scope of the exceptional jurisdiction that the CA preserved for awarding punitive damages and concludes that this will likely be a very limited jurisdiction. The conclusion in *PH Hydraulics* is a resounding affirmation of the orthodoxy that contract damages seek only to compensate and not punish. This does not deny that contractual breaches can sometimes implicate serious wrongdoing, but only that the avenues for achieving punitive and deterrent ends may typically lie elsewhere.

I. THE TRIAL

PH Hydraulics concerned a plain commercial dispute. The defendant (PH) was a manufacturer of heavy machinery for offshore use in the marine and oil and gas industry. In September 2007, it contracted with the plaintiff (Airtrust) to design and build a 300 tons reel drive unit (RDU). A typical RDU consists of a

[4] *Harris v Digital Pulse Pty Ltd* [2003] NSWCA 10, (2003) 44 ACSR 390.
[5] *Whiten v Pilot Insurance Co* [2002] SCC 18, [2002] 1 SCR 595.

large reel installed between two symmetrical towers. One or both of the towers comprises a motorised drive system that controls the spooling or unspooling of cables, wires and the like. At the time of the contract, Airtrust had informed PH that it was purchasing the RDU for lease to Trident Offshore Services ('Trident') to lay undersea umbilical in the Bass Straits of Australia. Seven months later, the RDU was delivered and mounted on board the *Maesk Responder*. It set sail on its maiden voyage in Australian waters. Catastrophically, the RDU broke down on this first voyage. The hydraulic drive motor and gear assembly on one of the towers broke loose from its mounting and fell in the course of the umbilical laying operation. Fortunately, no one was injured.

Airtrust successfully sued for breach of contract. At the end of a 'technically challenging trial',[6] Chan Seng Onn J concluded that the RDU was not of merchantable quality, not fit for the purpose for which it was intended to be used, not designed and manufactured adequately, and did not meet the relevant industry standards and certifications stipulated in the contract. Examples of PH's spectacular failure include poor design parameters and assumptions, inadequate bolting arrangements, under-designed brakes, gears and bearing arrangement, poor manufacturing processes, failure to check for compliance with drawings, and failure to perform required design calculations of critical components.

Importantly, Chan J also found that PH had been fraudulent in the discharge of its obligations. Under the contract, PH was required to provide a 'full certification' for the RDU. It sought to obtain this certification from ABSG (a third-party freelance certifying agency) and engaged a freelance structural engineer, Dr Liu, to perform the STAAD.Pro analysis[7] that was integral to ABSG's review of the RDU's structural design. ABSG issued the certification but was, in Chan J's assessment, misled into doing so by PH's dishonest representations. First, PH and Dr Liu had dishonestly represented that no wind load need be considered in the STAAD.Pro analysis because the RDU's spooler was to be housed in an enclosed cabin on board the ship. This was, in Chan J's assessment, 'absolutely false' since it must have been obvious to both PH and Dr Liu that the 300-ton reel could not be, and was not intended to be, operated within an enclosed cabin on board the vessel.[8] PH and Dr Liu had lied because they knew that the RDU would not pass the unity check if traverse wind loads were not excluded from the analysis.[9] Secondly, Dr Liu had dishonestly modelled certain bolted joints of the RDU as ball joints without making any calculations to ascertain if it would be appropriate to do so. For Chan J, to treat bolted

[6] *Airtrust (Hong Kong) Ltd v PH Hydraulics & Engineering Pte Ltd* [2015] SGHC 307 [8] ('*PH Hydraulics HC*').

[7] A structural analysis performed using the STAAD.Pro software.

[8] *PH Hydraulics HC* (n 6) [228].

[9] ibid [229].

joints as fully rotatable ball joints was an 'absurd engineering assumption' that could only be explained as 'a deliberate and dishonest effort to try to get a pass for the unity checks'.[10] Third, Dr Liu had erroneously modelled the RDU reel as being *fixed* in the X direction. In fact, it was constructed to *slide* traversely in the X direction when the ship rolls to its port or starboard side. Had the actual design been disclosed to ABSG, it would have rejected the RDU's design as unacceptable.[11] Taken together, Chan J was satisfied that these misrepresentations were fraudulent rather than grossly negligent since PH and Dr Liu must have known the RDU's actual design. This was not a case of an innocent mistake made in the course of a rushed job, nor was Dr Liu so ignorant or incompetent as to be unable to appreciate the significance of the errors.[12] Finally, PH had misled Airtrust into believing that it had obtained a full certification when ABSG provided only a partial certification.[13] PH would have known that ABSG did not issue a full certification since it had only instructed to ABSG to carry out a limited review of the RDU's design that could not have supported the issuance of a full certification.

The establishment of fraud at trial was significant for two reasons. First, it enabled the plaintiff to avoid an exclusion clause (Clause 25[14]) that would have limited its recovery to the value of the RDU without any claims for consequential loss of profits.[15] Second, it justified the award of punitive damages. Relying principally on Canadian authorities,[16] Chan J took the view that punitive damages may exceptionally be awarded for a breach of contract that is 'to highlight reprehensible, shocking or outrageous that the court finds it necessary to condemn and deter such conduct'.[17] In his view, PH's conduct met this threshold. In addition to the fraudulent misrepresentations, PH had instructed a junior engineer to copy and modify a RDU design that was untested and had not been certified by any third-party agency.[18] It had also procured important components for the RDU without checking their conformity with specifications.[19] The workmanship was so poor that it could not answer Airtrust's criticisms.[20]

[10] ibid [238].
[11] ibid [243].
[12] ibid [245].
[13] ibid [248].
[14] The clause stated that '*Neither party shall be liable to the other for any consequential or indirect losses* (whether or not foreseeable by either Party at the date hereof) including but not limited to *loss of profits*, products, and business interruption or economic losses arising out of or as a result of the performance of the work and regardless of the cause or reason for the said loss or damage and regardless of whether the same may arise as a result of the negligence of the other.'
[15] *PH Hydraulics HC* (n 6) [255].
[16] *Whiten* (n 5); *Brown v Waterloo Regional Board of Commissioners of Police* (1982) 136 DLR (3d) 49.
[17] *PH Hydraulics HC* (n 6) [264].
[18] ibid [266].
[19] ibid [269].
[20] ibid [271].

The totality of evidence paints a picture of blatant irresponsibility in the design, engineering and manufacture of the RDU.[21]

II. THE APPEAL

On appeal, PH accepted the trial judge's findings of contractual breaches but successfully challenged the inferences of fraud. Andrew Phang JA, delivering the court's sole judgment, agreed with PH that the trial judge's findings of fraud were unjustified both in fact and in law. In respect of the wind load representation, Phang JA thought there was insufficient evidence of ABSG having been misled, and of PH and Dr Liu's dishonest intent.[22] He also did not think that Dr Liu was dishonest or reckless in modelling the bolted joints as ball joints since the rigidity a bolted joint could fairly be said to be somewhere between a fixed and a fully rotational joint.[23] On this view, PH and Dr Liu could only be said to have been grossly negligent at the highest.[24] Similarly, the learned judge acknowledged that PH was negligent, or even grossly negligent, in failing to verify if ABSG had carried out the relevant review required for a full certification, but did not think the evidence as a whole supported the conclusion that it had no intention to secure a full certification from the start. Overall, therefore, the evidence did not meet the high threshold of knowledge or recklessness required for proof of dishonesty. However, Phang JA made clear that while this characterisation of PH's conduct (as negligent or grossly negligent) substantially weakened the case for punitive damages, it did not completely demolish it. Whether the punitive award could be upheld on the facts as established would depend on the antecedent questions of whether punitive damages can be awarded for breach of contract at all and, if so, what conduct would justify the award.

Turning to this substantive issue, Phang JA concluded that punitive damages should not, as a general rule, be available for breach of contract. His Honour cited four reasons. First, the consensual nature of contracts militates against the imposition of punitive damages. Since contract law is concerned with upholding the parties' agreements, the law should refrain from imposing an 'external' normative standard by way of a punitive award.[25] The same objection does not arise in the context of tort law. As the function of tort law is to delineate normative standards of behaviour between strangers, a punitive award may sometimes be justified to signify the denunciation of conduct that falls well below that

[21] ibid [272].
[22] *PH Hydraulics* (n 1) [39]–[41].
[23] ibid [46]–[47].
[24] ibid [50].
[25] ibid [72].

threshold level.[26] Phang JA did not explicitly address this point, but one could add that this distinction between contracts and torts is not undermined only because some torts do emanate from voluntary or consensual conduct. Yet when the provenance of the contract and tort obligations is similar, that does not alter the fact – as Phang JA emphasised – that the standards for *breach* are different in the two contexts. For purposes of torts, a breach is established by reference to a normative standard *external* to the parties. If, as is suggested here, the external standard imposed for torts is usually a threshold baseline standard, the moral quality of tortious breaches will generally be more serious than that of contractual breaches. For these reasons, the argument from uniformity – that the same range of remedial options ought to be available for both torts and contracts – was unpersuasive.

Second, there is no 'remedial gap' that requires the recognition of punitive damages. In Phang JA's view, there can be no remedial gap once it is accepted that punishment is not a legitimate aim of contractual enforcement.[27] And if it is thought that remedies with punitive or deterrent effects are needed in the contractual sphere, this gap is adequately filled by the availability of alternative remedies (such as *Wrotham Park* damages, account of profits and aggravated damages) that may nevertheless have incidental punitive and deterrent effects.[28]

Third, the criteria by which to identify punishable breaches are particularly elusive since self-serving conduct is very much a norm in commercial dealings.[29] It follows that even deliberate or cynical breaches of contracts whether for profit or other self-interests would not usually be regarded as punishable conduct.

Finally, the court cited strong policy considerations that favour the exclusion of punitive damages. One legitimate concern is that increased availability of punitive damages 'may add to its length, complexity and costs and confer upon plaintiffs an undue advantage in forcing large (or larger) settlements.'[30] In addition, in so far as the risks of recurrent reprehensible conduct typically occurs in situations of power imbalance – such as insurance, employment and consumer transactions – such risks may be better managed by regulation than by the award of punitive damages. This is because the regulator is often 'in a better position to assess the wider social as well as economic impact of a particular sanction and would therefore be better able to devise a suite of remedial responses (including, but not limited to, penal sanctions).'[31]

[26] ibid [74].
[27] ibid [78] and [84].
[28] ibid [79], [82] and [84].
[29] ibid [86].
[30] ibid [104].
[31] ibid [106].

For completeness, Phang JA considered the arguments that favour the award of punitive damages for breach of contract but did not find them compelling. Indeed, Phang JA was highly critical of *Whiten v Pilot Insurance Company*,[32] pointing out that the decision did not adequately distinguish between the different contexts of tort and contract, engendered uncertainty in so far as it failed to identify satisfactory criteria for imposing punitive damages and confused judicial with legislative function in presuming that courts have a legitimate role in inflicting punishment in the civil context. An alternative argument is that punitive damages are justified where the defendant breaches an express or implied duty of good faith, but Phang JA would consider such breaches a neutral factor at best, for it does not necessarily follow that any failure to act in good faith is, by itself, punishable conduct.

For all these reasons, Phang JA concluded that 'there ought to be a general rule that punitive damages cannot be awarded for breach of contract.'[33] Significantly, however, His Honour did not completely foreclose the possibility of punitive awards in a purely contractual context. In his view, there may still arise 'a truly exceptional case' where a contractual breach is so outrageous that would justify a departure from the general rule.[34] 'Never say never' is therefore a prudent way forward despite the weight of considerations against punitive awards in the contractual context.[35]

III. PRACTICAL HURDLES

A claimant in the shoes of Airtrust invariably faces an uphill task in their quest for punitive damages. Several reasons account for that. The first is the sheer technical complexity of the dispute. Scientific complexity increases costs, uncertainty and risks of error in adjudication.[36] At trial, Chan J had to hear evidence from no less than seven expert witnesses in a 'hot tub' format and 17 factual witnesses in a 19-day trial.[37] The paradox inherent in this process is that the judge is called upon, as a non-expert, to evaluate the evidence of the experts.[38]

[32] *Whiten* (n 5).

[33] *PH Hydraulics* (n 1) [135] (emphasis in original removed).

[34] ibid [136].

[35] ibid [136].

[36] Disputes of extreme complexity is a growing phenomenon both in arbitration (see J Risse, 'An Inconvenient Truth – the Complexity Problem and Limits to Justice' (2019) 35 *Arbitration International* 291) and litigation (see Sundaresh Menon CJ, 'The Complexification of Disputes in the Digital Age', speech delivered at the 26th Goff Arbitration Lecture, 9 November 2021).

[37] *PH Hydraulics HC* (n 6) [8].

[38] VP Hans and MJ Saks, 'Improving Judge & Jury Evaluation of Scientific Evidence' (2018) 147 *Daedalus* 164, 165.

While Chan J's background in industrial engineering[39] eliminated serious risks of error, inevitably there will still be gaps in evidence, knowledge or understanding that would predispose findings in the defendant's favour for want of proof.[40] In the final analysis, Chan J did find in the claimant's favour, but this vindication was achieved only through a protracted battle over a mass of information, and which was only a first but insufficient step in justifying punitive damages.

A second practical hurdle that stood in the way of Airtrust's claim was the asymmetry in access to evidence. As the specialist with knowledge and control of the entire design and construction process, PH had clear advantage in marshalling the evidence. While Airtrust eventually gained access to critical evidence, the process was drawn-out and haphazard. This was most clearly observed in relation to the evidence pertaining to fraud. Airtrust did not plead fraud in its initial statement of claim and did not even know of the existence of Dr Liu (who, as noted above, was a key source of the allegedly dishonest representations) until the witnesses were cross-examined at trial.[41] This underscores the evidential odds faced by a party alleging egregious conduct even in cases where the parties were of roughly equal bargaining power.

In addition to the difficulties of proof, a claimant alleging fraud would also have to surmount a high standard of proof.[42] *PH Hydraulics* was not a case that fell clearly on either side of the line. Although the CA ultimately found that the high standard of proof in respect of PH's fraudulent intention had not been met, it did not in any way contradict the trial court's findings of its appalling failures in the design and manufacture of the RDU.[43] Indeed, the defaults were of such alarming severity that one would reasonably sympathise with the view that this was a case of deliberate breach of contract with reckless disregard of the obvious and serious risks of disastrous consequences.[44] So it was against such astounding failure that Chan J weighed the evidence concerning the defendant's (in the form of its agents) states of mind. Seen in this light, the CA's refusal to characterise the defendant's conduct as fraudulent (whilst acknowledging that it could possibly have been grossly negligent[45]) was a close call of judgment. It illustrates the high bar that has to be surmounted even before the issue of punitive award arises for consideration.

[39] Chan Seng Onn J had tertiary and postgraduate education in science and industrial engineering respectively before embarking on legal education and career: <www.judiciary.gov.sg/who-we-are/justice-chan-seng-onn> accessed 7 May 2023.

[40] eg, Chan J conceded that it was not possible to prove which of the RDU's design flaws caused its catastrophic failure because there were simply too many variables as to what could have gone wrong to cause the incident: see *PH Hydraulics HC* (n 6) [206].

[41] *PH Hydraulics* (n 1) [34].

[42] *Wee Chiaw Sek Anna v Ng Li-Ann Genevieve* [2013] SGCA 36, [2013] 3 SLR 801 [30].

[43] Examples include the failure to make calculations for many critical components of the machine, the failure to take into account important factors such as vessel roll, wind load and fatigue, and the serious under-design of the braking system, sub-frame housing and bearings.

[44] Respondent's submissions on appeal filed on 25 April 2016, [75].

[45] *PH Hydraulics* (n 1) [59].

IV. COMPENSATION AND PUNISHMENT

The conventional starting point for understanding contract damages is encapsulated by Lord Hoffmann in *Co-operative Insurance Society v Argyll Stores (Holdings) Ltd*, that 'the purpose of the law of contract is not to punish wrongdoing but to satisfy the expectations of the party entitled to performance.'[46] This orthodox vision of contract damages is founded on a clear divide between compensation and punishment, and that one purpose is served to the exclusion of the other. Underpinning this vision is the more fundamental conceptual divide applicable across private law – that compensation and punishment are 'as incompatible as oil and vinegar'.[47]

In practice, however, damages may simultaneously serve multiple functions. For example, it is well recognised that even compensatory damages may discharge deterrent and punitive functions,[48] which would explain why punitive damages are awarded for torts 'if, but only if' compensatory damages are inadequate to *punish* the defendant.[49] In like vein, commentators have observed that punitive goals are sometimes 'smuggled' into overtly compensatory remedies such as damages for mental distress.[50] Conversely, claimants concerned with under-compensation may attempt to recover extra-compensatory damages to make up for the perceived shortfall. A plea for punitive damages may sometimes be motivated by the desire to augment (otherwise inadequate) compensatory damages.[51]

In the United States, where punitive damages are available for 'a wide variety of actions',[52] commentators have long observed a crossover or 'substitution' phenomenon in judicial decisions, viz, a blurring of the punitive–compensatory distinction such that punitive elements are built into compensatory damages (such as damages for emotional distress) particularly where the option for a separate penal award is closed off.[53] What this suggests is that decision-makers

[46] *Co-operative Insurance Society v Argyll Stores (Holdings) Ltd* [1998] 1 AC 1 (HL) [15] cited by Phang JA in *PH Hydraulics* (n 1) [62].

[47] *Cassell & Co Ltd v Broome* [1972] AC 1027 (HL) 1077.

[48] J Goudkamp and E Katsampouka, 'Punitive Damages: Ten Misconceptions' in E Bant et al (eds), *Punishment and Private Law* (Oxford, Hart Publishing, 2021) 204–05.

[49] *Rookes v Barnard* [1964] 1 AC 1129 (HL) 1227–28.

[50] W Courtney and J Goudkamp, 'Punishment and Private Law' in E Bant et al (eds), *Punishment and Private Law* (Oxford, Hart Publishing, 2021) 17; Goudkamp and Katsampouka, 'Punitive Damages' (ibid) 204.

[51] In *Borders (UK) Ltd v Commissioner of Police of the Metropolis* [2005] EWCA Civ 197, the English Court of Appeal countenanced an award of exemplary damages that bore compensatory elements.

[52] JY Gotanda, 'Punitive Damages: A Comparative Analysis' (2004) 42 *Columbia Journal of Transnational Law* 391, 392. There is also evidence that punitive awards are more prevalent than previously thought to be: see T Eiserberg et al, 'The Decision to Award Punitive Damages: An Empirical Study' (2010) 2 *Journal of Legal Analysis* 577.

[53] CM Sharkey, 'Crossing the Punitive-Compensatory Divide' in BH Borstein et al (eds), *Civil Juries and Civil Justice* (New York, Springer, 2008) 79, 80.

(including jurors, attorneys and judges) are likely to regard the different damages categories to be 'fungible'[54] so that 'Compensatory damages can punish, just as punitive damages can compensate.'[55] Such 'leakage' between damages categories has been explained as a manifestation of the equifinality principle viz, that decision-makers deploy different means to achieve a desired outcome.[56] More recently, commentators have argued that this substitution phenomenon provides a further reason to enlarge the jurisdiction to award punitive damages in private law, so as to avoid the creation of 'perverse incentives … for judges to search out alternative and often inferior mechanisms of punishment.'[57]

On a close inspection, one could detect in *PH Hydraulics* clues of an attempt to shift damages across categories. It seems reasonably clear that Airtust's plea for punitive damages was motivated, at least in part, by the concern of under-compensation. Clause 25 of the contract, which excluded liability for consequential loss, obstructed Airtrust's attempt to recover lost profits. If Clause 25 had not been operative, Airtrust would have sought to recover: (a) the purchase price paid for the RDU; (b) the rental profits that it would have earned by leasing the RDU to Trident; (c) the revenue that it would have earned by investing the rental profits; and (d) the costs expended in litigating the claim. Though item (b) was an indirect or consequential loss falling under the second limb of *Hadley v Baxendale*,[58] it would (but for clause 25) have been recoverable since PH was at all times aware of the intended lease of the RDU to Trident. Item (c), on the other hand, was likely too remote since there was no evidence that PH knew that the rental profits made from the RDU would be applied to generate other profits.[59] Eventually, of course, the CA held that items (b) and (c) could not be recovered as they comprised consequential damages excluded by clause 25. It also declined to order costs on an indemnity basis.[60] In consequence, Airtrust succeeded only in recovering item (a) and a fraction of the costs expended under item (d). For Airtrust, this was a highly unsatisfactory outcome. Despite the undisputed conclusion that PH had performed its contractual obligations in a 'blatantly irresponsible'[61] manner, Airtrust must be content with a limited recovery that falls significantly short of its true loss.

[54] J Klick and CM Sharkey, 'The Fungibility of Damage Awards: Punitive Damage Caps and Substitution' (working draft 2007) <https://papers.ssrn.com/sol3/papers.cfm?abstract_id=912256> accessed 7 May 2023.

[55] T Baker, 'Transforming Punishment into Compensation: In the Shadow of Punitive Damages' (1998) 1 *Wisconsin Law Review* 211, 212.

[56] MC Anderson and RJ MacCoun, 'Goal Conflict in Juror Assessments of Compensatory and Punitive Damages' (1999) 23 *Law and Human Behavior* 313.

[57] J Goudkamp and E Katsampouka, 'Punitive Damages and the Place of Punishment in Private Law' (2021) 84 *MLR* 1257, 1293.

[58] *Hadley v Baxendale* (1854) 9 Exch 341.

[59] *PH Hydraulics* (n 1) [156].

[60] ibid [158].

[61] *PH Hydraulics HC* (n 6) [272].

Cast in this light, *PH Hydraulics* was a failed attempt to recoup some losses through the punitive route. But the import of this failure extends beyond a single claimant's inability to optimise recovery. By laying down a '*general rule that punitive damages cannot be awarded for breach of contract*',[62] the CA effectively closed off, or at least severely curtailed, the use of punitive damages to enhance compensatory awards. The interesting question that follows is whether this will engender the substitution phenomenon just discussed. Will decision-makers – deprived of the option to overtly express their punitive intent – attempt to smuggle punitive objectives into compensatory awards?

Although the substitutive effect of damages can be observed in all areas of private law, there are reasons to suspect it is less significant in the context of contractual disputes. Of particular relevance is the fact that much of the literature documenting the substitutive effect had focused on *tort* law, where the claimants are more likely to recover damages for non-pecuniary loss, such as physical injury, pain and suffering, emotional distress and injury to dignitary interests. It is the 'elasticity' inherent in non-pecuniary damages that provides room for the leakage of punitive goals into compensatory damages. To the extent that claims for contractual disputes may involve far fewer incidents of personal injury, there may be much less scope for recourse to non-pecuniary loss. Moreover, aggravated damages are not recoverable for breach of contract[63] and damages for mental distress are likewise not recoverable as a general rule[64] although exceptionally they may be available for contracts formed with the object of providing pleasure, relaxation or peace of mind.[65] Where the claimant is a corporation, which was the case in *PH Hydraulics* and would also be typical of the vast majority of commercial disputes, there is even less scope for recovery of non-pecuniary loss. A company, not having the anthropomorphic features of a physical body, mind and emotions, is incapable of suffering pain, mental distress and loss of enjoyment.[66] These considerations suggest that, in the preponderance of commercial disputes involving businesses, the claimant's damages would be confined to demonstrable *financial* loss. The exclusion of punitive damages is unlikely, therefore, to spur attempts to punish outrageous through the compensatory back door.

In any event, the fact that compensatory damages may on occasion be pressed to serve punitive functions is not a particularly pertinent reason for explicitly incorporating punishment as a remedial goal. In *PH Hydraulics*, the CA noted[67] the incidental punitive effects that may reside in certain categories

[62] *PH Hydraulics* (n 1) [135] (emphasis in original).

[63] *Kralj v McGrath* [1986] 1 All ER 54 (QB) 60.

[64] *Addis* (n 2).

[65] *Jarvis v Swan Tours* [1973] QB 233 (CA); though it suffices if the object of pleasure or peace of mind is a major or important part of the contract but not its sole object: *Farley v Skinner* [2001] UKHL 49, [2002] 2 AC 732.

[66] V Wilcox, *A Company's Right to Non-Pecuniary Loss* (Cambridge, CUP, 2016) 127–31.

[67] *PH Hydraulics* (n 1) [80]–[83].

extra-compensatory damages, viz, *Wrotham Park* damages,[68] account of profits and damages for mental distress but did not regard that as a factor favouring the award of punitive damages. Instead, Phang JA cited these categories of damages to make the point that to the extent that there exists a limited role for contractual damages to deter or punish, this remedial 'gap' would be adequately filled by access to such extra-compensatory damages.[69] In other words, the substitutive effects of these remedies were a reason for *not* enlarging the role of punishment in the context of contracts. This analysis (rightly, it is submitted) underscores the important distinction between the *effects* and *purposes* of civil remedies.[70] The fact that a remedy may have observed punitive effects does not convert it into a punitive remedy aimed at punishment, nor does it signify that such a remedy is needed. Ultimately, punitive damages should only be awarded for breach of contract if it is justified on normative grounds, and if it can be aligned with and advances the institutional functions of contracting.

In sum, *PH Hydraulics* was a case that contained elements illustrating the practical fluidity of the different categories of damages that litigants (or their counsels) seek to exploit to their advantage. However, the effect of the CA decision was to constrain the opportunities for such exploitation, thereby reinforcing the orthodox compensate-not-punish paradigm.

V. CONTRACT AND TORT

At common law, punitive damages are an accepted feature of tort law[71] but are not usually available for breach of contract[72] or equitable obligations.[73]

[68] In *Turf Club Auto Emporium Pte Ltd v Yeo Boong Hua* [2018] SGCA 79, [2018] 2 SLR 655, the Singapore Court of Appeal confirmed that *Wrotham Park* damages are available as a 'residual' remedy in cases where the breach is of a negative covenant, damages are not otherwise adequate and the hypothetical bargain would not have been irrational. However, it declined to restrict the remedy to breaches of contractual rights that are economically valuable assets: *cf One Step (Support) Ltd v Morris-Garner* [2018] UKSC 20, [2018] 2 WLR 1353.

[69] *PH Hydraulics* (n 1) [76] and [84].

[70] K Barker, 'Punishment in Private Law – No Such Thing (Any More)' in E Bant et al (eds), *Punishment and Private Law* (Oxford, Hart Publishing, 2021) 42.

[71] With England being the most restrictive regime as the award is still subject to the 'categories' test laid down in *Rookes v Barnard* (n 49).

[72] Punitive damages are not awarded for breach of contract in England (*Addis* (n 2)), Australia (*Gray v Motor Accident Commission* (1998) 196 CLR 1 (HCA)), New Zealand (*Paper Reclaim Ltd v Aotearoa International Ltd* [2006] NZCA 27, [2006] 3 NZLR 188) and Singapore (*PH Hydraulics* (n 1)). Canada is a prominent exception: see *Whiten* (n 5).

[73] This appears to be the position in England: see, eg, *Mosley v News Group Newspapers Ltd* [2008] EWHC 1777 (QB), [2008] EMLR 20 and JD Heydon, MJ Leeming and PG Turner, *Meagher, Gummow & Lehane's Equity: Doctrines and Remedies*, 5th edn (Sydney, LexisNexis Butterworths, 2015) [23-600]; and also in Australia (*Harris v Digital Pulse Pty Ltd* [2003] NSWCA 10, (2003) 56 NSWLR 298). However, punitive damages are recoverable for equitable wrongs in New Zealand (*Aquaculture* v *New Zealand Green Mussel Co Ltd* [1990] 3 NZLR 299 (CA)) and Canada (*Norberg v Wynrib* (1992) 92 DLR (4th) 449 (SCC)).

This uneven availability of the remedy across different private law actions is often thought to be unsatisfactory. If punitive damages serve to punish and deter wrongdoing, why should it not extend to all causes of action so long as the conduct in question is of a quality that warrants censure and disapprobation?[74] The CA did not accept this reasoning in *PH Hydraulics*. Instead, it endorsed[75] the conventional view[76] that contracts and torts are distinct legal phenomena: the former are voluntary obligations whilst the latter are obligations imposed by law. This conceives of contractual autonomy as the *raison d'être* of contract law. Parties should be free – by means of 'voluntary agreement' – to regulate their legal relationships *themselves*.[77] The notion of punishment is 'antithetical to the very nature of contract law in general and to its remedial structure in particular' in so far as it seeks to regulate the relationships by reference to standards *external* to those agreed by the parties.[78] In contrast, it is consistent with the aims of tort law to empower courts to 'impose standards of normative behaviour between complete strangers'.[79] Making punitive damages available for torts is not therefore objectionable as there may be occasions when the remedy is needed to denounce conduct falling short of such normative standards.

This is a familiar conception of the tort–contract divide that conforms to the dominant 'freedom of contract' paradigm. But it is also criticised for straightjacketing contracts into a single paradigm of 'voluntary obligations'. In fact, contracts are a spectrum of diverse phenomena,[80] so the sheer variety makes 'the idea that all of them share characteristics making punitives inappropriate seems inherently implausible.'[81] Moreover, while freedom of contract is indisputably foundational to modern contract law, it is not unbridled. Like tort law, contract law comprises mandatory features.[82] The objective

[74] Thus, the Law Commission has argued for extending punitive damages to equitable wrongs: see Law Commission, 'Aggravated, Exemplary and Restitutionary Damages' (Law Com No 247, 1997) 110–11. See also A Burrows, 'Remedial Coherence and Punitive Damages in Equity' in S Degeling and J Edelman (eds), *Equity in Commercial Law* (Sydney, Lawbook Co, 2005). Those who favour the award of punitive damages for breach of contract have similarly cited this concern for consistency as justification: See, eg, N McBride, 'A Case for Awarding Punitive Damages in Response to Deliberate Breaches of Contract' (1995) 24 *Anglo-American Law Review* 369; R Cunnington, 'Should Punitive Damages be Part of the Judicial Arsenal in Contract Cases?' (2006) 26 *Legal Studies* 369; and A Tettenborn, 'Punitive Damages for Breach of Contract: What's so Special About Contract Claims?' (2005) <https://papers.ssrn.com/sol3/papers.cfm?abstract_id=938700> accessed 7 May 2023.

[75] *PH Hydraulics* (n 1) [68].

[76] As Lord Goff observed in *Henderson v Merrett Syndicates Ltd* [1995] 2 AC 145 (HL) 194, 'the tortious duty is imposed by general law, and the contractual duty is attributable to the will of the parties'.

[77] *PH Hydraulics* (n 1) [72].

[78] ibid.

[79] ibid [74].

[80] P Atiyah, *Essays on Contract* (Oxford, Clarendon Press, 1986) 5–8.

[81] Tettenborn (n 74).

[82] A Robertson, 'On the Distinction between Contract and Tort' in A Robertson (ed), *The Law of Obligations: Connections and Boundaries* (London, UCL Press, 2004). See also Cunnington (n 74) 375–76.

approach to contractual formation and interpretation, the doctrines of implied term, frustration and illegality, the rule against penalties as well as the limited availability of injunctive reliefs, are all manifestations of the law's endeavours at infusing norms of behaviour into the process of contractual bargaining, performance and enforcement. Even if voluntariness is confined to the act of contracting,[83] it may still be said that the freedom to form contracts does not necessarily entail freedom to dictate the remedies for breach.[84] Ultimately, the principles dictating what damages may be awarded upon breach are judicial policies determined by the court rather than parties' intention.[85] Freedom of contract does not, by itself, justify an absolute ban on punitive damages for breach of contract.

The CA's reasoning in *PH Hydraulics* does not fully explain why the act of voluntary agreement would necessarily exclude the court's regulation by imposing punitive damages. An important clue is found in Phang JA's observation that 'the common law of contract has largely been 'tolerant of a certain amount of self-interested behaviour'.[86] This implies that it is not the mere fact of agreement but the *prevailing contracting norm of promoting self-interests* that makes it incongruent for courts to impose punitive damages for breach. Phang JA subsequently confirmed this when he observed that if a contract contained an express or implied duty of good faith, 'the argument that the contracting parties are justified in performing the contract in a way that prioritises their self-interest falls away.'[87] Yet even the breach of such a term is a 'neutral factor' at best and something more is needed to justify the imposition of punitive damages.[88] Another situation where parties may be taken to have excluded the prioritisation of self-interests occurs where they agree to penalties for breach. Here, Phang JA was quick to emphasise that the penalty rule reflected the law's 'distaste for deterrent damages in contract',[89] thus suggesting

[83] Gardner noted this is the proper understanding of voluntariness: see J Gardner, *Torts and Other Wrongs* (Oxford, OUP, 2019) 342.

[84] 'It is bad logic to argue that because a contractual duty arises out of an agreement of two individuals the judicial response to breach of that duty must also be determined by the agreement of those two individuals.': see McBride (n 74) 383.

[85] Robertson (n 82) 101–03.

[86] *PH Hydraulics* (n 1) [71], citing S Rowan, 'Reflections on the Introduction of Punitive Damages for Breach of Contract' (2010) 30 *OJLS* 495, 504.

[87] *PH Hydraulics* (n 1) [134].

[88] ibid. Although Phang JA recognised that in jurisdictions such as Canada where punitive damages can be awarded for breach of contract, the development of a general duty of honesty in contractual performance in *Harish Bhasin v Larry Hrynew and Heritage Education Funds Inc* [2014] 3 SCR 494 might enable the Canadian courts to 'award punitive damages in response to a greater variety of contractual breaches' (*PH Hydraulics* (n 1) [132]). See also E Andrews, 'Lex Punit Mendacium: Punitive Damages and *Bhasin v Hrynew*' (2017) 7 *Western Journal of Legal Studies* 1.

[89] *PH Hydraulics* (n 1) [73], citing N Andrews et al, *Contractual Duties: Performance Breach, Termination and Remedies* (London, Sweet & Maxwell, 2011) para 20-024. In Singapore, the Court of Appeal has affirmed the traditional *Dunlop* test and declined to endorse the legitimate interest standard laid down in *Cavendish Square Holding BV v Makdessi* [2015] UKSC 67, [2016] AC 1172: see *Denka Advantech Pte Ltd v Seraya Energy Pte Ltd* [2020] SGCA 119, [2021] 1 SLR 631.

that the law's antipathy towards agreed punishment would prevail even over party autonomy.[90] Viewed as a whole, the CA's reasoning implies that the real distinction between contracts and torts lies in the contracting parties' acceptance of self-serving behaviour as the baseline contracting norm. Indeed, this norm is so robust that it is not easily displaced by agreement. Self-serving conduct that falls below (higher) contractual standards is not (without more) deemed reprehensible and punishable. Parties who do not wish to bear the risks of counterparty default will have the option of hedging against such risks through specific arrangements, although attempts to impose penalties disproportionate to the loss clauses are prohibited.

So construed, the endorsement of the classic voluntary-imposed distinction in *PH Hydraulics* was a means to highlight the different *standards* of conduct set by contracts and torts. This difference arises from the fact that tort and contract are two discrete, structurally dissimilar domains intended for different ends. Tort law is primarily concerned with identifying basic norms or ethical rules to guide and regulate inter-personal dealings.[91] To this end, the method of tort law is to identify a particular protectable interest and determine the conduct that would constitute an improper invasion of that interest. The standard of conduct so identified thus constitutes the baseline that one must not transgress in dealing with others. In contrast, contract law seeks to construct and maintain a fair legal infrastructure to facilitate transactions. As such, contractual obligations are not usually concerned with threshold conduct. They are formed to acquire benefits, the performance of which often exceeds that baseline standard. A breach of such 'higher' standard of conduct, even if motivated by selfish reasons, is not generally seen as a wrong deserving of punishment.[92] Thus, a deliberate failure to deliver goods purchased for resale is not of the same moral quality as a deliberate act to injure another or his or her property. So while the failure to meet the tort standard may sometimes be seen to be wrongful, the failure to meet the contract standard is less likely to have the same moral quality.[93]

[90] Although it should be noted that an *agreed* punishment is distinct from a court-imposed punishment so the prohibition of the former does not necessarily also justify the exclusion of the latter. I am grateful to Eleni Katsampouka for this observation.

[91] P Cane, *The Anatomy of Tort Law* (Oxford, Hart Publishing, 1997) 24–25.

[92] Diamond makes the point in more florid terms: 'Bad faith breach of contract, if defined as an intentional breach motivated by crass economic self-interest, has been, despite a clamoring of moral credos to the contrary, a judicially accepted staple of our system of commercial law. While some have condemned the willful contract breaker as a repulsive, evil aberration, woefully disrupting moral quietude, a close scrutiny of commercial practice, makes it transparently clear that our system not only sanctions such bad faith breaches, but with limitations, actually encourages them.': T Diamond, 'The Tort of Bad Faith Breach of Contract: When, if at all, should it be Extended Beyond Insurance Transactions?' (1981) 64 *Marquette Law Review* 425, 433.

[93] Rowan (n 86) 506–07, citing G Virgo, 'Restitution for Breach of Contract' in *The Principles of the Law of Restitution* (Oxford Scholarship Online, September 2015) 21, that 'breach of contract cannot be considered to be of the same magnitude of wrongfulness as committing a tort or crime or even a breach of fiduciary breach'.

It is true, of course, that this understanding of the distinction would still not justify an absolute ban of punitive damages in the contractual sphere since *some* contractual breaches may involve conduct that falls short of the threshold standard. Nevertheless, it is arguable that punitive damages are of greater relevance in the realm of torts since torts are more likely than contractual breaches to involve serious wrongdoing.

The obvious practical importance of maintaining a sharp division between torts and contracts is, of course, to confine punitive damages to torts to the (almost complete) exclusion of contracts.[94] This is a defensible remedial framework that conceives of torts and contracts as serving distinct but complementary roles.[95] Doubtless there will be situations where a breach of contract involves particularly culpable wrongdoing that warrants judicial censure, but that does not create a 'remedial gap' if the appropriate redress can be achieved through the law of torts. In *ACB v Thomson Medical Pte Ltd* ('*Thomson Medical*')[96] the Singapore Court of Appeal departed from *Rookes* to hold that punitive damages may now be awarded for all torts unconstrained by the 'categories test'. The touchstone for the award of punitive damages is 'conduct [that] is so outrageous that it warrants punishment, deterrence and condemnation'.[97] Importantly, inadvertent conduct would also qualify as there may be occasions when the negligent conduct is 'so beyond the pale that it is properly characterised as outrageous'.[98] Such an approach would be consonant with the broader purposes of punitive damages, viz, to promote societal welfare through deterrence and vindication.[99] *Thomson Medical* thus evinces a judicial attitude open to a broader application of punitive damages in appropriate cases in the realm of torts. That would mitigate the risks of any remedial lacuna arising as a result of denying punitive damages for breach of contract.

In summary, this section has sought to demonstrate that while the CA in *PH Hydraulics* had identified the party autonomy as the key factor that distinguished contracts from torts, the more critical consideration was the distinct contracting norm that prioritises self-interested conduct. The (real or perceived)

[94] Where there is concurrent liability in tort and contract, the claimant would generally be free to prosecute the more advantages cause of action. Technically, therefore, suing in tort would allow the claimant to seek punitive damages even if the same were not available for breach of contract. However, the contractual matrix on which the tort is founded is often a pertinent factor in the application of the tort principles. For instance, it was held in *Wellesley Partners LLP v Withers LLP* [2015] EWCA Civ 1146, [2016] 2 WLR 1351 that where tortious and contractual duties of care coexist, the contractual test for remoteness of damage should apply. I thank James Goudkamp for bringing this case to my attention.

[95] *PH Hydraulics* (n 1) [75].

[96] *ACB v Thomson Medical Pte Ltd* [2017] SGCA 20, [2017] 1 SLR 918.

[97] ibid [176].

[98] ibid [201].

[99] ibid [200].

dominance of this norm leaves very little room for the punishment of 'outrageous' breach in the sphere of contracts. At the same time, however, any residual risk of remedial inadequacy in cases of exceptionally oppressive conduct is addressed by a more expansive approach to punitive damages in torts.

VI. NEVER SAY NEVER

Despite being emphatic that 'there ought to be a general rule that punitive damages cannot be awarded for breach of contract', the CA in *PH Hydraulics* was ultimately unwilling to rule out the *possibility* of a case involving 'a particularly outrageous breach' that warrants a departure from the general rule.[100] This was a surprising twist given the forceful reasons that Phang JA enumerated for excluding punitive damages immediately prior. However, Phang JA was quick to stress that 'it would take a truly exceptional case to persuade this court that punitive damages should be awarded for breach of contract' given the need to surmount the 'many reasons of principle and policy … against doing so.'[101] The resulting tension has attracted both critics and supporters. Hickey thought it unsatisfactory to preserve a limited discretion with no guidance on the criteria for punitive awards, for in doing so it 'perpetuated the very uncertainty that [the court] criticized.'[102] Barnett, on the other hand, agreed with the CA in *PH Hydraulics* that 'a blanket ban is not merited'[103] because there will invariably be some cases where self-interested behaviour is not the governing norm.[104] On balance, the latter view is the more persuasive (though less elegant) as it reflects the varied nature of contracts. Contracts voluntarily formed to advance self-interests is the dominant but by no means exclusive paradigm.

If an exception is at all possible, what criteria would govern its ambit? Once it is accepted that an intentional, self-serving breach is not punishable behaviour, it is clear that invectives such as 'malicious', 'wanton', 'reprehensible', 'contumelious' or 'outrageous' are generally unhelpful as they provide no firm guidance beyond depicting a heightened sense of moral indignation. Criteria yoked to community standards of ethical behaviour or business norms[105] fare no better as these descriptions still leave too much room for subjectivity. Even

[100] *PH Hydraulics* (n 1) [135]–[136].

[101] ibid [136].

[102] SJ Hickey, 'Punitive Damages for Breach of Contract: A Singaporean Perspective' (2017) 46 *Common Law World Review* 239, 243.

[103] K Barnett, 'Exemplary Damages in Contract Law' in E Bant et al (eds), *Punishment and Private Law* (Oxford, Hart Publishing, 2021) 225.

[104] ibid 237.

[105] D Venour, 'Punitive Damages in Contract' (1988) 1 *Canadian Journal of Law and Jurisprudence* 87, 102–03.

a test based on targeted harm or malice[106] seems impracticable as the distinction between manifest bad faith and aggressive self-preservation would often be elusive. Another approach is to confine the remedy to instances involving vulnerable plaintiffs in unequal or dependent relationships, such as employees, insured persons and consumers.[107] As noted in *PH Hydraulics*, however, regulation may often be the more appropriate means to ameliorate such risks as legislatures are better placed to assess the wider social and economic ramifications of sanctions.[108]

More recently, in *Turf Club Auto Emporium Pte Ltd v Yeo Boong Hua*[109] ('*Turf Club*'), the Singapore Court of Appeal observed, in passing, that punishment and/or deterrence could perhaps be justified in a case where the contract 'involves a public interest which goes beyond the private interests of the parties themselves.'[110] This was said in the context of the Court's attempt to rationalise *Attorney-General v Blake* ('*Blake*'),[111] which of course concerned the different remedy of an account of profits. It is important to note that the Court had also (in *Turf Club*) expressed significant reservations as to whether the *Blake* remedy should even be adopted in Singapore.[112] These remarks underscore the CA's conservative stance towards punitive damages as is manifest in *PH Hydraulics*. Nevertheless, the very tentative endorsement of public interests as a ground for imposing extra-compensatory damages provides a hint as to the type of conduct that the Court might consider punishable in the commercial context.

Attempts to justify punitive damages by reference to public interests are not new. Indeed, the first of the *Rookes* categories – involving the oppressive, arbitrary or unconstitutional action by the servants of the Government – may be understood as a special category singled out for the protection of 'public interests in an efficient and reliable operation of the principles of legality and the rule of law'.[113] In this vein, Sharkey has argued that punitive damages ought to be rationalised as a form of 'societal damages' to 'redress harms caused by defendants who injure persons beyond the individual plaintiffs in a particular case'.[114] This approach has obvious appeal since the objectives of punishment and deterrence are traditionally associated with the protection of public interests in criminal law. But even if one puts aside the familiar 'windfall' objection,

[106] Tettenborn (n 74).
[107] See, eg, Hickey (n 102) 243–44. Barnett similarly argues that punitive damages are appropriate for 'agency problem' cases, 'where one party agrees to act in another's interests pursuant to the contract, all the risk lies on the other party's side and it is in the interests of the first party to breach, and it is difficult to detect the breach before it occurs' (Barnett (n 103) 251).
[108] *PH Hydraulics* (n 1) [106].
[109] See n 68.
[110] ibid [254].
[111] *Attorney-General v Blake* [2000] UKHL 45, [2001] AC 268.
[112] *Turf Club* (n 68) [254].
[113] V Janečk, 'Public Interest Damages' (2020) 40 *Legal Studies* 589, 596.
[114] C Sharkey, 'Punitive Damages as Societal Damages' (2003) *Yale Law Journal* 347, 351–52.

this rationalisation raises challenging questions on how the qualifying public interests are to be identified. In a broad sense, the public is always interested in the proper regulation of contracts,[115] but such interests would surely not justify the grant of punitive interests on every occasion of breach.

If 'public interest' should qualify as a sufficient criterion and justification factor, it is likely that the CA in *Turf Club* had in mind a very narrow conception of public interests. This is because the comment was made in the context of the unique facts of *Blake*. There, the interest at stake was that of national security, which was unequivocally 'public'. The claimant – the Attorney-General – was also a 'public' claimant responsible for safeguarding state interests. These features bring the case very close to a criminal prosecution but for the civil cause of action. Where a breach of contract is prosecuted by a private claimant, it is less clear that the award of punitive damages is appropriate even if it raises serious public concerns (such as widespread and systemic fraud or threats to health and safety). As the CA intimated in *PH Hydraulics*, legislative reform would generally be the superior solution since the adversarial litigation process is rarely the appropriate forum for regulating complex commercial or market activities.[116] The court risks overstepping its judicial function if it intervenes inappropriately.

The definitional difficulties canvassed in this section suggest that though the CA had left open the *possibility* of imposing punitive damages for breach of contract, this will likely be a very limited jurisdiction. In Phang JA's words, 'hardly ever'[117] would be an apt description of the availability of punitive damages for breach of contract.

VII. CONCLUSION

Those who support the wider availability of punitive damages for breach of contract typically concede that the remedy is not appropriate in the preponderance of contract cases. Their arguments for departing from the traditional ban are usually premised on contracts involving parties vulnerable to being exploited by counterparties with superior expertise or financial muscle. *PH Hydraulics*, however, was not such a case. Unfortunately for the claimant, both parties to the contract were businesses of roughly equal bargaining position. In hindsight,

[115] W Lucy and A Williams, 'Public and Private: Neither Deep nor Meaningful?' in K Barker and D Jensen (eds), *Private Law: Key Encounters with Public Law* (Cambridge, CUP, 2013) 52.

[116] An example of an unsuccessful judicial reform occurred in *Hii Chii Kok v Ooi Peng Jin London Lucien* [2017] SGCA 38, [2017] 1 SLR 492, where the Singapore Court of Appeal altered the test for determining the standard of care that medical officers must exercise in giving advice to patients. However, this development caused considerable uncertainty and anxiety among doctors. In response, Parliament consulted widely among the medical profession and enacted legislation to restore a more physician-centric approach in determining the standard of care for medical advice.

[117] *PH Hydraulics* (n 1) [136].

Airtrust could certainly have done more to protect itself against the risks of PH's default. Though deplorable, PH's irresponsible conduct was not of such depravity as to provoke the revolutionary instincts of the judges. Another lesson to draw from *PH Hydraulics* is the need to consider contractual remedies in context. It is but one means – and a fairly limited one – of regulating commercial behaviour. Recurrent or systemic misconduct is better tamed by legislation. With these considerations in mind, it is no wonder that orthodoxy rules.

Index

Introductory Note

References such as '178–79' indicate (not necessarily continuous) discussion of a topic across a range of pages. Wherever possible in the case of topics with many references, these have either been divided into sub-topics or only the most significant discussions of the topic are listed. Because the entire work is about 'punitive damages' the use of this term (and certain others which occur constantly throughout the book) as an entry point has been restricted. Information will be found under the corresponding detailed topics.

www.ingramcontent.com/pod-product-compliance
Ingram Content Group UK Ltd.
Pitfield, Milton Keynes, MK11 3LW, UK
UKHW021705230926
475560UK00015B/308

9 781509 967001